Electronic Governance and Cross-Boundary Collaboration:

Innovations and Advancing Tools

Yu-Che Chen
Northern Illinois University, USA

Pin-Yu Chu
National Chengchi University & Taiwan E-Governance Research Center, Taiwan

Information Science
REFERENCE

Senior Editorial Director: Kristin Klinger
Director of Book Publications: Julia Mosemann
Editorial Director: Lindsay Johnston
Acquisitions Editor: Erika Carter
Development Editor: Hannah Abelbeck
Production Editor: Sean Woznicki
Typesetters: Keith Glazewski, Natalie Pronio, Jennifer Romanchak, & Milan Vracarich, Jr.
Print Coordinator: Jamie Snavely
Cover Design: Nick Newcomer

Published in the United States of America by
Information Science Reference (an imprint of IGI Global)
701 E. Chocolate Avenue
Hershey PA 17033
Tel: 717-533-8845
Fax: 717-533-8661
E-mail: cust@igi-global.com
Web site: http://www.igi-global.com

Library of Congress Cataloging-in-Publication Data
Electronic governance and cross-boundary collaboration: innovations and advancing tools / Yu-Che Chen and Pin-Yu Chu, editors.
p. cm.
Includes bibliographical references and index.
Summary: "This book will provide research-based policy and management recommendations for innovative e-governance, focusing on recent developments that will shape the future of e-governance"--Provided by publisher.
ISBN 978-1-60960-753-1 (hardcover) -- ISBN 978-1-60960-754-8 (ebook) -- ISBN 978-1-60960-755-5 (print & perpetual access) 1. Internet in public administration. 2. Internet in public administration--International cooperation. I. Chen, Yu-Che. II. Chu, Pin-Yu, 1965-
JF1525.A8E424 2011
352.3'802854678--dc22
2011008675

British Cataloguing in Publication Data
A Cataloguing in Publication record for this book is available from the British Library.

Table of Contents

Detailed Table of Contents

Tzeng and Hu's chapter identifies critical issues facing cross-boundary integration and collaboration for e-government services. The authors use a focus-group approach to examine electronic public service integration in Taipei, Taiwan, and are able to uncover certain relevant issues, such as legal and institutional constraints, information privacy and security, trust, data ownership, nature of service, and technical readiness.

The government information sharing framework proposed by Estevez, Fillottrani, Janowski, and Ojo provides a multidimensional and operational framework for cross-boundary integration of government information. Moreover, this framework--which encompasses technological, organizational, inter-organizational, and environmental dimensions--can serve as an implementation template for addressing issues in e-governance information integration.

Sung's chapter offers executive insights into government-wide integration and collaboration for e-governance. He highlights the critical role of cross-boundary integration in moving to e-governance, capitalizing on his extensive leadership experience in guiding government-wide e-government projects in Taiwan. He offers practical implementation strategies, such as managing interdependence and adapting to environmental changes to move e-governance forward.

The analysis of Belgium's design and implementation of government-wide cross-boundary e-governance in Leyman's chapter offers important insights. It reinforces citizen-centric information and services as the core value and design principle of e-governance. The author's design of an e-government system has an identity and access management system at its core, and this helps integrate electronic services from various government departments.

Chang and Obi's chapter proposes and empirically tests a user-centric model of e-governance, with an emphasis on user satisfaction with e-services. The authors surveyed citizens as e-governance service users in Taipei and Tokyo. Their findings suggest the positive impact that citizens' experience in public affairs has on the perceived quality of e-services. In contrast, the perception of risks associated with the use of IT-enabled government services negatively impacts the perception of e-service quality.

The focus on civil servants and the inclusion of organizational variables in Chiang's chapter further expand our understanding of users and multiply the dimensions considered in modeling users/citizens. The survey of Taiwanese civil servants gives insight into cross-boundary e-governance systems that have civil servants as the target users. Empirical findings raise the importance of attitudes and norms in determining intention to accept online service delivery.

Citizen centricity should be an important design principle for successful e-governance, as the critical review of Thailand's e-government plan in Tubtimhin's chapter suggests. Such principle provides justification and momentum for the integration between the front and end-office e-government applications as well as the vertical and horizontal integration for successful e-governance.

Section 3
Evaluation Instrument and E-Governance Assessment

Morgeson's chapter fills an important lacuna in our knowledge concerning the impact of e-governance from the user's perspective. This external perspective provides a more balanced e-government performance measurement model that can put adequate weight on user experience. Morgeson brings to focus what matters to users/citizens/customers.

In their chapter, Hsiao, Chu, and Lee address an under-studied but critical group of stakeholders in successful e-governance: businesses. Moreover, the authors make a significant contribution to the development of an outcome-oriented e-governance model that advances the theory and practice of e-governance assessment. The notion of public trust, satisfaction, and adoption, as well as costs and benefits, are included in the outcomes.

The chapter by Huang, Lee, and Hsiao empirically studies the use of online surveys as instruments for evaluating e-governance. Using online surveys to gauge user experience of e-governance has the advantages of low cost and speedy response. The authors draw on their combined experience with conducting online surveys to evaluate e-governance, and they are able to identify several challenges, such as low response rates, difficulties in achieving representativeness, and challenges posed when working with government agencies.

Rodríguez-Bolívar, Caba-Pérez, and López-Hernández's chapter applies the CapGemini methodology to the evaluation of municipal e-government services in select Latin American and Caribbean (LAC) countries. This study fills the knowledge gap with regards to the performance of e-government in nineteen LAC countries such as Argentina, Ecuador, Paraguay, Peru, Cuba, and Brazil, to name a few.

Wood's chapter uses e-government stages theory to critically examine the e-government of U.S. county governments. Wood adapted and integrated several models of e-government development to develop a stage theory, which proves to be productive in tracking the development of e-governance, identifying areas for improvement, and formulating developmental strategies.

Relly's chapter examines the institutions for electronic governance in India and China. Viewing laws and regulations focused on government information access (open government) as the core institution for e-governance is instructive because access to government information is one of the main conditions for meaningful citizen participation, both offline and online. This study underscores the great potential of e-governance in both countries, even amidst challenges posed by political systems and infrastructure.

Shiang, Lo, and Wang's empirical investigation of the implementation of freedom of information regulations provides valuable lessons on national implementation. Their analysis of the five-year implementation of Taiwan's Freedom of Information Act underscores the importance of back-office support.

Sanchez and Ganapati's study of the role of the Internet in diasporic Iranian and Eritrean communities underscores both the innovative use of the Internet for political mobilization and the importance of political and institutional relationships in mediating the influences exerted by these communities. This chapter expands this edited volume's coverage to include the Middle East and Africa.

Yang's chapter provides a timely and insightful discussion of the nature and challenges of e-governance in China. Based partly on a review of relevant studies and policy statements, the study reveals China's commitment to modernizing its administration via the use of information and communication technology.

Yang, Zhang, and Tang's chapter explores various e-governance issues and provides a timely assessment and forecast. This chapter advances our knowledge of e-governance in two ways. First, it provides a broad review of Internet use as it relates to electronic governance in China, a country with the largest online population in the world (beginning in 2008). Second, this chapter reviews studies of e-government websites in China and provides an illustration of the development of e-governance in the public sector.

Pan, Chen, and Wang's chapter pushes the envelope of e-governance by examining an innovative Web 2.0 public governance application in Taiwan. The authors first present a framework for assessing government use of Web 2.0 by synthesizing the research literature on the value of public governance offered by Web 2.0. Using this framework, they conduct an empirical study of the central government's Vision 2020 Web site, which utilizes Web 2.0 features to facilitate the interaction between the elite and the general public in the process of envisioning Taiwan's future.

Chen's contribution to this volume, an analysis of the U.S. federal government implementation of Government 2.0, further enhances our knowledge with regard to utilizing Web 2.0 to improve public governance. The United States is at the forefront of technological innovation. The long-standing tradition of open government also provides the institutional foundation for online civic engagement. This chapter provides a framework and specific policy and management recommendations for countries aiming to pursue Government 2.0.

Preface

IMPERATIVES OF ELECTRONIC GOVERNANCE AND CROSS-BOUNDARY COLLABORATION

In the next decade, the shift from electronic government to e-governance will be one of the most important trends in the government use of information and communication technologies (ICTs). Using ICTs, electronic governance can transform the relationship between government and citizens, especially in the realm of the production and delivery of public services and information, as well as the practice of democratic governance. Governments should utilize ICTs to integrate information and services as well as to provide citizens with personalized information and services that traditionally have been provided by various departments. Moreover, electronic governance is concerned with actively engaging citizens in the making of public policy and program decisions. Such engagement reaches all corners of a society, as citizens voice their concerns individually or collectively via organizations in the public, private, and non-profit sectors.

The growing importance of electronic governance and cross-boundary collaboration results from the confluence of various factors. The development of ICTs is a significant driving force. The advancement of Internet technologies and the development of communication infrastructure (including cellular and smart phones) both enable citizens and government to interact online and via mobile devices. The growth in the number and increasing sophistication of online populations in developed countries and around the world speak to the importance of delivering public information and services online. Moreover, the recent growth of Web 2.0 has begun a new chapter in interactivity and engagement. Governments with more advanced technologies and an active online citizenry have begun to experiment with new ways of interacting with citizens for policy making and service delivery.

Another factor is the increasing recognition of the need for types of cross-boundary collaboration that can create public value. Providing citizen-centric public information and services requires both the horizontal and vertical integration of government information and services. A citizen receives a myriad of infrastructure, health, social, and human services from government; a progressive government is responsible for integrating those services for individual citizens, as opposed to requiring citizens to juggle the services of numerous departments. As advances in ICTs make horizontal and vertical integration possible, the increasing reliance on non-governmental organizations for public service production further elevates the importance of cross-boundary collaboration across the public, private, and non-profit sectors. ICTs play an important role in lowering the cost of such collaboration and monitoring the performance of the complex webs of organizations that provide public services.

Significant challenges lie ahead for the realization of the potential of citizen-centric democratic governance via the use of ICTs. One of these hurdles is the gap in our knowledge with regard to the theory and practice of electronic governance. One main reason for this gap is the fast-paced technological changes. For instance, the recent growth of Web 2.0, increase use of "smart" devices (i.e. smart phones and i-Pad), and expanded use of cloud computing all have implications for government-citizen interaction in a democracy. The next reason for the knowledge gap is the complexity of integration needed for successful e-governance and the resulting difficulty in studying complex problems. Such complexity originates from competing political interests, organizational goals, and technological systems and standards. Finally, scholarly attention to electronic governance has not kept pace with new technological developments and growing complexity judged by the number and quality of relevant journal articles.

Thus, the primary goal of this edited volume is to advance our knowledge about the theory and practice of electronic governance with a focus on cross-boundary collaboration. In particular, this edited volume makes a contribution to the following areas. First, it provides policy and implementation frameworks for e-governance cross-boundary collaboration and integration. Second, it enhances our understanding of the behavior of various e-governance stakeholder groups. Third, it advances our knowledge of evaluation tools and techniques that can be used to improve e-governance performance. Fourth, it examines online citizen participation, paying special attention to recent Web 2.0 developments, while examining certain electronic governance issues such as information access, politics, and institutions. Lastly, this edited volume draws from international experiences to provide diversity in institutional contexts and relevance to countries around the globe.

The main target audiences of the volume are scholars and practitioners interested in improving the theory and practice of electronic governance. That is, scholars and students in the field of public administration/affairs, public policy, political science, and information science focus on the role of Information Technology in public affairs will benefit from this volume. As for practitioners who may be interested in this volume, these include those in government responsible for implementing e-government and e-governance projects and those in non-governmental organizations that engage government in democratic governance issues. Almost all of the chapters will have specific policy and management lessons relevant for practitioners.

THEMES AND INSIGHTS

This edited volume treats several interrelated themes, the first of which centers on cross-boundary integration and collaboration. The chapters organized under this theme shed light on government implementation frameworks for information and technology integration, thus illuminating the analysis of implementation experience. The next theme complements the first, supplementing it with the perspective of e-governance users. The third section incorporates the perspectives of service providers and users, focusing on the evaluation of outcomes and performance, and evaluation criteria and tools, all of which are essential to improving e-governance performance. The subsequent section investigates the larger infrastructural, institutional, political, and organizational conditions required for successful e-governance; it strongly emphasizes a range of international experiences, which broadens the institutional contexts examined here. Finally, the last section examines growth trends in the online population as well as the use of Web 2.0. This discussion is particularly useful for scholars and practitioners who aim to advance the field of e-governance. What follows is a more in-depth discussion of the above mentioned themes, featuring brief introductions to the chapters found in this volume.

Cross-Boundary Integration and Collaboration

Tzeng and Hu's chapter identifies critical issues facing cross-boundary integration and collaboration for e-government services. The authors use a focus-group approach to examine electronic public service integration in Taipei, Taiwan, and are able to uncover certain relevant issues, such as legal and institutional constraints, information privacy and security, trust, data ownership, nature of service, and technical readiness. The issues listed above have been empirically grounded, confirming their relevance, even in a non-Western context. Moreover, Tzeng and Hu argue for the importance of leadership and incentives in addressing barriers to cross-boundary collaboration for e-governance. Thus, a policy recommendation points to the need for a careful analysis of both the supply and demand of cross-boundary e-government services. This deliberative approach will help anticipate and remove barriers to e-governance integration and collaboration.

The government information sharing framework proposed by Estevez, Fillottrani, Janowski, and Ojo provides a multidimensional and operational framework for cross-boundary integration of government information. Moreover, this framework--which encompasses technological, organizational, inter-organizational, and environmental dimensions--can serve as an implementation template for addressing issues in e-governance information integration. Furthermore, the emphasis on capacity building, as marked by stages of maturity of experience in sharing, infrastructure support, and information strategy, is especially instructive for implementation. Thus, the recommended framework improves the conceptual clarity and implementation effectiveness of government information sharing. To illustrate the framework's relevance, the authors apply it to cases in Australia, the United Kingdom, the United States of America, New Zealand, and Estonia. The international reach of the case studies, which are located in four continents, further increases the framework's applicability.

Sung's chapter offers executive insights into government-wide integration and collaboration for e-governance. He highlights the critical role of cross-boundary integration in moving to e-governance, capitalizing on his extensive leadership experience in guiding government-wide e-government projects in Taiwan. He offers practical implementation strategies, such as managing interdependence and adapting to environmental changes to move e-governance forward. Specific activities for strategy implementation include the promotion of common standards, articulation of service value, and strengthening of control and coordination mechanisms. The two implementation cases, namely e-government services platform and e-housekeeper services, offer rich examples of practicing cross-boundary integration.

The analysis of Belgium's design and implementation of government-wide cross-boundary e-governance in Leyman's chapter offers important insights. It reinforces citizen-centric information and services as the core value and design principle of e-governance. The author's design of an e-government system has an identity and access management system at its core, and this helps integrate electronic services from various government departments. This design has implications for Europe as a whole. A viable model for integration of e-government, Leyman argues, should be a federated one. The federated structure is in alignment with the institutional framework of the European Union, and this European perspective further sheds light on cross-broader collaboration of electronic governance.

Citizen/User Centric E-Governance

Chang and Obi's chapter proposes and empirically tests a user-centric model of e-governance, with an emphasis on user satisfaction with e-services. The authors surveyed citizens as e-governance service users in Taipei and Tokyo. Their findings suggest the positive impact that citizens' experience in public affairs has on the perceived quality of e-services. In contrast, the perception of risks associated with the use of IT-enabled government services negatively impacts the perception of e-service quality. Interestingly, citizens' expectation does not bear a statistically significant relationship with satisfaction, when the perception of e-service quality is controlled for. The main contributions of this study include underscoring the importance of first understanding the user when designing and implementing e-governance services and providing a comprehensive user-centric model of e-service satisfaction. Specific policy lessons drawn from both cities underscore the need for broad-based positive civic engagement and the importance of mitigating perceived risks associated with e-services.

The focus on civil servants and the inclusion of organizational variables in Chiang's chapter further expand our understanding of users and multiply the dimensions considered in modeling users/citizens. The survey of Taiwanese civil servants gives insight into cross-boundary e-governance systems that have civil servants as the target users. Empirical findings raise the importance of attitudes and norms in determining intention to accept online service delivery. The relevance of attitudes and norms speaks to the role of the organizational culture as a key driver in adopting online service delivery. A surprising finding is that technical skill level is not an important factor for determining adoption, when several other factors such as risks and attitude are controlled for. Perhaps, technical skill acts as a threshold and a tech-savvy civil service has passed that threshold and is thus inconsequential in adoption decisions.

Citizen centricity should be an important design principle for successful e-governance, as the critical review of Thailand's e-government plan in Tubtimhin's chapter suggests. Such principle provides justification and momentum for the integration between the front and end-office e-government applications as well as the vertical and horizontal integration for successful e-governance. Thailand's effort to develop comprehensive ICT and e-government plans over the last decade highlights some challenges and opportunities shared by other developing countries in improving e-governance. The improvement needed in accessibility, infrastructure, ICT literacy, business process, organizational design, management, and assessment will help propel Thailand and other countries to the next level of citizen-centric e-governance.

Evaluation Instruments and E-Governance Assessment

Morgeson's chapter fills an important lacuna in our knowledge concerning the impact of e-governance from the user's perspective. This external perspective provides a more balanced e-government performance measurement model that can put adequate weight on user experience. Morgeson brings to focus what matters to users/citizens/customers. These include basic elements such as navigation, search, and look and feel, all of which can have significant implications for user online experience of government. These elements, along with investigation of U.S. federal government websites, serve as the foundation for an assessment framework that incorporates citizen (external) perspectives. Such an e-government performance assessment framework for government-wide adoption can serve as an important tool to monitor and improve e-government services.

In their chapter, Hsiao, Chu, and Lee address an under-studied but critical group of stakeholders in successful e-governance: businesses. Moreover, the authors make a significant contribution to the development of an outcome-oriented e-governance model that advances the theory and practice of e-governance assessment. The notion of public trust, satisfaction, and adoption, as well as costs and benefits, are included in the outcomes. A large, government-wide empirical study, coupled with integration of relevant bodies of literature, lend a strong theoretical and practical grounding to the model. The authors' study of a labor insurance system in Taiwan yielded over 4,000 valid responses; thus, it can offer insights into the validity of an evaluation instrument. This chapter will be particularly relevant for those interested in conceptualization and operationalization of e-governance impact.

The chapter by Huang, Lee, and Hsiao empirically studies the use of online surveys as instruments for evaluating e-governance. Using online surveys to gauge user experience of e-governance has the advantages of low cost and speedy response. Data are collected in electronic format and ready for prompt analysis. The authors draw on their combined experience with conducting online surveys to evaluate e-governance, and they are able to identify several challenges, such as low response rates, difficulties in achieving representativeness, and challenges posed when working with government agencies. The authors propose several ways to increase response rates and to achieve a higher level of representativeness, such as offering surveys immediately upon completion of e-governance transactions and weighting to represent underlying demographics. Securing cooperation from government agencies to conduct survey and evaluation of e-governance activities, as suggested by the authors, will require building a long-term partnership between the research team in academia and the targeted government agency. These are important lessons for not only research teams, but also government agencies that are considering using online surveys in evaluating e-governance.

Rodríguez-Bolívar, Caba-Pérez, and López-Hernández's chapter applies the CapGemini methodology to the evaluation of municipal e-government services in select Latin American and Caribbean (LAC) countries. This study fills the knowledge gap with regards to the performance of e-government in nineteen LAC countries such as Argentina, Ecuador, Paraguay, Peru, Cuba, and Brazil, to name a few. Empirical investigation focuses on capital cities that can serve as good barometers of development progress. These LAC countries represent an area of potential growth in the application of e-government. Moreover, the utilization of an established methodology, CapGemini, provides for a systematic and comparative evaluation of e-government and policy lessons. In general, there is significant scope for development. Another important policy lesson is the need for public administration reforms to foster more open and participatory government. Such basic reforms will help realize the type of e-inclusion which the next stage of e-government calls for.

Wood's chapter uses e-government stages theory to critically examine the e-government of U.S. county governments. Wood adapted and integrated several models of e-government development to develop a stage theory, which proves to be productive in tracking the development of e-governance, identifying areas for improvement, and formulating developmental strategies. One defining feature of more advanced e-government is the maturity of integration and civic engagement. Wood evaluates the e-government performance of a random sample of 100 counties in two time periods, 2007 and 2010. The results suggest a more cautionary approach to the highly anticipated e-government benefits. Limited development is present particularly in the area of civic engagement.

Institutional and Political Aspects of E-Governance

Relly's chapter examines the institutions for electronic governance in India and China. The theoretical lens adopted is institutionalism. Viewing laws and regulations focused on government information access (open government) as the core institution for e-governance is instructive because access to government information is one of the main conditions for meaningful citizen participation both offline and online. The large populations and economic dynamism of India and China elevate the importance of this empirical investigation. This study underscores the great potential of e-governance in both countries, even amidst challenges posed by political systems and infrastructure. The comparison between China and India reveals how "engines" of e-governance development can differ: China relies more on government and academia, while India is more reliant on grassroots movements. India is facing profound challenges in terms of literacy rates and infrastructure development, while this is less so for China. A common theme is the critical importance of political support and infrastructural development (institutional and physical) in efforts to realize the potential of e-governance.

Shiang, Lo, and Wang's empirical investigation of the implementation of freedom of information regulations provides valuable lessons on national implementation. Their analysis of the five-year implementation of Taiwan's Freedom of Information Act underscores the importance of back-office support. An indicator of progress can be seen in the fact that most public agencies in Taiwan have a designated section focused on meeting freedom of information regulations. Interestingly, freedom of information requests via established channels are rare. Such requests, when filed and processed, are mostly via opinion e-mail boxes of public agencies. This finding points toward the need for a comprehensive look at how citizens interact with government when obtaining government information. The research, moreover, highlights the importance of strong back-office support of implementation.

Sanchez and Ganapati's study of the role of the Internet in diasporic Iranian and Eritrean communities underscores both the innovative use of the Internet for political mobilization and the importance of political and institutional relationships in mediating the influences exerted by these communities. This chapter expands this edited volume's coverage to include the Middle East and Africa. The uses of social networking, blogging, and other new media are examples of the innovative use of new Internet technologies in electronic governance. The ability to mobilize diasporic communities in various host countries and connect with fellow countrymen in their homeland demonstrates the Internet's ability to connect people across time and space. The authors discern three factors that mediate the impact of such political mobilization on polity, including the diasporic communities' relationships with home governments, their ability to create linkages, and their power relations with homeland populations.

Yang's chapter provides a timely and insightful discussion of the nature and challenges of e-governance in China. Based partly on a review of relevant studies and policy statements, the study reveals China's commitment to modernizing its administration via the use of information and communication technology. However, the orientation is administrative in nature, with a heavy emphasis on control. As a result, the Chinese government faces significant challenges in meeting the increasing public demand for online participation in policy-making. But China's emphasis on government control is likely to mean that it may miss opportunities to engage citizens online. Yang argues that to advance e-governance, the Chinese government needs to conduct a critical examination of guiding values (control vs. engagement). In fact, this is an important lesson for any country aiming to develop its e-governance capacity.

New Frontier in E-Governance

Yang, Zhang, and Tang's chapter, entitled "Internet Use and Governance in China," explores various e-governance issues and provides a timely assessment and forecast. This chapter advances our knowledge of e-governance in two ways. First, it provides a broad review of Internet use as it relates to electronic governance in China, a country with the largest online population in the world (beginning in 2008). The authors provide a review that covers the political and social implications of Internet use in a developing country, using credible, national statistics acquired from the China Internet Network Information Center. Second, this chapter reviews studies of e-government websites in China and provides an illustration of the development of e-governance in the public sector. The authors are able to identify various areas for improvement, especially the need for integrating e-government systems at all levels of government. China's experience charts a new territory in terms of how government can capitalize on its citizens' fast-growing Internet use. The use of Internet for civic engagement, an essential component for e-governance, depends on democratization and institutional changes.

Pan, Chen, and Wang's chapter pushes the envelope of e-governance by examining an innovative Web 2.0 public governance application in Taiwan. The authors first developed a framework for assessing government use of Web 2.0 by synthesizing the research literature on the value of public governance offered by Web 2.0. Using this framework, they conduct an empirical study of the central government's Vision 2020 Web site, which utilizes Web 2.0 features to facilitate the interaction between the elite and the general public in the process of envisioning Taiwan's future. The authors argue that the government must engage citizens with Web 2.0 technologies—it is a growing technology, and trust can be gained with active engagement. The main policy and management lessons concern the need to focus on ease-of-use to achieve a higher level of engagement, as well as the need for leadership to facilitate back-end integration. This study offers a much-needed analytical framework and management recommendations for advancing e-governance, just as more countries are beginning to formulate and implement plans to take advantage of Web 2.0 technologies for public governance.

Chen's contribution to this volume, an analysis of the U.S. federal government implementation of Government 2.0, further enhances our knowledge with regard to utilizing Web 2.0 to improve public governance. The United States is at the forefront of technological innovation. The long-standing tradition of open government also provides the institutional foundation for online civic engagement. This chapter provides a framework and specific policy and management recommendations for countries aiming to pursue Government 2.0. An adequate framework for Government 2.0, the author states, needs to be comprehensive; it must encompass policy/managerial, organizational, and technological dimensions. This chapter also highlights certain critical success factors, such as having policy guidance and supporting institutions, providing incentives and resources, and developing and promoting government-wide technical standards for better implementation.

MAIN CONTRIBUTIONS AND OPPORTUNITIES

This edited volume makes several contributions to the advancement of electronic governance. First, it provides insights into the theory and practice of improving electronic governance. To move to the next level of maturity, electronic governance needs to address challenging issues surrounding cross-boundary collaboration, civic engagement, institution-building, and innovative technologies (i.e. Web 2.0). Collectively, the chapters in this volume address these issues. Second, this volume provides useful frameworks for implementation and evaluation, such as frameworks for cross-boundary integration of government Information Systems, citizen-centric e-governance services, and evaluation of e-government performance. These frameworks are grounded in the research literature and critical investigation of existing practice.

Another main contribution of this volume is the coverage of countries that are either emerging or leading in the implementation of e-governance. China, India, and Latin American countries are charting courses in electronic governance. Several chapters in this volume provide in-depth examination of the challenges and opportunities respective to each country. Several chapters also offer a critical examination of leading examples of e-governance and thus are able to provide policy lessons relevant for those countries at the beginning stages of development. Web 2.0 in the United States, citizen-centric systems in Belgium, and government-wide integration in Taiwan are such examples. Collectively, these chapters also underscore the importance of political/managerial commitment, institutional support, performance evaluation, and citizen-centric service and engagement in e-governance success.

Future research should examine the implementation and evaluation frameworks suggested here, but applied in various contexts. Also, future studies can focus on the efforts of developing countries to advance e-governance based on this volume's rigorous empirical investigations of e-governance integration and civic engagement. Furthermore, e-governance performance evaluation is another productive area of future research; diminishing public resources and calls for accountability both require tracking and improving e-governance performance. Moreover, scholars and practitioners should begin to monitor the impact of the rapid development of Web 2.0 and Semantic Webs, not to mention, the impact of the increasing connectivity and openness offered by "smart" mobile devices. Clearly, government is in a position to lead the effort to develop technical standards that are able to ensure interoperability and identity management schemes that can foster citizen trust.

Yu-Che Chen
Northern Illinois University, USA

Pin-Yu Chu
National Chengchi University, Taiwan

Acknowledgment

The editors are grateful for the generous assistance and support of various organizations and individuals. Without their dedication, this project could not come to a successful completion. Taiwan Electronic Governance Research Center (TEG) is our most significant institutional supporter. It provided both personnel and financial support in the formulation and implementation of this volume. Dr. Jay N. Shih deserves a special mention as he was instrumental in founding TEG. Moreover, Dr. Yu-Hsien Sung, the leading e-government official in Taiwan, has provided significant support for this project via TEG.

The editors would like to recognize several members of the Editorial Advisory Board. We thank Charles Schweik for providing his insight into improving the quality of this volume. Chris Reddick was kind in sharing his experience with developing an edited volume.

Moreover, we would like to thank our assistants for their timely and outstanding service. Dr. Chu would like to thank Luo-Wei Li, Chih-Cheng Kung, and Li-Jung Yang for their thorough administrative assistance during various phases of the book development. Jianchuan Zhang assisted Dr. Chen in implementing the electronic review process and in putting together the final package for submission. Zhang's attention to details is much appreciated.

Chu's deepest gratitude goes to her family for their unflagging love and support. She would like to thank her parents for providing her with the opportunity to be where she is. She would like to thank her husband, Yehliang, and her sweetest daughter, Yang, because they have been her biggest support throughout her professional career.

Chen would like to express his gratitude for his family. The loving memory of his father has propelled him in pursuit of excellence and quality. He appreciates the support of his mother and elder brother. Li-Fen Lu, his wife, and Wesley, his toddler son, have provided much needed balance.

Yu-Che Chen
Northern Illinois University, USA

Pin-Yu Chu
National Chengchi University, Taiwan

Section 1
Cross-Boundary Integration and Collaboration

Chapter 1
To Cross or not to Cross the Boundaries? A Reflection on Electronic Public Service Integration

Kuan-Chiu Tseng
Tamkang University & Taiwan E-Governance Research Center, Taiwan

Lung-Teng Hu
National Taipei University & Taiwan E-Governance Research Center, Taiwan

ABSTRACT

Parallel with the rapid evolution of information and communication technologies, customer service delivery is confronting a radical transformation in both the public and private sectors. One-stop service delivery with inter-organizational integration, even joined-up with government, has become an appealing vision, as well as a desideratum of future public service provision. However, while a significant body of literature on business process reengineering and inter-organizational system presents the possibility of ubiquitous public service delivery, some governmental organizations remain reluctant to adopt this model.

This chapter aims to deal with the following questions. Is electronic cross-boundary service integration a desirable vision of e-governance? If so, why isn't everyone jumping on this bandwagon? What are the potential factors which the proponents of electronic cross-boundary governance should take into account which may influence departmental adoption of electronic public service integration? Is electronic cross-boundary governance a one-size-fit-all solution? This chapter seeks to answer the questions with a case study of Taipei online e-services provided by the Taipei City government. Because Taipei online e-services attempts to provide a digital platform by which citizens in Taipei City are able to complete most applications, requests, payments, even tracking requests, it is regarded as a system which threads multiple service operational procedures as well as databases across departmental boundaries. The vision raised by Taipei online e-services is very close to the promise offered by e-governance proponents.

DOI: 10.4018/978-1-60960-753-1.ch001

Still, certain services cannot be completed online fully. Most service deliveries which cannot be fully completed online fall into the departments which are significantly associated with the government's economic performance as well as citizens' quality of life, such as economic development, urban development, land, transportation, civil affairs, social welfare, and finance. In fact, the departments indicated above have to collaboratively interact with each other in order to provide citizen services.

To explore the reasons why certain services could not be digitally integrated and fully provided online, some focus-group interviews were conducted with key officials of the municipal departments mentioned above. Governmental insiders were able to offer some compelling factors which critically influence the integration of e-services. Surprisingly, some officials raised challenges: Is it merely rhetoric or is it imperative to integrate full services across departmental boundaries under e-governance? Research results and implications for electronic cross-boundary governance will be discussed in this chapter.

INTRODUCTION

Typically, a one-stop service center is "an umbrella organization that operates on top of existing functional departments in order to maximize the convenience and satisfaction of users through service integration" (Ho, 2002, pp. 436). Due to the fact that specialization and information silos are two of the key factors behind the occurrence of fragmented responses (Linden, 2010, p. 19), one-stop service with inter-organizational integration, even joined-up government (Perri 6, 2004; Pollitt, 2003), has become an appealing vision as well as a desideratum of future public service. For example, Choudrie and Weerrakody (2007) believe that the achievement of horizontal integration among local authorities in the e-government context can better deliver e-services to citizens.

With the rapid evolution of information and communication technologies (ICTs), customer service delivery is being confronted with a radical transformation in both the public and private sectors. This chapter focuses on this issue: Is the electronic cross-boundary governance (ECBG) a one-size-fit-all solution? There are various stages of e-government, each of which reflects a degree of technical sophistication or maturity (Moon, 2002, p. 426): (1) simple information dissemination (one-way communication); (2) two-way communication (request and response); (3) service and financial transactions; (4) integration (horizontal and vertical integration); and (4) political participation. This implies that governments have to deal with the numerous and significant impediments to the integration of government information and services (Coursey & Norris, 2008, p. 525). A report notes that unless governments endeavor to transform themselves into integrated entities through developing integrated back-office infrastructures, they will find it difficult to fully respond to the needs of their citizens (UN, 2008, p. 16). It would be valuable, therefore, to examine what and how potential factors would affect the process at different stages of e-government evolution, especially those more sophisticated features.

Although citizen-centered service is an emerging issue in e-government (Alshawi & Alalwany, 2009; Bertot, Jaeger, & McClure, 2008; Ho, 2002; Schedler & Summermatter, 2007), scholarly literature reminds us that government actions are mediated by many factors, each of which restricts ICTs' ability to transform society (e.g. institutional arrangements, budget scarcity, group conflict, cultural norms, and prevailing patterns of social and political behavior) (Fountain, 2001). Thus technology innovation in the public sector tends to be incremental rather than transformational (West, 2004, p.14). With this in mind, certain researchers have used different theoretical lens to examine the causes of the diffusion of e-government innovations. According to research findings, for example, Korteland and Bekkers (2007), suggest that to understand e-government innovation diffusion in the public sector requires attending to both the logic of consequence and the logic of appropriateness. Moon and Norris (2005) find that managerial innovativeness orientation is one of the most compelling determinants of municipal e-government adoption. Ho and Ni (2004) confirm that the support of political leadership and concerns about staff workload are significant factors in e-government adoption decisions.

The authors focus on electronic public service integration across departments or agencies. Correspondingly, ECBG can be defined as initiatives which intend to bridge silo information systems to connect government agencies as well as to help agencies share, exchange, and integrate information resources by the application of ICTs. ECBG can be observed through a platform that attempts to provide integrated public services. That is, citizens can have access to the e-service that links, to some extent, the front office and back office via the introduction of ICTs when accompanied by the redesign of the business processes. A strong body of literature on inter-organizational system and business process redesign has noted the possibility of ubiquitous public service delivery. However, some governmental organizations are not adopting this model.[1] This chapter aims to address the following questions: Is the electronic cross-boundary service integration a desirable vision under the promise of e-governance? If so, why isn't everyone jumping on this bandwagon? What are the potential factors, which the proponents of electronic cross-boundary governance should take into account, which may influence departmental adoption of electronic public service integration?[2]

The authors seek to answer these questions with a case study of Taipei online e-services provided by Taipei City government. Taipei online e-services is attempting to provide a digital platform by which citizens in Taipei are able to complete most applications, requests, payments, and even tracking requests. It is regarded as a system which threads multiple service operational procedures and multiple databases across departmental boundaries. The vision raised by Taipei online e-services is very close to the promise offered by e-governance proponents. However, certain services cannot be fully completed online. The service deliveries which cannot be fully completed online belong to departments that are significantly associated with government economic performance as well as citizen quality of life, such as economic development, urban development, land, transportation, civil affairs, social welfare, and finance.[3] In fact, the participating departments indicated above have to collaboratively interact with each other in order to provide citizen services.

In the initial discussion below, the authors will review the literature regarding inter-organizational system and business process redesign.[4] Then we will describe the research design, review the methods of data collection and analysis, and introduce relevant background information for the case study. Then we will present the case analysis and its implications. Finally, we will provide a brief conclusion.

LITERATURE REVIEW

Inter-Organizational System (IOS)

The inter-organizational system (IOS), as defined by Kumar and van Dissel (1996, p. 279), is an ICT-based system that transcends legal enterprise boundaries. The conceptual evolution of IOS can be traced to Barrett and Konsynski, who in 1982 denoted it as an inter-organizational information sharing system, while the term "inter-organizational system" was first coined by Cash and Konsynski to refer to an automated information system shared by two or more organizations (Hong, 2002). Hong (2002) describes IOS as a networked information system which extends beyond traditional organizational boundaries. Similarly,

Boonstra and de Vries (2005) also consider IOS as ICT-based systems which enable organizations to share information and business processes across organizational boundaries. Accordingly, IOS is a networked ICT-based system that organizations can use to share data and information across boundaries. Yet, the principle of organizational design primarily depends on professional divisions. Moreover, privacy and information security are always core concerns in information system installment. Then, what is the compelling trigger of IOS development? Due to the dramatic effect of transaction cost reduction related to information use and exchange among partner organizations, the radical development of IOS is derived from the desires of competitiveness enhancement and efficiency improvement, since both the public and private sectors can benefit from this logic (Volkoff, Chan, & Newson, 1999). Gradually, increasing attention has been paid to the application of IOS in the public sector, especially to bring about electronic cross-boundary service integration with the aim of public value creation (Schooley & Horan, 2007). In turn, e-governments worldwide are experiencing the tendency of information integration across jurisdictional, functional, and organizational boundaries (Fedorowicz, Gogan, & Williams, 2007).

Clearly, the major function of IOS is to reduce the costs of duplicated database implementation and maintenance as well as to achieve the benefits of better information quality and higher service efficiency (Gil-Garcia, Chengalur-Smith, & Duchessi, 2007). To arrive at a collaborative e-government initiative (Klievink & Janssen, 2009), proponents of IOS not only foresee the possibility of interagency information integration and networked service provision in the public sector, but they also expect IOS initiatives to bridge organization silo systems and turfs. By aligning with IOS in the public sector, collaborative organizations can unify system platforms and formal standards, and shorten business processes to speed up information exchange and sharing, and then further achieve the expected benefits of better services, operational savings, and increased program effectiveness (Gil-Garcia et al., 2007). Broadly speaking, the electronic cross-boundary service integration in government with IOS attempts to expedite information sharing as well as to co-produce public services effectively through collaborative networks (Fedorowicz et al., 2007), even through symbiotic networks (Volkoff et al., 1999).

While IOS optimists promote an appealing scenario featuring electronic cross-boundary public services, pessimists reveal the challenges sometimes left unacknowledged. According to Schooley and Horan (2007), the utilization of IOS in the governmental context has three issue dimensions that need to be addressed: operational, organizational, and governance dimensions. In addition to the operational dimension, the lack of shared goals, lack of agreement on cooperation and trust, as well as cultural differences pose as critical factors in the organizational dimension. Meanwhile, there are issues related to unclear lines of inter-organizational authority and accountability. This tends to impede information sharing and integration (Schooley & Horan, 2007). In summary, the application of IOS, like any IS implementation, is obviously much more than a simple technical issue.

A collaborative e-government initiative always involves multiple organizational participants. However, each participant has its motivation to join the initiative. In this regard, the motivations of participants should be sufficiently reflected in the project by aligning their technical, political, economic and operational occasions (Fedorowicz et al., 2007). As suggested, the use of IOS often results in political struggles (Homburg, 2000). Power and interests are dominating determinations of IOS shape and use (Boonstra & de Vries, 2005). Independence of partner organization, formal authority, controls over technology, and inter-organizational alliances and networks are all the possible factors shaping the progress of IOS

(Boonstra & de Vries, 2005). The offer of proper incentives and the avoidance of excessive harm in the data ownership of participating organizations are critical for the success of IOS initiatives as well (Homburg, 2000). In addition, it has also been found that the lack of coordination among governments and resistance to change by government officials are the most common barriers in European e-government development experiences (Eynon & Dutton, 2007). Bensaou (1997) also suggests the importance of relationships and governance structure in an IOS project. Fedorowicz et al. (2007) look at the factor dimensions of external environment, agency context, and collaborative network in an emergency service IOS initiative, and found that IOS initiatives should be initiated with the alignment interests and resources of participating organizations. Further, they suggest a need for multiple champions during the evolution of IOS initiatives. Consequently, the societal, political and economic demands and interests of the partnering organizations absolutely cannot be ignored. In contrast, there should be someone in charge to reconcile these interests. Luna-Reyes, Gil-Garcia, and Cruz (2007) similarly hold that if the institutional designs, organizational structures, and business processes do not support and are unfriendly towards inter-organizational collaborative information sharing, then the building of IOS cannot succeed. Accordingly, calculations of advantages, domain dominance, degree of interdependence, and transaction costs are extremely crucial factors in information sharing across organizational boundaries (Boonstra & de Vries, 2005).

Business Reengineering Redesign (BPR)

Although successful back-office integration will result in new processes (UN, 2008, p. 158), successful electronic boundary-spanning governance also relies on new processes—whether through business process reengineering or change. According to Hammer and Champy (1993), the key aspect of business process reengineering is the fundamental and radical change of business processes to achieve dramatic improvements. Business-process change in the public sector mostly means unification of business processes, automation of some activities and elimination of some others (Stemberger & Jaklic, 2007, p. 222). Although there are certain differences between process reengineering and change, both are included here in the definition of redesign.

E-government implementation is not only technological, it also involves organizational and business process redesign (Beynon-Davies, 2005). According to Stemberger and Jaklic (2007), e-government cannot be successfully implemented without redesign in business processes that are performed inside government institutions. Also, Lam (2005) argues that organizational barriers, such as pace of government reform and legacy government processes, should be addressed if the aim is to achieve a mature level of e-government. A clear fact, hence, is that redesign of interagency processes and the provision of the appropriate technical infrastructure both have been identified as critical elements, especially in striving for citizen-centered e-government (Hughes, Scott, & Golden, 2006).

As mentioned, achieving a mature and sophisticated level of e-government requires integration (Coursey & Norris, 2008; Lam, 2005; Moon, 2002; UN, 2008). Since e-government projects in practice are not always able to fully implement transactional processes, part of the value added by e-government is not sufficiently utilized. Researchers intend to present the BPR procedure or methodology suitable for the public sector. The UN (2008, p. 158) delineates common steps in managing the development and implementation of new processes.[5] Becker, Algermissen, and Niehaves (2006) provide guidelines in the form of a procedural model for e-government-indicated BPR projects. The authors note that the development of a reference process model as a store of domain knowledge, to some degree, can reduce the complexity of e-government projects and also simplify their implementation via an orientation around reference processes.

Nevertheless, BPR in the field of electronic boundary–spanning governance is not an easy task, especially when practiced in the public sector. Successful BPR in the public sector usually has to fulfill the following conditions (McAdam & Donaghy, 1999, p. 48): (1) top management support, commitment and understanding of BPR; (2) communication; (3) empowerment; (4) alleviation of downsizing fears; (5) preparedness for organizational change; (6) choosing the redesign team; (7) enlisting customer and stakeholder support. In a case study, Weerakkody, Baire, and Choudrie (2006) note that technical complexities, such as the need to integrate business processes across government agencies, can present the most significant challenges to implementing fully integrated e-government services. The authors maintain that a legacy of bureaucracy and established illogical routine tasks can prevent the government from expediting its e-government initiative.

Furthermore, based upon the general framework of Kettinger, Teng, and Guha (1997), Stemberger and Jaklic (2007) note that if we need to redesign business processes in the government sector, the following issues should be addressed: (1) organizational structures are rigid, project resources are scarce, senior management commitment is difficult to achieve, several processes are predominantly intra-functional, the culture supports the status quo, readiness for radical redesign is low in public institutions; (2) some processes are governed by laws and many processes are partially semi-structured or even unstructured, so they vary greatly in comparison with business; (3) although customer-oriented management and simplification of procedures are imperative and constitute the central aim for BPR in the public sector, the goal usually is not to attract new customers but to keep current ones.[6] Finally, Stemberger and Jaklic (2007) conclude that radical redesign in the execution of business processes are not suitable for the public sector.

Similarly, Hughes et al. (2006, pp. 84-86) observe that a complete understanding of the intricate and bureaucratic processes which combine to form citizen services is necessary to the identification of the process or elements of processes that can be redesigned or left unchanged. Put differently, the point is to investigate the unique nature of processes within the public sector so that information system platforms can be developed to accommodate less efficient processes rather than platforms that require unobtainable process redesign. Thus, it is not surprising that some would suggest that the definition of such collaborative processes may be problematic, unless it were possible to fully grasp the domain knowledge of the workflow of each government agency and fully comprehend what is achievable with the technology (Lam, 2005, p. 521).[7]

Following this logic, Willcoeks and Smith (1995) remind us that since IT-enabled BPR programs are likely to marginalize attention to human, social and political processes, management of the politics of change needs to be put at the core of BPR activity.[8] In a case study, Hesson and Al-Ameed (2007, p. 362) similarly observe that one obstacle can be seen in the reluctance of decision makers to relinquish or reduce some of their authority. Other factors such as resistance to change, and job redundancy resulting from change and financial resource change also need to be taken seriously. In summary, it is clear that the BPR literature indicates that while IT is one of the key elements in redesigning business processes, other factors such as structural change, organizational change and human resources should not be neglected.

RESEARCH METHOD

Case Selection

In this paper, the authors choose the Taipei e-services online (TESO) as the subject of our case study. The reason we have chosen TESO is because, firstly, the contents of TESO essentially correspond with the topic of electronic boundary-spanning governance, in both aspects of horizontal integration and vertical integration in governmental systems. Secondly, TESO has been established for eight years by the Taipei government, and it is a pioneering and the most famous case of its kind in Taiwan. After the TESO initiative, many central and local government authorities gradually adopted this technology innovation for their citizens. In short, the TESO initiative no doubt is a representative case and the research findings will be meaningful and significant for the larger research community in the e-government field.

Focus Group Interview

A focus group interview, which was held on October 6, 2009, was utilized to gather empirical data. *Focus group* is a type of collective *interview which is carried out by the author as a moderator in a* non-structured manner with a small group of respondents. The moderator intends to create an easy and comfortable atmosphere that evokes participant self-disclosure (Krueger & Casey, 2009, p. 4). In this method, group dynamic and interaction is a valuable and distinctive product. To be specific, the authors would gain sufficient insights by listening to a group of people if they can express their arguments and respond to each other's opinions freely. To attain this aim the authors have to identify the interviewees and develop the interview protocol surrounding the research interests before the meeting.

An interesting fact is that not all of the service items in this case can be dealt with digitally. That is, in terms of the business process, some are processed thoroughly via Internet and others are not, due to their attribute differences. To understand the nuances among service items, the rationale for sample selection should be taken into consideration. After reviewing the service item list of TESO, a total of nine authorities (i.e. Department of Economic Development, Department of Urban Development, Department of Land, Department of Transportation, Department of Information Technology, Department of Civil Affairs, Department of Social Welfare, Department of Finance, and Research Development and Evaluation Commission) were identified and selected due to the fact that all of them statistically contribute much of the cross-boundary services. However, most of these services are "semi e-services" and "non e-services" for citizens.

In other words, not all of the services were provided digitally. This, to some extent, contradicts our original concept of e-services, and the representatives from the agencies would help solve the puzzle of hindrances to "full e-services". Therefore, based upon the logic of purposive sampling, twenty-two public officers (most of whom were mid-level managers) belonging to nine agencies or bureaus were invited through formal written requests made by the authors to join our focus group interview. Accordingly, the issue of who should participate in the discussion was completely decided by each of the authorities. Except some section chiefs, most of participants were staff responsible for specific application services. The authors tried to separate them into two groups for convenience and efficiency of discussion. With the help of these governmental insiders, we would be able to discover and concentrate on the potential barriers to the full e-services across departmental boundaries.

The interview protocol was also developed to elicit and promote discussion about the challenges facing public managers and their attitudes toward e-services. Table 1 shows our questions, all of which focus on the reasons why thus far

Table 1. Focus group interview protocol

In the first place, as far as you know, what local government authorities are in charge of the TESO initiative? What is the main purpose of TESO? What tasks do you have to undertake in this initiative?
Secondly, so far a large portion of service items in the TESO initiative still cannot fulfill the dream of delivering so-called "full e-services", what do you think of the obstacles to it? In addition, according to your observations, how and to what extent can these obstacles be overcome?
Thirdly, since a lot of service items in this initiative have to be approved by the higher level government authority or reviewed by parallel government authorities in terms of the business process, do you believe that it would be possible to redesign the business process and shorten the process time through the introduction of ICTs?
Fourthly, because many service items are operationally in relation to vertical integration or horizontal integration, do you believe that it would be possible to redesign the business process and reduce the documents and forms provided by applicants via the integration or sharing of databases?
Finally, as far as you know, can you introduce certain databases that have already been shared among government agencies?[9] What do you think of the current status of database sharing? Also, if hindrances do exist, in your opinion, how should they be tackled?

we have yet to actualize the vision of delivering public services completely online.

Obviously, the above questions are designed to help us discover the barriers to electronic public service integration.

Regarding data analysis, the results of the *focus group* interview were permitted to be archived through a digital voice recorder and then converted into transcripts within two weeks. On average, the interviews lasted about two hours, which was enough to complete the interview process. With the help of research assistants, the transcripts were used for data analysis and coding. The analysis process closely followed the logic of grounded theory (Corbin & Strauss, 2008), and the main task involved grouping different kinds of codes or categories into a new one on a hierarchical and systematic basis. The findings were further examined in detail by the other author. One of the authors was in charge of grasping and developing the storyline of the case, and the other assisted by checking the related categories to make sure that they fit data closely. In this way external validity would be enhanced.

Case Description

Taipei is one of the most advanced cities in the world, particularly in terms of information technology infrastructure and wireless broadband applications. Since 1999, the Taipei City government has dedicated most of its resources to the value of "frequent the Net, free up the roads" in order to build up a digitized city. Under this vision, the "Taipei E-Services Online" (TESO) was one of the major initiatives launched in 2002 by the Taipei City government. The program goal of TESO is to provide a more efficient, convenient, and time-saving service platform for the public through the implementation of the Internet and ICTs. In this regard, TESO was created as a web-based, one-stop service portal. By integrating numerous individual online services into a single portal, TESO successfully integrated 64 pilot online services in December 2006. Residents in Taipei City are able to submit requests, pay bills, or merely download application forms from the TESO website. To date, TESO has been providing 28 categories and 471 items of e-services, ranging from civil affairs, finance, police affairs, transportation, education, to health. Among the 471 e-services provided by TESO, 102 items can be completed online, while 369 items should be partially complemented offline.[10] In addition to tracing the progress of e-service requests online, 25 standard services can also be tracked online by citizens. By July 31, 2008, TESO had accumulated 6,850,000 hits and there had been 92,128 e-service requests completed, as well as 3,868,574 application forms downloaded from the TESO website.[11]

The primary logic behind TESO aims at not only connecting back offices and databases but also integrating business processes across individual departments through a single portal in order to provide seamless and integrated e-services. Even the Taipei City government is incrementally approaching its goals.[12] There are still a number of hurdles that TESO confronts. In some sense the status quo remains: there are certain department databases that have yet to be integrated, or even connected to TESO—they still function independently. Moreover, a great number of service items requiring external review, requiring approval or authorization by upper authorities, or requiring conjunct inspections with other authorities can hardly be done digitally through the entire process from start to conclusion.[13]

Nevertheless, the authors wanted to explore the deeper structural reasons beyond the phenomenon that is already known. The authors intend to argue that there shall be critical determinants that strongly influence those Taipei departments that are not jumping on the bandwagon of electronic public service integration. The case analysis and discussions will be presented in the next section.

CASE ANALYSIS AND IMPLICATIONS

Case Analysis

As described previously, TESO is an online platform which integrates e-services across departmental boundaries with a single portal. The digital services offered by the Taipei City government through TESO fall into two categories, full online services and partial online services. While the partial online services require applicants to download application forms and submit them in person, the full online services allow citizens to complete the entire process of application or payment through the Internet. Generally, the full online services are characterized as uncomplicated service items and primarily belonging to a single agency's jurisdiction rather than requiring collaboration between departments.

TESO actually evolved out of the "Documentary Certificate and Transcript Free" system, which attempts not only to streamline the processes of applications and requests, but also simultaneously to alleviate the citizen's burden of providing documentation. Therefore, the system connects databanks most related to the basic information needed for certain online applications, such as household registration, land administration, zoning ordinance and land use designations, fire fighting, and building administration. With the "Documentary Certificate and Transcript Free" system, public officials can easily request information for processing citizen requests at the back end without paper documents. Thus, various online services are provided by TESO based upon the extended implementation of the "Documentary Certificate and Transcript Free" system.

Because the scope or number of full online services offered by TESO is constantly being extended and increased, collaborative needs across departmental boundaries, as contrasted with single-agency service provision, are dramatically emerging. Accordingly, there are still a number of issues of concern to the city government, namely, "To what extent should the full online services be broadened?" or "Is every single item of public service exactly feasible for full online provision?" In order to address these issues as well as to make clear the critical factors below the surface which may affect the willingness of related departments to collaborate with each other, we will focus on the services which are collaboration-intensive. Which is to say, we will examine services which require approvals or authorizations by upper authorities, services such as permit issuance which needs conjunct inspections with other authorities. Based on the focus groups interviews with public officials of the Taipei City government, we discovered the following influential factors:

Constraints of Laws and Rules

Certainly, prerequisites and requirements of administrative procedures are constrained by laws and rules, whether the procedures are operated in brick-and-mortar buildings or in virtual platforms. For example, even if the administrative agency were intending to promote full online services, its success would still be constrained if the legal climate does not provide for adjusting required documentation and proof requirements. On the other hand, one of the incentives of online services is to cut out unnecessary procedures and improve administrative efficiency. Still, simplification of procedures to some degree requires top management authorization and if authorization is not achievable, then the major incentive cannot be realized. In turn, there is no motivation for both citizens and official users to speed up the development of online e-services.

"In terms of the service items #81, #83, and #86 in land administration, it is for sure that these services can never be fully online if the related laws are not able to be revised." (TP-LD-01)

"Actually, we have checked the whole procedure of this (policing) service. We found that the key point is that it is required to be approved by the commissioner. Therefore, the procedure cannot be shortened if there is no chance to revise the law." (TP-RD-01)

Individual privacy is strictly protected by law and accountability is imposed on public employees if any personal information is disclosed illegally. Therefore, the concern with government oversight of information privacy becomes one of the barriers to online service development.

"It is quite simple that if any execution is subject to violation of Article 33 of the Tax Collection Act, no information is allowed to be provided." (TP-IT-01)

Lack of Database Integration

One of the prerequisites of streamlined e-service is the integration of back offices and databases. Particularly, an effective back-office integration should be both horizontally and vertically aligned. However, the challenges confronting TESO include many issues. On the one hand, TESO only covers the residential data of Taipei City. Which is to say, it is hard for Taipei government workers to access information across municipalities via TESO. Applicants sometimes need to provide such documents themselves. Moreover, some of major databanks in the central government have yet to be connected. As a result, Taipei government workers cannot easily search for needed information across databases. They have to go back and forth, checking each related database. Thus, in terms of horizontal and vertical database integration, TESO is facing various obstacles.

"Taking household registration as an example, what we can access is only the information belonging to the Taipei City government. If a citizen comes to me to apply for welfare subsidy, I am sorry to say that I could not approve it instantly, because we have to check whether the applicant has any family member in other counties as well as their income statuses. However, we don't have the authority to reach the databases in other county governments." (TP-IT-01)

"Frankly, it is not easy to build up a city-wide governmental databank. Nevertheless, it is still not good enough for our usage, because we always need decision-making support of nation-wide data." (TP-SW-01)

"I feel so frustrated that the databases of household registration and land administration in the Ministry of the Interior, though they are highly associated with each other, have not been connected or integrated." (TP-CR-01)

Concerns of Personal Privacy and Information Security

Undoubtedly, individual privacy protection and information security are constantly regarded as the main considerations in information technology and e-government development. There is no exception in the implementation of TESO. While citizens may be concerned with the security of governmental databases, public employees, even heads of agencies, also seriously consider the safety of data sharing and transfer; they are usually reluctant to share databases. Specifically, in terms of the establishment of e-services across departments, there is always a tension between information security and convenience of data sharing.

"Citizens' tax information is regarded as highly confidential. Accordingly, the Tax Collection Act rigidly obligates tax agencies to protect individuals' private information. Anyone who violates the Act may be charged with criminal conduct. On the other hand, we establish isolated internet and intranet and minimize the degree of data sharing in order to prevent the risk of unintended information disclosure." (TP-FT-02)

"The most we worry about is the divulgence of individual privacy. No matter how much high-tech facilities you use, there is always the possibility of risk of information divulgence." (TP-SW-02)

Trust, Risk, and Responsibility

Distrust in digital databases of public employees, as well as risk and responsibility aversion, form another obstacle to transboundary e-services. In the case of TESO it is notable that though the "Documentary Certificate and Transcript Free" system has come into effect for already several years, some agency employees occasionally ask applicants to provide updated documents that might be found in the previous system merely because the public employees feel less confident in the system. They seem to prefer to avoid potential risks of administrative accountability by requesting residents to provide proof. Moreover, some administrative agencies intend to refuse digital proofs or certificates (e.g. digital receipts) because of misgivings toward the authenticity of digital documents. Apparently, civil servants are more confident in written-form documents and are more likely to endorse their validity. They believe that the acceptance of written-form documents is useful for diminishing any risk to their carrying out of their responsibility.

"I think that it is hard to address the issue of endorsement between agencies. Sometimes I believe that it is impossible to promote the idea of 'documentary certificate and transcript free', despite the collaboration between public agencies, because many public officials simply do not want to take the responsibility." (TP-CP-01)

"The situation has changed. Nowadays, we, as opposed to the applicant, have to search for the required information to process the application. However, who do you think should be responsible if the information typed into the application form is incorrect? I think it will be the public official rather than the applicant. This is the key issue!" (TP-RD-01)

Readiness of Information Technology and Techniques

Obstacles to e-service can never be solved without the support of sufficient information technologies. Though there is no difficulty in creating a single portal on the website at the customer end, the most determinative part still relies on the technical support at the back end. To streamline the e-services across departments, TESO has to align the recent official document system with an online digital signature system. Furthermore, the conduct principles of digital files, as well as the validation and verifications of digital seals and receipts, are critical drivers of administrative agency acceptance, especially in the case of government financial and accounting units. Finally, improving an online payment system and ensuring its security will also be needed for full online service.

"It inevitably refers to whether we have the digital signature function. However, it is much more complicated to install it in public organizations." (TP-RD-01)

"If one day we all use full online services, then the key point shall be that how we would verify the validity of digital seals and how we would make sure which agency issued that digital seal." (TP-CR-01)

Resistance to Power Release by Agency Heads

Beyond certain exceptions, the largest obstacle to collaboration among agencies is usually resistance from top authorities. In the viewpoint of agency heads, data sharing or database sharing can be seen as relinquishing departmental power. Evidently, convincing department heads to open their turfs and share database ownership with others is a highly political issue and extremely difficult. It is clear, therefore, that political issues are the most difficult to address of the many obstacle to providing full online service.

"I certainly know that the staff who are in charge of the promotion of collaborative e-services are toiling. But the key point is top official's resistance to release of authority. If this block cannot be overcome, there is no possibility to talk about any collaboration among agencies." (TP-IT-01)

Attributes of Business Cases

Presently, the full online services of TESO are simple applications. In contrast, the applications that cannot be conducted online are constrained by a variety of reasons. First, application processing needs a certain number of required documents, or the required documents cannot be uploaded online. Second, some applications cannot be processed online thoroughly and safely. In the former case--which frequently happens in land administration, zoning ordinance, land use designations, or building administration businesses--when citizens or applicants attempt to submit the required documents online they may have to scan proposals with blueprints, layout drawings, or architectural designs as digital files. Such requirements for submitting an application challenges both the agency and the applicant, specifically their software and hardware resources. Therefore, rather than uploading scanned documents, both government agencies and applicants prefer downloading forms and submitting them in person. Besides, even the Taipei City government has provided the "Documentary Certificate and Transcript Free" system, which is dedicated to alleviating the burden of providing documentation. In some cases, citizens still have to provide certain required documents (e.g. lease contracts or agreements signed by stakeholders) which are not stored in databanks but are provided by applicants. Therefore, this requirement of additional document provision results in another obstacle to full online service. Participants of the focus-group interviews made the following comments:

"He may submit his proposal. If he wants to submit it online, that's fine, but he must have a scanner and scan hundreds-of-page of his proposal, then upload it online. Then, he might think it is much easier if he submit his proposal in paper rather than digital files." (TP-PM-01)

"For example, if an applicant has a thick proposal or a number of required documents to submit, then he/she needs to scan the proposal or documents as digital files, and upload them via the system with attached files. This whole process not only

challenges the applicant but also is a challenge for us." (TP-RD-01)

"Taking the application of Certificate of Parking Business Registration as an example, we may need the applicants to provide owner IDs, lease contracts or agreement of usage and so on. All of these documents need to be submitted by the applicants in written form." (TP-PM-02)

On the other hand, in the latter case, partial online services may also result from the concerns of availability and safety of virtualized processing. According to the participants of the focus-group interviews, there are various application permits requiring not only reviews of paper documents but also on-the-spot investigations or inspections of applicants. For example, citizens who apply for subsidies or nationality may need to complete the investigations of personal status. On-the-spot inspections are necessary for the applications relating to prostitution or the casino business. Official seals are required for religious field registrations. Arbitrational meetings need the participation of the persons involved. For these cases, the procedures and reviews cannot be conducted completely via online systems. Moreover, there are a number of relatively sensitive cases, such as personal identity, which invokes concerns with information security and privacy. In such cases, the applicants still must submit application forms and pick up certificates or identifications in person. Therefore, logically, most full online services are for less sophisticated businesses and applications.

"Like cases of building recalls, we may need him/her to provide contracts, agreement of negotiation, and something like this; we only can process the case with all of these documents, but they are not searchable in the database." (TP-LA-01)

"We have to review the company's official seals. However, we haven't digitized this function so far. Therefore, we still need them in original copies." (TP-ED-01)

"Regarding our major function of receiving and reviewing the applications of subsidies for senior citizens, the most important part of the review is assessing the status of applicants. Undoubtedly, the review largely depends upon personal interviews rather than written reports." (TP-SW-02)

Attributes of Users

Clearly, the digital divide caused by limitations in the capacity, facility, and habits of the applicant is yet another critical factor affecting the digital projects of public agencies. First, agencies may have no intention to develop full online services if certain potential users, such as the aged, low-income households, or taxi drivers, lack the digital capacity or facility to go online and take advantage of digital services.

"It is still unpopular for taxi drivers who like to access our service via the Internet. Therefore, we almost have no full online services for them." (TP-PT-01)

"The people whom the Department of Social Welfare is serving are relatively disadvantaged. Frankly, most the disadvantaged people do not have computer and related facilities at home. Therefore, it is less meaningful for us to provide full online services." (TP-SW-01)

Secondly, applicant preferences and behavior also drive the development of online services. Certain applicants may feel less comfortable going online and will prefer going to agencies and submitting applications in person. Meanwhile, some applicants may think that the risk of compromising confidential information could be minimized if they can hand in documents personally. Moreover, some businesses retain professional agents as representatives to deal with applications. Such businesses would prefer not to have to worry about the complexities and inconveniences of uploading large files.

"Because land administration is a very specialized field, it is quite difficult for ordinary people to handle the procedures via the Internet by themselves. Applicants may delegate agents to prepare those sophisticated documents." (TP-KT-01)

"Like the application of certificate of parking business registration, the owners usually ask agents to hand in required documents in person because they are afraid of divulging personal information." (TP-PM-02)

"The applicants who are preparing complicated documents always prefer to come to our agency in person simply because they are afraid that their applications might be withdrawn or be asked to provide additional proofs." (TP-LD-01)

Implications

Returning to our research question focusing on why certain services could not be digitally integrated and fully provided online, our findings indicate several factors, such as, the constraints of legal mandates, barriers to database sharing and integration, privacy and information security, trust, occupational risks and accountabilities, information technology readiness, reluctance to release the ownership of database among heads of departments, the characteristics of the service items, and the characteristics of the applicants. What can we learn from this case study?

On the one hand, some of the factors described above have been frequently noted by numerous scholars (e.g. Scholl & Klischewski, 2007; Schooley & Horan, 2007; Lam, 2005; Stemberger & Jaklic, 2007), such that they may not attract special attention. Laws and regulations, for example, may hinder achievement of e-service integration, and the best way to address this problem would be to amend them and even set up a more comprehensive legal framework. Moreover, concerning barriers to database sharing and integration, the jurisdictions between central and local governments and turf battles among local government agencies seem to be alive, and a major reason why agencies are not communicating among each other. Of course, blurring lines of responsibility or obscuring conflicts of interest may further exaggerate this kind of problem. Also, issues such as privacy and information security and agency accountability can be seen as two sides of a coin. That is, many administrators, in terms of bureaucratic personality (i.e. risk avoidance), would hesitate to embrace the e-service innovation until they can ensure that the rights of certain applicants or innocent third parties would not be violated by related e-government initiatives. The point here is that the more a bureaucrat intends to take self-protective actions, the less convenient and integrated the services that the agency will provide in terms of collaborative government.

To put it *bluntly*, the stakeholders within the government sector (i.e. policy makers and policy implementers) must work together to find ways to institutionally reduce tension and enhance balance or optimize their competing values, norms and pressures. Otherwise, it will be unrealistic to expect that the obstacles would vanish by themselves. Furthermore, due to the separation of powers, not all of the obstacles mentioned above could be removed easily. Thus, the initiator may need to calculate implementation cost and effectiveness. To be specific, the initiator has to answer the following questions: What kind of e-service integration do citizens/applicants eagerly desire in terms of convenience? What kind of e-service integration do administrators really need in terms of efficiency and effectiveness? What kind of e-service integration can be implemented smoothly and feasibly in terms of policy jurisdiction or legislation? Without identifying service items in advance, it would be rather difficult to make achievements. At the same time, top management should not take it for granted that subordinate bodies can self-organize in response to emerging challenges. On the contrary, top managers actually have an obligation to set reform agenda, prioritize e-government projects and initiatives to align with the vision of so-called joint-up government. They must allocate adequate resources to support and encourage their subordinate bodies to boldly diminish potential barriers in the midst of change.

Yet, on the other hand, surprisingly, our findings reveal that administrative practices seem more complex than we have imagined or expected. As mentioned, to a large extent not all of the service items in reality can be processed digitally, specifically in cases in which applicants are required by specific laws or regulations to present many validating documents (e.g. identification, certification, reference for proposal). Similarly, this is also the case for citizens who find that it takes much time and energy to scan and then submit related supporting materials to certain local government authorities. Aside from this, several service items are operationally far beyond the scope and procedure of document review. Which is to say, agencies have extra duties and responsibilities to thoroughly conduct field investigations or face-to-face reviews and secure the rights and benefits of specific applicants or third parties. In brief, "operational compatibility" of e-services should not be disregarded.

Though these challenges can be properly addressed, government authorities also confront another tough issue, especially in the field of social welfare. Not all applicants already possess the capability, preference or habit to go online. This is a fact that policy makers have to face. The idea of "digital divide" *refers* to the citizen's *inability* to utilize information technology smoothly. From the viewpoint of innovation diffusion, public administration and management always find it more difficult to induce all citizens to widely accept e-services unless they can be convinced that information technology can contribute substantially to the improvement of everyday life.

Under such circumstances it is not surprising that during the focus group discussion certain public administrators would hold conservative and even cynical attitudes toward the policy of providing full e-services online. For example, some officials raised this radical question: Is it rhetoric or an imperative to integrate full services across the departmental boundaries under the bandwagon of e-governance?

Put differently, subordinate bodies are faced with multiple realities of public service. Most importantly, they do not simply consider how to overcome the challenges of low e-service usage rates, but also reflexively consider whether it is worthwhile to comprehensively promote boundary-spanning e-services integration. The point here is that for many public administrators recognizing and fulfilling the individual requirements of the political community seem to be more pragmatic and significant than just blindly complying with policy objectives.

To be specific, in our case study when departments or agencies perceive that it is no longer possible to encourage certain target groups to take up technology innovation adoption, the agencies would consciously pay less attention to the policy of digitally integrating services across departmental boundaries. This is the case whether the technological, institutional and organizational barriers are removed or not. Thus, we argue that both the "supply-side" and "demand-side" are crucial in the world of electronic cross-boundary service integration. Policy makers and initiators should take care to avoid falling into the myth of continuously increasing full e-service usage rates or marketing its performance. Instead, they ought to attend to how many citizens actually utilize e-services and whether and to what extent they are really satisfied. These two factors are what should incentivize and legitimize government authorities that embrace full e-service.

Above all, the initiator of the TESO (i.e. Taipei RDEC) should reconsider the assumption that the more e-government services, the higher citizen satisfaction. The authors think that not all of the cross-boundary collaboration should be treated equally and provided online. It seems that the departments should professionally evaluate the supply-side and demand-side necessity, practically balance cost and effectiveness, and then decide whether to genuinely work together or not. Also, for the initiator of the TESO, these obstacles to inter-organizational information integration should be seriously considered, otherwise those departments would not likely ride this bandwagon.

CONCLUSION

E-government is coming of age and many suggest that e-government will be used by governments to provide interactivity, transaction, integration, and engagement. Governments around the world are striving to streamline current public services across departmental boundaries via the introduction of ICTs, though there is still a long way to go. In view of this reality, this chapter has focused on this question: What are the potential factors which the proponents of electronic cross-boundary governance should take into account and which may influence departmental adoption of electronic public service integration?

We have sought to address this question with a case study of Taipei's TESO, using the focus-group interview. Our research findings suggest at least eight barriers to the implementation of full e-services online: the constraints of legal mandates, the barriers to database sharing and integration, privacy and information security, trust, occupational risks and accountabilities, information technology readiness, reluctance to release the ownership of database among heads of departments, the characteristics of the service items, and the characteristics of the applications.

Some of these factors have already been identified in previous research, and to a large extent these factors are especially relevant to traditional boundary-spanning management. For example, key factors such as laws and regulations, risk aversion and turf battles have been typically found in the literature on inter-organizational collaboration (e.g. Alexander, 1995; Alter & Hage, 1993; Peters, 1998; Wilson, 1989). The authors find that the provision of ICTs alone will not make the dream of boundary-less government a reality. Non-technology factors (i.e. institution and incentive) will no doubt play a vital role. Bear in mind that top management still exerts a powerful stimulating effect upon the intention of related departments to work together authentically.

In addition, scholars in e-government research should not neglect the fact that complex application requirements and the social construction of e-services do matter. The findings suggest that many e-service items are actually not suitable for inclusion in the category of full online services, and also applicants are not all endowed with necessary knowledge, skills, abilities or desire to enjoy these innovation services. This substantially provides administrators with pretty good excuses for being reluctant to comply with simplistic visions of easy electronic cross-boundary service integration. Thus, the inhibiting forces include "operational feasibility" and "client demands". The authors especially highlight the importance of demand-drive, which has seldom been illustrated in the literature.

For researchers, more case studies should be conducted in order to cross-validate our findings. For practitioners, it is accordingly unwise to blindly enhance the percentage of full online services while overlooking the option of simultaneously providing multiple application channels (e.g. submitted in person, via mail, via fax, or via phone). This strategy would be more realistic and intelligent in the realm of public services. In our opinion, successful electronic cross-boundary service integration should provide citizens with a variety of choices instead of attempting to completely replace traditional application methods.

ACKNOWLEDGMENT

The data used in this chapter is from a project sponsored by the Taiwan e-Governance Research Center (TEG) and supervised by the Research, Development and Evaluation Committee (RDEC) of the Executive Yuan in Taiwanese central government. The project number is 0972461343. The authors are also thankful to Mr. Chih-Kai Chang and Mr. Rong-Chih Huang, for their assistance in the research project implementation.

REFERENCES

Akhavan, P., Jafari, M., & Ali-Ahmadi, A. (2006). Exploring the interdependency between reengineering and Information Technology by developing a conceptual model. *Business Process Management Journal, 12*(4), 517–534. doi:10.1108/14637150610678104

Alexander, E. R. (1995). *How organizations act together: Interorganizational coordination in theory and practice*. Philadelphia, PA: Gordon and Breach.

Alshawi, S., & Alalwany, H. (2009). E-government evaluation: Citizen's perspective in developing countries. *Information Technology for Development, 15*(3), 193–208. doi:10.1002/itdj.20125

Alter, C., & Hage, J. (1993). *Organizations working together*. Los Angeles, CA: Sage.

Attaran, M. (2004). Exploring the relationship between information technology and business process reengineering. *Information & Management, 41*, 585–596. doi:10.1016/S0378-7206(03)00098-3

Becker, J., Algermissen, L., & Niehaves, B. (2006). A procedure model for process oriented e-government projects. *Business Process Management Journal, 12*(1), 61–75. doi:10.1108/14637150610643760

Bensaou, M. (1997). Interorganizational cooperation: The role of information technology. An empirical comparison of U.S. and Japanese supplier relations. *Information Systems Research, 8*(2), 107–124. doi:10.1287/isre.8.2.107

Bertot, J. C., Jaeger, P. T., & McClure, C. R. (2008). Citizen-centered e-government services: Benefits, costs, and research needs. In S. A. Chun, M. Janssen, & J. R. Gil-Garcia (Eds.), *The Proceedings of the 9th Annual International Digital Government Research Conference: Partnerships for Public Innovation* (pp.137-142). Montreal, Canada: Digital Government Society of North America.

Beynon-Davies, P. (2005). Constructing electronic government: The case of the UK inland revenue. *International Journal of Information Management, 25*, 3–20. doi:10.1016/j.ijinfomgt.2004.08.002

Boonstra, A., & de Vries, J. (2005). Analyzing inter-organizational systems from a power and interest perspective. *International Journal of Information Management, 25*, 485–501. doi:10.1016/j.ijinfomgt.2005.08.006

Choudrie, J., & Weerrakody, V. (2007). Horizontal process integration: The perspective of a UK local authority. *International Journal of Electronic Government Research, 3*(3), 22–39. doi:10.4018/jegr.2007070102

Corbin, J., & Strauss, A. (2008). *Basics of qualitative research* (3rd ed.). Los Angeles, CA: Sage.

Coursey, D., & Norris, D. F. (2008). Models of e-government: Are they correct? An empirical assessment. *Public Administration Review, 68*(3), 523–536. doi:10.1111/j.1540-6210.2008.00888.x

Fedorowicz, J., Gogan, J. L., & Williams, C. B. (2007). A collaborative network for first responders: Lessions from the CapWIN case. *Government Information Quarterly, 24*, 785–807. doi:10.1016/j.giq.2007.06.001

Fountain, J. E. (2001). *Building the virtual state: Information Technology and institutional change*. Washington, DC: Brookings Institution Press.

Gil-Garcia, J. R., Chengalur-Smith, I., & Duchessi, P. (2007). Collaborative e-government: Impediments and benefits of information-sharing projects in the public sector. *European Journal of Information Systems, 16*, 121–133. doi:10.1057/palgrave.ejis.3000673

Hammer, M., & Champy, J. (1993). *Reengineering the corporation*. London, UK: Nicholas Brealy.

Hesson, M., & Al-Ameed, H. (2007). Business process reengineering in UAE public sector: A town planning case study. *Business Process Management Journal, 13*(3), 348–378. doi:10.1108/14637150710752281

Ho, A., & Ni, A. Y. (2004). Explaining the adoption of e-government features: A case study of Iowa County Treasurers' offices. *American Review of Public Administration, 34*(2), 164–180. doi:10.1177/0275074004264355

Ho, A. T. K. (2002). Reinventing local governments and the e-government initiative. *Public Administration Review, 62*(4), 434–444. doi:10.1111/0033-3352.00197

Homburg, V. (2000). The political economy of information exchange politics and property rights in the development and use of interorganizational Information Systems. *Knowledge, Technology, &. Policy, 13*(3), 49–66.

Hong, I. B. (2002). A new framework for interorganizational systems based on the linkage of participants' roles. *Information & Management, 39*, 261–270. doi:10.1016/S0378-7206(01)00095-7

Hughes, M., Scott, M., & Golden, W. (2006). The role of business process redesign in creating e-government in Ireland. *Business Process Management Journal, 12*(1), 76–87. doi:10.1108/14637150610643779

Kettinger, W. J., Teng, T. C., & Guha, S. (1997). Business process change: A study of methodologies, techniques, and tools. *Management Information Systems Quarterly, 21*(1), 55–81. doi:10.2307/249742

Klievink, B., & Janssen, M. (2009). Realizing joined-up government: Dynamic capabilities and stage models for transformation. *Government Information Quarterly, 26*, 275–284. doi:10.1016/j.giq.2008.12.007

Korteland, E., & Bekkers, V. (2007). Diffusion of e-government innovations in the Dutch public sector: The case of digital community policing. *Information Polity, 12*, 139–150.

Krueger, R. A., & Casey, M. A. (2009). *Focus groups: A practical guide for applied research*. Thousand Oaks, CA: Sage Publications.

Kumar, K., & van Dissel, H. G. (1996). Sustainable collaboration: Managing conflict and cooperation in interorganizational systems. *Management Information Systems Quarterly, 20*(3), 279–300. doi:10.2307/249657

Lam, W. (2005). Barriers to e-government integration. *The Journal of Enterprise Information Management, 18*(5), 511–530. doi:10.1108/17410390510623981

Linden, R. M. (2010). *Leading across boundaries: Creating collaborative agencies in a networked world*. San Francisco, CA: Jossey-Bass.

Luna-Reyes, L. F., Gil-Garcia, J. R., & Cruz, C. B. (2007). Collaborative digital government in Mexico: Some lesions from federal Web-based interorganizational information integration initiatives. *Government Information Quarterly, 24*, 808–826. doi:10.1016/j.giq.2007.04.003

McAdam, R., & Donaghy, J. (1999). Business process re-engineering in the public sector: A study of staff perceptions and critical success factors. *Business Process Management Journal, 5*(1), 33–49. doi:10.1108/14637159910249135

Moon, M. J. (2002). The evolution of e-government among municipalities: rhetoric or reality? *Public Administration Review*, *62*(4), 424–433. doi:10.1111/0033-3352.00196

Moon, M. J., & Norris, D. F. (2005). Does managerial orientation matter? The adoption of reinventing government and e-government at the municipal level. *Information Systems Journal*, *15*, 43–60. doi:10.1111/j.1365-2575.2005.00185.x

Olalla, M. F. (2006). Information technology in business process reengineering. *International Advances in Economic Research*, *6*(3), 581–589. doi:10.1007/BF02294975

6P. (2004). Joined-up government in the western world in comparative perspective: A preliminary literature review and exploration. *Journal of Public Administration Research and Theory*, *14*(1), 103-138.

Peters, B. G. (1998). Managing horizontal government: The politics of co-ordination. *Public Administration*, *76*, 295–311. doi:10.1111/1467-9299.00102

Pollitt, C. (2003). Joined-up government: A survey. *Political Studies Review*, *1*, 34–49. doi:10.1111/1478-9299.00004

Schedler, K., & Summermatter, L. (2007). Customer orientation in electronic government: Motives and effects. *Government Information Quarterly*, *24*(2), 291–311. doi:10.1016/j.giq.2006.05.005

Scholl, H. J., & Klischewski, R. (2007). E-government integration and interoperability: Framing the research agenda. *International Journal of Public Administration*, *30*, 889–920. doi:10.1080/01900690701402668

Schooley, B. L., & Horan, T. A. (2007). Towards end-to-end government performance management: Case study of interorganizational information integration in emergency medical services (EMS). *Government Information Quarterly*, *24*(4), 755–784. doi:10.1016/j.giq.2007.04.001

Stemberger, I. M., & Jaklic, J. (2007). Towards e-government by business process change: A methodology for public sector. *International Journal of Information Management*, *27*, 221–232. doi:10.1016/j.ijinfomgt.2007.02.006

Teo, H. H., Wei, K. K., & Benbasat, I. (2003). Predicting intention to adopt interorganizational linkages: An institutional perspective. *Management Information Systems Quarterly*, *27*(1), 19–49.

The United Nations. (2008). UN e-government survey 2008: From e-government to connected governance. New York, NY: UN Publishing Section. Retrieved May 26, 2010, from http://unpan1.un.org/intradoc/groups/public/documents/un/unpan028607.pdf

Volkoff, O., Chan, Y. E., & Newson, E. F. P. (1999). Leading the development and implementation of collaborative interorganizational systems. *Information & Management*, *35*, 63–75. doi:10.1016/S0378-7206(98)00087-1

Weerakkody, V., Baire, S., & Choudrie, J. (2006). E-government: The need for effective process management in the public sector. In R. H. Sprague, Jr. (Ed.), *Proceedings of the 39th Hawaii International Conference on System Sciences - Volume 04* (pp. 74-83). Los Alamitos, CA: IEEE.

West, D. M. (2004). E-government and the transformation of service delivery and citizen attitudes. *Public Administration Review*, *64*(1), 15–27. doi:10.1111/j.1540-6210.2004.00343.x

Willcoeks, L., & Smith, G. (1995). IT-enabled business process reengineering: Organizational and human resource dimensions. *The Journal of Strategic Information Systems*, *4*(3), 279–301. doi:10.1016/0963-8687(95)96806-J

Wilson, J. Q. (1989). *Bureaucracy: What government agencies do and why they do it*. New York, NY: Basic Books.

ADDITIONAL READING

Burn, J., & Robins, G. (2003). Moving towards e-government: A case study of organizational change processes. *Logistics Information Management*, *16*(1), 25–35. doi:10.1108/09576050310453714

Cheng, T. C. E., & Chiu, I. S. F. (2008). Critical success factors of business process re-engineering in the banking industry. *Knowledge and Process Management*, *15*(4), 258–269. doi:10.1002/kpm.316

Roy, C., & Séguin, F. (2000). The institutionalization of efficiency-oriented approaches for public service improvement. *Public Productivity & Management Review*, *23*(4), 449–468. doi:10.2307/3380563

Soliman, K. S., & Janz, B. D. (2004). An exploratory study to identify the critical factors affecting the decision to establish Internet-based interorganizational information systems. *Information & Management*, *41*, 697–706. doi:10.1016/j.im.2003.06.001

Sutanto, J., Kankanhalli, A., Tay, J., Raman, K. S., & Tan, B. C. Y. (2008). Change Management in Interorganizational Systems for the Public. *Journal of Management Information Systems*, *25*(3), 133–175. doi:10.2753/MIS0742-1222250304

KEY TERMS AND DEFINITIONS

Business Process Redesign (BPR): According to Hammer and Champy (1993), the key aspect of business process reengineering is the fundamental and radical change of business processes to achieve dramatic improvements. However, business process change in the public sector mostly means unification of business processes, automation of some activities and elimination of some unnecessary ones (Stemberger & Jaklic, 2007: 222). In this chapter, business process reengineering and business process change are both included in the definition of BPR.

Electronic Cross-Boundary Governance (ECBG): ECBG an be defined as initiatives which intend to bridge silo information systems among government agencies as well as to facilitate agencies that share, exchange, and integrate information resources by the application of ICTs.

Electronic Public Service Integration: This refers to a platform that attempts to provide integrated public services that citizens use to access specific e-services which link, to some extent, the front-office and back-office, via ICTs and redesigned business processes.

Interorganizational System (IOS): IOS is an ICT-based system shared by two or more independent organizations (Schooley & Horan, 2007).

Jointed-Up Government: This is a phrase which denotes the aspiration to achieve horizontally and vertically coordinated thinking and action. Through this coordination it is hoped that a number of benefits can be achieved. For instance, it becomes possible to offer citizens seamless rather than fragmented access to a set of related services (Pollitt, 2003).

ENDNOTES

[1] The authors have no intention to argue that we should have more e-government services in terms of number and complexity. The only

thing we note is that most research (e.g. UN, 2008) has emphasized providing integrated e-services when government authorities intend to enhance citizen satisfaction and administrative effectiveness. However, there might be numerous obstacles to integrated e-services and only a few researchers in the field of public management have ever solved the puzzles.

2 The authors intend to identify the factors that may hinder the provision of electronic cross-boundary services. In other words, our research subject is those e-government services which inherently require cross- departmental collaboration.

3 These departments have already provided certain cross-boundary services, according to the Taipei City government publication (i.e. Handbook of Citizen Application Processing Time Limits). Unfortunately, many services still cannot be processed digitally. The authors believe there is much room for improvement, specifically on the back-office side. Thus, we would like to inquire into the potential obstacles to ECBG by conducting focus group interview at a later time.

4 In most literature, BPR is seen as one of the obstacles to the inter-organizational system (IOS). This is a typical viewpoint from the private sector. On the contrary, in the public sector BPR should be given special consideration. That is, success in e-service integration depends not only on the information system, but it also is related to the business process. To be specific, the issue of BPR in the public sector broadly refers to the constraints of laws and rules which make BPR very difficult to actualize, and this issue would be neglected if not treated independently.

5 This include: (1) identifying the desired outputs from the system post implementation; (2) categorizing the desired outputs into essential and desirable; (3) prioritizing the desired outputs and by time frame (immediate, medium-term and long-term); (4) obtaining "sign-off" on outputs from key stakeholders; (5) designing new processes to deliver required outputs (focusing on immediate and essential); (6) engaging operational staff in designing /reviewing process maps; (7) producing and testing individual processes with the relevant staff and with system capacity; (8) obtaining business 'sign-off' on new processes; (i) designing or modifying the existing quality assurance and control processes to fit in with the new requirements and system; (9) ensuring there are appropriate security protocols/regulatory integrity; (10) implementing new processes; (11) reviewing and amending processes post implementation in consultation with staff and users.

6 Customers are very often obligated to use these services, e.g. when someone wants to establish a sports society it has to be registered by the state.

7 Information technology (IT) can be considered an important enabler of BPR. Whereas, traditionally, organizations have used IT to automate existing processes, currently, organizations are using IT not just to speed up routine processes, but to redesign those processes in order to achieve dramatic improvements in productivity (Akhavan, Jafari, & Ali-Ahmadi, 2006, p. 531). To be specific, IT allows an organization to alter processes in two ways: collaboration grade increase and medication grade decrease through the implementation of shared databases and communication technologies (Olalla, 2000, p. 588). IT helps in meeting the objectives of reengineering in three ways: by providing information across functional levels and establishing easy communication, improving the process performance, and finally by helping the reengineering effort by modeling,

optimizing and assessing its consequences (Attaran, 2004, p. 595).

8 They identified the top five most persistent barriers to BPR programs: middle and line management resistance, loss of commitment/non-enthusiastic support from the top, prevailing culture and political structure, and lower-level employee fear and resistance (Willcoeks & Smith, 1995, p. 296).

9 Each of the departments usually has built its own databases (e.g. household registration and conscription information system, land administration information system, taxation information system, land use zoning information system, etc.) for years, yet the interoperability among these systems might not be sufficient for several reasons.

10 As mentioned, among the 471 e-services currently provided by TESO, 102 items can be completed online, while 369 items are provided either semi-online or offline. The authors, based on a scrutiny of descriptions in the "Handbook of Citizen Application Processing Time Limits" published by the Taipei City government, found that the services which demand more collaborative effort between agencies (i.e. external reviews, approval by upper authorities, or conjunct inspections with other authorities) are more apt to be semi-online or offline provisions. Taking services of urban development as an example: the application for a copy of the illustrated compendium of construction license is provided fully online; the application for the postponement of construction beginning (or completion) of a large-scale billboard's miscellaneous license which needs approval or authorization by upper authorities could only be provided semi-online; and the application for alteration of usage license which requires reviews of external agencies is provided offline only. Even most cases fit this illustration. Indeed, there are a few services which require cross-agency collaborations but are provided fully online. For example, applicants applying for the assistance for women and families in dire conditions can complete the process fully online either by providing digital proofs of tax and income themselves or through the Social Affairs Department's request of electronic data exchange with the Financial Data Center at the Ministry of Finance. In this regard, if a cross-departmental service, which can be validated by digitized documents, were to be supported by digital data exchange, then it would not need external review or approval by other authorities, and thus would more likely be provided fully online.

11 Please refer to the Taipei E-Service Online website at: www.e-services.taipei.gov.tw.

12 It is clear that the Research Development and Evaluation Commission at the Taipei City government (Taipei RDEC), which acts on behalf of the mayor, exerts great pressure on departments to work together to provide electronic cross-boundary services. Those departments, for example, that usually have established functional databases (e.g. land use zoning information system) in a certain policy area are required to provide internet access to each other in order to maximize the benefits of data sharing. In this regard, the main role played by the Taipei RDEC requires regularly scrutinizing progress and then deciding whether to impose a penalty.

13 This statement was a preliminary finding drawn from a scrutiny of descriptions in the "Handbook of Citizen Application Processing Time Limits" published by the Taipei City government. The authors were inspired to discover the deeper structural reasons beyond this preliminary finding, and eager to understand why those barriers to advanced cross-boundary services identified in the paragraph still could not be overcome by electronic devices and efforts.

Chapter 2
Government Information Sharing:
A Framework for Policy Formulation

Elsa Estevez
United Nations University, China & Universidad Nacional del Sur, Argentina

Pablo Fillottrani
Universidad Nacional del Sur, Argentina & Comisión de Investigaciones Científicas, Argentina

Tomasz Janowski
United Nations University, China

Adegboyega Ojo
United Nations University, China

ABSTRACT

Information sharing (IS) is a key capability required for one-stop and networked government, responding to a variety of intra-organizational, inter-organizational, or cross-national needs like sharing service-related information between parties involved in the delivery of seamless services, sharing information on available resources to enable whole-of-government response to emergencies, etc. Despite its importance, the IS capability is not common for governments due to various technical, organizational, cultural, and other barriers which are generally difficult to address by individual agencies. However, developing such capabilities is a challenging task which requires government-wide coordination, explicit policies and strategies, and concrete implementation frameworks. At the same time, reconciling existing theoretical frameworks with the IS practice can be difficult due to the differences in conceptions and abstraction levels. In order to address such difficulties, this chapter proposes a conceptual framework to guide the development of Government Information Sharing (GIS) policies, strategies, and implementations. By integrating theoretical frameworks and the GIS practice, the framework adopts a holistic view on the GIS problem, highlights the main areas for policy intervention, and provides policy makers and government managers with conceptual clarity on the GIS problem.

DOI: 10.4018/978-1-60960-753-1.ch002

INTRODUCTION

Electronic Government (e-Government) refers to the use of Information and Communication Technologies (ICT), particularly the Internet, as a tool to achieve better government (OECD e-Government Studies, 2003). Accordingly, e-Government is not an aim in itself but a tool leading to better policy outcomes, higher quality of public services, more efficient government processes, more efficient use of public funds, higher citizen engagement, etc. While different maturity models exist to assess the level of e-Government development, all models agree that at the highest maturity level, called data-sharing or seamless government, government agencies are able to share information.

Information Sharing is a key capability required for one-stop and networked government. For example, sharing service-related information between parties involved in the delivery of seamless public services, sharing information on critical resources to enable whole-of-government responses to emergencies, etc. Government Information Sharing initiatives attempt to "unlock" data on fragmented information technology infrastructures spanning multiple agencies, making it readily discoverable and accessible to authorized users for direct consumption or further processing. Contexts for IS range from intra-organizational - for instance sharing citizen data among functional units within a single government agency; through inter-organizational - for instance the delivery of seamless services involving cross-agency processes; to inter-governmental - for instance the exchange of health or security surveillance data among neighboring countries or among different states in a federal government system.

Traditionally, most IS initiatives are functionally oriented or program-specific, referring for instance to health, environment or security areas. The shortcomings of program-specific Information Sharing which lacks an overarching framework have been highlighted extensively, with evidence, particularly in the context of counter-terrorism efforts (Office of the Director of National Intelligence, United States of America, 2008). Also regional integration efforts and globalization are generating more dynamic and complex cross-border IS scenarios. For example, global flu-pandemic, global financial crisis, delivery of pan-European services, and the emerging Pearl River Delta cooperation in Asia, etc. all require more generic and cross-boundary IS capabilities.

Developing the capabilities that enable agile responses to events as well as effective sharing of program-specific information, is both important and difficult. Existing literature presents various approaches to GIS. These include the development of information sharing strategies, integration of IS and interoperability initiatives, development of enterprise architecture programs, etc. For instance, the Federal Enterprise Architecture (FEA) (Office of Management and Budget, USA) by the US Government and Information Interoperability (Australian Government Information Management Office, 2006) by the Government of Australia have been directly designed to enable GIS.

This chapter presents a review of the theories underpinnings GIS as well as country-specific frameworks developed over the recent years, as a basis for defining a Government Information Sharing Framework (GISF). This conceptual framework has two main objectives: (1) provide a holistic framework for understanding IS in government and (2) articulating strategies for enabling GIS. Concerning the former, GISF captures and relates the main GIS concepts at intra-organizational, inter-organizational and inter-governmental levels. Concerning the latter, GISF identifies the core IS intervention areas, conceptualizing IS according to different stages of maturity in the IS practice. All these contribute to the definition of IS policies, strategies and concrete implementations. Finally, the chapter evaluates IS challenges in different organizational contexts and points at the emerging solutions to some of them. Overall, the chapter addresses the needs of policy and decision makers in government:

for better understanding of the nature and scope of GIS, for access to guidelines and know-how for developing the required IS capabilities, and for awareness of the core issues in implementing IS strategies.

The rest of the chapter is organized as follows. Following the Introduction, the section on Foundations of Government Information Sharing presents existing GIS theories. With such foundations in place, the section on Cases in Government Information Sharing presents and evaluates country experiences in developing IS frameworks, followed by the section about the Government Information Sharing Framework (GISF) to address the theory-practice gap and provide a unifying model for GIS. The Validation section applies GISF to the country cases and the final section contains some conclusions.

FOUNDATIONS OF GOVERNMENT INFORMATION SHARING

The review of the relevant research literature reveals two main theoretical models underpinning GIS and a number of focused studies into various aspects of GIS, particularly those related to policy and strategy development. These models and studies are presented here as theoretical foundations of GIS.

Two most influential theoretical models of GIS were published several years ago. The first (Dawes, 1996) provides (see Figure 1) a learning cycle of government agencies involved in the IS practice. Based on the results of a survey conducted among public managers from the New York state government, the model assesses the extent to which the IS-related benefits and barriers identified from literature are reflected in the IS practice. It depicts how a sharing experience is triggered by a pressing problem suitable for an IS-based solution. While participants enter the experience with their own perceptions of potential benefits and risks, the sharing experience is shaped by the underlying policy and management frameworks of the organization concerned. In turn, the sharing produces insights that help improve the framework, promoting benefits and mitigating risks of future sharing experiences. The model also proposes information stewardship and usefulness principles to drive the definition of the IS policy framework

While the first model focuses on IS within one agency, the second model (Landsbergen and Wolken, 2001) draws on the authors' work on interoperable systems in a networked environment. Depicted in Figure 2, the model is structured into stages. At Stage 1, the model considers the experience of individual agencies that share information, as in the Dawes's model. The learning

Figure 1. Theoretical Model for Government Information Sharing (Adapted from Dawes, 1996)

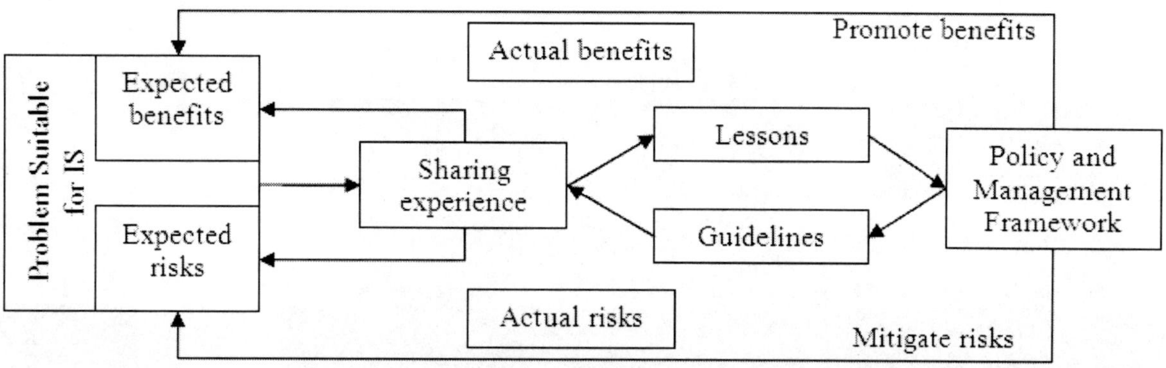

processes of these isolated experiences are driven by the expectations of the benefits and risks of participating agencies. Based on the experiences by individual agencies, the model proposes to build the interoperability infrastructure in support of Information Sharing – Stage 2. The proposed infrastructure comprises three elements: (1) Technical – elements to ensure hardware and software compatibility, availability of standardized processes and the integration of best practices into such processes; (2) Interoperability Policy Architecture – architectural elements such as the meta-data infrastructure to facilitate access to information, inter-agency contracts to ensure the fulfillment of information requirements among government agencies of the same (horizontal) or different (vertical) levels and others; and (3) Institutional – institutional elements such as the clearinghouse of best IS practices and a formbook of contracts that identify different alternatives for allocating risks and responsibilities when sharing information. Finally, Stage 3 identifies the required changes to be introduced in policies, laws, and management practices. In addition, the model identifies five IS-enabling tools: (1) meta-data to identify the presence, nature and quality of information; (2) laws and policies to specify timing and conditions upon which government agencies should make their information available; (3) economic and budgetary mechanisms to identify IS costs and benefits; (4) the extent of shared information; and (5) managerial tools to provide incentives and controls for IS processes.

In the following, we present some research studies into various aspects of GIS such as: (1) principles for defining IS policies and roles; (2) social and technical processes underpinning IS and related elements; (3) classification of IS initiatives as well as barriers and strategies for IS; and (4) other conceptualizations as well as challenges to IS in view of the organizational boundary concept. Finally, we discuss various technical aspects of IS as well as the IS knowledge areas.

Defining the principles that will guide the IS culture in government is one of the first steps for the formulation of IS policies and strategies. The Insider's Guide to Using Information in Government (Center for Technology in Government, 2001) identifies democratic principles as the foundation for information policies, and classifies such policies into these that promote information stewardship and these that promote information use. The principle of stewardship recognizes information as a public good, focusing on information accuracy, integrity, preservation and protection. The principle of usefulness recognizes government information as an asset, focusing on the potential benefits gained from its proper use. In upholding both principles, a government can play various roles: regulator, collector, producer,

Figure 2. Expanded Theoretical Model for GIS (Adapted from Landsbergen and Wolken, 2001)

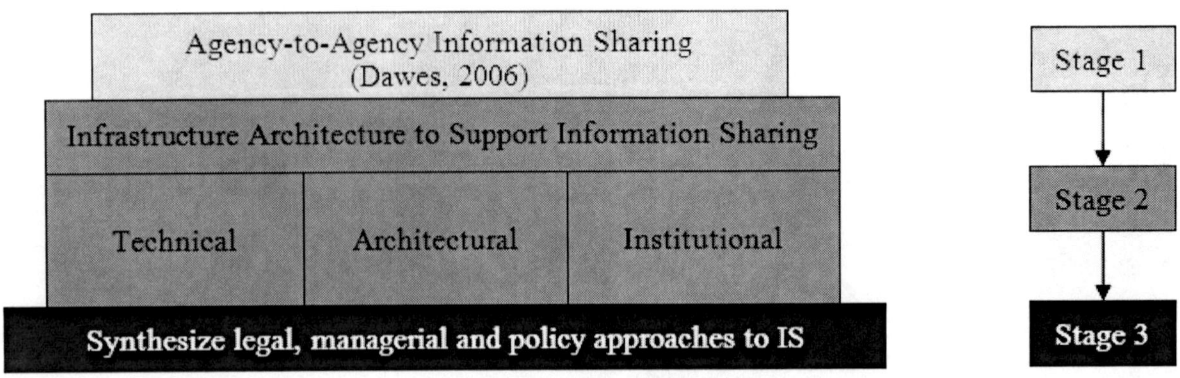

provider or user (Center for Technology in Government, 1999).

The IS problem can be defined through various perspectives. In particular, (Pardo, Cresswell, Dawes, & Burke, 2004) argues that the technical and social processes involved in IS can be characterized according to four perspectives: (1) Technological – standards, metadata, interoperability platforms, ontologies, data quality attributes and others; (2) Organizational – business and decision processes and their required adjustments; (3) Inter-organizational – the creation and maintenance of inter-organizational relationships, negotiation processes, commitments, trust-building, risk-reductions, resource conflict resolution and others; and (4) Political – legislations to enable collaboration and IS including economic models to help agencies identify IS costs and benefits. Complementing such perspectives and based on a similar study of social and technical aspects of inter-organizational information integration (Gil-Garcia, Pardo, & Burke, 2010), four inter-related elements of IS were identified: trusted social networks, shared information, integrated data and interoperable technical infrastructure. Regarding trusted social networks, a key requirement is a clear definition of the responsibilities of members: exercise of authority, diversity of participating organizations and their goals, and experiences (Pardo, Burke, Gil-Garcia & Guler, 2009).

Learning the lessons from the inter-organizational information integration initiatives, particularly in the criminal justice enterprise, (Gil-Garcia, Schneider, Pardo, & Cresswell, 2005) presents: (1) classification of integration initiatives – focusing on meeting specific needs and on building capacity, while considering intra-organizational, inter-organizational and inter-governmental perspectives; (2) barriers to integration – resistance to change, IT and data incompatibility, organizational diversity and multiple goals, and political complexities of the governance system; and (3) useful strategies to facilitate integration, such as retaining autonomy of the involved agencies, establishing and operating governance structures, ensuring strategic partnerships, carrying out a comprehensive and long-range planning, building the understanding of business processes, securing financial resources, and securing leadership and legislative support.

The challenges of inter-organizational IS give rise to the concept of organizational boundaries. While exploring the meaning of this concept, (Zheng, Yang, Pardo, & Jiang, 2009) identifies vertical and horizontal directions for IS and multiple dimensions – organizational, geographical, personal, developmental and process-related, and defines a theoretical framework for understanding the boundaries in IS initiatives. In addition, various IS challenges in government were identified and classified based on the case studies from China (Jing & Zhang, 2009) resulting in a five-layered model: (1) Individual Expectations – expected benefits and risks; (2) Organizational Readiness – top management support, IT capacity, cost and security; (3) Inter-Agency Partnership – trust and compatibility; (4) Upper-Level Managerial Agencies – cross-agency collaboration and authority; and (5) External Environment – laws, policies and political awareness about IS.

Finally, most researchers recognize the need for combining social and technical aspects of IS, with technical aspects including interoperability, data standards and specific technology applications, while social and organizational aspects including trust building, knowledge sharing and privacy (Gil-Garcia, Chun, & Janssen, 2009). Consequently, the major knowledge areas for IS include leadership, trust, perceptions and measures of success, inter-organizational relations, organizational change, and governance structures (Pardo & Tayi, 2007).

Table 1 presents a summary of the research contributions presented in this section to understand the GIS domain, including: authors, types of IS initiatives studied, research focus and contribution, and the tools identified in support of IS initiatives.

CASES OF GOVERNMENT INFORMATION SHARING INITIATIVES

This section presents government-wide IS initiatives from Australia, United Kingdom, United States of America, New Zealand and Estonia, most of them relying on interoperability frameworks to enable and support IS. These countries were selected because of the maturity level of their interoperability frameworks and the availability of public documentation about them. The choice provides us not only with the geographical diversity but also with a range of experiences. The UK first published its framework in 2001, and the framework has undergone several revisions since then. The frameworks of Australia, New Zealand and USA have had at least 2 versions, while the Estonian framework has been released recently in 2007. As we focus this chapter on interoperability frameworks, government enterprise architectures like the US Federal Enterprise Architecture (FEA) or Germany's Standards and Architectures for Government Applications (SAGA) are outside our consideration.

Australia

In order to ensure that government agencies maximize the opportunities for IS – cooperation of people, processes and systems to deliver seamless and customer-centric services, and promote system integration and reuse, the Government of Australia defined the Australian Government Interoperability Framework (AGIF). AGIF identifies the principles, standards and methodologies to support agencies in the delivery of integrated and seamless services. It covers technical aspects as well as guides, principles and business processes underpinning government services.

A foundation for IS between all levels of Australian government, AGIF includes the National Government Information Sharing Strategy (Australian Government Information Management Office, 2009) that identifies best practices, policies, tools and advices, and makes them available to all agencies.

Table 1. Foundations of Government Information Sharing – Summary of Research Contributions

Authors	Initiative	Focus and Contributions	Identified Tools
Dawes	intra-organizational IS	principles, benefits, barriers	inventories, data definitions, standards, clearinghouses
Landsbergen, Wolken	interoperable systems in networked environments	benefits, barriers, infrastruc-ture support, and legal, policy and managerial approaches	meta-data, inter-agency contracts, economic models, best practices, contract formbooks
Pardo, Cresswell, Dawes, Burke	inter-organizational IS, technical and social processes	IS dimensions, components and their relationships	metadata inventories, data sharing, agreements, economic models
Gil-Garcia, Schneider, Pardo, Cresswell	inter-organizational IS, technical and social processes	classification of IS initiatives, IS barriers and strategies	trusted social networks, interoperable technical infrastructures
Zheng, Yang, Pardo, Jiang	multi-organizational IS	organizational boundaries	IS directions and dimensions
Jing, Zhang	inter-organizational IS in China	IS challenges	IS challenges
Gil-Garcia, Chun, Janssen	IS and integration	combination of technical and social aspects	data standards, trust building, knowledge sharing, privacy regulations
Pardo, Tayi	inter-organizational information integration	knowledge areas	trust, leadership, success measures, interagency relations, organizational change, governance structure

AGIF is structured into a three-level hierarchy: (1) Business – addresses legal, commercial, business and political concerns; (2) Information – describes information and process elements that convey business meaning; and (3) Technical – proposes technology standards. The levels support each other in order to facilitate the delivery of the whole-of-government objectives.

The *Business Level* is described in the Business Process Interoperability Framework (BPIF) (Australian Government Information Management Office, 2007). In order to support the redesign of government business processes and ensure information interoperability, BPIF provides a set of tools:

- *Roadmap*: Six stages to facilitate progression towards interoperability: Plan, Agree, Discover, Map and Model, Implement, and Monitor and Review, with interactive progress and feedback employed throughout each stage towards business process interoperability.
- *Capability Maturity Model*: To identify the current level of business process interoperability within an agency and to define strategies for achieving a desired level, the Fisher's model (Fisher, 2004) has been adapted. The model introduces a five-stage hierarchy: (1) Siloed – ad hoc, vertical structure with agency-specific arrangements; (2) Tactical Collaboration – hierarchical structure with controls and efficiency measures; (3) Reuse – mixed vertical and horizontal structures with some multi-agency process controls in place; (4) Shared Services – mixed but strongly horizontal structures with efficiency and effectiveness as key performance indicators; and (5) Service-Oriented – network structure and cross-agency controls embedded in government business.
- *Case Studies*: Describing initiatives undertaken by agencies to improve business process management and interoperability, e.g. showcasing an internal business process approach practiced in a given government department or a multi-agency project executed government-wide.

In order to model business processes, BPIF suggests to use emerging standards like Business Process Execution Language – BPEL (OASIS, 2007), Unified Modelling Language – UML (OMG, 1997-2010) or Business Process Modelling Notation – BPMN (OMG, 1997-2010). It also provides criteria for selecting appropriate modelling tools and applications for each context.

The Business Level is also supported by the National Collaboration Framework (NCF) (National Collaboration Program Team, 2005), a series of reusable agreements between Federal, State and Local agencies to facilitate collaboration between jurisdictions for service delivery, and a knowledge base to assist such agencies in effective implementation of cross-jurisdiction projects.

The *Information Level* is defined by the Information Interoperability Framework (IIF) (Australian Government Information Management Office, 2006) to make sure that the information generated/held by government is managed as a national strategic asset. The framework defines a plan for IS which includes critical actions (enablers) underpinning successful achievement of Information Interoperability: (1) forming partnerships with agencies that have business needs to share information; (2) using a 'create once, use many' approach with authoritative sources of information and clearly defined accountability and ownership arrangements; (3) adopting a common business language and standards – metadata, thesauri, information object standards and links to business process; (4) establishing appropriate governance arrangements – responsibilities, roles, compliance regimes, measures of success and best practice models; (5) understanding the policy and legal frameworks governing information exchange including legal issues, security checklists and privacy guidelines; and (6) developing and using tools that facilitate the transfer of reliable information across agency boundaries in terms of best practice guides, Information Sharing protocols and Memoranda of Understanding.

IIF introduces an information management lifecycle (Figure 3) comprising the following steps:

1. *Planning*: Identification of information requirements relevant to any work activity – identifying potential uses of information, adopting standard concepts and definitions for recording data and items, and considering potential barriers to making the information available to others; ongoing third-party consent issues should be addressed.
2. *Create and Collect*: Information is created, collected, captured and accessed in a variety of ways and from a variety of sources to address business needs. Prior to creating new information holdings, agencies should undertake a review to determine if the information required can be sourced from an existing collection.
3. *Organize and Store*: Once created and collected, information should be organized and stored to enable consistent treatment (e.g. to best reveal patterns and trends) and to enable easy access to support business needs, e.g. applying appropriate metadata so that information can be annotated and discovered effectively.
4. *Access and Use*: Conditions related to access and use should ensure that information is used appropriately, carried out responsibly and consistent with the source. Access should be restricted to the authorized entities, considering existing legal, policy and administrative obligations.
5. *Maintenance*: The information lifecycle includes effective maintenance and disposal of information. With this is mind, agencies should liaise with information users when considering terminating, disposing of, or making content changes to collections, and conduct audits of security, quality, accessibility and compliance with access and use conditions.

It is important to observe that information reuse is part of information lifecycle, meaning that the agencies must consider not only their immediate information requirements, but the value of information to other users including their rights and responsibilities. These must be considered at all stages of the lifecycle.

The information level includes GovDex (GovDex Team, 2010), a collaborative tool for managing cross-agency projects and for storing shared information, models and resources. GovDex consists of a collaborative workspace, a repository of projects and standards, and a collection of tools and methods, providing a secure, private, web-based space for government agencies to manage projects and their stakeholders, share documents and information, and manage secretariat responsibilities. GovDex currently hosts over 450 communities and over 11000 registered users across all levels of government.

Figure 3. The Information Lifecycle in IIF

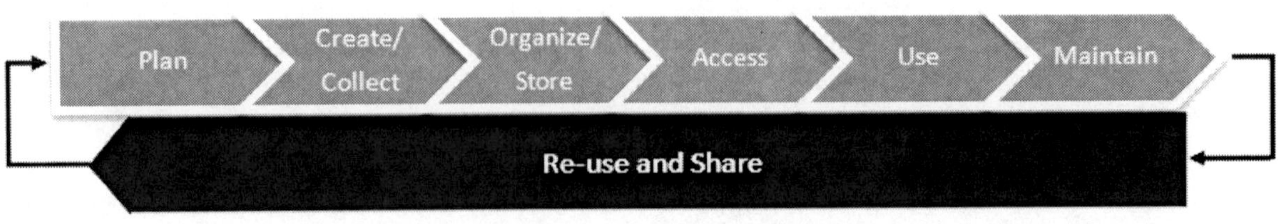

The *Technical Level* contains the Technical Interoperability Framework (TIF) (Australian Government Information Management Office, 2005). TIF prescribes a common language, conceptual model and standards to facilitate interoperability between agencies. It divides the technical domain into a series of topics as a way to categorize standards and recognize linkages to the network and service layers. It catalogues both open and proprietary standards, with preference given to the former. The categories are:

- *Security*: Covers standards and technologies which role is to support secure interoperation: data encryption, public key infrastructure supporting public and private encryption/decryption keys, digital signatures, and secure transmission protocols. Examples are: SSL, S/MIME ESS and X.509.
- *Interconnection*: Covers standards and technologies for connecting systems including basic connection protocols such as HTTP, HTTPS and FTP; web service message exchange protocols like SOAP; and service description languages like WSDL.
- *Data Exchange*: Contains standards and technologies to facilitate data exchange through appropriate structures and encodings: email protocols like SMTP and X.400, resource syndication protocols like RSS, data markup languages such as XML, and basic character-set encodings like UNICODE.
- *Discovery*: Covers standards and technologies supporting the discovery and location of resources: metadata standards to support consistent description of resources such as RDF, Dublin Core, UDDI and DNS; and directory standards such as LDAP.
- *Presentation*: Covers standards related to the presentation of information, allowing data to be interpreted and presented in consistent ways between systems: HTML and XHTML; a range of image and streaming media formats like GIF, PDF, JPEG and MPEG; document encoding formats like RTF; and a range of specialized mark-up languages like languages for mobile devices.
- *Metadata for Process and Data Description*: These standards are concerned with sequencing of operations and their execution dependencies, including a range of workflow description languages and emerging web service coordination and choreography languages such as BPEL4WS. They also support descriptions of data semantics, data structures and data relationships, including modelling standards like UML, Entity-Relationship Diagrams, Flowcharts and XML Schema.
- *Naming*– This category covers basic primitives for defining consistent names for resources, like URI, URL, XML Namespaces, ISO 3166 (country codes), and ISO 8601 (date and time representations).

The usage of standards is classified into: Fading – standards that while still used, are receiving less support or are being superseded; Emerging – standards that do not have widespread use but are expected to receive more usage in the future; and Current – standards that have a strong and ongoing support.

United Kingdom

The e-Government Interoperability Framework (e-GIF) was defined by the UK Government to set out the government's policies and specifications for achieving interoperability and coherence in the usage of ICT systems across the public sector. The framework adopted some basic design principles like alignment with the Internet; adoption of XML as the primary standard for data integration and management; and adoption of an Internet browser as a key interface. The framework also defines policy frameworks covering the issues of security, confidentiality, delivery and others.

e-GIF is divided into two layers: (1) the framework itself which covers high-level policy statements, technical policies, and management, implementation and compliance regimes; and (2) the e-GIF registry which includes the e-Government Metadata Standard (e-GMS), the Government Data Standards Catalogue (GDSC), XML schemas, and the Technical Standards Catalogue (TSC). While the first layer is similar to the Technical Level and part of the Information Level of the Australian AGIF, there is no equivalent in e-GIF to the Business Process level. The second layer is a collection of concrete standards.

The e-GIF Framework is presented in five sections:

1. *Policy and Scope*: The objectives and drivers of the framework, and its architecture and scope.
2. *Technical Policies*: Equivalent to the Australian IIF, but only contains general standards with specific ones left to the regularly updated TSC document. The standards are classified into: Interconnection – includes S/MIME, TSL/SSL, FTP, DNS, SOAP, UDDI and WSDL; Data Integration – includes XML, XML Schema, XSL Transformation, RDF and UML; Content Management Metadata – specifies e-GMS for metadata as well as ANSI/NISO Z39.84 for identifiers; e-Service Access and Channels – includes specifications of e-service access using different channels; and Standards for Business Areas – for e-learning, e-health, finance, commerce, workflows, web services and others.
3. *Implementation Support*: It covers processes by which e-GIF and the tools needed to implement it will be developed, applied and maintained. Priorities are defined for production of XML Schemas. It also includes the GovTalk website (Cabinet Office, 2010) that supports the whole initiative and incorporates management processes so that the government can consult and take decisions.
4. *Management Process*: The Management Process outlines the roles and responsibilities of the central government and other public sector and industry organizations.
5. *Change Management and Compliance Regime*: It shows how to manage the update process of e-GIF so that it meets the requirements of all stakeholders and is aligned to the potential of new technologies and markets. The Compliance Regime provides general guidance on what compliance means and how it is enforced, intended to inform all those involved in the development and provision of public sector systems and services of their responsibilities and timetables for conforming to e-GIF.

The e-GIF Registry comprises e-GMS, GDSC, TSC and XML Schema vocabulary and developer guides. e-GMS describes the core vocabulary required for effective retrieval and management of official information. Each element in this vocabulary contains details related to particular aspects of an information resource, e.g. title or creator. Based on the Dublin Core (Dublin Core Metadata Initiative, 1995-2010) and now ISO 15836, it is meant as a superset of all elements and refinements needed throughout the UK public sector. e-GMS contains GCL (Government Category List), an older taxonomy for indexing government web pages. GDSC has two parts: (1) the rationale, approach and rules for setting up and agreeing upon the metadata to be used in schemas and other interchange processes; and (2) data types and data items standards. TSC defines the minimum specifications conforming to the e-GIF technical policies covering the domains of interconnectivity, data integration, content management metadata, e-services access, and specifications for miscellaneous business areas like e-health or e-learning. These categories are the same as those included in the Technical Policies.

United States of America

The National Information Exchange Model (NIEM) (US Department of Justice and US Department of Homeland Security, 2010) was designed to develop, disseminate and support enterprise-wide IS standards and processes across the whole of the justice, public safety, emergency and disaster management, intelligence, and homeland security enterprises at all levels and across all branches of the US government. It is a framework to identify IS requirements; to develop standards in support of IS; and to provide technical tools and assistance in the development, discovery, dissemination and reuse of information. The vision for NIEM is to be the standard of choice for intergovernmental information exchange, with common exchange formats, processes, tools and methodologies to improve public safety and homeland security. NIEM represents a partnership, initially between the US Department of Justice and the US Department of Homeland Security and soon engaging other agencies covering justice, intelligence, immigration, emergency management, international trade, and infrastructure protection domains.

From the technical point of view, NIEM introduces the following concepts:

- *Data Component*: Information exchanged between agencies can be broken down into individual data components representing real-world objects or concepts. For example, information about people, places, material things and events. Components that are frequently and uniformly used in practice are specified in NIEM and can be reused by practitioners for information exchange regardless of the business context. Some sources of data components include data models, databases, data dictionaries, schemas and exchanges. For the purpose of consistent definition, these objects and constructs are represented in NIEM using XML Schema. The model, however, is independent of any particular technology and could be depicted in any number of representations, including Resource Definition Framework (RDF), Web Ontology Language (OWL), etc. to facilitate interoperable information sharing. To effectively exchange information, a common semantic understanding of the data among participating agencies is required, and the data must be formatted in a semantically-consistent manner.
- *NIEM Core*: The data components that are universally shared and understood among all, or almost all, domains are identified as universal components (e.g. person, address or organization). To become a universal component, consensus by all domains is required on the semantics and structure of the component. Once established, the core set of NIEM universal components is stable and small.
- *Domain*: It refers to a business enterprise broadly comprising the agencies, units of government, operational functions, services and information systems, all organized or affiliated to meet common objectives. The NIEM domains are organized to facilitate governance, and each has a level of persistency. Each domain traditionally includes a cohesive group of data stewards who are subject-matter experts, have some level of authority within the domains they represent, and participate in the processes related to harmonizing conflicts and resolving data-component ambiguities. Domain examples include justice, intelligence, immigration and emergency management.
- *Community of Interest (COI)*: COI is a collaborative group of users who exchange information in pursuit of shared goals, interests, missions or business processes and who therefore must have a shared vocabulary for the information exchanged. COIs are formally constituted through an

organizational charter, a memorandum of understanding (MOU), articles of incorporation, or the Federal Advisory Committee Act (FACA).

- *Information Exchange Package Documentation (IEPD)*: The information that is commonly or universally exchanged between participating domains can be organized into information exchange packages (IEPs) in the form of XML Schemas. An example is data associated with an arrest, including not only personal identification data regarding the individual arrested but also information about the person's alleged offense, the location of the offense, the arresting officer, etc. The IEP represents a set of data that is actually transmitted between agencies for a specific business purpose e.g. initiating a charging document by the local prosecutor, and includes the XML instance that delivers the payload of information. Additional information can be further documented through IEPD, which also contains data describing the structure, content and other artefacts of the information exchange. An IEPD supports a specific set of business requirements in an operational setting.

The formal definitions of these concepts, together with the technical principles and rules governing their use are presented in the document NIEM Naming and Design Rules (NIEM Technical Architecture Committee - NTAC, 2008). The document includes the relationships between NIEM to XML Schema and conformance rules. It is declared that the NIEM conceptual model follows the RDF semantics – each piece of data is represented through the subject-predicate-object triples, but this is an informal statement. In the end, data components are presented as instances of XML Schema declarations, and RDF is not used. From the organizational point of view, NIEM includes a set of operational and governance procedures, documentations, tools, training materials and technical assistance described in the NIEM Concepts of Operations (ConOps) (NIEM Program Management Office - NPMO, 2007).

New Zealand

Inspired by e-GIF, the Government of New Zealand defined the New Zealand e-GIF (NZ e-GIF). Since then, NZ e-GIF has evolved independently from e-GIF becoming a significant tool to promote collaboration and efficient use of resources among government agencies in New Zealand. Its version 3.3 consists of three documents (State Services Commission, 2008):

- *Policy*: Outlines the policy behind NZ e-GIF and its development, covering design principles, compliance regime, and procedures for extension and evolution.
- *Resources*: Covers the history of the framework, reference lists and URLs for all standards.
- *Standards*: A collection of standards organized into four structural layers – Network, Data Integration, Business Services, and Access and Presentation; and four aspects orthogonal to these layers – Security, Best Practice, Governance and Management (see Figure 4).

The four structural layers are:

1. *Network*: It covers the details of the data transport, such as network protocols. A crucial area for interoperability, NZ e-GIF applies a subset of the Internet Protocol suite, like IP v4, IP v6, LDAP version 3, FTP, HTTP version 1.1 and WebDAV.
2. *Data Integration*: This layer facilitates interoperable data exchange and processing, comprising standards that allow data exchange between disparate systems and data

Figure 4. New Zealand e-Government Interoperability Framework (NZ e-GIF) Technical Architecture

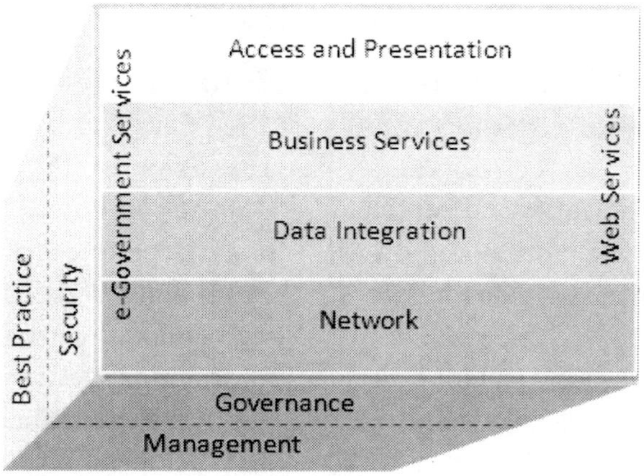

analysis on receiving systems, for example UTF-8, HTML, XML, GZIP and TAR.

3. *Business Services*: This layer supports data exchange between business applications and information contexts. Some standards in this layer are generic, covering multiple business information contexts like RDF and NZGLS (New Zealand Government Locator Service). Others work with data integration standards to define the meaning of data, mapping data to usable business information. For example, an agency could format a stream of name-and-address data in XML (Data Integration) using the business rules of xNAL (Business Services) to create a representation of name-and-address information, or use GML (Geographic Markup Language) to describe geographically oriented data.
4. *Access and Presentation*: This layer covers how users can access and present systems, compiled in New Zealand Government Web Standards and Recommendations (State Services Commission, 2009). It contains prescriptions of website contents, "about this site" sections, printing options, etc.

The following aspects apply to all structural layers:

- *Security*: This aspect crosses all layers to reflect the fact that security must be designed into a system, and not added as a layer on top of it. NZ e-GIF contains security standards designed to offer different levels of security, for example HTTPS, SSL or S/MIME. It also refers to a series of standards and policy statements (NZSITs) that provide advice and direction on the levels required.
- *Best Practice*: As published standards do not alone ensure interoperability but merely offer a common approach to managing and understanding the context of information exchange, this section contains Best Practices, Codes of Practice, and other general or sector-focused guidance. Included in this section are standards and local conventions that support best practices, rather than the actual data exchanges. Agencies use these standards, not necessarily with direct dependence on the standards of other agencies with whom they interoperate, but to support interoperability in general. DRM, WSBPEL, XSLT, UML, XMI, SAX and DOM all belong to this category.
- *e-Government Services*: The actual NZ e-GIF-compliant implementation of the

IT infrastructure which the ICT Branch of the State Services Commission makes available to public sector agencies for their use. Examples include: Metalogue – a web-based metadata repository, and Government Logon Service (GLS) – high-quality online authentication service providing users with a common logon to access all online services provided by participating agencies.

- *Web Services*: This aspect includes the standards related to web services like UDDI, WSDL and SOAP, facilitating the connection and integration of web-based applications over the Internet. Using best practice implementations, agencies can agree on interoperable service delivery to customers.

Underpinning these layers are governance and management specifications included in the Policy document. In addition, NZ e-GIF introduces five standard compliance levels: (1) Future Consideration – the standard is not yet reviewed, customized or having any successful implementation in the New Zealand government, yet it is probably necessary for public sector IT systems; (2) Under Development – the standard is under assessment by more than one government agency, e.g. having an active working group, a proof of concept or a pilot implementation with associated documentation; (3) Recommended – the standard emerges from development, review or a Working Group process with implementation documentation and evidence of successful interoperability and data exchange experiences, it is generally more recent and founded upon newer technologies or standards; (4) Adopted – normally upgraded from the Recommended status, the standard is mandatory, well established in the public sector ICT, and has complete supporting documentation and implementation processes; and (5) Deprecated – the standard has been abandoned for, or superseded by, better solutions at the Adopted or Recommended levels.

Estonia

The Estonian IT Interoperability Framework (Ministry of Economic Affairs and Communications, Department of State Information Systems, 2005) aims at providing guidance for elaborating common concepts used in the country-wide information systems and the organization of public procurement. The framework assumes that the operations performed by civil servants, entrepreneurs, local residents and software are all regarded as services, and the whole state information system is a service-centred organization (see Figure 5). End-users access the services in a common service space (CIT), interested in the service and not in the organization providing it. A service can access several information systems (IS) from different agencies. In order to achieve interoperability, service descriptions are compiled by service providers and published in the administrative system (RIHA). Taxonomies are also part of RIHA UDDI, presenting the characteristics and indicators of services. The service description is also published in free text on the web (in RIHA, by the service provider, or elsewhere).

The framework is divided into three aspects:

1. *Organizational Interoperability*: It refers to the ability of an organization to provide services to other organizations, or to their clients, by making use of information systems. It is associated with activities carried out by organizations and agreements between them, and ensured by legislation or agreements.
2. *Semantic Interoperability*: It refers to the ability of organizations to consistently understand the data exchanged, assuming a presentation mechanism for such data. Semantic interoperability has been recently updated to include a domain glossary using OWL (W3C, 2004) and a semantic descrip-

Figure 5. A view on the Estonian Information System – A Service Space based on the Support Systems Administered by RIHA (Adapted from Ministry of Economic Affairs and Communication, Department of State Information Systems, 2005)

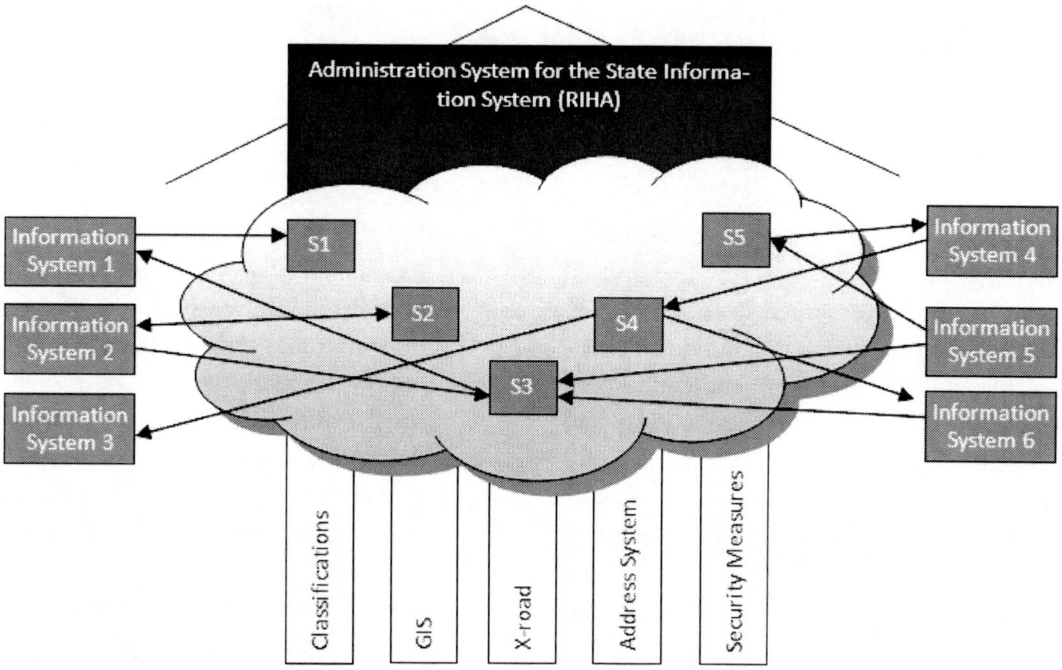

tion of operations and databases using WSDL (W3C, 2001).

3. *Technical Interoperability*: It denotes the infrastructure and software interoperability. Infrastructure interoperability is the ability of hardware acquired by different organizations to work in a connected way. Software interoperability is the ability of software in different organizations to exchange data.

This framework is complemented by the semantic interoperability methodology (Ministry of Economic Affairs and Communication, Department of State Information Systems, 2007a) and (Ministry of Economic Affairs and Communication, Department of State Information Systems, 2007b). The methodology is implemented using a variety of W3C recommendations - XML, XSD, WSDL, SA-WSDL, RDF and OWL, and OMG standards - UML2 and XMI.

GOVERNMENT INFORMATION SHARING FRAMEWORK (GISF)

In order to understand the concepts, issues and initiatives related to GIS previous sections reviewed the theory and practice in this domain. In particular, two theoretical models complemented by relevant research results were presented in the Foundations of Government Information Sharing section. While the models define the main dimensions of the GIS problem and provide the relevant concepts, tools, examples, components and solutions in each dimension, we also observe that before these models can be applied in practice, they must address the circumstances of individual organizations. As shown in the previous section, GIS initiatives vary in scope, depth, resources and level of support. While some GIS frameworks are just collections of standards, others include organizational and inter-organizational techniques and tools. We argue that despite the amount of knowledge available in the domain, a comprehensive framework that depicts the main concepts and guidelines for effective implementation of GIS initiatives is still missing. Such a framework could guide governments, particularly those beginning with IS initiatives, in how to enable IS within, across and beyond organizational boundaries.

This section introduces the Government Information Sharing Framework (GISF) – a revised version of the model presented in (Estevez, Fillottrani and Janowski, 2010) that builds on existing literature and experiences. The framework comprises two views: GISF Abstract View and GISF Detailed View.

The Abstract View is structured into a table with four rows representing dimensions and three columns representing maturity stages, as depicted in Figure 6. The dimensions follow (Pardo, Cresswell, Dawes, & Burke, 2004) after renaming the political into environmental dimension to extend its scope:

1. *Technological*: ICT-related concepts supporting or affecting IS;
2. *Organizational*: elements of an organization supporting or relevant to IS;
3. *Inter-organizational*: IS-related concepts concerning several organizations; and
4. *Environmental*: the environment affecting government IS, usually addressed at the political level.

Following (Landsbergen and Wolken, 2001), the Abstract View identifies three maturity stages in GIS:

1. *Experience Sharing*: the concepts that should be considered in early stages of government information sharing, serving to lay the foundations for GIS;
2. *Infrastructure Support*: the concepts that define the components that are accessible to the whole public administration, like infrastructure, GIS facilitation and promotion, etc.; and
3. *Information Strategy*: the concepts to define, enable and maintain the GIS environment.

For each pair of dimensions and maturity stages, we have the relevant GIS concepts, as shown in Figure 6.

The Detailed View identifies the concepts within each GIS dimension and maturity stage. The view, depicted in Figure 7, includes the core Government Information Sharing package that

Figure 6. Government Information Sharing Framework – Abstract View

concepts		MATURITY STAGES		
		1 - Experience Sharing	2 - Infrastructure Support	3 - Information Strategy
DIMENSIONS	Environmental	benefits risks	laws regulations	strategy engagement
	Inter-Organizational	scope	partnerships trust	governance community
	Organizational	roles	processes people	capacity-building function
	Technological	unit data component	standards attributes	repositories ontologies

contains one concept for each IS dimension (rows in the Abstract View). The detailed concepts are grouped into three packages according to different GIS maturity stages (columns in the Abstract View), informed by literature review and country experiences. The following four sections explain each package one by one.

Package 1: Government Information Sharing

This package introduces the concept of GIS and captures the four dimensions of GIS in order to relate them to the remaining three packages.

By GIS we understand all activities aimed at obtaining, maintaining, using and safeguarding information, performed collaboratively by people, processes and systems in the government sector. The four dimensions of GIS that are identified in this package are Technological, Organizational, Inter-Organizational and Environmental.

Package 2: Experience Sharing

The package includes the body of concepts that should be considered in early stages of GIS, a foundation for GIS. Some concepts, like Principle and Lifecycle, serve general purposes and cannot be analyzed from the GIS dimension perspective alone. Others like Benefit, Barrier and Risk are related to the Dimension concept and provide a basis for further classification.

Figure 7. Government Information Sharing Framework – Detailed View

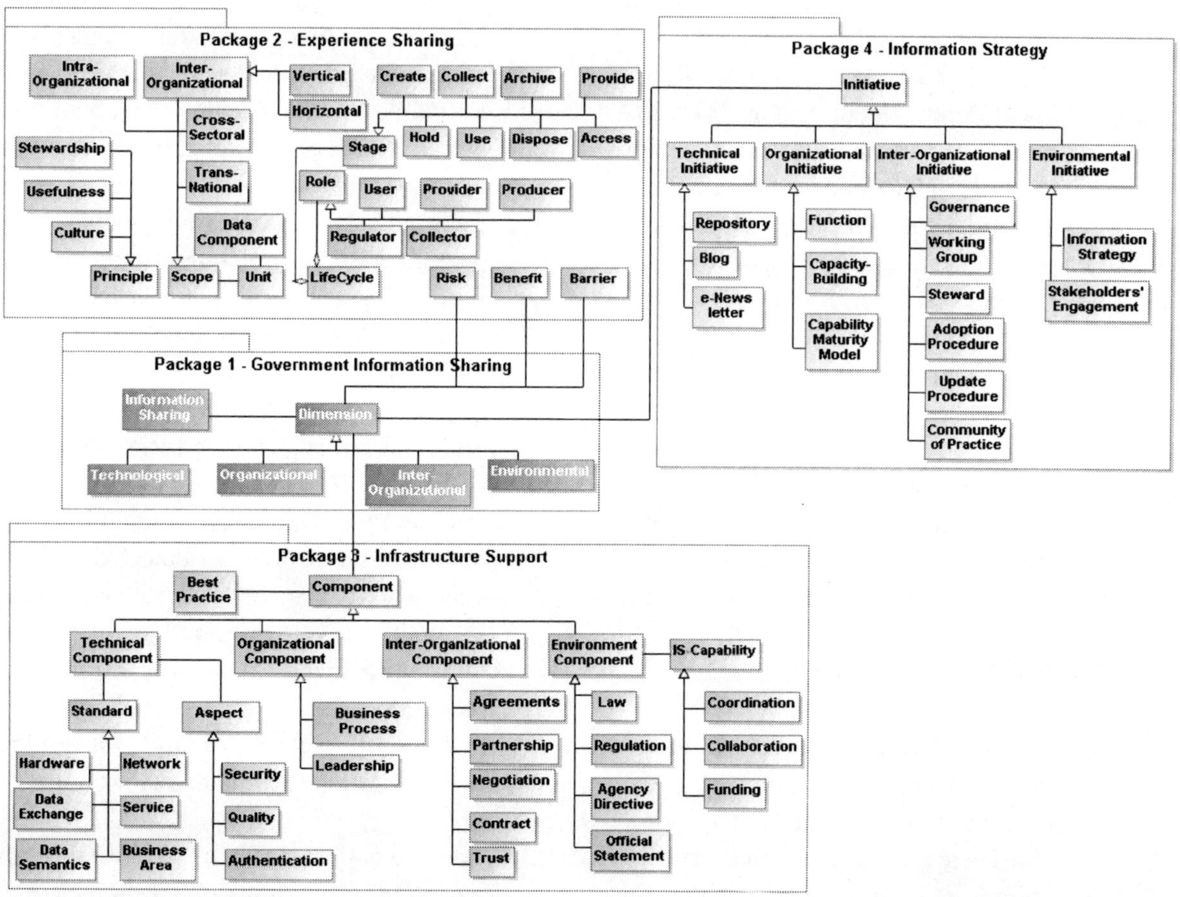

The concepts in this package are described as follows:

1. *Scope*: It determines the functional areas and the organizations involved in and affected by a GIS initiative, with four types of initiatives identified as follows:
   - Intra-Organizational: an initiative that affects all functional areas within an organization. For example, a GIS initiative involving all departments of a government agency.
   - Inter-Organizational: an initiative involving different agencies at the same (horizontal) or different (vertical) government levels. For example, a GIS initiative affecting all government agencies under a Ministry (horizontal) or a GIS initiative affecting federal, state and local government agencies (vertical).
   - Cross-Sectoral: an initiative affecting different organizations from the public, private and third sectors. For example, a GIS initiative involving a specific industry sector, including the government agency responsible for the sector and various companies operating in this sector.
   - Trans-National: an initiative affecting different public administration systems.
2. *Unit*: An organization involved in the GIS initiative, the lowest organizational structure involved in or affected by the initiative. A unit has GIS-related authority and responsibilities.
3. *Principle*: A comprehensive guiding assumption for GIS. Examples include:
   - Stewardship: a conservative principle to ensure that government agencies work to protect the accuracy and integrity of the information they collect and disseminate (Center for Technology in Government, 1999), and promote the fiduciary responsibility of all government agencies in managing such information.
   - Usefulness: an expansive principle that focuses on the value of information as a public asset (Center for Technology in Government, 1999);
   - Culture: the recognition that GIS denotes behavior and not technology (United States Intelligence Community, 2008) emphasizing the holistic/integrated approach required by GIS.
4. *Life-cycle*: identifies different activities and responsibilities required for GIS. Each activity is viewed as a stage and the following stages are defined: (1) Create – bringing to existence new information, for example registering a new company; (2) Collect – gathering or assembling information maintained by others, for example the agency responsible for public health collecting data about common illnesses encountered in public hospitals; (3) Hold – keeping created or collected information, for example maintaining citizen records; (4) Use – making use of information for a given purpose, for instance using statistics on common illnesses to design public health policies; (5) Archive – storing information for future use, for example archiving police, arrest and criminal records of citizens; (6) Dispose – destroying information, for example removing information about common illnesses detected over ten years ago; (7) Access – allowing an entity to obtain access to information, for example allowing citizens to access information related to public tenders; and (8) Provide – making information available, for instance broadcasting parliament sessions online.

While executing different activities of the information lifecycle, units play different roles:

(1) Regulator – ensuring compliance with GIS-related laws, regulations and established rules, for example an agency acting as a regulator of intellectual property rights; (2) Collector – gathering information from other entities, for example Justice collecting information from Police; (3) User – making use of information, for example Immigration Departments using information provided by Police; (4) Producer – producing information, for example the Statistics department collecting information on costs of living; and (5) Provider – supplying information, for example the local government disseminating tourism information to visitors.

5. *Data Component*: data representing a physical or abstract concept from the real world. For example, citizen, industry, holiday, etc. Data components are the target of GIS.
6. *Benefit*: useful consequences of a GIS initiative. Different categories of benefits are:
   - Technical: a benefit that improves the efficiency of providing ICT solutions, like adopting standards and metadata that enable heterogeneous applications to exchange data;
   - Organizational: addressing an organizational issue like increasing the quality, quantity and availability of data. For example, one benefit of implementing the National Spatial Data Infrastructure (NSDI) reported by the Federal Geographic Data Committee is that the savings obtained from data sharing can be used for other areas and that the released resources can be reallocated to serve quality control, data management or further data collection (Federal Geographic Data Committee, 2006);
   - Inter-Organizational: a benefit received by more than one organization, like improved professional relationships or broadened collaborative networks; and
   - Environmental: assisting public administrations in delivering better governance, for instance better understanding of economic and demographic trends by sharing data (Dawes, 1996).
7. *Barrier*: types of obstacles typically encountered while pursuing GIS, such as:
   - Technical: hardware and software incompatibility;
   - Organizational: lack of human and institutional capacity for GIS;
   - Inter-Organizational: any barrier that requires the involvement of several organizations to provide a solution, like inter-agency agreements for managing shared data; and
   - Environmental: a barrier related to the overall environment or the governance system, for example protecting the policy-making power of administrative agencies (Dawes, 1996).
8. *Risk*: possible threats affecting GIS initiatives, classified into:
   - Technical: unauthorized disclosure of sensitive or personal information managed by government (United States Intelligence Community, 2008), for instance the risk that a government agency discloses personal information to the spouse of a citizen without his or her permission;
   - Organizational: competition for resources between agency-focused and whole-of-government demands (Dawes, 1996), for example an agency having all its IT human resources working on internal projects and not being able to allocate time for developing new joined GIS projects;
   - Inter-Organizational: difficulties to share values such as trust, for ex-

ample an agency B duplicating the process of collecting and maintaining data that is already collected by an agency A, because B has no trust in the data provided by A or A is unwilling to share this data; and

- Environmental: societal consequences of not sharing government information. For example, the commission created in the US to investigate the 9/11 attacks illustrated several examples where the lack of effective GIS between federal, state and local agencies resulted in the failure of authorities to intercept the attack (The 9/11 Commission, 2004).

Package 3: Infrastructure Support

Two main concepts in this package are: Component – an element that can be present in a GIS-support infrastructure; and Best Practice – a technique, methodology, practice, procedure or other element that through experience or research has been proven to lead to good GIS results. Components can be further classified following GIS dimensions:

1. *Technical Component*: a solution to an ICT-related GIS problem. Two types of Technical Components are Standards and Aspects:
   - Standards: adopted conventions, protocols and rules necessary for infrastructure or software interoperability, grouped into: (1) Hardware – channel-specific standards for computers, digital TV, mobile phones, smart cards, etc. For example, the Minimum Hardware Configurations NASA Technical Standard (National Aeronautics and Space Administration, 2008) specifies a minimum configuration to purchase software components: processors, memory, mass storage, displays, graphics cards, interfaces, sound, optical drives, network interfaces, removable storage, smart card readers, etc. (2) Network – communication and data transport protocols, for example the File Transfer Protocol (FTP) standard (The Internet Engineering Taskforce - IETF, 1985). (3) Data Exchange – Standards for data representation, transformation and naming, for instance the ISO 3166 Codes (International Organization for Standardization, 1999) for representing the names of countries. (4) Data Semantics – Standards representing the meaning of data, for example the DoD Enterprise Architecture Data Reference Model (US Department of Defense, 2005) providing descriptions of 33 subject areas with definitions of the main data entities in each area. (5) Service – service and process description languages including access and presentation, for example the BPEL4WS (WS BPEL TC, 2003) language for modeling business processes and interaction protocols. (6) Business Areas – common business objects and standards for domain-specific transactions, for example the Business Reference Model of the US Federal Enterprise Architecture (FEA) that defines the lines of business (LoB) and their supporting internal operations. Such LoB help to focus on government functions instead of functional areas responsible for their execution, promoting collaboration across the government.
   - Aspects: cross-cutting technical concerns relevant to standards, grouped into: (1) Security - the elements supporting secure interoperation, for

example NZ e-GIF (State Services Commission, 2008) recommending Web Services Security (WSS) (OASIS, 2002) as a technical foundation to ensure secure exchange of messages. (2) Quality - ensures that the information is correct and complete, with indicators for measuring reliability and efficiency. For example, Guideline # 32 of the Guidelines for Juvenile Information Sharing (Office of Juvenile Justice and Delinquency Prevention, 2006) issued by the US Office of Juvenile Justice and Delinquency Prevention recommends designing procedures to ensure that the information disclosed by participating agencies is accurate and complete. (3) Authentication - specifications for digital signatures and digital rights. For example, the International Standard ISO/IEC 9594-8 – ITU-T Recommendation X.509 (ITU, 2005) that defines a framework for public key certificates and attribute certificates has been adopted by many countries as part of their GIS initiatives.

2. *Organizational Component*: supporting organizational aspects of GIS, in particular the issues of Business Processes and Leadership:
    - Business Process: a set of coordinated tasks and activities executed by persons and software that enable the accomplishment of GIS-related goals. GIS requires that business processes of various organizations are understood and mutually adjusted, with common processes identified, reengineered and provided as part of the infrastructure. For example, the interoperability approach by the Government of Australia addresses the harmonization of common business processes for service delivery (Australian Government Information Management Office, 2007).
    - Leadership: a functional role that enforces the organizational, process and cultural changes necessary for GIS. For example, in the US the role is fulfilled by the Chief Information Officer (CIO). The Clinger-Cohen Act created the Federal CIO position within the Office of the Management and Budget (OMB) reporting directly to the OMB Director, as well as the CIO function in every federal agency.
3. *Inter-Organizational Component*: elements like Agreements, Partnerships, Negotiations, Contracts and Trust, all used to create, support or maintain relationships between organizations:
    - Agreement: an arrangement between organizations regarding a course of action related to GIS. For instance, the Internal Revenue Service in the US has written agreements with all 50 states for sharing information on the regular basis – monthly, quarterly and annually, usually called Fed/State Agreements (Internal Revenue Service, 2009).
    - Partnership: a formalized agreement between public and non-public organizations specifying collaboration rules and defining precise roles and responsibilities of parties. For example, the Public-Private Partnership Program established by the US National Institutes of Health aims at facilitating collaboration between public and private sectors to improve public health through biomedical research. The program is responsible for defining partnership policies related to data sharing, data access, intellectual property, participation,

governance and decision-making processes, among others (Office of Science Policy - National Insitute of Health, 2010).

- Negotiation: a process by which the organizations involved in a specific issue resolve matters of dispute by holding discussions and making commitments which are formalized in agreements. For example, the Statement on Information Sharing and Personal Data Protection between the European Union and the US (US Department of Homeland Security, 2008) explicitly mentions the need for negotiation. Both parties agree that due to the incompatibility of laws, the processing of personal information in specific areas should be made according to specific conditions and considering safeguards for the protection of privacy, personal data and personal liberties. Such conditions would be defined through the negotiation of a GIS agreement.
- Contract: a document that formalizes an agreement between parties. Contracts can be modeled as a "formbook" similar to those used by lawyers to specify common practices. An example is "A Model Contract for Health Information Exchange" (The Markle Foundation, 2006), modeling the terms and conditions that collaborating entities can use for GIS within the health domain.
- Trust: the confidence required by the parties for effectively sharing information. Creating inter-organizational relationships for IS between public and non-public organizations requires negotiation and development of commitments primarily relying on trust. For example, one of the goals of the Information Sharing Strategy of the US Intelligence Community (United States Intelligence Community, 2008) is to establish a common trust environment. The goal is to establish uniform identity management, information security standards, information access rules, user authorization, auditing, and access control to promote trust.

4. *Environmental Component*: a component that exists or should be developed in the environment to facilitate, enforce or enable GIS initiatives, including capabilities and legal instruments:
   - Capability: the capacity for executing GIS initiatives in collaboration with others, including Coordination, Collaboration and Funding. (1) Coordination is the act of ensuring harmonious functioning of parties for obtaining the most effective results related to GIS. For example, the Interagency Threat Assessment and Coordination Group (ITACG) (ITACG, 2010) was established within the Information Sharing Environment (ISE) (Information Sharing Environment Office of the Director of National Intelligence, 2010) to facilitate the sharing of terrorism information among five communities: Intelligence, Law Enforcement, Defense, Homeland Security and Foreign Affairs. Within the ISE, the aim of ITACG is to improve the sharing of terrorism information with state, local, tribal, and private sector officials. (2) Collaboration refers to the act of working jointly with others. For example, the new GIS model proposed

by the IS Strategy of the Intelligence Community (see Figure 8) seeks greater collaboration between the Intelligence Community stakeholders and partners (United States Intelligence Community, 2008). (3) Funding includes the mechanisms to ensure the presence of financial resources for executing GIS projects. For example, the US Office of Justice Programs provides information on several funding mechanisms for developing or improving GIS (US Department of Justice, Office of Justice Programs, 2004). It explains sources of funding that can be used for criminal justice GIS projects and some mechanisms used for distributing funds to the states.

- Legal Instrument: laws, regulations, agency directives and other official statements underpinning GIS initiatives. (1) Laws comprise the body of rules and principles that govern GIS, enforced by a political authority. For instance, the UK Data Protection Act regulates the processing of information related to individuals, including obtaining, holding, using and disclosing such information (United Kingdom, 1998). (2) A Regulation is an official rule to control the behavior of those to whom it applies. For example, the regulation published by the U.S. Financial Crimes Enforcement Network (FinCEN) (US Department of Treasury, 1990) specifying agreements with foreign jurisdictions, enabling agencies of such jurisdictions to submit information requests concerning financial investigations to the financial institutions in the US through FinCEN. (3) An Agency Directive is an order or instruction given by a government agency. For example, the directive number 501 of the Intelligence Community establishes policies for discovering, disseminating and retrieving intelligence-related information collected or produced by the Intelligence

Figure 8. US Intelligence Community GIS Model (Adapted from Office of the Director of National Intelligence, United States of America, 2008)

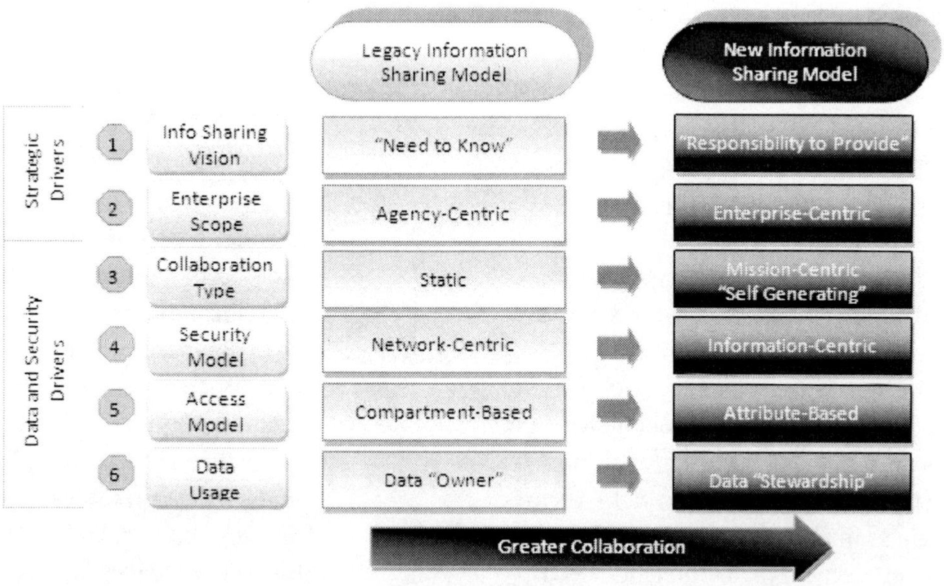

Community (Office of the Director of National Intelligence, 2009).

Finally, Best Practices refer to the solutions that have proven successful in solving GIS-related problems. Best Practices are orthogonal to the dimensions of GIS and their transfer requires customization to local conditions. For example, the Federal Emergency Management Agency of the US Department of Homeland Security created a national online network for sharing lessons learnt, best practices and innovative ideas for emergency response and homeland security. The initiative is called Lessons Learned Information Sharing (LLIS.gov) (US Department of Homeland Security, 2010).

Package 4: Information Strategy

The Information Strategy Package contains initiatives to enable and sustain IS among government agencies. The initiatives are again grouped into four GIS dimensions:

1. *Technical Initiatives*: any project delivering an ICT-related resource in support of GIS, like repositories, blogs, e-Newsletters, etc.
    - A Repository is a collection of electronic resources with services provided for adding new resources and for discovering and retrieving existing ones. Usually, repositories of standards and metadata are created by GIS initiatives, for example the e-GIF registry. Repositories also include data to be used by organizational units, activities in which the units are involved, and their roles.
    - A Blog is a specialized website that enables information exchange and sharing, and opinion-making on specific topics of interest to various government stakeholders. For example, the US Homeland Security Department implemented Blog@HomelandSecurity (US Department of Homeland Security, 2009), a blog for publishing daily activities of the Department and receiving citizen opinions. The Blog was implemented as part of the Open Government Initiative, aimed at publishing and improving the quality of government information, creating and institutionalizing the culture of open government, and enabling policy frameworks for open government.
    - E-Newsletter is an online medium for disseminating information, such as agency experiences with GIS initiatives; for example the National Information Exchange Model (NIEM) Newsletter (NIEM, 2009).
2. *Organizational Initiatives*: any GIS-related project that affects the organizational structure, functions, processes and responsibilities of a functional area. Examples include projects that establish information-related functions within organizational structures, build human and institutional capacity, and measure and assess the GIS maturity stage:
    - Function: recognizing information as an asset that must be managed, such initiatives assign the responsibility for information management within agencies. For example, the Queensland Government Enterprise Architecture (QGEA) Information Standard defines principles for implementing custodianship processes of information assets in government. The standard defines custodians as the officers responsible for implementing and maintaining information assets to ensure their quality, security, integrity, correctness, consistency, privacy, confidentiality and accessibility. Custodians are also responsible

for classifying and categorizing specific information assets (Queensland Government Chief Information Officer, 2010).

 - Capacity-Building: such initiatives aim at building human and institutional capacity to ensure that the responsibility for information management is performed effectively. For example, a capacity-building initiative introducing participants to the US National Information Exchange Model (NIEM). The initiative includes an online course that teaches XML-related concepts required for understanding NIEM, implementation concepts, and steps enabling information exchange with NIEM (NIEM, 2010).
 - Capability Maturity Model: a model for assessing the state of practice related to IS of an organizational unit. For example, the UK Cabinet Office created an Information Assurance Maturity Model (IAMM) to improve the information risk management (CESG - The National Technical Authority for Information Assurance, 2010) with five maturity levels.

3. *Inter-Organizational Initiatives*: any project affecting collaboration between or producing deliverables used by government units. This includes inter-organizational GIS initiatives to establish Governance, Working-Groups, Stewards, Adoption Procedures, Update Procedures, Communities of Practice and others, described as follows:
 - Governance: the system for leading and managing GIS initiatives. For instance, the US Department of Homeland Security established the IS governance framework comprising: (1) Information Sharing Governance Board (ISGB) as the higher-level decision-making body for all GIS and collaboration issues related to the Department, (2) the Information Sharing Coordination Council (ISCC) as the implementing body on the GIS issues, and (3) the Shared Mission Communities (SMC) comprising members of a shared mission that support ISCC and ISGB in gathering IS requirements and implementing solutions (Office of Science Policy - National Insitute of Health, 2010).
 - Working Groups: expert groups responsible for GIS-related issues, such as standards, metadata and other resources adopted by agencies. For example, the Global Justice Information Sharing Initiative (US Department of Justice, Office of Justice Programs, 2010) that advises the US Attorney General on justice, IS and integration initiatives has defined the following working groups: (1) Global Infrastructure and Standards Working Group - GISWG, (2) Global Intelligence Working Group - GIWG, (3) Global Outreach Working Group - GOWG, (4) Global Privacy and Information Quality Working Group - GIPQWG, and (5) Global Security Working Group. In particular, GPIQWG assists government agencies, institutions and justice entities in ensuring that personal information is appropriately collected, used and disseminated within the justice information systems (Global Privacy and Information Quality Working Group (GPIQWG), 2010).
 - Stewards: persons responsible for managing and coordinating IS initiatives across government. For example, ISCC, part of the governance

structure of the US Department of Homeland Security (DHS) (US Department of Homeland Security, 2009) comprises IS officers representing 22 offices of DHS. Such officers, responsible for GIS actions in their own units, are IS stewards.
    - Adoption Procedures: required for adopting government-wide practices by agencies. For example, the procedure by the Hertfordshire police (Hertfordshire Constabulary, 2008) aims at raising awareness about IS need and providing a uniform approach and general guidance for IS.
    - Update Procedures: keep standards and practices up-to-date with innovations introduced by new technologies. For instance, the policy document of the NZ e-GIF outlines procedures for extending the framework by submitting new standards.
    - Communities of Practice: groups of experts that share interests in GIS initiatives. An example is the Shared Mission Communities (US Department of Homeland Security, 2009), part of the governance framework defined by the U.S. Department of Homeland Security.
4. *Environmental Initiatives*: any project introducing a new GIS or GIS-supporting practice. Such projects are usually promoted by senior government officials since they require strong political support. Two examples are Information Strategy and Stakeholder Engagement:
    - Information Strategy: a plan for implementing IS or information-related policies. An example is the Information Sharing Strategy defined by the United States Intelligence Community (United States Intelligence Community, 2008). IS strategy includes the IS vision, model, goals and objectives, implementation plan and the governance system.
    - Stakeholder Engagement: a process that identifies and involves stakeholders, e.g. through a consultation process, in providing feedback about IS-related government policies. For example, the Stakeholder Engagement Policy by the Department of Local Government, Sport and Recreation of the Queensland Government specifies six principles for stakeholder engagement: inclusiveness, reach-out, mutual respect, integrity, affirming diversity and adding value.

VALIDATION

The Government Information Sharing Framework (GISF) presented in the previous section aims at refining and integrating existing theoretical and practical models for GIS. In order to demonstrate its completeness and flexibility, we applied GISF to describe and carry out a comparison between the five national GIS frameworks. The result is shown in Table 2.

Most frameworks concentrate on the Environmental and Technological dimensions and put less emphasis on the Organizational one. Australian AGIF is the most complete framework which includes: a roadmap for business process interoperability captured by the GISF's business process component at the maturity Stage 2, a capability maturity model captured as the GISF's organizational initiative at Stage 3; and case studies captured as best practices at Stage 2. In addition, the Australian NCF is an example of the GISF's inter-organizational initiative at Stage 3. The AGIF's Information Level describes enablers such as leadership, partnerships, and legal and policy frameworks, captured as organizational, inter-organizational and environmental components at

Stage 2, and an information lifecycle with roles and stages included in the GISF's Stage 1. The GovDex repository is an example of the technical initiative at Stage 3. AGIF's Technical Level enumerates technical standards and aspects, like those at the GISF's Stage 2. Finally, the Australia's IS Strategy is a concrete example of the GISF's environmental initiative at Stage 3.

The UK's e-GIF covers inter-organizational and technological concepts at the GISF's Stage 3, but the environmental and organizational concepts arrive only up to the Stage 2. The US's NIEM describes elements on the three levels of the environmental, inter-organizational and technological dimensions, while in the organizational dimension there are only references to capacity building and function concepts from the GISF's Stage 3. Similarly, the Estonian framework covers all three stages in the technological dimension, the first two stages in the environmental and inter-organizational dimensions, but in the organizational dimension the only described element is best practices at the GISF's Stage 2. New Zealand's NZ e-GIF, like the Australian framework, is well distributed over the three levels in the four dimensions, but the coverage of the concepts is less complete.

CONCLUSION

This chapter introduced the theory and practice of government information sharing (GIS) in order to capture the related concepts, issues and initiatives. From the theoretical point of view, GIS requires a multidisciplinary approach to understand the related issues, concepts, tools, requirements and visions, and the consideration of several perspectives on the problem. We also note that the nature of the problem may change depending on the circumstances of the organizations involved. From the practical point of view, national frameworks and experiences show that the GIS initiatives vary greatly in scope, depth, support and resources. Some frameworks are just collections of suggested technical standards, whilst others also include organizational and inter-organizational techniques and tools.

We also proposed the Government Information Sharing Framework (GISF) as a refined and updated version of the Landsbergen and Wolken's model, with more refined classification of the Stages 2 and 3. In order to classify and analyze practical GIS frameworks, the Landsbergen and Wolken model is the most complete among all models described in the Foundations of Government Information Sharing section. However, there is still no simple and clear way of organizing and understanding GIS with this model. The Stage 2 in this model is Supporting Infrastructure and its classification into technical, interoperability policy architecture and institutional is not clear, with the second apparently the outcome of the other two. In fact, the original work only suggests possible actions in these categories, without a model of the concepts involved. In addition, Stage 3 is merely described as "synthesize legal, managerial, and policy approaches to interoperability sharing", whereas the frameworks like AGIF and NZ e-GIF provide concrete examples at this stage that need a more detailed characterization. More recent theoretical works like (Pardo, Creswell, Dawes and Burke, 2004) and (Gil-García, Jun, Janssen, 2009) propose a refined structure of these concepts but from a limited perspective and not related to the overall model.

In a summary, despite the amount of knowledge available in the GIS domain, a comprehensive framework to capture the main concepts and guidelines for effectively implementing IS in government is missing. In order to fill the gap, the Government Information Sharing Framework (GISF) was proposed with two abstraction levels and with real-life examples to illustrate each concept of the framework. In addition, the validity of GISF was assessed though the comparison of the five national GIS frameworks.

Table 2. Applying GISF for Comparing Five National GIS Frameworks

			MATURITY STAGES		
		Countries	1: Experience Sharing	2: Infrastructure Support	3: Information Strategy
DIMENSIONS	Environmental	Australia	risk, benefit, barrier, usefulness, culture	regulation, agency directive, official statement, capabilities	information strategy
		UK	benefit, principle	official statement	------------------------
		US	benefit	agency directive, capabilities	stakeholder engagement
		NZ	benefit, usefulness, culture	official statement, agency directives, capabilities	stakeholder engagement
		Estonia	benefit, usefulness, culture	official statement agency directive	------------------------
	Inter-Organizational	Australia	vertical, horizontal scope	agreements, partnership	governance, working groups, update procedure, community of practice
		UK	horizontal scope	agreements	governance update procedure
		US	horizontal scope	trust, partnership	governance, working groups, update procedure, community of practice
		NZ	vertical, horizontal scope	agreements, partnership, trust	working groups
		Estonia	vertical, horizontal scope	agreements, laws, partnership	------------------------
	Organizational	Australia	stages, roles, usefulness	business process best practice	capability maturity model capacity building
		UK	roles	business process	------------------------
		US	------------------------	------------------------	capacity building, function
		NZ	------------------------	business process, leadership, best practice	capacity building
		Estonia	------------------------	best practice	------------------------
	Technological	Australia	------------------------	hardware, network, data exchange, business area, security, authentication	e-newsletter
		UK	data component	hardware, network, data exchange, security, authentication	repository vocabulary
		US	unit, data component	data exchange, network, data semantics, business area, security, authentication	vocabulary
		NZ	data component	hardware, network, data exchange, data semantics, security, quality, authentication	repository vocabulary e-newsletter
		Estonia	unit, data component	network, data exchange, data semantics, service, security, authentication	repository ontology

The chapter has made three contributions to the GIS literature. First, it improved conceptual clarity of information sharing in the government context vis-à-vis related government initiatives such as interoperability. Second, it identified the areas of concern and examples of concrete GIS initiatives for policy makers and government managers. Third, through the proposed framework, a number of interesting research problems associated with cross-border information sharing could be identified.

As explained in the introduction section, GIS is a key capability for raising e-Government to its highest maturity level – Seamless Government. In particular, Information Sharing across organizational boundaries is a key requirement for delivering seamless public services to be accessed through one-stop government portals. The proposed framework could serve as a tool for government decision-makers and practitioners to better understand the domain and to identify key areas for policy intervention.

Future work includes developing a methodology for strategic planning for GIS, refining the areas and concepts for policy intervention, identifying the areas and concepts of GISF that should be adapted to the local conditions, and proposing guidelines for carrying out this localization.

REFERENCES

W3C. (2001, March 15). *Web services description language (WSDL) 1.1.* Retrieved August 30, 2010, from http://www.w3.org/TR/wsdl

W3C. (2004, February 10). *OWL Web ontology language.* Retrieved August 30, 2010, from http://www.w3.org/ TR/ 2004/ REC-owl-features-20040210/

Australian Government Information Management Office. (2005, July). *Australian government technical interoperability framework.* Retrieved August 27, 2010, http://www.finance.gov.au/ publications/ australian-government-technical-interoperability-framework/ docs/ AGTIF_V2_-_FINAL.pdf

Australian Government Information Management Office. (2006, April). *Australian government information interoperability framework - Sharing information across boundaries.* Retrieved August 27, 2010, from http://www.finance.gov.au/ publications/ agimo/ docs/ Information_Interoperability_Framework.pdf

Australian Government Information Management Office. (2009, August). *National government information sharing strategy - Unlocking government assets to benefit the broader community.* Retrieved August 27, 2010, from http://www.finance.gov.au/ publications/national-government-information-sharing-strategy/ docs/ ngiss.pdf

Australian Government Information Management Office. (2007, July). *The Australian government business process interoperability framework: Enabling seamless service delivery.* Retrieved Auguust 27, 2010, from http://www.finance.gov.au/ publications/ agimo/ docs/ Business_Process_Interoeprabiltiy_Framework.pdf

Cabinet Office. (2010, May 29). *Gov talk.* Retrieved August 30, 2010, from http://www.cabinetoffice.gov.uk/ govtalk.aspx

Center for Technology in Government. (1999, October 1). *What rules govern the use of information?* Retrieved August 27, 2010, from http://www.ctg.albany.edu/ publications/ reports/ what_rules_govern/ what_rules_govern.pdf

Center for Technology in Government. (2001, April 10). *Insider's guide to using information in government, policy area.* Retrieved August 27, 2010, from http://www.ctg.albany.edu/ static/ usinginfo/ Policy/ policy.htm

CESG - The National Technical Authority for Information Assurance. (2010, May). *HMG IA maturity model*. Retrieved August 30, 2010, from http://www.cesg.gov.uk/ products_services/ iacs/ iamm/ index.shtml

Dawes, S. (1996). Interagency information sharing: Expected benefits, manageable risks. *Journal of Policy Analysis and Management, 15*(3), 377–394. doi:10.1002/(SICI)1520-6688(199622)15:3<377::AID-PAM3>3.0.CO;2-F

Der Beauftragte der Bundesregierung für Informationstechnik. (2008, August 24). *Standards and architecture for e-government*. Retrieved August 30, 2010, from http://www.CIO.bund.de/ cln_164/ DE/ Standards/ SAGA/ saga_node.html

Dublin Core Metadata Initiative. (1995-2010). *DCMI home: Dublic Core (R) metadata initiative*. Retrieved August 30, 2010, from http:// dublincore.org

Estevez, E., Fillottrani, P., & Janowski, T. (2010). *Information sharing in government - Conceptual model for policy formulation*. 10th European Conference on eGovernment, Limerick, Ireland.

Federal Geographic Data Committee. (2006, September 29). *Benefits - Federal Geographic Data Committee*. Retrieved August 30, 2010, from http://www.fgdc.gov/ framework/ handbook/ benefits

Fisher, D. (2004, September). *The business process maturity model - A practical approach for identifying opportunities for optimization.* Retrieved August 27, 2010, from http://www.bptrends.com/ publicationfiles/ 10-04% 20ART% 20BP%20 Maturity%20 Model%20-%20 Fisher.pdf

Gil-Garcia, J. R., Chun, S. A., & Janssen, M. (2009). Government information sharing and integration: Combining the social and the technical. *Information Polity, 14*(2).

Gil-Garcia, J. R., Pardo, T. A., & Burke, B. (2010). Conceptualizing information integration in government. In Scholl, J. (Ed.), *Electronic government, information, technology and transformation*. M.E. Sharpe.

Gil-Garcia, J. R., Schneider, C. A., Pardo, T. A., & Cresswell, A. M. (2005). *Interorganizational information integration in the criminal justice enterprise: Preliminary lessons from state and county initiatives*. 38th Hawaii International Conference on System Sciences (p. 8). IEEE Computer Society.

Global Privacy and Information Quality Working Group (GPIQWG). (2010). *Privacy and information quality*. Retrieved August 30, 2010, from http://www.it.ojp.gov/ default.aspx? area=globalJustice& page=1151

GovDex Team. (2010). *The Australian government collaborative workspace - Govdex*. Retrieved August 27, 2010, from http://www.govdex.gov.au/

Hertfordshire Constabulary. (2008, October). *Standard operating procedure title: Information sharing - Procedure number: P60105_1.* Retrieved August 30, 2010, from http://www.herts.police.uk/ FOI/ corporate_support_policies/ P60105_Procedure.pdf

Information Sharing Environment Office of the Director of National Intelligence. (2010). *Information sharing environment*. Retrieved August 30, 2010, from http://www.ise.gov/Homepage.aspx

Internal Revenue Service. (2009, December 22). *Fed/State information sharing*. Retrieved August 30, 2010, from http://www.irs.gov/ govt/ liaisons/ article/ 0,id=133087,00.html

International Organization for Standardization. (1999). *ISO 3166 code lists.* Retrieved August 30, 2010, from http://www.iso.org/ iso/ country_codes/ iso_3166_code_lists.htm

ITACG. (2010, September 03). *Interagency thread assessment and coordination group.* Retrieved August 30, 2010, from http://www.ise.gov/ITACG.aspx

ITU. (2005, August). *X.509.* Retrieved August 29, 2010, from http://www.itu.int/ itu-t/ recommendations/ rec.aspx?rec=X.509

Jing, F., & Zhang, P. (2009). *A field study of G2G information sharing in Chinese context based on the layered behavioral model.* 42st Hawaii International International Conference on Systems Science (HICSS-42 2009). IEEE Computer Society.

Landsbergen, D. Jr, & Wolken, G. Jr. (2001). Realizing the promise: Government Information Systems and the fourth generation of Information Technology. *Public Administration Review, 61,* 206–220. doi:10.1111/0033-3352.00023

Ministry of Economic Affairs and Communication, Department of State Information Systems. (2007a, February 25). *Instructions for the semantic description of databases and operations performed by databases,* version 1.1. Retrieved August 30, 2010, from http://www.riso.ee/ en/ files/ EstonianGov_Semantic_Description-Instructions_v1.1c.pdf

Ministry of Economic Affairs and Communication, Department of State Information Systems. (2007b, April 08). *Methodology for the semantic interoperability of databases and operations performed by databases.* Retrieved August 30, 2010, from http://www.riso.ee/ en/ files/ EstonianGov_Semantic_Description-Methodology_v1.2.pdf

Ministry of Economic Affairs and Communications, Department of State Information Systems. (2005). *Estonian IT interoperability framework.* Retrieved August 30, 2010, from http://www.riso.ee/ en/ files/ framework_2005.pdf

National Aeronautics and Space Administration. (2008, June 24). *Minimum hardware configurations.* Retrieved August 28, 2010, from http://www.nasa.gov/ pdf/ 324312main_STD-2805L.pdf

National Collaboration Program Team. (2005, May 05). *The National Collaboration Framework (NCF) - An introduction.* Retrieved August 27, 2010, from http://www2.finance.gov.au/ e-government/ service-improvement-and-delivery/ national-collaboration-framework/ docs/ NCP-Overview_Document_-_5_tiers.pdf

NIEM. (2009, August). *NIEM newsletter.* Retrieved August 31, 2010, from http://www.niem.gov/ newsletter200908-2.php

NIEM. (2010). *The NIEM practical implementer's course.* Retrieved August 29, 2010, from http://www.niem.gov/ elearning.php

NIEM Program Management Office - NPMO. (2007, January 9). *NIEM concepts of operations.* Retrieved August 30, 2010, from http://www.niem.gov/ files/ NIEM_Concept_of_Operations.pdf

NIEM Technical Architecture Committee - NTAC. (2008, October 31). *National information exchange model naming and design rules.* Retrieved August 30, 2010, from http://www.niem.gov/ pdf/ NIEM-NDR-1-3.pdf

OASIS. (2002). *OASIS Web services security (WSS).* Retrieved August 30, 2010, from http://www.oasis-open.org/ committees/ tc_home.php?wg_abbrev=wss

OASIS. (2007, April 11). *OASIS Web services business process execution language (WSBPEL) TC*. Retrieved August 27, 2010, from http:// www.oasis-open.org/ committees/ tc_home.php? wg_abbrev=wsbpel

OECD e-Government Studies. (2003). *The e-government imperative.* OECD Publishing.

Office of Juvenile Justice and Delinquency Prevention. (2006, October). *Guidelines for juvenile information sharing*. Retrieved August 30, 2010, from http://www.ncjrs.gov/ pdffiles1/ ojjdp/ 215786.pdf

Office of Management and Budget. USA. (n.d.). *Federal Enterprise Architecture (FEA)*. Retrieved August 30, 2010, from http://www.whitehouse.gov/ omb/ e-gov/ fea/

Office of Science Policy - National Insitute of Health. (2010, June 10). *NIH public private partnerships program*. Retrieved August 30, 2010, from http://ppp.od.nih.gov/

Office of the Director of National Intelligence. (2009, January 21). *IC directive 501 - Discovery and dissemination or retrieval of information within the intelligence community*. Retrieved August 30, 2010, from http://www.dni.gov/ electronic _reading_room/ ICD_501.pdf

Office of the Director of National Intelligence, United States of America. (2008, February 22). *United States intelligence community - Information sharing strategy.* Retrieved August 27, 2010, from http://www.dni.gov/ reports/ IC_Information_Sharing_Strategy.pdf

OMG. (1997-2010). *Object Management Group - UML*. Retrieved August 27, 2010, from http:// www.uml.org/

OMG. (1997-2010). *Object Management Group/ Business process management Initiative*. Retrieved August 27, 2010, from http://www.bpmn.org

Pardo, T. A., Burke, B., Gil-Garcia, J. R., & Guler, A. (2009). Clarity of roles and responsibilities in government cross-boundary information sharing initiatives: Identifying the determinants. *Proceedings of 5th International Conference on e-Government,* (pp. 148-155). Boston, MA: Academic Publishing Limited.

Pardo, T. A., Cresswell, A. M., Dawes, S. S., & Burke, G. B. (2004). Modeling the social & technical processes of interorganizational information integration. *Proceedings of the 37th Hawaii International Conference on System Sciences - 2004* (pp. 1-8). IEEE.

Pardo, T. A., & Tayi, G. K. (2007). Interorganizational information integration: A key enabler for digital government. *Government Information Quarterly*, *24*(4), 691–715. doi:10.1016/j.giq.2007.08.004

Queensland Government Chief Information Officer. (2010, February 08). *Information asset custodianship (IS44) - Current information standards*. Retrieved August 30, 2010, from http:// www.qgcio.qld.gov.au/ QGCIO/ architectureandstandards/ informationstandards/ current/Pages/ InformationAssetCustodianship.aspx

State Services Commission. (2008, February). *New Zealand e-government interoperability framework (NZ e-GIF),* version 3.3. Retrieved August 30, 2010, from http://www.e.govt.nz/ library/ e-gif-v-3-3-complete.pdf

State Services Commission. (2009). *Web standards - E-government in New Zealand*. Retrieved August 30, 2010, from http://www.e.govt.nz/ standards/ web-standards

The 9/11 Commission. (2004, July 22). *The 9/11 Commission report.* Retrieved August 30, 2010, from http://www.9-11commission.gov/ report/ 911Report.pdf

The Internet Engineering Taskforce - IETF. (1985). *File transfer protocol (FTP).* Retrieved August 30, 2010, from http://tools.ietf.org/ html/rfc959

The Markle Foundation. (2006, October). *A model contract for health information exchange.* Retrieved August 30, 2010, from http://www.connectingforhealth.org/ commonframework/ docs/ M2_ModelContract.pdf

United Kingdom. (1998). *Data Protection Act.* Retrieved August 30, 2010, from http://www.opsi.gov.uk/ acts/ acts1998/ ukpga_19980029_en_1

United States Intelligence Community. (2008, February 22). *Information sharing strategy.* Retrieved August 30, 2010, from http://www.dni.gov/ reports/ IC_Information_Sharing_Strategy.pdf

US Department of Defense. (2005, August 20). *DoD enterprise architecture data reference model,* v 0.04. Retrieved August 30, 2010, from http://cio-nii.defense.gov/ docs/ DoD_DRM_v04_5Aug.pdf

US Department of Homeland Security. (2008, December 12). *Statement on information sharing and personal data protection between the European Union and the United States of America.* Retrieved August 30, 2010, from http://www.dhs.gov/xlibrary/assets/usa_statement_data_privacy_protection_eu_12122008.pdf

US Department of Homeland Security. (2009). *The blog@HomelandSecurity.* Retrieved August 30, 2010, from http://blog.dhs.gov

US Department of Homeland Security. (2009). *Information sharing mechanisms to improve homeland security.* Retrieved August 30, 2010, from http://www.whitehouse.gov/ omb/expectmore/ issue_summary/ issueDetailedPlan_24.pdf

US Department of Homeland Security. (2010). *Lessons learnt-Information sharing.* Retrieved August 30, 2010, from https://www.llis.dhs.gov/ index.do

US Department of Justice and US Department of Homeland Security. (2010, August 19). *National information exchange model (NIEM).* Retrieved August 29, 2010, from http://www.niem.gov/ index.php

US Department of Justice, Office of Justice Programs. (2004, October). *Justice information sharing initiative.* Retrieved August 30, 2010, from http://it.ojp.gov/documents/ Infoshare_102004 _PlusAcronymGlossary.pdf

US Department of Justice, Office of Justice Programs. (2010). *Global justice information sharing initiative.* Retrieved August 30, 2010, from http:// www.it.ojp.gov/global

US Department of Treasury. (1990). *Financial crimes enforcement network.* Retrieved August 30, 2010, from http://www.fincen.gov/ about_fincen/ wwd/

WS BPEL TC. (2003, May). *Business process execution language for Web services,* version 1.1. Retrieved August 30, 2010, from http://www.ibm.com/ developerworks/ library/ specification/ ws-bpel/

Zheng, L., Yang, T.-M., Pardo, T. A., & Jiang, Y. (2009). Understanding the "boundary" in information sharing and integration. *Proceedings of the 42nd Hawaii International Conference on System Sciences - 2009* (pp. 1-10). IEEE.

Chapter 3
Cross-Boundary Collaboration of E-Governance in Taiwan

Yu-Hsieh Sung
Research, Development, and Evaluation Commission, Taiwan

ABSTRACT

To bolster e-government's chronic promotion of seamless services to all citizens, the Taiwan government will continue to focus on developing from the e-government to e-governance, which reflects the value of citizen-centric innovative service for better governance through information and communication technologies. With efforts over the past score years, the development of e-government has reached a certain limit, general public aspiration of one-stop services and swift services is still invariable. The integration and cross-boundary collaboration become the most momentous countermeasures to fulfill services from e-government to e-governance.

INTRODUCTION

There are four parts of this chapter based on Taiwan experience in the public sector which will be briefly described. The first part address the e-Government has reached a certain limits in spite of e-Government services have acquired many significant achievements, and cross-boundary collaboration is the key for next stage e-Government. Secondly, explains the theory and principles of cross boundary management and examines the link between the interdependence among agencies and cross boundary collaboration. Thirdly, elaborates the cross boundary management issues which bridge over the varied perplexity. Lastly, this chapter illustrate the e-Government cross-boundary collaboration in terms of two cases, those are Government Services Platform, and so-called "e-Housekeeper Services."

DOI: 10.4018/978-1-60960-753-1.ch003

BACKGROUND

Taiwan has been well known for its e-Government achievements over the past two decades. Taiwan is also well-regarded as a leading e-Government benchmark in international reports and studies. For example, Brown University of the United States has ranked Taiwan at first place three times in the global-e-Government surveys from 2001 to 2008 (West, 2008). The idea and process of building e-Government in Taiwan can be traced back to 1997. E-government projects in Taiwan were initiated by the Research, Development and Evaluation Commission (RDEC) under the Executive Yuan (the Cabinet). Taiwan government had set four stages as a roadmap for developing e-Government (details described in the Figure 1), which include: infrastructure development and penetration (1998~2000), on-line services development (2001~2004), integrated/ubiquitous government (2005~2007), and intelligent government (starting 2008). Through successful implementation of e-Government projects, Taiwan has achieved fruitful results. With above-mentioned processes as infrastructure, individual application, service online of e-Government, it has already marched into the phase of integration and innovations in Internet applications so that there have been milestone breakthroughs and developments in terms of service convenience, reduction in the volume of documents and transcripts, enhancement of administrative efficiency for public business, and active disclosure and transparency of government as well as the stimulation of networking service. Consequently, those e-services that were found dispersed in various government agencies in the past have been combined to simplify service workflow and integrate systems, and the efforts have, aside from helping to continuously enhance the efficiency of government service, also focused on effectiveness as the government heads towards integrated internet service to meet citizen's need (Sung, 2007).

THE DEVELOPMENT OF E-GOVERNMENT HAS REACHED A CERTAIN LIMIT

Taiwan has had more than 10 years experiences in developing e-Government projects since it was first introduced in 1997. To continue the ongoing implementation of e-Government, Taiwan government enacted a series of e-Government projects since 1997. Various government websites had been set up and almost all government application forms and services are available on-line. Moreover, a new master plan has been planned starting from shaping a new vision of integrated e-services after 2011. However, are those on-line services really meeting the citizen's demand?

The aim of e-Government by using information and communication technologies (ICT) is to provide the public better information and services. To transform and improve the traditional service is a continuous concern and needs to be supervised and controlled with care. During the last decade, Taiwan government just as many other countries in the world has placed great effort and resources in building an e-Government and earned certain achievements. Various e-Government applications such as e-taxation, e-procurement, electronic document interchange and many others started with "e-" are common in many countries. However, Taiwan government is not satisfied with what has been achieved. Obviously, the advantage of e-Government is providing fast and convenient services that save time and money. If the general public is not enjoying the benefits, the investment would not be worthy. Many citizens suggest that they would like to have more integrative services instead of visiting different government web sites for services. Then, for the next stage e-Government development, it ought to be so called "citizen-centric" (which means application developed from the standpoint of citizen). Therefore, Taiwan government need to promote the idea of using e-Government services by effectively integrating cross-agency services that meets the needs

Figure 1. The road map of e-government of Taiwan (Source: Sung, Y. H. (2007))

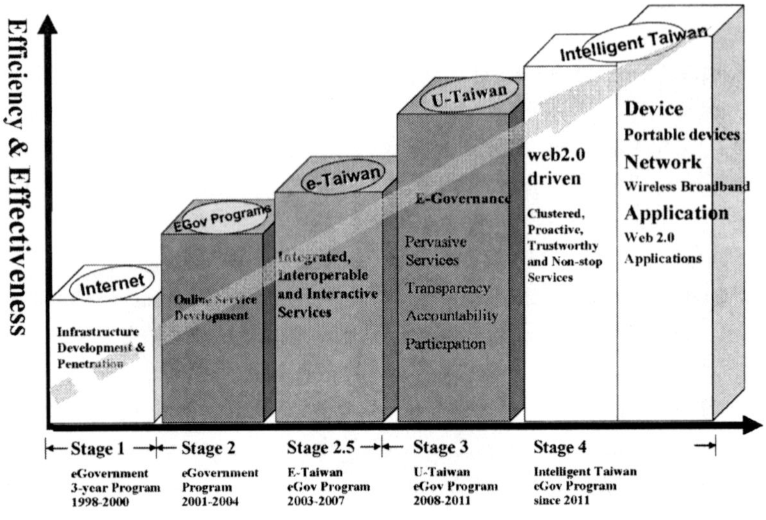

of citizens. The fulfillment of this step needs to tackle the challenge of not only adopting advanced ICT, but also paying attention to the classic problem of collaboration among different agencies. It also involves organization culture factors and procedural changes. Cross boundary task forces should be formed to build up consensus among co-workers from different agency and to re-design standard operation procedures from the point of view of citizen. Development of more innovative cross-agency e-services is necessary to meet the need of the general public (Sung, 2009). But, what kind of cross boundary e-services have the greatest chance to succeed remains the main problem? We need to understand the basics of cross boundary management in public sector.

Governments have traditionally been organized to respond to the requirements of general social functions and to meet people's collective needs, and, as such, divide their resources, distribute their resources and manage the performance of their operations based on those criteria. However, social problems do not occur according to how governments have divided their resources, especially when one bears in mind radical environmental and societal change. Therefore, those problems are defined as having boundary-spanning essence. Besides, there is a so-called issue related to cross boundary management in organizations that is in complete contrast to the issue related to result-oriented management applied in the traditional design of division of labor. However, in practice, the division of labor in an organization often becomes an obstacle, neglected in the quest to achieve its goals. So, the core issue of cross boundary management should be to focus on how an organization can best benefit from its division of labor and reach solutions to boundary-spanning collaboration. In the past, governments had been traditionally organized in order to control and issue commands to their members of staff, thus handling affairs through their vertical and horizontal hierarchies. However, boundaries between agencies will become increasingly blurred and ambiguous in the future because more and more public affairs must be handled in a cross boundary manner. Therefore, governments in many countries have nowadays addressed the issue about how a government may effectively deal with boundary-spanning issues among different agencies. Besides, more and more government reformers have started to suggest that governments use ICT to improve their cross boundary management to ease problems regarding the division of labor in their organizations (Sung, 2006).

PRINCIPLES OF CROSS BOUNDARY MANAGEMENT

This part examines how government manages cross boundary relationships among different agencies, and adapts to environmental changes in order to reduce coordination costs with the best-designed structure. Moreover, how ICT play the role to drive the adaptation and result in structural change? As long as we understand the essence of cross boundary management, we can easily apply it to the integration of e-Government services.

Theoretical Base for Cross Boundary Management

Organization theorist Thompson believed that the establishing, merging or the abolition of structures, has to start with the review of organization functions (Thompson, 1967). The organization function is the soundest measurement for the mission of an organization. In examining an organization, one has to identify its functions, and then realize why design the structure to exercise the functions. Which functions can be done away with? Which functions could be done better outside the organizational scope? How should an organization be designed and organized in order to make it function and put them into practice? Based on the above, we should start with the basic functions an organization should have, and discuss them within the structure of an organization. The question of how to make an organization perform at its best in the process of organizational structure design includes the questions of how to put necessary functions together and to departmentalize them, and the question of how to reduce coordination cost among agencies as you deal with organization design.

Management of Interdependence Beyond Agency Boundary

When an organization has decided its functions, the designation of its functional activities is also confirmed, and this is the starting point for departmentalization. Thompson emphasized putting functional activities that are continually interdependent into the same agency first, in other words, identifying their sequential relationships and group them together. Secondly, grouping reciprocal interdependent relationships should be considered accordingly. In other words, for those output of a certain unit is the input for other units should be integrated into one agency. Lastly, it is the relationship of pooled interdependence can be put together, this is to say, two units run their function independently but if one needs to work with the other, then the two can combine. In sum, the possibility of combining together depends on whether the new combination can bring down the coordination cost among different units. Using similar analogy, if the agencies involved do have sequential, reciprocal or pooled interdependence, those agencies have more chance to manage cross boundary collaboration successfully. Although functional scopes are expected to use different methods of combination to define its scope of function, they cannot indefinitely be incorporated into the same one big organization. One has to consider the degrees of inter-unit cooperation (low communication and operating cost), economies of scale formed between units, and total cost of organization internal collaboration as a whole. Thompson suggests first to deal with the ones that are sequentially interdependent and adopt them into the scope of cross boundary management, secondly, those that are reciprocally interdependent, and lastly the pooled interdependent. In the public sector, in incorporating different functions into the same organization, one can take into consideration the above-mentioned order of interdependence. These are the theoretical bases for understanding how to manage the cross boundary interdependence among ministries/agencies under the Cabinet, or bureaus/sections under the ministry.

To be sure, putting all related units in the same agency is the best solution. However, if some units cannot be in the same agency due to high coordination cost, then a hierarchy will then be another solution. If a hierarchical system is not possible, a temporary task force can be formed as a solution, this also explains that when an organization is departmentalized, there is still cross boundary management issues. It is the result of departmentalization but also why there are so many types of committee and task-forces co-existing to strengthen inter-unit cooperation and coordination. Moreover, if we consider the impact of ICT on cross boundary management, it does help to reinforce sequential, reciprocal or pooled interdependent relationship among agencies because they are already get used to send emails, share web applications, or use same data bases, etc. That will even tighten their interdependent relationships.

Re-Adjust Cross Boundary Management to Adapt to the Environment

All organizations face the problem of uncertainties in their environment, and such uncertainties make public administrator unable to control and project how the resource is used and circulated. Therefore under the circumstances where the environment is complicated and unstable and resources few, cross boundary management becomes a challenge. Besides the inherent complication and uncertainty, the degree of dynamism and pace of change require an organization to react promptly. Therefore in order to effectively manage the environment, to minimize uncertainty, an organization needs an adaptive organizational structure to respond to the needs of the functional change in such an environment. In other words, the re-adjustment of the organizational structure becomes a means to adapt to the external environment. Thompson believes that when an organization faces an uncertain environment, the degree of departmentalization efforts tends to be higher than in a stable environment. Therefore, it is generally agreed that the more complicated and fast-paced an environment the organization faces, the less formal the structure of the organization should become. Inversely, when the environment is stable, and of the same nature, it is generally agreed that an organization adopting stable structure, centralized authority and a broader Standard Operating Procedure is more efficient.

CROSS BOUNDARY MANAGEMENT ISSUES FOR E-GOVERNMENT DEVELOPMENT

Once we understand the nature of cross boundary management, there are still several issues need to be addressed in the development of next stage e-Government which require building up incentives and overcome the challenges for cross-boundary collaboration. It will start with technical issues, then ultimately reach the basic question of the evolvement of cooperation among different agencies. There are fours things need to keep in minds when dealing with cross boundary management (Sung, 2008):

Adopting Web Service Platform

Through adopting the basic framework of web service platform and integrating cross boundary citizen-centric application services, the government can thus provide one-stop, integrated services to the public using a single Internet platform. The platform is the solution for putting all kinds of sequential, pooled and reciprocal interdependences among various agencies together for cross boundary collaboration. Public satisfaction can be increased while costs for constructing government information systems can be reduced to achieve the best results from cross boundary integration.

Promoting Common Standards

To facilitate the integration of information systems and reduce operational costs, common standards should be promoted and related information processing guidelines will be enforced. The government plans to promote open software as one of bases for e-Government services, which will serve as the service platform for innovative, integrated cross boundary services and support the integration of information application systems among agencies. This will accelerate the integration of agency's internal resources and alleviate the difficulties in providing integrated e-services.

Expanding Service Value

From the point of view of the general public or private enterprises, the government not only have to integrate inter-agency work flow vertically but also integrate the service flow of different agencies horizontally to create an innovative cross boundary service flow to replace the current segmented service flow and realize the ideal integrated, one-stop services. For example in Taiwan, three brand new e-housekeeper (for the general public, more on the following case introduction), e-helper (equivalent to e-housekeeper but for private enterprises services) and e-secretary (e-housekeeper counterpart aimed at government employee) were being developed and provide value-added services to satisfy the integrative needs of the general public.

Control and Coordination Mechanism

After establishing the platform and adopting common standards among agencies, a control and coordination mechanism needs to set up to ensure the continuous operation of this cross boundary management. Regular meeting, dedicated task force, and many other management techniques should be employed to maintain the balanced collaboration. This is very important for agencies retaining certain interdependent relationships which they don't have jurisdiction with each others.

E-GOVERNMENT PRACTICE FOR CROSS-BOUNDARY COLLABORATION

To utilize ICT to improve administrative efficacy of various interdependence among government agencies, to enhance public service quality and to support government reform, and finally to provide better services to the general public are the major concerns of Taiwan government. To develop innovative and integrative one-stop services and collaboration among government agencies for information exchange is critical for future success. It is not just e-Government applications, but also towards the optimal goal of e-Governance. Two typical cases in Taiwan for above purpose are as follows (RDEC, 2010):

Developing E-Government Services Platform (GSP) for Better Integration of Information Services

In order to integrate government information services, to coordinate with agencies of all levels, to breakthrough existing work bottleneck and promote cross boundary e-services, the standardized e-Government Services Platform (GSP, as shown in Figure 2) is set up in collaboration with advanced technologies and skills. Taiwan government has recognized the importance of customer-oriented and user-centric service concepts. GSP is thus set up in accordance with the principles of cross boundary management to serve as the foundation of e-Government. The major objective is to provide the general public a convenient online service delivery "one-stop window". No matter where the people are, they could have access to government services as long as they are connected to the Internet. E-Government service platform hopes to offer the general public integrative services, which greatly streamlines the government operation procedures, to link all kinds of serial, reciprocal, and pooled interdependence among agencies together and brings up the best results.

Taiwan government has invested USD 30 million since GSP project was launched in 2003. To enhance the government's administrative efficiency and provide innovative, useful and valuable services to citizens, more and closer cross-agency cooperation and collaboration are required and it is critical to integrate the various information systems used among government agencies. On the technical side, the RDEC has implemented GSP that provides a very convenient and helpful environment for developing and implementing cross-agency service integration. GSP follows the Service Oriented Architecture, and consists of 11 modules such as account management, service integration, directory service, and e-payment, etc.. At this entry site, the general public now could access to 5,089 websites of government agencies and suggestion mailbox, download 8,729 application forms, and connect to 2,501 online services. The number of visits of the portal website has exceeded 17 million monthly.

Agencies can also build cross-agency web services easier on GSP. Currently, GSP has supported the development of various cross-agency cluster services. The most difficult issues have been culture and human factors instead of technical ones. How to nurture a culture for successful cooperation and collaboration among government agencies is a critical factor for the project's success. Along with the portal site, GSP is the gateway to integrate and exchange needed information for the various agencies in order to provide innovative one-stop service. Those various innovative services are classified into 12 categories: e-travel, e-business, e-care, e-health, e-employment, e-household, e-taxation, e-military service, e-housing, e-public safety, e-foreigner service, e-mainland policy service. Using the service platform, agencies are able to handle different interdependence effectively. For those citizen-centric services, they all include agencies with some kinds of interdependence which ensure successful implementation. The experience told us if there are no clear interdependences among agencies involved, there is less likely to be successful to implement cross boundary application.

Figure 2. Government service platform of Taiwan's e-government (Source: Sung, Y. H. (2008))

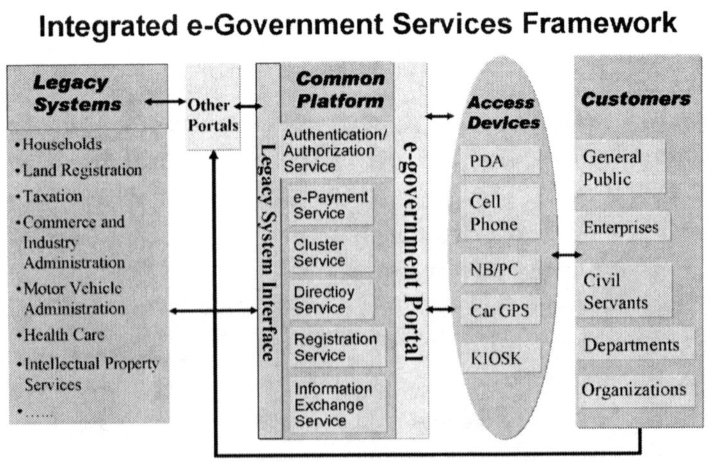

Developing Citizen-Centric E-Government Services

"E-Housekeeper" service (for details please refer to Figure 3), the most popular citizen-centric service in Taiwan, is aimed at providing effective management of citizens' daily affairs. The public generally needs to visit separate government websites with their various inquires, and may have to visit different agency websites for different information and to make payments. To address this inconvenience, Taiwan government has gathered all billing and notification information into a single one-stop window website called e-Housekeeper. This project is designed to collect all types of information relevant to people's daily lives such as payments, reminder letters and messages from the pertinent government agencies. Issues such as vehicle inspection orders, traffic tickets, parking fees, etc. are all loaded to the single website. The service thus not only informs users instantly of new issues, but also automatically reminds users of payment messages and pay-by dates. The e-Housekeeper service has been in operation since 2008. There are more than one hundred and sixty thousand of members subscribe this service till 2010. In the future, the e-Housekeeper service will not only indicate when payments are due, but will also keep people informed through the assistance of a personal information manager.

Clearly, the e-Housekeeper serves as a gateway to integrate and exchange pooled information for the various agencies in order to provide citizen-centric one-stop service. The general public will be benefited by this project that can help them pay their water bills, electricity bills, parking fee, telephone bills, or obtain vehicle registration services and make registration of their properties. This requires lots of efforts in cross agency coordination and proves to be a successful application for serial, reciprocal, and pooled interdependence management. The successful implementation of this service is done by a task force organized by RDEC. It identified agency interdependence from the start which ensured there are incentives for agencies to collaborate, thereafter pushed for cross boundary coordination. Of course, there were arguments when integrating different information systems. The solution was to adopt common standards and use universal platform.

CONCLUSION

Through the continuous efforts of pushing the next stage e-Government, the "e" concept has been integrated with government administration altogether. However, we should not merely emphasize ICT to approach new style of Taiwan e-Government project, we also have to lift the

Figure 3. Cross boundary application: e-housekeeper service (Source: Sung, Y. H. (2008))

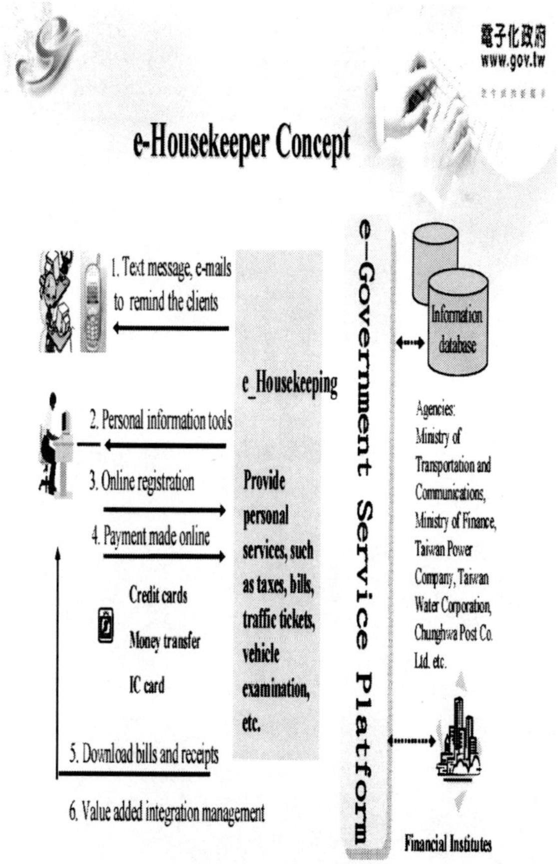

attention to e-Governance level which means more commitment for citizen-centric e-services. We definitely recognized that the next step for Taiwan government development is to continuously evolve, requires better management of agency interdependence, and leverage the level of e-Government to e-Governance. To achieve the extra-ordinary goal, any public administrators need to know the nature of cross boundary management and apply it to e-Government projects in order to get best results for e-Governance.

REFERENCES

Government Reform and Innovation. (n. d.). Retrieved September 1, 2010, from http://www.rdec.gov.tw/ mp.asp? mp=14

Sung, Y. H. (2006). Reforming government organization and information system to provide integrated services. [RDEC]. *Research, Development and Evaluation Commission Bi-monthly, 30*(6), 35–43.

Sung, Y. H. (2007). How has Taiwan achieved the world highest e-government standard? In Obi, T. (Ed.), *E-governance: A global perspective on a new paradigm* (pp. 75–80). Tokyo, Japan: IOS Press.

Sung, Y. H. (2008). *Digital government*. Lujhou, China: National Open University.

Sung, Y. H. (2009). Service quality between e-government users and administrators. *Journal of E-Government Policy and Regulation, 32*, 241–248.

Thompson, J. (1967). *Organizations in action*. New York, NY: McGraw-Hill.

West, D. (2008). *The Brookings Institution*. Retrieved September 1, 2010, from http://www.brookings.edu/

Chapter 4
E-Government Implementation in Belgium and its Link with the European Dimension

Frank Leyman
Federal Public Service for ICT, Belgium

ABSTRACT

Information and communication technologies have become the core element of managerial reform, and electronic government (e-government) has played an extremely important part in public governance. With respect to availability of e-services for businesses and citizens, Belgium has considerably improved its position in international benchmarks. Belgium has increasingly focused on reducing administrative burden, developing cross-boundary collaboration, and achieving many important user-related goals. This chapter describes the development of The Federal Public Service for ICT (FEDICT), and its various modules and functions in details. In addition, it discusses how FEDICT helps to reach the goal of a user-centric and cross-boundary e-government in Belgium, and its relationship with other European countries.

INTRODUCTION

With the rapid evolution of information and communication technologies (ICTs), customer service delivery is being confronted with a radical transformation in the public sectors. ICTs have become the core element of managerial reform, and electronic government (e-government) will play an extremely important part in future governance. Indeed, ICTs have not only opened up many possibilities for improving internal managerial transparency and efficiency and the quality of public service delivery to industries and citizens, but also contributed to dramatic changes in re-

DOI: 10.4018/978-1-60960-753-1.ch004

engineering (Anderson, 1999), politics (Nye, 1999), government institutions (Fountain, 2001), performance management (Brown, 1999), etc.

E-government, in response to the rapid development of the Internet and increased use of ICTs, is one of most interesting concepts introduced in the field of public governance in the twentieth century. E-Government development has been dispersed throughout various countries, with significant differences in approach, scope and speed due to considerable variations in size of administrations and resources dedicated to e-government. In Belgium, E-Government development began to take off at the end of the 1990s. With respect to availability of e-services for businesses and citizens, Belgium has considerably improved its position in international benchmarks since then. According to the European Commission Benchmark of European Online Public services, Belgium evolved from a fully online availability of 50% in 2006 to 60% in 2007. Belgium ranks among the leader in a wider European Union comparison of online sophistication of basic public services for businesses (OECD, 2008).

There are various stages of e-government, each of which reflects the degree of technical sophistication or maturity: (1) simple information dissemination (one-way communication); (2) two-way communication (request and response); (3) service and financial transactions; (4) integration (horizontal and vertical integration); and (5) political participation (Moon, 2002: 426). In order to move to the next stage of e-government, developing a user-centric and cross-boundary e-government in Belgium is an essential challenge, as in other European countries. On the one hand, developing a user-centric e-government depends heavily on being aware of the different needs people have when interacting with public authorities and institutions. That is, it is crucial to focus on the interests of demand side rather than on supply side and on technological capabilities. On the other hand, developing a cross boundary e-government depends heavily on horizontal and vertical integration of public services and simplification of users' interactions with public authorities.

Belgium is aiming to pursue e-government not as an end in itself, but rather as an enabler for wider public sector development. Belgium has increasingly focused on enabling administrative burden reduction, developing cross-boundary collaboration, and many important user-related goals. This paper describes the development of The Federal Public Service (FEDICT), and its various modules and functions in details. We also discuss how FEDICT helps to reach the goal of a user-centric and cross-boundary e-government in Belgium, and its relationship with other European countries.

GEOGRAPHICAL AND POLITICAL STRUCTURE IN BELGIUM

Belgium is a kingdom situated in the heart of Europe in between France, The Netherlands, Luxembourg and Germany. The country has about 10.6 million citizens on a rather small area of 30.528 km^2. 60% speak Dutch, 40% French and less than 1% German. Flanders is relatively flat and has a coastline, while the Walloon Region has a much more accentuated landscape especially in the southeast of the country where the Ardennes is situated.

Belgium became independent in 1830. Between 1970 and 1993, the country evolved into a more efficient federal structure. This occurred through five state reforms (in 1970, 1980, 1988-89, 1993 and 2001). As a result, the first Article of the Belgian constitution reads today: "Belgium is a federal state, composed of communities and regions". The power to make decisions is no longer the exclusive preserve of the federal government and the federal parliament. The leadership of the country is now in the hands of various partners, who independently exercise their authority within their domains.

The redistribution of power occurred along two lines. The first line relates to language and, in a broader sense, to everything related to culture. The result was several communities. The concept of "community" refers to persons that make up a community and the bond that unifies them, namely their language and culture. Belgium sits across the fault line that separates German and Latin cultures. This explains why the country has three official languages: Dutch, French and German. As a result, Belgium today, has three communities: the Flemish Community, the French Community and the German-speaking Community. These communities therefore correspond with the population groups.

The second line of state reform was historically inspired by economic interests. The Regions, which aspired to more economic autonomy, conveyed these interests. The establishment of the three regions was the result: the Flemish Region, the Brussels Capital Region and the Walloon Region. Up to a certain level they can be compared with the American states or the German "Länder". The country is further divided into 10 provinces and 589 municipal councils.

The Federal State

Figure 1 shows the geographic location of Belgium. The Federal State nevertheless retains important powers, for example in the area of foreign affairs, national defense, justice, finance, social security, important parts of national health and domestic affairs. However, the communities and the regions also have the power to establish and maintain foreign relations.

Reconciling regional and cultural identities within a federal structure is easier said than done. Yet, it has the advantage of taking the decision process closer to the population. The result is a more sharply defined political structure with a greater emphasis on the quality of life. Nevertheless, these differences make Belgium the charming little country what it is. The diversity between the cultures creates a certain attraction for visitors.

Today all powers have been distributed over the political entities. For example, defence is

Figure 1. Geographic location of Belgium. Source: from FEDICT

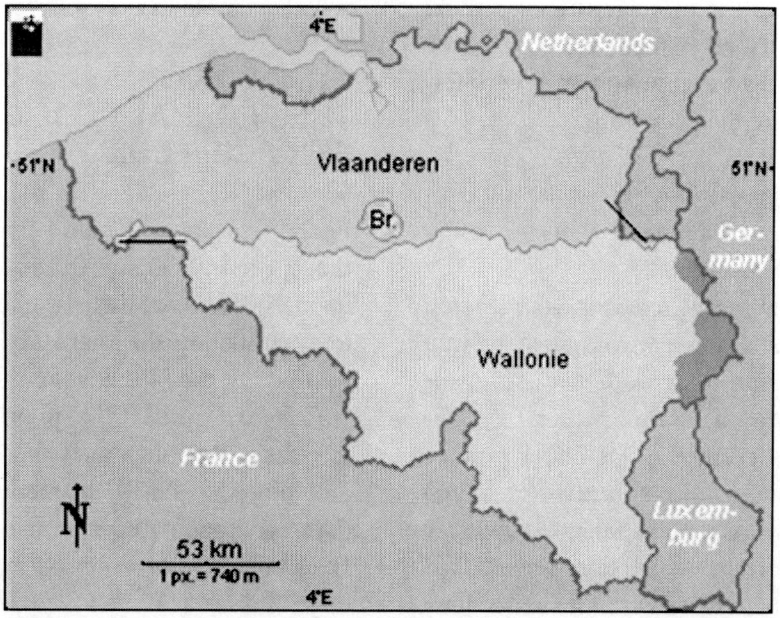

handled by the Federal level, there where education is handled at Community level. This means that Prime Minister has nothing to say when it comes down to a law for schools. It is the Head of the Community who has the last word on this matter. This political situation, which makes Belgium unique, also creates an additional complexity with regards to building e-government services and, as a consequence, makes e-governance more difficult.

For the Belgian citizen it is very difficult to have a complete view on who is responsible for what. He/she "does not know" or "doesn't want to know". It is up to public authorities to organise themselves in such a way that it is transparent to the citizen. E-government must enable one virtual government consistent to the customers with full respect for every single competence. One could say that even within the Belgian territorial borders, a cross-boundary e-government collaboration, be it here between Federal level, Regions and Communities, is needed.

The day that Belgium decided to go for a federal model, it also allowed that each of the entities was free to define its own e-government strategy with its own budget, priorities and speed of implementation. Very soon we would see divergence and less alignment of programmes. As this can only lead to more confusion for the citizens and industry, all parties decided to agree on a set of pre-agreed e-government principles. These principles are the following:

- Only launch an e-service when the full end-to-end solution is available. This means no phased implementation.
- Be fully transparent towards your citizen when it comes down to usage of private data. This means that we tell in clear language when we have used which (private) data for what purpose. (Open book policy)
- Limit the administrative formalities. When converting an existing paper based application into an electronic version, we verify if the process is still needed, if it can be done easier, faster or simpler. In some cases we even delete the application.
- No extra cost. This means that an electronic version of an application should not cost any Euro more to the citizen compared to the paper based process. (No digital divide)
- Use authentic unique data sources (virtual government). In view of better efficiency we decided never to duplicate databases, but to only work with authentic sources. This avoids working with non up-to-date data or wrong information. There is only one entity that is responsible for a particular database. It is the only door at which to knock if you need that data. They are also the only ones accountable for the quality of the data.
- Respect of privacy: everything that is being built needs to be in full accordance with the rules of respect of privacy.
- No digital divide: it goes without saying that any e-government service that is being built, should not make the digital divide bigger than it already is. This means that we cannot force people to invest in electronic equipment just to be able to access a service. So all e-services also need to be available in the non-electronic way.

THE FEDERAL PUBLIC SERVICE: FEDICT

Fedict is a young Federal Public Service (FPS) that specializes in e-government. When it was set up in 2001, Fedict focused mainly on developing and maintaining the foundations of e-government. Nowadays, the FPS devotes more attention to the various aspects of ICT support and developing e-government applications, as well as to campaigns and projects aimed at encouraging society to adopt computerization. It also actively promotes Belgium internationally as a region of ICT knowledge and innovation. Over the years, Fedict has based itself more on the requests and needs of its customers: private citizens, other public services and businesses. This evolution has gone hand in hand with an important shift: the emphasis placed previously on developing foundations and technical support has been replaced by an enhanced focus on services. These days, Fedict no longer responds solely to the purely technical needs of its customers: it now applies a holistic approach that is directed towards processes. To build further on the success of e-government, Fedict believes that it is essential to take an end-to-end approach in managing the administrative processes between the various public services (horizontal perspective). With this in mind, e-government does not restrict itself to being the "electronic version of existing government services": its aim is to improve the provision of services and create new relationships between the authorities, citizens and businesses.

In practical terms, Fedict focuses its approach on three closely related areas: (1) Computerization of the State; (2) Computerization of Society; and (3) Development of an ICT Innovation and Knowledge Region.

The Computerization of the State encompasses the full offering of services relating to the foundations, as well as the introduction of e-government applications and their integration into the various administrative processes. In this regard, Fedict conducts projects in collaboration with various public bodies by providing them with active support and by considering Information Security as one of the main spearheads of its mission.

The aim of the Computerization of Society is to encourage the use of e-government applications. Fedict's policy in this area covers six aspects:

- To narrow the digital divide, given that access to the digital world creates more social opportunities and generates a greater feeling of wellbeing.
- To focus on the interests of users rather than on technological capabilities.
- Not to resort to interventionism, but rather to conduct campaigns aimed at stimulating the market and promoting the use of information and communication technologies.
- To work with the private sector on the campaigns mentioned above.
- To provide a stimulus to the Belgian ICT sector by incorporating Belgian products in campaigns and promoting highly successful achievements on the international stage.
- To combine general national campaigns with targeted programs in order to provide greater depth to the case for a specific target audience.

The development of Belgium as an ICT region has two aims: one, to assist Belgian ICT companies to win new markets in other countries and, two, to arouse the interest of foreign companies and encourage them to invest in Belgium. The overall objective is to develop a Belgian knowledge society. Fedict is supporting and speeding up this development by introducing projects and services linked to new technologies in the area of computerizing the State and society – and by publicizing these initiatives via a range of different channels.

The Citizen's Perspective

The overall approach for (intra muros) cross-boundary e-government collaboration rests on a technical back-office system that is fully citizen centric oriented. This approach is symbolized by Figure 2, in which six distinguished elements have been implemented.

COMMON BACK-OFFICE

Fedict's e-government strategy is supported by a number of basic services, or elementary building blocks. Particularly, "authentic sources" are an important concept of e-government (see Figure

Figure 2. The overall approach for (intra muros) cross-boundary e-government collaboration. Source: from FEDICT

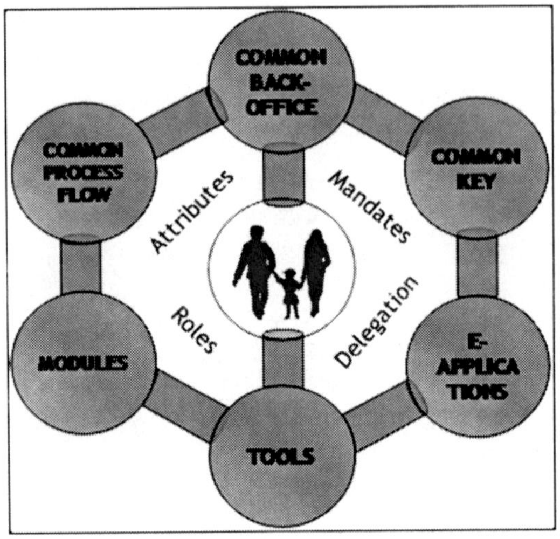

3). It entails the different federal government departments that gather information from citizens, companies and civil servants, storing and managing it in their own databases. This database or "authentic source" can be consulted by other FPSs that need the information. It means that the customer in question, be it a company or a private person, only needs to submit the information once. This simplification is one of the basic principles of Fedict's e-government strategy.

Figure 3. Building Blocks. Source: from FEDICT

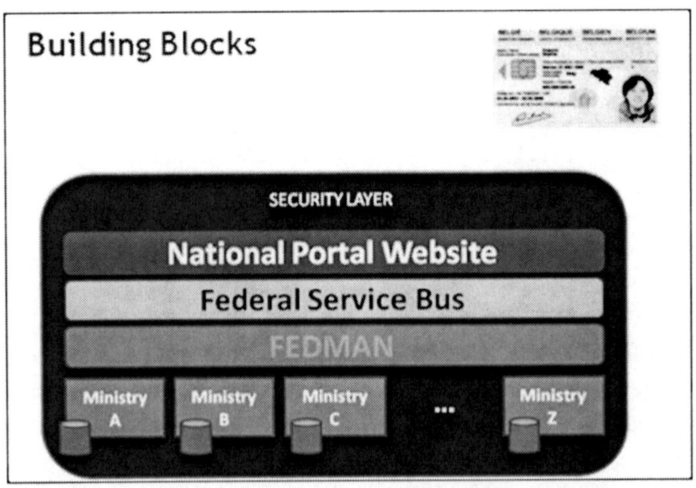

Fedict ensures that the necessary "authentic sources" are operational and accessible and that the exchange of information between the different departments goes smoothly. This is the foundation of e-government: conceiving a fundamentally new and integrated way of working, including the rethinking of work processes, procedures, structures and laws.

In the implementation of e-government applications, 80% of the work is behind the scenes and is more process- than ICT related. Essential for "an 'authentic source" is that the responsible department is able to guarantee the accuracy, completeness and authenticity of the data so that the other government departments can be sure to have correct, reliable and recent information. Furthermore, an authentic source can only be accessible to authorized people and organizations. In this way privacy and the confidentiality of the data can be guaranteed.

Several "authentic sources" are operational at the moment (see figure 4). The FPS for the interior manages the National Register, which contains the basic details of all Belgian nationals registered with a local authority or embassy. The Crossroads Bank for Social Security (CBSS) contains the Bisregister with the basic details of all people in Belgium without Belgian nationality who are registered with the social security services. The Crossroads Bank for Enterprises (CBE) is in the hands of the FPS for the Economy, SMEs, Middle Classes and Energy and contains the basic details of all Belgian enterprises. And finally there is the Central Balance Sheet Office of the National Bank of Belgium, which does not fall under the authority of the federal government but is a very important legal 'authentic source'. An "authentic source" for geographic data will be added in the future. This will be compiled in co-operation with the land registry office, the National Geographic Institute and the three regions. An 'authentic source' with details of, among others, legal advisors (notaries), medical doctors and architects is also being compiled (see Table 1).

The FedMAN Federal Network

To exchange information electronically, the federal government departments need to be connected. For this purpose Fedict has built the FedMAN high-speed network (Federal Metropolitan Area Network). The network connects all FPSs in Brussels. Today, 80,000 civil servants have access to FedMAN via 24 access points. For an expansion to government departments outside Brussels the FedWAN concept (Federal Wide Area Network) is currently being examined. It is intended to directly connect the bigger Belgian cities with FedMAN. FedMAN works at a speed of 1 gigabit per second. The guaranteed availability (more than 99.5%) is possible because the network has been made entirely redundantly.

The FedMAN network is used for:

- The structured exchange of data
- Sending e-mail messages between the different FPSs
- Consulting the websites and web services of the FPSs
- Consulting the federal FedDS 'White Pages' (Federal Directory Services): the FedDS is used to look up contact details of civil servants
- Sending large files via FTP (File Transfer Protocol)

FedMAN offers government departments' safe, central access to the Testa network (Trans European Services for Telematics between Administrations) of the European Union and to the Internet. Crucial for a reliable information exchange is the security of FedMAN. The network is protected against viruses, spam (unwanted e-mails) and intruders. Access by civil servants working remotely is also guaranteed secure thanks to SSL VPN. FedMAN is in its second version in the meantime. FedMAN II, operational since 1 March 2006, has ten times the capacity of the first version and makes additional services, such as Voice over IP (calling via FedMAN) and shar-

Figure 4. Authentic sources. Source: from FEDICT

Authentic source

- Is the source of the information
    - oWith respect of all laws on data protection
- Is accessible with the unique key of an object
    - oCitizen, enterprise, car...
- Is the source of the information
- Contains the data of that object
    - oGenerally there are more authentic sources for one object
- Is under the responsibility of an administration (distributed model)
- Collect, update, archive, make available

Table 1. Service with citizen's perspective

Elements	Systems	Functions
Common back -office	Authentic sources	Entails the different federal government departments that gather information from citizens, companies and civil servants, storing and managing it in their own databases.
	FedMAN federal network	Connect the federal government departments to exchange information electronically.
	UME and FSB	To structure the exchange of authentic information via the federal FedMAN network.
	Federal portal site	Brings together all the information and services of the federal government
	User and access right management	The identity and access rights of users are strictly monitored, There are four levels defined of access security.
	eID	eID is an essential building block in Fedict's e-government strategy.
	Information security management	The information systems of the federal government need to be properly protected to guarantee reliability and stability.
Common key	eID	eID is to be seen as a "key" to open a door and nothing more, gives you access to online applications.
e-Applications	At Federal level	Social Security: declaring employees status Mobility: requesting car license plates Online consultation of your National Register file (https://mijndossier.rrn.fgov.be) VPN (teleworking) Online tax declaration e-notary: signing and deposit of purchase acts e-procurement e-invoicing for public sector
	At Regional level	Flemish Parliament: submitting and electronically signing decrees, questions and resolutions Academy of Fine Arts Flemish Region: enrolment via eID Vlaamse Huisvestingsmaatschappij: enrolment via eID
	At local level	e-loket: Requesting certificates (vb. marriage, birth, etc.) Requesting change of address School enrolments Enrolment/access to libriaries Access to swimming pools Access to container parks
Tools	Quick install	Install a card reader to your PC
	My.belgium.de	Converts all possible applications into a personalised version.
	eID middleware	Consult all flat data and technical data related to the eID that is in your card reader
	Open book policy	All cardholders of a Belgian eID can consult online all data that the National Register (Ministry of Interior) is keeping on their account.
	www.checkdoc.be	Any external person can check the validity of Belgian passports and identity cards.
Modules	FAS	Federal Authentication Service via eID.
	e-LOKET	Tool to allow municipalities to offer electronic services to its citizen in a secure way.
	e-DEPOT	Service to allow notaries to faster register acts.
	PersonService	Web-service to allow fast query about physical persons in the public registers.
	DIGIFLOW	User interface the Public Sector uses to get access via the FSB to company data.
	IAM	Identity and Access Management.
	MAGMA	Delegation of powers between two legal entities in order to allow the second to operate online transactions in the name of the first (accountants, social representatives, etc).
	e-PAYMENY	Service to allow public authorities to offer electronic transactions.
Common process flow	Three examples for using these systems	The principles of using the systems.

ing datacenter infrastructure between government departments possible. This benefits availability.

The Federal Service Bus: UME and FSB

Exchanging authentic information via the federal FedMAN network needs to be structured. Fedict has developed the UME (Universal Messaging Engine) for this, a service that simplifies the exchange of information between the federal portal site and the different government applications and between the applications themselves. Now, UME is fully integrated in FSB, the Federal Service Bus that uses Web Services in a Service Oriented Architecture to achieve the same goal while adhering to international standards. Every day the FSB exchanges more than several 10s of thousands structured messages. The FSB is a service that allows information to get to the right application safely. Moreover, by using open standards such as XML and http(s), data can be exchanged between heterogeneous systems: the FSB makes sure the information is converted into the right format. This means the IT infrastructure of the different departments can be different without affecting communication.

FSB provides a single stop shopping solution to get to data from the authentic sources: the Crossroads bank for Enterprises, the Crossroads bank for Social Security and the National Register and has (among others) connections to the Finance department, the Justice department, the National Bank of Belgium, the Belgian Notaries, the Bailiffs, different eHealth partners, Police – on – web and the Business-one-stop-shops.

To increase ease of use, Fedict has also developed the Digiflow web application. With this application different FSB data flows can be connected. This application is currently used for two contexts: Public Procurement and for checking dossiers of regularization of illegal immigrants. Four different certificates can currently be requested: a certificate from the Social Security Office to ensure a company has paid all its contributions, extracts of the Balance Sheet from the National Bank, a certificate of non-bankruptcy of the Belgian Federal Crossroads bank of Enterprises, and a certificate from the Federal Treasury department to see if the enterprise is to be compliant with the VAT regulations. Further attestations and contexts are in preparation.

Federal Portal Site

Government departments are now connected to each other via FedMAN and are able to exchange UME data from authentic and other sources via the federal mail service. The work behind the scenes – the so-called "back office", which remains hidden from the user – is almost ready. Now a platform is needed where customers are able to consult the various services (the "front office"). This is why Fedict has built the www.belgium.be portal site. It brings together all the information and services of the federal government. The site has been constructed intuitively from the user's point of view. This means all customers can quickly and easily find their way around. The site is also accessible to poor-sighted people and was one of the first government sites to be awarded the AnySurfer label.

The convenience and the user-friendliness of the federal portal site are essential, of course. The federal portal site is made up of a static and a dynamic part. The static part contains information of all FPSs. The content of this part is managed by a work group representing all FPSs. The dynamic part contains a wide range of applications and services for civil servants (budget reporting, requesting certificates, etc.), private citizens (electronic tax return, elections site, etc.) and companies (modifying information in the Crossroads Bank for Enterprises, Dimona, income tax at source, etc.). Some applications were developed by Fedict for, and in co-operation with, other FPSs which manage the service after development. The applications are constructed as much as possible using reusable components so that when Fedict develops a new application it doesn't have to start from scratch again.

Work is currently underway on a new federal portal site, the underlying architecture of which will be decentralized. The applications are technically disconnected from the portal site to simplify maintenance and management. Also, more information is shared with the existing government department websites which means this information does not have to be provided separately again by the different departments. For the end user the site offers higher usage comfort because he or she will get better information more quickly.

User and Access Right Management

Privacy laws mean that access to information and services is restricted. The identity and access rights of users are strictly monitored. There are four levels defined of access security:

- **Level 1:** corresponds with public access. No password required.
- **Level 2:** a password is required for some services.
- **Level 3:** a password and a token are required for some services. A token is a card with 24 identification codes. Every time a service is accessed, one of the identification codes is requested. There are tokens for private citizens and tokens for civil servants. Users can apply for their token via the federal portal site.
- **Level 4:** some services are only accessible with an eID or electronic identity card. Fedict is responsible for management of the tokens and is an important player in the development of the eID. It also makes software available to integrate these security tools in applications that want to use it.

Fedict is currently developing a system of authentication in which it is not the identity of the user that has priority, but his or her quality, such as his or her position as a legal advisor (notary), medical doctor or bailiff. The mandate management system, whereby a third person (e.g. an accountant or a legal advisor (notary)) can act on behalf of a private citizen or a company, is also being expanded. And finally, Fedict is working on a shared authorization concept whereby a user is able to access the services of various FPSs simultaneously. This can be interesting in processes where several FPSs are involved.

The Electronic Identity Card (eID)

The highest level of access security on the federal portal site uses the eID or electronic identity card. This means the eID is an essential building block in Fedict's e-government strategy. The eID contains a chip that allows the cardholder's identity details to be read with a card reader and the necessary software. The eID's functions are threefold:

- **Efficient consultation and transfer of identity details:** by inserting the card in the card reader the party consulting the details has faster and easier access to them. And they are guaranteed to be correct;
- **Authentication:** for every application or website for which a user needs to prove his or her identity, the eID is a universal way to do so in a secure way. Authentication via the eID is PIN code protected and therefore cannot be used by just anyone, not even when the card is lost;
- **Electronic signature:** the eID enables the cardholder to put a legally valid signature under electronic documents. As with a written signature it gives the document authenticity (it is actually the cardholder who signed it), integrity (nothing has been changed in the document since the cardholder signed it) and irrefutability (the card holder cannot deny that he or she was the person who signed the document).

The number of possible applications for the eID is virtually endless. Nowadays it is deployed in applications used by the federal government and other authorities: to apply for and sometimes sign all kinds of electronic declarations, for identification in the case of electronic registrations and applications, as a library pass and entry to a recycling park. Thousands of other applications are imaginable, also for private purposes. It is an important responsibility of Fedict to stimulate the market for this and to promote applications that integrate the eID.

Information Security Management

A major point in Fedict's e-government strategy is mastering security of information. Naturally the information systems of the federal government need to be properly protected to guarantee reliability and stability. But because e-government also opens up these systems to the outside world, even greater security efforts are necessary: the risk of confidentiality and privacy violation has increased greatly. Fedict has worked out a global information security strategy for the whole federal government. Creation of a consultation platform was given priority and Fedict acts as its secretariat. It has also provided a forum for those who are responsible for information security in the different FPSs. The aim of the forum is to harmonize the management of information security in the different federal government departments. Fedict gets the various FPSs to conduct risk analyses and use this information to launch security procedures. Fedict will assist if necessary by providing methodology, advice, training and support in the implementation of safety measures. Another aspect of Fedict's security program is service continuity. As all components of the e-government architecture (networks, datacenters, etc.) must be robust and redundant, Fedict also advises the FPSs when drawing up a "disaster recovery plan" to get the service operational quickly again in the event of a problem.

ONE UNIQUE ELECTRONIC KEY: THE BELGIAN E-ID

The second important aspect of this citizen centricity model is the unique electronic key that we have issued for all Belgian citizen and foreign residents (all those who have an official address in Belgium). They all have received an eID. Since September 2009, all Belgians aged 12 and over are mandatory to have an eID (8.1 million cards), and the citizens are obliged to carry it with them at all times as of 15 year. For the children younger than 12 year, parents can order a kids-ID on a voluntary basis. This card is to be seen as a "key" to open a door and nothing more. It gives you access to online applications. The data that is residing on the chip (and which is also printed on the card) is the minimum minimorum to identify a physical person. All additional data related to that person are to be consulted online in one or the other authentic source. The eID is more and more used today, with hundreds of new applications developed both in the private and public sector. Furthermore, Fedict is working on initiatives to encourage use of the eID: the eID label for card readers, documentation for developers to correctly integrate the eID, the availability of free read software for the eID, the distribution of card readers, etc. For more information about the electronic identity card, please go to: www.eid.belgium.be.

LOTS OF E-APPLICATIONS

With regards to e-applications, Belgium took the approach not so much to build applications, but more to facilitate the development of applications. The government has created the necessary toolboxes and developer kits (downloadable from the website) so that anybody who wishes to develop an application and wants to use the eID as login system can do so.

The government sees how many people have downloaded the software, but they don't know how many applications they developed with it. The latest survey gave a figure between 500 and 600 applications. In order to make some promotion about these applications, the government developed an interactive map of Belgium where all applications are visualized by clicking on the city or municipality. (http://map.eid.belgium.be/). Table 1 lists some interesting applications.

LOTS OF TOOLS AT YOUR DISPOSAL

As already mentioned in the section above, the government has built several tools to allow developers to build secure websites and applications. Some examples of websites that have made use of the overall back-office, by collecting fiscal data linked to Belgian citizens, and by visualizing it on the front-office side in a specific way (see Table 1):

Quick Install: The software is downloadable for free from the government website. Once installed it allows citizens to read what is on the chip of their cards. It also allows citizens to identify themselves at those websites that request authentication. Finally it will also allow citizen to place an electronic signature if needed (see Figure 5).

My.belgium.be: By logging into this Belgian portal website and by using his or her eID to identify him or herself, this website converts all possible applications into a personalized version. This means that, via a single sign on procedure, citizens can get (today up to 70 online transactions with) their personal data linked to those topics. In the back-office citizens' personal data will be automatically linked to these websites and become personalized. It makes it much easier to communicate with government. Some of the screens can be pre-filled-in with your data. Please note that the government has taken a decision not to ask you data that they already have somewhere in their authentic sources (see Figure 6).

eID middleware: This Open Source middleware allows citizens to consult all flat data and technical data related to the eID that is in their card reader. The exact versions of the different software and OS can be consulted. Any citizen

Figure 5. eID Quick Install. Source: from FEDICT

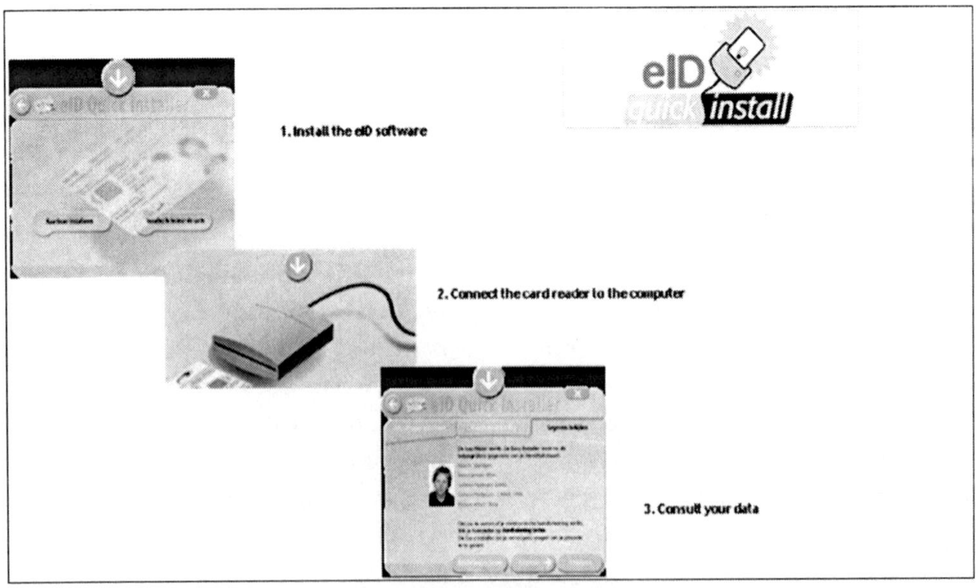

can read all data related to the two certificates, the key lengths, etc.

Open book policy: Via the website https://mondossier.rrn.fvog.be all cardholders of a Belgian eID can consult online all data that the National Register (Ministry of Interior) is keeping on their accounts. The complete history of all documents related to the cardholder can be consulted. Even more interesting is the list of those civil servants that have consulted citizens' data, when and for what purpose. As a Belgian citizen he or she has the right to ask questions about these consultations in case he or she finds them not normal.

www.checkdoc.be: Via this website any external person can check the validity of Belgian passports and identity cards. Belgian citizens just need to type in the card/passport number and the system will make an online consultation of the authentic source and tell them if this document is genuine or not. The system replies with a red or a green light. None of the data out of the authentic source will be transmitted.

LOTS OF MODULES AT YOUR DISPOSAL

Besides the different tools that have been described above, we prepared also a list of little modules that can easily been taken from the shelf and inserted into the website you want to build. Here is a list of some of these modules: Federal Authentication Service (FAS), e-LOKET, e-DEPOT, PersonService, DIGIFLOW, Identity and Access Management (IAM), MAGMA, e-PAYMENY, etc. (see Table 1)

Standard Usage: Standard Process Flows

Last but not least, besides all these technical elements, you also need to agree on a common way to use and consult. Therefore it is of utmost importance that everybody uses the system in the same way. The principle is the following (see Figure 7).

Figure 6. My.belgium.be. Source: from FEDICT

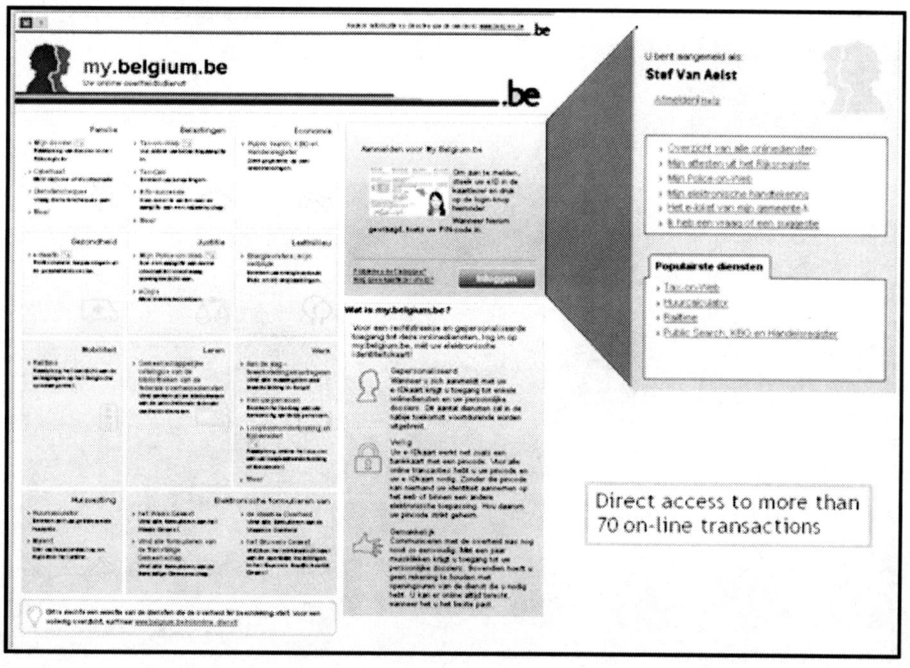

Belgian citizens always access via a web application. The consultation/collection of data is then done via the FSB (Federal Service Bus) who will guide them through the FEDMAN network to reach one or more authentic sources. Here are some examples to make this process clear:

Example 1: Citizen Files a Complaint "Theft"

Imagine a Belgian citizen bicycle has been stolen and he or she needs to make a declaration at the nearest police station. Thanks to the application "Police-on-web" he or she can do this declaration online, Figure 8 shows this online declaration process.

The Federal authentication service for eID (FAS) will allow his or her to login and identify him or herself. Once that is done he or she will be able to fill in an electronic form. This form has been made with the "e-FORM" module. Via the FSB the filled in electronic declaration will be sent to the Police repository. In return (and via the same FSB) the citizen will get a ticket number back from the police department, that will be his or her prove of "declaration of theft". With that he or she can then go to his or her insurance company to get compensated for the loss.

Example 2: Civil Servant Verifies Legal Info about Company X for a Tender

As Figure 9 shows, the situation where a civil servant can verify is a company X is complying with all necessary legal requirements to be able to reply to a tender. Typical requirements are related to the fact that this company is up-to-date with its payments of VAT, social security, etc. In this case, the civil servant will also login into the web telemarc by using his/her eID and by typing the correct PIN. Once the authentication is done, the request about company X can be introduced. Via the FSB all requested data will be collected out of the different authentic sources and pulled up towards the civil servant (who in this case will have the authority to do such queries).

Example 3: Hospital Declares a New Birth

The third example is the case where a hospital doctor can do an electronic declaration of birth (see Figure 10 the doctor will start by identifying himself with his eID (by way of the FAS module). An electronic declaration form will be filled in and sent out to different instances. The BPM within

Figure 7. Standard process flows standard usage. Source: from FEDICT

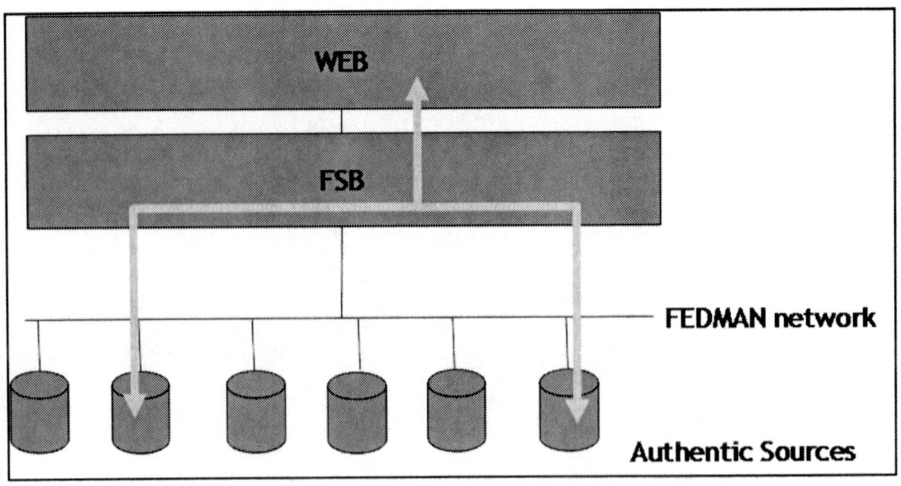

Figure 8. Example 1: citizen files a complaint "theft." Source: from FEDICT

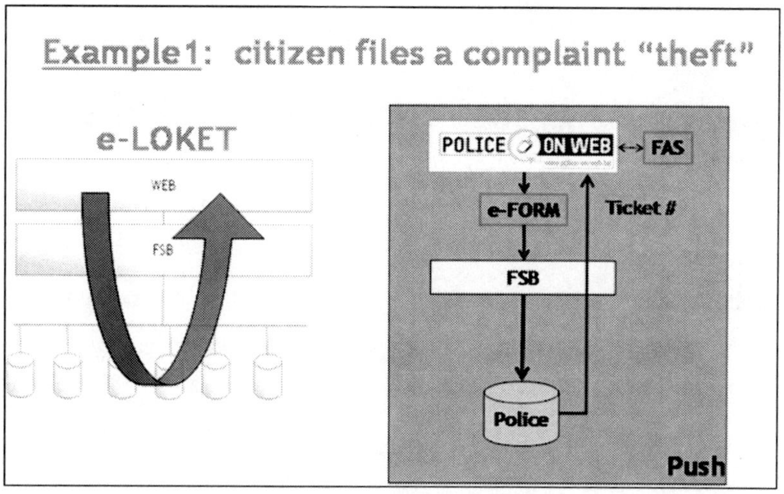

the Federal Service Bus knows which data needs to be forwarded/pushed to which destination.

Besides the National Register (Internal Affairs), who will create a unique national register number, some information is also forwarded for statistics reasons, for social security or for automatic grants rights. One final remark on this Standard Usage: it can very well be that information flows from federal level towards a regional or local level (see Figure 11). Each level might use its own FSB. In that case a secure and trust connection is made between the different Service Busses.

FUTURE DEVELOPMENTS

We all know that, when it comes down to identity, a physical person not only has a name, a place and date of birth and an address. He or she also has an extensive list of attributes that can be linked to him or her. On top of that this person can also

Figure 9. Example 2: civil servant verifies legal info about Company X for a tender. Source: from FEDICT

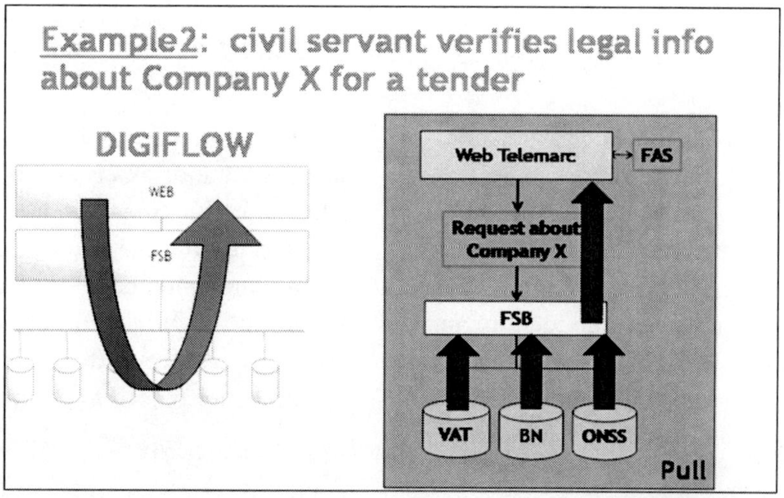

Figure 10. Example 3: hospital declares a new birth. Source: from FEDICT

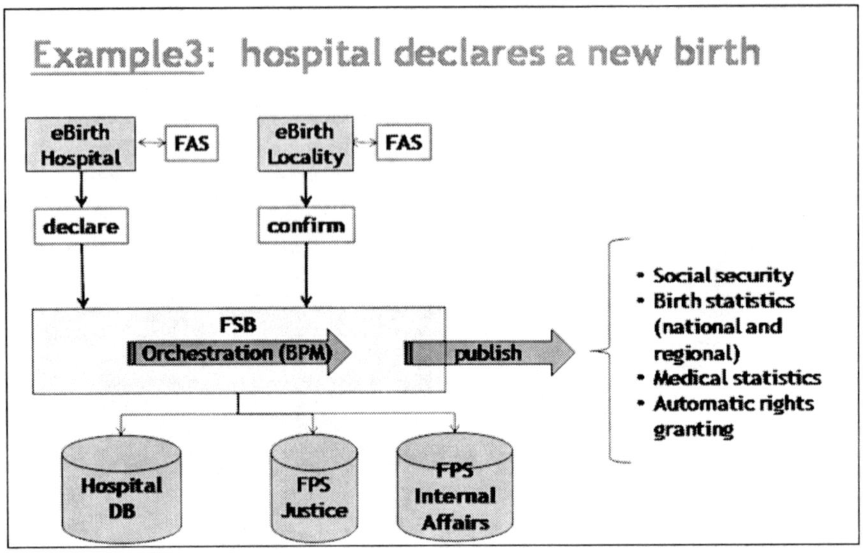

Figure 11. Identity and Access Management system, IAM. Source: from FEDICT

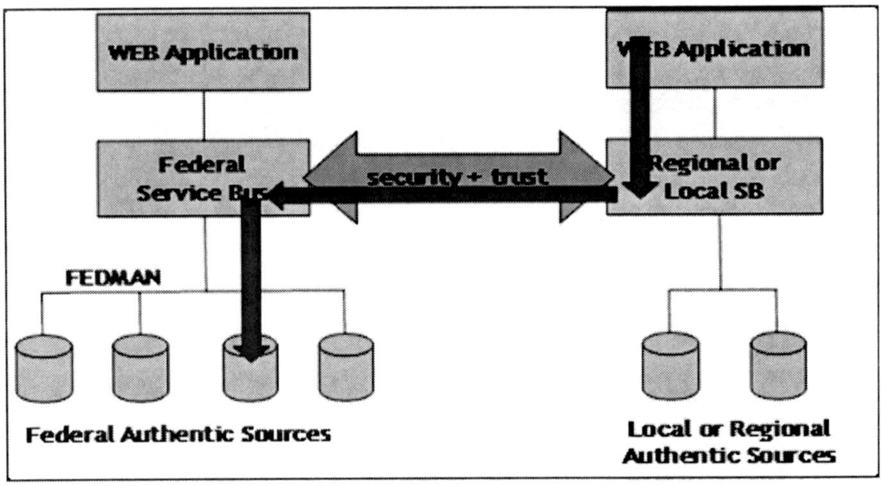

play different roles, have a job, be part of a community, etc. By linking the attributes, mandates, delegations and roles to a particular person, we all of a sudden can start using the same infrastructure describing in this paper, into the economical/industry world. Therefore we need an Identity and Access Management system (IAM, see Figure 12). Building this IAM is a huge task and it will take two to three years before it is fully implemented (See Figure 13).

This is what Belgium is building for the moment as a major extension to the existing back-office infrastructure. Building this IAM is a huge task and it will take two to three years before it is fully implemented. However, we do not think it is up to the public authorities to start feeding that particular repository. There are other instances better placed to do this:

Figure 12. Identity and Access Management system, IAM. Source: from FEDICT

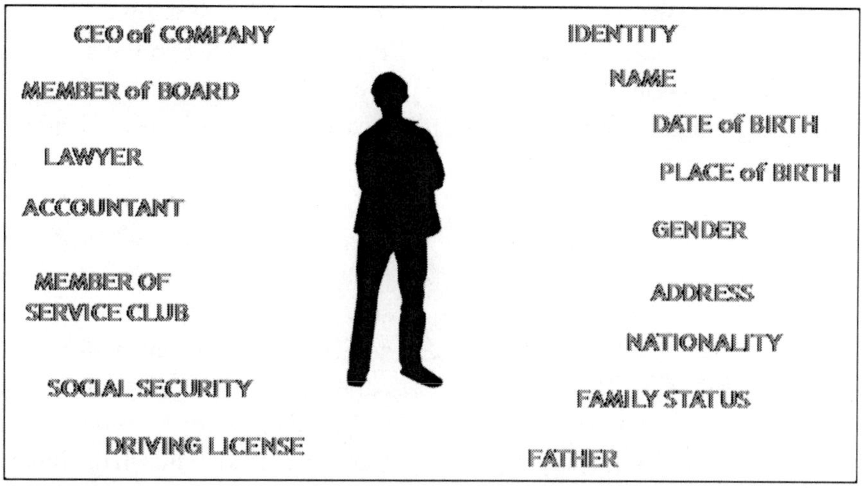

Figure 13. e-Government as a catalyst. Source: from FEDICT

IAM as an e-government catalizer:

- "As Is"
  - oStrong Identification & Authentication Services

oTargeted User Management functionalities build within the context of 3 target groups (Civil servants, enterprises and citizens)

- **Under construction**
  - oExtended sets of functionalities organized as "Generic Services"
    - Extended Authentication, Attribute and Attribute collection workflow

Extended User and Role Management (Delegation, Mandates, etc.)

- oFederal Governance Organization and Mechanisms

oFedict as the Partner for International Exchanges (Belgian IDP Hub)

- A human resources director of a private company is best placed to declare who within the company has decision rights and signature rights.
- The federation of notaries in Belgium is best placed to say if a person is a real notary and still in function.
- The boss of a company is best placed to state to who he/she has given certain delegations to act on his/her behalf.
- The chairman of a service club is best placed to state you as a member of his club.

Most of all, all the elements described in this paper permit Belgium to be very citizen focused because of the essences of common and secure back-office infrastructure, common electronic key, common rules of usage, common tools and modules, and common legislation. The political landscape also drive Belgium towards no centralized system, full political liberty of development by the ministries (but also accountability), liberty of choice of hardware and software, and a future proof solution.

THE EUROPEAN DIMENSION

Belgium, being in the heart of Europe (and being geographically very small), immediately has to do with a big part of its economy generated by non-Belgian entities. It is therefore important that the national back-office infrastructure gets plugged to other national/regional back-offices cross-border. This is why the Belgium model is made in such a way that it is extendable on the upper side as well as on the lower side. On the lower side we are integrating the regional and municipal levels.

On the upper side, Belgium is building the gateway towards other countries. First initiatives have been set up with its neighboring countries for typical border applications. Nowadays Europe has taken several initiatives to organize this cross-border interoperability at an EU level. They did this by setting up Large Scale Pilot projects (LSP) in some top areas such as eID, e-Procurement, e-Health, and the Service Directive (one-stop-shop for creation of companies abroad).

The concept is the following: the European Commission suggested that the Member States regroup in a temporary consortium to build an architecture that would make interoperability possible (a federated model), to be tested by a number of well defined pilots. These 3-year pilot projects are sponsored for 50% by the Commission and for 50% by the participating Member States. Figure 14 describe the overall goal.

Four major pilots and Consortia have been set up:

STORK (https://www.eid-stork.eu/)**:** STORK is the pilot that looks at eID interoperability. The aim of the STORK project is to establish a European eID Interoperability Platform that will allow citizens to establish new e-relations across borders, just by presenting their national eID. Cross-border user authentication for such e-relations will be applied and tested by the project by means of five pilot projects that will use existing government services in EU Member States. In time however, additional service providers will also become connected to the platform, thereby increasing the number of cross-border services available to European users. Thus in the future, people should be able to start a company, get your tax refund, or obtain your university papers without physical presence; all people will need to access these services is to enter their personal data using their national eID, and the STORK platform will obtain the required guarantee (authentication) from their government.

The role of the STORK platform is to identify a user who is in a session with a service provider, and to send his data to this service. Whilst the service provider may request various data items, the user always controls the data to be sent. The explicit consent of the owner of the data, the user, is always required before his data can be sent to the service provider.

PEPPOL (http://www.peppol.eu/)**:** The objective of the PEPPOL (Pan-European Public e-Procurement On-Line) project is to set up a pan-European pilot solution that, conjointly with existing national solutions, facilitates EU-wide interoperable public e-procurement. The vision of the PEPPOL project is that any company and in particular SMEs in the EU can communicate electronically with any European governmental institution for the entire procurement process. The final outcome of PEPPOL will be an inter-operational environment build upon national systems and infrastructures supporting the full cycle of e-procurement activities.

Figure 14. e-Government as a catalyst. Source: from FEDICT

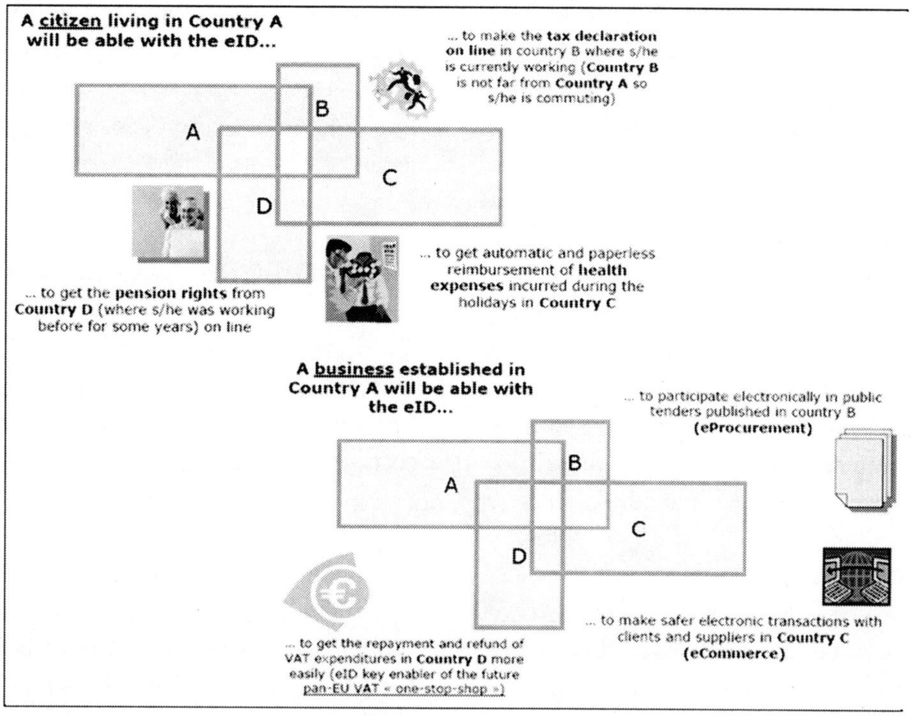

The pilots that will be developed in PEPPOL will support any economic operator in the EU and the European Economic Area (EEA) to respond to any published public tender notice electronically and to govern the entire procurement process from their own national infrastructure to any another national infrastructure. Thereby PEPPOL will focus on the engagement and participation of SME companies to public e-procurement.

EPSOS (http://www.epsos.eu/)**:** European Patients Smart Open Services - epSOS, (previously known as S.O.S. - "Smart Open Services open eHealth initiative for a large scale European pilot of patient summary and electronic prescription) is a Europe-wide project organized by 27 beneficiaries representing twelve EU-member states, including ministries of health, national competence centers and numerous companies. This makes it the first European eHealth project clustering such a large number of countries in practical cooperation.

The overarching goal of epSOS is to develop a practical eHealth framework and an Information & Communication Technology (ICT) infrastructure that will enable secure access to patient health information, particularly with respect to basic patient summaries and e-prescriptions between different European healthcare systems. To achieve this goal, the national entities cooperating within epSOS test both services in pilot applications, which interconnect national solutions. The approach, which is based on advanced and distinct use cases and associated infrastructural components, aims to deliver both a methodological process and durable implementations: building blocks. These building blocks will form the basis for a longer term, pan-European approach to develop interoperable service solutions.

The project is structured into work packages (WPs) which analyze the current situation in the participating countries, explore the legal questions, develop technical specifications covering all basic components of secure use of personalized health data, and finally set up the test environment where the findings can be validated in a close to real life situation.

SPOCS (http://www.eu-spocs.eu/)**:** SPOCS, which is the acronym for "Simple Procedures Online for Cross-border Services", is a pilot project launched by the European Commission which aims to remove the administrative barriers that European businesses face before offering their services abroad. SPOCS is expected to further enhance the quality of electronic procedures completion and has been designed for businesses that have an interest in cross-border activities. It will allow them to meet all the administrative obligations through a single contact point that is available online in all EU Member States now.

It will initially involve at least two professional categories of service providers and its results will be widely promoted to raise awareness and to encourage innovative solutions for administrative simplification. A special effort will be placed on the dissemination of open specifications, the sharing of knowledge and best practices, as well as the encouragement for further cooperation. A wide range of organizations is represented among the partners in order to ensure that the value chain - from decision makers to service providers and IT solutions – is well balanced, and to allow contributions from different backgrounds.

SPOCS will have the advantage to already benefit from the results achieved by its "sister projects" STORK (on electronic identity) and PEPPOL (on electronic procurement), in relation to mutual recognition for the use of electronic identity and signatures.

The pilot project will be implemented in different phases and a special emphasis will be drawn on the development of common specifications and tools for electronic services, such as technical and semantic interoperability, the promotion of electronic documents (e-documents) and the creation of a services directory. At all stages, SPOCS will be carried out openly to facilitate consensus by public administrations, their suppliers and partners, industry and standardisation bodies. Nevertheless, it's worth mentioning that the national systems will not be replaced, but will only take into account common specifications to ensure cross border interoperability.

DISCUSSIONS AND CONCLUSION

E-governance and Cross-boundary Collaboration is in Belgium made possible thanks to a well organized common back-office infrastructure, respecting the political situation as well as all non-technical aspects linked to respect of privacy and confidentiality. On an international level, a similar approach is ongoing thanks to the different pilot initiatives of the European Commission. Cross-border interoperability is only possible within the EU borders if a federated model is chosen. A model with a central IT infrastructure and central management would be not politically sellable, nor would it be an option on security level. It would be too inviting for criminal attack.

The downside of this option is that a consensus amongst 27 Member States on a technical, contractual and political level is needed in order to get a joined federated architecture organized. And that is not all. A nice EU architecture is also needed, but that does not mean that TRUST will be a fact. Today, all EU countries have their own national legislations and have defined their different levels of trust. None of these 27 countries have the same levels of trust. Therefore it is important to converge towards (probably) four commonly accepted levels of trust. Interfacing of each of the countries needs to be done. Afterwards, you also need to have an EU cross-border legislation in place to hope for a minimum of trust. Finally, I suspect that still bilateral discussions will be needed before full trust can be installed.

Although this last paragraph might give a negative impression, the author feels confident that Belgium will get there soon. The technical aspects are well under way and the discussion on the legal framework has started. The four Large Scale Pilots that have been described will boost the realization of this trust environment. In other words: "The future is bright…"

REFERENCES

Anderson, K. (1999). Reengineering public sector organizations using information technology . In Heeks, R. (Ed.), *Reinventing government in the information age* (pp. 312–330). New York, NY: Routledge.

Brown, D. (1999). Information Systems for improved performance management: Development approaches in U.S public agencies . In Heeks, R. (Ed.), *Reinventing government in the information age* (pp. 113–134). New York, NY: Routledge.

Fountain, J. (2001). *Building the virtual state: Information Technology and institutional change*. Washington, DC: Brookings Institution.

Moon, M. J. (2002). The evolution of e-government among municipalities: Rhetoric or reality. *Public Administration Review*, *62*(4), 434–443. doi:10.1111/0033-3352.00196

Nye, J. S. Jr. (1999). Information technology and democratic governance . In Kamarck, E. C., & Nye, J. S. Jr., (Eds.), *Democracy.com? Governance in networked world* (pp. 1–18). Hollis, UK: Hollis Publishing Company.

OECD. (2008). *OECD e-government studies: Belgium*. Paris, France: Organization for Economic Co-operation and Development.

Section 2
Citizen-Centric E-Governance

Chapter 5
Global Comparative Study on the Relationship between User's Traits and Public E-Service Quality

Chih-Hao Chang
Waseda University, Japan

Toshio Obi
Waseda University, Japan

ABSTRACT

The study in this chapter aims to understand the relationship between user intrinsic factors and perceived e-service quality, as well as consequent satisfaction. From an interdisciplinary perspective, five major and influential factors are generated, and related hypotheses are formed according to previous research. Two leading-edge cities in terms of e-service implementation, Taipei and Tokyo, are adopted to examine the hypotheses. Because of the limitation of sample size, a sophisticated yet accountable statistical methodology called Partial Least Square (PLS) is employed in this study. The results point toward five intrinsic factors being partially significant in the Taipei and Tokyo cases, respectively.

While much of e-government or e-service research has focused on system or internal efficiency improvement, this study tries to raise another important topic regarding user traits, user perception of quality, and causality. Meanwhile, by integrating different kinds of theories and perspectives, namely sociology, management and informatics, a comprehensive blueprint can be fully discussed. The findings contribute to our knowledge of theoretical development in e-governance, service marketing, and policy marketing. In addition, the empirical results can be used as a general principal reference for other cities planning to implement e-services and can be used as specific evaluation criteria by which the two cities in the cases studies can further understand their users.

DOI: 10.4018/978-1-60960-753-1.ch005

INTRODUCTION

In this information age, information and communication technologies (ICTs) have been widely adopted in every aspect of daily life. In the context of present-day information society, the public administration sector certainly cannot remove itself from the comprehensive influences caused by ICTs. Many scholars have been proposing various concepts combining both ICTs and public administration, such as "digital/electronic democracy", "digital/electronic government", "Teledemocracy", "information polity", "electronic republic", "digital/electronic governance" and so on. These concepts, in one way or other, illustrate that ICTs are going to innovate new approaches in governance, posing an unprecedented challenge and stake in terms of the design and practice of public policy, and eventually facilitating a major progress in forming the value of democracy.

Discussions have promised that ICTs would provide opportunities to change political and societal environments and to create a new type of governance and life style. However, many scholars also agree that new governance models cannot be created by merely implementing ICTs. In fact, during the process of dealing with public affairs, other than ICTs, economical, societal, political and cultural factors will influence the practice of public administration. Therefore, incorporating ICTs into the processes of the public sector without any modifications to the system or environment contexts does not guarantee a real transformation of government by means of ICTs (Donk & Snellen, 1998).

More and more government agencies have already utilized websites or portals, just as the private sector has done. The use of websites or ICTs in the public sector is now a global phenomenon and public servants around the world are adopting novel ways to leverage ICTs to better serve their constituents. As these websites have been seen as the first step toward e-government, they are rapidly becoming a new aspect of governments. Many citizens now have a brand new experience of interacting with their governments online, either to communicate their opinion on current issues, to request or submit an application or to petition a government act.

Moreover, the concept of marketing has long been adopted by the private sector, and has proven to be a great success. In the public sector, some have argued that it is unnecessary to implement policy marketing to the public as the nature of policy and public service is somewhat different from commercial business. Nevertheless, since the 1970s, more and more scholars have begun to adopt the concept of marketing within government or non-government organization. The concept of "social marketing" was born under the context of transferring the value and perspective to general public and making them accept or adopt it as a norm. Based on that context, many countries now have their own e-government systems or applications in order to make social communication easier. However, though government has built a sophisticated electronic mechanism to help it serve its citizens online, the usage of electronic government service by citizens is still at a relative low level. It has been proven that the information system was found to be underutilized or sometimes abandoned because of the lack of user acceptance in the last decade. Thus, the urgency lies in exploring where and who the target users might be.

"The Waseda World e-Government Ranking", conducted since 2005, contains six major elements which are believed to constitute a well-designed and sophisticated e-government ecosystem. From the e-governance perspective, this represents a process of knowledge delivery and user participation through e-channels. With the usage of web 2.0 technology, a full e-participation can be realized easily in cyberspace. In this context, the ranking system will introduce the new element of "e-participation" in order to complement the description of the e-government ecosystem, and in order to understand user traits vis-à-vis e-service usage.

WASEDA WORLD E-GOVERNMENT RANKING

"The Waseda World e-Government Ranking" has been conducted annually since 2005. Over the past few years, the research team has been diligently tracking developments and trends in the e-governments of select countries, while continuously improving on the ranking methodology. The following section will illustrate the evolution and logic so as to give an overview of the ranking system.

The Evolution

Over the past few years as "The Waseda World e-Government Ranking" has been conducted, there have been constant changes made to improve the quantity and quality of the ranking. The ranking is based on a principle of executing a comprehensive and systematical survey. Under this principle, improvement has been made every year. In its inception in 2005, the e-Government initiatives of twenty-three countries were surveyed with only four dimensions. The following year, nine new countries were included together with two new indicators, which were "management optimization" and "promotion of e-government". In its third year, Fiji and India were added for the first time. To date, forty countries are now monitored in this ranking system.

Although seven indicators remain, including the newly added "e-participation", the titles, definitions and contents of the original indicators have been redefined. One of the most significant modifications made in 2008 to the evaluation methodology was the replacement of the previously used five-point scale with the check-list format, which provides a higher degree of differentiation among surveyed countries. For example, the definition of the first sub-indicator 'Introduction to CIO', rather than be defined by a scale of 0 to 5, was broken down into five distinct items, with each item getting one point. Hence, this eliminated any possible ambiguity and enhanced the evaluation.

The Formula of an Ideal E-Governance System

The implementation of e-Governance can be seen as an ecosystem. In an ecosystem, there are several factors that could, and would, affect the healthiness and richness of the system. For example, sufficient rainfall provides the required water source for the survival of species. Water that is not used will eventually evaporate into the sky and thus complete the cycle. In order to achieve the goal of e-governance, government CIOs or other related departments are eager to establish an ideal system based on this ecosystem pattern, and the participation by users will somehow reflect the efficiency of the whole system. From this point of view, six main mechanisms in an e-Governance ecosystem are proposed, namely ICT preparedness, ICT usage, EA ICT Model (enterprise architecture ICT model), information provision capability, policy marketing, and resource allocation (Obi, 2009).

"ICT preparedness" resembles the environment, which is the availability of ICT. It refers to measuring a stakeholder's ability to leverage ICT and its related applications. Here, the stakeholders does not refer to just the government itself but also citizens and businesses.

"ICT usage" corresponds to the users of resources in the environment, indicating how the public sector uses available ICT technologies. "ICT usage" in the public sector focuses on how to measure government's ability in using ICT and its related applications.

"EA ICT model" is akin to the physical rules of nature, which in the case of e-government, is the method and rule of ICT that ensures that it runs efficiently. EA is a methodology for standardizing service procedures and information systems, and creating highly efficient organization through optimizing the organization (METI[1]). It is also the basic principle for actualizing the highly efficient management of organizations. It can be seen as a way to achieve the internal effectiveness and efficiency of governmental operations.

"Information provision capability" correlates to the visibility of the beauty of the environment, which in turn refers to the availability and richness of content provided by the government to the public through ICT. Information provision capability stresses the importance of the transparency and richness of e-government information. This is essential in order to involve citizens in the process of decision making. Under the rational choice tradition, the quality and quantity of information provision are critical for a government's e-governance.

"Policy marketing" mirrors the measures promoting the environment, which is related to how the government promotes its e-government to the public. "Policy marketing" would be one of the main purposes of e-government. Policy promotion through ICT increases the efficiency and transparency of government services, which in turn reduces the transaction cost between the government and its stakeholders.

Finally, "resource allocation" acts as a CIO that governs overall measures of the e-government implementation process. In the following paragraph, a detailed explanation of the six main mechanisms of e-government is presented. Government resource allocation is essential to sustain the e-government mechanism, with government CIOs being the most likely candidate for making effective decisions regarding the allocation of limited resources. The CIO is expected to integrate management strategy with IT investment in order to achieve a balance between the business strategy, organizational reform, and management reform.

The six elements are indispensable to an ideal e-governance system, and together can create a synergy invaluable to the whole system. A well-designed system with these six elements ought to stimulate user participation in public affairs or the policy making process. As a result, the goal of e-governance will be accomplished under the framework mentioned above.

AN EXPLORATORY STUDY OF E-PARTICIPATION FROM THE PERSPECTIVE OF USER TRAITS

Despite some significant modifications made in the current survey to increase reliability, the research team for "The Waseda World e-Government Ranking" has to admit that its system still has some limitations and obstacles that need to be addressed in any subsequent survey. One possible angle is to look at the prospective opportunities presented by e-participation and e-democracy brought on by the introduction of new technologies. Some countries are starting to take advantage of Web 2.0 to establish interaction with stakeholders and engaging them in decision-making through online polls, surveys, blogging, and so forth. Strong motivation from citizens and other stakeholders to be fully integrated into the social and political life of their communities will keep fostering the advent of new interaction modes between government and citizens. The strengthening of democratic processes by ICT brings to the forefront the importance of electronic municipal services. The efforts of decentralization in e-government strategies can be clearly viewed to date in countries with strong democratic cultures, especially in Scandinavia, where municipalities enjoy considerable independence. Provision of municipal services online is even more important as it helps bridge the digital divide among rural and central areas, which is an issue of vital importance for the developing world. The shift from administration to social and political services, and as a consequence the shift from federal to local e-government, need to be captured by the next survey to produce an effective differentiation between the countries (Obi, 2009).

In order to reach the goal of e-participation, citizen attitudes and behavior toward the transformation brought by ICTs need to be understood. With the increase of social communication between government and its citizens via ICT, as well as the importance of the New Public Management movement, we are eager to understand the factors affecting citizen e-service satisfaction, especially the intrinsic factors. The purpose of the following section is to explore these intrinsic factors from the viewpoint of marketing, particularly with reference to the service marketing theory and from the information system perspective. Additionally, the concept of New Public Management movement will also be discussed in order to clarify the characteristics of public e-service.

E-service can be defined as the electronic provision of a service to customers (Saanen, Sol, & Verbraeck, 1999). Madlberger and Kotzab (2001) suggest that the definition of e-business, and thereby e-service, is a complex issue. They base their eventual definition on an understanding of business transactions and they define, "electronic commerce as electronic business via public or private networks including electronic publishing, electronic banking, and electronic retailing". They go on to further refine this by suggesting that there are two separate aspects to electronic business, as with the non-electronic business world, namely, business-to-business and business to consumer. Boyer, Hallowell, and Roth (2002) define e-service as follows:

The e-service encounter is the initial landing on the home page until the requested service has been completed or the final product has been delivered and is fit for use. (pp. 175-88)

These definitions, while helpful, are clearly based on private sector assumptions. In order to define e-service in the context of the public sector, it is helpful to examine a definition of e-government. Lenk and Traunmüller (2002) have noted that while e-government was coined as a term after e-commerce, it addressed an Internet reality that is very different from that of commerce. They suggest that the common understanding of e-government is fairly simplistic and focus on "simple transactions between identifiable customers (citizens, enterprises) on one side, and a multitude of government organizations on charge of registering objects, issuing passports, collecting taxes or paying benefits on the other".

In seeking to define e-service in a public sector context, it seems sensible to draw upon literature from both the private sector and e-government. In this study, the definition derived by Boyer et al. (2002) as stated above will be employed. The following section is going to extract user traits that might affect perceptions of e-service from various perspectives.

Engagement Tendency from Civic Engagement Perspective

First, the civic engagement perspective is concerned with obtaining response and support for public affairs from citizens. Government has to find an effective way to involve citizens in public affairs through electronic means, and these means have become a significant feature of public administration nowadays. Moreover, civic engagement also emphasizes the agency of individuals and the equality in the political relationship between citizens and government.

The tendency of engaging in public affairs, or so-called civic engagement, has multi-dimensional definitions, depending on the scope and field. Civic engagement refers to the ways in which citizens participate in the life of a community in order to improve conditions for others or to help shape the community's future (Adler & Goggin, 2005). In Putnam's classic book, "*Bowling Alone*", he indicated that civic engagement is a basic foundation for building "Social Capital". The forms of civic engagement contain official and unofficial social activities. The former includes visiting friends, playing poker with friends or other similar activities, while the latter is to engage in community service and political engagement (Putnam, 2000).

The interactive effect between technology usage and citizen's tendency toward public affairs engagement has been viewed as ambiguous, due to limitations in methodology and observation of raw data (Norris, 2001). Even so, two perspectives can be generated by existing literature, one is optimism and the other is pessimism or skepticism. Norris (2001) has proposed mobilization and reinforcement hypotheses based on skepticism. The mobilization hypothesis holds that technology is able to provide an opportunity to those who would like to be involved in public affairs. On the other hand, the latter hypotheses hold that technology will increase the digital divide because only a portion of the citizenry can access information and that portion will dominate technological resources. Similarly, Carpini's research (2000) also indicate that technology can increase civic engagement for those who are interested in public affairs, or has been involved in public affairs. But, conversely, for those who are not interested in public affairs, the technology is useless or ineffective. In general, most researchers agree that technology causes the reinforcement effect rather than mobilization effect, at least up to date. Citizens who are engaged in the real world will extend their experience to the virtual world by using technology.

According to Norris' reinforcement hypotheses, it is said that the experience with or tendency toward civic engagement of citizens may have a positive effect towards encouraging them to use public e-service to access information, furthering daily contact once they have the ability to get online and the network environment is ready. Moreover, public e-service may not be the only tool for citizens to engage in public affairs. Actually, e-service itself is a kind of "public sphere" in which citizens can engage. The public sphere refers to an ideal speech situation in which citizens engage in open-ended conversations that are neither strategic nor self-interested, and are focused on issues of common interest (Habermas, 1996). In this context, citizens with the tendency to engage in public affairs would be willing to utilize public e-service as their means of civic engagement.

Technology Readiness and Anxiety from the Information System Perspective

Second, if we take public e-service as a system with sophisticated ICTs combinations, then the approach shall take on the information system perspective. Although ICTs have brought numerous benefits to users in many ways, they still frustrate some users as they interact with the system. From this point of view, much research has focused on how ICTs can be employed by users and how to improve system efficiency and effectiveness. For example, a famous model proposed by Davis (1989) called the "Technology Acceptance Model" (TAM) has been supported by its explanatory power and parsimony of theory and also supported by many empirical studies (Davis, 1989).

The concept of "technology readiness" was proposed by Parasuraman in order to reinforce the explanation of the traditional triangle model of service marketing. It can be viewed as an overall state of mind resulting from a gestalt of mental enablers and inhibitors that collectively determine a person's predisposition to use new technology (Parasuraman & Grewal, 2000) or can refers to people's propensity to embrace and use new technologies for accomplishing goals in home life and at work (Liljander, Gillberg, & Van Riel, 2006; Parasuraman & Colby, 2003). Similarly, based on the user competency perspective, McClure (1994) said that Internet surfers should possess some type of literacy, such as computer and network literacy, if they want to solve problems through technology. However, compared to McClure's viewpoint, the "technology readiness" viewpoint is much closer to the concept of human psychology essentially and further from the concept of acquired ability (Walczuch, Lemmink, & Streukens, 2007).

Technology readiness consists of four dimensions, which are optimism, innovativeness, discomfort and insecurity. It serves as an insight into a person's own motivation and inhibitions regarding the adoption of technology, but not competency (Parasuraman & Colby, 2003). Optimism refers to a positive view of technology and a belief that it offers people increased control, flexibility, and efficiency in their lives. Innovativeness is a tendency to be a technology pioneer and thought leader. Discomfort refers to a perceived lack of control over technology and a feeling of being overwhelmed by it. Insecurity is the distrust of technology and skepticism about its ability to work properly.

Somewhat related to technology readiness, another concept known as "computer anxiety" is defined as "the fear, apprehension and hope people feel when considering use or actually using computer technology (Meuter, Ostrom, Bitner, & Roundtree, 2003). Meuter et al. (2003) extended this theory into the idea of "technology anxiety", which focused on a user's state of mind regarding general technology tools. "Computer anxiety" is more narrowly focused on anxiety related to personal computer usage. Furthermore, technology anxiety is a contrasting concept, relative to technology readiness, which specifically is defined as people's willingness and ability to use technology-based tools.

In the "Technology Acceptance Model" (Davis, 1989), people's attitude toward technology usage has been discussed widely, based on perceptions of ease of use and performance, and these perceptions are affected by individual innovativeness, or so-called "technology readiness". Citrin, Sprott, Silverman, and Stem Jr. (2000) have note that individual domain-specific innovativeness will produce an interference effect relative to Internet usage and online shopping. In addition, Dabholkar and Bagozzi (2002) have found that the characteristic of inherent novelty seeking, which is similar to technology readiness, will attenuate the positive relationship between perception of performance and attitude toward using technology-based self-services.

In addition, Dabholkar and Bagozzi (2002) have employed the term "self-efficacy" to explain the user's attitude toward using technology-based self-services. Generally speaking, users with greater self-efficacy will have more confidence in their ability to use technology-based self-services. In this case, high self-efficacy is quite similar to low technology anxiety, and perceived ease of use may not be that important to them as to those with low self-efficacy. Yi and Hwang (2003) have noted that application-specific self-efficacy and computer self-efficacy will have a positive effect on ease of use and actual system use, respectively. Moreover, Meuter et al. (2003) have shown that the level of technology anxiety will influence the experience of using technology: the lower the technology anxiety, the higher the satisfaction toward technology-based self-services.

To summarize, technology readiness and technology anxiety are both states of mind in terms of technology usage. Compared to other extrinsic factors which influence the usage of e-service, such as information access, information ability and information literacy, the intrinsic factors, such as technology readiness and technology anxiety, are able to provide more explanation because the ratio of citizens who are capable of using the Internet is generally increasing in some countries or areas[2]. In other words, as the ability of technology utilization reaches a specific level, user intrinsic factors will become more influential than extrinsic factors.

Need for Interaction and Perceived Risk from Service Marketing Perspective

Last but not least, in order to capture the complexities resulting from the growing infusion of technology into serving customers, this study focuses on the service marketing perspective as well. Parasuraman (1996) supplemented technology influence into the traditional service triangle (Kolter, 1994) and labeled it the "Service Pyramid". The "Service Pyramid" concept focuses on the transformation of technology toward each player in the service triangle. Particularly, the technology process which the customer experiences will be totally different from traditional human contact, though the outcome for the customer is usually the same. Therefore, Self-Services Technology (SSTs) related literature can be employed because comprehensive discussions are available (Dabholkar, 1996; Parasuraman, 1996; Meuter, Ostrom, Roundtree, & Bitner, 2000; Lin & Hsieh, 2006, 2007). Additionally, the concept of service quality and customer expectation will be introduced in order to form a measurement model to test the user perceptions of public e-service.

The concept of"Service encounter" is considered a key element affecting customer perceptions of service quality, and some have termed it "the moment of truth". It has been defined broadly as a period of time during which a consumer directly interacts with a service. This includes the interaction between customer and service delivery systems, including service employees, facilities, and other tangible factors (Bitner, 1990). However, much research indicate that a loyal customer is derived from the human contact quality between customer and service employee. Thus, the face to face interaction between customer and service employee is considered a core factor in terms of service marketing.

Dabholkar (1996) used the idea, "need for interaction with a service employee" to illustrate this phenomenon. The interaction within a service delivery environment is very important to some consumers (Bateson, 1985). Moreover, in the case of self-service technology usage, users needing interaction with service employees will avoid using self-service technology like ATMs, and vice versa. Similar concepts and findings have been proposed by Meuter et al. (2000) as well.

Also, within the need for interaction with service employee there exists the moderating effect that impacts the perceptions of ease of use of consumers on their attitude towards use of technology-based self-services (Dabholkar & Bagozzi, 2002). As mentioned above, an individual with a greater need for interpersonal contact tends to avoid machines. Instead, they would rather interact with service employees. Therefore, for those who have high interpersonal contact need, the perceived ease of use of service should be strengthened in order to be adopted.

Accordingly, being a technology-based service, public e-service may have the same effect. Citizens who have the need for interaction with public servants will not use public e-service actively. The reason may be that, on one hand, the intrinsic tendency of human contact makes the citizen comfortable, so the citizen values this kind of contact. On the other hand, if a long-term relationship has been established between public servant and citizen, the citizen would tend to contact the public servant directly. In this case, public e-service would become merely a complement for on-site service and not a substitution.

The concept of perceived risk refers to the feeling of uncertainty regarding possible negative consequences of using a product or service (Featherman & Pavlou, 2003). The formal definition is a combination of uncertainty plus seriousness of outcome involved and the expectation of losses associated with purchase, which acts as an inhibitor to purchase or use (cited from Featherman & Pavlou, 2003).

Generally speaking, the major categories of perceived risk can be thought of as performance and psychosocial (Cunningham, 1967). Cunningham further typified perceived risk according to six dimensions. These are performance, financial, opportunity/time, safety, social and psychological loss. In addition, an overall measure of perceived risk was proposed to illustrate the occurrence of a trade-off behavior (Featherman & Pavlou, 2003). A luxury may reduce social risk by increasing financial risk, for example.

In the marketing literature, perceived risk has been regarded as one of the most important factors influencing consumer behavior (Bauer, 1960; Cunningham, 1967). In the context of e-service or self-service technology, many discussions have been focused on psycho-social and performance risks, and a new factor has been introduced, privacy risk (Featherman & Pavlou, 2003).

Furthermore, Dabholkar and Bagozzi (2002) have adopted the idea of social risk to explain the concept of "self-consciousness" in terms of using technology-based self-services. Self-consciousness refers to a person's view of himself/herself as a social object, with an acute awareness of other people's perspectives about themselves. The research has noted the interesting fact that an individual with greater self-consciousness will hesitate to use technology-based self-services. In other words, persons who perceive high social risk may be reluctant to use technology-based services. The outcome was also in line with Bateson's research (1985) in terms of risk.

To sum up, compared to e-services provided by the private sector, public sector e-services contain much more confidential and personal information. Therefore, it is no surprise that citizens may perceive more risk when they use public e-services. Similarly, citizens with a risk avoidance tendency will hesitate to use a public e-service in which the personal information may be hacked or stolen, not to mention the inherent negative attitude towards government information architecture, which is often associated with uncertainty and insecurity.

EMPIRICAL ANALYSIS

According to the above discussion, there are five intrinsic factors extracted from various perspectives that might affect the user's willingness to use e-services and further impact the perceptions of service quality. The five intrinsic factors are: technology readiness, technology anxiety, engagement tendency, need for interaction with service employee and perceived risk. Furthermore, a comprehensive and integrated conceptual framework was proposed in order to explore the relationship among user intrinsic traits, expectations and attitude towards e-service under the context that the user has already adopted e-service. This section will explore the relationship between user satisfaction in using e-service as derived from perceptions of quality, and the consequence this has on satisfaction with the government.

First, five components based on the above discussion were extracted to represent user's traits: technology readiness, technology anxiety, need for interaction with service employee, engagement tendency and perceived risk. These factors have been considered as key elements affecting user's technology adoption in private sectors. Furthermore, these factors are derived not just from information system related researches, but also notably from researches done on service marketing and public administration.

In addition, the Expectancy-Disconfirmation model (Oliver, 1980) of satisfaction theory claims that the users already form their opinion of e-service before using it and this constitute as an expectation. The gap between expectation and actual perceived quality will cause users to form their satisfaction regarding e-service. Using the Expectancy-Disconfirmation model, Van Ryzin (2005) tested citizen's satisfaction regarding local public policy and the result showed that even though expectation is non-significant as perceived disconfirmation existed, the issue of expectation should be considered in order to obtain more evidence. Furthermore, the satisfaction regarding e-service will even affect satisfaction regarding government overall (Van Ryzin & Immerwahr, 2007). Therefore, based on the above discussion, this study proposes a conceptual framework (see Figure 1) that accounts for the factors of user traits, namely: perceived e-service quality, e-service expectation and satisfaction with e-service.

Methodology

In order to verify that these factors really do have an effect on e-service behavior and intention, an empirical analysis was conducted. Two cities, Tokyo and Taipei, were selected in accordance with the above discussion.

Figure 1. Conceptual framework of this study

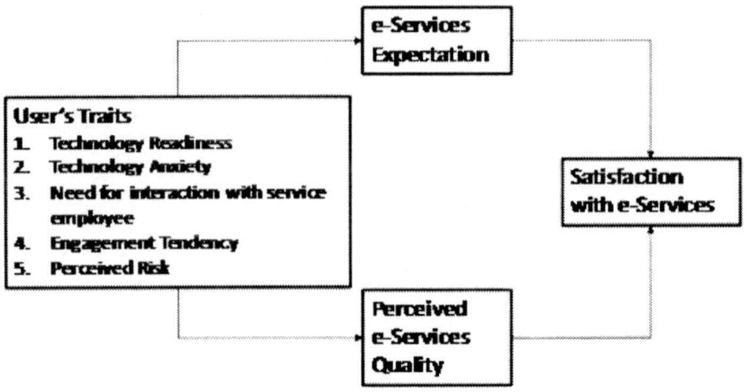

Since the focuses of this study are on user traits vis-à-vis the usage of e-services, the provision of e-services and the quality of e-service system are to be considered first. In light of the Waseda e-government ranking survey, Japan and Taiwan are selected because of their sophisticated systems. Japan and Taiwan ranked 6th and 10th in the 2010 survey, respectively, and ranked 2nd and 4th within the category of East Asia. Regarding their e-services provision, both Japan and Taiwan are among the top 10 countries in the survey. Moreover, considering the usage of e-services, this study focused on the capitals of these countries as targets. Not only are the e-services offered in the capital cities more mature, but users there are more experienced than in other local cities.

The Tokyo municipal government initiated an ICT-based project called e-City for its 3.3 million citizens in 2001. The project consisted of three major parts, which were infrastructure, application and government. In terms of government, the Tokyo municipal government established a subproject called *"e-City Project"*, and focused on four initiatives, both internally and externally. One of the initiatives was to enhance user perceptions of e-service for both inhabitants and enterprises, and great success was achieved. Moreover, Tokyo citizens are considered to possess high technology readiness, thus they are highly capable of using technology-based services or products.

In 1999, the Taipei city government (TCG) initiated a project called "CyberCity," a new virtual city project that included not only an ICT infrastructure deployment but also application development. With a total area of 272 square-kilometers and a population of 2.62 million, Taipei has an average population density of 9,700 persons per square-kilometer. With this geographic limitation, TCG resolved to establish a new virtual city in order to make Taipei the leading frontier of digitalization. To date, Taipei has earned accolades for its ICT deployment. For example, TCG won the best prize for ICT deployment in the public sector, WCIT 2002[3]. It was also awarded the best intelligent community of the year in December 2003, as well as the Intelligent Community Award 2006 by WTA[4]. Therefore, Tokyo's *"e-City"* and Taipei's *"CyberCity"* projects were chosen as research focus, and a survey was conducted among their respective users who had previously used government e-service.

The main purpose of this study is to explore how user traits will affect attitude and satisfaction with e-service, and consequently attitude towards government. Thus, the study result can be used as a reference for the "e-participation" indicator of "The Waseda World e-Government Ranking". The key construct is user traits and there are five factors: technology readiness, technology anxiety, engagement tendency, need for interaction and risk tendency. Furthermore, e-service quality is measured by five variables: responsiveness, reliability, customization, user interface and overall (see Table 1). Before developing multi-item scale measurements for these constructs to test the relevant research hypotheses, an explicated operational definition of these constructs are needed in order to achieve empirical testability, verifiability, and conformability.

A seven-point Likert scale was employed; most similar studies have been conducted in the same fashion. Ambiguity in responses can be avoided with better discriminability. The scale was measured from 1, "strongly disagree," to 7, "strongly agree". In addition, content validity (also known as logical validity) refers to the extent to which a measure represents all facets of a given social construct. In this study, all measurements are derived from previous research, which meant that the measurements in this study do have adequate content validity.

Regarding the analytical method, Partial Least Square (PLS) method was adopted. The Partial Least Square (PLS) method (Chin & Newsted, 1999) is a useful alternative to Covariance-based SEM. PLS can be a powerful method of analysis because of the minimal demands on measurement scales, sample size, and residual distributions (Chin & Newsted, 1999). Hence, this method is usually termed "soft modeling". The PLS model can be specified by an arrow scheme and each latent variable (LV) is indirectly observed by a block of manifest variables (MVs). LS (Least Squares) estimation is distribution-free, except for predictor specification, and does not require independent observations. Predictor specification can be summarized as a linear conditional expectation relationship between dependent and independent variables, and LS modeling based upon predictor specification is prediction-oriented (Wold, 1985). That is, the variance-based approach of PLS shifts the orientation from casual model/theory testing to component-based predictive modeling (Chin & Newsted, 1999). In some situations, there are many variables but not necessarily as many samples and observations. PLS is considered especially useful for constructing predictive equations in such situations (Garthwaite, 1994) and the sample range of minimal recommendations is from 30 to 100 cases (Chin & Newsted, 1999). Due to the limitation of the field survey, a total of 102 and 105 cases were obtained in Taipei and Tokyo, respectively, during the testing period. Therefore, the PLS method was adopted to analyze the data.

This study utilized the *SmartPLS* software developed by Ringle, Wende, and Will (2005) at the University of Hamburg and it has been adopted in many academic research studies. *SmartPLS* is Java-based, which means that it is independent from the user's operating system and that only raw data can be analyzed. The model is specified by drawing the structural model for the latent variables and by assigning the indicators to the latent variables via "drag and drop". The output is provided in HTML, Excel or Latex format, as well as a parameterized path model. Bootstrapping and blindfolding are the resampling methods available. A special feature of *SmartPLS* is the finite mixture routine (FIMIX). Such an option might be of interest if unobserved heterogeneity is expected in the data (McLachlan & Peel, 2000). Regarding the resampling method, bootstrap has been adopted for this study. The bootstrap samples are built by resampling with replacement from the original sample. The procedure produces samples consisting of the same number of units as in the original sample. The number of re-samples has to be specified. The default is "100", but a higher number (such as "200") may lead to more reasonable standard error estimates. In this study, the number "300" is used to resample the cases.

Results

The research findings (see Figure 2 and Figure 3) partially support the proposed framework in the public e-service context. First, with regard to engagement tendency, need for interaction with

Table 1. Construct and measurement

Construct	Operational definition	Item and number		Source
Technology Readiness	Constituted by optimism, innovativeness, discomfort and insecurity which is considered overall as the tendency of people are willing to use technology-based service.	Optimism	4	Parasurama and Grewal (2000)
		Innovativeness	3	
		Discomfort	3	
		Insecurity	3	
Technology Anxiety	The fear, anxious and aspire as people are using or going to use technology-based services.		5	Meuter et al. (2003)
Engagement Tendency	People's experience in terms of involving in public affairs.		4	Kahne et al. (2002, 2005)
Need for Interaction	People would like to interact with service employee rather than using technology-based service anytime and anywhere.	Need interaction with service employee	3	Dabholkar (1996)
Perceived Risk	The risk or insecurity that people perceived as they use technology-based service.		3	Featherman and Pavlou (2003)
Expectation	People's expectation toward e-service before they use it		1	Ryzin (2005)
Perceived e-Service Quality	People's evaluation toward e-service in terms of responsiveness, reliability, customization, security, user interface and overall aspect.	Responsiveness	3	Van Riel et al. (2003)
		Reliability	3	
		Customization	3	
		Security	3	
		User Interface	3	
Satisfaction with e-Service	An overall attitude toward e-service after using it.		3	Van Riel et al. (2003)

service employee and perceived risks were found to significantly affect user perceptions of e-service quality in both cities. On the other hand, the effects of technology readiness and technology anxiety were supported only in the case of Taipei. Before using e-service, user technology readiness and need for interaction with service employee were key factors affecting expectations of e-service, for the Taipei case, while the need for interaction with service employee and perceived risk were the same in the Tokyo case. The results indicate that the five extracted traits--engagement tendency, technology readiness and anxiety, need for interaction and perceived risk--were significant with regard to affecting user perceptions of e-service quality, in the Taipei case. On the other hand, only three traits--engagement tendency, need for interaction with service employees and perceived risk--were significant for the same independent variable in the Tokyo case.

The comparison of these two cases indicates that the effect of technology readiness and technology anxiety remain ambiguous. Though there is no clear evidence that technology based characteristics, such as technology readiness and technology anxiety, are related to a country or a

Figure 2. The path analysis of Taipei case

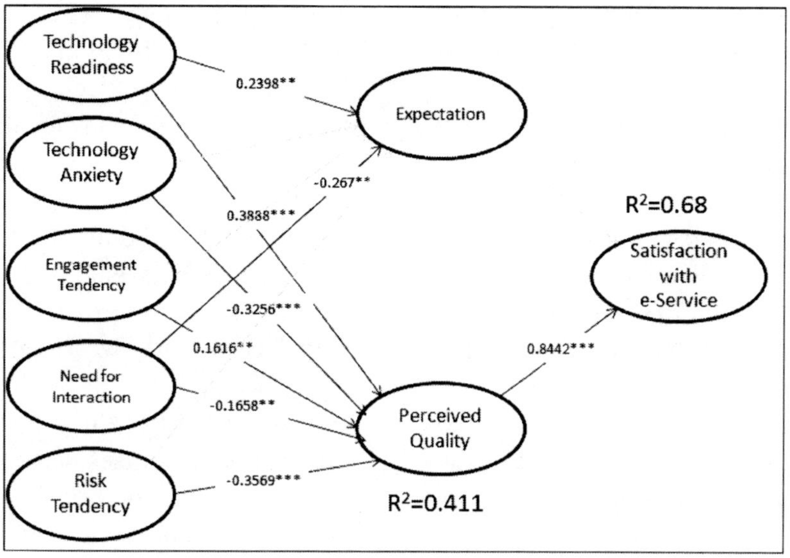

race, cultural factors seem to have some relationship. For example, Elliott, Hall, and Meng (2008) have assessed differences in American and Chinese students with respect to level of "technology readiness". Their findings indicate that Chinese students exhibit a lower propensity to embrace and use new technology, as compared to American students. Similarly, some differences between the Taipei and Tokyo cases do exist. However, cultural factors were not included in this empirical study as the research focused solely on the relationship between user traits and perceptions of e-service quality in a specific context. Nevertheless, the importance of cultural factors cannot be ignored and may be suggested as a topic for further research.

Figure 3. The path analysis of Tokyo case

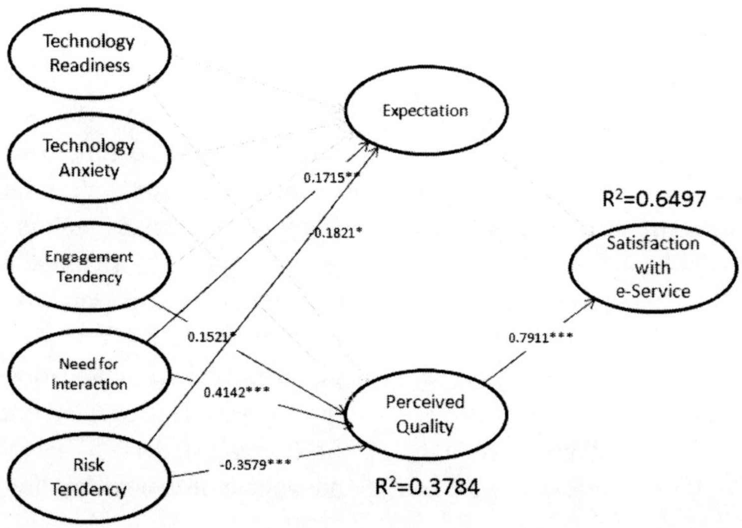

In scholarly research, the TAM-based approach is often used to describe user technology behavior through two contextual variables, perceived ease of use and perceived usefulness, which can then be used to explain further reactions like intention to use, satisfaction and so on. These two variables do make a lot of contribution toward explaining human behavior in terms of technology acceptance. However, even though this model, to some extent, reflects the sophistication of the system, it fails to show the real reason why people are willing to use technology.

Furthermore, the results reveal people's real concerns toward e-service. In the Taipei case, users with high technology readiness have higher expectations toward e-service, compared to those with lower technology readiness. While in the Tokyo case, users with high perceived risk might have lower expectation than those with low perceived risk. In other words, the findings somehow indicate that the reasons for user interest in e-service, between these two cities, differ. Users in Taipei may be concerned whether they are capable of using the system, while users in Tokyo may be concerned with the risks of using the system. Moreover, both cases show that the need for interaction with service employees is another key factor affecting expectation. Yet, the results contradict the proposition of SSTs. This is a possible explanation: on the one hand, most users do not have much opportunity to deal with government, so though they have the need to interact with service employees, they will still want to switch their transaction or interaction to electronic means. On the other hand, though users prefer to be served in person, their experience tells them that e-service might be better.

In summary, these two case studies were employed to test the five major factors which might affect user perceptions of using public e-service and perceptions of quality, both of which would in turn affect perceptions of satisfaction. Though these two cases told different stories, because of the differences in context, the result is still significant in determining a set of key factors in public e-service usage. In addition, a unique variable introduced in this study, engagement tendency, has been proven significant in both cases. The results imply that ICTs are able to enhance mobilization, especially by those who are active in public affairs in real life and the results also confirm the concept of cyber skepticism.

Solutions and Recommendations

The purpose of this study is to explore potential traits influencing user perceptions of public e-service quality and user satisfaction with e-service. The results of the study will be further used to introduce an e-participation perspective to "The Waseda World e-Government Ranking". The five traits concluded and tested in this research have their own managerial implications. First, from the perspective of policy marketing, in spite of the limited ability in locking target customers (Snavely, 1991), government agencies still need to know who and where the "customers" are. At the core of Snavely's policy marketing model, the concept of target customer does exist, along with other facilitators like service, policy analysis, human resource and so on. But, thus far no one has been able to offer a way to identify them for a specific service or policy.

Moreover, according to diffusion of innovations theory (Rogers, 1995), innovation would be diffused among different members within the societal system as time passes. These members can be categorized by the time series of innovation adoption, namely innovators, early adopters, early majority, late majority and laggards. Rogers has also noted the importance of individual traits on innovation diffusion related research. The main idea of diffusion of innovations theory emphasizes the importance of early adopters who play the role of "opinion leaders" by spreading the news of the advantage of new technology.

The characteristics of target customer toward public e-service were defined by five factors in this study, and the relationship between user characteristics and perceived quality were confirmed. In other words, government agencies are able to establish who their target customers are based on these characteristics, and then proceed to design and plan marketing actions with these users in mind. These users will then spread their positive experiences to other early majorities, which might form the most influential group. Nevertheless, even when these characteristics were understood, it is another matter trying to seek out these groups in reality. However there is a solution available. Community marketing, for example, might be the best way for government agencies to find their target users. Most Internet users will organize communities based on shared interests, and those users who are active in virtual communities usually possess high technology readiness, low technology anxiety, or even high engagement tendency. With community marketing tools, or the so called Web 2.0, it is relatively easy to get involved and participate in public affairs for both government and citizens.

Another issue which might be related to government's internal administration is that the two factors, need for interaction with service employee and perceived risk, are confirmed to be related to perceived quality and further satisfaction. For government, when designing the e-service architecture, the very first step will be to reduce the system risk as perceived by users. Apparently, this point is slightly different from commercial service, as users do not trust public e-service, probably because of privacy concerns. Meanwhile, the more interaction with employees the users have, the more they are able to understand e-service. Thus, government agencies should educate or provide necessary help to users before or when they are using the system.

FUTURE RESEARCH DIRECTIONS

While much of the research on e-government or e-service has focused on system or internal efficiency improvement, this study tries to raise another important topic regarding user traits and user perceptions of quality as well as examining the causality from the perspective of e-governance. Thus, by integrating different kinds of theories and perspectives--namely sociology, management and informatics--a comprehensive blueprint can be fully discussed. The findings contribute to our knowledge of the theory of e-governance, service marketing, and policy marketing.

In addition, the study also provides profiles and clearer understanding of two cities in Asia on the leading-edge of e-service. The empirical results can be used as a general reference for other cities that are going to implement e-service and the results can help these cities better understand their users, based on the specific evaluation of the two cities surveyed here.

Despite the care given to this study, there are several limitations that should be noted and addressed in future research. First, this research has empirically tested the e-service usage of two cities, and it did not select any specific e-service from the target cases. As there are a great variety and diversity within e-services, the characteristics of each e-service could possibly influence the results in some way. Future empirical studies should select and focus on a particular e-service which is available in both cases to eliminate any possible variance.

A panel study is needed. A panel study is a longitudinal study that involves collecting data from the same sample of individuals over time. In such a study, the factor of expectation should be considered as an early variable at a particular time point. The study should be conducted before the users actually use the system. However, due to time limitations, this methodology was not adopted for the present study. Perhaps, this is why expectation was insignificant for satisfaction with e-service. Further research will be advised to conduct a panel study in order to understand the effect of expectation.

For this study, each case had a sample size of just over 100, which is acceptable by the methodology of PLS (partial least square) which this study employed. However, PLS is used to discriminate the relationship between variables, but does nothing for cluster analysis. The users in this study should be subject to grouping according to their traits, which would then be meaningful for describing the behavior of each group, for the purposes of scholarly research and practical application.

CONCLUSION

By conducting a sophisticated survey of two e-service systems, *"e-service online"* of Taipei's *"CyberCity"* project and *"e-Tokyo online service"* of Tokyo's *"e-City"* project, the proposed factors and their relationships were tested thoroughly. The results partially supported the proposed hypotheses in the public e-service context. First, engagement tendency, need for interaction with service employee and perceived risk were found to affect user perceptions of e-service quality significantly, while technology readiness and technology anxiety were only supported in the case of Taipei. Before using e-service, user technology readiness and need for interaction with service employee were key factors affecting user expectations toward e-service, for the Taipei case. For the Tokyo case, the need for interaction with service employee and perceived risk had the same effect. Undoubtedly, user perceptions of e-service quality do affect satisfaction with e-service, both in the Taipei and Tokyo cases. However, only in the Taipei case was there a link between satisfaction with e-service and government. Surprisingly, user expectations toward e-service did not have any effect on the satisfaction with e-service, as illustrated in the "Expectancy-Disconfirmation model".

E-governance definitely does bring a lot of benefits, not only to the government itself, but also to other stakeholders, such as citizens and enterprises. The transparency of information enables users to become more effective, responsive, interactive and accountable. Internally, government is able to manage its employees and systems through a more effective and productive method. Externally, a better service can be provided to both citizens and enterprises. As a result, effective and productive employees, citizens (or enterprises), government and technology constitute a so-called "Service Marketing Pyramid" within the public sector. Under this logic, the only objective of e-government for each party is to provide or be served by better services through technology. Yet, among e-government studies, there are few studies addressing user traits in relation to public e-service, and very little research conducted using a comprehensive and integral approach to explore this issue.Therefore, this article employs the perspective derived from service marketing, information system and public administration in order to discern user traits that might impact e-service usage. Furthermore, this empirical research has adopted the concept of TAM to describe user behavior and accompanying perceptions of e-service quality. With a sophisticated survey conducted on two e-service systems, Taipei e-service online and e-Tokyo online service, the proposed model was tested thoroughly.

REFERENCES

Adler, R. P., & Goggin, J. (2005). What do we mean by "civic engagement"? *Journal of Transformative Education*, *3*(3), 236–253. doi:10.1177/1541344605276792

Bateson, J. E. G. (1985). Self-service consumer: An exploratory study. *Journal of Retailing*, *61*(3), 49–76.

Bauer, R. A. (1960). Consumer behavior as risk taking. In Hancock, R. S. (Ed.), *Dynamic marketing for a changing world* (pp. 389–393). Chicago, IL: American Marketing Association.

Bitner, M. J., Booms, B. H., & Tetreault, M. S. (1990). The service encounter: Diagnosing favorable and unfavorable incidents. *Journal of Marketing*, *54*(1), 71–84. doi:10.2307/1252174

Boyer, K. K., Hallowell, R., & Roth, A. V. (2002). E-service: Operation strategy - A case study and method for analyzing operational benefits. *Journal of Operations Management*, *20*(2), 175–188. doi:10.1016/S0272-6963(01)00093-6

Carpini, M. X. D. (2000). Gen.com: Youth, civic engagement, and the new information environment. *Political Communication*, *17*, 341–349. doi:10.1080/10584600050178942

Chin, W. W., & Newsted, P. R. (1999). Structural equation modeling analysis with small samples using partial least squares. In Hoyle, R. H. (Ed.), *Statistical strategies for small sample research* (pp. 307–341). Thousand Oaks, CA: SAGE Publications.

Citrin, A. V., Sprott, D. E., Silverman, S. N., & Stem, D. E. Jr. (2000). Adoption of Internet shopping: The role of consumer innovativeness. *Industrial Management & Data Systems*, *100*(7), 294–301. doi:10.1108/02635570010304806

Cunningham, S. M. (1967). The major dimensions of perceived risk. In Cox, D. F. (Ed.), *Risk-taking and information handling in consumer behavior* (pp. 82–108). Boston, MA: Harvard University Press.

Dabholkar, P. A. (1996). Consumer evaluations of new technology-based self-service options: An investigation of alternative models of service quality. *International Journal of Research in Marketing*, *13*, 29–51. doi:10.1016/0167-8116(95)00027-5

Dabholkar, P. A., & Bagozzi, R. P. (2002). An attitudinal model of technology-based self-service: Moderating effects of consumer traits and situational factors. *Journal of the Academy of Marketing Science*, *30*(3), 184–202.

Davis, F. D. (1989). Perceived usefulness, perceived ease of use, and user acceptance of Information Technology. *Management Information Systems Quarterly*, *13*(3), 319–340. doi:10.2307/249008

Elliott, K. M., Hall, M. C., & Meng, J. (2008). Student technology readiness and its impact on cultural competency. *College Teaching Methods & Styles Journal*, *4*(6), 11–22.

Featherman, M. S., & Pavlou, P. A. (2003). Predicting e-service adoption: A perceived risk facets perspective. *International Journal of Human-Computer Studies*, *59*, 451–474. doi:10.1016/S1071-5819(03)00111-3

Garthwaite, P. H. (1994). An interpretation of partial least squares. *Journal of the American Statistical Association*, *89*(425), 122–127. doi:10.2307/2291207

Habermas, J. (1996). *Between facts and norms: Contributions to a discourse theory of law and democracy*. Cambridge, MA: MIT Press.

Kahne, J., Chi, B., & Middaugh, E. (2002). *City works evaluation summary*. Los Angeles, CA: Constitutional Rights Foundation.

Kotler, P. (Ed.). (1994). *Marketing management: Analysis, planning, implementation and control*. Englewood Cliffs, NJ: Prentice-Hall.

Lenk, K., & Traunmuller, R. (2002). Preface to the focus theme on e-government. *Electronic Markets, 12*, 145–147. doi:10.1080/10196780232024590l

Liljander, V., Gillberg, F., & Van Riel, A. (2006). Technology readiness and the evaluation and adoption of self-service technologies. *Journal of Retailing and Consumer Services, 13*(3), 177–191. doi:10.1016/j.jretconser.2005.08.004

Lin, J. C., & Hsieh, P. L. (2006). The role of technology readiness in customers, perception and adoption of self-service technologies. *International Journal of Service Industry Management, 17*(5), 497–517. doi:10.1108/09564230610689795

Lin, J. C., & Hsieh, P. L. (2007). The influence of technology readiness on satisfaction and behavioral intentions toward self-service technologies. *Computers in Human Behavior, 23*(3), 1597–1615. doi:10.1016/j.chb.2005.07.006

Madlberger, M., & Kotzab, H. (2001). Adapting the Internet as distribution channel for stationary retailers: The American case. *Electronic Markets, 11*(1), 64–74. doi:10.1080/101967801511054 65

McClure, C. R. (1994). Network literacy: A role for libraries? *Information Technology and Libraries, 13*(2), 116–117.

McLachlan, G. J., & Peel, D. (2000). Mixtures of factor analyzers. In P. Langley (Ed.), *Proceedings of the Seventeenth International Conference on Machine Learning* (pp.599-606). San Francisco, CA: Morgan Kaufmann.

Meuter, M. L., Ostrom, A. L., Bitner, M. J., & Roundtree, R. (2003). The influence of technology anxiety on consumer use and experiences with self-service technologies. *Journal of Business Research, 56*(11), 899–906. doi:10.1016/S0148-2963(01)00276-4

Meuter, M. L., Ostrom, A. L., Roundtree, R. I., & Bitner, M. J. (2000). Self-service technologies: Understanding customer satisfaction with technology-based service encounters. *Journal of Marketing, 64*, 50–64. doi:10.1509/jmkg.64.3.50.18024

Norris, P. (2001). *Digital divide: Civic engagement, information poverty, and the Internet worldwide*. Cambridge, UK: Cambridge University Press.

Obi, T. (2009). Waseda University international e-government rankings. *I-Ways: The Journal of E-Government Policy and Regulation, 32*(3), 129.

Oliver, R. L. (1980). A cognitive model of the antecedents and consequences of satisfaction decisions. *JMR, Journal of Marketing Research, 17*, 460–469. doi:10.2307/3150499

Parasuraman, A., & Colby, C. (2003). *Techno-ready marketing: How and why customers adopt technology*. New York, NY: The Free Press.

Parasuraman, A., & Grewal, D. (2000). The impact of technology on the quality-value-loyalty chain: A research agenda. *Journal of the Academy of Marketing Science, 28*(1), 168–174. doi:10.1177/0092070300281015

Parusuraman, A. (1996, October). *Understanding and leveraging the role of customer service in external, interactive, and internal marketing*. Paper presented at the meeting of the Frontiers in Service Conference, Nashville, TN.

Putnam, R. D. (2000). *Bowling alone: The collapse and revival of American community*. New York, NY: Simon & Schuster Inc.

Ringle, C. M., Wende, S., & Will, A. (2005). *SmartPLS 2.0*. Retrieved September 1, 2010, from http://www.smartpls.de

Rogers, E. M. (1995). *Diffusion of innovation* (4th ed.). New York, NY: The Free Press.

Saanen, Y. A., Sol, H. G., & Verbraeck, A. (1999). Snapshots of e-commerce's opportunities and threats. *Electronic Markets*, *9*(3), 181–189. doi:10.1080/101967899359085

Snavely, K. (1991). Marketing in government sector: A public policy model. *American Review of Public Administration*, *21*(4), 311–326. doi:10.1177/027507409102100403

van de Donk, W. B. H. J., & Snellen, I. Th. M. (1998). Towards a theory of pubic administration in an information age? In Snellen, I. Th. M., & van de Donk, W. B. H. J. (Eds.), *Public administration in information age: A handbook* (pp. 3–19). Amsterdam, The Netherlands: IOS Press.

Van Riel, A., Semeijn, J., & Janssen, W. (2003). E-service quality expectations: A case study. *Total Quality Management*, *14*(4), 437–450. doi:10.1080/1478336032000047255

Van Ryzin, G. G. (2005). Testing the expectancy disconfirmation model of citizen satisfaction with local government. *Journal of Public Administration: Research and Theory*, *16*, 599–611. doi:10.1093/jopart/mui058

Van Ryzin, G. G., & Immerwahr, S. (2007). Importance-performance analysis of citizen satisfaction surveys. *Public Administration*, *85*(1), 215–226. doi:10.1111/j.1467-9299.2007.00641.x

Walczuch, R., Lemmink, J., & Streukens, S. (2007). The effect of service employees' technology readiness on technology acceptance. *Information & Management*, *44*(2), 206–215. doi:10.1016/j.im.2006.12.005

Wold, H. (1985). Systems analysis by partial least squares. In Nijkamp, P., Leitner, H., & Wrigley, N. (Eds.), *Measuring the unmeasurable* (pp. 221–251). Boston, MA: Martinus Nijhoff.

Yi, M. Y., & Hwang, Y. (2003). Predicting the use of Web-based Information Systems: Self-efficacy, enjoyment, learning goal orientation, and the technology acceptance model. *International Journal of Human-Computer Studies*, *59*, 431–449. doi:10.1016/S1071-5819(03)00114-9

KEY TERMS AND DEFINITIONS

E-Governance Ecosystem: The ecosystem is constituted by six main mechanisms namely ICT preparedness, ICT usage, EA ICT Model (enterprise architecture ICT model), Information provision capability, policy marketing, and resource allocation.

Technology Readiness: Constituted by optimism, innovativeness, discomfort and insecurity which is considered overall as the tendency of people are willing to use technology-based service.

Technology Anxiety: The fear, anxious and aspire as people are using or going to use technology-based services.

Engagement Tendency: People's experience in terms of involving in public affairs.

Need for Interaction: People would like to interact with service employee rather than using technology-based service anytime and anywhere.

Perceived Risk: The risk or insecurity that people perceived as they use technology-based service.

Expectation: People's expectation toward e-service before they use it.

Perceived e-Service Quality: People's evaluation toward e-service in terms of responsiveness, reliability, customization, security, user interface and overall aspect.

Satisfaction with E-Service: An overall attitude toward e-service after using it.

ENDNOTES

1 Ministry of Economy, Trade and Industry, Japan

2 According to the survey conducted by Ministry of Public Management, Home Affairs, Post and Telecommunications of Japan, 74.9% of Japanese are capable of using Internet in 2005, whereas 69.4% in 2003. As well as in Taiwan, the same ratio is growing from 61.1% in 2004 to 65.6% in 2007.

3 World Congress of Information Technology

4 World Teleport Association

Chapter 6
Trust and Public Services in E-Government Based on Customer Orientation

Li-chun Chiang
National Cheng Kung University & Taiwan E-Governance Research Center, Taiwan

ABSTRACT

This chapter aims to identify the role of risk perception and trust in civil servants' intention to deliver e-services in e-government. The research method is based on theories on perceived behaviors and technology acceptance. The research uses questionnaires to examine civil servants' intention to adopt digitalized services in e-government and seeks to measure perceived usefulness of e-services, subjective norm, self-efficacy, technology facilitating conditions, trust towards Information Systems, and perceived risk from the perspective of service marketing (e.g., SSTs, self-service technologies). Structural equation modeling is used to further analyze the data and to design a theoretical model predicting the individual's intention to trust e-services in e-government. The research results indicate that perceived usefulness cannot directly influence behavioral intention without an attitude of acceptance towards digitalized administration. Further, civil servants do not have high risk perception in using online public services.

INTRODUCTION

The purpose of e-government is the utilization of information technology (IT) to provide efficient, timely and accessible means of linking citizens to the public sectors. The proliferation of e-government can be attributed to the delivery capability of government information, resources and services through 24/7 Web access (Holden, Norris, & Fletcher, 2002). Maintaining online access to e-government to provide services is part of government, especially for those officials who

DOI: 10.4018/978-1-60960-753-1.ch006

are charged with implementing public services. Therefore, it is important to explore the intention of administrators to adopt online service delivery. Their values and perceptions influence their attitudes and behavior, and determine whether they can successfully execute public service delivery. Whether, civil servants trust the new technology, management, and services will impact the benefits and risks of e-government.

In this study, the Theory of Planned Behavior (TPB) and the Technology Acceptance Model (TAM) are used to examine administrator acceptance of online service delivery, which can result in a larger base of administrator share (Brown, Chervany, & Reinicke, 2007; Wu & Chen, 2005). TPB can be used to explore the influence of an individual's attitudes and personality on personal behavior while considering individual perceptions in social systems (Ajzen, 1991). TAM has been applied to understand and predict user attitude, adoption, and use of IT (Davis, 1989). Based on these two research models, the study used questionnaires to examine the intentions of officials to adopt online service delivery in e-government, by measuring perceived usefulness and perceived ease of use of e-services, subjective norm, self-efficacy, technology facilitating conditions, trust towards information systems, and perceived risk. The two crucial objectives of this research are (1) to illustrate the relationships between key factors and behavioral intentions, and (2) to clarify variables in online services delivery which could provide a framework for policies cultivating information trust and perceived risks of e-government. Questionnaires to be analyzed by the Structural Equation Model were designed based on TPB and TAM, and sent to those who have worked in the Tainan City government. This was done to explore official perceptions of online services delivery and to help us understand their intention to maintain online services in Taiwan. Structural Equation modeling was used to further analyze the data and to design a theoretical model predicting individual intention to maintain e-services in e-government. The research results are expected to illuminate the nature of cyber trust and the relationships among the influential factors that inform e-services.

This research is a quantitative study, and proceeds as follows: Section two reviews the theoretical arguments and some existing findings related to trust, perceived risk, TAM and TPB. Section three illustrates the research design, including research model and hypotheses, research methods (i.e. sampling and measurement). Section four presents the data analyses and hypotheses. Section five discusses research findings. Finally, section six draws conclusions and provides suggestions aimed at strengthening administrator's intention to maintain online service delivery in Taiwan.

BACKGROUND

User attitudes towards accepting and trusting information technology have been an important issue in discussing security and perceptions of trust towards information technology. Since Davis (1989) provided the Technology Acceptance Model (TAM) and showed the theoretical basis for actual use depends on behavioral intention, the attitude construct in TAM represents attitude toward the behavior of using technology (Wixom & Todd, 2005). Davis (1989) provided two important concepts in TAM: (1) perceived usefulness refers to user feelings of improved performance when using technology; (2) perceived ease of use is concerned with user perceptions of degree of exertion needed to use technology. Using TAM, Igbaria, Guimaraes, & Davis (1995) examined the role of organizational factors on personal computing acceptance and found that these factors indirectly influenced usage through ease of use and perceived usefulness. Therefore, in this study ease of use and perceived usefulness are selected as two main factors to test user's intention of IT acceptance, following the TAM model. Gefen, Karahanna, and Straub (2003) have noted that consumer trust is as important to online commerce, thus showing an agreement with the widely accepted TAM concepts of perceived usefulness and perceived ease of use.

Ajzen (1991) provides a theory of planned behavior (TPB) that plays a major role in initiating new technology use by organizations and in investigating the acceptance process. According to the TPB model, human action is influenced by three dimensions: (1) behavioral beliefs about the possible and proper outcomes of the behavior and the evaluations of these outcomes (i.e., behavioral beliefs producing a favorable or unfavorable attitude toward the behavior); (2) normative beliefs about the normative expectations of others and motivations to comply with these expectations (i.e., normative beliefs result in perceived social pressure or a subjective norm); and (3) control beliefs about the presence of factors that may facilitate or impede performance of the behavior and the perceived power of these factors. Control beliefs give rise to perceived behavioral control (i.e., individuals self-evaluate the cause and consequences of behaviors). Attitude refers to an individual's positive or negative feelings about performing the target behavior (Chen, Fan, & Farn, 2007). Quadahi (2008) studied employee resistance to a new information system (IS) and found that attitudes toward adopting IS are related to psychological characteristics of the potential adopters, including, open-mindedness, self-efficacy and interest in information technology. Lu, Zhou, and Wang (2009) studied user behavioral intentions toward IM usage, and they noted that the subjective norm and perceived behavioral control have significant impacts on usage behavior. Taylor and Todd (1995) noted that facilitating conditions and self-efficacy are two elements that inform perceived behavioral control to determine user behavioral intention. That is, 'facilitating conditions' reflect the availability of resources needed (such as time, money, equipments) and 'self-efficacy' (i.e., an individual's self-confidence in the ability to perform a behavior). van Beuningen, Ruyter, Wetzels, and Streukens (2009) argue that self-efficacy increases the financial performance perceptions of novice customers, service value evaluations, and future usage intentions.

TAM only employs two variables to explain behavioral intention. In addition, a user's behavioral intention toward accepting information technology will also be affected by other factors, such as attitude, subjective norm, perceived behavioral control over necessary resources and skills (Fishbein & Ajzen, 1975; Ajzen, 1991). Further, while TPB provides the basic theoretical framework in analyzing IT adoption, it does not shed light on what attitudinal beliefs would affect a user's attitude toward IT (Wu & Chen, 2005). Venkatesh, Morris, Davis, and Davis (2003) formulated a unified Theory of Acceptance and Use of Technology (UTAUT) to explain user acceptance of information technology. The theory included four core constructs: performance expectancy (perceived usefulness), effort expectancy (perceived ease of use), social influence (subjective norm), and facilitating conditions (perceived behavioral control). Lee, Kim, Rhee, and Trimi (2009) examined the intrinsic and extrinsic motivations that affect Chinese user acceptance of Instant Messaging (IM) based on TPB and TAM, and they found that perceived usefulness and perceived enjoyment significantly influence user attitudes towards IM, which in turn impacted their behavioral intention.

In addition to TAM and TPB, this study incorporates the concept of self-service technology (SSTs), from the perspective of service marketing. That is, self-service technology allows customers to shape their own service encounters via the interaction of electronic service interfaces or machines, rather than by interacting with a firm's service personnel (Chen, Chen, & Chen, 2009:1248). In that sense, trust and perceived risk are two influential factors in discussing online services.

Therefore, in this study, the factors of perceived ease of use and perceived usefulness from the TAM model, and attitude, subjective norms and perceived behavioral control from the TPB model, are used to explore user behavioral intention to accept online public services.

RESEARCH DESIGN

Research Structure

According to the Theory of Planned Behavior, Behavioral Intention, Attitude, Subjective Norms, and Perceived Behavioral Control are the four behavioral variables which form a structural equation model expressed as Figure 1.

Research Hypotheses and Research Questions

According to Venkatesh et al. (2003) and Chen et al. (2007), perceived ease of use and perceived usefulness significantly influence personal intention towards acceptance of technology. The main reason civil servants accept online public services are that they find them useful. Therefore, the following hypotheses are suggested:

H_1. Perceived ease of use will have a positive effect on the perceived usefulness of online public services.

H_2. Perceived usefulness will have a positive effect on attitude toward accepting digitalized administration.

H_3. Perceived usefulness will have a positive effect on the behavioral intention toward accepting online public services.

Davis (1989), Igbaria et al (1995) and Wu and Chen (2005) argue that a more positive attitude toward IT usage would lead to greater behavioral intention toward acceptance of online public services. Attitude is evaluated as behavior which is favorable or unfavorable, and further includes the concepts of egoism and altruism. Baston and Coke (1981) argue that egoism and altruism are antecedents to attitude. Furthermore, both concepts should influence attitudes toward IT usage. Thus, the following hypothesis is proposed:

H_4. Attitude toward accepting digitalized administration will have a positive effect on

Figure 1. Research structure

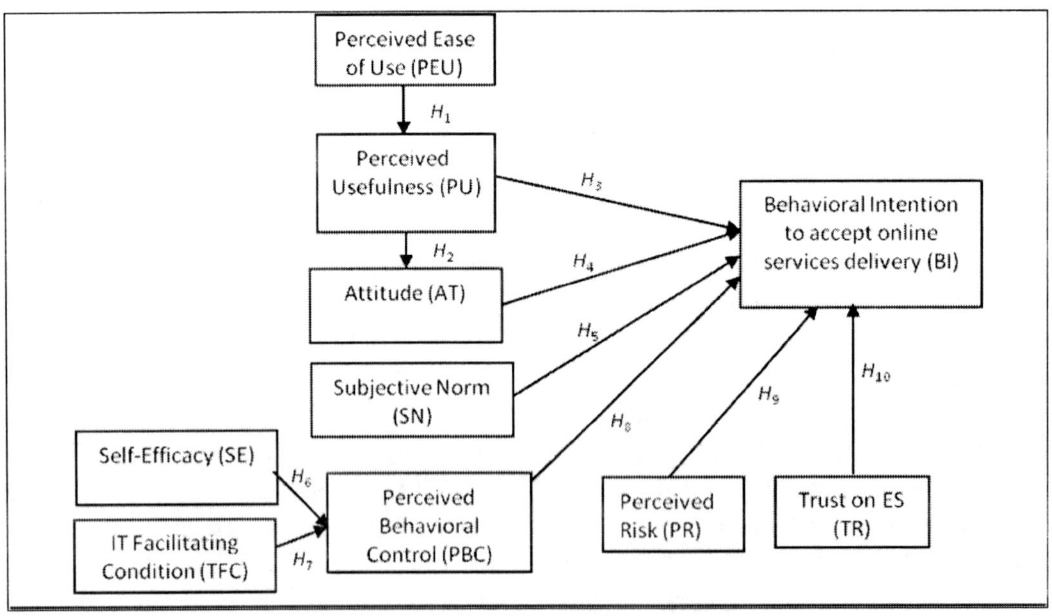

behavioral intention toward accepting online public services.

According to Premkumar, Ramamurthy, and Liu (2008) and Wu and Chen (2005), subjective norms refer to user perceptions of whether other important people perceive they should engage in the behavior. Lee, Kim, Rhee, and Trimi (2009) argue that many Internet users choose to use one kind of instant messaging only because the kind of IM that their friends use and recommend to them. Therefore, this hypothesis is suggested:

H_5. Subjective norm is positively related to the behavioral intention to accept online public services.

Ajzen (1991), Venkatesh et al. (2003) and Quadahi (2008) argue the relationships among self-efficacy, IT facilitating condition and perceived behavioral control do influence user acceptance of online services. Therefore, based on the theoretical and empirical support from the literature, the following hypotheses are suggested:

H_6. Self-efficacy will have a positive effect on perceived behavioral control to accept online public services.

H_7. IT Facilitating conditions will have a positive effect on perceived behavioral control to accept online public services.

H_8. Perceived behavioral control will have a positive effect on behavioral intention to accept online public services.

Using new technology may involve both benefits and risks to the end-user, and before deciding to adopt the technology the individual may want to weigh risks and benefits (Horst, Kuttschreuter, & Gutteling, 2007). Users may not have confidence in using technology or computer programs, in part, because of lack of knowledge regarding security. Trust is defined as the willingness to believe in the reliability, honesty, worthiness and capability of another entity (Chadwick & Basden, 2001; Lekkas, 2003). Therefore, these hypotheses are suggested:

H_9. Perceived risk has a positive effect on behavioral intention to accept online public services.

H_{10}. Trust will have a positive effect on behavioral intention to accept online public services.

The following research objectives have been designed to test the above study hypotheses: where perceived usefulness (PU) is influenced by perceived ease of use (PEU); attitude regarding online services delivery (AT) reflects the influence of PU and behavioral intention to accept online services delivery; perceived behavioral control (PBC) is affected by self-efficacy (SE) and IT facilitating condition (TFC); subjective norm (SN), PBC, trust (TR) and perceived risk (PR) influences behavioral intention to accept online services delivery (BI). Each dimension was measured using a 5-item scale (from 1: "strongly disagree" to 5: "strongly agree").

Ease of use is an indication of the user's ability to operate online services without difficulty. Respondents answered with four items related to ease of use as follows:

1. Using digitalized services is easy for me.
2. I easily adapted to online services.
3. Digitalized service for me is an easy way to deliver public services.
4. It is easy to operate information systems to deliver public services.

Perceived usefulness is the determinant of user beliefs that using online services improves public services delivery. Respondents answered three questions related to perceived usefulness:

1. Digitalized public services are helpful for me to improve public services delivery (such as timeliness).

2. Using digitalized services is convenient for me to communicate with citizens.
3. Digitalized services are a useful way for me to service citizens.

Attitudes toward using digitalized services indicate user action and preference for digitalized public services. Attitudes of intention are captured in the following items:

1. Using digitalization to deliver public services is a good idea.
2. I like using digitalization to deliver public services.
3. Using digitalization to deliver public services is wise thinking.
4. Using digitalization to deliver public services is a happy experience.

Subjective norms is defined as an individual's perception of social normative pressures, or relevant beliefs of others concerning whether an individual should or should not perform a certain behavior.

1. My application of digitalized services is influenced by my colleague's perception that I should use digitalized public services.
2. An individual who can influence me can affect my desire to use digitalized public services.
3. The opinions related to digitalized public services which come from the media will influence me to use digitalized public services.
4. The newspapers I read related to digitalized public services will influence me to use it.

Self-efficacy is defined as people's beliefs about their capabilities to produce designated levels of performance that exercise influence over events affecting their lives. Self-efficacy beliefs determine how people feel, think, motivate themselves and behave (Bandura, 1994). Respondents answered three questions related to self-efficacy:

1. I feel comfortable when using digitalized public services.
2. I can easily operate digitalized facilitations to execute public services.
3. Without anyone's help, I can use digitalized facilitations to execute public services.

Perceived behavioral control is defined as an individual's perceived ease or difficulty with regard to performing a particular behavior (Ajzen, 1988). Respondents answered three questions related to perceived behavioral control:

1. I can appropriately use digitalized facilitations to execute public services.
2. I am capable of using digitalized equipments to execute public services.
3. I have enough knowledge and skills to execute digitalized public services.

Perceived risk is the indicator of danger or loss in the e-voting system or process. Perceptions of risks are measured through three questions:

1. The e-voting system fits in with the principle of secrecy.
2. The results produced by the e-voting system are accurate.
3. The e-voting system should be reliable.

Trust in the e-voting system (TEV) is defined as the belief in and acceptance of the e-voting system. Trust is captured in these questions:

1. According to my understanding of digitalization, I believe it can provide good service to citizens.
2. According to my understanding of digitalization, I believe that it can help citizens accept public services.
3. According to my understanding of digitalization, using digitalized services is trustworthy.

Behavioral intention is defined as an indication of an individual's readiness to perform a given behavior. It is assumed to be an immediate antecedent of behavior (Ajzen, 2002).

1. I am willing to frequently use digitalization to execute public services.
2. I am willing to continuously use digitalization to execute public services.
3. If there is any way to use digitalization to execute public services, I make efforts to use it to service citizens.

In addition to the above mentioned questions in this research, there are several demographic questions related to sex, education, age, service years and training.

Research Analysis

The study was implemented between March 15 and April 15, 2009. The sample of 217 participants included 145 females (66.80%) and 72 males (32.90%). Most participants were between the ages of 31 and 45 years old. 73.30% of civil servants had bachelor degrees. Most participants were familiar with using computers; 96.30% of the participants had 4 or more years of computer experience. 74.20% of participants have worked in Tainan city government for over 4 years. Thus, they were not unfamiliar with digitalized administration in e-government. All demographic information on the respondents is shown in Table 1.

The analytical procedures utilized a two-step approach. The first step used the analysis of the measurement model and the second step tested the structural relationships among latent constructs (Anderson, & Gerbing, 1988; Hair, Anderson, Tatham, & Black, 1998). The aim of the two-step approach was to assess the reliability and validity of the measures before using them in the full model. In terms of the threshold reliability of the measures, 0.60 is a recommended value for a reliable construct (Hu & Bentler, 1995). As Table 2 shows, the composite reliability values range from.70 to.87 (Cronbach's $\alpha \geq 0.60$), which fall at or above the acceptable value.

As shown in Table 4, the structural model reflecting the assumed linear, causal relationships among the constructs is tested with the data collected from the validated measures (Bagozzi & Yi, 1988; Bentler, 1990; Jöreskog & Sörbom, 1992; Hair, et al., 1998; Hu & Bentler, 1995). The model fit indices are within accepted thresholds: χ^2 to degrees of freedom ratio of 1.91 ($\chi^2 = 811.09$; df = 424), AGFI = 0.77, NFI = 0.94, CFI = 0.81, and RMSEA = 0.07), suggesting adequate model fit.

Table 1. Demographic data

	Terms	Frequency	Percentage (N=217)
Sex			
	Male	72	32.90
	Female	145	66.80
	Total	217	100
Age (Years Old)			
	21-25	18	8.30
	26-30	32	14.70
	31-35	39	18.00
	36-40	33	15.20
	41-45	32	14.70
	46-50	29	13.40
	51-55	26	12.00
	Over 55	8	3.70
	Total	217	100
Education			
	High School	27	12.40
	College	48	22.10
	University	111	51.20
	Graduate School	29	13.40
	Total	215	99.10
	Missing	2	0.90

continued on following page

Table 1. continued

Years of using Computers (years)			
	Less than 1yr	1	0.50
	1-3	7	3.20
	4-6	23	10.60
	7-9	43	19.80
	10-12	55	25.30
	13-15	42	19.40
	16-18	18	8.30
	Over 19	24	11.10
	Total	213	98.20
	Missing	4	1.80
Working Years (years)			
	Less than 1yr	21	9.70
	1-3	35	16.10
	4-6	29	13.40
	7-9	36	16.60
	10-12	13	6.00
	13-15	14	6.50
	16-18	20	9.20
	Over 19	47	21.70
	Total	215	99.10
	Missing	2	0.90

The results of the analysis are shown in Figure 2 and Table 3. One out of the ten paths exhibit a *p*-value less than 0.05, and the remaining one is not significant (0.05 level of significance). A review of the findings considered the usefulness factors. As shown in Figure 2, ease of use does present a negative effect on perceived usefulness ($t = -2.56$, $p \leq 0.05$). Thus, hypothesis 1 is supported. Perceived usefulness shows a significant effect on attitude of IT acceptance ($t = 4.56$, $p \leq 0.05$), but it does not show a significant effect on behavioral intention to accept online public services ($t = 1.22$; $p \geq 0.05$). Thus, hypothesis 2 is supported. Conversely, hypothesis 3 is not confirmed. Perceived usefulness influences behavioral intention through attitude of acceptance of digitalized administration. Thus, the factor of attitude is a medium between perceived usefulness and behavioral intention.

Attitude and subjective norm both present strong influences on behavioral intention toward accepting online public services ($t = 11.12$ and $t = 7.62$, respectively, $p \leq 0.001$). Thus, hypotheses 4 and 5 are supported. Self-efficacy and IT fa-

Table 2. The composite reliability of variables

Terms	Items	Cronbach's Alpha	AVE
Perceived of Ease Use	4	0.84	0.68
Perceived Usefulness	3	0.82	0.51
Attitude	4	0.85	0.60
Subjective Norms	4	0.82	0.54
Perceived Behavior Control	3	0.85	0.61
Self-Efficacy	3	0.82	0.60
Technology Facilitating	2	0.62	0.50
Perceived Risk	3	0.71	0.50
Trust	3	0.76	0.53
Behavioral Intention	3	0.87	0.56

Note:
[a] N = 217; Cronbach α should exceed 0.60 (Hu & Bentler, 1995).
[b] Cronbach, L. (1951). Coefficient alpha and the internal structure of tests. Psychometrika, 16, 297-334.
[c] Hair, J.F., Anderson, R.L., Tatham, W.C. & Black, W.C. (2006) Multivariate data analysis (6th ed.). Englewood Cliffs, New Jersey: Prentice Hall.

Figure 2. Research Results. Note: Chi-square = 811.09; df = 424; p ≦ 0.05; p** ≦ 0.001; RMSEA = 0.07*

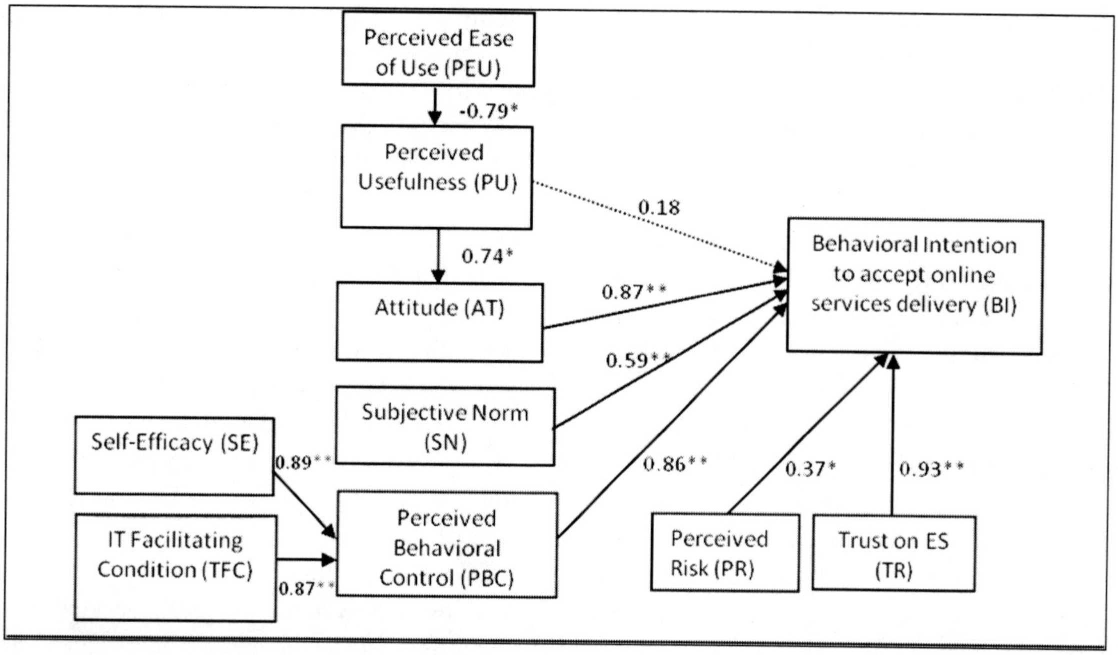

Table 3. The results of hypotheses

Items	Hypotheses	Results
H_1	Perceived ease of use will have a positive effect on the perceived usefulness of online public services.	Supported
H_2	Perceived usefulness will have a positive effect on attitude to accept digitalized administration.	Supported
H_3	Perceived usefulness will have a positive effect on the behavioral intention to accept online public services.	rejected
H_4	Attitude toward accepting digitalized administration will have a positive on behavioral intention to accept online public services.	Supported
H_5	Subjective norm is positively related to the behavioral intention to accept online public effect services.	Supported
H_6	Self-Efficacy will have a positive effect on perceived behavioral control to accept online public services.	Supported
H_7	IT Facilitating Condition will have a positive effect on perceived behavioral control to accept online public services.	Supported
H_8	Perceived behavioral control will have a positive effect on behavioral intention to accept online public services.	Supported
H_9	Perceived risk has a positive effect on behavioral intention to accept online public services.	Supported
H_{10}	Trust will have a positive effect on behavioral intention to accept online public services.	Supported

cilitating condition both show strong effects on perceived behavioral control (t = 8.44 and t = 9.90, respectively, $p \leq 0.001$). Perceived behavioral control has strong influence on behavioral intention toward accepting online services (t = 10.22, $p \leq 0.001$). Thus, hypotheses 6, 7 and 8 are supported.

Perceived risk and trust both show significant influences on behavioral intention toward accepting online public services (t = 4.00 and t = 9.91, respectively, $p \leq 0.05$). Thus, hypotheses 9 and

10 are also supported. Trust may influence the intention to use a system. If people have no trust, they will not accept a system.

Consequently, as Figure 2 shows, hypotheses 1 and 2 receive empirical support and hypothesis 3 is not confirmed. Through perceived usefulness as a medium, ease of use can influence attitude toward accepting information technology both directly and indirectly. Attitude of IT acceptance, subjective norm and perceived behavioral control ties in significantly and positively affect behavioral intention toward accepting online public services. This supports hypotheses 4, 5 and 8. In addition, the effects exhibit positive and significant influence among self-efficacy and IT facilitating condition toward perceived behavioral control. This supports hypotheses 6 and 7. Perceived risk and trust also shows positive and significant influences on behavioral intention toward online service acceptance. Thus, hypotheses 9 and 10 receive empirical support.

Solutions and Recommendations

The findings of this study indicate that user attitude and trust are important factors that influence perceptions of online service delivery. In terms of attitude, all respondents perceived e-services as a good way to provide public services, which is also confirmed by Quadahi (2008). Notably, with perceived usefulness as a medium, ease of use can influence attitudes toward accepting information technology both directly and indirectly. Perceived behavioral control is an influential factor, even more than perceived risks. That is, civil servants are willing to control their own behavior toward IT use, rather than face the risks presented in IT use. Moreover, hardware or software and other relative IT equipment are required for civil servants to execute online public service, which agrees with the research of Taylor and Todd (1995) as well as Lu, Zhou, and Wang (2009).

Civil servants have confidence in self-efficacy when asked about their viewpoints concerning online public services delivery. They do not pay more attention to IT risks. That is, Internet security is easily ignored when they use information systems or other relative systems to execute public services delivery. Therefore, the government should enhance education and outreach regarding Internet security for the benefit of civil servants. In addition, information systems and related equipment designed for digitalized administration should first be evaluated for usefulness, then evaluated according to ease of use. The majority of civil servants have high educational attainments, and so they would not find it difficult to learn and use IT. If a system is not useful for delivering online public services, then regardless of the relative ease of use, civil servants will avoid spending too much time on it to complete their work and thus place even more burden on public service delivery. Therefore, IT designers or programmers should take note of this point when designing information systems or programs for civil servants.

FUTURE RESEARCH DIRECTIONS

This paper focused on describing trust and public services in e-government especially with regard to the behavioral intention of civil servants' acceptance of online service delivery. This study examined IT acceptance, attitudes, subjective norms, perceived risks and perceptions of trust and how they affect civil servant behavioral intentions toward accepting online service delivery. To move this line of research forward, the author hopes to extend and use the initial findings presented in this study to conduct focused in-depth interviews with some of the survey participants to explore the relationship between digital confidence and public services in e-government. In subsequent research, the author wishes to conduct a similar study of civil servants in China and Taiwan to compare and contrast the extent of IT related trust practices, factoring in gender, education, specialty and workplace for different agencies practicing e-government.

CONCLUSION

The research findings of this study indicate that digitalized administration may be easy to use, but civil servants do not always perceive usefulness. Perhaps, civil servants are required to fill out many online administrative forms and thus their administrative load does not decrease in light of digitalized administration. Second, the research finding has shown that perceived usefulness cannot directly influence behavioral intention without a medium, such as attitude of accepting digitalized administration. Which is to say, civil servant perceptions of the usefulness of digitalization do affect attitudes and behavioral intentions toward accept digitalized administration. Third, the research finding has shown that civil servants do not have high risk perception in accepting online public services.

Perceived ease of use and usefulness significantly influence user attitudes toward accepting digitalization in public service delivery. If the information systems used to operate public services are required conveniences for officials, then officials are willing to accept digitalization for public services delivery. As the results shown in Figure 2 suggest, attitude is the strongest factor that influences civil servant behavioral intention toward accepting online public administration. In addition, intention to accept digitalization is influenced by subjective norms, such as opinions related to digitalization for public services delivery as communicated by colleagues, television, and newspapers. Thus, these third party entities are an important factor that influences civil servant intentions. An individual's capacity to use digitalized equipment and control systems also influences behavioral intention toward accepting digitalization for public service delivery. Thus, the government should provide enough digitalized knowledge and skills for officials before they start using the systems for public service delivery.

In sum, in order to improve civil servant perceived risks, the government has the responsibility to design training programs or outreach related to threats to IT security, such as piracy, privacy, viruses and hackers. This can help civil servants improve their knowledge, management, and skills in risk perception.

ACKNOWLEDGMENT

This research was supported in part by Taiwan Information Security Center at National Cheng Kung University and National Science Council in Taiwan under the Grants NSC 98-2219-E-006 -001.

REFERENCES

Ajzen, I. (1991). The theory of planned behavior. *Organizational Behavior and Human Decision Processes*, *50*(2), 179–211. doi:10.1016/0749-5978(91)90020-T

Ajzen, I. (2002). Perceived behavioral control, self-efficacy, locus of control, and the theory of planned behavior. *Journal of Applied Social Psychology*, *32*, 665–683. doi:10.1111/j.1559-1816.2002.tb00236.x

Anderson, J. C., & Gerbing, D. W. (1988). Structural equation modeling in practice: A review and recommended two-step approach. *Psychological Bulletin*, *103*(3), 411–423. doi:10.1037/0033-2909.103.3.411

Bagozzi, R., & Yi, Y. (1998). On the evaluation of structural equation models. *Journal of the Academy of Marketing Science*, *16*(1), 74–94. doi:10.1007/BF02723327

Bandura, A. (1994). Self-efficacy. In Ramachaudran, V. S. (Ed.), *Encyclopedia of human behavior* (*Vol. 4*, pp. 71–81). New York, NY: Academic Press.

Batson, C., & Coke, J. (1981). *A source of altruism and helping behavior: Social, personality and developmental perspective*. New Jersey: Erlbaum.

Bentler, P. M. (1990). Comparative fit indexes in structural models. *Psychological Bulletin*, *107*(2), 238–246. doi:10.1037/0033-2909.107.2.238

Brown, S. A., Chervany, N. L., & Reinicke, B. A. (2007). What matters when introducing new Information Technology. *Communications of the ACM*, *50*(9), 91–96. doi:10.1145/1284621.1284625

Chadwick, D. W., & Basden, A. (2001). Evaluating trust in a public key certification authority. *Computers & Security*, *20*(7), 592–611. doi:10.1016/S0167-4048(01)00710-6

Chen, C. D., Fan, Y. W., & Farn, C. K. (2007). Predicting electronic toll collection service adoption: An integration of the technology acceptance model and the theory of planned behavior. *Transportation Research Part C, Emerging Technologies*, *15*, 300–311. doi:10.1016/j.trc.2007.04.004

Chen, S. C., Chen, H. H., & Chen, M. F. (2009). Determinants of satisfaction and continuance intention towards self-service technologies. *Industrial Management & Data Systems*, *109*(8-9), 1248–1263. doi:10.1108/02635570911002306

Davis, F. D. (1989). Perceived usefulness, perceived ease of use, and user acceptance of Information Technology. *Management Information Systems Quarterly*, *9*, 319–340. doi:10.2307/249008

Davis, F. D., Bagozzi, R. P., & Warshaw, P. R. (1989). User acceptance of Information Technology: A comparison of two theoretical models. *Management Science*, *35*(8), 982–1003. doi:10.1287/mnsc.35.8.982

Fishbein, M., & Ajzen, I. (1975). *Belief, attitude, intention, and behavior: An introduction to theory and research*. Reading, MA: Addison-Wesley.

Gefen, D., Karahanna, E., & Straub, D. W. (2003). Trust and TAM in online shopping: An integrated model. *Management Information Systems Quarterly*, *27*(1), 51–90.

Hair, F. Jr, Anderson, R. E., Tatham, R. L., & Black, W. C. (1998). *Multivariate data analysis* (5th ed.). Basingstoke, UK: Macmillan.

Holden, S. H., Norris, D. F., & Fletcher, P. D. (2002, January). Electronic government at the grass roots: Contemporary evidence and future trends. *Proceedings of the 36th Hawaii International Conference on System Sciences*, Hawaii.

Horst, M., Kuttschreuter, M., & Gutteling, G. M. (2007). Perceived usefulness, personal experiences, risk perception and trust as determinants of adoption of e-government services in The Netherlands. *Computers in Human Behavior*, *23*(4), 1838–1852. doi:10.1016/j.chb.2005.11.003

Hu, L., & Bentler, P. M. (1995). Evaluating model fit. In Hoyle, R. H. (Ed.), *Structural equation modeling: Concepts, issues, and applications* (pp. 76–99). Thousand Oaks, CA: SAGE.

Hung, S. Y., & Chang, C. M. (2005). User acceptance of WAP services: Test of competing theories. *Computer Standards & Interfaces*, *27*(4), 359–370. doi:10.1016/j.csi.2004.10.004

Igbaria, M., Guimaraes, T., & Davis, G. B. (1995). Testing the determinants of microcomputer usage via a structural equation model. *Journal of Management Information Systems*, *11*(4), 87–114.

Lee, S. M., Kim, I., Rhee, S., & Trimi, S. (2006). The role of exogenous factors in technology acceptance: The case of object-oriented technology. *Information & Management*, *43*(4), 469–480. doi:10.1016/j.im.2005.11.004

Lekkas, D. (2003). Establishing and managing trust within the public key infrastructure. *Computer Communications, 26*, 1815–1825. doi:10.1016/S0140-3664(03)00077-X

Lu, Y. B., Zhou, T., & Wang, B. (2009). Exploring Chinese users' acceptance of instant messaging using the theory of planned behavior, the technology acceptance model, and the flow theory. *Computers in Human Behavior, 25*(1), 29–39. doi:10.1016/j.chb.2008.06.002

Ouadahi, J. (2008). A qualitative analysis of factors associated with user acceptance and rejection of a new workplace Information System in the public sector: A conceptual model. *Canadian Journal of Administrative Sciences, 25*(3), 201–213. doi:10.1002/cjas.65

Premkumar, G., Ramamurthy, K., & Liu, H. N. (2008). Internet messaging: An examination of the impact of attitudinal, normative, and control belief systems. *Information & Management, 45*(7), 451–457. doi:10.1016/j.im.2008.06.008

Taylor, S., & Todd, P. A. (1995). Understanding Information Technology usage: A test of competing models. *Information Systems Research, 6*(2), 144–176. doi:10.1287/isre.6.2.144

van Beuningen, J., de Ruyter, K., Wetzels, M., & Streukens, S. (2009). Customer self-efficacy in technology-based self-service assessing between- and within-person differences. *Journal of Service Research, 11*(4), 407–428. doi:10.1177/1094670509333237

Venkatesh, V., Morris, M. G., Davis, G. B., & Davis, M. D. (2003). User acceptance of Information Technology: Toward a unified view. *Management Information Systems Quarterly, 27*(3), 425–478.

Wixom, B. H., & Todd, P. A. (2005). A theoretical integration of user satisfaction and technology acceptance. *Information Systems Research, 16*(1), 85–102. doi:10.1287/isre.1050.0042

Wu, I. L., & Chen, E. L. (2005). An extension of trust and TAM model with TPB in the initial adoption of on-line tax: An empirical study. *International Journal of Human-Computer Studies, 62*(6), 784–808. doi:10.1016/j.ijhcs.2005.03.003

ADDITIONAL READING

Boyne, G. A., & Law, J. (2005). Setting public service outcome targets: Lessons from local public service agreement. *Public Money & Management, 25*(4),.253-260.

Byrd, T. A., & Turner, D. E. (2001). An exploratory analysis of the value of the skill of IT personnel: Their relationship to IS infrastructure and competitive advantage. *Decision Sciences, 32*(1), 21–54. doi:10.1111/j.1540-5915.2001.tb00952.x

Carmeli, A. (2004). Strategic human capital and the performance of public sector organizations. *Scandinavian Journal of Management, 20*, 375–392. doi:10.1016/j.scaman.2003.11.003

Cheney, P. H., & Lyons, N. R. (1980). Information systems skill requirements: A survey. *Management Information Systems Quarterly, 4*(1), 35–43. doi:10.2307/248866

Cherchye, L. (2001). Using data envelopment analysis to assess macroeconomic policy performance. *Applied Economics, 33*, 407–416. doi:10.1080/00036840122353

Chiang, L. (2007). IT assets, organizational capabilities, and firm performance: How resource allocations and organizational differences explain performance variation. *Organization Science, 18*(5), 763–780. doi:10.1287/orsc.1070.0306

Chin, W. W., Gopal, A., & Salisbury, W. D. (1997). Advancing the theory of adaptive structuration: The development of a scale to measure faithfulness of appropriation. *Information Systems Research, 8*, 342–367. doi:10.1287/isre.8.4.342

Cohen, W. M., & Levinthal, D. A. (1990). Absorptive capacity: A new perspective on learning and innovation. *Administrative Science Quarterly*, *35*(1), 128–152. doi:10.2307/2393553

Darais, K. M., Nelson, K. M., & Reich, B. H. (2002, January). *Identifying the dependent variables of IT personnel transition*. Proceedings of the 35th Hawaii International Conference on System Sciences, Hawaii.

Dimitriadis, S., & Kyrezis, N. (2010). Linking trust to use intention for technology-enabled bank channels: The role of trusting intentions. *Psychology and Marketing*, *27*(8), 799–820. doi:10.1002/mar.20358

Eckardt, S. (2008). Political accountability, fiscal conditions and local government performance-cross-sectional evidence from Indonesia. *Public Administration and Development*, *28*, 1–17. doi:10.1002/pad.475

Feng, Y. J., Lu, H., & Bi, K. (2004). An AHP/DEA method for measurement of the efficiency of R&D management activities in university. *International Transactions in Operational Research*, *11*, 181–191. doi:10.1111/j.1475-3995.2004.00450.x

Gao, J. (2009). Governing by goals and numbers: A case study in the use of performance measurement to build state capacity in China. *Public Administration and Development*, *29*, 21–31. doi:10.1002/pad.514

Hair, J. F., Black, W. C., Babin, B. J., Anderson, R. E., & Tatham, R. L. (2006). *Multivariate data analysis*. New Jersey: Personal Prentice Hall.

Harkness, W., Kettinger, W. J., & Segars, A. H. (1996). Sustaining process improvement and innovation in the information services function: Lessons learned at the Bose corporation. *Management Information Systems Quarterly*, *20*(3), 349–368. doi:10.2307/249661

Hecht, A. (1997). *Restructuring Municipal Financial in Israel*. Jerusalem: The Floersheimer Institute for Policy Studies.

Horan, T. A., Abhichandani, T., & Rayalu, R. (2006, January). *Assessing user satisfaction of e-government services: Development and testing of quality-in-use satisfaction with advanced traveler information systems* (ATIS). Proceedings of the 39th Hawaii International Conference on System Sciences, Kauai, Hawaii.

Jöreskog, K., & Sörbom, D. (1992). *LISREL 8: Structural Equation Modeling with the SIMPLIS Command Language*. Hillsdale: Erlbaum Associates.

Kaufman, R. J., & Sougstad, R. (2008). Risk management of contract portfolios in IT services: The profit-at-risk approach. *Journal of Management Information Systems*, *25*(1), 17–48. doi:10.2753/MIS0742-1222250102

Kyereboah-Coleman, A., & Amidu, M. (2008). The link between small business governance and performance: The case of the Ghanaian SEM sector. *Journal of African Business*, *9*(1), 122–143. doi:10.1080/15228910802052880

Lee, D. M. S., Trauth, E. M., & Farwell, D. (1995). Critical skills and knowledge requirements of IS professionals: A Joint academic/industry investigation. *Management Information Systems Quarterly*, *19*(3), 313–340. doi:10.2307/249598

MacAdam, R., & Walker, T. (2004). Evaluating the best value framework in UK local government services. *Public Administration and Development*, *24*(3), 183–196. doi:10.1002/pad.275

Melitski, J. (2003). Capacity and e-government performance. *Public Performance & Management Review*, *26*(4), 376–390. doi:10.1177/1530957603026004005

Melkers, J., & Willoughby, K. (2005). Models of performance-measurement use in local governments: Understanding budgeting, communication, and lasting effects. *Public Administration Review, 65*(2), 180–190. doi:10.1111/j.1540-6210.2005.00443.x

KEY TERMS AND DEFINITIONS

Attitude: An individual's positive or negative feelings about performing the target behavior (Chen, Fan, & Farn, 2007).

Egoism: An excessive or exaggerated sense of self-importance (Sources from Wikipedia, the free encyclopedia).

Risk Perception: The subjective judgment that people make about the characteristics and severity of a risk (Sources from Wikipedia, the free encyclopedia).

Self-Efficacy: As the belief that one is capable of performing in a certain manner to attain certain goals or as a person's belief about their capabilities to produce designated levels of performance that exercise influence over events that affect their lives (Sources from Wikipedia, the free encyclopedia).

Technology Acceptance Model (TAM): Two important concepts of TAM: (1) perceived usefulness refers to users' feelings of improved performance when they use the technology; (2) perceived ease of use is concerned with users' perceived exerted efforts when using the technology (Davis, 1989).

The Theory of Planned Behaviors (TPB): A theory designed to predict and explain human behavior in specific contexts (Ajzen, 1991).

Trust: Relationship of reliance. It allows us to form relationships with others and to depend on others—for love, for advice, for help with our plumbing, or what have you. Trust always involves the risk that the trusted person will not pull through for the trusting person (Sources from Wikipedia, the free encyclopedia).

Chapter 7
Thailand Citizen Centric E-Government Service:
Maturity and Challenges

Jirapon Tubtimhin
Ministry of Science and Technology/International Academy of CIO (IAC), Thailand

ABSTRACT

Thailand started its race for e-government with the consecutive IT2000, IT2001, and followed by the first ICT Master Plan during 2002-2008, a key policy framework planning to incorporate 5 key "e" strategy flagships: e-government, e-commerce, e-industry, e-education, and e-society, in order to lead the country toward knowledge economy by 2010. E-government development has been reflected through various projects and initiatives, especially some prominent online initiatives. These public service showcases for certain extent and appropriate condition have proved that "citizen centric" approach has been a critical factor for their achievements.

The country's current ICT master plan aims at the end of the plan in 2013 for being "Smart Thailand" where sustainable ICT implementation will be based on IT-literate-human capacity in all levels of society and on the good governance foundation in all development sectors as well as the accessible-to-all infrastructure. Key government bodies to drive implementation of the country master plan range from policy level of Ministry of ICT (MICT) to implementation level, including every single ministry and department under its supervision. Results of an e-government maturity survey in 2004 revealed that the overall e-services development in early years lacked attention on integration among government agencies, whereas the e-government maturity model used in the survey placed the "integration" level among the 5 stages in an order of advancement. These are: information, interaction, interchange transaction, integration, and intelligence. A later survey in 2008 showed maturity improvement, which contributed, for a certain extent, to citizen centric activities and projects. Challenges are among how to cater such leverages which could secure them from the burden of big investment and of falling into the pitfall of fast-moving ICT.

DOI: 10.4018/978-1-60960-753-1.ch007

The current ICT master plan has put more attention on the governance factor since there have been lessons learnt during the first master plan implementation: a lack of properly conducted governance caused most project misconducts and less citizen engagement. Therefore e-governance has been underlined both in terms of front and back-end services. Likewise, challenges toward success for the next phase of e-government are to define clearly the governance elements in both vertical and horizontal dimensions. Most importantly, "citizen centricity" is crucial in all those angles to keep the online activities in high record of citizen community attention. Above all, the e-government development efforts must lead the country toward a smarter and more sustainable condition and environment.

E-GOVERNMENT, DEFINITION AND EVOLUTION

E-Government has been prone to public attention regarding ICT development in public sector when the World Bank defined e-Government as the use of information and communication technologies or ICT to enhance efficiency, effectiveness, transparency and accountability to service delivery to citizens (World Bank) (Halachmi, 2004). While at the same time United Nations referred e-Government to the use of ICT in public sector to enhance efficiency and effectiveness as well as to enhance relationship between public organization and citizens and later evolved to the use of ICT such as Wide Area Networks, the Internet, and mobile computing by government agencies (UN) (Halachmi, 2004). While OECD noted that e-Government refers to the use of ICT and particularly the Internet, as a tool to achieve better government (OECD) (Halachmi, 2004).

In fact e-Government evolved from the dot com era of e-Commerce when business sectors flocked into the internet world to succeed their business transaction during the past decade. Public sector then cached up this phenomenon and started turning on to reinvent itself into "Electronic Service Delivery" or ESD which has been emerging all over the world to date.

SHIFTING TO THE SECOND GENERATION E-GOVERNMENT PARADIGM

The report of United Nations, UN E-Government Survey 2008 (the United Nations [UN], 2008), From E-Government to Connected Governance, took an important note on e-Government development that paved direction of ICT development of public organization into the Second Generation e-Government Paradigm where value creation for citizens has to be called for attention. The report emphasized about the whole concept e-Government as noted that "The emerging ICT-for-development approach towards public sector transformation is creating new perceptions about government and governance. The twin objective of achieving further improvements in service delivery and efficacy in government functioning is bringing about a rethinking of the role of ICT. Governments are increasingly looking towards *e-government-as-a-whole concept* which focuses on the provision of services at the front-end, supported by integration, consolidation and innovation in back-end processes and systems to achieve maximum cost savings and improved service delivery". While stressed on public domain integration helps enhance value to public service to citizen quoted as mentioning "Within the ambit of the whole-of-government approach, the focus of the second generation e-government initiatives has shifted from the provision of services to the use of ICTs to increase the *value* of services. As indicated, the approach to public sector service delivery has evolved over time from the traditional model of government dispensing services via traditional modes to an emphasis on e-government and eservices *per se,* to an integrated approach for enhancing the *value of services to the citizen.* In many countries around the world, public sector development strategies are being revisited to address the question: how can the *value of the public services* be enhanced?

FROM E-GOVERNMENT TO E-GOVERNANCE

Recent survey of Accenture revealed an important notion of next phase e-Government development which can confirm the UN recommended direction to care for citizens' value which implies requiring citizens' participation and engagement. Accenture addressed in its findings that "to date it is about time to move from e-Government to e-Governance". According to the survey during the event Global Cities Forum in 2009, by Accenture, Institute for Health and Public Service Value, result of the survey (Accenture Institute for Health & Public Service Value Project Team, 2009) indicated that public service value governance is the key factor. New generation of public organization needs to have a framework which implies to include publicly engaged model of governance. The model reflects the following four elements containing governance items which citizen centricity will be key development approach.

Outcomes

Focusing on improved social and economic conditions for citizens such as health, learning and safety and not merely on the amount of services provided or on efficiency with strategies: focusing performance management on actual improvements in people's social and economic conditions; continually improving the customer experience by soliciting service user and customer feedback; improving the efficiency and effectiveness of public service provision. (*Performance; Feedback; Efficiency and Effectiveness)*

Balance

Balancing choice and flexibility with fairness and common good, being mindful that narrow application of either can widen gaps between those who are able to take advantage of service improvements and those who are not with strategies: conducting customer segmentation analysis and using customer insight to target services appropriate; ensuring that more citizens can access and use digital media channels and providing support to those who cannot. (*G2A, G2B, G2C, G2D...G2Z; Accessibility)*

Engagement

Engaging, educating and enrolling citizens as co-producers of public value by eliciting their views, helping clarify their perceptions and enabling them to make best use of government resources and to contribute to improving their own quality of life with development strategies: enabling citizens to engage with each other through social networking technologies; enabling citizens to participate in their governance through digital media; educating citizens and encouraging participation through online training and learning resources. (*Engagement and Participation*)

Accountability

Clarifying accountability, being more transparent about government actions and performance, and facilitating public recourse by providing accessible means to remedy problems with government and public services with following development strategies: increasing transparency and accountability by developing web-based tools to report on results achieved; enabling citizens to report problems and resolve complaints through online channels. (*Accountability, Transparency and Online Consultation)*

What learned reflected from the survey also revealed that "People do indeed want to become more engaged in their governance. They want to be more informed and to have a bigger say in how government acts to make their life better." This input reflects "Next Journey to e-Governance" regarding to development of "Citizen-Centric Vision of Governance" will need the following actionable activities and processes:

- To develop flexible service delivery mechanisms and effective enterprise tools that enable front-office staff to assemble networks of service providers around citizens' needs.
- ERP and BPM solutions, for instance, enable citizen-centric public services by providing decision makers with enhanced business insight and greater control over the flow of resources and information.
- To deliver more responsive, flexible public services, these IT solutions must be part of a broader change program to establish a customer-centric culture in the front office.
- This change program should provide staff with enhanced client service skills and a comprehensive understanding of service delivery mechanisms.

Additionally to the above mentioned, the journey needs to have tailor services and communications to meet user needs and preferences, strengthening and fostering of the capacity to innovate by creating a sense of ownership within the workforce and lastly aiming for success in terms of improved service quality and increased citizen trust in government.

To this end, with the framework of governance parameters, e-Government has been evolving to the next phase where citizens are the center of development in achieving the ultimate goal of public service i.e. good governance environment which will cater sustainable economic and social development of each single economy in the globe. Governance characteristics defined by UNESCAP are depicted in the below picture. The UNESCAP good governance characteristics include accountability, transparency, responsiveness, equity and inclusion, effectiveness and efficiency, follows the rule of law, participation and consensus oriented.

THAILAND PACES OF E-GOVERNMENT DEVELOPMENT

Thailand started its e-Government development with the policy frameworks of IT 2000 and 2010 ("Thailand IT 2010 Framework, 2001-2010", http://www.nectec.or.th). The ICT policy frame works were then translated into the country's ICT Master Plan to lay down e-Government architecture during 2002-2008 (National Electronics and Computer Technology Center [NECTEC], National Science and Technology Development Agency [NSTDA], & Ministry of Science and Technology [MOST], 2003). The IT2000 set target to lay basic foundation of ICT Infrastructure including human resource development. Whereby the IT2010 (2001-2010) which was set forward to achieve the ultimate goal of building up the country to the level of knowledge based economy and three specific goals: 1) to raise the technological capability of Thailand from "dynamic IT adopter" nation to "a potential leader", 2) to increase the proportion of knowledge workers and 3) to increase a contributable sum of knowledge-based industries to the country growth. To achieve these goals, IT2010 has

Figure 1. ICT Development Program, Flagships and Infrastructure in IT 2010. Source: National Electronics and Computer Technology Center (NECTEC). (2010). Retrieved September 15, 2010, from http://www.nectec.or.th

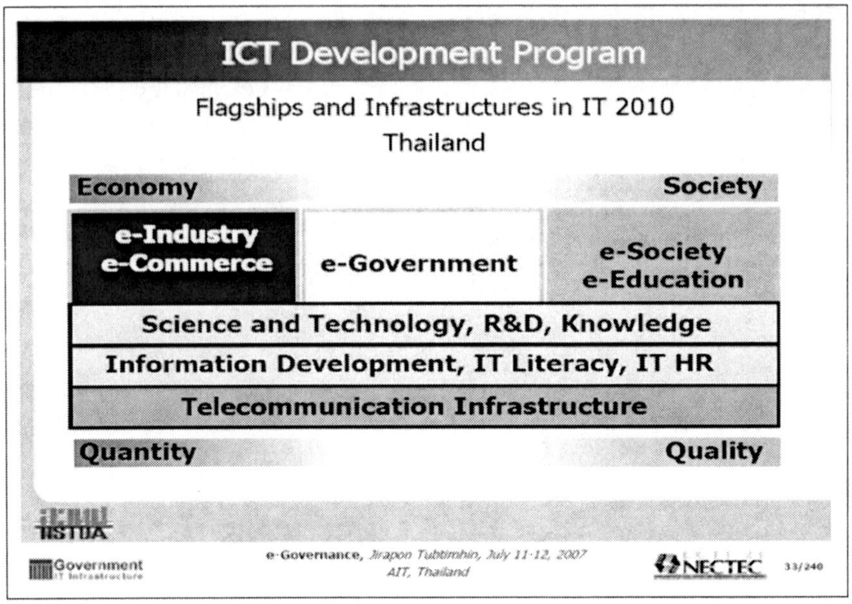

identified five main flagships: e-Government, e-Education, e-Commerce, e-Society and e-Industry as the country's e-development initiatives.

Interpretation of the IT2010 has been depicted through the country's first ever ICT Master Plan (2002-2006 and extended until 2008) with key objectives: to apply ICT to increase competitiveness, to develop a knowledge-based society, to apply ICT for sustainable development, and to develop business around the ICT industry. The second ICT master plan has currently been endorsed by the cabinet and ready for deployment during the years 2009-2013 (Ministry of Information and Communication Technology [MICT], 2010). The succeeding master plan's ambition is to further develop the country to a so called "Smart Thailand" where sustainable ICT implementation will be based on IT-literate-human capacity in all levels of society and on the good governance foundation in all development sectors as well as the accessible-to-all infrastructure.

THE 2ND COUNTRY ICT MASTER PLAN, DRIVING TOWARD SMART THAILAND (MICT, 2010)

"Driving toward Smart Thailand through ICT" is the vision aimed in 2013 when at the end of 2nd Thailand ICT Master Plan. "Smart Thailand" refers to a society that develops and uses ICT in a smart manner and adheres to the principles of the sufficiency economy philosophy. People at all levels of society should be smart and information literate. This leads to benefits for themselves and society as a whole. ICT should be managed with *smart governance* in order to support the development of a knowledge- and innovation-based society and economy that are sustainable and stable.

To achieve this target the 2nd ICT Master Plan has defined some key principles including firstly the Master Plan aims for the development of a knowledge-based society, which is consistent with the development objectives set forth in the National Economic and Social Development Plan, which is the key national development framework as well as the Master Plan seeks to ensure continuity within the policy framework of IT 2010 and the 1st ICT Master Plan by continuing to emphasize the development and application of ICT for e-Commerce and e-Industry, e-Education and e-Society, and e-Government for the *promotion of good governance in government administration and services*. In addition, it also places a priority on carrying forward activities in the 1st Master Plan that have not achieved their targets, in order to demonstrate rapid progress.

The 2nd Master Plan also emphasizes addressing two current weaknesses as a first priority, namely: 1) developing people who are smart and information literate and 2) managing ICT at the national level in accordance with the *principles of good governance*. In addition, it also places a priority on accelerating the development of the high-speed network with universal access and reasonable prices. This is considered key infrastructure for the development of the knowledge economy and society that is dependent on ICT as a driver, and is an area in which Thailand still lags behind many other countries.

Among ICT strategies defined under the 2nd Master Plan, strategy number 4 provides public organization to pursue its knowingly 2nd phase e-Government development following the 1st phase during the 1st ICT Master Plan. In this 2nd phase public agency is encouraged to use ICT as tools in order to enhance governance in its front office and back office operations. Therefore, each agency has to elaborate its potential areas of development which are lining up along both vertical and horizontal dimensions both of which actions and related activities can be enhanced by applying citizen-centric approach. Comparisons of Thailand ICT strategies under the 1st and 2nd ICT Master Plan are as details in Table 1.

CURRENT STATUS OF THAILAND E-GOVERNMENT

E-Government development of the country during the early ICT framework and plan some

Table 1. Comparisons of Thailand ICT strategies under ICT Master Plan I & II

ICT Master Plan I (2002-2008)	ICT Master Plan II (2009-2013)
Strategy 1: Development of the ICT industry into a regional leader	**Strategy 1:** Develop ICT professionals and general human resources who are information literate
Strategy 2: Utilization of ICT to enhance the quality of life and society	**Strategy 2:** Improvement of National ICT governance
Strategy 3: Reform and enhancement of the capability on ICT research and development	**Strategy 3:** Develop ICT infrastructure
Strategy 4: Reinforcement of social capacity for future competition	**Strategy 4:** e-Governance
Strategy 5: Development of entrepreneurs capacity for the expansion of international markets	**Strategy 5:** Enhance competitiveness of the ICT industry to add economic values and increase earnings
Strategy 6: Utilization of ICT in Small and Medium Enterprises (SMEs)	**Strategy 6:** Use ICT to build sustainable competitiveness for Thai industries
Strategy 7: Utilization of ICT in government administration and services	

Source: Ministry of Information and Communication Technology. (2010, April 28). Thailand ICT masterplan 2. Retrieved September 15, 2010, from http://www.mict.go.th/ewt_news.php?nid=74

Posted by: Office of Permanent Secretary, Ministry of ICT, Thailand

successful pilot projects (National Electronics and Computer Technology Center [NECTEC], 2001) under the country's e-Government initiatives included e-Revenue (Revenue Department), e-Investment (Board of Investment), e-Statistics (National Statistics Office), e-Economics (NESDB), e-Commercial Registration (Department of Business Development) and e-Parliament as for good examples were accomplished at a certain extent. At the same time some urgent projects were specified under the first ICT master plan targeting for implementation of some key infrastructure components essentially for e-Services integration, including GDX/GNX (Government Data/Network Exchange), Web Portal, One Stop Services, Government Intranet, and Government Certification Authentication systems. Eventually these prioritized projects had not been paid much attention enough to succeed as planned. Noticeably, the then government had made much more decisions on the quick-win-self-centered projects such as government official e-mail directory, rather than the integration-oriented infrastructure and citizen-centered ones.

Under the framework of IT2010 and succeeded by the first ICT Master Plan during 2002-2008, e-Government has been promoted and developed as a driving and balancing development mechanism for the other two wings of "e" sectors, i.e. the economy sectors: e-Commerce and e-Industry; and the social sector which comprised e-Education and e-Society. The second version of the country ICT Master Plan has succeeded to cover an implementation period of 2009-2013. The current master plan aims to take over those pending projects under the 5 "e" flagships with more focus strategies. Firstly, the new plan will emphasize on human capacity buildings for ICT development across the board, including ICT personnel in all level of government sector, ICT workforce for targeted ICT industries such as animation software per'se and ICT literacy for all the country's societies and communities.

The second emphasis is to put more attention on the so called "Governance" factor. There have been lessons learnt during the first plan implementation that, lacking of incorporating good governance elements objectively led to under utilization and less citizen engagement which needed citizen centricity as an essential part. Hence e-Governance has been underlined as key strategy for e-Government project implementation in all development sectors. ICT governance is also been defined to incorporate into public sector e-Government implementation project both in terms of front and back-end services. ICT infrastructure is definitely addressed as usual as the previous plan as one of the main strategies in the second country ICT master plan to assure that all sectors of society will not be left out of the information society.

Thailand through ICT related authorities at this end has realized that presently the country is in the new phase of ICT and e-Government development in paving way for fulfilling of substantial aims on economic and social development. Current and future development based on its e-Governance framework must incorporate citizens as center of development to altogether step forward to leapfrog its maturity level of e-Government services development and to keep abreast with the international development arena.

AIMING FOR A STEP FORWARD

E-Government Ranking and Benchmarking

The latest UN survey in this year of 2010 (the United Nations [UN], 2010) revealed that Thailand was ranked 76 out of 191 countries in the overall score table, after Singapore, Malaysia and Brunei Darussalam among ASEAN region comparison. The benchmarking target has been defined in the second ICT master plan which aims to leverage the country ICT ranking to a certain level at the

Figure 2. International ICT / e-Government Rankings. Source: National Electronics and Computer Technology Center (NECTEC). (2010). Retrieved September 15, 2010, from http://www.nectec.or.th

International ICT/e-Government Rankings

Index/ Country	World Competitiveness Scoreboard 2009 (2008) 57 (55)	Networked Readiness Rankings 2008-2009 (2007-2008) 134 (127)	Digital Opportunity Index ปี 2005-2006 (181)	e-Readiness Ranking 2009 (2008) (70) Economist Intelligence Unit	E-Government Readiness ปี 2010 (2009) (192)	IT Industry Benchmarking 2008 (2007) (66 (64) ประเทศ)	Waseda University International e-Government Rankings 2010 (52,51) (40, 34)
Thailand	**26 (27)**	**47 (40)**	**82**	**49 (47)**	**76 (64)**	**42 (41)**	**25 (21,20)**
Japan	17 (22)	17 (19)	2	22 (18)	17 (11)	12 (2)	6 (5,5)
Korea	27 (31)	11 (9)	1	19 (15)	1 (6)	8 (3)	7 (6,4)
Taiwan	23 (13)	13 (17)	7	16 (19)	NA	2 (6)	10 (8,10)
India	30 (29)	54 (50)	124	58 (54)	119 (113)	48 (46)	28 (24,29)
Singapore	3 (2)	4 (5)	5	7 (6)	11 (23)	9 (11)	1 (1,2)
Malaysia	18 (19)	28 (26)	57	38 (34)	32 (34)	36 (36)	24 (22,18)
Viet Nam	N.A.	70 (73)	126	64 (65)	90 (91)	61 (61)	34 (31,31)
Denmark	5 (6)	1 (1)	3	1 (5)	7 (2)	5 (8)	13 (N.A.)
Norway	11 (11)	8 (10)	12	4 (11)	6 (3)	14 (14)	18 (12,13)
Sweden	6 (9)	2 (2)	9	2 (3)	12 (1)	4 (7)	9 (3,9)
Finland	9 (15)	6 (6)	11	10 (13)	19 (15)	13 (13)	12 (9,8)
UK	21 (21)	15 (12)	10	13 (8)	4 (10)	3 (4)	2 (4,12)
Australia	7 (7)	14 (14)	22	6 (4)	8 (8)	7 (5)	5 (13,7)
South Africa	48 (53)	52 (51)	86	41 (39)	97 (61)	37 (37)	27 (25,27)
Mexico	46 (50)	67 (58)	66	40 (40)	56 (37)	46 (46)	29 (20,28)
USA	1 (1)	3 (4)	20	5 (1)	2 (4)	1 (1)	2 (2,1)

end of the plan, below Figure 2 shows table of Thailand rankings within various key International ICT / e-Government Rankings compared to some selected countries.

Rankings in International ICT / e-Government arena depicted that Thailand in most cases were placed in the 2nd and 3rd quartiles of the reference tables. It's ambition to move upward into the 1st quartile especially in the table of NRR or Networked Readiness Ranking is not too far to go as long as it keeps its stable paces of development under the good framework of e-Governance under citizen centric direction. Parameters used by all ranking institutions touch base on the UNESCAP governance components in different angles of indices.

The latest 2010 United Nations E-Government rankings take into account various roles for e-government in addressing the ongoing world financial and economic crisis. UN further addressed in the report that the public trust that is gained through transparency can be further enhanced through the free sharing of government data based on for instance open standards. The ability of e-government to handle speed and complexity can also underpin regulatory reform. While technology is no substitute for good policy, it may give citizens the power to question the actions of regulators and bring systemic issues to the fore. Similarly, e-government can add agility to public service delivery to help governments respond to an expanded set of demands even as revenues fall short.

In general, Thailand in its race to climb up the target ranking table, the country have to prove that the government have made great stride in development of online services, especially under citizen centricity conditions. At the same time it has to make costs associated with telecommunication infrastructure competitive enough to cater all segments of citizens. Human capital must be consistently developed as planned in the country's 2nd ICT Master plan which divide into 2 target groups i.e. ICT professionals and ICT users including the general public. However, effective strategies and legal frameworks can compensate significantly, in terms of infrastructure and human capital costs even in least developed countries. In addition, the country has to be appropriately able to harness the potential of expanded broadband access in developed regions and mobile cellular networks in developing areas. The 2010 United Nations E-Government rankings are based on five indices including E–Government Development Index, Online Service Index and its Components, Telecommunication Infrastructure Index and its Components, E–Participation Index and Human Capital Index.

According to Waseda University 2010 World e-Government Rankings (T.Obi Research office, 2010), trends observed this year were the special attention governments have given to Green ICT / Environmental ICT issues. Other trends observed were the uses of Government 2.0 mash-ups using Web 2.0 technology. In particular, there was an increase in real time SNS or Social Network Software applications such as Twitter in government sites. This has led to another trend which is the increase in the quality and depth of e-participation between users and governments. Stronger linkages between local and central government were also implemented. Cloud computing was another topic of great interest to many governments with a view towards reducing operating costs as well as their carbon footprint. Thailand as developing country can take the Waseda observations into their cautious consideration to gain some advantages that ICT is poised to the local conditions to date. Applying social networking and media could help leverage community centric development with more or less reasons in building up a clustered interest group to voice out loud through the public channel where they belong. This phenomenon would gain more open society and promote democracy and at the same time would help alleviate the current incidents of organizing physical political rallies claimed violence as wide-spreading all over the country. Trends over environmental issues in relation to ICT are obviously important that the country must be considerate upon required local condition benchmarked with affordable international standards and practices.

Current Status of e-Government Maturity Level

E-Government development needs interactions between public organization and its stakeholders including citizen (G2C), Business (G2B), Government (G2G) and Employee (G2E) on public services rendering to them. Implementing E-government is a continuing process, and most often the development is conceptualized in stages. The widely known maturity model suggested by Layne and Lee(Layne & Lee, 2001) who sees E-government as an evolutionary phenomenon, from which E-government initiatives should be derived and implemented (Almarabeh & AbuAli, 2010). They assume four stages of a growth model for E-government: (1) Cataloguing, (2) Transaction, (3) Vertical integration, and (4) Horizontal integration. Presently, the maturity model evolved into a more IT enable approach which allows two way communication and citizen centricity than in the beginning IT adopter one. The latest generic model being used widely and similar to the one used in the UN e-Government rankings is as shown in the Figure 3.

In 2008 Thailand by Ministry of ICT conducted a survey study as part of the MICT's project, "Survey of Present Status of e-Government Development" ("Survey Report of e-Government Survey Project, 2008", http://www.mict.go.th) reflected that the country will need to

Figure 3. e-Government Maturity. Source: National Electronics and Computer Technology Center (NECTEC). (2010). Retrieved September 15, 2010, from http://www.nectec.or.th

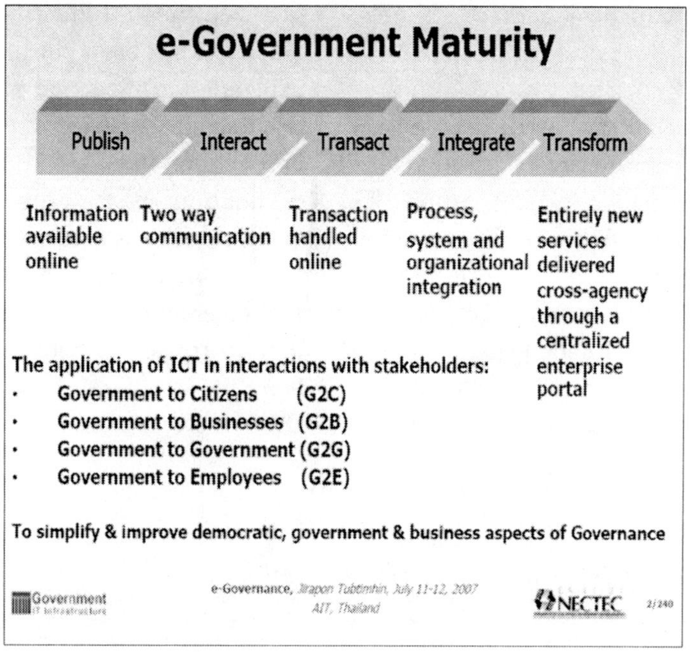

leapfrog its ICT and e-Government development if the country is to raise its benchmarking to a higher position in the international ranking arena. Presently, according to the survey, the country's development maturity in terms of e-Government services is still not that far from the last survey conducted in 2004 when it was hosted by MICT and NECTEC ("Public Sector Website Survey Project, 2004", http://www.mict.go.th & www.nectec.or.th). The overall e-Services development at present lacks attention of integration among related government agencies, where maturity model used in the survey placed the "Integration" level among the 5 stages in order of advancement, Information, Interaction, Interchange Transaction, Integration and Intelligence. The 5 maturity stages of e-Government services development in concept together with depiction of results from the survey (Sunalai & Tubtimhin, 2009) are as follows:

5 Maturity stages used in the "Survey of Present Status of e-Government Development" hosted by Ministry of ICT comprises of:

- **Information:** To reflect during the early stage of e-Government development when information is major item to be published on the web (see Figure 4).
- **Interaction:** Interactive mode is introduced when in later stage needs to have such as search engine to facilitate information inquiries and web board and etc (see Figure 5).
- **Interchange Transaction:** This stage counts when a complete transaction service can be rendered to customer by using internal integrated data of organization (see Figure 6).
- **Integration:** This stage renders cross-boarder integration service to client (see Figure 7).

- **Intelligence:** To render personalized service that uses CRM technique to help recognize the customers' behavior (see Figure 8).

The latest survey in 2008 showed that most public agencies have been aware of priority of e-Government services in their ICT development agenda. In overall picture found in the survey, majority has achieved an advanced Information maturity, where the "Interaction" stage comes second. Among many ministries such as Ministries of Finance, Industry, Commerce, Interior, Agriculture, Science and Technology, Communications have deployed e-Services application in the level of "Interchange Transaction". This is a good sign of a step forward in terms of integration though the effort has been put limitedly within own organization at the same time its own experience from inside will pave way for linking cross-border from outside.

Leading ICT deployed agencies such as taxation agencies, agencies issuing ID card and license including driving license have already implemented cross-border integrated applications in rendering e-Services for citizens. On the other hand, most public agencies are still relying on their "Silo" database system which they believe an ob-

Figure 4. Chart 1: Information. Source: Survey Report of e-Government Survey Project, 2008. (n.d.). Retrieved September 15, 2010, from http://www.mict.go.th

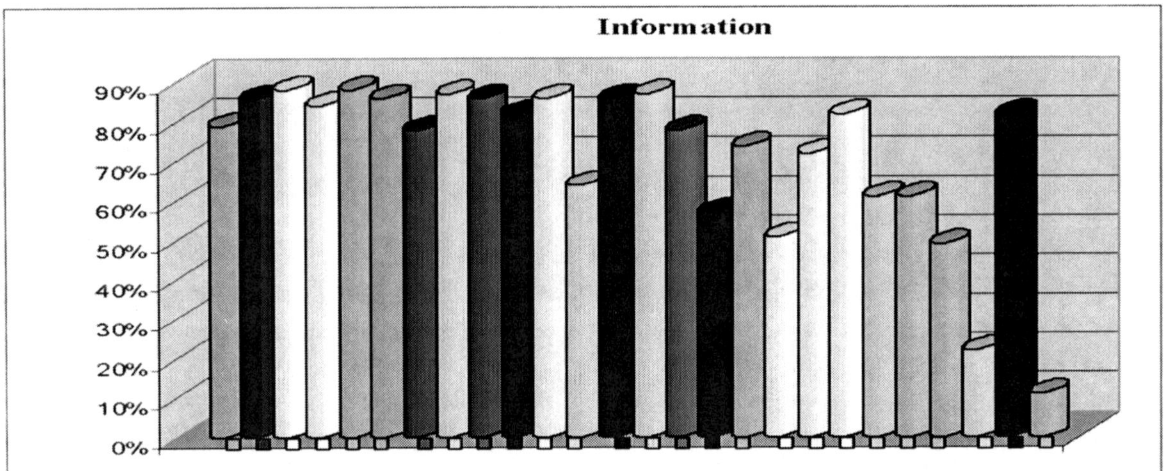

Figure 5. Chart 2: Interaction. Source: Survey Report of e-Government Survey Project, 2008. (n.d.). Retrieved September 15, 2010, from http://www.mict.go.th

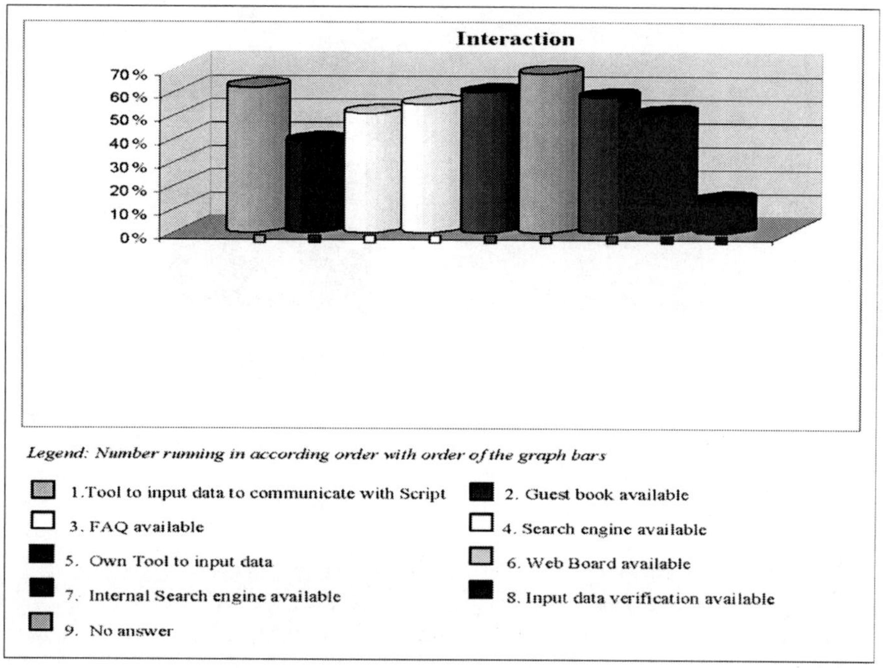

Figure 6. Chart 3: Interchange Transaction. Source: Survey Report of e-Government Survey Project, 2008. (n.d.). Retrieved September 15, 2010, from http://www.mict.go.th

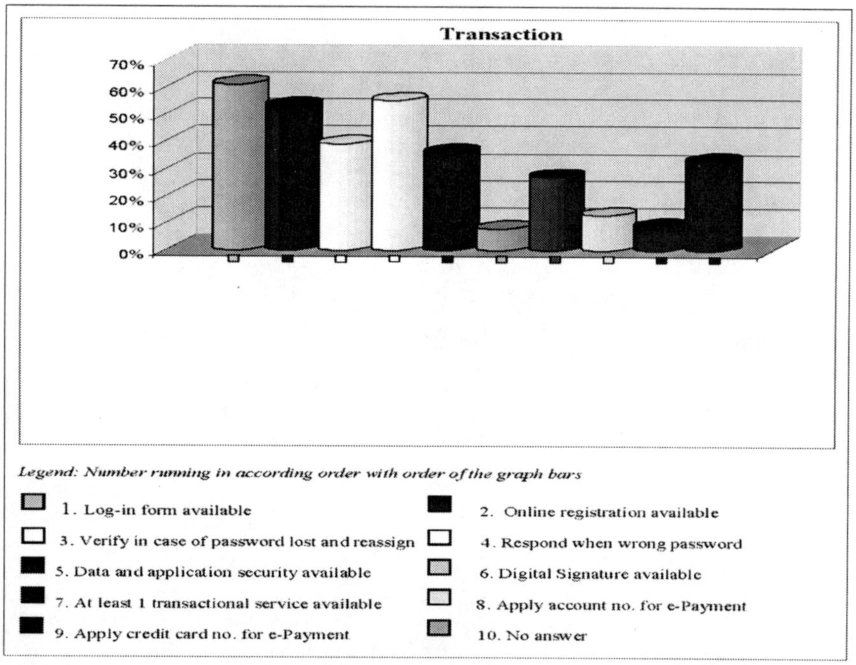

Figure 7. Chart 4: Integration. Source: Survey Report of e-Government Survey Project, 2008. (n.d.). Retrieved September 15, 2010, from http://www.mict.go.th

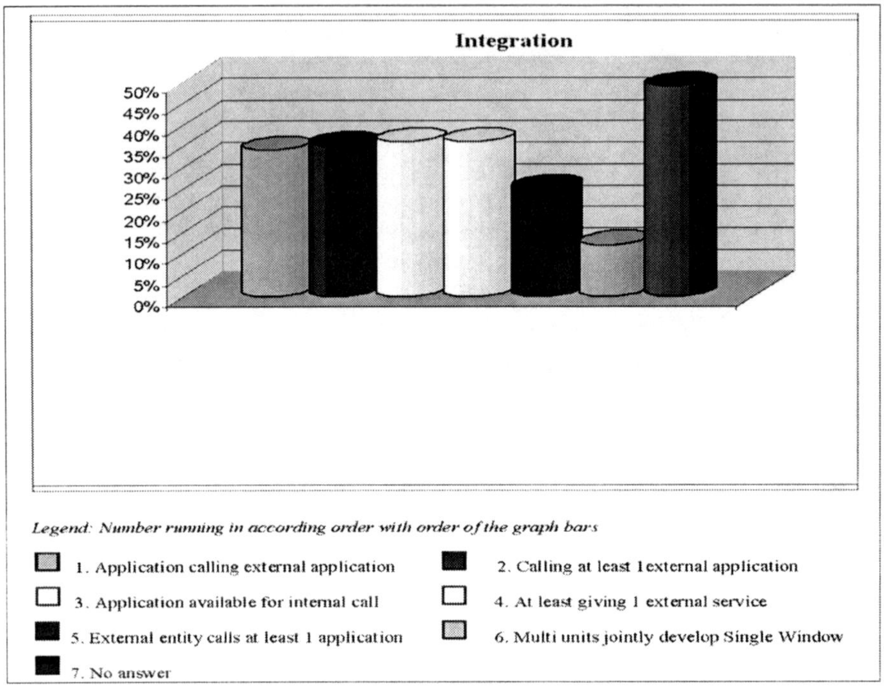

Figure 8. Chart 5: Intelligence. Source: Survey Report of e-Government Survey Project, 2008. (n.d.). Retrieved September 15, 2010, from http://www.mict.go.th

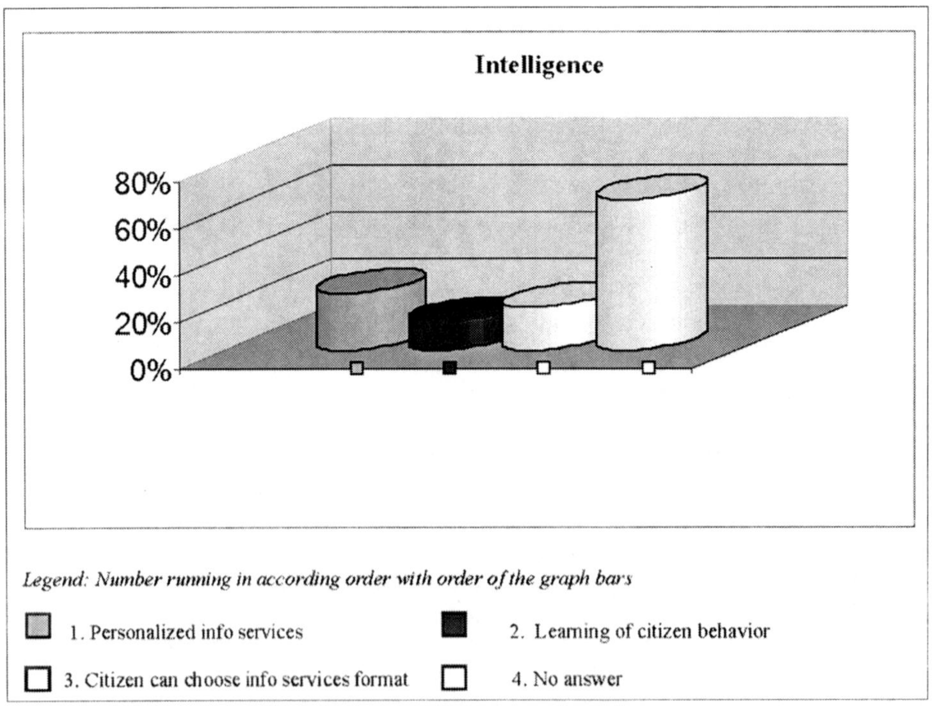

stacle for data integration. Likewise, present ICT development systems of government agencies are based on multi standards and platforms which need right solutions toward data, network, process and security integration. Under these circumstances, government agencies create duplication of budget and resources on ICT development. Human capacity and capability especially in the area of network administration as well as other technical works are still weak points of the government sector. The country has to tackle all of these obstacles in order to leverage the maturity level of ICT and e-Government development.

E-Government Roadmap toward Transformed Government

An ultimate goal of the study under the MICT's project, "Survey of Present Status of e-Government Development" ("Survey Report of e-Government Survey Project, 2008", http://www.mict.go.th) in 2008 indicated that in order for Thailand to achieve its ambitious goal of ICT and e-Government leverage into a higher maturity level as well as higher places in international ranking in the foreseeable time frame, and moving forward into a transformed government status, the country has to leapfrog its own development into a right direction and track. Therefore e-Government development roadmap of the country was redefined and set forth to move forward from e-Government to connected Government, m-Government and u-Government towards the so-called "Transformed Government" during the period of 2010-2014 e-Government Action Plan for Leapfrog Development.

The so-called Ministry of ICT implementation project GIN or Government Information Network has fulfilled for a certain extent to connect all government agencies with shared ICT infrastructure within the government domain as the good kick-off for being connected government defined by the United Nations. The rest efforts lie upon the content and transaction of public services to be enabled upon the GIN.

In the context of m-Government, the country planned to put very much attention to the content side of development on top of its effort of building up such an environment of an m-Government to leap-frog its maturity of ICT and e-Government development.

As for the u-Government, related parties are to take much more serious attention on the ubiquitous conditions which allows people in anywhere to access to government e-Services by using any devices or access channels under proper bandwidth of communications.

Under the above mentioned implementation scheme, the country will be moving forward from e-Government to connected government which means the country will have every public domain connected and integrated, hence accomplishing the "Integration" maturity level. The development target will gradually be able to move further into an m-Government and then u-Government before finally transform into a transformed government that will improve drastically in its services delivery to citizen which will lead the country to sustainable information society.

HIGHLIGHTS OF INITIATIVES AND PROJECTS

Resulted from the public sector reform in 2002 when Thailand's Ministry of ICT has been founded, through. the first and second national ICT Master Plan during 2002-2009, various key e-Government projects and initiatives have been implemented and deployed across all over ministries and related agencies. These high priority projects/initiatives have been considered to be a new face lift of the country ICT and e-Government development and still in the development pipelines ready to be leveraged to a higher scale of e-Governance extent plus citizen centered approach if well defined according to the second ICT Master Plan' s e-Governance strategy. The projects / initiatives (MICT 2009) in line with UNESCAP governance factors are as followings:

E-Citizen Smart Cards Project

The project is to issue smart ID cards for 63 million people, 25 million smart cards have been delivered since 2005 and the rest has been planned for the following years. The smart ID cards of Thai citizens when fully applied in e-Services to citizen will help facilitate governance in public services in terms of efficiency, effectiveness and accountability at least to count.

Related Smart Card Applications/Projects

The Applications and Projects are in the pipelines for development including Security System: PKI and Root CA, Identification Card for Access Control and access to e-Government services.

GFMIS (Government Financial Management Information System)

The project renders integrated financial management system including current account status of the country. The system has been gradually developed to the extent that can provide the government with current and historical financial data and information of the country and ready for decision making as well as to manage current account over fiscal earning and spending.

Ministerial and Departmental Operation Centers (MOC, DOC, POC)

The operation center at the level of Ministry (MOC), Department (DOC) and Provincial (POC) aimed to help executives to efficiently and effectively access to the right information in the right time for their decision makings. Data and information integration is the key success of the OC.

E-Auction

This system allows public agency to gain transparency in price bidding as part of its procuring or tendering process. The system has been used widely used across the board public agencies throughout the country including local administration. There is still requirement among users to enhance the system within the context of ICT governance to make the system transparent and accountable enough to fit the local conditions of all stakeholders.

E-Logistics (Single Window Portal for Importer-Exporter Facilitation)

The electronic system aims to integrate the whole value chain regarding logistics systems of the country in order to facilitate import and export procedures resulting in costs saving, higher efficiency, accountability, competitiveness and boosting economy as a whole.

E-Port, E-Gate, E-Toll

These initiatives are import parts of the e-Logistics project which aims at efficiency and effectiveness of the sea-port services. The projects of e-Port, e-Gate, e-Toll have been implemented in the pilot site of Laem Chabang Seaport which is the biggest platform for imports and exports via the ocean of the country.

E-Healthcare

The healthcare service developments especially the front & back office systems for hospitals throughout the country have been aware across the board. More and more champion in terms of service innovation are always be found in this sector made it good cases and practices to the others these days in terms of community/citizen driven implementation where engagement and participation are important factors.

E-Security

The e-Security initiative especially in the context of network security service has been more and more important toward building trust and accountability on e-Government services.

E-Services

E-Services of public agencies have been continuingly promoted by related authorities. Ministry of ICT developed the Government Information Network for being main channel to render e-Service of all agencies both among central and regional public sites. At the same time most agencies now realizes the use and application of Web Services as well as SOA to enhance their services effectively.

Thailand E-Government Interoperability Framework (Th-eGIF)

The TH-eGIF project is to facilitate data sharing and integration among public agencies. An e-Document Flow project has been piloted among interest group of public agencies for proof of concept coordinated by Ministry of ICT. This project is hopeful among public organizations to bridge different ICT platforms toward connected government in terms of data integration and sharing.

CCTV and Monitoring System

Physical security is an important agenda of the country while integration of the use of CCTV and Monitoring System among public agencies are gradually aware to gain efficiency and effectiveness of the systems usage. Central management to integrate in terms of content and system management are essential in the long run to build up efficiency, effectiveness and accountability of the system.

Government Information Network (GIN)

GIN project aims for being main government network backbone to render e-Service to citizens of all agencies throughout the country. Currently until the end of fiscal year of 2009 the project has completed connection down to the level of local administration to include all provinces of the country made it ready to be government channel to render services to citizens all over the nation.

Thai Tele-Centers

The project of Thai Tele-Center aims to promote the less opportunity communities within the country to have their own community ICT asset accessible to high speed internet. Objectives of community usages include the use of ICT and internet for their own livelihood such as for learning, chatting, and marketing of community products as for good examples. The center is planned to leverage to e-Community level where more ICT tools and resources will be provided and promoted.

E-Province

To develop totally 13 common systems to support provincial level authorities, provincial offices and provincial governors for 5 provinces in the first phase including Khonkaen, Mahasarakam, Roi-et, Karasin and Udornthani as pilot sites. The developed systems can fulfill and support the specified member domains in the target provinces in their daily operation in general and at the same time to assist and facilitate related users in their works including in rendering data and/or report for their governors in such a new way of "faster service" and "just-in-time". This project covers a full cycle of ICT development including conducting surveys, requirement analysis on both operational and management levels in the targeted provincial units as inputs for developing the targeted application systems to support their operations and to facilitate data/information exchange among the units within own province and across member provinces as well.

E-Municipality

E-Municipality has been promoted among major cities and towns in Thailand. Green Bangkok WiFi is free internet for Bangkok population in downtown areas. Cities if Chiangmai, Pattaya, Udon Thani, Songkla are among role models for e-Municipality development including e-Services based on single ID number such as ID card renewal, driving license issuance, birth, death and land registrations are among popular services to citizens.

SUMMARY OF THAILAND E-GOVERNMENT DEVELOPMENT STATUS AND AIMS: CASE STUDIES

A Case Study of Nakhonchaisi Hospital in Thailand: A Shift from "Function Centric" to "Patient Centric" (Tubtimhin, 2010)

Shifting to a "Citizen Centric" Healthcare Service and Key Benefits

A success case of community hospital called Nakhonchaisi has been recognized widely in Thailand when the hospital has succeeded its important core value of its healthcare service through the *"Humanized Care"* system derived from its Case Management initiative. This key method bears to maintain a high standard level of healthcare resulted from a shifting from *"Disease Fixing Centric"* to the *"Patient Caring Centric"* implied *"Citizen Centric"* approach. The "Humanized care" system can respond directly to a personalized need of each patient. Case management helps hypertensive patients to reach the standard goal from 70% to 89% while at the same time

Table 2.

UN e-Government Maturity Model				
Emerging	Enhanced	Interactive	Transactional	Connected/ Transformed
Maturity Model used by Ministry of ICT				
Information	Interaction	Interchange Transaction	Integration	Intelligence

also helps reduce the hypertensive crisis from 14.06% to 2.86% and the loss of cases being followed up is reduced from 3% to 1%. Some other interesting records to reveal herewith are number of DM patients who are sugar level controllable increases from 39% to 47% and the number tends to be continuingly increasing. This phenomenon implies decreasing of losses of lives and of disabilities such cases as malfunction of nephropathy decreases from 20.16% to 15.67%, malfunction of retinopathy decreases from 24.60% to 17.03% and deterioration of neuropathy decreases from 30.21% to 22.04%, resulted in the aged people of the community with chronic diseases are able to maintain their lives as peacefully as the others and better quality of lives is expectable as well.

Key Implementation Steps

Nakhonchaisi Hospital started its race for hospital quality development since 2002 and was certified in 2008 by Institute of Hospital Quality Development and Certification. To increase efficiency and quality for such specific elderly group under DM and Hypertension conditions, the management team planned for development of service rendering system as well as knowledge and skill of related segment of human resources. Commencing by development of their mindset toward organization by building up common value of "to love organization, starting by loving your teammate" in order to create "Cross-Functional Teamwork", fine tuning related services for quality, fast action, desirable adoption and admiration of service delivery of the customers.

Table 3.

e-Government Development Status and Future Aims		
Function (Supply) Based Thailand has been starting its footprint of e-Government since the first policy framework IT 2000 which was later leveraged to IT 2010 that giving birth of ICT Master Plan as during 2002-2008 to include Public Information Infrastructure while result of this very first agenda of e-Government development reflected from e-Service has been rather limited on autonomous agency than cross agency service. First survey in 2004 on maturity of e-Service via website confirmed this limited integration phenomenon. Figures showed that 87% of Thai public agencies fell into Information Presence or Emerging, 77% were in the level of Interaction, 72% were at the Transaction Service and a niche of 7% catered Intelligence level of e-Services. Highlighted projects /initiatives include:	**Citizen Centric (Demand) Based** E-Service integration has gradually come into picture with various citizen centric projects like Web Portal across Thai ministries, to name a few: Min of Science and Technology, Min. of Industry, Min of Commerce, Min of Interior. However, such portal at national level has not yet been aware to take into serious account. Survey on e-Service Maturity in 2008 revealed some improvement comparing to the previous survey conducted in 2004 especially in such essential element to facilitate online e-Services i.e. e-payment while the desire level of integration has been achieved, amounted to 13% out of about 250 public agencies at department level and at Intelligence level of 12%.	**Citizen/Social Driven** Roadmap defined by Ministry of ICT for e-Government development during 2010-2014 aims at: Phase 1: By 2010 e-Government service cross border agency is to be enhanced. Phase 2: By 2011 m-Government by mobile phone is to be promoted. Phase 3: By 2012 m-Government by using other mobile devices is to be promoted. Phase 4: By 2013 u-Government, e-Service is render via any devices and anywhere. Phase 5: By 2014 Transformed Government is aimed to render fully online service where demand avails.

With an intention in developing the hospital services for responding to needs and expectations of its community members consistently, a wide range of innovative initiatives and activities regarding to the hospital administration have been developed as followings:

E-Services and ICT Application initiatives: By knowledge management system together with ICT, the hospital introduced an automation system called "e-Medical Record". This electronic channel service has turned into a new era of e-Document. Under this system, a function of the traditional medical record was scrapped, resulted in reducing from 7 to 3 officers for handling the new e-Record. At the same time, patient's record information retrieval becomes faster while registration via internet is also possible these days by applying the available smart ID Card. Moreover this can help reduce service processing steps as well as waiting time, transferring of patient and

Table 4.

Projects/Initiatives	Projects/Initiatives	Projects/Initiatives
• Every Public Agency website • MOC/DOC • e-Revenue (e-Tax Filing) • e-Registration (for Company) • e-Parliament • e-Auction • Smart Cards • e-Transaction Law, Computer Crime Law • GFMIS • e-Port, e-Gate, e-Toll • e-Information Services • CCTV and Monitoring System • Government Information Network • Counter Service/ Service Links • Back Office Systems • Chief Information Officer	• PKI/CA • e-Logistics (Single Window) • e-Healthcare for Hospitals • e-Security Services • e-Information Services • Th-eGIF • Counter Service/ Service Links • Thai Tele-centers • e-Municipality • e-Province	• Collective Intelligence • Service Innovation • Common Infra, Services, Applications • Sourcing: Virtualization, Cloud Computing • Chief "Innovation" Officer

paper consumption. Whereby, the application of One Stop Services are also scaled up to cover all function of OPD including the dental, disease examination, emergency, family and community medication so that the customers will be happy with one stop service benefits.

Multi-functional Person: Under the new paradigm shift, the hospital personnel has been trained to be single person multi tasking approach which also creating a new organizational culture of handling duty when any individual can do a multiple job in relation to rendering service to customers. This phenomenon reflects cross functional services as well as coordination of works both inside and outside one's domain and in all means creating happily constructive environment within the hospital.

Workload Management: As for efficiency and effectiveness, the hospital has implemented a technique of distribution of workloads management. The method allows balance of ratio between patient and officer on duty in every mean time. On the other hand, to avoid congestion situation in the morning times, afternoon services especially for the elderly under chronic conditions with the appointment services scheme of "coming on time getting it on time" along with special track arrangement allows the hospital to guarantee service delivery time for this critical case within 25 minutes.

Case Management: The initiative of case management is the hospital's proud service innovation. It is a remarkable milestone of the hospital to shift from *"Function Centric"* to *"Patient Centric"* approach of medication for the elderly under chronic conditions. The new way opens a new fold of hospital caring system terming as "Humanized Care" system. Under the system a nurse-case manager is assigned to a patient to coordinates with a multi-disciplined medication team including such as a doctor, a pharmacist and a nutrition specialist to plan for taking good care of each chronic patient in tuning, directing and monitoring health condition of the patient. Nowadays, the hospital with this initiative of the "Case Management" the doctors and staff today can manage efficiently and effectively in the cases of chronic diseases over the elderly. Case management system can respond directly to a personalized need of each chronic patient which helps maintain the high standard level of medical care over hypertensive patients to reach the standard goal and reduce the hypertensive crisis. The loss of cases being followed up is also reduced while DM patients are sugar level controllable, implied decreasing of losses of lives and of disabilities such as malfunction of nephropathy, malfunction of retinopathy and deterioration of neuropathy. We are delighted to reveal that these days the elderly members of our community under chronic disease conditions are able to live their lives as comfortably as the other members and within the same limit and expectation of quality standard.

Previous Situation

Nakhonchaisi Hospital is a concisely 30-bed community hospital located in the suburban area of Nakhonpathom Province, Thailand. Majority of Nakhonchaisi's population live up their lives in agriculture, and stay at a certain distance away from the only hospital of this district. Quite a number of them commute to see a doctor there by boat. Even there exists a bus service but with multi connecting stations cause longer journey than expected. The hospital provides primary medical services to 66,384 community members. Among them, according to a certain survey on health condition evaluation, 1,200 people of age over 35 have been found under Diabetes Mellitus (DM), 800 with high blood pressure (Hypertension) and some 23.26 percent of them or 15,440 members are of high risk under DM and Hypertension conditions.

90% of the above mentioned patients are old ages that need their relatives to get along and have to leave for the hospital at around 4:00-5:00 a.m. before dawning in order to arrive early enough to be able to secure for the limited quota of the day for the check-ups. They are left alone waiting in the long queue and at the same time the rendering service has unavoidably many steps, each taking a long time, for example, 4-6 hours for some severe cases to conclude the service process. The incidences cause very much effect to the patients in waiting because their conditions such as cases of foot infection and tends to be cut, cases of renal failure and cases of Hypertension with paralyzed condition that needs permanent assistance, and all cases normally need promptly intensive care but they have to be sitting in destiny of pains and tears while waiting in long queue for the services.

Nakhonchaisi Hospital receives more than 136,000 visits annually or about 500 visits per day for all kinds of medical services. More than 80% of the patients regularly come to the hospital in the morning, but there are only 3 doctors who oversee 300 outpatients during the morning period. Since the doctor per patient ratio is not well balanced, it is not only resulting in a long waiting time for the patients but also a shorter service time which is usually within the limit of 5 -10 minutes, for a physician to examine such a chronic disease patient. This leads to a low quality care and is poised to a higher level of complication of these seriously chronic cases. To date, few patients are treated within standardized level of care and attention. Statistics in 2006 reveals that 67% of the patients with DM and 38% with Hypertension are uncontrollable caused by penetration of other chronic deceases which are in high risks of their lives, disabilities, physical degeneration, and dis-functionality of important body organs that affect directly to their quality of life as well as mentality of their relatives, family and community as a whole.

Objectives of the hospital reform program include:

- Reduction of service processing and delivery time especially on wasting time for unnecessary steps.
- Leveraging to a better quality of treating the patients under chronic disease.
- Reduction of disability and death rates caused by condition complications and threatening conditions of chronic diseases especially DM and Hypertension.
- Key strategies used to achieve above objectives are as follows.
- A paradigm shift of all level of personnel through the process of organization development including: to promote participation throughout the whole hospital staff, to change organizational culture and to implant mindset of good services.
- Applying knowledge management and IT aiming for e-Service Delivery in the process of re-designing of new services.
- Applying an approach of Humanized care within the hands of nurse-case managers for the target aged group under DM and Hypertension cases and building up a prototype model for a proof of concept.

A Case Study of Thai Tele-Center: A Community Tele-Center to Focus on Community Needs and Participation

Ministry of Information and Communication Technology or MICT, Thailand set up a constructive policy to enhance opportunities for members of communities over the whole country to access knowledge and to use ICT as tools in their own ways of living. The policy particularly aims to narrow the digital gap and enable local leaders, and the community members from all age groups to apply knowledge and ICT in their Community Tele-center, which is established by the ministry, to their day-to-day life style in order to improve the quality of life and promote the community development.

Concepts of Community Tele-Center

Community Tele-center has become a brand new learning center that attracts considerable attention from people throughout the world communities as a result of advances in ICT that has contracted this contemporary world into a single society known as "a global village." To make use of ICT as another tool for development is, thus, so significant that any communities can no longer avoid.

Characteristics of Community Tele-Center

Characteristics of community Tele-center to build up community strength are as follows:

- To operate in accordance with the directions of the community development and to promote greater unity of community members and bring benefits to them clearly and fairly according to the level of participation.
- To be able to provide knowledge, appropriate technology, and guidance on how to manage equipments, materials and labor in the community.
- To aim at promoting the ability of the community in administration and involving the community members in administration.
- To take information or activities concerning community environment and ecosystem into consideration in order to keep pace with current trends toward environment.
- To have simple operating procedures in order for the center to be able to allocate duties and responsibilities among members all over the community.
- To offer holistic information essential for community utilization.

Participatory Management Approach

The setup community Tele-center focuses on needs and participation of community members as well as related organizations as followings:

- Both community leaders and members together with related organizations receive equal opportunities to express opinions on establishing a Tele-center.
- Members are given opportunities to propose activities they are interested in.
- Decision making on any activities will be based on majority vote. Members are encouraged to participate in group discussion and collaborate in the project plan and implementation accordingly to the concluded solution.
- Members are divided into groups responsible for appropriate duties in order to help each other planned tasks concerning operating a community Tele-center.

Success Cases: Using Community Center to Market the Community Products

The bright idea of utilizing the Tele-center to market community member products has been succeeded in two different locations. First case was in the north-eastern province of Roi-et in Pathumrat District, where a community member posted her product of souvenir doll in a community website and used the center email to transact her sales to a Japanese client in Japan that she never had any idea to know him without the opportunity given by the center. The second center which has the same experience is in the province of Satul located in the southern part of the country. In this case a local producer in Kampaeng district used the community website in the Tele-center to learn and observe market behavior of her target in order to develop and customize her own decoration items made from pearl to the needs of her target customers. These two successful cases are eligible to be good practices for the other centers to follow. On the other hand, the Tele-centers of this kind can fulfill the founding objectives of related parties including MICT and counterpart community in serving community members' livelihood and sustainable living.

Provision of Facilities

Ministry of ICT started the Thai Tele-center project in 2007, in 2007 and 2008 totally 20 and 40 Tele-centers were established respectively and concluded to the total of 200 in 2009. Each Tele-center is equipped with 5-20 desktop computers depending on the small, medium and large sizes. One server for each is provided plus installation of free broadband internet for one year. Location depends on the community's own choice and in most cases have been located in community temples, schools and where deemed appropriate. MICT sets target to install totally about more than 500 Tele-centers in the level of district level of administration. First batch of responsible personnel of each center is to join training courses provided by MICT.

CHALLENGES AND OPPORTUNITIES FOR DEVELOPING SUCCESSFUL CITIZEN-CENTRIC E-GOVERNMENT

As defined in the 2nd ICT master Plan of the country, to be Smart Thailand at the end of the plan in 2013, Thailand realizes that it has to act smarter in all aspect to create the development conditions that will help shape up the e-Government of the country to accomplish good governance driven by the use of ICT i.e. entering e-Governance era across the board public sector agencies. In all dimension of e-Governance development, citizen centricity is the key development approach that public organization, to date, be aware of. In this new paradigm of e-Government development and in order for developing successful citizen-centric e-Government, following challenges and opportunities still exist for Thailand to act smarter in the following years to come.

Smarter Organization

Central Agency

To set up an e-Government central agency to handle centralized policies, procedures, processes and systems that free from any intervention as well as to closely cooperate and collaborate with other central units including the Bureau of Budget, Office of Civil Service Commission, Office of Public Sector Development Commission and National Economics and Social Development Board for central policy and guidelines upon management of budget, workforces and other resources. Most importantly this central agency is to handle the coherent integration of government infrastructure, systems, and processes as well as channelize effective communications across government.

Next Wave of Public Organization

To cater the right demand of setting up proper organization for Next Generation of e-Government as defined by the World Bank (Sudan, 2008) which is composed of six qualifications as followings:

- Whether centralized or de centralized?: Federated
- Whether focused on technology or the business?: Business
- Whether public or private?: More public, more focus on public-private partnerships
- Whether large or small?: Small with a large network or relationships
- Whether doer or influencer?: Enabler and facilitator
- Whether hierarchical or flat?: Matrix organization

Smarter Business Processes

Processes to be Redesigned/ Change in Mindset

Organization for Next Generation of e-Government as defined by the World Bank has to emphasize on business processes of its own domain rather than paying attention to only technology. Public sector will be more active as facilitator and promoter on service innovation based on citizen needs and toward improving service quality.

Citizen and Business Portals

To enhance transaction services by connecting government agencies infrastructure, to serve the near-term e-services, that set forth ranging from National Web Portal, Single Window for Logistics System, Secured Government Intranet and Secured Payment Gateway as priorities.

Smarter Integration

Standards-Interoperability

To share and integrate resources and systems in order to utilize the advantage of common systems such as the 13-digit ID number for increasing more integrated e-Services in the rest agencies which never used this unique ID number for cross agency applications. Government agencies are entitled to use common standards framework especially THeGIF, throughout the government to shorten development time and ensure compatibility.

Common IT Infrastructure

In addition to standards and interoperability, there must be a proper framework or measures to adopt a common IT infrastructure for the government whereas Identify and reform regulatory schemes that make interaction with the government onerous are also essential.

Smarter Security and Trust

Increased Citizen Trust

In the efforts of building trust to the e-Government services, the government in collaboration with private domain to set up a root-PKI system in order to integrate PKI and e-Signature that offering services by various providers at present. Moreover, the government has to promote and develop the utilization of Smart ID cards that issued to more than 40% of the Thai citizens already. Moreover To encourage government agencies to fully implement the ICT laws which are effective already as well as to provide procedures and guidelines as well as technical assistance to the agencies where facing problems in their implementations to be confident that every rule of law has been exercised accordingly

Increased Systematic Security

The government should endorse the followings (Almarabeh & AbuAli, 2010): (1) Designate a senior official responsible for computer security. (2) Continually assess systems to make sure that security precautions are being implemented. (3) Define framework on backup information regularly and store backups in a separate location. (4) When it comes to personal information, keep information collection to a minimum and do not disclose personal information without express prior consent. (5) Provide ongoing training to employees on computer security. (6) Evaluate performance of system managers in adhering to sound security Practices.

Smarter People on ICT

ICT Literacy

To neatly categorize ICT capacity development to cover ranging from building awareness to every quarter of society, enhancing ICT literacy for people especially in the rural area, changing government mindset toward better service delivery to citizen and ICT governance for all. In addition, Strengthening and fostering of the capacity to innovate by creating a sense of ownership within the workforce community will help enhance citizen centricity approach.

CIO, Chief Information Officer as e-Governance Chief

Sooner or later, every organization has to prepare to implement good e-Governance. A compelling direction will see the roles of the Chief Information Officer or CIO become as significant as that of the Chief Executive Officer or CEO, since they have to take responsibility for the organizations' good governance. CIO according to Wikipedia is a job title for the board-level head of Information Technology or IT within an organization. The CIO typically reports to the CEO or Chief Executive Officer. The prominence of the CIO position has risen greatly as IT has become a more important part of business. In some organizations, the CIO may be a member of the executive board of the organization. CIO provides senior executives insights and in-depth knowledge of IT thus has to be in charge of the e-Governance of organization.

Smarter Management

Budget Priority

To prioritize and handle budget especially on cross-agency integration projects that need longer than a year timeframe to execute.

Effective Partnership with Private Sector or Public-Private-Partnership

To take Public-Private-Partnership or PPP into account as an effective mechanism for matching core competencies as well as investment funds between public agencies and counterpart companies towards e-Government services deployment.

Smarter Assessment

SENSE Assessment Model (Auffret, 2010)

In carrying out assessment on e-Government project, a model developed for rural and urban e-Government project assessment called SENSE is applicable among developing economies. Best practices from Andhra Pradesh, Sao Paulo, Fairfax County in the US and other successful rural and urban projects can be synthesized in a framework to help in assessing the likelihood of project success in advance of formal project approval. Abbreviated as SENSE, the framework can also provide a roadmap for ongoing governance and project assessment in design, development, implementation and governance of e-Government projects.

- Strength: Project strength as a result of high level commitment, organizational ability to complete, deployment model, price and cost, scalability, and compatibility and consistency with enterprise architecture.
- Engagement: Broad and meaningful engagement of citizens, government stakeholder groups and other relevant stakeholder groups.
- Need: Meets tangible need of the citizens and provides a significant enhancement over existing service levels.
- Sustainability: Planned and in practice business model so that the initiative is financially supported (self-sufficient or dedicated funding) over the long term.
- Evolution: Planned enhancements and how the initiative fits in with overall e-Government plan for the region.

SENSE can be applied for any e-Government projects across the board of all level of administrations because it is touching bases with related practical aspects of the projects.

Smarter Accessibility

Online Public Services for All

Governments must serve all members of society irrespective of their physical capabilities. Online public services will have to be designed with appropriate interfaces under the principle of universal design. For substantial implementation, following actions must be endorsed: (1) design applications that accommodate the disabled, such as an audio option for the blind, (2) establish as a legal requirement that the government must adopt technology to assist the disabled, (3) Set performance criteria and measure progress.

Universal Access Framework

Related government authorities must cooperate with National Telecommunication Committee in providing access to all as defined in the country constitution including following actions: (1) provide communal access through available village computer centers or kiosks, (2) combine access with training, (3) Provide incentives to the private sector to donate equipment and training, (4) Emphasize local language and content tailored to different communities, (5) use profit oriented entrepreneurs to build and sustain access points in small and lagging behind communities.

CONCLUSION

E-Government development currently has reached next phase where governance factors become essential part public organizations aim for. Citizen centricity plays important role in enhancing public services online in entering e-Governance era as the next phase of e-Government development. Accenture, through its recent survey revealed this phenomenon with conclusion that new generation of public organization needs to have a framework which implies to include publicly engaged model of governance. The model includes well defined elements essentially considered as success factors towards e-Governance implementation. The factors include (1) *outcomes* which are to focus on *Performance; Feedback; Efficiency and Effectiveness*, (2) *Balance* of Accessibility through social network/media in creating *stakeholder segmentation: G2A, G2B, G2C, G2D,...G2Z,* 3) *Engagement* and participation of *citizens as co-producers of public value*, (4) *Accountability, Transparency and Online Consultation* are to aim more.

Thailand in its endeavor on e-Government development, the country issued their ICT policy frameworks i.e. IT2000 and IT2010. Based upon the frameworks, the first ever ICT master plan as a blueprint during 2002-2006 for Thailand ICT and e-Government development was laid with the goal of leading the country towards knowledge based society. To achieve the goal the country's first ICT master plan put into high public attention on 5 strategic flagships including e-Commerce, e-Industry, e-Government, e-Education and e-Society as foundation for other e-Strategies. Followed by the second ICT Master Plan to succeed what founded and assessed during and after the 1st plan, the 2nd version plan is now emphasizing to implant e-Governance across the board of ICT and e-Government development of the country. As parallel action, good governance for ICT application and usage or in other word, ICT governance has been national ICT agenda. ICT infrastructure development for all is still put as one of the key strategy among the six major strategies of the 2nd plan. At the same time ICT literacy for citizen and ICT workforce development are also put as one of the key ICT strategies. The ultimate outcome is to build up the country to become "Smart Thailand" by 2013.

Considering baseline of the country's e-Government, firstly in terms of benchmarking, international tables of rankings showed that Thailand in most cases are in the 2nd and 3rd quartile of the tables. The country now set target to leverage itself as levied in the 2nd ICT master plan to reach the 1st quartile of NRR at the end of the plan of 2013. Secondly, in terms of e-Government maturity, during the mid point of the 1st ICT master plan when it was in 2004, the country conducted a survey and evaluated maturity status of e-Government services through website and founded that maturity level of major ministries has reached in average mid-level of the Interchanged Transaction stage out of 5 levels which in consecutive order are Information, Interaction, Interchanged Transaction, Integration and Intelligence. The maturity level remained quite the same when in 2008 MICT conducted the same type of survey on status of e-Government services and found the truth. Lastly is in terms of ambitious e-Government leap-frog defined in the set roadmap under Ministry of ICT supervision on ICT and e-Government development during 2009-2013. Under a certain implementation planning scheme the country set target to move forward from e-Government to connected government, m-Government, u-Government and ultimately towards transformed government in 2013. In achieving all these targets with the well set of the above mentioned baselines, the country sets forth to move forward into e-Governance direction as well defined in ICT master plan 2nd version and coupled by a citizen centric approach implementation projects and initiatives which are all lined up readily to accomplish good governance over public services as a whole. case studies of citizen centric development projects in healthcare sector and community Tele-center are depicted as proof of concept and be good practices for other domains to follow suit.

Challenges and opportunities for developing successful citizen-centric e-Government are elaborated in order for Thailand to act "Smarter" in the following years until 2013 which include (1) *Smarter organization* in the context of central agency and next wave of public organization, (2) *Smarter business processes* in terms of processes to be redesigned/change in mindset, citizen and business portals, (3) *Smarter Integration* within the context of standards-interoperability, common IT infrastructure, (4) *Smarter security and trust* in the context of increased citizen trust, increased systematic security, (5) *Smarter people on ICT* within the context of ICT literacy, CIO, Chief Information Officer as e-Governance Chief, (6) Smarter management in the context of budget priority, effective partnership with private sector or public-private-partnership (7) *Smarter Assessment* and (8) *Smarter accessibility* in the context of online public services for all and universal access framework.

REFERENCES

Accenture Institute for Health & Public Service Value Project Team. (2009, November 12). *From e-government to e-governance: Using new technologies to strengthen relationships with citizens*. Retrieved September 15, 2010, from http://www.accenture.com/Global/Research_and_Insights/Institute_For_Public_Service_Value/From-e-Government-to-e-Governance.htm

Almarabeh, T., & AbuAli, A. (2010). A general framework for e-government: Definition maturity challenges, opportunities, and success. [from http://www.eurojournals.com/ejsr.htm]. *European Journal of Scientific Research, 39*(1), 29–42. Retrieved September 15, 2010.

Auffret, J. P. (2010). Rural and municipal e-government initiatives in developing countries: Best practices and a framework for success. *Journal of E-Governance, 33*(3), 139–143.

Halachmi, A. (2004). *E-government theory and practice: The evidence from Tennessee (USA)*. Retrieved September 28, 2010, from http://unpan1.un.org/intradoc/groups/public/documents/un/unpan019248.pdf

Ministry of Information and Communication Technology. (2010, April 28). *Thailand ICT master plan 2*. Retrieved September 15, 2010, from http://www.mict.go.th/ewt_news.php?nid=74

National Electronics and Computer Technology Center (NECTEC). (2001). *E-government project 2002-2003*. Ratchathewi, Thailand: NECTEC. Retrieved September 15, 2010, from http://www.nectec.or.th

National Electronics and Computer Technology Center (NECTEC). National Science and Technology Development Agency (NSTDA), & Ministry of Science and Technology (MOST). (2003). *Thailand Information and Communication Technology (ICT): Master plan (2002-2006)*. Ratchathewi, Thailand: National Electronics and Computer Technology Center. Retrieved September 15, 2010, from http://www.mict.go.th

National Electronics and Computer Technology Center (NECTEC). (2010). *Website*. Retrieved September 15, 2010, from http://www.nectec.or.th

Public Sector Website Survey Project. (2004). *Website*. Retrieved September 15, 2010, from http://www.mict.go.th

Sudan, R. (2008). *Next generation organization models for e-government*. Washington, DC: The World Bank's Development Bookstore. Retrieved September 15, 2010, from http://web.worldbank.org/

Sunalai, A., & Tubtimhin, J. (2009). Thailand e-government: A step forward into the right track. In J. Tubtimhin, & R. Pipe (Eds.), *Global e-governance - Advancing e-governance through innovation and leadership, volume 2: Global e-governance series* (pp. 3-25). Fairfax, VA: IOS Press.

Survey Report of e-Government Survey Project. (2008). *Survey report*. Retrieved September 15, 2010, from http://www.mict.go.th

Thai Telecentre. (n.d.). *The origin of a community telecenter project*. Retrieved September 15, 2010, from http://www.thaitelecentre.org/thai/index.php?option=com_content&view=article&id=44&Itemid=54&lang=en

The United Nations. (2008). *E-government survey 2008: From e-government to connected governance*. New York, NY: UN Publishing Section. Retrieved September 15, 2010, from http://unpan1.un.org/intradoc/groups/public/documents/un/unpan028607.pdf

The United Nations. (2010). *United Nations e-government survey 2010: Leveraging e-government at a time of financial and economic crisis*. New York, NY: UN Publishing Section. Retrieved September 15, 2010, from http://www2.unpan.org/egovkb/global_reports/10report.htm

T.Obi Research Office. (2010). *The 2010 Waseda University world e-government ranking*. Tokyo, Japan: T.Obi Research Office.

Tubtimhin, J. (2010). Community driven healthcare service, a case study of Nakhonchaisi hospital in Thailand. In Pipe, R. (Ed.), *Journal of E-Governance*. Fairfax, VA: IOS Press.

Section 3
Evaluation Instrument and E-Governance Assessment

Chapter 8
E-Government Performance Measurement:
A Citizen-Centric Approach in Theory and Practice

Forrest V. Morgeson III
American Customer Satisfaction Index, USA

ABSTRACT

The emergence and rapid spread of electronic government in the United States over the past decade, as well as across much of the globe, has created a need for better, more robust methods of measuring this system's performance. In this chapter we discuss several issues surrounding performance measurement of e-government websites. We outline two types of performance measurement – internal and external measurement – and emphasize the importance of external, citizen-centric performance measures in the e-government context. Following a brief case study illustrating the value of this type of performance measurement, we conclude the chapter by recommending a unified system of e-government performance measurement spanning levels and types of government in the United States. Such a system would best position not only the U.S. government, but many political systems currently implementing and expanding e-government services to realize the goals of improved citizen perceptions of service quality, government efficiency, government responsiveness, transparency, trust, and so forth, through e-government.

INTRODUCTION

The emergence and rapid spread of electronic government (i.e. "e-government" or "digital government") in the United States over the past decade, as well as across much of the rest of the world during this time, has created a need to rigorously measure this system's performance. As a relatively new and still-developing mode of communication and citizen-government interaction, one that is quickly being integrated into a growing number of government services and

DOI: 10.4018/978-1-60960-753-1.ch008

activities, measuring the success of e-government in fulfilling its objectives and realizing its potential is vital. In this chapter we discuss several issues surrounding performance measurement of e-government, focusing on these issues as they relate to the deployment of e-government in the U.S. at the federal level.

The chapter proceeds as follows. After discussing the current state of e-government, with a particular emphasis on both the perceived benefits and enduring shortcomings of this technology, we turn to a discussion of two types of performance measurement – internal and external performance measurement. While recognizing the relevance of internal performance measurement, we emphasize the importance of external, citizen-centered performance measurement for the e-government domain, where persistent shortcomings and poor performance relative to the private sector, along with rapidly evolving technology and an increasingly demanding group of consumers, necessitate an understanding of user (i.e. citizen) perceptions of this system.

Next, we examine e-government website satisfaction data from the American Customer Satisfaction Index (ACSI) as evidence of the informational and process-improvement value of external performance measurement. This exercise not only reveals important lessons about which websites are performing well (and which poorly), but also illuminates systematic cross-category differences, suggesting that some types of websites are likely to have a more difficult time satisfying their citizen-users. More importantly, this exercise evidences the value of performance benchmarking in identifying top performers within and across categories, which in turn can aid bureaucrats seeking models of improvement for their e-government offerings. Finally, we conclude the chapter by recommending a unified, standardized system of external e-government performance measurement spanning levels and types of government in the United States. Such a system would best position not only the U.S. government, but many political systems currently implementing and expanding e-government services to realize the goals of improved citizen perceptions of service quality, government efficiency, government responsiveness, transparency, trust, and so forth, through e-government.

THE STATE OF E-GOVERNMENT TODAY

Since first appearing in the late 1990's, e-government has been credited with creating – or at minimum, holding the potential to create – innumerable social benefits. Collectively, these benefits have been presented as the central justification for the adoption and expansion of e-government, and a corresponding reduction of other modes of citizen-government contact and types of services, such as reducing the number of physical locations, call centers or customer service personnel. Given this, the realization of the promised benefits of e-government is more than a trivial matter; indeed, the success of e-government will ultimately be judged relative to the ability of this medium to realize its perceived potential.

The purported benefits of e-government have been discussed extensively and are by now well known (Bertot & Jaeger, 2006; Chadwick & May, 2003; Edmiston, 2003; Gasco, 2003; Moon, 2002; Roy, 2003; Thomas & Streib, 2003; West, 2007). In the first instance, e-government has long been heralded as a vital new mode of government-to-citizen (G2C), government-to-business (G2B), and intergovernmental communication (G2G) for reasons of *enhanced efficiency and cost-savings* (Moon, 2002). The efficiencies and revenue savings generated by the speed, ease and accessibility of e-government were perhaps most responsible for winning the first generation of advocates and converts to this technological medium, and the centrality of this value can be seen (at least in the United States) in supporting legislation like the *E-Government Act of 2002* (E-Government Act,

2002). From this perspective, e-government appears to be realizing its potential extremely well; by one estimate, e-government saved the U.S. federal government more than $500 million in the 2007 fiscal year alone (Nagesh, 2008).

Yet enhanced efficiency and cost savings are not the only justifications for the development of e-government, as a number of less tangible benefits of this new technology have also been proposed. E-government has been viewed as an effective means for government to *improve the quality of services* delivered to citizens, and possibly even provide service quality on par with the private sector (E-Government Act, 2002; Morgeson & Mithas, 2009). As a consequence of this improved service quality and government performance, some have suggested that e-government may also prove instrumental in improving overall *citizen trust* in government, a value that has been mostly on the decline over the past several decades in western democracies like the United States (Morgeson & Mithas, 2009; Morgeson, VanAmburg & Mithas, 2011; Parent, 2005; Tolbert & Mossberger, 2004; West, 2004). E-government has further been praised as an important tool for enhancing *democratic participation* and civic engagement ("e-democracy"), a mode of communication that could bring citizens "closer" to elected officials and legislative processes (Norris, 2007). Similarly, e-government has been viewed as a means of democratizing traditionally less democratic processes like *administrative rulemaking* through a more open and inclusive mechanism termed "e-rulemaking" (Morgeson 2005; Schlosberg et al., 2007). *Electronic voting* ("e-voting") now has many advocates as well, due to its potential to expand citizen participation in elections, and has even been recommended for adoption across the entirety of the European Union (Treschel and Mendez, 2005). Finally, e-government has even been viewed as *environmentally beneficial*, with many processes once responsible for the consumption of large quantities of paper, energy, physical space and other resources now being moved online.

Given these and a variety of related benefits of e-government, it is not surprising that governments in the United States at all levels – city, county, state and federal – have integrated e-government into most of their interactions with citizens. The technology has likewise been adopted to varying degrees by a large number of both developed and developing countries across the globe (United Nations, 2010). The range of services ("e-services") many citizens can now receive from their governments through the Internet and a vast assortment of government websites is expansive, and grows more so every day. Processes once completed through assorted other means – such as paper filing and mailing tax returns, applying for government benefits, seeking a government-subsidized loan, searching for data, reports or news and information distributed by the government, contacting an elected or appointed government official, or seeking government employment, among myriad other tasks and objectives – can now be completed via e-government websites. Indeed, due to the sheer number and magnitude of the changes produced by e-government, it is little wonder that some have credited this technological medium with creating a "new face of government," with fundamentally and irrevocably altering the way citizens and government connect and interact now and in the future (Thomas & Streib, 2003).

Yet the exuberance directed toward e-government notwithstanding, its implementation has not been without significant difficulties, and along with these difficulties have come questions about the true potential of this medium. More specifically, while few would dispute the tangible benefits of e-government (i.e. its ability to help governments save money), e-government's success in realizing the intangible benefits often attributed to it has recently come under closer scrutiny. For instance, evidence indicates that government lags the private sector in developing effective, high-quality websites, a result suggesting that e-government is not yet providing the best services possible or living up to the lofty standards set by private corporations and the free market (Morgeson & Mithas, 2009). Indeed, some U.S. federal agencies now acknowledge that private sector websites are far more advanced than their e-government counterparts, and are taking steps to copy the model provided by these websites (Weigelt, 2006). Others have suggested that the citizen trust enhancing benefits of e-government have been oversold, and that relatively weak e-government performance and user satisfaction may be behind this problem (Morgeson, Mithas & VanAmburg, 2011; West, 2004). Still others have suggested that e-government initiatives aimed at enhancing democracy have been very limited and slow to be implemented (Mahrer & Krimmer, 2005). Finally, early applications of e-voting have revealed significant problems with this technology, throwing its future into question in many once-enthusiastic democratic nations (Ozimek, 2008). All in all, the enduring shortcomings of e-government have caused some to scale back their expectations of this new technology considerably.

The relatively poor performance of e-government appears to have several causes, and this diversity of sources only adds to the difficulty in resolving these problems. For example, e-government deployment in the U.S. federal system continues to be a largely piecemeal effort, due to functional separation between both levels of government and distinct government agencies, with minimal cooperation and technological harmonization resulting in significant variation between and across agencies and units of government in their e-government offerings (Mahler, 2004; Morgeson & Mithas, 2009; West, 2004; West, 2007). Some have argued that the problems of e-government may be endemic to government itself, that among bureaucratic managers a disincentive may exist for the successful deployment of IT in general (Fountain, 2001). From this perspective, if e-government were to truly succeed its efficiencies would only result in reduced budget appropriations and/or power for agencies, and thus public managers have been slow to implement (or at least publicize the benefits) of e-government. Finally, these and related problems are only exacerbated by the fact that IT as a whole is evolving quickly; not only must government improve to match the performance of the private sector, but at the same time integrate and assimilate the constant stream of changes and advances emerging in this area.

While the precise nature, extent and causes of the shortcomings of e-government are open for debate, all of these problems point to the importance of rigorous systems of *e-government performance measurement*. As a tool for gauging success and realizing improvements within public and private organizations alike, as well as various systems, programs, and policies implemented by these organizations, performance measurement provides a useful means for both overcoming the perceived deficiencies of e-government as it stands today, and carefully monitoring this expanding service-delivery mechanism as it grows and becomes an even more important part of government in the future. In the next section we discuss performance measurement more fully, and particularly as this practice applies to e-government.

E-GOVERNMENT PERFORMANCE MEASUREMENT: AN INTERNAL OR EXTERNAL APPROACH?

Following the lead of the for-profit private sector, governments at all levels, along with a large number of other public and non-profit organizations, have begun to measure and manage their performance (Behn, 2003; Hatry, 2006; Holzer & Yang, 2004). Performance measurement, which we will define here as the "regular measurement of the results (outcomes) and efficiency of services or programs," comes in many shapes and sizes (Hatry, 2006, 3). Likewise, the justifications for performance measurement among federal agencies are many, and the basic goals and purposes driving this practice have been understood differently (Behn, 2003).

Measurement and publication of performance data is valuable, some have suggested, because it provides citizens with the information needed to hold elected officials and bureaucrats responsible for their performance, thereby facilitating a more meaningful type of democratic accountability (Wholey & Newcomer, 1997). Performance data also provides a feedback mechanism between government agencies and their citizens, customers and other stakeholders similar to that of the free market private sector, a mechanism and "network of communication" that is otherwise lacking for most government agencies and programs (Fornell et. al., 2005; Wholey & Hatry, 1992). Moreover, performance data allows public managers the ability to more accurately gauge the quality of services (and other goods) they are delivering, and to acquire the information needed to reform and retool sub-optimal processes (Wholey & Hatry, 1992). Finally, performance measures are sometimes regarded as useful proxies for or determinants of trust in government, indicators of public support for both the political system as a whole and its distinct units (Bouckaert & Van de Walle, 2003).

But setting these justifications aside, perhaps the most significant and commonly referenced purpose driving government performance measurement is its usefulness for *benchmarking*. Over the last decade, the practice of performance benchmarking, an idea borrowed from the quality management approaches of the private sector, has increasingly been viewed as applicable to and important for government (Keehley et. al., 1996; Kouzmin et. al., 1999). Performance benchmarking aims "to identify competitive targets which render the weak points of the benchmarking organization visible and to establish means of improvement," and it is this purpose of benchmarking – to realize better government through comparison across units of government, identification of best practices, and consequent process or service quality improvements – that has been the focus of most government agencies (Kouzmin et al., 1999, 123).

In relation to the varieties of performance data utilized in the practice of performance benchmarking within government, two general perspectives on how to conduct performance measurement are identifiable: *internal* and *external* performance measurement (Brown & Coulter, 1983; Hatry, 2006; Kelly & Swindell, 2003). While both internal and external performance measurement are practiced by government agencies, internal measures tend to dominate.[1] These measures of performance "may be thought of as internal measures…because they come from a definition of effectiveness derived and monitored by administrators" (Kelly & Swindell, 2003, 610). In essence, internal performance measures are labeled as such because they rely on *internal criteria* of performance and *internal actors* (i.e. professionals working within an organization measuring its performance) to evaluate success in meeting these criteria. Ranging from comparisons between the projected and actual accomplishment of an overall mission (e.g. "has program X met its goal of reducing poverty, increasing literacy, etc.?"), to internally verifiable evaluations of finite aspects of service delivery relative to established goals (e.g. an agency setting a goal of 40 days for application processing, and comparing average actual delivery time with this goal), internal performance measures in government rely on bureaucrats – and in some instances, related but distinct oversight institutions and actors, such as the U.S. Congress or the Office of Management and Budget – to evaluate performance. One popular type of internal performance measurement is performance-based budgeting, where program effectiveness relative to budget allocation (e.g. people served per dollar spent) provides the critical metric of success, and where future budget allocations may be driven by a determination of successful performance (Swiss 2005).

On the other hand, instead of focusing on strictly internal criteria or internal actors to judge performance, external performance measurement focuses on clients, citizens, users or other stakeholders external to an organization – but directly affected nonetheless by the organization's performance – as the means of gauging success. That is, external measures of performance diverge from internal measures both in who evaluates organizational success and in the criteria used to evaluate success. External performance measures typically ask relevant external groups to evaluate various program activities – usually through surveys of individuals within these groups – related to the services they have experienced (such as perceptions of customer service delivered, perceptions of the ease or efficiency of application processes, the accessibility of information disseminated, etc.). Because the respondents surveyed will usually have had direct experience with the agency or program under investigation, they are able to provide perceptions based on these experiences that can prove useful to organizations attempting to improve their processes, their service offerings, and so forth.

Within government, both internal and external measures of performance have been advocated as useful tools, instrumental in furthering a number of the critical goals mentioned above. Relatively recent legislation – most notably the *Government Performance and Results Act of 1993* – has mandated performance measurement of both types at the federal level of government in the U.S., resulting in a huge increase in the number of federal agencies now involved in performance measurement, benchmarking and management of one kind or another (GPRA, 1993). The more recent adoption of the "Program Assessment Rating Tool" directed by the OMB, which uses a relatively unified assortment of performance measures to gauge the success of a large number of federal programs, has only reinforced the federal government's commitment to performance measurement (Office of Management and Budget, 2008).

In relation to e-government, and in particular the most ubiquitous form of e-government –government websites – the nature of some internal and external measures of performance can be easily illustrated. Figure 1 provides a list (although certainly not an exhaustive one) of some internal and external performance metrics, in several different categories, that can be (and are) implemented to gauge the performance of an e-government website.

As Figure 1 suggests, an internal system of e-government website performance measurement would be conducted by professionals (bureaucrats) working within the organization and their internal analysis, most likely including IT professionals responsible for the creation and maintenance of the website, as well as the agency's chief information officer (CIO) and related senior managers. Using their internal criteria, these individuals would rate their website on the basis of questions like those outlined in Figure 1. For instance, one basic question would ask if the website includes all of the necessary pages, content and information. Further, is the website logically sequenced, and are all page links functioning properly? Are contact points (such as email addresses) provided, and do they route the user to the correct person within the agency? Does the website effectively aid in the accomplishment of the overall mission of the agency? Is the number of users of the website growing, and are customers transitioning from alternative modes of communication to the website? Again while not exhaustive, answers to these and related questions would provide evidence – performance data – of the quality and performance of an e-government website, as well as offering insight into critical areas where improvement is still needed.

On the other hand, external measures of e-government website performance would, as mentioned earlier, focus on the users of these websites (rather than internal actors) to gain similar but distinct performance data through survey data collection. Usually taking the form of a random sample of users of the website, such a survey seeks feedback from these users helpful

Figure 1. Internal and external measures of e-government website performance

	Website Navigation/ Organization	Website Information	Interactivity/ Customer Service	Overall Website Performance	Website/ Channel Growth
Internal (Internal Analysis)	Arrangement/ sequence of pages; Inclusion of all necessary pages; Functionality of links	Content analysis; Completeness of information	Inclusion of email addresses; Channeling queries to correct addresses	Average time on website (?); Accomplishment of mission	User growth rate (?); User conversion rate
External (User Perceptions)	Ease of navigation; Ability to understand page layout	Ability to find the information needed; Ability to understand information provided	Ability to find correct email recipient; Question answered quickly/ accurately	User satisfaction	Likelihood to reuse website; Likelihood to recommend website

in overcoming enduring problems (or detecting sources of strong performance) of the website. For instance, these users might be asked if the website was easy to navigate, easy to use to find information or points of contact, the understandability of information contained on the website, and so forth. Typically, external performance measures will also include proxies for overall website performance such as user satisfaction, as well as future-oriented measures like the user's likelihood to reuse and recommend the website. Similar to internal performance measures, the information gained from this data would help officials detect areas of success, as well as areas where additional work is still needed.

Before proceeding to discuss the relative merits of one of these two types of performance measurement vis-à-vis e-government, it should be noted that the two perspectives are not and should not be considered entirely distinct or mutually exclusive (Ostrom, 1973; Ostrom 1999). Indeed, in many ways internal and external measures of performance should be viewed as complementary. For example, linking internal assessments of website navigation to external perceptions of ease of navigation among users could provide invaluable information to IT professionals attempting to offer the best, easiest user experience. Analyzing differences between how IT professionals view the informational content of a website they maintain to how users view the same website's information content, to take another example, could begin a process of critical system reevaluation. Similarly, there is tremendous value in linking the satisfaction expressed by users to actual growth rates in the number of users or to success in converting offline users to the online medium, as such a linkage would allows a bureaucratic agency to determine the "bang for the buck" (or in this instance, the "bang for the byte") in seeking improved website user satisfaction. While these are just a few examples, linking internal and external measures of performance often provides greater and more useful information than either of these types taken in isolation.

Be this as it may, there are strong reasons to emphasize the critical importance of one of these types for e-government, *external performance measurement,* over the other, particularly as many governmental organizations have neither the manpower nor the budget to effectively adopt and actively monitor multiple performance metrics simultaneously. In the first instance, Figure 1 hints at the difficulty of interpretation of some common internal measures of website performance when applied to the public sector (Ostrom, 1999). It is, for example, difficult to interpret a metric such as average user time spent on the website in the context of government. For the private sector more time spent on the website is usually considered a positive outcome, as it means users are being lured to buy (or at least consider buying) additional merchandise or services. But for government this could indicate either a positive user experience or an inefficient website requiring unnecessary user time and creating user dissatisfaction, depending on the nature and purpose of the website. Similarly, user growth rate in the private sector is almost always a positive outcome, as it indicates new customers (or converted customers) and new sources of potential revenue. But in the public sector user growth rate could be driven by entirely external factors (such as the creation of a new program, temporary growth in the number of citizens requiring a particular service due to a rare emergency, and so forth) that have little to do with the actual quality of the website.

Additionally, internal performance measures are sometimes subject to manipulation by the actors tasked with measuring performance, calling into question their objectivity and usefulness in process improvement. That is, it is naturally tempting for an IT professional who created a website to overstate the success of his or her own creation, and thus independent validation through external measures can provide a clearer, more accurate picture of performance. What is more, the speed with which things change on the Internet (and for the "new economy" in general) necessitates a nearly-constant understanding of the shifting needs and demands of website users, particularly when compared to the relatively slow pace of the old economy which afforded consumers far less power (Fornell, 2007). As one IT CEO recently put it, "things change fast in today's world and you've got to keep up or get left behind" (Jarboe, 2010). While internal performance measures (and the general expertise of IT professionals) may help identify some of these shifting demands relatively quickly, the input of users is often a far faster and more efficient means for detecting changes. Finally, as many of the suggested benefits of e-government are tied to citizen perceptions (citizen trust, enhanced democracy, increased transparency, etc.), understanding these perceptions – and not solely the second-order perceptions of internal actors far removed from their citizen-customers – is vital. In the final analysis, e-government has been praised in large part for its ability to transform citizen perceptions (West, 2004), so understanding these perceptions and how e-government is meeting user demands would seem to matter most.

For these reasons and more, performance measurement of e-government in general, and external performance measurement in particular, is more important now than ever. In the next section, we illustrate the value of one such external measure, examining citizen satisfaction with a large cross-section of U.S. federal government websites.

CASE STUDY: MEASURING AND BENCHMARKING CITIZEN SATISFACTION WITH U.S. FEDERAL WEBSITES

In what follows, we provide an example of external performance measurement and benchmarking of e-government performance data. Using a sample of U.S. federal government website satisfaction scores derived from surveys of users of these websites, data provided by the American Customer

Satisfaction Index (ACSI) project and ForeSee Results, Inc., a partner of the ACSI responsible for the e-government, e-business and e-commerce portions of the project, this brief case study provides evidence of the uses and value of external performance measurement data.

A few words on the data included in the sample analyzed below are necessary. The data, as mentioned above, come from the ACSI e-government study. As part of the goal of measuring customer satisfaction with the goods and services produced and consumed across the U.S. economy, the ACSI measures user satisfaction with federal government services, including satisfaction with a large number of federal e-government websites. The ACSI utilizes a general and standardized survey instrument and modeling methodology that facilitates cross-measure, cross-category comparison, an essential aspect of any study intended for performance benchmarking (Fornell et al., 1996; Fornell et al., 2005).

The satisfaction index score for each measured website reflects a mean (average) score on a 0-100 scale, from low to high satisfaction. The mean score for a website is derived from a sample of interviews with a large number of recent users of these websites, with each *n*th interviewee picked randomly upon visiting the website and being asked to immediately participate in the survey via a "pop-up" window. While the total number of respondents for each measured website varies, typically hundreds (at minimum) of users are interviewed and asked about their satisfaction with the website (along with other relevant user perceptions) during data collection. The satisfaction index score, a latent variable comprised of three distinct satisfaction questions included in the ACSI model, is a portion of a larger structural equation statistical model examining satisfaction as well as determinants and outcomes of satisfaction (Fornell et al., 1996; Fornell et al., 2005). Full analysis of this model allows for identification not only of relative performance and benchmarking of scores over time and across agencies, websites, units of government, and so forth, but also assists in identifying the areas of improvement that will most effectively and efficiently increase user satisfaction. An example of this statistical model as it is applied to e-government websites is found in Appendix A.

Including all e-government websites measured during the 2008 calendar year, the sample analyzed includes a total of 401 distinct federal agency/department website satisfaction index scores.[2] These federal websites cut across several distinct categories, including employment and career recruitment websites (e.g. the Department of Labor and Department of State's career sites), homepage and portal websites (e.g. the main websites for the Centers for Disease Control and the Federal Bureau of Investigation), e-commerce and transactional websites (e.g. the application page for the Social Security Administration and the online catalog for the U.S. Mint), and news and information websites (e.g. the page for Medline Plus and other health information resources).[3] While for some websites satisfaction scores are calculated once each quarter, generating four data points for the website each year, for the sake of brevity we pool the data and analyze all website index scores for the 2008 calendar year together. Table 1 provides descriptive statistics for the overall sample, as well as each underlying category. A brief analysis of these results follows.

As shown in Table 1, the average satisfaction score across the full sample of website satisfaction measures is 73.3 on the 0-100 scale.[4] However, satisfaction is not constant across the various categories of websites. News and information websites score lowest at 72.1, while e-commerce/transaction websites score highest at 77.2, a gap of 5.1 points. Results from *t*-test analysis of significant difference between these two scores shows this difference to be statistically significant ($t = 4.65; p = 0.00$), indicating that federal e-commerce/transaction websites are providing significantly higher user satisfaction when compared to news and information e-government websites. While

Table 1. Sample statistics

	N	MIN	MAX	MEAN	SD	SE
Full Sample	401	53	90	73.3	7.030	0.351
News/Information	228	53	87	72.1	7.145	0.473
Main/Portal	104	57	84	73.5	6.220	0.610
E-Commerce/Transaction	53	64	90	77.2	7.293	1.002
Career/Recruitment	16	74	81	76.9	2.413	0.603

it is difficult to pinpoint the source of these different satisfaction levels, it is in keeping with comparable results from the private sector, where e-commerce websites (e.g. Amazon.com, eBay.com, etc.) provide, on average, significantly greater satisfaction than news and information websites (e.g. CNN.com, ABCNews.com, etc.). Nevertheless, it appears that the type of service or function being offered by an e-government website matters in how satisfied users are likely to be.

There is also a considerable range of 37.0 from lowest (53) to highest (90) satisfaction score among the full sample of individual websites. In other words, it appears that e-government is not being implemented equally – or at least equally successfully, in the minds of users – across all federal government agencies. Some web pages are performing at an extremely high level in satisfying users, including the Social Security's "Retirement Estimator" webpage (with a score of 90) and Health and Human Service's "Medline Plus" website (86). On the other hand, some e-government websites perform much lower in terms of user satisfaction, with some scoring in the low 50's. This finding suggests that there remains significant variation in user satisfaction with e-government websites.

What is more, within the different categories of e-government websites there exists a significant range from low to high performing website, indicating that the variance in user satisfaction with websites cannot be explained entirely by differences in the functions or purposes of these websites. The range is smallest for career recruitment websites (7.0, from 74 to 81), although this is likely due (at least in part) to the relatively small number of websites measured in this category. E-commerce and transactional websites range 26.0, from a high of 90 (the Social Security Administration's "Retirement Estimator") to a low of 64. News and information websites show an even greater range of 34.0, from a high of 87 (the Department of Defense's "America Supports You" website) to a low of 53. Homepage and portal websites have a range between these two categories at 27.0, from a high of 84 (for a National Institutes of Health website) to a low of 57. While these findings show, as mentioned above, that levels of user satisfaction do not vary solely on the basis of the category of e-government website, it also provides essential information for improving performance among lower-scoring websites. That is, through this simple performance benchmarking exercise, we have identified several high performing websites (from the Social Security Administration, the National Institutes of Health, the Department of Defense, etc.) in various categories that could serve as models of best practices for lower scoring websites in the same category.

In sum, this very brief exercise in analyzing e-government performance measurement data offers several lessons useful to bureaucrats (and others) interested in this system's performance. First, these results show that the *type of service or function being offered* by an e-government website matters in terms of user satisfaction. Second, however, the variance in user satisfaction with websites *cannot be explained solely on the basis of differences in the functions or purposes of these websites*. Thus, while some e-government website functions seem to be "tougher" in terms of providing satisfaction, with news and information websites at something of a disadvantage relative to e-commerce and transactional e-government websites, it does not excuse the poor performance of some websites relative to others in the same category. Finally, and perhaps most importantly, this exercise shows how performance measurement and benchmarking can *identify top performers within and across categories*, and in turn provide bureaucrats seeking improvements for their e-government websites with exemplars and best practices useful in realizing these improvements. In this sense, performance measurement can certainly assist in optimizing e-government performance and in helping bureaucrats realize the potential of e-government.

CONCLUSIONS: TOWARDS A UNIFIED E-GOVERNMENT PERFORMANCE INDEX

Measuring the performance of e-government, both in general and particularly in reference to the citizen-facing portions of e-government like agency websites, is a matter of considerable importance. This is especially true for e-government, as it appears poised to cover a larger and larger number of citizen contacts with government in the near future. Further, the enduring shortcomings and challenges facing e-government only reinforce this point. If e-government is to realize its considerable potential, the ability to detect where it is performing well, and where it may need additional improvement, is critical. This reality holds true both for governments like the United States, where e-government is well-developed and widely implemented, to countries just now beginning to implement or expand e-services.

In this chapter we have emphasized the importance of external performance measurement for e-government. Once again, this recommendation is not intended as a wholesale rejection of internal performance measurement, but rather as recognition that in the realm of e-government, where things do change quickly, where citizen perceptions matter most and users have greater power, and where government resources often limit the quantity of performance measurement that can be accomplished, external measurement may provide the single best approach.

Our analysis of a sample of federal website satisfaction scores illustrates the value of external performance measurement and performance benchmarking. These results show that satisfaction with e-government websites varies both across individual agencies and across type of website. Not only does this analysis suggest that some websites require improvements to meet the demands of users, and that e-government is not yet performing equally well across different government agencies, but also that some high-performing websites present themselves as models for other (i.e. poorer-performing) websites to follow. This case study shows, in other words, the value of performance measurement of e-government in general, identifying both high performance and exemplars for improvement in performance.

The value of e-government performance measurement demonstrated here would seem to suggest the adoption of a more robust system of such measurement, I would argue. This imperative has not been entirely lost on regulatory agencies involved with these measures in the United States and elsewhere. For instance, the Office of Management and Budget's (OMB) recent guidance on the "Program Assessment Rating Tool" (a directive aimed at encouraging and harmonizing performance measurement across the U.S. federal government) explicitly encourages "agencies to provide the means by which their programs may be benchmarked internationally or across agencies, which provides one indicator of program quality" (Office of Management and Budget, 2008, 74). Likewise, the United Nations has become heavily involved in monitoring the deployment of e-government cross-nationally through its survey of national e-government systems and its annual "E-Government Readiness Index" (United Nations, 2010).

Be this as it may, performance measurement, much like e-government itself, remains a largely disorganized, piecemeal effort. While nearly every federal agency utilizes some type of performance metric (although many only because they are required to do so), these measures vary widely from one agency to another, and agency commitment to examining and acting on these measures varies considerably as well. In turn, benchmarking and comparing performance is a difficult task (if not impossible, in many instances), and the kind of organizational learning facilitated by this practice is not being maximized. Given this, one recommendation (both for the U.S. federal government and for governments at all levels and cross-nationally) vis-à-vis e-government performance measurement is worth exploring: implementation of a *centralized, unified system of e-government performance measurement spanning levels and types of government.* Such a system would provide the most effective means for utilizing performance measurement to realize meaningful improvements in e-government. Such a system could, for instance, best position government to realize the long-stated goals of improved citizen perceptions of service quality, efficiency, government responsiveness, transparency, and so forth, through e-government. Perhaps most importantly, improvements in these areas could help realize a vital outcome many have connected to e-government: improved citizen trust in government through improved government performance.

REFERENCES

Behn, R. (2003). Why measure performance? Different purposes require different measures. *Public Administration Review, 63*(5), 586–606. doi:10.1111/1540-6210.00322

Bertot, J. C., & Jaeger, P. T. (2006). User-centered e-government: Challenges and benefits for government websites. *Government Information Quarterly, 23*, 163–168. doi:10.1016/j.giq.2006.02.001

Bouckaert, G., & Van de Walle, S. (2003). Comparing measures of citizen trust and user satisfaction as indicators of "good governance": Difficulties in linking trust and satisfaction indicators. *International Review of Administrative Sciences, 69*(3), 329–344.

Brown, K., & Coulter, P. (1983). Subjective and objective measures of police service delivery. *Public Administration Review, 43*(1), 50–58. doi:10.2307/975299

Chadwick, A., & May, C. (2003). Interaction between states and citizens in the age of the Internet: E-government in the United States, Britain, and the European Union. *Governance: An International Journal of Policy and Administration, 16*(2), 271–300.

DeLone, W. H., & McLean, E. R. (1992). Information Systems success: The quest for the dependent variable. *Information Systems Research, 3*(1), 60–95. doi:10.1287/isre.3.1.60

E-Government Act. (2002). *E-Government Act.* (Pub. L. No. 107-347, 116 Stat. 2899).

Fornell, C. (2007). *The satisfied customer: Winners and losers in the battle for buyer preference.* New York, NY: Palgrave Macmillan.

Fornell, C., Johnson, M. D., Anderson, E. W., Cha, J., & Bryant, B. E. (1996). The American customer satisfaction index: Nature, purpose and findings. *Journal of Marketing, 60*(4), 7–18. doi:10.2307/1251898

Fornell, C., Van Amburg, D., Morgeson, F. V. III, Bryant, B., Anderson, G., & Johnson, M. (2005). *The American customer satisfaction index at 10 years*. Ann Arbor, MI: The Stephen M. Ross School of Business.

Fountain, J. E. (2001). *Building the virtual state: Information Technology and institutional change*. Washington, DC: Brookings Institution Press.

Hatry, H. P. (2006). *Performance measurement: Getting results*. Washington, DC: Urban Institute Press.

Holzer, M., & Yang, K. (2004). Performance measurement and improvement: An assessment of the state of the art. *International Review of the Administrative Sciences, 70*(1), 15–31. doi:10.1177/0020852304041228

Jarboe, G. (April 8, 2010). Rip Van Winkle: "Things change fast in today's world." Retrieved from http://blog.searchenginewatch.com/100408-093526.

Keehley, P. S., Medlin, S., MacBride, S., & Longmire, L. (1996). *Benchmarking for best practices in the public sector*. San Francisco, CA: Jossey-Bass.

Kelly, J., & Swindell, D. (2002). A multiple indicator approach to municipal service evaluation: Correlating performance and citizen satisfaction across jurisdictions. *Public Administration Review, 62*(5), 610–621. doi:10.1111/1540-6210.00241

Kelly, J. M., & Swindell, D. (2002). Service quality variation across urban space: First steps towards a model of citizen satisfaction. *Journal of Urban Affairs, 24*(3), 271–288. doi:10.1111/1467-9906.00127

Kouzmin, A., Loffler, E., Klages, H., & Kakabadse, N. (1999). Benchmarking and performance measurement in public sectors. *International Journal of Public Sector Management, 12*(2), 121–144. doi:10.1108/09513559910263462

Mahler, J. (2004). Influences of organizational culture on learning in public agencies. *Journal of Public Administration: Research and Theory, 7*(4), 519–540.

Mahrer, H., & Krimmer, R. (2005). Towards the enhancement of e-democracy: Identifying the notion of the "middleman paradox". *Information Systems Journal, 15*(1), 27–42. doi:10.1111/j.1365-2575.2005.00184.x

Moon, M. J. (2002). The evolution of e-government among municipalities: Rhetoric or reality? *Public Administration Review, 62*(4), 424–433. doi:10.1111/0033-3352.00196

Morgeson, F. V., III. (2005). Reconciling democracy and bureaucracy: Towards a deliberative-democratic model of bureaucratic accountability. (Doctoral dissertation, University of Pittsburgh, 28 March 2005).

Morgeson, F. V. III. (2011). Comparing determinants of website satisfaction and loyalty across the e-government and e-business domain. *Electronic Government: An International Journal, 8*(2/3), 164–184. doi:10.1504/EG.2011.039835

Morgeson, F. V. III, & Mithas, S. (2009). Does e-government measure up to e-business? Comparing end-user perceptions of U.S. federal government and e-business websites. *Public Administration Review, 69*(4), 740–752. doi:10.1111/j.1540-6210.2009.02021.x

Morgeson, F. V. III, VanAmburg, D., & Mithas, S. (2011). Misplaced trust? Exploring the structure of the e-government-citizen trust relationship. *Journal of Public Administration: Research and Theory, 21*(2), 257–283. doi:10.1093/jopart/muq006

Nagesh, G. (February 7, 2008). *OMB touts savings from e-gov initiatives.* GovExec.com. Retrieved from http://www.govexec.com/dailyfed/0208/020708n1.htm

Norris, D. F. (2007). Electronic democracy at the American grassroots. In Norris, D. F. (Ed.), *Current issues and trends in e-government research*. Baltimore, MD: University of Maryland. doi:10.4018/9781599042831.ch008

Norris, D. F., & Lloyd, B. A. (2006). The scholarly literature on e-government: Characterizing a nascent field. *International Journal of Electronic Government Research, 2*(4), 40–56. doi:10.4018/jegr.2006100103

Norris, P. (2001). *Digital divide: Citizen engagement, information poverty and the Internet worldwide*. New York, NY: Cambridge University Press.

Office of Management and Budget. (2008). *Program assessment rating tool, guidance no. 2008-01*. Retrieved from http://www.whitehouse.gov/omb/assets/performance_pdfs/part_guid_2008.pdf

Ostrom, E. (1973). The need for multiple indicators in measuring the output of public agencies. *Policy Studies Journal: the Journal of the Policy Studies Organization, 2*, 85–91. doi:10.1111/j.1541-0072.1973.tb00132.x

Ostrom, E. (1999). Why do we need multiple indicators of public service outputs? In McGinnis, M. D. (Ed.), *Polycentricity and local public economies*. Ann Arbor, MI: University of Michigan Press.

Ozimek, J. (Novermber 9, 2008). Finland's flawed e-voting scheme - Blame the voters? *The Register*. Retrieved from http://www.theregister.co.uk/2008/11/09/finland_evoting/

Parent, M., Vandebeek, C. A., & Gemino, A. C. (2005). Building citizen trust through e-government. *Government Information Quarterly, 22*, 720–736. doi:10.1016/j.giq.2005.10.001

Schlosberg, D., Zavestoski, S., & Shulman, S. W. (2007). Democracy and e-rulemaking: Web-based technologies, participation, and the potential for deliberation. *Journal of Information Technology & Politics, 4*(1), 37–55. doi:10.1300/J516v04n01_04

Swiss, J. (2005). A framework for assessing incentives in results-based management. *Public Administration Review, 65*(5), 592–602. doi:10.1111/j.1540-6210.2005.00486.x

Thomas, C. W. (1998). Maintaining and restoring public trust in government agencies and their employees. *Administration & Society, 30*(2), 166–193. doi:10.1177/0095399798302003

Thomas, J. C., & Streib, G. (2003). The new face of government: Citizen-initiated contacts in the era of e-government. *Journal of Public Administration: Research and Theory, 13*, 83–102. doi:10.1093/jpart/mug010

Tolbert, C. J., & Mossberger, K. (2006). The effects of e-government on trust and confidence in government. *Public Administration Review, 66*(3), 354–369. doi:10.1111/j.1540-6210.2006.00594.x

Trechsel, A., & Mendez, F. (Eds.). (2005). *The European Union and e-voting: Addressing the European Parliament's Internet voting challenge*. London, UK: Routledge.

United Nations Department of Economic and Social Affairs. (2010). *United Nations e-government survey 2010: Leveraging e-government at a time of financial and economic crisis*. New York, NY: UN Publishing Section.

Welch, E. W., Hinnant, C. C., & Moon, M. J. (2004). Linking citizen satisfaction with e-government and trust in government. *Journal of Public Administration: Research and Theory, 15*(3), 371–391. doi:10.1093/jopart/mui021

West, D. M. (2004). E-government and the transformation of service delivery and citizen attitudes. *Public Administration Review*, *64*(1), 15–27. doi:10.1111/j.1540-6210.2004.00343.x

Wholey, J. S., & Hatry, H. (1992). The case for performance monitoring. *Public Administration Review*, *52*(6), 604–610. doi:10.2307/977173

Wholey, J. S., & Newcomer, K. E. (1997). Clarifying goals, reporting results. In Newcomer, K. E. (Ed.), *Using performance measurement to improve public and non-profit programs*. San Francisco, CA: Jossey-Bass.

KEY TERMS AND DEFINITIONS

E-Government: The use of information and communications technologies to improve the delivery of government services to citizens.

Performance Measurement: Methods employed to gauge the quality and/or efficiency of a particular process, or an organization as a whole.

Performance Benchmarking: The comparison of performance data between similar organizations with the goal of assessing relative performance and seeking strategies for improvement.

Citizen Satisfaction: The reported level of happiness/pleasure individuals receive from an encounter with government agencies or government services.

American Customer Satisfaction Index (ACSI): Originally founded at the University of Michigan, the ACSI measures customer satisfaction with the goods and services produced and consumed across the U.S. economy, including user satisfaction with local and federal government services.

ENDNOTES

1 The dominance of internal performance measures within government agencies has a variety of causes, but is primarily due to the ability of agencies using this method to keep the results out of the critical view of both the public and regulatory agencies. Yet the Freedom of Information Act and related "sunshine" legislation is making maintaining the secrecy of any performance data – whether internal or external – increasingly difficult.

2 While due to space limitations we do not reproduce the full list of ACSI e-government scores here, all of the individual federal website satisfaction scores are publicly available and can be viewed at: www.theacsi.org. It should also be noted that ForeSee Results, Inc. conducts a large number of federal e-government website measures on an opt-in, for-profit basis, but all scores posted on the ACSI website follow the same strict data collection and analysis methods of the larger ACSI project.

3 These e-government website categories are used by the ACSI to differentiate the sites into meaningfully unique groups, but certainly do not represent the only possible categorization of e-government sites.

4 Here we will not benchmark these e-government satisfaction results with the more-than 200 private sector, company-level satisfaction scores also produced each year by the ACSI. However, to put these scores in context, the private sector-wide National Average of all measures was 75.9 as of the fourth quarter of 2009. Moreover, the E-Business satisfaction average was 81.5 as of the second quarter of 2009, and the E-Commerce average was 81.4 as of the second quarter of 2009.

APPENDIX

*Figure 2. An example e-government performance measurement model**

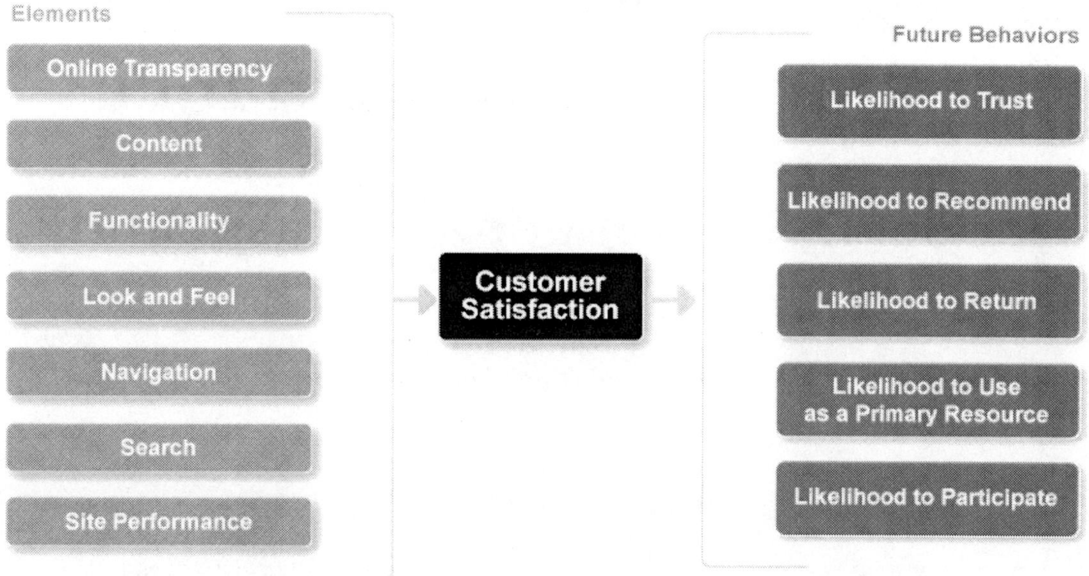

*Model picture reproduced with permission of ForeSee Results, Inc.

Chapter 9
Impact of E-Governance on Businesses:
Model Development and Case Study

Naiyi Hsiao
National Chengchi University & Taiwan E-Governance Research Center, Taiwan

Pin-yu Chu
National Chengchi University & Taiwan E-Governance Research Center, Taiwan

Chung-pin Lee
Tamkang University & Taiwan E-Governance Research Center, Taiwan

ABSTRACT

The success of e-government policies and projects hinges on a robust assessment strategy that provides not only a valuable understanding of the impacts on stakeholders, but also an effective feedback mechanism for mid-course corrections. This study examines the antecedents of the impact assessment of e-governance in the context of an integrated model. The model incorporates a wide variety of important factors from previous research into a single theoretical framework provided by the e-government value chain model and the Information System success model. A government-to-business (G2B) case is utilized to operationalize the model into survey questions. The current chapter presents the results of the G2B survey and summarizes the key findings from the impact assessment of G2B. The knowledge gained from this study will help pave a path for future e-governance initiatives and improve our understanding of the key factors affecting the success of e-governance.

INTRODUCTION

E-governance has been available and promoted for a long time, but a number of questions regarding its impacts remain unanswered. Most of the literature concerning e-governance research has focused on two basic problems. First of all, the e-governance impact literature has focused mainly on the supply side, taking the perspective of the government. Little has been written that directly addresses the demands or needs of users. Second, most e-government impact assessment studies are

DOI: 10.4018/978-1-60960-753-1.ch009

conceptual, or they are case studies examining the factors influencing the success or failure of e-government, such as infrastructure investments, system accessibility and service quality, usage and citizen satisfaction. Studies examining the nature and extent of e-governance impact assessment in the context of an integrated model are necessary.

Considering the importance of the demand side and the essence of impact assessment, this study proposes a theoretical framework and further elaborates the impact assessment of e-governance in the government to business (G2B) context. In section two, we review the history of e-governance development, the importance of e-governance impact assessment, and several essential theoretical models, such as the e-government value chain model (Heeks, 2006), the information system success model (DeLone & McLean, 2003) and e-SERVQUAL (Zeithaml, Parasuraman, & Malhotra, 2002). Based on the e-government value chain model and the information system success model, we introduce our theoretical framework, which covers three aspects of e-government, i.e., quality, usage, and impact, in section three. In section four, we use survey methodology to test this framework and make detailed assessments of three large-scale G2B programs. The concluding section discusses the key contributions of our research to the e-governance impact assessment literature.

LITERATURE REVIEW

In the field of information and communication technologies (ICTs) in the public sector, e-government is the first emergent concept recognized as an important development in the outreach from government to citizens since the early 1990s. The emergence of ICTs can be traced to the report, "Reengineering through Information Technology", produced by the Clinton Administration (Lenk and Traunmüller, 2002). E-government is usually presented as using ICTs to (1) provide citizens and businesses easy access to government information and services; (2) increase the quality of services by increasing their speed, completeness and process efficiency; and (3) provide citizens with the opportunity to participate in different types of democratic processes. According to the United Nations (UN, 2003), the major purpose of e-government is to use ICTs to transform its internal and external relationships. UN/ASPA (2001) identifies the five stages for quantifying the progress of e-government as emerging, enhanced, interactive, transactional, and seamless.

Recently, researchers have argued that the early concept of e-government is ambiguous and should be clarified. For example, Chadwick (2003) argued that applications of ICTs in the public sector have become a convergence of "e-democracy" and "e-government," and this convergence provides a broader understanding of how ICTs are reshaping public governance. In other words, e-government not only addresses service delivery but can also include e-democracy, which refers to the transformation of political systems (Mahrer and Krimmer, 2005; Bishop and Anderson, 2004). Backus (2001) used "e-governance," a composite term to represent the overall concept of the application of ICTs in the public sector. Marche & McNiven (2003) distinguished e-governance from e-government, with e-governance emphasizing methods of policy making, while e-government emphasizes policy execution and service delivery. Finger & Pécoud (2003) viewed e-governance as a dynamic concept that comprises three main functions: e-government, e-regulation, and e-democracy. Chiang, Chen, Huang, Chung, and Hsiao (2004) further described e-governance as "a key platform for integration and collaboration of social resources in which government follows principles of equity, transparency, efficiency, rule of law, and democracy, and adopts information and communication technologies to provide and promote e-infrastructure, information sharing, e-service, e-consultation, and decision participation, achieve efficiency and effectiveness, transparency and accountability, equity and rule of law, democracy and participation, and public trust and satisfaction."

We agree with the importance of clarifying the concept of ICT utilization in the public sector and define e-governance as follows: "A process of the authoritative allocation of values for a society in which government massively adopts information and communication technologies to provide and promote e-infrastructure, e-regulation, e-administration, e-service, and e-participation, and then achieve efficiency and effectiveness, transparency and accountability, equity and rule of law, democracy and participation, and public trust and satisfaction" (Huang, Chu, & Huang, 2008).

The Importance of E-Governance Impact Assessment

The success of e-governance hinges on a robust assessment strategy that provides not only a valuable understanding of the impacts of individual projects on stakeholders, including citizens, government employees, and businesses, but also an effective feedback mechanism for mid-course corrections. Governments worldwide are eager to understand the nature and extent of the impacts of e-governance. For this purpose, many institutions, such as the United Nations (UN) and Brown University, have begun gathering empirical data to evaluate e-governance in cities and countries. The UN has conducted five global e-government surveys to date (2003, 2004, 2005, 2008, and 2009). The studies assessed primary websites, such as national portals or official government home pages. The 2008 survey included 192 UN member countries. According to the UN's 2008 report (UN, 2008), this survey was "based on a questionnaire, which allocated a binary value to the indicator based on the presence/absence of specific electronic facilities/services available." The term "electronic facilities/services" refers to an e-government developmental stage model, as mentioned previously.

Although these indices are widely quoted in both academia and practice, these investigations are not only narrowly focused on e-government but also use an expert-centered perspective to deduce the performance of e-governance. However, these approaches fail to consider the impact on e-government stakeholders, resulting in a significant void (Heeks & Bailur, 2007; Huang & Lee, 2010). An e-government initiative will leave room for improvement due to a lack of understanding of the perspective of the target users (Saxena, 2005). Moreover, Bhatnagar (2007) pointed out that evidence of the outcomes of investment in ICTs by the public sector has not been fully established. Only a few studies have given attention to the impact of e-governance on users, neglecting related impact dimensions, such as political trust, political efficacy, and satisfaction. Contrary to these e-government studies, which evaluate e-government based on infrastructure and readiness and mainly focus on providers rather than receivers of services (Reddick, 2005), we propose a conceptual model that examines anecdotes of the impacts of e-governance and specifically addresses the importance of the user-centric e-governance impact assessment.

E-Government Value Chain

The significance of developing an e-governance impact assessment framework can be justified in the process of the e-government value chain (EVC) (Heeks, 2006; see Figure 1). The EVC refers to a model that illustrates how an e-governance initiative turns inputs into impacts and outcomes. The EVC model suggests that the process of creating e-government value starts from the precursors (the general environment, such as telecommunications infrastructure and human resource infrastructure) and inputs, such as the financial and political support provided by government for all of the requirements of e-government development. As a result, these precursors and government inputs, the so-called "readiness", produce quality governmental web channels or systems and enable e-government use/adoption by both external and internal customers. Finally, these adoptions/uses result in the desired outputs and outcomes for users, such as financial benefit or time saved. A comprehensive e-government assessment model should place equal emphasis on all elements within the value chain.

A well-developed e-government research field should cover all of the components in the EVC model. Early studies of e-governance performance, however, focused mainly on system evaluation and system adoption, such as the e-government website evaluation research conducted by the United Nations and Brown University, as well as the technology acceptance model, which applies to the reasoned action theory developed by Davis (1989). Even most existing e-government benchmarking studies, unfortunately, tend to focus only on the core/center of the value chain, ignoring the upstream (e.g., precursors and inputs) or even downstream (e.g., impacts, outcomes, and, to some degree, outputs) elements (Heeks, 2006; Huang & Lee, 2010). This limited focus makes it difficult to address the questions of whether e-government produces the desired value and how it does so. Heeks mentioned that the particular emphasis on intermediates is problematic because it cannot demonstrate actual adoption and use, the downstream measures. For example, a well-designed website/system can have a very low rate of use or yield unexpected outcomes.

Scholars have addressed the impact of e-governance on users from many perspectives in existing studies. For instance, impact assessment may include cost-benefit analysis, subjective expert assessment, and performance forecasts from the e-governance objective, but an impact assessment that focuses on user-oriented performance evaluation is rare. An OECD report, "E-government For Better Government" (OECD, 2005a), used cost-benefit analysis to identify the impact of e-government. That report viewed e-government

Figure 1. E-government value chain. Source: Heeks, 2006 (p.14)

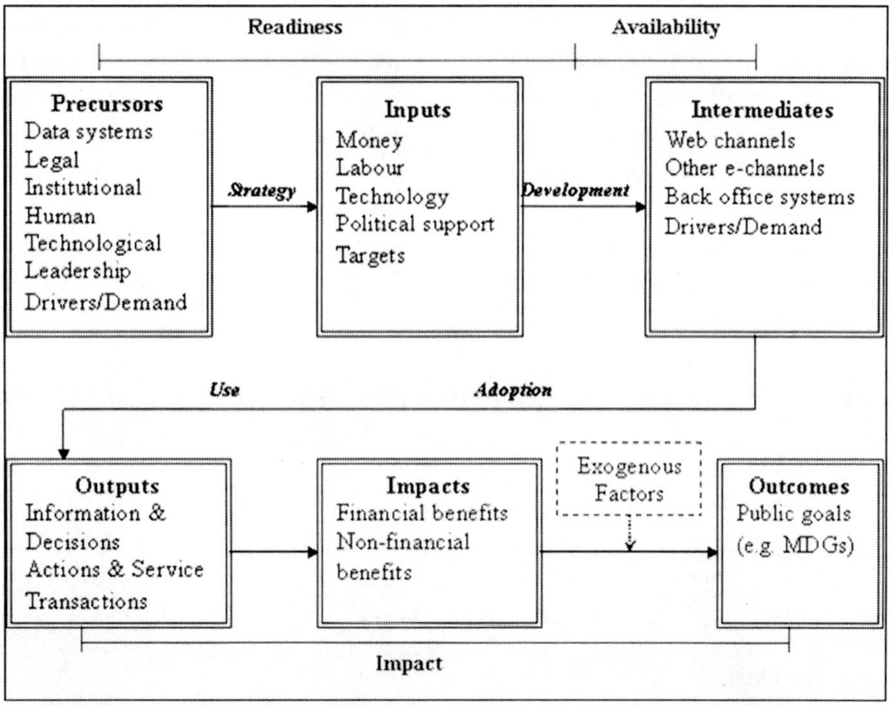

projects as a business model and laid out reasons why e-government should be estimated with cost and benefit indicators. According to this report, three types of costs and benefits resulted from e-government use (OECD, 2005b): direct financial costs and benefits, direct non-financial costs and benefits, and indirect costs and benefits.

Information System Success Model

Drawing from a review of 180 studies, DeLone and McLean (1992) developed a widely accepted information system success model, the so-called D & M Information Success Model. The original D & M model aimed to construct a framework for evaluating the performance of information systems. In their updated model (see Figure 2), DeLone and McLean (2003) proposed that information quality, systems quality, and service quality are three of the main factors affecting a user's willingness to use a system, their satisfaction with its use, and its level of impact. Particularly, they define the impact, "net benefits" in their model, of an information system as its influence on its users.

The updated model, which is based on empirical efforts that apply, test, or validate the original model, adds service quality to reflect the importance of service in information systems. It also uses a more parsimonious concept, net benefits, to substitute the individual and organizational impacts in the original model (DeLone & McLean, 2003). According to DeLone and McLean's own statistics, more than 300 articles have referred to or made use of the D & M model. For examples, Wang and Liao (2007) provided the first empirical test of the D & M model in the context of e-government. Except for the link from system quality to use, they found that the hypothesized relationships between the six success variables in the D & M model have significant support from the data. Petter and McLean (2009) used the meta-analysis method to aggregate 52 empirical studies that examine relationships within the D & M model and found support for the causal relationships in the model. The high popularity of the D & M model provides a rationale for incorporating it into our e-governance impact assessment framework.

E-SERVQUAL

The most common definition of service quality relies on a global consumer judgment of the superiority of the product or service (Parasuraman, Zeithaml& Berry, 1988), which includes the service provider's attitude and friendliness, the form and design of the physical environment, and the complexity of the service procedure (Gronroos, 1990). More specifically, Parasuraman, Zeithaml and Berry (1985) viewed customer-perceived service quality as the magnitude and direction of the discrepancy between service expectation and perceptions. They first developed a conceptual model of service quality, also called a gap model, and identified service quality as a function of four organizational gaps associated with

Figure 2. DeLone and McLean's updated IS Success Model. Source: DeLone and McLean (2003)

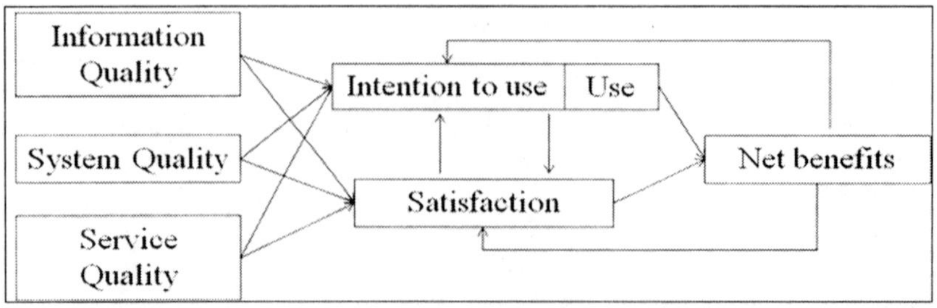

the design, marketing, and delivery of services. Parasuraman et al. (1988) developed an instrument, SERVQUAL, to assess service quality performance. SERVQUAL is a multiple-item scale consisting of five dimensions – tangibles, reliability, responsiveness, assurance and empathy – as well as 22 pairs of Likert-type items.

Zeithaml et al. (2002) followed Parasuraman et al. (1985) by developing e-SERVQUAL to measure e-service quality. Seven dimensions of e-services are included: efficiency, fulfillment, reliability, and privacy form the core e-SERVQUAL scale; responsiveness, compensation, and contact become salient when online customers have questions or encounter problems. Parasuraman, Zeithaml, and Malhotra (2005) developed E-S-QUAL and E-RecS-QUAL; the former contains the core e-SERVQUAL scale, and the latter contains the other three dimensions of the e-SERVQUAL scale. Similar scales for evaluating e-service quality have been developed. For example, WEBQUAL/eQual (Lociacono, Watson, & Goodhue, 2002) and eTailQ (Wolfinbarger & Gilly, 2003) are used to evaluate e-service quality in the service sector.

Some instruments that originated from the service sector have been employed to examine service quality in e-government services. For example, Barnes and Vidgen (2003) used WebQual, with dimensions including usability, information quality and service interaction, to assess the perceptions of users regarding the quality of a specific cross-national website provided via the OECD before and after a redesign process. They also used eQual (previously called WebQual) to analyze user perceptions of the quality of a national website provided by the UK government (Barnes & Vidgen, 2006). On the other hand, Horan, Abhichandani, & Rayalu (2006) constructed an EGOVSAT instrument, comprising utility, reliability, efficiency, customization, flexibility and sub-dimensions, to evaluate the satisfaction of users with the Advanced Travel Information System (ATIS), a form of the G2C (government to citizens) e-government service.

Public Trust

Public trust in government has declined in almost every country since 1960. Some believe the decline in public trust is due to dissatisfaction with public service or government performance (Van de Walle & Bouckaert, 2003; Christensen & Laegreid, 2005; Chanley, Virginia, Thomas, & Wendy, 2000). Because e-government has been recognized as a more efficient, effective, transparent, interactive and responsive digital means of public service, as well as an opportunity to improve public service performance, it has been proposed as a possible method for restoring public trust in government (Tolbert & Mossberger, 2006; Moon, 2003; Holzer, 2004; Parent, Vandebeek & Gemino, 2004; Welch & Hinnant, 2003). In other words, public trust is dependent on e-government use and must be included in the performance evaluation framework of e-government. According to the e-government 2020 Project funded by the European Commission, the trust of citizens is the second most important necessity for the future of e-government (Codagnone & Wimmer, 2007).

Tolbert and Mossberger (2006) theorized that public trust in government could gain strength through two approaches. The entrepreneurial approach claims that public trust in government could be facilitated through the satisfaction of citizens with e-services provided by the government. The participatory approach emphasizes the possibility that citizen participation in decision making through ICTs can elevate the trust of citizens in government. To date, however, the empirical results regarding whether e-government applications enhance the trust of citizens in government are mixed. Tolbert and Mossberger found a statistically significant relationship between the use of websites by governments and trust. They believe that e-government can increase process-based trust by improving the public's interactions with government. Welch, Hinnant and Moon (2005) also found a positive association between users' satisfaction with government websites and their trust in government. They believed that this result indicates that e-government is becoming increasingly embedded into citizen conceptions of government performance assessment. Moon (2003) argued that using government websites could enhance user satisfaction with government, which could in turn increase trust in government. Morgeson, VanAmburg & Mithas (2010), in contrast, found that e-government does not correlate with greater trust in the federal government. West (2004) found no significant effect of visiting federal government websites on public trust.

E-GOVERNANCE IMPACT ASSESSMENT FRAMEWORK

The current research integrates the e-governance value chain model proposed by Heeks (2006) and the D & M Model (2003) to propose a fundamental framework of e-governance impact (see Figure 3). The framework proposes to divide the e-governance impact assessment into three related causal blocks: QUALITY, USAGE, and IMPACT. We define each of these constructs and develop the theoretical rationale for the causal relationship in this framework below (see Figure 4).

QUALITY Dimension

QUALITY describes the quality of the website (system quality), the information quality, and the service quality. Quality of websites (or systems) refers to the measurements of the information processing system. The widely cited global e-government surveys conducted by the UN and Brown University focused on this dimension. The main indicators of system quality are website content (West, 2008; Holzer & Kim, 2007), accessibility, privacy protection, Internet security (Holzer & Kim, 2007; Panopoulou, Tambouris & Tarabanis, 2008), multilingual design (West, 2008), and usability (Holzer & Kim, 2007). Information quality refers to the output of the information system. Ahituv (1980) pointed out five required information features of an information system: accuracy, timeliness, relevance, aggregation, and formatting. Bailey and Pearson's (1983) integration is a very good base for conceptualizing the variables of information quality in an e-governance system. They proposed nine characteristics of information quality: accuracy, precision, currency, timeliness, reliability, completeness, conciseness, format, and relevance.

Finally, service quality plays a role in e-governance quality. In the updated model proposed by DeLone & McLean (2003), they argued that service quality, measured by the SERVQUAL measurement instrument from marketing, should

Figure 3. E-governance impact framework. Source: this study

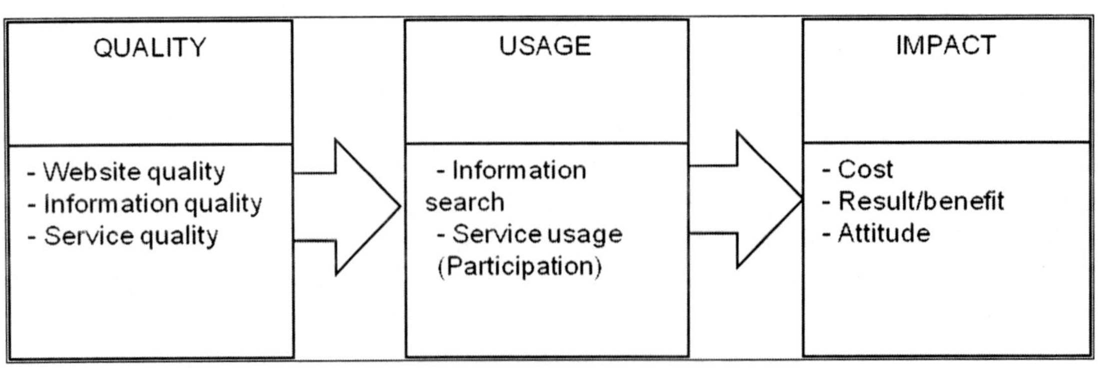

Figure 4. Conceptualization of the e-governance impact framework. Source: this study

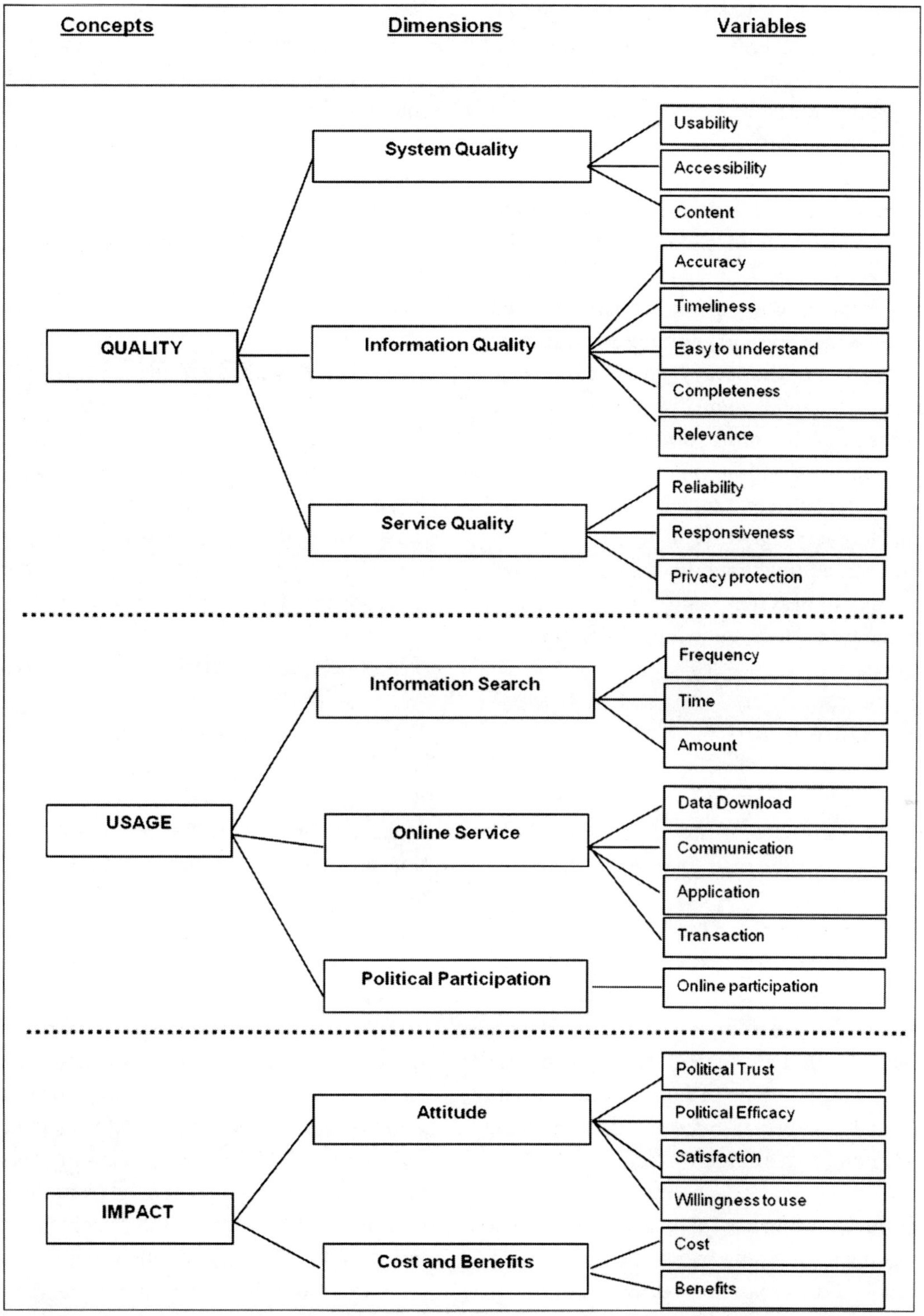

be added to the success model. According to Parasuraman et al. (1985), the SERVQUAL instrument items include tangibility, reliability, responsiveness, assurance, and empathy.

USAGE Dimension

The concept USAGE is similar to "adoption behavior" in the technology acceptance model (TAM) developed by Davis (1986). Because e-governance encompasses e-government (focused mostly on information and administrative service provision) and e-democracy (focused mostly on online civic engagement), we argue that the e-governance user application should enable searching for information, online service usage, and democratic participation. However, this does not mean that every e-governance system provides all of these three functions. In some cases, such as online tax-filing systems and e-procurement in Taiwan, the types of usage would fall only under online services.

IMPACT Dimension

The IMPACT construct encompasses the costs, benefits, and attitudes of the user. All of these impacts were addressed in OECD's report (2005b). According to OECD (2005b), the first type of impact of e-governance on users refers to the most immediate and easily quantified return. For a citizen or business, the first impact can be in the form of time and money saved by finding information online and using an online public service. The second type of impact relates to attitude, which includes user satisfaction and trust in government. According to Welch et al. (2005), the use of government websites has a positive association with citizens' satisfaction and trust in government. The study by Parent, Vandebeek, and Gemino (2004) pointed out that the use of e-government could significantly improve the trust and political efficacy of citizens. Tolbert and Mossberger (2006) found that local government website visits enhance citizens' trust in local government.

The e-governance impact framework proposed in the study can serve as the basis of any future integrated or single-system e-governance impact assessment. We believe that user-oriented performance impact can be more validly evaluated by adapting this framework to operationalize the assessment indicator of a particular e-governance case.

IMPACT ASSESSMENT FOR G2B

This study aims to develop a solid application of the e-governance impact framework proposed in Figure 4 to a government-to-business (G2B) case. This section first introduces the G2B case under evaluation and then describes the data collection methods employed and the survey results.

The G2B Case and Data Collection

We utilize the Labor Insurance System (LIS) provided by Taiwan's Council of Labor Affairs as the G2B application for our evaluation. The LIS serves as a one-stop online portal for business and non-profit organizations that apply for, inquire about, and process mandatory labor insurance for their employees. Launched in 1999 along with all online e-governance systems in Taiwan, the LIS is a popular alternative to the traditional paperwork required by labor insurance. Starting in 2002, the LIS advanced its efficiency and security by issuing electronic identification cards (EIDs) for organizations. More than 650,000 organizations have adopted the LIS for processing labor insurance affairs based on statistics from the Council of Labor Affairs from 2009, ranking it second among all G2B online applications.

We drafted the survey questions (see Tables 1-3) according to the conceptualizations of relevant dimensions and variables proposed in Figure 4 above. The items selected for the constructs in our model are mainly adapted from prior studies to ensure content validity. For example, information quality is evaluated in terms of the output of the information system, which refers to the ease of understanding and completeness of the information, which is operationalized using two items adapted from Barnes & Vidgen (2007). We used three items modified from Parasuraman et al. (2005) and Barnes and Vidgen (2007) to assess service quality: reliability, responsiveness, and privacy protection of the system. We used two items modified from Gibert, Balestrini, and Littleboy (2004) to measure the attitude of the customer toward the system: customer satisfaction and willingness to continue use. To further ensure the validity of the questionnaire, we invited ten expert business users to suggest possible revisions, which were made accordingly.

In 2009, with the assistance of the EID issuance unit in the Department of Commerce, an online invitation was distributed to all of the organizations registered on the LIS. The organizations were invited to browse the survey website to decide if they were interested in completing the survey questions. From August 17 to September 4, 8,580 organizations browsed the survey website; 4,684 of them finished the questionnaire, with 4,023 providing valid responses. Of the responding organizations, 60.5% are located in northern Taiwan. 39.1% have been in business for 10 years, and 33.6% have been in business for 11-20 years. In addition, nearly half of the responding organizations reported that more than 80% of their employees had adopted computerized systems, although less than half reported that they had independent IT units in their organizations. The sample statistics show that the organizations using the LIS, despite their various sizes and scales (in terms of number of full-time employees), have high-level digital literacy when dealing with general business concerns. The reliability measures in terms of Cronbach's alpha are above 0.7 for all dimensions.

Table 1. The survey results for the QUALITY dimension

	Very negative	Negative	Neutral	Positive	Very positive	Don't know
System Quality						
Readability of the LIS interface (n = 4,021)	73 (1.8%)	400 (9.9%)	1,691 (42%)	1,550 (38.5%)	201 (5%)	106 (2.6%)
Overall ease of use of the LIS (n = 4,018)	110 (2.7%)	436 (10.8%)	1,589 (39.5%)	1,581 (39.3%)	188 (4.7%)	114 (2.85%)
Information Quality						
Understandability of the online help (n = 4,015)	62 (1.5%)	350 (8.7%)	1,825 (45.5%)	1,516 (37.8%)	104 (2.6%)	158 (3.9%)
Completeness of the online help (n = 4,012)	55 (1.4%)	349 (8.7%)	2,150 (53.6%)	1,194 (29.8%)	82 (2%)	182 (4.5%)
Service Quality						
Reliability for fulfilling the task (n = 4,107)	71 (1.8%)	208 (5.2%)	904 (22.5%)	2,280 (56.8%)	419 (10.4%)	135 (3.4%)
Responsiveness for the questions asked (n = 4,019)	69 (1.7%)	323 (8%)	1,388 (34.5%)	1,640 (40.8%)	169 (4.2%)	430 (10.7%)
Effective privacy protection (n = 4,016)	50 (1.2%)	169 (4.2%)	1,225 (30.5%)	1,565 (39%)	134 (3.3%)	873 (21.7%)

Source: this study

The Results for the USAGE Dimension

Although the LIS has been widely adopted among the business and non-profit sectors in Taiwan, the usage frequency varies based on the responding organizations: 90% reported an online duration of less than 3 hours per week, which may be due to the highly routine nature of labor insurance matters. In addition, 2,677 organizations (66.5%) did not use online and phone help, although 2,711 organizations (67.4%) searched for information, such as related regulations and online functions. The results imply that the LIS online search and help functions are so mature and easily accessible that most adopting organizations do not have to ask for additional help by phone or email.

Further survey evidence about organizations' usage behavior is promising for the future of LIS. In particular, 85.1% (3,424) of the respondents believed that the online application and inquiry for labor insurance is a sustainable trend for future operation, and 52.3% (2,105) adopted the LIS due to sustained promotion from the government. The widespread adoption of the LIS implies that the G2B case examined here has met with at least initial success in its promotion. While labor insurance affairs are mandatory for all profit and non-profit organizations in Taiwan, the LIS has also gained the support of users in terms of usage outcome, which not all G2B and G2C e-governance applications currently have. The evaluation below concerning the QUALITY dimension may explain some of the success of the LIS.

The Results for the QUALITY Dimension

Table 1 summarizes the LIS users' quality perceptions. Overall, the responding organizations largely approved of the system, information, and service quality of the LIS, particularly its usefulness for fulfilling labor insurance tasks (67.2% positive). All quality measures received less than 15% negative evaluation. Ease of use (13.5% negative and 39.5% neutral) demonstrates room for improvement. Based on an inspection by the authors, the LIS interface appears outdated in its design, especially compared with newer websites.

The Results for the IMPACT Dimension

The impact measures summarized in Table 2 indicate mostly positive responses from the responding organizations regarding their experience adopting the LIS. Particularly, they perceive that only a small burden is necessary to adopt the LIS in terms of financial and manpower considerations and the risk taken. Though not sufficiently high in satisfaction, respondents showed less than 10% dissatisfaction, coupled with more than half indicating the possibility of continued use of the LIS. All measures of cost reduction earned more than 60% positive perceptions from the respondents, as did all measures of time and effort benefits. The responding organizations showed at least 40% positive and less than 15% negative evaluations for business flow integration and trust in the labor insurance and government.

Examining individual dimensions and variables also sheds light on the impact of LIS in more detail. Particularly, among the three types of resources allocated by the responding firms to adopt the LIS, the privacy risk stands out compared with financial and manpower investments. Although that finding appears consistent with most empirical evidence concerning e-government and the Internet, it may result from the nature of the LIS platform of handling personal data, such as salary and health status.

Correlation and Cross-Tabulation Analyses

A series of cross-tabulations revealed more instructive results and policy implications. Relative contributions to the overall satisfaction with the

Table 2. The survey results for the IMPACT dimension

Satisfaction						
	Very negative	Negative	Neutral	Positive	Very positive	Don't know
Satisfaction with online and offline help (*n* = 4,021)	56 (1.4%)	197 (4.9%)	1,738 (43.2%)	1,335 (33.2%)	115 (2.9%)	580 (14.4%)
Overall satisfaction with the LIS (*n* = 4,016)	63 (1.6%)	212 (5.3%)	1,510 (37.6%)	1,953 (48.6%)	127 (3.2%)	151 (3.8%)
Willingness to continuous use						
Willing to continue using the LIS (*n* = 4,016)	0-20%	20-40%	40-60%	60-80%	80-100%	
	378 (9.4%)	997 (24.8%)	2,636 (65.5%)	2 (0%)	3 (0%)	NA
Resources allocated						
	Very low	Low	Mid.	High	Very high	
Financial investment (*n* = 4,023)	1,004 (24.9%)	1,501 (37.3%)	1,472 (36.6%)	41 (1%)	5 (0.1%)	NA
Extra manpower allocated (*n* = 4,022)	914 (22.7%)	1,603 (39.8%)	1,460 (36.3%)	40 (1%)	5 (0.1%)	NA
Extra risk for privacy (*n* = 4,022)	306 (7.7%)	920 (22.9%)	2,554 (63.5%)	211 (5.2%)	31 (0.8%)	NA
Cost reduction						
	Very negative	Negative	Neutral	Positive	Very positive	Don't know
Labor cost reduced (*n* = 4,022)	40 (1%)	293 (7.3%)	1,072 (26.6%)	1,944 (48.3%)	563 (14%)	110 (2.7%)
Materials saved (*n* = 4,023)	52 (1.3%)	343 (8.5%)	1,019 (25.3%)	1,861 (46.2%)	673 (16.7%)	75 (1.9%)
Communication cost saved (*n* = 4,022)	26 (0.6%)	111 (2.8%)	642 (16%)	2,234 (55.5%)	947 (23.5%)	63 (1.6%)
Transportation cost reduced (*n* = 4,023)	20 (0.5%)	125 (3.1%)	517 (12.8%)	2,254 (56%)	1,033 (25.7%)	74 (1.8%)
Time and effort benefits						
	Very negative	Negative	Neutral	Positive	Very positive	Don't know
Manpower reduced (*n* = 4,022)	32 (0.8%)	147 (3.7%)	531 (13.2%)	2,339 (58.2%)	889 (22.1%)	84 (2.1%)
Faster service received (*n* = 4,022)	37 (0.9%)	135 (3.4%)	929 (23.1%)	2,238 (55.6%)	564 (14%)	119 (3%)
Overall convenience gained (*n* = 4,022)	40 (1%)	134 (3.3%0	638 (15.9%)	2,367 (58.8%)	763 (19%)	80 (2%)
Additional benefits						
	Very negative	Negative	Neutral	Positive	Very positive	Don't know
Business flow integration (*n* = 4,022)	60 (1.5%)	401 (10%)	1,735 (43.1%)	1,441 (35.8%)	168 (4.2%)	218 (5.4%)
Increasing trust in the labor insurance (*n* = 4,022)	41 (1%)	163 (4%)	1,528 (38%)	1,910 (47.5%)	222 (5.5%)	158 (3.9%)
Increasing overall trust in government (*n* = 4,023)	69 (1.7%)	264 (6.6%)	1,825 (45.3%)	1,500 (37.3%)	154 (3.8%)	211 (5.2%)

Source: this study

LIS resulted from the following quality measures (of those in Table 1), respectively ($p = 5\%$): ease of use (bivariate $r = 0.639$), usefulness ($r = 0.608$), online help understandability ($r = 0.582$), any question's being resolved effectively ($r = 0.578$), interface readability ($r = 0.573$), online help completeness ($r = 0.549$), and effective privacy protection ($r = 0.469$). These quality measures also affect the willingness of firms to utilize the LIS in the future, in approximately the same order. In addition, the overall satisfaction closely corresponds to firms' trust in the LIS ($r = 0.513$) and in the government overall ($r = 0.498$), with statistical significance ($p = 5\%$). Further practice and research are necessary to describe the causal model for e-governance impact assessment.

Some demographics and characteristics of the responding firms appear to affect the quality and impact measures in Table 1 and Table 2. First, firms with more employees relying on ICTs in their work (60% and above) tend to show more willingness to utilize the LIS when compared with those firms with the lowest proportion of these employees (less than 20%). More interestingly, firms with 60-80% computerized work show higher overall satisfaction than those with less than 20% and those with higher than 80%. We argue that the firms with the middle-to-high (60-80%) level of computerization may receive a relatively large "marginal benefit" from adopting the LIS compared with those above the 80% level. On the other hand, those with less than 20% of the workforce computerized require more scale and experience to receive the benefits contributed by the LIS.

In addition, the extent to which the firms rely on the e-business model in transactions with their external customers influences cost reduction. Particularly, the firms with the highest ICT-based interaction with their customers benefit from LIS adoption via more significant cost reduction, including labor, materials, communication and transportation, as shown in Table 2. Time and effort benefits, including manpower, faster service and overall convenience, correlate with the same e-business model developed by the surveyed firms.

DISCUSSION AND CONCLUSION

Most e-government impact assessment studies are either conceptual process models or case studies examining the factors contributing to the success or failure of e-government, such as infrastructure investments, system accessibility and service quality, usage and citizen satisfaction. This research further elaborates and elucidates the theoretical underpinnings of the relationships among those factors. This study integrates the e-governance value chain model proposed by Heeks (2006) and the information technology system success model proposed by DeLone and McLean (2003) to propose a conceptual model to examine empirical evidence of the impact of e-governance. The results indicate high levels of satisfaction.

The current study, as exhibited in Figure 4, proposes a framework derived from the literature to evaluate G2B e-governance, including dimensions of use, quality and impact. Taking the labor insurance system (LIS) as the case example, we apply the framework and evaluate the LIS by administering an online survey of organizations regarding their experience in adopting the LIS. Based on the survey results, we will now discuss in more detail future directions for system improvements, e-government policy implications, and approaches to future research on e-governance impact assessment.

System Improvements

The LIS interface, like many government websites, appears outdated in its design, especially compared to new websites. Because a website's visitor is the only person who clicks the mouse and, therefore, decides everything, user-centric design has become a standard approach for successful web design. The higher the cognitive load induced by a website and the less intuitive its navigation, the less willing users will be to remain at and continue to use the website. Visual design, usability, and stability are three important areas for improvement of the LIS interface and other government websites in general. In addition, the LIS platform inquires and provides information about people and businesses, such as salary and income. Although the Council for Labor Affairs claims that they have significantly improved the service efficiency, responsiveness and most of all, privacy protection of the LIS, the interactive design for process control and the information template for the privacy protection policy should be further enhanced.

Because specialization and information silos are two of the key factors behind the occurrence of fragmented responses (Linden, 2010), one-stop service with inter-organizational integration, even linked governments, has become a crucial element for cross-boundary electronic governance. Continuous process re-engineering and service integration across departments or agencies are challenging but necessary steps for the improvement of the LIS.

Policy Implications

Aside from the evidence provided by the survey, the most significant implication of the study lies in its conceptualization and operationalization of the impact of e-governance, including measurement and procedure. All governmental agencies that have delivered e-governance G2B services benefit from the measurement and procedure of comprehensive evaluation. We believe that bureaucrats, political executives, legislators, and mass media can obtain additional solid evidence about how well e-governance programs have been implemented. Such evidence would undoubtedly affect resource allocation in prospective e-governance policies and programs. The evidence and experience of the study also leads to the strong recommendation that all e-governance programs in the future should be required to implement plans for evaluation before they initiate the legal process of budget allocation and approval.

The evidence from the correlation analyses deserves note for the LIS and for e-governance practice in general. Based on the degree of overall satisfaction in the LIS, the public agencies providing online G2B services should aim to improve the usefulness, ease of use, and the online and offline help of online G2B systems. As evidenced in many previous studies, user-oriented functions, friendly system/website interfaces, and helpful customer services contribute to the fundamental success of any e-governance project.

Conclusion and Future Research

This paper makes several contributions to the e-governance literature. First, it provides empirical evidence of the impacts of G2B programs. Prior research on this topic has usually focused on theoretical discussions and implementation strategies surrounding e-government. Largely missing is the development of empirical evidence for generalization. Second, though the positive assessment of G2B has been reported in a limited way, related impact dimensions, such as political trust, political efficacy, and satisfaction, have been neglected. This paper brings together insights from the public administration and management information systems literatures and tests system, information, and service quality, usage, and the overall impacts of G2B. Third, to ensure validity, this study experimented with a new approach by inviting actual G2B users to thoroughly experience the selected G2B applications and report their findings. The study also held a series of validity focus groups to collect expert opinions and feedback about the survey questionnaires. Last, past research usually focused on one or two e-government programs, failing to offer a complete picture. This paper assesses three G2B programs, and the resulting findings will be valuable for understanding the complexity of various G2B programs and predicting the impacts of e-government.

The present study has several limitations that should be noted and addressed by future research. First of all, this study did not investigate the impact of changes in perception and behavior with regard to the usage of G2B services over a significant period of time. It is therefore recommended that further research examine whether, with increasing experience over time, there is any reduction in unnecessary lobbying or bribery in government procurement, thereby increasing trust in government. Second, in addition to earlier evaluations of e-government based on infrastructure and readiness, our assessment of e-governance mainly focuses on external user satisfaction. While citizen-centric evaluations of e-governance offer an important lens through which to assess the performance of e-government, another crucial but neglected dimension is the impact of e-governance on internal users, that is, the civil servants who provide services to the public. To consider the importance of internal and external customers, future research may require an impact assessment of e-governance on internal and external users. Finally, this paper does not cover the causal effects among service quality, system use, customer satisfaction, impact and outcome. Further investigation of the impacts of e-government should be carried out to develop causal e-governance performance models to fill a void in the existing literature.

ACKNOWLEDGMENT

This chapter was supported by the "Outsourcing Services Program of the E-governance Research Center" under the Research, Development and Evaluation Commission, Executive Yuan, Taiwan, R.O.C.

REFERENCES

Ahituv, N. (1980). A systematic approach toward assessing the value of an information system. *Management Information Systems Quarterly*, *4*(4), 61–75. doi:10.2307/248961

Backus, M. (2001). E-governance and developing countries: Introduction and examples. *IICD Research Report, 3.* Retrieved April 30, 2010, from http://www.ftpiicd.org/files/ research/reports/report3.doc

Bailey, J. E., & Pearson, S. W. (1983). Development of a tool for measuring and analyzing computer user satisfaction. *Management Science*, *29*(5), 530–545. doi:10.1287/mnsc.29.5.530

Barnes, S. J., & Vidgen, R. (2003). Measuring website quality improvements: A case study of the forum on strategic management knowledge exchange. *Industrial Management & Data Systems*, *103*(5), 297–309. doi:10.1108/02635570310477352

Barnes, S. J., & Vidgen, R. (2006). Data triangulation and Web quality metrics: A case study in e-government. *Information & Management*, *43*, 767–777. doi:10.1016/j.im.2006.06.001

Barnes, S. J., & Vidgen, R. (2007). Interactive e-government: Evaluating the website of the UK inland revenue. *International Journal of Electronic Government Research*, *3*(1), 19–37. doi:10.4018/jegr.2007010102

Bhatnagar, S. (2007). *Impact assessment study of computerized services delivery projects from India and Chile*. IT@WEB Staff working Papers. Retrieved April 28, 2009, from http://www.iimahd.ernet.in/ egov/documents/ impact-assessment-study-wbr.pdf

Bishop, P., & Anderson, L. (2004). *E-government to e-democracy: High tech solutions to no tech problems*. Paper presented at the Australian Electronic Governance Conference, Centre for Public Policy, University of Melbourne, Melbourne Victoria.

Chadwick, A. (2003). Bring e-democracy back in: Why it matters for future research on e-governance. *Social Science Computer Review*, *21*(4), 443–455. doi:10.1177/0894439303256372

Chanley, Virginia, A., Thomas, J. R., & Wendy, M.R. (2000). The origins and consequences of public trust in government: A time serious analysis. *Public Opinion Quarterly*, *64*, 239–256. doi:10.1086/317987

Chiang, M. S., Chen, T. Y., Huang, D. Y., Chung, K. J., & Hsiao, N. Y. (2004). *Utilizing ICTs to realize citizen participation: Vision, cases, and strategies*. Institute for the Information Industry.

Christensen, T., & Laegreid, P. (2005). Trust in government: The relative importance of service satisfaction, political factors, and demography. *Public Performance & Management Review*, *28*(4), 487–511.

Cristiano, C., & Wimmer, M. A. (Eds.). (2007). Roadmapping e-government research: Visions and measures towards innovative governments in 2020. *EC-funded Project eGovRTD2020*. Retrieved July 19, 2010, from http://www.egovrtd2020.org/ EGOVRTD2020/FinalBook.pdf

Davis, F. D. (1989). Perceived usefulness, perceived ease of use and user acceptance of Information Technology. *Management Information Systems Quarterly*, *13*(3), 318–339. doi:10.2307/249008

DeLone, W. H., & McLean, E. R. (1992). Information System success: The quest for the dependent variable. *Information Systems Research*, *3*(1), 60–95. doi:10.1287/isre.3.1.60

DeLone, W. H., & McLean, E. R. (2003). The DeLone and McLean model of Information System success: A ten-year update. *Journal of Management Information Systems*, *19*(4), 9–30.

Finger, M., & Pecoud, G. (2003). *From e-government to e-governance? Towards a model of e-governance*. Paper presented at the 3rd European Conference on e-Government, Trinity College Dublin, Ireland.

Gilbert, D., Balestrini, P., & Littleboy, D. (2004). Barriers and benefits in the adoption of e-government. *International Journal of Public Sector Management*, *17*(4), 286–301. doi:10.1108/09513550410539794

Gronroos, C. (1990). *Service management and marketing: Managing the moments of truth in service competition*. Lexington, MA: Lexington Books.

Heeks, R. (2006). *Benchmarking e-government: Improving the national and international measurement, evaluation and comparison of e-government*. Paper presented at iGovernment Working Paper, 18, Manchester, UK: University of Manchester.

Heeks, R., & Bailur, S. (2007). Analyzing e-government research: Perspectives, philosophies, theories, methods, and practice. *Government Information Quarterly*, *24*, 243–265. doi:10.1016/j.giq.2006.06.005

Holzer, M. (2004, May). *Restoring trust in government: The potential of digital citizen participation*. Paper presented at the Second Sino-U.S. International Conference: Public Administration in the Changing World? China, Beijing.

Holzer, M., & Kim, S. (2007). *Digital governance in municipalities worldwide -- A longitudinal assessment of municipal websites throughout the world*. Paper presented at The e-governance Institute, National Center for Public Performance, Rutgers, the State University of New Jersey, Campus at Newark.

Horan, T. A., Abhichandani, T., & Rayalu, R. (2006). *Assessing user satisfaction of e-government services: Development and testing of quality-in-use satisfaction with Advanced Traveler Information System (ATIS)*. Paper presented at the 39th Hawaii International Conference on System Sciences, Hawaii.

Hunag, C. M., Chu, P. Y., & Huang, T. Y. (2008). *Evaluation and analysis of e-governance in Taiwan (*G2G, G2E). Taiwan e-Governance Research Center. Taipei. Retrieved August 27, 2010, from http://www.teg.org.tw/research /view.do?id=24&language=en

Hunag, T. Y., & Lee, C. P. (2010). Evaluating the impact of e-government on citizens: A cost-benefit analysis. In Reddick, C. G. (Ed.), *Citizens and e-government: Evaluating policy and management* (pp. 37–52). Hershey, PA: IGI Global. doi:10.4018/978-1-61520-931-6.ch003

Lenk, K., & Traunmüller, R. (2002). Electronic government: Where are we heading? In Lenk, K., & Traunmüller, R. (Eds.), *Electronic government: First international conference, EGOV 2002* (pp. 1–9). New York, NY: Springer.

Linden, R. M. (2010). *Leading across boundaries: Creating collaborative agencies in a networked world*. San Francisco, CA: Jossey-Bass.

Lociacano, E., Watson, R. T., & Goodhue, D. (2002). WebQUAL: A measure of website quality. *Marketing Educators' Conference. Marketing Theory and Applications*, *13*, 432–437.

Mahrer, H., & Krimmer, R. (2005). Towards the enhancement of e-democracy: Identifying the notion of the middleman paradox. *Information Systems Journal*, *15*(1), 27–42. doi:10.1111/j.1365-2575.2005.00184.x

Marche, S., & McNiven, J. D. (2003). E-government and e-governance: The future isn't what it used to be. *Canadian Journal of Administrative Sciences*, *20*(1), 74–86. doi:10.1111/j.1936-4490.2003.tb00306.x

Moon, M. J. (2003). *Can IT help government to restore public trust? Declining public trust and potential prospects of IT in the public sector.* Paper presented at the 36th Hawaii International Conference on System Sciences.

Morgeson, F. V., III, VanAmburg, D., & Mithas, S. (2010, April). Misplaced trust? Exploring the structure of the e-government-citizen trust relationship. *Journal of Public Administration Research and Theory Advance Access*. Retrieved from http://jpart.oxfordjournals.org/ content/ early/2010/04/25/ jopart.muq006.abstract

OECD. (2005a). *E-government for better government*. OECD publishing.

OECD. (2005b). *Proposed outline for accessing e-government benefits*. OECD publishing. Retrieved February 18, 2008, from http://webdomino1.oecd.org/ COMNET/PUM/egovproweb.nsf/ viewHtml/ index/$FILE/ GOV.PGC.EGOV.2006.1.doc

Panopoulou, E., Tambouris, E., & Tarabanis, K. (2008). A framework for evaluating websites of public authorities. *Aslib Proceedings*, *60*(5), 517–546. doi:10.1108/00012530810908229

Parasuraman, A., Zeithaml, V. A., & Berry, L. L. (1985). A conceptual model of service quality and its implications for future research. *Journal of Marketing*, *49*(Fall), 41–50. doi:10.2307/1251430

Parasuraman, A., Zeithaml, V. A., & Berry, L. L. (1988). SERVQUAL: A multiple-item scale for measuring consumer perceptions of service quality. *Journal of Retailing*, *64*(1), 12–40.

Parasuraman, A., Zeithaml, V. A., & Malhotra, A. (2005). E-S-QUAL: A multiple-item scale for assessing electronic service quality. *Journal of Service Research*, *7*(3), 213–233. doi:10.1177/1094670504271156

Parent, M., Vandebeek, C. A., & Gemino, A. C. (2004). *Building citizen trust through e-government*. Paper presented at the 37th Hawaii International Conference on System Sciences. Retrieved February 18, 2008, from http://csdl2.computer.org/ comp/proceedings/hicss/2004/2056/05/205650119a.pdf

Petter, S., & Ephraim, R. M. (2009, April). A meta-analytic assessment of the DeLone and McLean IS success model: An examination of IS success at the individual level. *Information & Management*, *46*(3), 159–166. doi:10.1016/j.im.2008.12.006

Reddick, C. G. (2005). Citizen interaction with e-government: From the streets to servers? *Government Information Quarterly*, *22*, 38–57. doi:10.1016/j.giq.2004.10.003

Saxena, K. B. C. (2005). Towards excellence in e-governance. *International Journal of Public Sector Management*, *18*(6), 498–513. doi:10.1108/09513550510616733

The United Nations. (2003). *World public sector report 2003: E-government at the crossroads*. New York, NY: UN.

The United Nations. (2008). *United Nations e-government survey 2008: From e-government to connected governance*. New York, NY: UN.

The United Nations /ASPA. (2001). *Benchmarking e-government: A global perspective*. Retrieved April 30, 2010, from http://unpan1.un.org/intradoc/ groups/public/documents/un/unpan021547.pdf

Tolbert, C. J., & Mossberger, K. (2006). The effects of e-government on trust and confidence in government. *Public Administration Review*, *66*(3), 354–369. doi:10.1111/j.1540-6210.2006.00594.x

Van de Walle, S., & Bouckaert, G. (2003). Public service performance and trust in government: The problem of causality. *International Journal of Public Administration*, *26*(8-9), 891–913. doi:10.1081/PAD-120019352

Wang, Y. S., & Liao, Y. W. (2008, October). Assessing e-government systems success: A validation of the DeLone and McLean model of Information Systems success. *Government Information Quarterly*, *25*(4), 717–733. doi:10.1016/j.giq.2007.06.002

Welch, E. W., & Hinnant, C. C. (2003). *Internet use, transparency, and interactivity effects on trust in government*. Paper presented at the 36th Annual Hawaii International Conference on System Sciences (HICSS'03), Hawaii, USA.

Welch, E. W., Hinnant, C. C., & Moon, M. J. (2005). Linking citizen satisfaction with e-government and trust in government. *Journal of Public Administration: Research and Theory*, *15*(3), 371–391. doi:10.1093/jopart/mui021

West, D. M. (2004). E-government and the transformation of service delivery and citizen attitudes. *Public Administration Review*, *64*(1), 15–27. doi:10.1111/j.1540-6210.2004.00343.x

West, D. M. (2008). *Improving technology utilization in electronic government around the world*. Retrieved April 30, 2010, from http://psiplatform.net/content/ download/14972/187426/file/0817_egovernment_west.pdf

Wolfinbarger, M. F., & Gilly, M. C. (2003). eTailQ: Dimensionalizing, measuring, and predicting e-tail quality. *Journal of Retailing*, *79*(3), 183–198. doi:10.1016/S0022-4359(03)00034-4

Zeithaml, V. A., Parasuraman, A., & Malhotra, A. (2002). Service quality delivery through websites: A critical review of extant knowledge. *Academy of Marketing Science Journal*, *30*(4), 362–375. doi:10.1177/009207002236911

Chapter 10

Using Internet Survey to Evaluate the Effects of E-Government: The Case of Taiwan's Tax Return Filing System

Tong-Yi Huang
National Chengchi University, Taiwan

Chung-Pin Lee
Tamkang University, Taiwan

Naiyi Hsiao
National Chengchi University, Taiwan

ABRSTACT

This chapter examines the case of an online survey regarding the assessment of the tax return filing system in Taiwan. The aim is to illustrate the strengths and limitations of utilizing on-line surveys to evaluate the performance of e-government. Based on our findings, we propose suggestions pertaining to increasing the quality of the survey as well as how to collaborate with a government agency while conducting a survey concerning sensitive issues. This is pioneering, and perhaps is the first attempt to address the methodological and administrative issues of an on-line survey in collaboration with the public sector. We invite and encourage future efforts to confront such issues, to advance and enrich methodological discussions, and to make online survey a useful tool for evaluating government performance not only with regard to e-government effects but also on other programs.

INTRODUCTION

Since the last decade, governments worldwide have invested enormous efforts to construct the infrastructure of e-government systems, to streamline internal administrative processes, to provide information, and to deliver public services. Such efforts in e-government have consumed considerable resources in both advanced as well as developing countries and the evaluation of the effects of electronic governance has become an imperative task for practitioners as well as

DOI: 10.4018/978-1-60960-753-1.ch010

scholars. Traditional survey research techniques, such as face-to-face interviews, mail surveys and telephone interviews have been employed to evaluate e-government.1 As the number of people connected to the Internet is increasing rapidly, Internet survey has been used widely in the private sector. As a result scholars have invested enormous efforts in developing and comparing different internet survey designs (Christian, Dillman, & Smyth, 2007; Dillman, Phelps, Tortora, Swift, Kohrell, Berck, & Messer, 2009; Hoonalker & Carayon, 2009; Smyth, Dillman, Christian, & O'Neill, 2010). Such new techniques, however, are rarely applied to assessing e-government nor are they subject to systematic appraisal. In addition to the limits of ordinary online questionnaires, using this technique to evaluate e-government services would involve the public sector and, thus, would entail certain limitations beyond issues related to the private sector.

To remedy the lack of current literature focused on the methodological issues related to using the internet survey to evaluate e-government, this chapter examines the case of employing an Internet survey to assess the effects of Taiwan's Tax Return Filing System on its users. By examining the case in Taiwan, this chapter aims to explore the two problems that arise when online questionnaires are used in assessing the system of e-government. The first problem is with the limitations arising from the use of the ordinary Internet survey, and the second problem is with the difficulties brought about by the survey's use in the public sector. Such a methodological analysis is essential from three perspectives. First, a sound data collection method will enable the researcher to gather high-quality data, which is the foundation for a precise evidence-based assessment of the e-government system and its further reform. Second, methodological issues relating to the administration of the survey and project management have practical implications for practitioners as well as researchers. Third, the methodological case study of the online survey adds a public dimension to current analysis and contributes to methodological discussions in the survey research literature.

The next section will briefly review the literature available on internet surveying, with an emphasis on the benefits and limitations that have been identified by scholars. The third section describes how the survey was conducted, which is followed by an analysis of the limitations in the forth section. The last section discusses our findings and proposes suggestions for implementing Internet surveys to evaluate e-government systems.

BACKGROUND

The Internet has been gaining prominence as a medium of communication, a tool for entertainment, and a new frontier for survey research. As social science researchers look to Internet surveys to possibly replace the more traditional modes of surveying, it has become necessary to examine the literature available to identify what scholars are saying about this new development. Fricker and Schonlau (2002) state, "Internet-based surveys are now in vogue – those conducted via the Web in particular – because of three assumptions: (1) Internet-based surveys are much cheaper to conduct; (4) Internet-based surveys are faster; and (3) when combined with other survey modes, Internet-based surveys yield higher response rates than conventional survey modes by themselves" (p. 2). The following section is divided into two main categories, focusing on the benefits and the limitations of using the Internet to conduct surveys, while also addressing the three assumptions noted by Fricker and Rand.

Benefits

The first assumption presented is that internet-based surveys are cheaper than the more traditional modes. Kaplowitz, Hadlock, and Levine (2004) have argued that one of the potential advantages associated with the use of the internet-based surveys is in the cost savings that result from eliminating the printing and mailing of paper survey questionnaires. Another advantage in cost is in the time and labor saved when the returned survey data is already in electronic format.

The second assumption presented is that internet-based surveys are faster and this assumption can be supported in the faster response time found in multiple studies (Fricker & Schonlau, 2002). Couper, Traugott, and Lamias (2001) note, "A major advantage of Internet surveys, conducted via e-mail or the Web, is the speed with which completed questionnaires are returned" (p. 242). The delivery time is reduced when researchers do not have to wait for the postal service to deliver the questionnaires and then wait for the respondents to mail their completed forms back. Fricker and Schonlau (2002) found that the Internet survey not only cut down waiting time, it also reduced transcription errors made when converting the paper-based responses into electronic form.

The third assumption presented is that when combined with another mode of surveying, internet-based surveys can yield higher response rates than using a single conventional mode. This is supported by Kaplowitz, Hadlock, & Levine (2004), who have argued, "In a population in which each member has Web access, a Web survey application can achieve a comparable response rate to a questionnaire delivered by surface mail if the Web version is preceded by a surface mail notification" (p. 100). While not directly related to response rates, but still having an impact on the potential higher response rate, is the advantage that Crawford, Couper, and Lamias (2001) have noted, "One advantage of interactive Web surveys over passive Web surveys or traditional mail surveys is that the former method yields data from all person who began the survey, even if they fail to finish it" (p. 147). It is found that though abandonment does still occur with Internet-based surveys, it is not a complete loss as it would be with a mailed survey that is never returned.

An advantageous side effect found in regard to responses by those using internet-based surveys was the tendency for respondents to give answers that are less socially desirable than respondents who were randomly dialed for a telephone survey (Fricker, Galesic, Tourangeau, & Yan, 2005). This observation is supported by Hoonakker and Carayon (2009) who argue that one of the strengths of an Internet survey is its higher response quality.

Several studies have also noted that there are two major design benefits in Internet-based surveys: first, the ability to prompt a response and not accept "DK" as an answer and second, the audiovisual advantage. It has been noted that unlike a telephone survey, a prompt can be programmed into Internet-based surveys to trigger respondents to answer a question they had skipped, be it on purpose or accidentally (Fricker & Schonlau, 2002). It was found that by utilizing the creative capacity of the online Internet-based survey, the survey design could employ complex audio and visual illustrations, features that could not appear in paper questionnaires (Fricker et al., 2005).

As in most cases, for every benefit there is often a drawback that seems to negate it and studies show that while there may be potential benefits for Internet-based surveys, there are several limitations.

Limitations

In addressing the first assumption of Internet-based surveys being cheaper, it was found that when considering only postage and printing costs, e-mail and Web surveys almost by definition are cheaper than mail surveys. However, when the total costs of a survey are considered, including labor and other costs, Web surveys may or may not be cheaper depending on whether the additional expenses incurred with that mode, such as programmer costs, are offset by savings, such as postage and data entry costs (Fricker & Schonlau, 2002).

The second assumption is based on the timeliness of responses. It was found that Web surveys might only save time in the area of delivery and not in the actual fielding time or the necessary follow-up contact to remind and promote completion (Fricker & Schonlau, 2002).

The third assumption of using a mixed mode survey would actually be a limitation in this case. The survey would reduce the time-saving benefit because a mixed-mode survey would actually utilize either a telephone survey and an Internet-based survey, or a mail survey and an Internet-based survey, both combinations of which would take extra time.

Much of the literature has presented other limitations. For example, many studies have found that Internet-based surveys actually yield lower response rates than the more traditional modes. It was found that in comparison to the more commonly used paper surveys sent through the mail, Internet surveys actually rarely achieve a response rate equal to that of mail surveys (Fricker & Schonlau, 2002; Couper, Kapteyn, Schonlau, & Winter, 2007; Kaplowitz et al., 2004; Couper, 2000).

It has been found that without the presence of an interviewer to prompt or motivate respondents to complete the survey, break-offs or abandonments are high with Internet-based surveys and self-administered surveys in general. Crawford et al. (2001) noted, "There is no interviewer present to motivate respondents to continue with the survey, and new ways must be found to maintain motivation and interest" (p. 160).

Moreover, a major limitation that has been noted is the issue of population coverage. Fricker and Schonlau (2002) state, "Today the general population coverage for Internet-based surveys still significantly lags behind the coverage achievable using conventional survey modes" (p. 11). Couper (2000) found that it would be a challenge to find creative ways for Internet-based surveys to ensure that those who in the target population are included. There is an issue of limited access or the accidental exclusion of a percentage of the population that does not have access to or frequently access the Internet when it comes to Internet-based surveys (Orr, 2005). Ballard and Prine (2002) found, "The most significant response rate limitation of Internet surveys is that only individuals with computer network access may participate" (p. 486). Fricker et al. (2005) state that, "Compared to telephone or area probability samples, Web surveys offer relatively poor coverage of the general household population" (p. 372).

Another limitation found was the compatibility and universal availability of the required hardware and software to run the Internet-based surveys (Fricker & Schonlau, 2002; Orr, 2005; Couper, 2000). Surveys designed to run on certain browsers may not run or look visually as appealing on other browsers and connection speed can impact the timeliness of completion.

Compared to telephone surveys, it has been found that a limitation of Internet-based surveys is that this mode has nothing comparable to the random digit dialing that researchers utilize when creating a sample. Fricker et al. (2005) note, "There are no comprehensive lists of Internet users and no methods for sampling Internet users analogous to the methods used to generate random digit dial (RDD) samples" (p. 373).

Finally, another limitation often raised by those studying this area is that of privacy and security. Cho and LaRose (1999) say, "Privacy is a more sensitive issue for Internet surveys than for conventional survey media" (p.428). When using an e-mail survey, respondents often return their survey with an affixed return email address and an identifying name. Anonymity and confidentiality is more of a concern with Internet-based surveys (Orr, 2005; Couper, 2000).

To summarize, most literature on Internet surveys mainly focus on the benefits and limitations of this new survey method. The distinction between surveys conducted by the private sector and those by the public sector is seldom made. This void needs to be filled as the Internet has become an increasingly important component of the citizen's everyday life and the evaluation of government services through the Internet has become popular. Our discussion on ordinary Internet surveys, however, has shed some light on how Internet surveys relate to the public sector. Our brief literature review indicates that the effect of Internet surveying is not yet clear. Both benefits and limitations have been found when utilizing Internet surveys. Since Internet surveying has become a preferred way to measure the user-centric impact of e-government initiatives, it is necessary to pay more attention to the impact and effect of Internet surveys. The intent of this chapter is to use the case of "Taiwan's Online Tax Returning Filing System Impact Research," a part of a four-year research project on e-government impact sponsored by the Taiwan E-Government Research Center, to examine the benefits and limitations of using an Internet survey for an e-government impact assessment.

MAIN FOCUS

Evaluating Taiwan's Online Tax Return Filing System

Before analyzing the case, this section will first introduce Taiwan's Online Tax Return Filing System and then present the research process.

Taiwan's Online Tax Return Filing System

Taiwan's online tax return filing system originated out of the "Intermediate-range Action Plan for E-Government" and the online service for filing individual income tax returns was kicked off in 1998 as the core foundation of the nation's early-stages of the promotion of e-government (Hung, Chang, & Yua, 2006). At present, there are three approaches for filing one's income tax return in Taiwan.

- **Paper Tax Return:** The taxpayer fills out a tax return on paper.
- **2D Bar Code:** The taxpayer downloads (or obtains an optical disk from the National Tax Administration) and installs software for online tax return filing. Following the test calculation, the taxpayer still needs to print out the 2D bar code tax return and mail it or go in person to a local branch of the National Tax Administration to complete the process.
- **Online Tax Return Filing:** To file his or her tax return via the Internet, the taxpayer has to possess a citizen digital certificate, a citizenship card, the number of his or her household certificate, or a financial certificate.

Filing tax returns online is considered a key aspect of the promotion of Taiwan's e-government. According to the statistics of the Ministry of Finance, with respect to its usage, the number of those who filed their tax return online topped 3,120,000 in 2009 and almost doubled the number recorded in 2005, when the web-based application was first launched. This number accounts for 64% of Taiwan's tax payers and the number using the Internet to file tax is still growing, a remarkable record of online tax return filing in Taiwan's e-governance.

Research Process

In order to establish a comprehensive set of indicators for evaluating the effects of e-governance, and in accordance with the results of the review of prior research, our research team has developed a comprehensive user-oriented model. As Figure 1 demonstrates, the model encompasses three aspects of e-government: quality appraisal, user behavior, and influence. This comprehensive model is used for the evaluation of e-governance mainly based on the literature review above, and on the value-chain model created by DeLone and McLean (2003) and Heeks (2006), which was designed for information systems and e-government. Our research team used the impact evaluation framework for e-governance to assess the Taiwanese e-government's online service for filing tax returns, and we assessed the effects of e-governance more precisely via a case analysis of the e-government system. After the questionnaire was drafted, the team organized a focus group meeting, comprised of users and non-users, to modify the questionnaire. We used the experience of participants, hoping to measure precisely the influence of the online tax return filing service on the public. Following the participant discussion, and while communicating with the staff at the Financial Data Center (FDC), the survey questionnaire was generated. It contained sixty-five questions, including multiple-choice questions with one answer, multiple-choice questions with more than one answer, open-ended questions, and so forth.

Aside from the challenges faced with any survey, one key issue the research team immediately faced was the problem of data collection. After the design of the questionnaire was completed, the research team started to consider which system to adopt for data collection. One alternative was to commission the survey to a private company specializing in Internet surveys. The FDC, however, did not accept this option because of its serious concern with the problem of leaking the private information of citizens and also the public's trust in such a company. After several meetings, the research team and the FDC agreed to collect data through the survey system of the Information Center of National Cheng-chi University. This system is an experimental survey system which has limited function and an inferior layout compared with the system belonging to the private company. The capacity of the university system, in terms of sample size, is much less and also less stable. Despite the defects of this system, the research team and the FDC agreed that this system could gain the trust of the interviewees, because it was operated by a well-established Taiwanese public university.

The questionnaire was uploaded to the questionnaire system of National Chengchi University, with a survey period lasting from August 8 until August 30, 2009. The population of this survey consisted of those who had filed their 2008 individual income tax return online and left their email address, totaling 92,912 taxpayers. Due to the large number of taxpayers surveyed and the limited capacity of the system, the randomly selected 90,000 interviewees were divided into six groups by the research team and six survey websites were created to reduce the burden for a single survey website and to maintain a sound survey system. Furthermore, because online tax return filing involves personal data, taking data

Figure 1. E-Governance Impact Framework. Source: by author

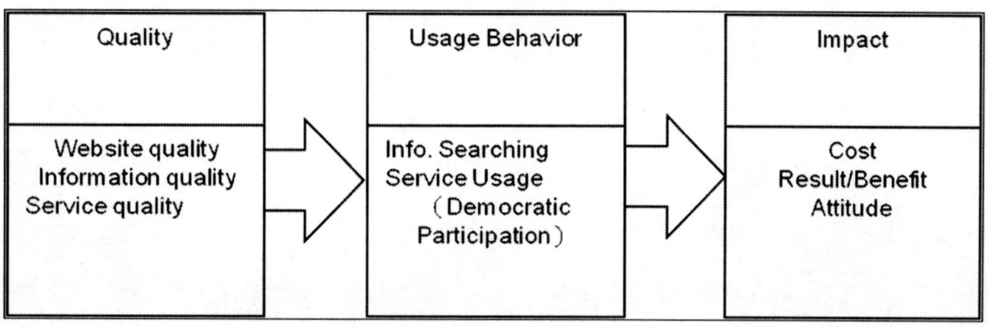

security into account, the team sought assistance in carrying out the survey from the FDC of the Ministry of Finance. The research team created six survey websites and on each website prepared approximately 17,000 sets of account numbers and codes, and then sent this data to the FDC, requesting it to design a mailing program to send out invitations for the participation in the Internet-based survey. The emailed invitation contained a website address for the online survey and an account number and code, requesting the receiver to click on the website address and use the account number and code to log into the survey system of National Chengchi University (NCCU) to fill out the questionnaire, as illustrated by Figure 2.

With respect to the schedule for conducting the survey, the first wave of invitations was sent out between August 8 and August 12, 2009 and 6,134 invitees had visited the websites to fill out the questionnaire by August 17, 2009. Following that, a second wave of email prompts was sent out between August 18 and August 21, 2009. In order to boost the attraction of the survey, a prize-drawing activity was organized. The prize included an e-PC, iPod, and convenience store certificate worth at least 200 NTD (about 7 USD). Those who were willing to participate in this activity were requested to leave the last four digits of their personal identification number and address. In light of prior experience with other projects in which a high volume of public complaints was received regarding the prize-drawing process, the sponsor of this research, the Research, Development and Evaluation Commission, cautioned the research team to pay attention to this matter. In response, the research team contacted the University Information Center and the Center conducted hourly checks of the system to ensure the stability of the system, especially on weekends. By August 30, 2009, 12,684 invitees had visited the websites to fill out the questionnaire. After excluding invalid samples, the team obtained 11,875 valid samples.

Analysis of the Case

The major benefit of Internet surveying expected by both researchers and practitioners is the lower

Figure 2. Internet Survey System of NCCU. Source: by author

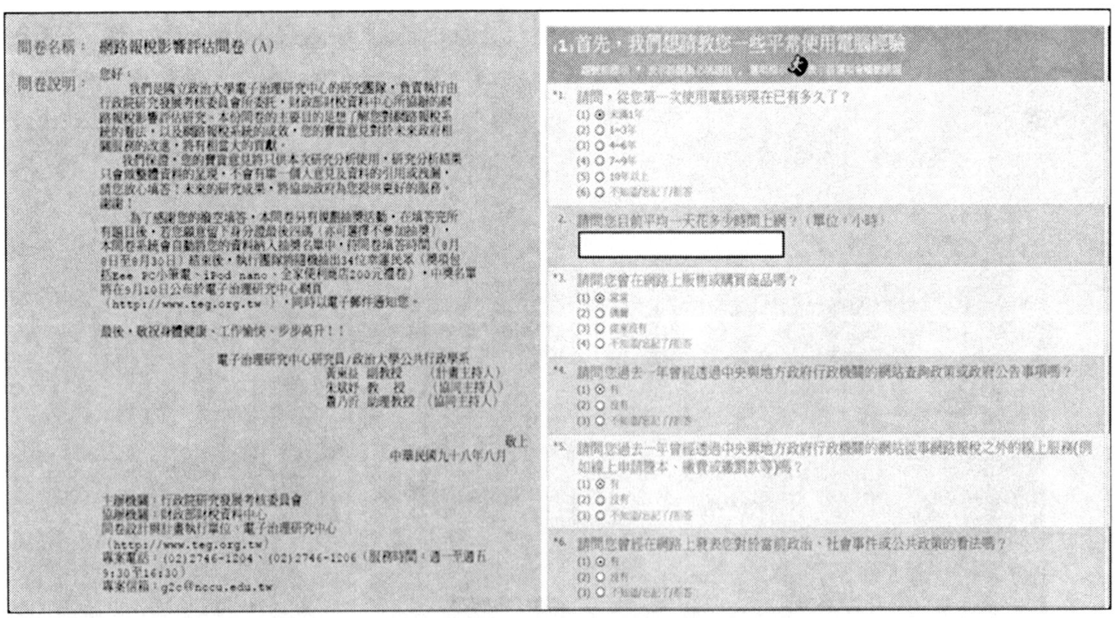

cost of completion time. In this case, the research team got more than ten thousand respondents within twenty-two days. We believe this result not only successfully mirrored the initial expectation, but it also anticipates a likely future for conducting large sample survey research. Another benefit we found in this case is that the method yielded a lower survey researching cost, compared with a traditional telephone survey or mail survey. In fact, the research team spent less than budgeted on this survey, with the exclusion of the prizes for respondents. We believe this advantage is a huge incentive to conduct Internet survey research. However, this does not mean that Internet surveying does not have challenges and limitations. With regard to this, we found at least two difficulties.

Difficulty 1: The Limits of Online Surveys

According to the literature in the field, Internet surveys are faced with many limitations, such as problems with coverage rate, response rate, privacy and security, and so forth. The main point of this section is to list several difficulties, already noted by scholars, which we encountered during the process of conducting our survey.

Coverage Rate of Sampling Frame

The problem of coverage is the most commonly mentioned issue regarding Internet surveys. This problem constitutes the most daunting challenge to our case. The circle in Figure 3 represents the total tax-filing citizens in Taiwan. The 90,000 interviewees of this survey were picked out of the 3,128,515 taxpayers who filed their income return via the Internet because they had left their email address. This number only accounts for 2.9% of those who had filed their tax returns on the Internet and 1.86% of the total number of citizens who filed their taxes in 2009. This kind of coverage rate is far too narrow and will threaten the representativeness of the sample.

Table 1. Schedule for conducting the online survey

Schedule for Conducting	Content	Explanation
Online Survey Time		
July 19th, 2009	The research team uploaded the online questionnaire to the online survey system of National Chengchi University.	
July 24th-July 27th, 2009	Team members were invited to test-use the questionnaire.	
August 8th-August 12th, 2009	The team created 90,000 sets of account numbers and codes at random.	
August 8th-August 12th, 2009	The invitations (first wave) were sent out and each invitee was given an independent set of account number and code.	The FDC sent out a total of 90,000 emails inviting a selection of participants to fill out the questionnaire.
August 17th, 2009	A list of the invitees who did not respond was created.	6,134 questionnaires were completed, and 93,866 questionnaires were still waiting to be filled out.
August 18th-August 21st, 2009	The second wave of email prompts was sent out.	
August 30th, 2009	The online survey was concluded on this day.	12,684 questionnaires in total were filled out.
August 31st-September 10th, 2009	The data regarding the online survey were organized.	After excluding invalid samples, the team obtained 11,875 valid samples.
September 10th, 2009	The results of the prize drawing were made public.	
September 17th, 2009	The emails for notifying those who had won a prize were sent out.	

Source: by author.

Response Rate

The survey questionnaires were sent by email to the interviewees during the five-day period between August 8 and August 12, 2009. Five days after the questionnaire emailing was completed, our team members began to organize the list of those who had not visited the websites and filled out the questionnaire. They found that the number of those who had returned the samples was 6,134 while the number of those who had not responded was 83,866. The team then turned over the latter issue to the FDC on August 18 and the FDC in turn sent out email prompts to those who had not responded during the period between August 18 and August 21. As illustrated in Table 2, except for the period between August 8 and August 12, when the invitation emails were first sent out, during the four-day period (18– 21) when the email prompts were sent out, the daily response rate was higher than for other dates. Hence a positive effect of sending out email prompts can be confirmed. The number of samples eventually returned was 12,670, translating into a response rate of merely 13.6%

Errors Arising from Anonymity

Due to the properties of online surveys, we could not ensure that the interviewees responding were the objects of our survey, although our survey attempted to confirm the identity of the interviewee as the original taxpayer by asking questions related to online tax return filing. The survey sent invitations to those taxpayers who had left their emails, but we were unable to confirm that the email address was not shared, for example, by other family members of the interviewee or that the email address was really owned by the taxpayer. Because we were faced with this type of potential error, as well as with the fact that the FDC did not give sufficient data to enable our team to make further confirmation, the representation of this survey's samples was somewhat limited.

The Limitation of Questionnaire Length

It is generally agreed that questionnaire length has a significantly negative effect on the response rate. The difficulty we found in this case was in the data quality (see Table 3). The willingness of respondents to keep answering questions signifi-

Figure 3. Coverage Scope of the Survey. Source: by author

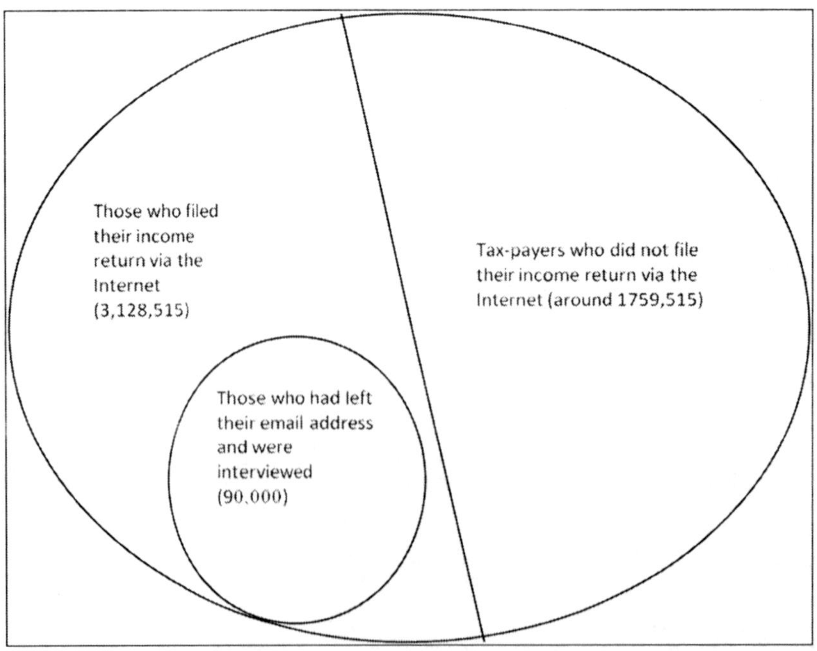

Table 2. Response rate by date

Date	registered interviewees	percentage	date	registered interviewees	percentage
8/8	55	0.5	8/20	1,354	11.4
8/9	19	0.2	8/21	1,425	12
8/10	925	7.8	8/22	405	3.4
8/11	2,144	18.1	8/23	275	2.3
8/12	1,545	13	8/24	561	4.7
8/13	707	6	8/25	311	2.6
8/14	336	2.8	8/26	184	1.5
8/15	126	1.1	8/27	147	1.2
8/16	111	0.9	8/28	101	0.9
8/17	208	1.8	8/29	74	0.6
8/18	159	1.3	8/30	71	0.6
8/19	632	5.3	total	11,875	100

Source: by author.

cantly dropped after the 38th question. In other words, the dropout rate increases quickly after that point. We believe that this is due to people's visual limitation. Reading from computer screens is not only tiring for the eyes but also much slower than reading from paper and most people do not like to read from a computer screen for too long.

Difficulty 2: Limits Caused by Its Involvement in Public Issues

The Privacy Concern and the Cooperation of the Government

The population of this study consisted of taxpayers who had filed their tax returns via the Internet and there are typically two methods of data collection that can be adopted: one is to set up a questionnaire on the taxation website so that the taxpayers can fill out the questionnaire in a pop up window right after filing their tax return, and the other is to use the method adopted by this research team, which was to work with the government and request a list of the population from which to sample for the survey. However, while working with the government, the team had to take into account the concerns of government agencies.

The first concern was with regard to the confidential nature of tax-filings. Afraid that the privacy of the public might be encroached upon, the FDC did not cooperate in providing the contact

Table 3. Analysis of drop-out respondents

Question number	Drop-out respondents
[1]	133
[4]	1
[6]	0
[7]	39
[20]	91
[23]	72
[24]	1
[26]	1
[38]	75
[40]	20
[42]	22
[44]	25
[46]	64

Source: by author.

information of the target population. Therefore, contact with the interviewees had to be carried out by the FDC, while the team was responsible for such tasks as designing the questionnaire, uploading it, creating the account numbers and codes, and maintaining the system. Also, due to such privacy concerns, the research team was not allowed to collaborate with a private company that specialized in Internet surveys. Instead, we had to use an experimental web-survey system designed by students of National Cheng-chi University. It was a system that was primitive in terms of survey function. The system was suggested because a highly-regarded university would easily gain public trust.

The second concern of the FDC was with regard to risk control and increases in its workload. One year before the survey was conducted, a newspaper reported that complaints from interviewees of a survey conducted by the RDEC had flooded the government. The complaints were about the stability of the system and the prize-drawing process at the survey's conclusion. The publicity of the event not only damaged the image of the government but also irritated public officials. Since then, government officials have been very cautious with regard to prize-drawings and the stability of the system. Aside from the risks arising from the survey, the public officials also reluctant to take on the workload accrued from the survey. Therefore, the research team had to take the burden of most of the survey, while the FDC mainly distributed the invitation through email.

The Problem with Public Trust

The FDC, the government agency assisting us, was very cautious about conducting this survey. Prior to the survey, the center had set up two telephone lines for the public to ask questions about the online questionnaire and the research team sent assistants to the FDC to answer the public's questions on the FDC's behalf.

During the three weeks when the survey was conducted, more than ten interviewees telephoned to make sure that the survey invitations had been sent by the FDC and were not email fraud. With respect to this question, the research team disseminated messages about the survey via the FDC at tax agencies across the country as well as on their websites and invited the public to confirm the event on the websites themselves to dispel any doubts or worries.

Solutions and Recommendations

Even though Internet surveys offers enormous potential to increase the efficiency of survey research by lowering costs, the limitations and challenges found in this study also make it clear that Internet surveys cannot completely replace traditional methods. The major limitations we found in this case, such as the population coverage problem and the privacy and trust issue, echo the concerns of prior studies.

When an online questionnaire survey is conducted, its quality can be influenced by such factors as the number of questions, the design of the questionnaire webpage, and the arrangement of compulsory questions. Based on the results of this research, the team offers the following suggestions for future Internet-based questionnaire surveys and for collaborating with the government in conducting surveys.

To improve the quality of the survey, we suggest the research team pay attention to the following issues: First, solve the sampling frame coverage problem. Currently the coverage of the sampling frame is extremely limited in our case. To solve this problem, several approaches can be experimented with. The research team can implement a pop-up window immediately after the user completes the tax filing. Furthermore, if a pop-up window is not feasible from a technical or administrative perspective, weighting according to aggregate data on demographic variables such as gender, education, residence area, as calculated from total tax filers, can be applied.

Second, the on-line questionnaire should be under 40 questions to increase the response rate. Obtaining successful samples is an important consideration for online surveys. In the team's experience, the interviewees began to skip questions more frequently after the 40th question, indicating that the interviewee's endurance vis-à-vis the number of questions or the duration of time began to decrease greatly with the increased number of questions. In order to ensure the overall quality of the returned questionnaires, we suggest that the number of questions should not exceed 40. With a proper number of questions, the quality of the returned data is further secured.

Third, open-ended questions should be avoided. Open-ended questions are more demanding in an Internet survey when compared to other data-collection methods, such as the telephone interview or face-to-face interview, because the participants need to type on a computer. According to the result of this research, among the questions skipped by many interviewees, open-ended questions were more frequently skipped than multiple-choice questions. Therefore, we suggest using more multiple-choice questions.

For collaborating with the government, we also suggest building a long-term partnership with the public sector. In the process of conducting the online survey, we discovered that government agencies were very discreet about cooperating with academic teams. Since this was the first time we worked with the FDC, the FDC was very cautious in the interaction because it intended to prevent the government image from being damaged during the survey. Online tax return filing, which was the subject of this research, poses a sensitive issue to the public, so the FDC, which is in charge of tax data, had to take actions to alleviate the public's concern that the security of their personal data might be compromised because of the survey. The FDC also requested the partner not only to take precautionary measures to prevent any complaint from interviewees, but also insisted that the team shoulder any work load generated by the survey.

As a result, we suggest that while conducting an online survey the research team should be rigorous in every step to control the quality of the survey. A team consisting of well-established experts and/or affiliated with a prestigious institution would be an indication of high quality and prestige. This would easily gain the trust of the agency and increase the agency's willingness to collaborate. Efforts also need to be invested in establishing a long-term cooperative relationship with the government agency to generate more sophisticated research, such as a trend study or panel study. The research team should try to convince the agency that the survey is beneficial for the agency, especially if the objective of the assessment of agency performance can serve as the foundation for evidence-based strategic planning. If the agency refuses to conduct the survey, the research team may make the survey possible through personal connections or through an official order from a superior. While conducting the survey, the research team should do its best to share the extra work the survey imposes and to reduce the risk that could arise from administrative or technical problems. The success or failure of the first experience would have a significant impact on the willingness to collaborate in the future.

FUTURE RESEARCH DIRECTIONS

In addition to continuing to systematically study the methodological and administrative issues related to regular on-line surveys, we advocate more in-depth research on conducting on-line surveys that evaluate government performance. First, we need to address the issues regarding the optimal business model, including "who" should conduct the survey and "how" to implement the survey. The second issue concerns the privacy of citizen data, i.e. under what conditions can the data be used for on-line survey? The third issue centers on discerning what factors contribute to citizen trust in the survey and citizen cooperation with the survey. Addressing these issues is essential if on-line surveys are to become a regular citizen consultation tool.

CONCLUSION

This chapter takes the case of an online survey of the performance of a Taiwanese tax return filing system to illustrate the strengths and limitations of utilizing on-line surveys and to evaluate the performance of e-government. Based on our findings, we offer suggestions pertaining to increasing the quality of the survey as well as pertaining to collaborating with a government agency in conducting such surveys that treat sensitive issues. This is pioneering, and is perhaps the first attempt to address the methodological and administrative issues entailed in an on-line survey that collaborates with the public sector. We invite more efforts to address these issues, to enrich methodological discussions, and to make online surveys a useful tool for evaluating government performance, not only with regard to e-government effects but also with regard to other programs.

REFERENCES

Ballard, C., & Prine, R. (2002). Citizen perceptions of community policing: Comparing Internet and mail survey responses. *Social Science Computer Review*, *20*(4), 485–493. doi:10.1177/089443902237324

Cho, H., & LaRose, R. (1999). Privacy issues in Internet surveys. *Social Science Computer Review*, *17*(4), 421–434. doi:10.1177/089443939901700402

Christian, L. M., Dillman, D. A., & Smyth, J. D. (2007). Helping respondents get it right the first time: The influence of words, symbols, and graphics in Web surveys. *Public Opinion Quarterly*, *71*(1), 113–125. doi:10.1093/poq/nfl039

Couper, M. P. (2000). Web surveys: A review of issues and approaches. *Public Opinion Quarterly*, *64*(4), 464–494. doi:10.1086/318641

Couper, M. P., Kapteyn, A., Schonlau, M., & Winter, J. (2007). Noncoverage and nonresponse in an Internet survey. *Social Science Research*, *36*(1), 131–148. doi:10.1016/j.ssresearch.2005.10.002

Couper, M. P., Traugott, M. W., & Lamias, M. J. (2001). Web survey design and administration. *Public Opinion Quarterly*, *65*(2), 230–253. doi:10.1086/322199

Crawford, S. D., Couper, M. P., & Lamias, M. J. (2001). Web surveys: Perceptions of burden. *Social Science Computer Review*, *19*(2), 146–162. doi:10.1177/089443930101900202

DeLone, W. H., & McLean, E. R. (2003). The DeLone and McLean Model of Information System success: A ten-year update. *Journal of Management Information Systems*, *19*(4), 9–30.

Dillman, D., Phelps, G., Tortora, R., Swift, K., Kohrell, J., & Berck, J., & Messer[REMOVED HYPERLINK FIELD], B. (2009). Response rate and measurement differences in mixed-mode surveys using mail, telephone, interactive voice response (IVR) and the Internet. *Social Science Research*, *38*(1), 1–18. doi:10.1016/j.ssresearch.2008.03.007

Fricker, R. D., & Schonlau, M. (2002). Advantages and disadvantages of Internet research surveys: Evidence from the literature. *Field Methods*, *14*(4), 347–367. doi:10.1177/152582202237725

Fricker, S., Galesic, M., Tourangeau, R., & Yan, T. (2005). An experimental comparison of Web and telephone surveys. *Public Opinion Quarterly*, *69*(3), 370–392. doi:10.1093/poq/nfi027

Heeks, R. (2006). Benchmarking e-government: Improving the national and international measurement, evaluation and comparison of e-government. *iGovernment Working Paper, 18,* 1-33.

Hoonakker, P., & Carayon, P. (2009). Questionnaire survey nonresponse: A comparison of postal mail and Internet surveys. *International Journal of Human-Computer Interaction, 25*(5), 348–373. doi:10.1080/10447310902864951

Hung, S. Y., Chang, C. M., & Yua, T. J. (2006). Determinants of user acceptance of the e-government services: The case of online tax filing and payment system. *Government Information Quarterly, 23*(1), 97–122. doi:10.1016/j.giq.2005.11.005

Kaplowitz, M. D., Hadlock, T. D., & Levine, R. (2004). A comparison of Web and mail survey response rates. *Public Opinion Quarterly, 68*(1), 94–101. doi:10.1093/poq/nfh006

Orr, S. K. (2005). New technology and research: An analysis of Internet survey methodology in political science. *Political Science and Politics, 38*(2), 263–267.

Smyth, J., Dillman, D., Christian, L., & O'Neill, A. (2010). Using the Internet to survey small towns and communities: Limitations and possibilities in the early 21st century. *The American Behavioral Scientist, 53*(9), 1423–1488. doi:10.1177/0002764210361695

ENDNOTE

1 These attempts include e-government assessment surveys conducted by World Internet Project, Pew Foundation and International City/Council Management Association (ICMA).

Chapter 11
Municipal E-Government Services in Emerging Economies:
The Latin-American and Caribbean Experiences

Manuel Pedro Rodríguez Bolívar
University of Granada, Spain

Maria del Carmen Caba Pérez
University of Almería, Spain

Antonio Manuel López Hernández
University of Granada, Spain

ABSTRACT

This chapter examines and discusses the approach taken by local governments in developing countries to using the Web as a means of providing e-services. In particular, we focus on the capital cities of Latin American and Caribbean (LAC) countries to discover whether their public administrations are using the Internet to transform how they interact with citizens through the delivery of online public sector services, thus advancing a benchmarking process. An empirical study was carried out of e-government services in these cities, focusing on the content of e-services by applying the CapGemini (2009) methodology, which has been widely used in prior research. Our findings confirm the existence of a wide variety of e-services among the cities examined, with many of these local administrations remaining unaware of the possibility of using Internet to facilitate the delivery of public sector services. Therefore, there is great scope for improvement in the field of e-government. Reforms in public administration are needed in order to make government more participative and open. Likewise, setting effective policies to ensure e-inclusion is the key to the future of LAC's new empowered societies, with a more visible voice and more chances to express their concerns.

DOI: 10.4018/978-1-60960-753-1.ch011

INTRODUCTION

There is increasing public awareness of the need to endow public sector bodies with effective, efficient management systems, rationalizing the use of financial resources and improving the performance of public services. Public administrations need to be made more efficient (Rocheleau & Wu, 2002) and more transparent (Piotrowski & Van Ryzin, 2007), building an operative framework which facilitates competitiveness, provides more information and enhances participation in public life (Fieldman & Khademian, 2007).

In response to increasing demands by their citizens, numerous countries have implemented changes in public administration, applying the principles of New Public Management (NPM), adopting tools providing greater transparency and increasing citizens' involvement in the decision-making process (Bonson et al., 2006).

The implementation of Information and Communication Technologies (ICTs) in public administrations (e-government) is considered to be among the most important items on current political agendas with respect to transforming and modernizing public administrations (Jaeger, 2003; Borins, 2001; Chan & Chow, 2007). E-government can often act as a conducting mechanism to accelerate the decentralization of public administration, promoting the adoption of new technologies in order to meet NPM objectives, thus meeting social demands efficiently and effectively (Welch & Hinnant, 2002) and, at the same time, improving the capacity of governments to supervise activities (Thorson et al., 2005). In addition, the implementation of ICTs in public administrations could reduce both administrative costs and the time devoted to repetitive tasks by civil servants (Yen & Evans, 2005), offering greater transparency to public administration (Wong & Welch, 2004; Ya & Tat-Kei Ho, 2005), improving the current performance of public sector services (Hartley, 2005) and expanding the access to services, thanks to the 24 hours a day, 7 days a week availability of the Internet (West, 2004; Scott, 2006).

Accordingly, in recent years, public administrations have created official websites, viewing e-government as an Internet-driven activity that improves citizens' access to government information, services and expertise, thus enhancing their participation and satisfaction with the government (United Nations and the American Society for Public Administration, 2002). The Internet is now one of the tools most widely used by the public to access government financial information (Borins, 2002), and the most common form of e-government initiatives has been to establish a government-run website or portal (Joseph & Jeffers, 2009). Thus, many public administrations use ICTs both to offer the digitalization of procedures –public services– and to introduce a website oriented towards economic transparency, allowing users free, easy and appropriate access to fiscal and economic information on the management of public finances.

Nonetheless, although e-government has been promoted over many years, by a variety of international bodies (see, for example, G-7, 1997; OCDE, 1998), developments in the implementation of ICTs in public administrations have been slower than the technical advances made. Moreover, although public administrations have developed websites and leading edge cities have invested, albeit in a fairly finite set of functions (Kaylor et al., 2001), their efforts to improve performance regarding public sector services and online government information remain irregular (Paris, 2005). In fact, e-government has been penetrating national government much more rapidly than local government (Edmiston, 2003; Streib & Willoughby, 2005). In this regard, although e-government has been adopted by many municipal governments, it is still at an early stage and has failed to obtain many of the outcomes promised in e-government rhetoric (Moon, 2002). Studies such as that of Shackleton et al. (2004) indicate that apart from Web based information provision, little progress has been made in the transition to electronic service delivery in most areas of local government. In general, only immature web sites with limited transactional services have been achieved, although in the area of participatory government, local e-government is often far more innovative than at higher levels (Shackleton et al., 2004).

Most previous studies have focused on local governments in developed countries, especially in the USA (Edmiston, 2003; Reddick, 2004), Australia (Shackleton et al., 2004) and municipalities with a high online population (Holzer & Kim, 2006 and 2008; Holzer, 2007). However, there is a gap with respect to e-government in developing countries, and very few studies have examined the Latin American and Caribbean (LAC) region. In recent years, public administrations in this region have made great efforts to implement and benefit from ICTs. This is now a high priority for LAC governments, and programmes are being developed to implement ICTs in diverse areas, through plans, specific actions, legislation or, at the very least, strategy documents (United Nations, 2010). The main initiatives being taken are aimed at enhancing the transparency of management, reducing corruption, improving the internal and external efficiency of public administration, especially as concerns the provision of services, and promoting and expanding citizens' participation (Welp, 2008). Thus, since the 1990s, countries such as Argentina, Chile, Colombia, Mexico and Uruguay have undertaken initiatives on e-government, which are being followed by many other countries in the region (United Nations, 2010).

Nonetheless, although most Latin American countries have begun e-government initiatives in which great emphasis is placed on improving national managerial and administrative processes and the quality of online services offered, the enhancement of methods for citizens' interaction has taken a back seat (Betancourt, 2006).

In view of the foregoing comments, this chapter examines and discusses the approach taken by local governments in developing countries to using the Web as a means of providing e-services, thus enhancing accountability and performance management. Specifically, we focus on the capital cities of LAC countries to discover whether their public administrations are using the Internet to transform the way in which interact with citizens through the delivery of online public sector services, thus contributing to encouraging a benchmarking process. To achieve this aim, we analyze the online public sector services provided by these municipal governments.

This chapter is organized as follows. Section 2 analyzes the online provision of public sector services, aimed at enhancing the relationship with citizens, improving the efficiency of these services and better meeting citizens' needs. Section 3 describes the state of the art of e-government initiatives and legislative changes that have been made in LAC countries. Section 4 then proposes a research methodology to analyze online public services, and applies it to the LAC capital cities. Finally, the main results obtained are discussed and some conclusions are drawn.

EFFECTS OF E-GOVERNMENT ON PUBLIC SECTOR SERVICES

Nowadays, most local governments are urged to provide efficient and effective e-government information and services, to enhance accountability and performance management (Shackleton et al., 2004). E-government represents a transformation of public management, enabling administrations to achieve greater information transparency, with implications regarding the fulfilment of their responsibilities in this field (Rodríguez et al., 2007), and providing a new form of interaction with the various parties affected, enabling citizens to acquire a crucial level of involvement (Hughes et al., 2006; Löfstedt, 2007). Improvements in effectiveness and efficiency and the provision of a better service to citizens are among the fundamental justifications of this process (MAP, 2007).

Over the last twenty years, progressive and well prepared national ICT programmes have established a strong foundation for transforming public services. This has been coupled with a holistic e-government framework that addresses not only technology, but also management, process, governance, social and cultural issues to deliver accessible, integrated, and value added e-services to stakeholders (James, 2003; Sin, 2007). National governments are responsible for the welfare of a whole country, while local governments are more likely to render services to readily definable groups whose services are more community focused (Shackleton et al., 2004), although the evidence suggests that the dominant stakeholder in development is the bureaucratic administration rather than citizens or politicians (Flak et al., 2005). In any case, ICTs have made it possible, among other benefits, to increase productivity, to reduce administrative burdens (González et al., 2007), to increase transparency, to improve communication and citizens' participation (Tolberg & Mossberger, 2006) and, in short, to offer more and better services (MAP, 2007).

Although there is potential at all levels of government for improving public services, reducing costs, and enhancing the democratic process, e-government is penetrating national government much more rapidly than local government. The main obstacles to greater adoption of e-government seem to be marketing and privacy issues, equity and financing (Edmiston, 2003). Developing e-government services does require the investment of a considerable volume of financial resources, and this could be problematic in view of the severe budgetary constraints often imposed on public administrations. Therefore, the evolution of such services might be significantly advanced if governments could find the necessary financial resources outside their general fund provision, for example, by means of user fees. Citizens and businesses would probably be more prepared to pay for online transactions if they were aware of the time and resource costs involved in completing a traditional transaction with government agencies (Chen & Thurmaier, 2008).

The latter conclusion is reinforced by the fact that, with ICTs, governments can customize services based on users' preferences and needs (Ho, 2002), which would largely enable such needs to be met (Bonham et al., 2001). The design of public services is an essential element in the subsequent evaluation of their efficiency, and thus e-government initiatives need to be taken into account in the design of e-services; therefore, the attitudes of public sector workers and the organizational culture in this process are aspects of crucial importance (Åkesson & Edvardsson, 2008).

Nevertheless, there seems to be a gap between citizens' and governments' perspectives on issues of e-government implementation and use (Tassabehji et al., 2007). The focus for citizens is usage and trust, where trust is considered to be the safety, security and privacy of information and confidence in e-government services (West, 2004). For governments, the focus is on managing security resources such as IT infrastructures, personnel and finances, but also on improving customer services and the politics of information sharing across different departments and organizations (Tassabehji et al., 2007). Research has highlighted the increased attention spent on privacy/security and services, and the need for further attention in the area of usability, content and citizen participation via municipal websites (Holzer & Kim, 2008).

The possibility of delegating control to stakeholders in the design of e-government services has been one of the principal approaches taken to increasing perceived satisfaction. According to Mills and Krantz (1979), giving customers greater control over how the service process is conducted is likely to enhance customer satisfaction. Cook et al. (2002) went further, contending that service providers should show their commitment to customer choice by allowing the customer to control the process. Similarly, Hughes et al. (2006) argued that allowing citizens some control over personal data and its use may help alleviate fears relating to centralised data storage. Perceived control has been found to have a positive impact on perceived service quality. Accordingly, the nature of e-government services necessitates a closer working relationship among government stakeholders, and this has led some authors to conclude that the development of meaningful, effective relationships between central government, government agencies and users of e-government services is crucial to successful e-government integration (Lam, 2005). Public managers should involve both employees and customers in projects and processes during the introduction of e-government services, developing and/or redesigning them to ensure that the benefits of ICT systems are fully realized (Åkesson & Edvardsson, 2008).

Prior research has shown that perceived usefulness, trust of the Internet, previous use of an e-government service and perceived ease of use all have a significant impact on a citizen's intention to use an e-government service (Carter, 2008). According to another study, the perceived usefulness is the most important factor in predicting e-government adoption (Benbasat & Barki, 2007). Since successful completion of an e-government service favours its adoption, government agencies should target potential first-time adopters. In this regard, an intuitive, user-friendly design should always be a priority for developers of e-government systems (Carter, 2008). There is an evident need to analyze issues of access, navigability, ease-of-use, and other aspects of web site design (Barnes & Vidgen, 2004; Potter, 2002; Smith, 2001). Nonetheless, the above analyses were made once public sector services had been uploaded to the public administrations' web sites; previously, there were no data available for comparing citizens' and governments' perspectives on issues of e-services implementation and usage. In this chapter, therefore, we focus on the content of online service delivery procedures, and trust future research will examine the contrasting views mentioned above. Moreover, many cities have yet to recognize the importance of involving and supporting citizen participation online, and citizen participation rates remain very low (Holzer & Kim, 2006 and 2008).

The above considerations are reflected in changes of outlook and of paradigms within public administrations. The implementation of ICTs in public administrations has produced a shift from the traditional bureaucratic paradigm, in which public managers emphasize internal productive efficiency, functional rationality and departmentalization, hierarchical control and rule-based management (Kaufman, 1977; Bozeman, 2000), to one of e-government, in which public managers focus on user satisfaction and control, flexibility in service delivery, and network management with internal and external parties (Ho, 2002). The application of e-government has been related to a transformation of government processes, of how they work, share information and deliver services to external and internal clients by harnessing ICTs to improve relationships with citizens and businesses and among different branches of government and to increase operational efficiency and automation.

Nevertheless, the e-government process is not the same in all countries and it does not affect all citizens in the same way. It has been argued that, in evaluating e-government development, country specific assessment indicators are needed to enable cross-country comparisons (Flak et al., 2005). Indeed, governments need to overcome some problematic issues before e-government service delivery becomes a reality. First, e-government presents risks to civilian society through the possible creation of a digital divide, further increasing the disadvantage of already disadvantaged citizens (Dugdale et al., 2005; Ryder, 2007; James, 2008). Second, remote Internet service delivery, as in rural areas, is made to a wide variety of personal computers and Web browsers. Although most combinations of computers and browsers may be compatible with the e-government service delivery system, some may not be able to support the security and privacy features required by the government system. For this specific issue, free distribution of the latest versions of the most common browsers may provide a stopgap solution (Lawson-Body et al., 2008). Third, although the Web has become a major tool for delivering government services, many local governments have yet to benefit from its potential for cost savings and improved citizen communication and e-services, due to inadequate financial, managerial and technical support, increased staff demands, and the difficulty of integrating e-government capabilities into existing information technology operations at the grass roots (ICMA, 2005).

In view of these aspects, this chapter investigates the implementation of ICTs in online public sector services as part of the move to increase accountability and performance management at a municipal level. To date, research has mainly focused on American municipalities (Edmiston, 2003; Reddick, 2004), on Australian ones (Shackleton et al., 2004) and on those whose online population is high (Holzer & Kim, 2006 and 2008; Holzer, 2007). Moreover, studies differ as to which characteristics of online service provision are of interest. Some limit themselves to the meta characteristics of web sites, focusing on issues of access, navigability, ease-of-use, and other design aspects (Barnes & Vidgen, 2004; Potter, 2002; Smith, 2001). Others focus on content, and exclude design considerations (eEurope 2001), while another indicated the need to evaluate five components of e-government at municipal level (Holzer & Kim, 2006 and 2008; Holzer, 2007): (1) Privacy/Security; (2) Usability; (3) Content; (4) Services; and (5) Citizen Participation. In this chapter, we examine e-services in capital city municipalities in Latin American and Caribbean countries (LAC), an area that has not previously been analyzed in detail. Indeed, little prior research has focused on municipalities in developing countries. This initial approach to analyzing the development of e-government services in LAC countries makes use of the well-known CapGemini (2009) methodology.

GOVERNMENTAL PROMOTION OF WEB-BASED PUBLIC SERVICES IN LATIN AMERICA AND THE CARIBBEAN

Numerous LAC governments are taking steps to favour the online provision and management of public services. In all these countries, to a greater or lesser extent, programmes and initiatives have been developed to implement ICTs in diverse areas, including plans, specific actions, legislation or, at the very least, strategy documents, all of which highlights the arrival of this question on the political agenda (United Nations, 2008). The principal initiatives that have been developed by these countries in the field of ICTs have been aimed at increasing management transparency, reducing corruption, promoting and expanding citizens' participation and improving the internal and external efficiency of the public administration, from the user's perspective, especially as regards the provision of services (Welp, 2008).

The countries in this region have all approved legislation to favour citizens' access to public services via the Internet, using ICTs, and have created organizations to work towards this objective (Table 1). With respect to e-government, many LAC governments signed the Santo Domingo Declaration on Good Government and Development in the Knowledge-Based Society, at the 2006 General Assembly of the Organization of American States, while in 2007, the Ibero-American Charter on Electronic Government was approved at the 9th Ibero-American Conference of Ministers on State and Public Administration Reform (Pucón, Chile: 31 May-1 June, 2007). This Charter was adopted at the 17th Ibero-American Summit of Heads of State and Government in Santiago de Chile on 10 November 2007 (Resolution No. 18).

Table 1. Organizations and legislation to promote the online management of public services in LAC countries

Country	Organization	Legislation
Argentina	Secretariat for Public Management	Decree No. 378/2005 approving the strategic guidelines for the National Plan on E-Government
Bolivia	Agency for the Development of E-Government and the Information and Knowledge-Based Society (AGESIC)	Decree No. 450/009, of 28 September 2009, approving the Principles and Strategic Guidelines for E-Government.
Brazil	Secretariat for Information Logistics and Technology (SLTI) Executive Committee for E-Government (CEGE)	Resolution No. 12, of 14 November 2002, creating the Portal for Government Information and Services (E-Government)
Chile	Ministry of the Secretariat-General of the Presidency and the Committee of Ministers for Digital Development	Presidential Directive No. 005, of 1 May 2001 on E-Government
Colombia	Intersectoral Commission on Information Policies and Management for the Public Administration (COINFO)	Decree No. 1151, of 14 April 2008, establishing the General Guidelines for E-Government Strategy
Costa Rica	Technical Secretariat for E-Government of the Presidency of the Republic (STGD) and Intersectoral Commission on E-Government and the Technical Secretariat for E-Government	Law No. 8229, of 4 March 2002. Law to Protect the Citizen from Excessive Administrative Requirements and Procedures
Cuba	Ministry for Computing and Communications (MIC)	Decree-Law No. 199/1999, of 25 November 1999, establishing and regulating the System for the Security and Protection of Official Information
Ecuador	National Connectivity Commission and Special Technical Commission for E-Government	Executive Decree No. 2471, Official Register No. 507, of 19 January 2005, approving the Regulations for the Law on Transparency and Access to Public Information
El Salvador	National Commission on the Information Society	Legislative Decree No. 1038/2006, of 18 May 2006. Law on Governmental Ethics.
Guatemala	Presidential Commission for the Reform, Modernization and Reinforcement of the State and its Decentralized Organizations (COPRE)	Law on Access to Public Information. Decree No. 57, 2008, of the Congress of the Republic of Guatemala
Honduras	Presidential Commission for the Modernization of the State (CPME). Governmental Committee on Infotechnology (CGI)	Law on Transparency and Access to Public Information, No. 170-2006
Mexico	Office for E-Government and Information Technology Policies (UGE-PTI) of the Secretariat for the Public Administration. Intersecretarial Commission for the Development of E-Government (CIDGE)	Federal Law on Transparency and Access to Governmental Public Information, of 11 June 2002.
Nicaragua	Nicaraguan Council of Science and Technology (CONICYT)	Law on Access to Public Information. No. 621, of 2007
Panama	Secretariat of the Presidency for Governmental Innovation. e-Panama Committee - Standing Committee for Modernization in the field of New Information and Communication Technologies	Law on Transparency, No. 6-2002, of 23 January 2002. Law No. 65 of 30 October 2009, creating the National Authority for Governmental Innovation
Paraguay	Paraguayan National Commission for the Information Society (CNSI). Inter-institutional Commission to develop, promote and implement E-Government in Paraguay	Law No. 1028/1997 on Technology and Science. National Information Society Development Plan for Paraguay.
Peru	National Government Office for E-Government (ONGEI)	Ministerial Resolution No. 274-2006-PCM (Presidency of the Council of Ministers), of 26 July 2006, approving the National Strategy for E-Government. Project: "Master Plan for E-Government", of March 2009
Dominican Republic	National Commission for the Information and Knowledge Society (CNSIC). Presidential Office for Information and Communication Technology (OPTIC)	Law No. 200/2004, of 28 July 2004. General Law on Free Access to Public Information. Presidential Decree No. 551-09, of 29 July 2009, promoting the technological development of the Dominican Republic.
Uruguay	Agency for the Development of E-Government and the Information and Communication Society (AGESIC)	Decree No. 450/009, of 28 September 2009, establishing principles and strategic guidelines for E-Government
Venezuela	National Centre for Information Technologies (CNTI), within the Ministry for Science, Technology and Intermediate Industries	Organic Law on Science, Technology and Innovation (published in the Official Gazette No. 38.242 of 3 August 2005). Technical Standards for ODF and PDF open format documents and National Assembly web portals (Official Gazette No. 39.109, of 29 January 2009)

Source: Own elaboration, from official websites, April 2010.

These international agreements grant citizens a right that facilitates their participation in public management and enhances their relations with the public administrations. They also contribute to making administrations more transparent and encourage them to uphold the principle of equality, while promoting both effectiveness and efficiency. Furthermore, as an indirect strategic goal, they seek to achieve the construction of an information, knowledge-based society, one that is inclusive, people-focused and aimed at positive development. However, according to the (UN, 2010), e-government in Latin America is not highly developed and, indeed, is tending to regress (Table 2). Central America is the only region in the Americas that registered a regional average below that of the world average, though some countries in this region scored above it.

On the other hand, the situation of LAC countries varies widely; some countries (Mexico, Costa Rica, El Salvador, Guatemala, Nicaragua, Argentina, Brazil, Peru, Venezuela, Ecuador, Bolivia and Paraguay) received lower scores in the 2010 Survey than in 2008, while others (Colombia, Chile, Uruguay, Panama and Honduras) rose in the rankings (Table 3). Particularly significant are the cases of Mexico and Colombia. Mexico experienced the most significant drop in global rankings, falling by 19 positions between 2008 and 2010; it is currently ranked 56th globally. The degeneration of Mexico's e-government situation is mainly attributed to the much lower score received for online services, which dropped from 0.7057 to 0.4413. In contrast, Colombia (0.6125) enjoys the highest global ranking in the region in the 2010 Survey, climbing 21 positions from the 2008 Survey. The Colombian national portal features a variety of online services, especially in the public service delivery procedures section, which allows citizens to search by department or region.

Table 2. E-Government development index value (Americas Region)

Region (Americas)	2010	2008
Caribbean	0.4454	0.4480
Central America	0.4295	0.4604
North America (United States and Canada)	0.8479	0.4808
South America	0.4869	0.5072
Regional average	0.4790	0.4936
World average	0.4406	0.4514

Source: Adapted from UN (2010)

The e-government development index (UN, 2010) is complemented by an e-participation index. E-participation is a tool that enables governments to dialogue with their citizens (Macintosh, 2006). The possibility of achieving higher levels of participation and citizen involvement through the use of ICTs is widely recognized by many governments as a valuable opportunity to enrich democratic processes and to open more channels to social engagement, thus enabling an administration that is more transparent and better capacitated to take citizens' needs into account (European Commission, 2009a). However, policy-makers and governments involved in the process should not ignore the fact that the path towards e-participation is rife with challenges that must be overcome before the potential benefits can be obtained. Digital inclusion, or e-inclusion, (European Commission, 2009b) is a crucial precondition for e-participation; in the case of e-participation it is of much more importance than regarding other eGovernment-related issues (Archmann & Castillo, 2009; FreshMinds, 2009).

Many governments have enhanced their national and ministerial websites to incorporate interactive tools and strengthen citizens' e-participation. As citizens become more empowered, they enter a different relationship with government, characterized by enhanced effectiveness and a more direct response by governments to citizens' needs. The e-participation index is indicative of how governments create an environment in which citizens can be more active and supportive

Table 3. E-government development in LAC countries

LAC Rank 2010	Country	E-government index value		World e-government ranking	
		2010	2008	2010	2008
1	Colombia	0.6125	0.5317	31	52
2	Chile	0.6014	0.5819	34	40
3	Uruguay	0.5848	0.5645	36	48
4	Argentina	0.5467	0.5844	48	39
5	Mexico	0.5150	0.5893	56	37
6	Brazil	0.5006	0.5679	61	45
7	Peru	0.4923	0.5252	63	55
8	Venezuela	0.4774	0.5095	70	62
9	Costa Rica	0.4749	0.5144	71	59
10	El Salvador	0.4700	0.4974	73	67
11	Panama	0.4619	0.4718	79	83
12	Dominican Republic	0.4557	0.4943	84	51
13	Ecuador	0.4322	0.4840	95	75
14	Cuba	0.4321	0.3990	96	42
15	Bolivia	0.4280	0.4867	98	72
16	Paraguay	0.4243	0.4654	101	88
17	Honduras	0.4065	0.4048	107	110
18	Guatemala	0.3937	0.4283	112	99
19	Nicaragua	0.3630	0.3668	118	117

Source: Adapted from UN (2010)

of their governments. This index assesses how governments interact via popular Web 2.0 tools such as blogs, chat rooms and SMS as well as communication technologies such as Facebook, Twitter and other social networking tools (UN, 2010). Table 4 shows the 2010 data on the evolution of this index in LAC countries.

Thus, Colombia heads the e-Participation index in LAC countries, followed by Mexico, Chile and Guatemala, although only Colombia is in the top 30 of the world ranking. The UN Report highlights the Best Practices implemented in Chile. This country placed more emphasis on obtaining feedback and inputs from citizens and also included more e-participation tools such as blogs, discussion forums, social networking sites, polls and citizen feedback (UN, 2010:85). The most striking cases are those of Nicaragua and Guatemala, which are at the bottom of the 2010 e-government ranking for LAC countries, but nevertheless are among the highest ranked regarding e-participation (UN, 2010).

Citizen-focused governance is particularly relevant at the local level, where individuals are most likely to come into contact with public agencies. To what degree are local governments providing supporting information, actively consulting with citizens through online channels, and involving them in decision-making as a matter of course? Holzer & Kim (2006, 2008) examined municipal use of the Internet to foster civic engagement and citizen participation in government. Their analysis

Table 4. E-participation index in LAC countries (2010)

LAC Rank	Country	E-participation index value	World e-participation ranking
1	Colombia	0.4429	26
2	Mexico	0.3714	32
3	Chile	0.3429	34
4	Guate-mala	0.3143	36
5	Nicaragua	0.3000	39
6	Brazil	0.2857	42
7	Uruguay	0.2571	48
8	Argentina	0.2000	58
9	Bolivia	0.2000	58
10	Costa Rica	0.2000	58
11	Domini-can Re-public	0.1857	64
12	Peru	0.1714	68
13	Ecuador	0.1571	76
14	Venezuela	0.1429	82
15	Honduras	0.1286	86
16	Cuba	01143	97
17	El Salva-dor	0.0714	117
18	Paraguay	0.0143	157
	Panama	Wd	Wd

Source: adapted from UN (2010); Wd: Without data

looked at ways in which public agencies at the local level involve citizens (for example, do municipal websites allow users to provide online comments or feedback to individual agencies or elected officials?). Table 5 shows the participation results obtained for the LAC cities analyzed.

In view of the above, we considered it timely to observe whether the process of greater approximation between citizens and local government in LAC countries is apparent in the provision of online services, as a first stage towards favouring e-inclusion.

THE ANALYSIS OF MUNICIPAL ONLINE PUBLIC SERVICES IN LAC COUNTRIES

Sample Selection and Definition of Areas of Public Services and Procedures

As this study is of an exploratory nature, its main concern is to describe the degree of maturity and development of the different areas of services offered on the websites of LAC capital cities. These cities were selected for study because they concentrate a high volume of citizens and, therefore, deliver a large number of public sector services, which could justify making public sector services available online. During April 2010, the website of each of the 19 LAC cities was consulted and the online public services provided were analyzed. The following cities were included: Buenos Aires (Argentina); Sucre (Bolivia); Brasilia (Brazil); Bogotá (Colombia); San José (Costa Rica); Santiago (Chile); Havana (Cuba); Quito (Ecuador); San Salvador (El Salvador); Guatemala (Guatemala); Tegucigalpa (Honduras); Mexico City (Mexico); Managua (Nicaragua); Panama City (Panama); Asuncion (Paraguay); Lima (Peru); Santo Domingo (Dominican Republic); Montevideo (Uruguay) and Caracas (Venezuela).

Before analyzing the research methodology employed, let us clarify some concepts concerning these public services and the procedures involved. We analyzed the administrative procedures to be followed, via the municipal website, by any citizen, business or organization wishing to obtain a document, to fulfil an obligation, to obtain a permit or to enjoy a right. Thus, we studied the degree to which the websites enabled users to perform the functions necessary to obtain public services, and thus avoid unnecessary physical presence and paperwork.

For example, our analysis of online public services related to vehicle transit considered the

Table 5. Results in LAC Citizen Participation

LAC Cities Rank 2007	City (Country)	Score		World Citizen Participation ranking	
		2007	2005	2007	2005
1	Caracas (Venezuela)	5.45	0.00	20	78
2	San José (Costa Rica)	4.36	2.18	26	46
3	Mexico City (Mexico)	2.91	0.36	42	70
4	Buenos Aires (Argentina)	2.55	1.45	46	55
5	Sao Paulo (Brazil)	2.54	2.00	48	49
6	Bogotá (Colombia)	2.00	0.55	51	67
7	Santiago (Chile)	1.64	0.00	57	78
8	Lima (Peru)	1.45	1.09	62	63
9	Montevideo (Uruguay)	0.91	0.36	68	70
10	La Paz (Bolivia)	0.73	0.55	71	67
11	Guatemala City (Guatemala)	0.73	0.18	71	74
12	Guayaquil (Ecuador)	0.55	0.18	75	74
13	San Salvador (El Salvador)	0.55	1.64	75	51
	Panama City (Panama)	Wd	0.55	Wd	67

Source: Adapted from Holzer & Kim (2006, 2008); Wd: Without data

degree of online maturity and development of procedures to obtain documents such as car parking permits in general, or for businesses or residents, and reserved areas for goods loading/unloading, whether temporary or permanent.

As many different public services can be addressed via the municipal website, the public services offered there were segmented by areas of municipal activity. In LAC countries, municipal areas of competence may vary considerably, due to differing levels of decentralization (ROLAC, 2007), and so we believe this form of analysis of the services offered on the website, by creating a higher degree of homogeneity, facilitates comparison of the city websites examined. For this reason, the services provided are not considered individually, but are grouped into 11 areas of activity (see Table 6).

METHODOLOGY OF RESEARCH

As noted previously, this is an initial approach to studying the maturity of online public sector services in LAC, and so we focused on analyzing the content of the online service delivery procedures. Thus, taking note of the study by Layne & Lee (2001), the model of e-Government development is considered to be comprised of four stages, which could be simplified to two basic ones: cataloguing and transaction, on the one hand, and vertical and horizontal integration, on the other. Cataloguing and transaction are based both on the possibility of organizing and distributing information to citizens and on that of performing transactions via electronic means. Integration, on the other hand, involves the joint provision of functions and services at different administrative levels within a public organization.

Table 6. Areas of municipal activity

	AREAS OF PUBLIC SERVICES
Courts of justice, security and transport	Justice, public safety and transport, protection and civil defence, fire services, traffic control and street parking.
Housing and town planning	Housing, town planning and control, and the public promotion of new housing construction.
Community welfare	Services aimed at improving the quality of life in general, such as sanitation, water supply and distribution, waste collection, treatment and disposal, street cleaning, cemeteries and funeral services.
Environment	Protection and enhancement of the environment, forestry replanting, the prevention of forest fires and the maintenance of beaches and coastlines.
Social services and social welfare	The promotion of gender equality, support and social reinsertion for the disadvantaged; social services, services for dependent persons; social assistance, homes for the elderly and similar facilities.
Employment, economic development and tourism	Promoting employment, improving, supporting and regulating agriculture, livestock farming, fish factories, industry and commerce, as well as promoting, supporting and developing the tourist industry.
Healthcare	Preventing and curing disease, and maintaining immunization levels within the population; hospitals, clinics and healthcare institutions of all kinds, including first aid centres, emergency medicine points, spas and analytical laboratories; public health services; control and supply of medicines and sanitary products; public hygiene and food safety.
Education	Education of all kinds, and complementary services such as school transport, grants and other forms of assistance.
Culture and sport	Culture and sport, including libraries, museums, archives, culture centres, cultural and leisure activities, exhibition centres, conference halls, zoological gardens, bands and other musical formations, local celebrations of popular origin, conservation of the historical and artistic heritage, sports facilities of all types, and the promotion and publicity of sports events.
Finance	Financial and fiscal administration, including cash management, the management, inspection and collection of taxes, the preparation and updating of fiscal registers, the resolution of economic-administrative appeals, and the fiscal ombudsman service.
Services of a general nature	Municipal register of inhabitants, electoral processes, hiring and contracting, statistics, inscription in diverse registers, legal services and citizens' participation.

As it is the two first stages that enable us to observe the reality of individual organizations, various authors (such as Accenture, 2003; Layne & Lee, 2001; Cap Gemini, 2007, 2009; Moya, 2003) have established a consensual methodology for evaluating the degree of maturity and development of online services.

In the present study, based on the methodology proposed in previous research, we develop this double level of analysis, to measure both the online availability and the online service development of the areas of public service provided online by the LAC capital cities. The aim of this exercise is to determine the degree of maturity of e-services in these countries.

With respect to the analysis of online availability – the first level of analysis – we believe that in general, in accordance with their particular characteristics, it is possible to distinguish four distinct levels of maturity of online public services (Cap Gemini, 2007, 2009):

- **Information**: Represents the minimum level of maturity of online public services. Includes the data required for these services to be provided, and in particular all the steps and procedures involved in carrying out a given procedure.
- **Interaction:** In this phase of development, there exists the possibility of downloading forms to be presented later. Thus, the citizen can undertake administrative procedures via the electronic availability of standard models from this Administration. At this point, the citizen may:

a. Print out and present the completed forms at the traditional municipal registry.
b. If possible, and if he/she wishes, perform the presentation via the Internet, with full legal validity. In this latter case, the Administration needs to have electronic record procedures to accept applications for a procedure to be initiated.

- **Transaction:** The maximum level of development of the web-based service, enabling a bidirectional relation (citizen-administration, administration-citizen), thus facilitating the complete development of the service via the Internet. Depending on the particular characteristics involved, some services conclude with a notification by the Administration, while others, for the service to be provided, require the citizen to make a payment. Specifically:
  a. Secure electronic notifications: in a totally electronic way, administrative actions are notified to the interested parties, with full legal effect. Citizens receive these notifications at a specified email address.
  b. Payments via the Internet: the public administration must adopt the necessary measures to make an online payment system available to citizens.
- **Targeting/Automatization:** This provides an indication of the extent to which front- and back-offices are integrated, data is reused and services are delivered proactively. In general, they are services that could be delivered either in an automated or a personalized way.

As the level of interaction described above can be subdivided into two areas, depending on whether the initiation of the procedures for the provision of a public service is implemented via paper-based or electronic formats, for practical purposes, the four levels of development described are normally divided into five stages – with stage 0 merely reflecting that the service referred to is not present on the Internet (Cap Gemini, 2007, 2009).

- **Stage 0.- Absence of service:** Total absence of any publicly-accessible website administered by the service provider. Alternatively, the service provider does have a website, but the latter offers no possibility of obtaining relevant information, or performing any interaction or transaction concerning the service in question.
- **Stage 1.- Information:** Information describing the necessary procedure for obtaining the public service is available online.
- **Stage 2.- Unidirectional interaction:** The website offers the possibility of obtaining, via forms downloaded from the Internet, the documents (forms) in paper format, necessary for initiating the service provision procedure. Also considered as corresponding to Stage 2 is the situation in which an electronic form may be obtained for online completion, when this must then be printed out and presented, physically, to the corresponding municipal office.
- **Stage 3.- Bidirectional interaction:** The website offers the possibility of electronically introducing data, using an electronic form to initiate the service provision procedure online. This stage requires an authentication of the person (physical or legal) who is requesting the service.
- **Stage 4.- Totally electronic processing:** The website offers the possibility of processing the public service in a totally electronic way. No other formal procedure is required of the applicant – neither paper documents nor his/her physical presence in public offices.
- **Stage 5.- Targeting and proactivity in services:** In this phase, the public organi-

zation has the capacity to personalize the service, or to anticipate the possible demand for services by citizens, making use of personal data, previously recorded on databases. This, for example, would be the case when, some weeks before the expiry of a national ID card, the relevant public organization sent a message reminding the citizen of this fact and of the need to renew the document in question. It would also be the case of the automatic performance of tax liability calculations by the public administration when it has the necessary information to do so, and without the taxpayer having to request any action; or when a public library provides an information service on its new acquisitions.

The first three stages are classed as "no full online availability", while the final two are termed "full online availability", as they enable the provision of the complete online service.

Following the methodology of Cap Gemini (2007, 2009) another aspect analyzed concerns "online services development", which refers to the degree of development of public services provided online by the city in relation to the potential level of development that could have been achieved if the complete service transaction had been performed online, thus providing an overview of the areas of public services in which these cities are making a greater or lesser effort to make online services available to their citizens. Obviously, the characteristics particular to each public service will largely determine the possibilities of its online provision, but in any case, a public organization that is developing its services on the Internet should aim to achieve the highest possible degree of development in this respect.

Accordingly, we compared the degree of interaction currently being achieved on the websites of these capital cities (Stages 1, 2, 3, 4 or 5), with respect to the range of services included within each of the areas defined, with the level of interaction that should be reached. To test the level of interaction that could be achieved, for each of the services included in a given area, we followed the proposal made by Cap Gemini (2009), in which certificates, copies, authorizations, registrations, applications, appeals and similar services are considered to be able to reach, at the most, the fourth stage. On the other hand, public service delivery that involves the renewal of obligatory documents, or taxes that citizens must pay every year, are considered capable of reaching stage five.

Finally, to ensure reliability, each capital city website was assessed separately by the three authors, to ensure the greatest objectivity. In cases where significant variation (±10%) existed between evaluators' results, the websites were re-analyzed. The evaluators were also given comprehensive written instructions on assessing and analysing the online services.

ANALYSIS OF RESULTS

Characterization of the Object of Study

Before analyzing the content and maturity of online public sector services in LAC, we located and characterized the official websites of the sample cities concerning the provision of online public sector services. Our aim was to determine the number of procedures or public sector services provided and to show how they are identified on the websites. To do so, the existence of an official municipal website was determined, using both general search engines and specific pages listing the websites of local governments in LAC. Through this process, we identified the websites of 18 of the 19 cities analyzed; it was not possible to locate one for the city council of Havana using either Google, Altavista or Lycos. Thus, practically all LAC capitals employ ICTs to achieve greater proximity between citizens and the local administration.

However, it should be noted that although Asunción (Paraguay) has a website, it does not provide information on the procedure to be followed regarding the public services offered by the local administration. With the exception of Caracas (Venezuela), all of these cities considered it useful to give special prominence on their websites to the services provided by the local administration, with the inclusion of a specific area on the home page (see Table 7).

9 of the 17 local administrations analyzed segment services by areas of activity, so that they are readily identifiable to the user; the others offer a simple list of services. However, the number of such areas of activity varies widely, from the 31 identified by Buenos Aires (Argentina) to just 8 in the case of Bogotá (Colombia). Note, too, that 5 of these cities highlight on their home page the services that are most frequently requested by citizens, thus facilitating their rapid identification.

Overview of Online Public Services Offered

On analyzing the online procedures and services offered that may reach Stage 4, that of totally electronic processing, the first aspect to be observed is the great diversity in the numbers offered by these LAC cities, ranging from just 1 in Tegucigalpa to 869 in Bogotá (Figure 1). The latter city offers the most online public service delivery procedures, followed by Mexico City and Buenos Aires (Figure 1).

Table 7. Structure of online services offered on the websites of LAC capital cities

City Authority	Buenos Aires (Argentina)	Sucre (Bolivia)	Brasilia (Brazil)	Bogota (Colombia)	Santiago (Chile)	San José (Costa Rica)	Quito (Ecuador)	San Salvador (El Salvador)	Guatemala (Guatemala)	Tegucigalpa (Honduras)	Mexico City (Mexico)	Managua (Nicaragua)	Panama (Panama)	Asuncion (Paraguay)	Montevideo (Uruguay)	Lima (Peru)	Caracas (Venezuela)	Santo Domingo (Dominican Reuublic)	Havana (Cuba)
Has a website	x	X	x	x	x	x	x	x	X	x	x	x	x	x	x	x	x	x	-
It provides information about procedures or services	x	X	x	x	x	x	x	x	X	x	x	x	x	-	x	x	x	x	-
It has a section to access all the services offered	x	X	x	x	x	x	x	x	X	x	x	x	x	-	x	x	-	x	-
The services offered are separated by areas	x	-	x	x	x	-	-	-	X	-	x	x	-	-	x	x	-	-	-
If so, how many areas are available?	31	-	12	8	17	-	-	-	24	-	23	10	-	-	7	15	-	-	-
The most-frequently requested services are identified	x	-	-	-	-	-	-	-	X	-	x	x	-	-	x	x	-	-	-
The services of other administrations are included	x	-	x	x	-	-	-	-	-	-	-	-	-	-	-	-	-	-	-

The large number of possibilities offered by Bogota on its website is due, in the first place, to the fact that the city changed its organizational strategy, signing agreements to create municipal offices to simplify matters for citizens and businesses, providing a single location for services to be provided and procedures performed, not just regarding local matters, but also national and private concerns. This strategy was later expanded to enable online access to services – not only in the municipal field, via the city's website, but also national and private, so that in the future citizens and businesses may be able to access online services without needing to be familiar with the internal structure of all the administrative functions and with their physical location.

Another area of great diversity concerns the services about which the cities provide online information, this being largely due to differences in the degree of decentralization of municipal services (ROLAC, 2007). Our empirical study shows that the competences of city halls in LAC countries with respect to service provision differ considerably; for example, areas such as education, health and town planning are in some cases strictly local concerns, while in others they are local/national, or local/provincial, or solely national or provincial.

One goal of our analysis was to determine which areas of services are currently being prioritized by the LAC cities. Figure 2 shows that of the total number of public service delivery procedures offered on municipal web sites (2939), the area of "employment, economic development and tourism" is most prominent, accounting for 21.54%, followed by "social services" with 11.41%. Therefore, among the services that are suitable for provision via the Internet, priority is being given, in the first place, to those aimed at stimulating and promoting employment, at promoting, supporting and developing commercial activities, at public transport, and at services to promote, support and develop tourism. Second in priority are services related to the promotion of gender equality, the promotion and social reinsertion of the disadvantaged, social services, services for dependent persons and social assistance, homes for the elderly and others of a similar nature.

Services related to education, of all kinds, and complementary services, such as school transport,

Figure 1. No. of online services provided on the LAC capital cities' websites

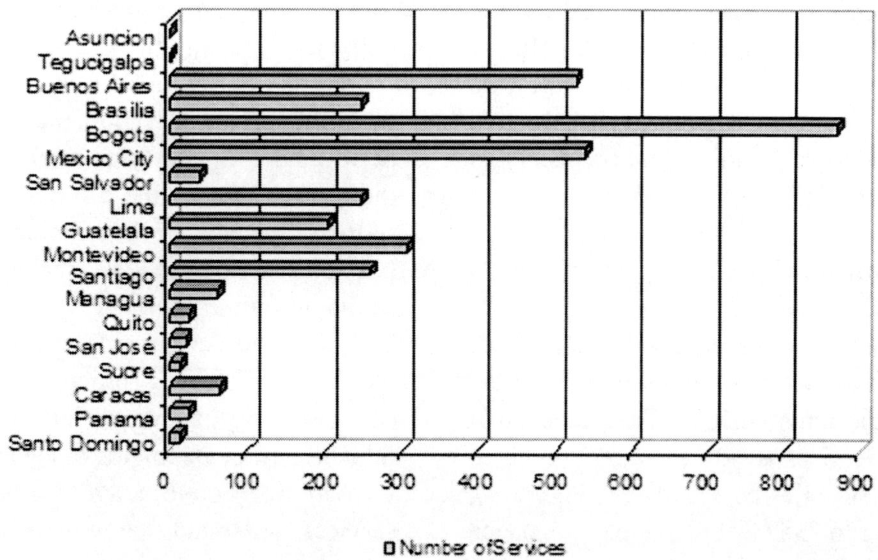

Figure 2. Extent of online services, by areas

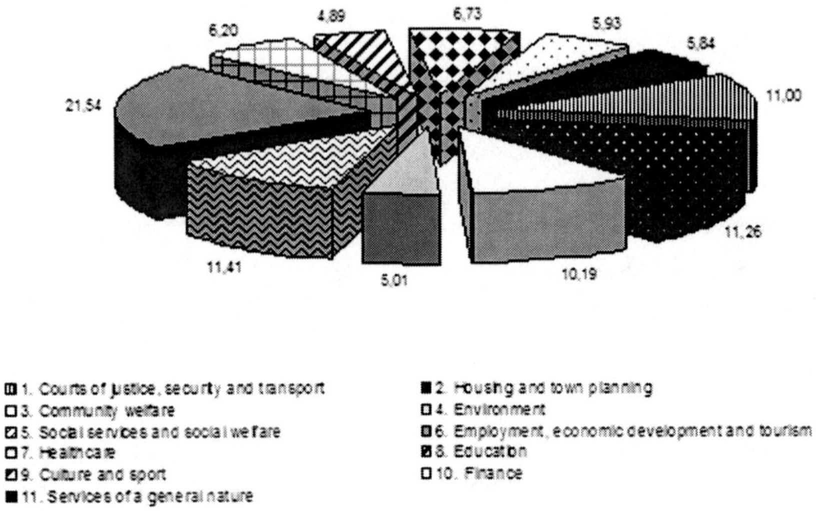

grants and other forms of assistance, are less visible on the municipal websites studied, accounting for just 4.89% of the total.

The analysis of the LAC capital cities by service areas shows which of these correspond to public service delivery procedures given highest priority. It can be seen that the cities providing facilities for the greatest number of public service delivery procedures (Bogotá, Mexico City and Buenos Aires), focus mainly on those related to "employment, economic development and tourism" and "social services" (see Figure 3), while the cities enabling fewest public service delivery procedures (Panama City, Caracas and Sucre), are fundamentally concerned with services related to housing and town planning, and financial and fiscal administration.

Online Availability

According to the results obtained, the level of information, the first stage in our classification, representing the minimum level of development of online public services, is most commonly reflected in the group of cities analyzed (see Figure 4), corresponding to 73.2% of all the public service delivery procedures mentioned on municipal websites. In most cases, the data necessary for the performance of these procedures is provided, with details of all the steps and proceedings required in each case.

With respect to the interaction stage, by which the citizen is enabled to initiate administrative proceedings via the online availability of standardized forms, we found that there were more possibilities for downloading forms for subsequent presentation at municipal offices (10.3%) than for a full online public service delivery procedures, with total legal validity (2.6%).

Turning to the highest level of development of online service provision, the totally electronic performance of the transaction, which enables the user to achieve the full development of the service by means of the Internet, we found this possibility in only 13.9% of the services made available online by the LAC cities (Figure 4). Therefore, the current proportion of services that require no other formal procedure of the applicant (i.e., paper documents and/or physical presence in public offices) remains fairly low.

With respect to Stage 5, the targeting of services, we found that none of the LAC cities

Figure 3. Capital cities of the LAC countries and online services by areas

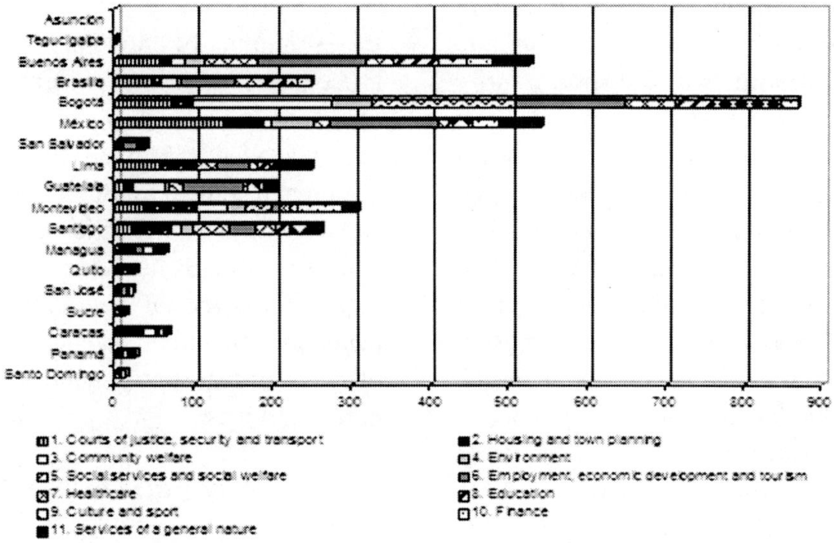

in question, to date, provides the possibility of personalizing the service, or of anticipating citizens' possible demand for services by making use of personal information previously recorded on municipal databases.

Analysis of the stages achieved for each area of services reveals that, in most cases, the public service delivery procedures remain in Stage 1, providing merely a description of the procedure established for performing the action or for receiving the service in question. Services related to housing or town planning go somewhat further, with 25.4% reaching Stage 2. In this case, users are offered the possibility of downloading the paper documents needed to initiate the service procedure. It is noteworthy that the services and proceedings included in the area of "social services" (6.55%) provide the greatest possibilities of bidimensional interaction (Stage 3), by facilitating the electronic inputting of data via an online form for initiating the necessary procedure to obtain the service.

Figure 4. Online availability of services

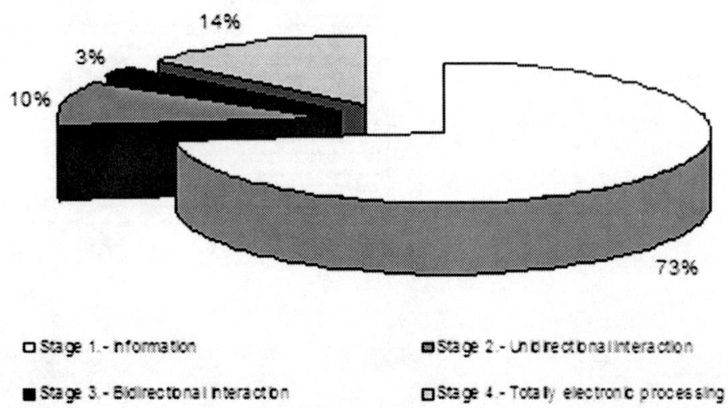

Nevertheless, the areas offering the possibility of performing most actions and receiving most public services by a totally electronic procedure (Stage 4), are those of "employment, economic development and tourism" and of "justice, security and urban transport" (Figure 5).

The analysis, for each LAC city, of the level of online availability achieved with respect to the service areas included on their websites (classifying each service area as either "no full online availability" or "full online availability"), showed that for most of these cities, their service areas corresponded to the description of "no full online availability". Table 8 shows the total number of public services, by area and by country, available online, for which at least information is available on the procedures to be followed to obtain the service, with the number of services with full online availability being shown in brackets. Therefore, the number of services with "no full online availability" is the difference between the first and the second of these numbers. For example, Mexico City offers 136 procedures with respect to Courts of justice, security and transport, of which 115 have full online availability; thus, only 21 have no full online availability.

It is striking that although Bogotá offers the largest number of online public service delivery procedures, it does not present the highest level of full online availability. This classification is, in fact, headed by Mexico City, followed (though at a great distance) by Buenos Aires, Bogotá and Brasilia. In the other cities examined, this possibility is virtually non-existent, with users being required to carry out the traditional procedure of paper documents and physical presence at public offices in order to perform proceedings and obtain public services.

In Brackets, Full Online Availability

Online Services Development

Having analyzed the results obtained in the first level of analysis, we then focused on the "Online services development" of the different areas of services offered online by the LAC cities. By multiplying each public service delivery procedure in each area by the level of development currently

Figure 5. Online availability by areas

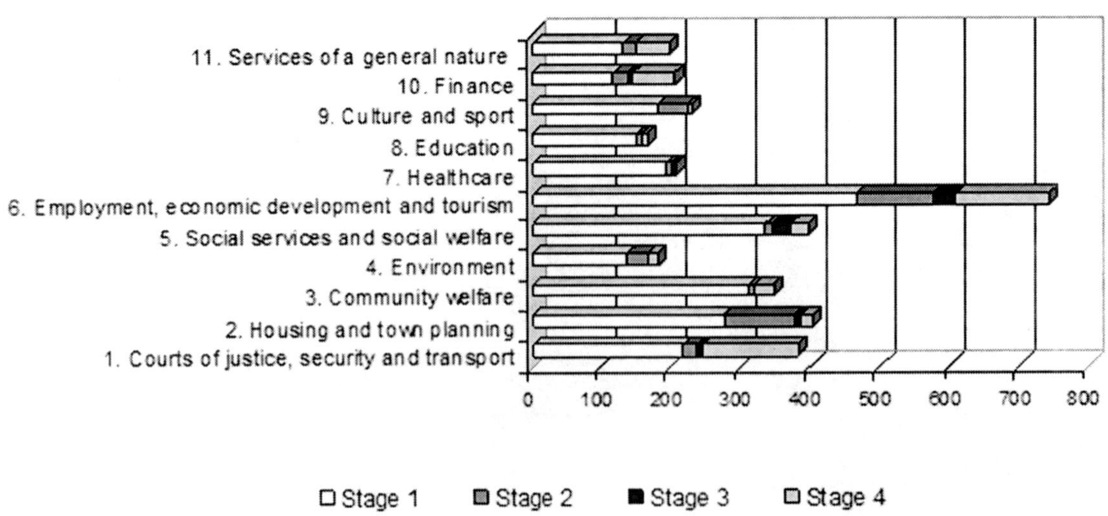

Table 8. Full online availability

	1. Courts of justice, security and transport	2. Housing and town planning	3.Community welfare	4. Environment	5.Social services and social welfare	6. Employment, economic development and tourism	7.Healthcare	8. Education	9. Culture and sport	10. Finance	11. Services of a general nature	total
Santo Domingo	0	5 (1)	2	0	0	1	0	0	0	5	0	13 (1)
Panama	0	10	5	1	0	4	0	1	2	2	0	25 (0)
Caracas	0	36	14	2	0	2	0	0	0	6	6	66 (0)
Sucre	0	13	0	0	0	0	0	0	0	0	0	13 (0)
San José	0	4	2	1	0	7	0	2	1	4	0	21 (0)
Quito	0	15	1	0	3	4	0	0	0	2 (2)	0	25 (2)
Managua	0	20	2	3	0	11	0	0	0	8	15	59 (0)
Lima	3	45	3	0	26	91	10	16	7	7	25	233 (0)
Santiago	22	49	12	15	46	33	26	16	25	2	13	259 (0)
Montevideo	34 (2)	69	38	23	33	10	13	0	10	54 (4)	7 (5)	291(11)
Guatemala	12	9	42	6	16	77	6	0	13	6 (4)	18	205 (4)
El Salvador	1	9	0	0	0	16	0	0	0	1	8	35 (0)
Mexico City	136 (115)	52	10 (2)	53 (3)	21	136 (90)	15	0	30	33 (33)	54 (23)	540(266)
Bogotá	72 (5)	26 (1)	176 (11)	50 (1)	183 (21)	139 (15)	65 (2)	49 (6)	86 (1)	23 (3)	0	869(66)
Brasilia	44 (7)	14 (8)	21 (14)	3	0	69 (11)	39	24	17	17 (7)	0	248 (47)
Buenos Aires	57 (7)	20 (8)	18	25 (12)	40 (5)	131 (18)	64	61 (2)	37 (2)	26 (4)	54 (20)	553(78)
Tegucigalpa	0	0	0	0	0	0	0	0	0	1 (1)	0	1(1)

achieved, and comparing this with the level of interaction that could potentially be reached, we determined that it is the area of "finance" that achieves the highest value in this regard, with 46.78% of the maximum possible. This is followed by the area of "justice, security and urban transport", with 43.50%. The service area that presented the lowest value in this respect was that of "health", with 27.71%. The other service areas recorded an average "Online services development" value of 30% (Figure 6).

With respect to the "Online services development" achieved by the online services offered by each of the LAC cities (Figure 7), Mexico City presented the highest value (58.8%), followed by San José (Costa Rica), with 50%, although it should be noted that this city only provides 21 online services, while 540 are offered by Mexico City. Third place corresponds to Buenos Aires, whose 526 services achieve an average degree of online services development of 47.5%. The cities faring worst in this respect are Panama City (25 online services, and 24.35% development) and Sucre (13 services, and 25% development). Finally, note that Bogotá, which provides the highest number of online public service delivery

Figure 6. Online services development by areas

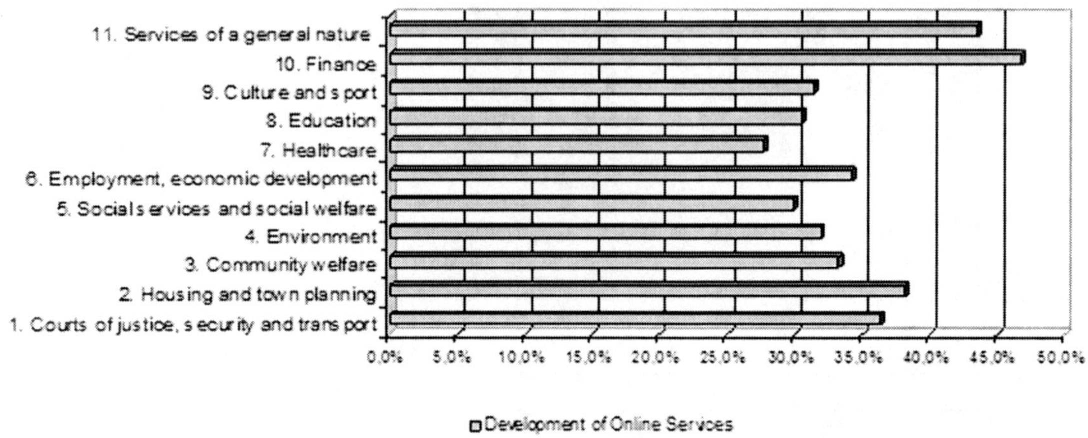

Figure 7. Online services development by cities

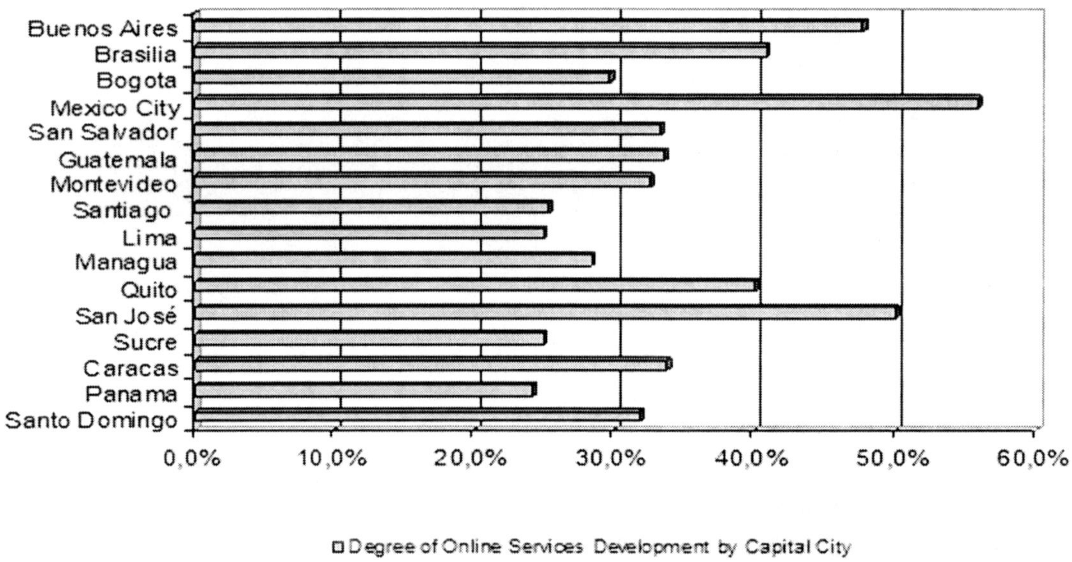

procedures (869), presents a fairly low average level of development, obtaining only 29.75% of the maximum score possible.

DISCUSSION AND CONCLUSION

This chapter examines the approach taken by local governments in developing countries to using the Web as a means of providing e-services, thus enhancing accountability and performance management. In particular, we focus on the public administrations of capital cities of LAC countries to discover whether they are using the Internet to transform the way in which they interact with citizens through the delivery of online public sector services, thus contributing to encouraging a benchmarking process.

In this context, although nearly 3000 e-services are offered in the LAC cities, the results obtained show there is considerable heterogeneity among the cities. In the first place, the public sector services offered vary widely from one city to another. Thus, some render public sector services that are offered by the Central Administration in other countries, for example, university studies. Secondly, the number of public sector services offered online also differs greatly, ranging from Tegucigalpa (Honduras), which only offers one online public sector service, to Bogotá (Colombia), which offers almost 900. This means that most LAC capital cities are still in the process of introducing e-government with respect to public sector services and that the development achieved in this process differs greatly. Differences in funding limitations and difficulty in hiring skilled IT personnel to implement e-services could also account for these disparities. Indeed, it is these latter two aspects that have been highlighted in previous studies (Norris et al., 2001; Edmiston, 2003; Streib & Willoughby, 2005; Chen & Knepper 2005; Coursey & Killingsworth 2005; Cresswell & Pardo 2001; Wood et al., 2009).

Among the different e-services offered, the area of employment, economic development and tourism, together with social services, contributes the highest number of online public sector services. By contrast, the public sector services linked to the area of education are those least commonly available in the LAC cities, although it is necessary to take into account the different competences at municipal level enjoyed by the cities in question, because some of these public sector services are rendered by regional or central administrations.

Analysis of the results city-by-city shows that those with fewest e-services are often focused on the rendering of public sector services included in the areas of housing and town planning, and of finance, especially regarding taxation. Thus, these cities are using the official website as a means of facilitating the receipt of funds from building licenses and from taxes on citizens. By contrast, the cities with the highest number of e-services are often focused on the area of employment, economic development and tourism and on that of social services. In other words, these cities are at a higher stage of e-government development, in regard to online public sector services, because they not only offer e-services to facilitate tax payments, but they focus on public sector services that directly affect public welfare. Nonetheless, there is much scope for improvement in all the cities examined. In addition, as prior research has indicated, the limited access of citizens to the e-services provided could restrict their usefulness (Ballard, 2001; Edmiston, 2003; Streib & Willoughby, 2005). Therefore, government should invest in IT infrastructure to allow citizens to have access to online public sector services.

As regards the current state of e-services development in the different areas of analysis, almost 75% of online public sector services only achieve Stage 1, in accordance with the terminology proposed by the Cap Gemini study. In this stage, only information about public sector services is provided online. When the e-services development reaches Stage 2, the municipal authorities promote a one-way interaction for initiating the process of obtaining online public sector services and achieving the full transaction of these services (this stage is currently reached by only 14% of online public sector services), but the two-way interaction stage and the targeting stage are almost non-existent. Indeed, the targetisation stage is not currently used by any of the cities examined.

Although Bogotá offers the highest number of e-services on its official website, few cities provide full online availability of their public sector services. Mexico City offers the greatest number of full online availability services, followed at a great distance by Buenos Aires.

The above-mentioned results reflect the low degree of development of e-services in LAC capital cities; although some of them offer a large number of e-services, in many cases these services cannot be completed on the web, which merely provides (one-way) information. Therefore, the official websites of the cities included in this analysis are being used as a means of information dissemination instead of allowing interaction and active participation by citizens.

Our analysis by areas of service shows that only in the area of employment, economic development and tourism and in that of justice, security and town transport is there the possibility of completing the full online transaction of public sector services; these services mainly correspond to driving taxes and licenses and to the provision of information about taxis and other forms of public transport. In the area of social services, citizens may effect a two-way interaction regarding e-services. This could be due to the social nature of the e-service, which requires a specific interaction. Finally, town planning and building services remain mainly in the one-way interaction stage. This finding could be due to several causes: firstly, these public sector services are often complex, and many documents must be completed, and so the municipal authorities focus on making it possible to initiate proceedings online. Moreover, the bureaucratic administration advocated of LAC (Ramió, 2001) requires citizens to be physically present at public offices to complete the public sector service. Secondly, town planning and building services are of great significance within the public sector services offered by local administrations, and represent an important source of funding for municipal budgets. Therefore, city administrators are interested in supplying information and documents for citizens to download, facilitating the possibility of initiating this kind of public sector services. In any case, these types of 'inefficiencies' are exactly what E-government has been shown to most effectively address.

Finally, although the public sector services included in the area of finance achieve the highest stage of online e-services development, these services are still at only 47% of their potential maximum level of maturity. Therefore, there remains wide scope for improvement. Indeed, the local administrations examined in this study appear to be unaware of the possibility of using the Internet to facilitate public sector services delivery. This circumstance could be due to the particular characteristic of post-bureaucratic administration in these LAC countries.

Comparison of the data on e-government development in LAC countries shows that, in most cases, the largest cities in the region are incorporating only very slowly into the provision of public services the strategies and policies of administrative modernisation related to the implementation of ICTs and of e-services that are being applied by central governments. Furthermore, comparison of the scant development of e-services in some of the cities examined with the score reported by previous studies for the same cities with respect to citizens' participation (Holzer & Kim, 2006, 2008) shows that many municipalities are still not making all possible use of ICTs to expand and enhance their levels of citizens' participation and to enrich the democratic process.

In conclusion, reforms in public administration are needed in order to make government more participative and open. Digitizing public sector services requires the prior development of public administrations' management systems, to facilitate the online provision of public sector services. But in this process of developing e-services, the risk of the "digital divide" should be taken into account; ensuring e-inclusion is of vital importance to ensure that no citizen is left behind in accessing new channels of participation and democracy. Setting effective policies to ensure e-inclusion is the key to the future of LAC's new empowered societies, with a more visible voice and more chances to express their concerns. Nonetheless, due to the financial constraints affecting these countries (Norris et al., 2001; Edmiston, 2003; Streib & Willoughby, 2005), the need to protect individual privacy (Streib & Willoughby, 2005), questions regarding the security of online information and electronic transactions (Streib & Willoughby, 2005), the difficulty in recruiting and maintaining skilled IT staff in governments (Chen & Knepper 2005; Coursey & Killingsworth 2005; Cresswell & Pardo 2001; Wood et al., 2009) and reasonable and equitable access to e-government resources (Ballard, 2001; Edmiston, 2003; Streib & Willoughby, 2005), it will be necessary to prioritize the development of the e-services that are suitable for online application and performance. In this regard, strategic planning for the progressive digitization of public sector services is needed.

In future research, a model could be proposed for designing online public sector services to increase their homogeneity, and an analysis performed of key factors in helping these cities raise their level of e-government development.

REFERENCES

Accenture. (2003). *El liderazgo de la administración electrónica-Desarrollo de una visión estratégica.* Retrieved February 2004 from http://www.accenture.com

Akesson, M., & Edvardsson, B. (2008). Effects of e-government on service design as perceived by employees. *Managing Service Quality, 18*(5), 457–478. doi:10.1108/09604520810898839

Archmann, S., & Castillo, J. (2009). *E-inclusion: Paving the way for e-participation.* Retrieved August 2010 from http://www.epractice.eu/files /eGov.%202.0-pave%20the%20 way%20for%20 e-Participation %20-%202009.pdf

Ballard, T. N. (2001). *All e-government is local, tech leaders say.* Retrieved September 10, 2010, from http://www.Govexec.com

Barnes, S. J., & Vidgen, R. (2004). Evaluating the website of the UK inland revenue. *Journal of Electronic Commerce in Organizations, 2*(1), 42–63. doi:10.4018/jeco.2004010104

Benbasat, I., & Barki, H. (2007). Quo vadis TAM. *Journal of the Association for Information Systems, 8*(4), 211–218.

Betancourt, V. (2006). *E-government: An opportunity for citizen participation in the era of digital development.* Retrieved April, 14, 2009, from http://www.apc.org/en/news/ all/world/e-government- opportunity-citizen- participation-era

Bonham, G. M., Seifert, J. W., & Thorson, S. J. (2001). *The transformational potential of e-government: the role of political leadership.* Paper presented at the Electronic Governance and Information Policy (Panel 9-1), 4th Pan-European International Relations Conference of the European Consortium for Political Research, University of Kent, Canterbury.

Bonsón, E., Escobar, T., & Flores, F. (2006). Online transparency of the banking sector. *Online Information Review, 30*(6), 714–730. doi:10.1108/14684520610716180

Borins, S. (2001). Public management innovation: Toward a global perspective. *American Review of Public Administration, 31*(1), 5–21. doi:10.1177/02750740122064802

Borins, S. (2002). On the frontiers of electronic governance: A report on the United States and Canada. *International Review of Administrative Science, 68*(2), 199–211. doi:10.1177/0020852302682003

Bozeman, B. (2000). *Bureaucracy and red tape.* Upper Saddle River, NJ: Prentice Hall.

CapGemini. (2007). *The user challenge- Benchmarking the supply of online public services, 7th measurement.* European Commission, General Direction of Information Society and Media. Retrieved January 2008 from http://ec.europa.eu/ information_society/ eeurope/i2010/docs/ benchmarking/ egov_benchmark_2007.pdf

CapGemini. (2009). *Smarter, faster, better e-government.* 8th Benchmark Measurement.

Carter, L. (2008). E-government diffusion: A comparison of adoption constructs. *Transforming Government: People. Process and Policy*, *2*(3), 147–161.

Chan, H. S., & Chow, K. W. (2007). Public management policy and practice in Western China: Metapolicy, tacit knowledge, and implications for management innovation transfer. *American Review of Public Administration*, *37*(4), 479–497. doi:10.1177/0275074006297552

Chen, Y.-C., & Knepper, R. (2005). Digital government development strategies: Lessons for policy makers from a comparative perspective. In Huang, W., Siau, K., & Wei, K. K. (Eds.), *Electronic government strategies and implementation* (pp. 394–420). Hershey, PA: Idea Group.

Chen, Y.-C., & Thurmaier, K. (2008). Advancing e-government: Financing challenges and opportunities. *Public Administration Review*, *68*(3), 537–548. doi:10.1111/j.1540-6210.2008.00889.x

Cook, L. S., Bowen, D. E., Chase, R. B., Dasu, S., Stewart, D. M., & Tansik, D. A. (2002). Human issues in service design. *Journal of Operations Management*, *20*(2), 159–174. doi:10.1016/S0272-6963(01)00094-8

Coursey, D. H., & Killingsworth, J. (2005). Managing e-government in Florida: Further lessons from transition and maturity. In Garson, G. D. (Ed.), *Handbook of public Information Systems* (2nd ed., pp. 335–351). New York, NY: Marcel Dekker/CRC.

Cresswell, A. M., & Pardo, T. A. (2001). Implications of legal and organizational issues for urban digital government development. *Government Information Quarterly*, *18*(4), 269–278. doi:10.1016/S0740-624X(01)00086-7

Dugdale, A., Daly, A., Papandrea, F., & Maley, M. (2005). Acessing e-government: Challenges for citizens and organizations. *International Review of Administrative Science*, *71*(1), 109–118. doi:10.1177/0020852305051687

Edmiston, K. D. (2003). State and local e-government: Prospects and challenges. *American Review of Public Administration*, *33*(1), 20–45. doi:10.1177/0275074002250255

European Commission. (2009a). *E-government: E-participation*. Retrieved August 2010 from http://ec.europa.eu/ information_society /activities/egovernment/ policy/eparticipation / index_en.htm

European Commission. (2009b). *E-inclusion*. Retrieved August 2010 from http://ec.europa.eu/ information_society/ activities/einclusion/ index_en.htm

Fieldman, M. S., & Khademian, A. M. (2007). The role of public management in inclusion: Creating communities of participation. *Governance: An International Journal of Policy. Administration and Institution*, *20*(2), 305–324.

Flak, F., Olsen, D. H., & Wolcott, P. (2005). Local e-government in Norway. Current status and emerging issues. *Scandinavian Journal of Information Systems*, *17*(2), 41–84.

FreshMinds. (2009). *Understanding digital inclusion - A research summary* [Electronic Version]. Retrieved August 2010 from http://research.freshminds.co.uk/ files/u1/shminds_report_ understandingdigitalinclusion.pdf

G-7. (1997). *Government strategies and the new Information Technologies*. Retrieved December 3, 2009, from http://www.open.gov.uk/ govonline/ golint ro.htm

González, R., Gasco, J., & Llopis, J. (2007). E-government success. Some principles from a Spanish case study. *Industrial Management and Data, 107*(6), 845–867. doi:10.1108/02635570710758752

Hartley, J. (2005). Innovation in governance and public services: Past and present. *Public Money and Management, 25*(1), 27–34.

Ho, A. T.-H. (2002). Reinventing local government and the e-government initiative. *Public Administration Review, 62*(4), 434–444. doi:10.1111/0033-3352.00197

Holzer, M. (2007). Global trends in municipal e-government: An online assessment of worldwide municipal Web portals. In Agarwal, A., & Ramana, V. V. (Eds.), *Foundations of e-government*. Computer Society of India.

Holzer, M., & Kim, S. T. (2006). *Digital governance in municipalities worldwide (2005): A longitudinal assessment of municipal websites throughout the world.* The E-Governance Institute National Center for Public Performance.

Holzer, M., & Kim, S. T. (2008). *Digital governance in municipalities worldwide (2007): A longitudinal assessment of municipal websites throughout the world.* The E-Governance Institute National Center for Public Performance.

Hughes, M., Scot, M., & Golden, W. (2006). The role of business process redesign in creating e-government in Ireland. *Business Process Management Journal, 12*(1), 76–87. doi:10.1108/14637150610643779

ICMA. (2005). *The municipality yearbook 2005*. Washington, DC: International City/County Management Association (ICMA).

Jaeger, P. T. (2003). The endless wire: E-government as global phenomenon. *Government Information Quarterly, 20*(4), 323–331. doi:10.1016/j.giq.2003.08.003

James, J. (2008). The digital divide across all citizens of the world: A new concept. *Social Indicators Research, 89*(2), 275–282. doi:10.1007/s11205-007-9156-9

James, Y. (2003). *E-government in Asia: Enabling public service innovation in the 21st century*. Times Edition.

Joseph, R. C., & Jeffers, P. I. (2009). E-government in the Caribbean nations. *Journal of Global Information Technology Management, 12*(1), 52–70.

Kaufman, H. (1977). *Red tape: Its origins, uses, and abuses*. Washington, DC: Brookings Institution.

Kaylor, C., Deshazo, R., & Van Eck, D. (2001). Gauging e-government: A report on implementing services among American cities. *Government Information Quarterly, 18*(4), 293–307. doi:10.1016/S0740-624X(01)00089-2

Lam, K. (2005). Barriers to e-government integration. *Journal of Enterprise Information Management, 18*(5), 511–530. doi:10.1108/17410390510623981

Lawson-Body, A., Keengwe, J., Mukankusi, L., Illia, A., & Miller, G. (2008). E-government service delivery performance: An adaptation of the balanced scorecard to the public sector. *Journal of Electronic Commerce in Organizations, 6*(2), 11–28. doi:10.4018/jeco.2008040102

Layne, K., & Lee, J. (2001). Developing fully functional e-government: A four stage model. *Government Information Quarterly, 18*(1), 122–136. doi:10.1016/S0740-624X(01)00066-1

Löfstedt, U. (2007). E-government services in local governments- A study of development in Swedish municipalities. *Journal of Organizational Transformation and Social Change, 4*(2), 157–176. doi:10.1386/jots.4.2.157_1

Macintosh, A. (2006). E-participation in policy-making: The research and the challenges. In Cunningham, P., & Cunningham, M. (Eds.), *Exploiting the knowledge economy: Issues, applications and case studies*. Amsterdam, Netherlands & Washington, DC: IOS Press.

Mills, R. T., & Krantz, D. S. (1979). Information, choice, and reactions to stress: A field experiment in a blood bank with laboratory analogue. *Journal of Personality and Social Psychology*, *37*(4), 608–620. doi:10.1037/0022-3514.37.4.608

Ministerio para las Administraciones Públicas (MAP). (2007). *Ley de acceso electrónico de los ciudadanos a los servicios públicos. Plan de actuación*. Madrid, Espana: Ministerio par alas Administraciones Públicas.

Moon, M. J. (2002). The evolution of e-government among municipalities: Rhetoric or reality? *Public Administration Review*, *62*(4), 424–433. doi:10.1111/0033-3352.00196

Moya Martinez, G. (2003). La administración pública en línea: Estudio sobre servicios públicos de los ayuntamientos de la región de Murcia basados en Web. *Anales de Documentación*, *6*, 187–202.

Norris, D. F., Fletcher, P. D., & Holden, S. H. (2001). *Is your local government plugged in? Highlights of the PTI/ICMA 2000 electronic government survey*. Retrieved April 6, 2009, from http://www.ipa.udel.edu/ localgovt/training/web/ egov2000survey_results.pdf

Organization for Economic Co-operation and Development (OECD). (1998). *Information Technology as an instrument of public management reform*. Madrid, Espana: Ministerio para las Administraciones Públicas.

Paris, M. (2005). Local e-government and devolution: Electronic service delivery in Northern Ireland. *Local Government Studies*, *31*(3), 307–319. doi:10.1080/03003930500095137

Piotrowski, S. J., & Van Ryzing, G. G. (2007). Citizen attitudes toward transparency in local government. *American Review of Public Administration*, *37*(3), 306–323. doi:10.1177/0275074006296777

Potter, A. (2002). Accessibility of Alabama government websites. *Journal of Government Information*, *29*(5), 303–317. doi:10.1016/S1352-0237(03)00053-4

Ramió, C. (2001). The problems of implementing new public management in Latin American administrations: State model and institutional culture. *Revista del CLAD Reforma y Democracia*, *21*(Octubre). Retrieved December 3, 2009, from www.clad.org

Reddick, C. G. (2004). A two-stage model of e-government growth: Theories and empirical evidence for U.S. cities. *Government Information Quarterly*, *21*(1), 51–64. doi:10.1016/j.giq.2003.11.004

Regional Office for Latin America and the Caribbean (ROLAC). (2007). *Participación municipal en la gestión de los servicios públicos, equipamientos sociales y tributos para alcanzar los OMD's en América Latina y el Caribe*. Río de Janeiro, Brasil: ROLAC, United Nations Human Settlements Programme.

Rocheleau, B., & Wu, L. (2002). Public versus private Information Systems. Do they differ in important ways? A review and empirical test. *American Review of Public Administration*, *32*(4), 349–397. doi:10.1177/027507402237866

Rodríguez Bolívar, M. P., Caba, C., & López, A. M. (2007). E-government and public financial reporting. The case of Spanish regional governments. *American Review of Public Administration*, *37*(2), 142–177. doi:10.1177/0275074006293193

Ryder, G. (2007). Debunking thc optimists - An evaluation of conventional wisdom about the digital divide and e-government in the British Isles. *Transforming Government: People. Process and Policy*, *1*(2), 112–130.

Scott, J. K. (2006). E the people: Do U.S. municipal government websites support public involvement? *Public Administration Review*, *66*(3), 341–353. doi:10.1111/j.1540-6210.2006.00593.x

Shackleton, P., Fisher, J., & Dawson, L. (2004). E-government services: One local government's approach. In Linger, H. (Eds.), *Constructing the infrastructure for the knowledge economy: Methods and tools, theory and practice* (pp. 581–592). Melbourne, VIC, Australia: Kluwer Academic/ Plenum Publishers.

Sin, C. Y. (2007). *Foundation of effective e-government: The Singapore experience. Harvard University: Belfer Center for Science and International Affairs (BCSIA)*. John F. Kennedy School of Government.

Smith, A. G. (2001). Applying evaluation criteria to New Zealand government websites. *International Journal of Information Management*, *21*(2), 137–149. doi:10.1016/S0268-4012(01)00006-8

Streib, G. D., & Willoughby, K. G. (2005). Local governments as e-governments: Meeting the implementation challenge. *Public Administration Quarterly*, *29*(1), 78–110.

Tassabehji, R., Elliman, T., & Mellor, J. (2007). Generating citizen trust in e-government security: Challenging perceptions international. *Journal of Cases on Electronic Commerce*, *3*(3), 1–17.

Thorson, S., Chung, J., & Ma, L. (2005). E-government in China: Bringing economic development through administrative reform. *Government Information Quarterly*, *22*(1), 20–37. doi:10.1016/j.giq.2004.10.001

Tolberg, C. J., & Mossberger, K. (2006). The effects of e-government on trust and confidence in government. *Public Administration Review*, *66*(3), 354–369. doi:10.1111/j.1540-6210.2006.00594.x

United Nations. (2008). *E-government survey 2008. From e-government to connected governance*. Retrieved April 14, 2009, from http://unpan1.un.org/intradoc/ groups/public/documents/ UN/UNPAN028607.pdf

United Nations. (2010). *United Nations e-government survey 2010. Leveraging e-government at a time of financial and economic crisis*. Retrieved April 24, 2010, from http://www2.unpan.org/ egovkb/global_reports/ 10report.htm

United Nations & American Society for Public Administration. (2002). *Benchmarking e-government. A global perspective*. Retrieved November 10, 2002, from http://www.npan.org/ egovernment2.asp

Welch, E. W., & Hinnant, C. C. (2002). *Internet use, transparency, and interactivity effects on trust in government*. Paper presented at the 36th Hawaii International Conference on System Sciences–2003, Hawaii, USA.

Welp, Y. (2008). América Latina en la era del gobierno electrónico. Análisis de la introducción de nuevas tecnologías para la mejora de la democracia y el gobierno. *Revista CLAD Reforma y Democracia*, *41*, 42–57.

West, D. M. (2004). E-government and the transformation of service delivery and citizen attitudes. *Public Administration Review*, *64*(1), 15–27. doi:10.1111/j.1540-6210.2004.00343.x

Wong, W., & Welch, E. (2004). Does e-government promote accountability? A comparative analysis of website openness and government accountability. *Governance: An International Journal of Policy. Administration and Institutions*, *17*(2), 275–297.

Wood, L., Bernt, P., & Ting, C. (2009). Implementing public utility commission websites: Targeting audiences, missing opportunities. *Public Administration Review*, *69*(4), 753–763. doi:10.1111/j.1540-6210.2009.02022.x

Ya Ni, A., & Tat-Kei Ho, A. (2005). Challenges in e-government development: Lessons from two information kiosk projects. *Government Information Quarterly*, *22*(1), 58–74. doi:10.1016/j.giq.2004.10.005

Yen, D. C., & Evans, D. (2005). E-government: An analysis for implementation: Framework for understanding cultural and social impact. *Government Information Quarterly*, *22*(3), 354–375. doi:10.1016/j.giq.2005.05.007

KEY TERMS AND DEFINITIONS

Benchmarking Process: It is the continuous process of measuring an entity's products, services, and practices against its toughest competitors.

E-Government: It is a term used to refer to the use of information and communication technology to provide and improve government services, transactions and interactions with citizens, businesses, and other arms of government.

E-Inclusion: e-Inclusion or digital inclusion, written eInclusion when referring to specific policies, is the term used within the European Union to encompass activities related to the achievement of an inclusive information society.

Emerging Economies: It is a term generally used to describe an economy with low to middle per capita income.

Full Online Availability: A core benchmark indicator used to assess the e-services against the fourth and fifth stages of the 5-stage maturity model.

Information Transparency: It is defined as the availability of online governmental information and access to this information.

Proactivity in Services: The public organization has the capacity to anticipate the possible demand for services by citizens, making use of personal data, previously recorded on databases.

Chapter 12
E-Government at the Grassroots:
Existing Challenges, Pending Opportunities

Lawrence E. Wood
Ohio University, USA

ABSTRACT

This chapter conveys the results of an empirical analysis designed to evaluate how e-government in practice, particularly at the local level, corresponds with e-government stages theory. At the same time, examining e-government activity through the lens of such theory provides insights regarding the e-government maturation process, in a way that informs our understanding of not only relatively recent trends, but perhaps expectations for the future as well. The research identifies major challenges associated with establishing even basic e-government activity in some locations, though the results across virtually all locations included in the analysis should serve as a cautionary tale in regards to some of the highly anticipated benefits of e-government, especially in the area of civic engagement. From a policy-oriented standpoint, the relatively straightforward nature of this analysis can serve as a framework for similar evaluations, especially as e-government opportunities, and indeed challenges, continue to evolve.

INTRODUCTION

Along with the growth of E-government activity at the turn of the millennium was the concomitant growth of what has now become a relatively substantial body of literature depicting "stages" of E-government activity (Coursey & Norris, 2008; Goldkuhl & Persson, 2006; Lee, 2010; Siau & Long, 2005; and see, for example, Baum & Maio, 2000; Capgemini, 2005; Hiller & Belanger, 2001; Howard, 2001; Layne & Lee, 2001; UN, 2008; UN & ASPA, 2002). The nature of these stages models is remarkably consistent, though various scholars, government agencies, and consulting

DOI: 10.4018/978-1-60960-753-1.ch012

firms have offered slightly different depictions in such regards. Perhaps surprisingly then, whether considered in terms of the overall consistency of such models or the opportunity to substantiate any given unique representation, relatively little empirical work has truly endeavored to fully interrogate the accuracy of these models.

This is not to say that 'E-government benchmarking' studies are anything other than pervasive, especially in terms of cross-sectional work. As noted by Janssen et al. (2004), such studies have been fairly common, though the nature of these studies has been highly inconsistent. Inherent in these inconsistencies has often been a lack of evaluation explicitly through a stages-based framework. Similarly, and as alluded to by Heeks and Bailur (2007), E-government scholars have been astonishingly remiss about conducting longitudinal analyses, which could be particularly informative to stages models. In general, it is difficult if not somewhat impossible to assess the dynamics of the E-government maturation process through a static approach to research.

With these types of issues in mind, the empirical study that serves as the framework for this chapter is based upon a longitudinal analysis that examined, in a stages based context, local government website activity in the U.S. The research was conducted amidst the understanding that the U.S. is considered to be one of the countries on the leading-edge of E-government (Chen & Hsieh, 2009; UN, 2010). It was therefore understood that obstacles identified through this analysis would perhaps likely exist at the local government level in other countries as well. Furthermore, the study was designed amidst the understanding that local governments provide essential services and functions that are unique to their scale of jurisdiction. They are also a particularly key point of contact for civic participation and grassroots concerns. In short, local government has a distinct and important role to play in specific areas of E-government. E-government research, however, has tended to focus on broader scales of analysis (Heeks, 2006).

In summary, the purpose of this chapter is twofold. First, it conveys the results of a cross-sectional and longitudinal analysis, based upon primary data collected by the author, that examined how E-government in practice corresponds with E-government stages models, with the understanding that these models often lack empirical verification. Secondly, and considering such matters somewhat in reverse, examining local level E-government activity through the lens of stages-based models was understood as a means to identify the nature of such activity. Through this overall analysis this chapter addresses some of the key themes serving as the basis for this edited volume, including the practice of measuring E-government performance and related theoretical concerns. Important considerations also arise in relation to online civic engagement and its challenges, as well the phenomena of cross-boundary collaboration.

BACKGROUND

Corresponding with the growth of E-government activity over the past 10-15 years has been, not surprisingly, the growth of E-government literature, including from academic scholars (e.g., Stowers, 1999; West, 2004), government agencies (e.g., U.S. OMB, 2005; UN, 2008), and consulting firms (e.g., Capgemini, 2005; Deloitte, 2000). Such literature has included visions and best practice scenarios for what E-government activities might effectively entail (e.g., Chen & Gant, 2001; Mele, 2005; Streib & Willoughby, 2005), case studies of agency experiences with implementing E-government (e.g., Allen, Juillet, Paquet, & Roy, 2001; Coursey & Killingsworth, 2005; Cresswell & Pardo, 2001), and seemingly countless content analyses of government websites (e.g., Huang & Chao, 2001; Scott, 2006; Stowers, 1999; West, 2006). Within this broader realm of literature, and whether considering the work of academics, consulting firms, or government agencies, has been a fairly substantial body of work that has endeavored to identify "stages" of E-government activity (e.g., Baum & Maio, 2000; Capgemini, 2005; Deloitte, 2000; Hiller & Belanger, 2001; M. Janssen & Veenstra, 2005; Layne & Lee, 2001; Sakowicz, 2004; UN, 2005; UN & ASPA, 2002). Identifying 'stages of growth' in relation to a particular phenomenon is not uncommon in academic work, such as in the case of theories related to cognitive (Piaget, 1954) or economic (Rostow, 1960) development; and as has been the case with E-government, various scholars have identified stages of E-commerce activity as well (e.g., McCarthy & Aronson, 2000/2001; Rao & Metts, 2003).

While the body of work related to E-government stages has become relatively substantial, it is also remarkably consistent. For the most part, and implicitly if not explicitly, the E-government stages literature somewhat consistently identifies what are sequential stages of E-government activity. Each stage incorporates increased levels of sophistication, and government agencies, for example, can be expected to incrementally move through these stages as their E-government activities grow and mature over time. In short, while there may be unique elements in relation to any given model or depiction, taken as a whole the stages of E-government as presented across different works are remarkably similar.

Moreover, the stages concept has found relatively widespread acceptance across the entire body of E-government literature as a whole. For example, the stages approach has served as a common point of reference in various works (e.g., Chatfield & Alhujran, 2008; Santana 2009; Seifert & Petersen, 2002; Wood, Bernt, & Ting, 2009; Yang & Paul, 2005), while other researchers have relied upon a stages framework to form the basis of their own empirical analyses (e.g., Kaaya, 2004; Parks & Schelin, 2005; Reddick, 2004). As previously suggested, however, these types of analyses have tended to be cross-sectional rather than longitudinal in nature, and they typically have not been conducted as a means to inform E-government stages theory per se. Relatedly, while the literature can be characterized as assuming that E-government activities tend to move through stages incrementally (e.g., McDonagh, 2002; Sakowicz, 2004; UN, 2005), the empirical research up to this point in time has done little to clearly inform such matters.

Stages of E-Government

Across the literature one can find as few as three (e.g., Howard, 2001) to as many as six (e.g., Deloitte, 2000) stages of E-government. While at first glance this might appear to be an indication that the literature is not entirely consistent, differences in depictions are typically more subtle than substantial. Nowhere is this more the case than in regards to the sophistication of website content. Indeed, virtually all stages models include at least some elements of government website activity as a basis for defining the E-government maturation process. Thus, while it is important not to conflate "E-government" itself to matters associated with government website activities alone, a pertinent consideration in relation to understanding the stages models as well as related analyses is the link between government website activity and what are considered to be the early stages of E-government. More generally, for a given government entity, E-government activity is depicted as having at least the possibility of evolving, maturing, or moving incrementally through stages, with these types of terminologies identifying, at least in part, the process of increasingly sophisticated website activities (cf., Claver-Cortés, Juana-Espinosa, & Tarí, 2008; Dawes, 2008; Layne & Lee, 2001).

Almost every model characterizes websites as being identifiable by three increasingly sophisticated levels of content, from a government entity having a website with only basic content, followed by more sophisticated 'interactive' content, and then even more sophisticated functionality that allows for online transactions. While there is not always entire agreement upon whether or not these types of increasing levels of sophistication should fall into two, three, or even four separate stages (c.f. Howard, 2001; Layne & Lee, 2001; UN, 2005), the idea of the maturation process being defined by basic presence, to something slightly more interactive such as the ability to download forms, to transactions that involve, for example, making online payments, is highly consistent across interpretations of E-government stages (e.g., Capgemini, 2005; Howard, 2001; Irani, Al-Sebie, & Elliman, 2006; Seifert & Petersen, 2002; Siau & Long, 2005; UN, 2005; West, 2004).

To further elaborate upon each of these individual levels of sophistication, as well as upon how E-government stages are defined in the context of this particular analysis, the literature almost invariably defines Stage I E-government as simply having a basic, online presence (e.g., Baum & Maio, 2000; Hiller & Belanger, 2001; UN, 2005). Though referred to by various names, such as "publishing" (Howard, 2001), "presence" (Baum & Maio, 2000), or "emerging presence" (UN, 2005), the overall consensus is that 'Stage I' E-government entails little more than simply having a website. Content at this stage may include, for example, hours of operation for government offices, mailing addresses, phone numbers, and perhaps some documents (Baum & Maio, 2000; Siau & Long, 2005; West, 2004). At this stage, the information included on a site is typically static.

What is often referred to as the "interaction" stage (e.g., Baum & Maio, 2000; Siau & Long, 2005), or some variation thereof (e.g., Capgemini, 2005; Hiller & Belanger, 2001; UN, 2005), is where matters tend to get slightly more indistinct, at least in content related terms. A general idea that often emerges from the literature is that the interactive stage involves a larger flow of information than occurs through simply having a Web presence, yet this flow of information still exclusively occurs in one direction: from the Website to the user. One content-related item that clearly differentiates Stage I from Stage II is the opportunity for users to download forms (Baum & Maio, 2000; Capgemini, 2005; Hiller & Belanger, 2001; Reddick, 2004; Seifert & Petersen, 2002; Siau & Long, 2005; UN, 2005). Thus, sites can be understood as "interactive" in terms of having, for example, forms for business or citizen-related needs, such as license application forms that would otherwise need to be mailed or picked up at an office if they were not available for download. In these regards Stage II can be differentiated from Stage I in terms of offering a greater degree of functionality and promoting more efficiencies in terms of costs, time, and effort.

The key element in the literature that typically differentiates Stage II from Stage III levels of sophistication is the nature of the interaction itself, where Stage III activity allows for actual online transactions to take place. Thus, while an interactive website provides the possibility to download a form, it is still necessary, for example, to return that form by mail. In the more mature "transaction" stage, the flow of online information is two-way, as opposed to one-way, in nature (Baum & Maio, 2000; Reddick, 2004; Siau & Long, 2005; UN, 2005). Typically referred to as such (e.g., Baum & Maio, 2000; Hiller & Belanger, 2001; Howard, 2001; Reddick, 2004), the "transaction" stage allows for tasks to be conducted and completed entirely online. Transactions may require having secure links and can include, for example, paying taxes or fines, renewing licenses, and submitting 'forms' through a website (Baum & Maio, 2000; Capgemini, 2005; Layne & Lee, 2001; Siau & Long, 2005; UN, 2005). While the issue of conducting a transaction can nominally be found in different numerical stages across different stage depictions in the literature, clear agreement nonetheless exists that this capability is evidence of websites being more mature than those that simply offer a downloadable form, for example (c.f., Howard, 2001; Layne & Lee, 2001; UN, 2005). Virtually every stages model differentiates between relatively less sophisticated "interaction" and the more complex "transaction" types of functionality, and the ability to conduct online transactions is understood to be an indication of advanced website capacity outside of the stages literature as well (e.g., Scott, 2006).

In short, the areas of basic presence, interaction, and transaction are clearly seen as being indicative of increasing levels of website sophistication, particularly in terms of website functionality. Although the overall tone of the literature suggests that government agency website activity will incrementally pass through these stages, typically the models are not especially explicit in these regards, often leaving open the possibility for a website to 'skip' a stage (e.g., Baum & Maio, 2000; Howard, 2001; Irani et al., 2006; Siau & Long, 2005). Some scholars clearly refer to such possibilities (e.g., Brown, 2007). Overall, however, widespread agreement exists regarding what qualifies as increasingly sophisticated functionality, at least in terms of relatively straightforward types of content and utility. It is beyond these relatively straightforward depictions of the initial stages of E-government, however, where less consistency in interpretation of E-government sophistication is found.

"ADVANCED" STAGES OF E-GOVERNMENT: INTEGRATION AND E-DEMOCRACY

The E-government stages literature somewhat invariably classifies issues related to the horizontal and vertical integration of E-government activity, as well as 'E-democracy' endeavors, as more advanced stages of E-government (e.g., Baum & Maio, 2000; Siau & Long, 2005; UN, 2005). However, concepts often associated with integration and E-democracy are typically far more ambiguous than those related to the levels of website functionality and their associated stages as defined in the previous section. While website phenomena associated with "integration" and "democracy" can appear to be entirely different phenomena than the content and functionality as described thus far, as at least somewhat identified in some literatures (e.g., Sakowicz, 2004; Ya Ni, 2006) and explicitly identified in others (e.g., Gisler & Spahni, 2001), opportunity exists for making connections between E-democracy types of ideals and the aforementioned, more functionality oriented phenomena that are typically used to characterize the initial stages of government website activity. Somewhat as an aside, it is perhaps of note that the tendency across the literature to implicitly if not explicitly equate E-government activity with government website activity is a matter that could be held to greater scrutiny. Among other things, this equivalency tends to blur some of the specifications of more advanced stages of E-government, where stages depictions tend to move beyond the more easily identifiable phenomena associated with website functionality.

To provide some clarification regarding both of these matters, and as can be generally understood through the literature, integration is the point where all government services are integrated and can be accessed through a single point of contact (Baum & Maio, 2000; Hiller & Belanger, 2001; Irani et al., 2006; Norris & Moon, 2005; Seifert & Petersen, 2002). Layne and Lee (2001) identify integration in terms of two separate stages, with one stage involving vertical integration among government units at different levels but with similar functions, and a more mature, horizontal integration stage, where government services are integrated across different functions. While a general sentiment in the literature has been that vertical and horizontal integration have yet to fully transpire (Norris & Moon, 2005; Reddick, 2004), some elements of integration are clearly evident and indeed quite common, at least in some instances (Capgemini, 2005; UN, 2005). Thus, at the farthest extreme, integration is best described as an ideal stage, and the extent to which government will ever achieve this stage is, as of yet, entirely unclear. On the other hand, and by some measures of integration, these sorts of processes are already taking place.

Thus, and more so than is the case with the Stage I through Stage III functionality as previously described, assessing levels of integration through examining government websites can be a matter of subjective interpretation. At the very least, the integration concept could use further clarification in the stages literature, especially considering the ways in which E-government activity has evolved since the time many of the works addressing these particular matters were published.

The same is true regarding notions of E-democracy. Again, this concept, which is also referred to as "political participation," "cyberdemocracy," and the like, is considered, whether along with or separate from integration, the most advanced stage of E-government (e.g., Baum & Maio, 2000; Hiller & Belanger, 2001; Siau & Long, 2005; UN, 2005). Like the concept of integration, some ideas associated with this issue are as of yet unachieved, while other phenomena are already occurring and being measured in stages-oriented analyses (e.g., UN, 2005). Ultimate, long-term goals related to E-democracy include notions of governments more fully and actively soliciting citizen participation in relation to public policy and regulation; widespread online voting; improved government transparency; greater citizen empowerment; and wholesale changes in governance more generally (Baum & Maio, 2000; Siau & Long, 2005; UN, 2005).

Yet while transformed governance remains, as of yet, an unachieved objective, specific examples of website content that can be related to some of the aforementioned issues reflective of greater transparency and citizen engagement are clearly available through some government websites at this time, including through online polls, the inclusion of meeting agendas or minutes, online voter registration, and simply the inclusion of public official email addresses (Baum & Maio, 2000; Gisler & Spahni, 2001; Reddick, 2004; Siau & Long, 2005; UN, 2005). Thus, the issue of E-democracy and similar concepts as they relate to E-government are arguably therefore in need of better specification, including when considering the stages literature as a whole. Some work, however, has identified the possibility of E-democracy types of activities occurring at different, increasingly more complex, levels, or in relation to various domains. For example, Gisler and Spahni (2001) classify E-Democracy activities in a way that largely mirrors the notions of basic presence, interaction, and transaction as previously described in relation to website activity (c.f., Baum & Maio, 2000; Gisler & Spahni, 2001; Hiller & Belanger, 2001; Siau & Long, 2005; UN, 2005). Other work offers similar, though less explicit, classification schemes (e.g., Capgemini, 2005; Sakowicz, 2004). Rather than presenting E-democracy as a single, more advanced, and somewhat elusive stage, expanding the definition to incorporate various phenomena, as has been done in such work, arguably allows for a more realistic and practical way to measure important activities associated with E-government. However, such differentiation has remained the exception rather than the norm in the literature.

With these and other issues in mind, this research was in part designed to lend empirical insight to the E-government stages literature, much of which to this point in time has been theoretical, rather than empirical, in nature (e.g., Baum & Maio, 2000; Hiller & Belanger, 2001; Layne & Lee, 2001; Lee, 2010). As suggested elsewhere, there is limited empirical work that has endeavored to substantiate E-government stages models (Claver-Cortés, Juana-Espinosa, & Tarí, 2008; Coursey & Norris, 2008; Siau & Long, 2005). While there is no substantial body of work that has been designed to test such theory, research that has taken such an approach offers evidence that stages models are somewhat poor predictors of the nature of E-government activity (e.g., Coursey & Norris, 2008). Yet for over a decade now the stages concept has served as a key theoretical basis for understanding the E-government 'maturation' process. Using the stages framework as a basis for this analysis, this work was designed to further inform such theory, while at the same time providing some insights regarding local level E-government activity, a phenomenon that has remained, somewhat similarly, relatively less empirically scrutinized in the literature compared to E-government activities at other scales.

METHODS

As noted elsewhere (Heeks & Bailur, 2007), much of the existing E-government research lacks methodological transparency, leaving the rigor, validity, and generalizability of such work at least somewhat in question. With this in mind, along with the understanding that elaborating upon a number of key issues is fundamental to comprehending this study's results, a somewhat detailed discussion of research design follows. First, one key element worth noting is that this study was conducted over two time periods, in particular as a means to identify the nature and extent of the maturation of website activity over time.

Initially, data were collected in 2007 as a means to ascertain the nature of the urban-rural E-government divide in relation to local government website activity in the U.S. At that time, inclusion of counties in the overall sampling frame was based upon a stratified random sampling design, particularly in relation to the metropolitan location and economic characteristics of counties. One set of sample counties was drawn from what can be considered highly affluent, highly populated metropolitan locations, while the other set was drawn from relatively depressed, highly rural, non-metropolitan locations. Further specification of the locational and economic characteristics of counties included in the sampling frame is as follows. In terms of metropolitan and non-metropolitan location, the U.S. federal government classifies any given county in the U.S. as being in either a metropolitan or non-metropolitan area (U.S. Census, 2008). Metropolitan counties include those that have large cities, specifically with populations of at least 50,000, though typically cities of much greater size, as well counties considered to be 'highly economically and socially integrated' with such cities. Counties classified as "non-metropolitan" are beyond the commuter sheds of these large urbanized areas. While non-metropolitan counties often include at least one or more relatively small urban areas, much if not all of their populations are classified as being "rural" and live outside such areas. Categorizing county-level economic conditions involved using an economic index similar to that utilized by various U.S. federal and state government agencies (Fullenbaum & McNeill, 1995). The index is based upon county unemployment rates, poverty rates, and per capita income. The non-metropolitan depressed counties included in the analysis had unemployment and poverty rates well above, and income levels far below, national averages, while the metropolitan affluent counties had economic characteristics that were exceptionally better than national averages.

The first stage of the analysis involved assessing whether or not a random sample of 50 metropolitan affluent counties as well as a random sample of 50 non-metropolitan depressed counties had websites. Specifically, over a six week period spanning June and July of 2007, a thorough search of the World Wide Web was conducted to see if these 100 county governments had a website, or what can be referred to as having at least a Stage I, basic presence, as commonly referred to in the E-government literature. Thereafter, websites from a random sample of 50 counties – 25 from metropolitan affluent counties as well as 25 from non-metropolitan depressed counties – that actually had sites were examined in relation to specific content.[1] The details of this content analysis are included in the latter parts of this section. This phase of the analysis was conducted as a means to determine, in a stages-based context, levels of website sophistication for county governments that actually had websites. These sites were also examined for content and functionality related to matters commonly associated with political engagement, or E-Democracy, elements of E-government. The content examined in this aspect of the research is explained in further detail below. The research conducted in 2007 set the basis for a follow-up analysis of the same counties, primarily as a means to determine whether or not county websites were advancing through stages of E-government activity, as much of the existing literature on such matters would generally suggest. Thus, the exact same analysis for the exact same counties included in the 2007 analysis occurred during a one-month period spanning March and April, 2010, allowing for an assessment of any changes that had taken place on any given county's website close to three years after the initial analysis had been conducted.

Nature of Content Analyzed

As discussed somewhat extensively in the literature review, there is fairly widespread agreement in terms of what can be understood as Stage I, II, and III levels of government website activity. Given that there are some inconsistencies regarding such matters, however, and as a means to provide clarity in regards to this particular empirical analysis, some elaboration regarding what was deemed to be Stage I, II, and III levels of website activity in this analysis is as follows. As commonly referred to in the E-government literature, Stage I activity can be understood as a government having, at the very least, a basic Web presence. As previously suggested, determining whether or not a local government had a Stage I presence involved a thorough search of the World Wide Web for what can be considered an official county government website. In some cases these sites were the only websites for a given county, though where appropriate, links were followed to specific county agency sites as a means to determine whether or not a given county had an online presence. In terms of the content analysis of actual websites, this aspect of the analysis was designed to assess the absence or presence of content and functionality related to, as defined in the literature review, interaction and transaction oriented content and functionality, or Stage II and Stage III levels of sophistication, respectively. In short, the content analysis involved searching for content that was somewhat clearly agreed upon in the literature as being indicative of increasingly more advanced content, with Stage II content involving one way interaction, such as the possibility to download a form, and Stage III functionality allowing for an online transaction to take place.

Thus, the content analysis was designed to assess the absence or presence of content and functionality related to, as defined in the literature review, Stage II and Stage III levels of maturity. Specifically, Stage II content included the following: citizen registration forms (in a downloadable format, such as a word document or a.pdf format); similarly, business permit forms; RFP/contract application forms for bidding on/applying for government contracts; job application forms; and archived meeting minutes, typically in the form of a Microsoft word or.pdf document, though in a few instances in audio or video format. Stage III applications included the following in terms of functionality: online payment; online registration for citizens (such as permits or licenses); online registration for businesses (again, such as for permits, licenses, or contracts); online job application capability; and an online survey or poll. It is of note that rather than including simply any type of Stage II or Stage III content and functionality, the information searched for in the content analysis was understood to provide clear efficiencies and/or utility to at least one stakeholder, such as a business or citizen stakeholder. The E-democracy oriented content searched for in the analysis included the following: contact information, including phone numbers, government office addresses, and elected official email addresses; meeting schedules, agendas, and minutes; voter registration information; local code/ordinance information; county budget information; listing of contract award recipients; and online surveys or polls.

Amidst various considerations, the content searched for in this analysis was based upon an assessment of content included in similar research, with at least some focus upon research that had examined county-level website activities in the U.S. (CDG, 2006; Eyob, 2004; Z. Huang, 2006; Kinder, 2002; NACO, 2000; Parks & Schelin, 2005; UN, 2005; West, 2006; Wilkinson & Cappel, 2005; Yang & Paul, 2005). Similarly, various resources were used as a guide for determining the civic engagement and political participation-related content and functionality that could at least somewhat reasonably be expected to be found on such sites (Baum & Maio, 2000; Gisler & Spahni, 2001; Sakowicz, 2004; Siau & Long, 2005; UN, 2005; Ya Ni, 2006). While discussions and justifications of categories included and not included in the content analysis could be extensive, it is instead noted here that final decisions about content to be included in the analysis were based upon not only the aforementioned objectives and resources, but a range of other considerations as well, such as if coding for a given category was seen to be overly subjective. Similarly, to provide a further example of reliability considerations that helped to guide the analysis, and as approached in related research (UN, 2005), qualitative interpretation was kept at a minimum. This practice is often the case in content analysis more generally (Holsti, 1969), and was seen as a means to improve reliability, especially given the longitudinal nature of the analysis. While each website was assessed in relation to each content category included on the coding sheet, the eventual analysis primarily involved determining whether or not a given website had at least one Stage II, as well as at least one Stage III, application. Finally, it is worth noting that the overall content analysis aspect of the research was based upon conventional content analysis methodology (Holsti, 1969; Neuendorf, 2002). A substantial amount of empirical E-government research has utilized this same methodological approach (e.g., Fagan & Fagan, 2001; Hale, Musso, & Weare, 1999; Z. Huang, 2006; Parks & Schelin, 2005; Stowers, 1999; West, 2006; Wilkinson & Cappel, 2005).

RESULTS

The analysis led to a number of key findings, many of which empirically inform E-government stages theory, while also providing further insights regarding the current realities of local E-government in the U.S. First, in terms of Stage I, basic presence, of the 100 counties randomly sampled in 2007, 62 had a website. By 2010, two of these counties no longer had a site, though 11 had added a site, bringing the total number of counties with a website to 71. Thus, of the 38 counties that did not have a site in 2007, 11 – or around 29 percent of that total – had added a site. While at first glance this finding would apparently support the idea that, at least in some instances, progress is being made in E-government activity at the local level, as will be discussed in further detail below, a further interrogation of these findings reveals some cause for concern.

More specifically, and in terms of the locational characteristics associated with Stage I E-government in particular, all but one of the metropolitan affluent counties included in the analysis had a website in 2007, and by 2010 this lone outlier that previously had not had a site had developed one. Thus, the changes in Stage I activity as previously described were almost exclusively a function of non-metropolitan counties commencing website activity at some time between the two periods studied (see Figure 1). Ten of these counties added sites, while two no longer had one, by 2010. A further examination of these newly established websites provided evidence supporting the idea that government website activity, at least at some scales, matures incrementally. It also revealed collaborative efforts across government scales. As noted as part of the methods section, metropolitan as well as county-level economic conditions are at least somewhat regional in nature, and the random sample of counties included in the 2007 analysis reflected these types of patterns. Kentucky, a state with an exceptionally high number of economically depressed counties compared to most other states in the U.S., had, as therefore might be expected, a relatively large number of economically depressed counties included in the initial sample of such counties. Six of the ten non-metropolitan depressed counties that had added a site by 2010 were in Kentucky, and, in fact, the one metropolitan county that had added a site was in Kentucky as well. As indicated in related research, what might be referred to as a 'state effect' can influence local level website activity (Greenberg, 2006; Huang, 2006), where issues such as particular enthusiasm for E-government activity at the state level, or collaboration across government units at the state and local scales, can, for example, support local level E-government initiatives within a state.

Clearly these types of collaborative efforts were at work in Kentucky, as all of the newly added websites in the analysis had been created through state auspices. On the surface these types of collaborative efforts would appear to be important, especially in instances where, for example, a local government has not yet achieved a basic website presence. However, while the metropolitan Kentucky county website was at a Stage II level of sophistication, all six of non-metropolitan Kentucky sites exhibited only Stage I levels of E-government activity. Assuming that Stage I website activity offers only limited utility, it would be an overstatement to suggest that collaborative efforts were yielding particularly notable improvements in E-government activity in these locations. On the other hand, to the extent that having any sort of website at all could potentially lead to more advanced activities in the longer term, movement into Stage I levels of E-government activity by these counties perhaps provides at least some cause for optimism. Trends were generally similar across the remaining four non-metropolitan counties that added websites as well, with each of these counties being in a different state. Three of these counties had websites that only included Stage I content. All in all, of the 11 counties that had created websites since 2007, nine exhibited only Stage I characteristics, with the remaining two sites exhibiting Stage II

Figure 1. Percent Counties by Location with Websites by Year

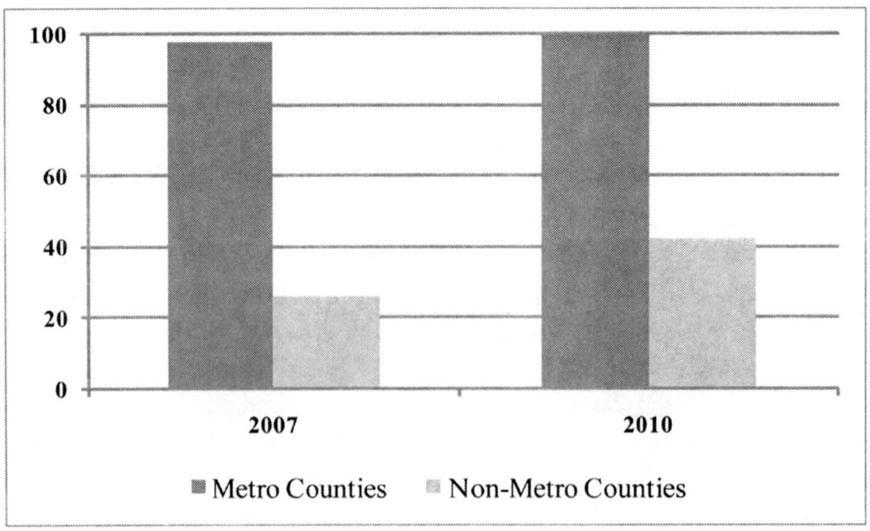

levels of E-government activity. Furthermore, it is perhaps of note that one of the counties that no longer had a website in 2010 was in Texas, and in 2007 that county's site was a result of collaborative efforts with a state-wide county government association. For at least this one county in Texas, these collaborative efforts had for some reason collapsed.

Finally, what should not be lost in relation to this aspect of the analysis is that close to three-quarters (27 out of 37) of the non-metropolitan counties that did not have a website in 2007 still did not have a site by 2010. Meanwhile, two counties in the 2007 non-metropolitan county sample no longer had a site. Only one of the non-metropolitan counties that had added a site demonstrated levels of sophistication beyond simply having a basic, online presence. Thus, while most counties that did not have a website in 2007 still did not have one in 2010, those that had added a site – 9 out of 10 – had made what can be described as an incremental move into Stage I E-government activity. As will be discussed in relation to various other findings in this analysis, tendencies of incremental movement – at least in instances where there was any movement at all – would turn out to be the norm. More generally, however, any movement through stages was rare.

Just Going Through a Stage?

As noted in the methods section, to further examine the nature of the website maturation process, the next phase of the analysis included a random sample of 50 counties that all had websites, meaning that each of these counties were, at the very least, at Stage I levels of E-government in 2007. At that time, all of the websites in the metropolitan counties had content indicative of at least a Stage II level of sophistication, with the majority of these counties actually including transactional, Stage III levels of functionality (see Figure 2). However, the non-metropolitan counties exhibited a completely different set of circumstances. By 2010, slightly less than half of these counties still only included Stage II levels of functionality, and only 20 percent exhibited Stage III levels of sophistication.

As alluded to in the previous section, between 2007 and 2010, the phenomena of either decline, stagnation, or at best incremental movement through one stage at a time was evident in this

Figure 2. Percent Counties by Stage II and Stage III E-government

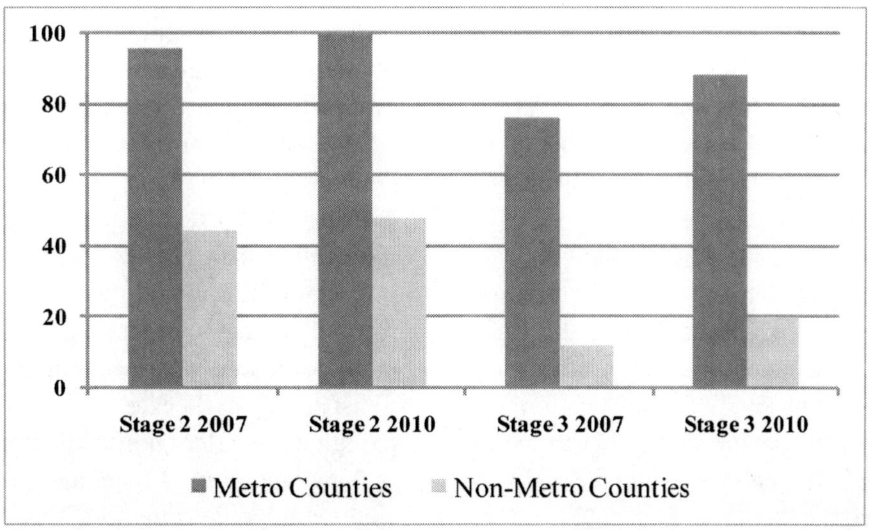

aspect of the analysis as well, particularly in relation to the non-metropolitan depressed counties. Of the 14 non-metropolitan county websites that could be characterized as being at a Stage I level of sophistication in 2007, only two of these sites had advanced beyond this stage by 2010 – one had advanced to Stage II, and another to Stage III. Nine of these websites remained in Stage I, while three of the counties included in the initial sample no longer had sites. In short, 12 of the 14 (86 percent) non-metropolitan counties that were only at Stage I levels of E-government in 2007 either remained at that level or no longer had a site close to three years later – suggesting a trend of stagnation, if not decline, rather than one of sequentially advancing through stages. Similarly, of the 11 non-metropolitan counties that were in Stage II in 2007, only one had moved to Stage III.

Across the entire analysis, and unlike some of the counties that only had a basic presence in 2007, any county that had achieved at least a Stage II level of sophistication in 2007 still had a website in the follow-up analysis. Yet of the 28 counties that were either in Stage I or Stage II, but not yet in Stage III in 2007, only six (21 percent) had advanced at least one stage, with only one of these advancing more than one stage. Similarly, and as referred to in the previous section, of the counties that did not have a website in 2007, far and away the majority of those that did have a website by 2010 only offered basic, Stage I E-government content. Thus, the overall analysis supports the idea that at least in some contexts, trends related to E-government maturation are characterized more by stagnation than by even incremental progress; and in the relatively rare instances where any sort of website maturation is taking place, the tendency, at least at this time, is more one of incremental change rather than skipping a stage. The level of sophistication that had been established by the county governments included in the 2007 analysis had, in the majority of cases, stayed the same.

Stages of E-Democracy

The E-democracy content included on the websites led to what might be considered some causes for concern as well. Taking all of the websites into account, the content and functionality made available in these regards followed the same sort of pattern as identified in relation to the previously discussed aspects of the research. Stage I, basic content information was the most likely E-democracy types of content to be available, followed by increasingly more sophisticated interactive, and then transaction-oriented, content (see Table 1). Specifically, the top four content categories included on the sites, such as phone numbers and voter registration information, could be understood as basic presence, Stage I content. The next most likely content available was information that could be understood as having Stage II characteristics, such as meeting minutes, local ordinance information, and county budgets, which were typically included as Microsoft word or.pdf files. Finally, what might be considered transactional content, such as online surveys and polls, was exceptionally rare. In instances where this functionality was available, the content tended to be superficial.

Perhaps surprisingly, less than half of the sites included public official email addresses. Such information requires no more than to be in the form of basic content, similar to that of contact phone numbers and addresses. This finding sheds a rather bleak light on what is typically understood as one of the more compelling, participatory democracy features of E-government. Apparently political officials, at least in these instances, more often than not feel disinclined to include information that would allow for a relatively direct form of contact. One small glimmer of improvement over time was in the area of government transparency, with categories showing the most, though nonetheless limited, increases in relation to the availability of meeting minutes as well as county budget information. These increases may

Table 1. E-democracy Content on Websites

	2007	2010
Contact Information - Phone Numbers	43	44
Contact Information – Address(es)	43	44
Meeting Schedules	37	37
Voter Registration Information	33	36
Meeting Agendas	32	32
Meeting Minutes (Text)	23	30
Local Code/Ordinance Information	28	29
County Budget Information	24	28
Elected Official Email Address(es)	24	23
Meeting Minutes (Audio/Video)	8	9
Listing of Contract Award Recipients	9	9
Online Survey/Poll	2	2

Note: The 2010 totals are for the 47 counties from 2007 that still had websites.

have been reflective of county governments experiencing tangible citizen demand for such information. On the other hand, contract awards listings – another issue that relates to government transparency – were included on less than 20 percent of the sites, and this category showed no improvement over time. In general, there was limited overall change in terms of E-democracy types of content included on the websites between 2007 and 2010, and key areas related to online civic engagement and political participation showed virtually no improvement at all. Like other elements of the analysis, a key conclusion that can be drawn from this aspect of the research is that, at least at this scale of government in the U.S., E-government activity is stagnating.

CONCLUSION

This analysis was framed in an 'E-government stages' based context, which over the past decade has served as a key theoretical basis for understanding the E-government maturation process. While the body of work related to this issue has become relatively substantial, much of it is also remarkably consistent, and can thereby provide a relatively straightforward approach to empirically examining web-based activities over time and across different government entities. Overall, a limited amount of E-government research has examined such activity at the local level, despite the unique importance of local government in regards to services as well as grassroots politics. Furthermore, despite the prevalence of E-government stages literature, an exceptionally scant amount of research has offered any empirical verification of the website maturation process, including at various political scales. More generally, and as suggested in other, scholarly-based E-government literature, longitudinal analyses have been rare in the overall body of E-government research to this point in time. The results of this research empirically inform an important theoretical area in the E-government literature, one that has received very little empirical attention. This research conveyed the results of a cross-sectional and longitudinal analysis that examined how E-government in practice corresponds with E-government stages models, with the understanding that these models often lack empirical verification. The results suggest that the stages literature may be a poor predictor of the E-government maturation process.

This chapter has addressed some of the key themes serving as the basis for this edited volume, including not only the practice of measuring E-government performance, but issues such as online civic engagement and its challenges, as well as possibilities associated with cross-boundary collaboration. Having utilized primary data to evaluate E-government maturation in a stages-based context, the results of this work offer findings for practical as well as theoretical consideration. In general, the findings should serve as a cautionary tale. Amidst various key findings, the analysis demonstrates that while many local governments have achieved a relatively high level of maturity in E-government activity, especially in terms of website functionality, others have not, and this research identifies major challenges associated with establishing even basic E-government activity in some locations. For many rural, low income areas that are already marginalized in socioeconomic terms, the current status of local E-government activity, and prospects for the future, seem unpromising. If it is in fact true that local government website activity tends to stagnate at a given stage, which seems apparent through this research, the short term, if not longer term prospects for relatively more advanced E-government applications being available in counties that are currently at, or have yet to enter, Stage I levels of E-government activity are seemingly limited.

Across all of the websites assessed in the study there was little evidence of innovation over the three year period of study, including in areas such as Web 2.0 applications. Furthermore, the results of this analysis can only lead to the conclusion that achieving more advanced, E-democracy ideals, regardless of issues such as urban-rural location, may be particularly difficult. In contrast to how E-democracy types of issues are often envisioned in the E-government literature, this chapter concludes that government websites may not necessarily be the key mediums for some of the political participation and civic engagement applications that are often seen as some of the ultimate goals of E-government. Instead, trends may point to phenomena such as social networking sites, which are ostensibly outside the realm of government, as being the settings where E-democracy ideals, at least to some extent and to this point in time, have the best opportunity to thrive. In short, the E-democracy visions that are pervasive in much of the E-government literature, to the extent that they are even being realized at all, are taking place outside of, strictly speaking, E-government activity. One would be challenged to find consistent success, not only at the local level but at any level, in regards to substantive online civic engagement and deliberative democracy types of activity taking place through government websites. Overall, these types of challenges, though opportunities as well, can only be expected to evolve over time in conjunction with the ongoing evolution of web-based technologies.

These and other findings may lead to conclusions about the necessity for some government entities, especially local governments which typically face considerable fiscal and staffing constraints, to further consider cross-boundary E-government collaborations. Such collaborations, however, will likely present their own challenges. It was evident through this study that collaborative efforts were, at best, only leading to limited benefits, and one county that had collaborated with a state-wide association to develop a website no longer had a site in 2010. Other collaborative efforts, such as between state and local governments in Kentucky, typically resulted in the local governments have nothing more than a basic, Stage I online presence, which tends to offer little, if any, stakeholder benefits. In a few instances the analysis revealed cross-boundary collaborations between private sector entities and local governments, as well as what might be referred to as 'quasi-governmental' website activity, with government information hosted on local Chamber of Commerce websites. Perhaps depending upon one's ideological viewpoint, these types of public-private website partnerships might be seen as innovative and efficient; or, conversely, viewed as private sector encroachment upon the public sector domain, which in turn can threaten matters associated with political accountability, citizen trust in government, and the democratic ideals that are central to how E-government is commonly idealized more generally.

In terms of broader theoretical considerations related to the E-government stages literature, the analysis made it apparent that differentiating by functionality in regards to simply having, or not having, an online presence; interactive content; and offering the ability to conduct transactions online is a reasonable way to differentiate between levels of website activity, at least in terms of content and functionality. Further proof of this came through, for example, all counties that had Stage III content having Stage II content as well. Overall the analysis suggested that, the stages of basic presence (or lack there-of); interaction, particularly in terms of online forms; and transactions, such as the ability to make online payments, has utility in terms of clearly differentiating levels of website activity. At the same time, the longitudinal analysis suggested that rather than maturing over time, levels of website sophistication have tended to stagnate, at least for the more rural counties included in the analysis. Overall, if there was any E-government maturation taking place at all in these types of counties, it tended to be incremental. Thus, in only a few instances did counties advance more than one stage during the period studied. Only two counties in the analysis went from having no website at all to having a website with Stage II levels of sophistication, while only one county went from Stage I to Stage III. In contrast to the overall tone of the E-government stages literature, which suggests that government agency website activity should mature over time, this analysis demonstrated that the current process is marked by stagnation, and in some instances even decline, for some counties. Any sort of incremental, stages-based website changes taking place at all during the period studied was the exception rather than the norm. The results of this analysis also suggest that E-democracy should not necessarily be considered its own, unique, and entirely advanced, stage. Though only a few models have differentiated in these regards, this analysis indicated that identifying political engagement, government transparency, and related types of content in relation to different levels of sophistication has utility as well as merit.

This study concludes that ongoing assessments and perhaps re-evaluations of E-government stages models, as well as appraisals of government activities through the lens of such models, can be a useful if not necessary element of E-government performance evaluation. This chapter has essentially outlined a relatively straightforward mechanism for measuring E-government performance, though with the understanding that these types of frameworks will need to be constantly evaluated to remain relevant. For public administrators, policy analysts, and scholars who want to effectively understand the nature, development, relevance, and challenges associated with E-government activity, similar types of empirical evaluations will be essential. In the meantime, the results of this research suggest that for some locations, even basic E-government activity remains a particular challenge, including in a country that is understood to be at the leading edge of E-government activity. Meanwhile, and even across the metropolitan, more affluent locations included in this study, some of the grand visions of the civic engagement elements associated with E-government are far from being realized. The results of this analysis suggest that for governments to truly play an active role in areas such as encouraging deliberative democracy will require not only candid evaluations of such matters, but exceptionally determined efforts towards realizing such objectives as well.

REFERENCES

Allen, B. A., Juillet, L., Paquet, G., & Roy, J. (2001). E-governance & government online in Canada: Partnerships, people, & prospects. *Government Information Quarterly*, *18*, 94–104. doi:10.1016/S0740-624X(01)00063-6

Baum, C. H., & Maio, A. D. (2000). *Gartner's four phases of e-government model*. Retrieved December 3, 2007, from http://www.gartner.com

Brown, M. M. (2007). Understanding e-government benefits: An examination of leading-edge local governments. *American Review of Public Administration*, *37*(2), 178–197. doi:10.1177/0275074006291635

Capgemini. (2005). *Online availability of public services: How is Europe progressing?* Capgemini for the European Commission Directorate General. Information and Society Media. Retrieved December 3, 2007, from http://ec.europa.eu/information_society/soccul/ egov/ egov_benchmarking_2005.pdf

Census, U. S. (2008). *Metropolitan and micropolitan statistical areas*. Retrieved June 2, 2007, from http://www.census.gov/ population/www/metroareas /metroarea.html

Center for Digital Government (CDG). (2006). *Digital counties survey*. Folsom, CA: The Center for Digital Government. Retrieved June 7, 2007, from http://www.centerdigitalgov.com/ contact.php.

Chatfield, A. T., & Alhujran, O. (2008). A cross-country comparative analysis of e-government service delivery among Arab countries. *Information Technology for Development, 15*(3), 151–170. doi:10.1002/itdj.20124

Chen, Y., & Gant, J. (2001). Transforming local e-government services: The use of application service providers. *Government Information Quarterly, 18*(4), 343–355. doi:10.1016/S0740-624X(01)00090-9

Chen, Y., & Hsieh, J. (2009). Advancing e-governance: Comparing Taiwan and the United States. *Public Administration Review, 69*, s151–s158. doi:10.1111/j.1540-6210.2009.02103.x

Choudrie, J., Weerakkody, V., & Jones, S. (2005). Realising e-government in the UK: Rural and urban challenges. *The Journal of Enterprise Information Management, 18*(5), 568–585. doi:10.1108/17410390510624016

Claver-Cortés, E., Juana-Espinosa, S., & Tarí, J. J. (2008). E-government maturity at Spanish local levels. *International Journal of Value Chain Management, 2*(1), 4–17. doi:10.1504/IJVCM.2008.016115

Coursey, D., & Norris, D. (2008). Models of e-government: Are they correct? An empirical assessment. *Public Administration Review, 68*(3), 523–536. doi:10.1111/j.1540-6210.2008.00888.x

Coursey, D. H., & Killingsworth, J. (2005). Managing e-government in Florida: Further lessons from transition and maturity. In Garson, G. D. (Ed.), *Handbook of public Information Systems* (2nd ed., pp. 335–351). New York, NY: Marcel Dekker/CRC.

Cresswell, A. M., & Pardo, T. A. (2001). Implications of legal and organizational issues for urban digital government development. *Government Information Quarterly, 18*(4), 269–278. doi:10.1016/S0740-624X(01)00086-7

Dawes, S. S. (2008). The evolution and continuing challenges of e-governance. *Public Administration Review, 68*(s1), s86–s102. doi:10.1111/j.1540-6210.2008.00981.x

Deloitte, R. (2000). *At the dawn of e-government: The citizen as customer*. New York, NY: Deloitte Research.

Eyob, E. (2004). E-government: Breaking the frontier of inefficiencies in the public sector. *Electronic Government, 1*(1), 107–114. doi:10.1504/EG.2004.004140

Fagan, J. C., & Fagan, B. D. (2001). Citizens access to on-line legislative documents. *Government Information Quarterly, 18*, 105–121. doi:10.1016/S0740-624X(01)00064-8

Ferber, P., Foltz, F., & Pugliese, R. (2004). *Cyberdemocracy v. e-government: The degree of interactivity on state legislative websites.* Paper presented at the 2004 Meeting of the American Political Science Association, Chicago, IL.

Fullenbaum, R., & McNeill, M. (1995). *Survey and comparison of distressed area definitions*. Washington, DC: Appalachian Regional Commission.

Gisler, M., & Spahni, D. (2001). *E-government*. Haupt.

Goldkuhl, G., & Persson, A. (2006). *From e-ladder to e-diamond - Re-conceptualizing models for public e-services*. Paper presented at the 14th European Conference on Information Systems, June 2006.

Greenberg, S. R. (2006). *State e-government strategies: Identifying best practices and applications*. Report for the Congressional Research Service. Retrieved June 14, 2007, from http://www.utexas.edu/lbj /pubs/isbn/egovernment

Hale, M., Musso, J., & Weare, C. (1999). Developing digital democracy: Evidence from Californian municipal Web pages. In Hague, B. N., & Loader, B. D. (Eds.), *Digital democracy: Discourse and decision making in the information age* (pp. 96–115). London, UK: Routledge.

Heeks, R. (2006). *Benchmarking e-government: Improving the national and international measurement, evaluation and comparison of e-government*. Manchester, UK: Institute for Development Policy and Management.

Heeks, R., & Bailur, S. (2007). Analyzing e-government research: Perspectives, philosophies, theories, methods, and practice. *Government Information Quarterly*, *24*, 243–265. doi:10.1016/j.giq.2006.06.005

Hiller, J. S., & Belanger, F. (2001). *Privacy strategies for electronic government*. The PricewaterhouseCoopers Endowment for The Business of Government, Arlington, VA. Retrieved June 19, 2007, from http://www.businessofgovernment.org /pdfs/HillerReport.pdf

Howard, M. (2001). E-government across the globe: How will "e" change government? *Government Finance Review*, *17*(4), 6–9.

Huang, C. J., & Chao, M.-H. (2001). Managing WWW in public administration: Uses and misuses. *Government Information Quarterly*, *18*(4), 357–373. doi:10.1016/S0740-624X(01)00085-5

Huang, Z. (2006). E-government practices at local levels: An analysis of U.S. counties websites. *Issues in Information Systems*, *7*(2), 165–170.

Irani, Z., Al-Sebie, M., & Elliman, T. (2006). Transaction stage of e-government systems: Identification of its location & importance. *Proceedings of the 39th Hawaii International Conference on System Sciences, 2006*.

Janssen, D., Rotthier, S., & Snijkers, K. (2004). If you measure it they will score: An assessment of international e-government benchmarking. *Information Polity*, *9*, 121–130.

Janssen, M., & Veenstra, A. F. v. (2005). Stages of growth in e-government: An architectural approach. *The Electronic Journal of E-Government*, *3*(4), 193–200.

Kaaya, J. (2004). Implementing e-government services in East Africa: Assessing status through content analysis of government websites. *The Electronic Journal of E-Government*, *2*(1), 39–54.

Kaylor, C., Deshazo, R., & Eck, D. V. (2001). Gauging e-government: A report on implementing services among American cities. *Government Information Quarterly*, *18*(4), 293–307. doi:10.1016/S0740-624X(01)00089-2

Kinder, T. (2002). Vote early, vote often? Democracy in European cities. *Public Administration*, *8*(3), 557–582. doi:10.1111/1467-9299.00318

Layne, J., & Lee, J. (2001). Developing fully functional e-government: A four stage model. *Government Information Quarterly*, *18*(2), 122–136. doi:10.1016/S0740-624X(01)00066-1

Lee, J. (2010). 10 year retrospect on stage models of e-government: A qualitative meta-synthesis. *Government Information Quarterly*, *27*(3), 220–230. doi:10.1016/j.giq.2009.12.009

McCarthy, R. V., & Aronson, J. E. (2000/2001). Activating consumer response: A model for website design strategy. *Journal of Computer Information Systems*, *41*(2), 2–9.

McDonagh, M. (2002). E-government in Australia: The challenge to privacy of personal information. *International Journal of Law and Information Technology*, *10*(3), 327–343. doi:10.1093/ijlit/10.3.327

Mele, V. (2005). Paradigm and practice: The innovative organization to deal with e-government. In Khosrow-Pour, M. (Ed.), *Practicing e-government: A global perspective* (pp. 289–309). Hershey, PA: Idea Group. doi:10.4018/978-1-59140-637-2.ch013

National Association of Counties (NACO). (2000). *2000 e-government survey*. Washington, DC: National Association of Counties.

Norris, D. F., & Moon, M. J. (2005). Advancing e-government at the grassroots: Tortoise or hare? *Public Administration Review*, *65*(1), 65–75.

Parks, J. D., & Schelin, S. H. (2005). Assessing e-government innovation. In Garson, G. D. (Ed.), *Handbook of public Information Systems* (2nd ed., pp. 615–630). New York, NY: Marcel Dekker/CRC.

Piaget, J. (1954). *The construction of reality in the child*. New York, NY: Basic Books. doi:10.1037/11168-000

Rao, S. S., & Metts, G. (2003). Electronic commerce development in small and medium sized enterprises: A stage model and its implications. *Business Process Management*, *9*(1), 11–32. doi:10.1108/14637150310461378

Reddick, C. G. (2004). A two-stage model of e-government growth: Theories and empirical evidence for U.S. cities. *Government Information Quarterly*, *21*(1), 51–64. doi:10.1016/j.giq.2003.11.004

Rostow, W. W. (1960). *The stages of economic growth: A non-Communist manifesto*. Cambridge, UK: University Press.

Sakowicz, M. (2004). *How to evaluate e-government? Different methodologies and methods*. United Nations Online Network in Public Administration and Finance. Retrieved December 2, 2007, from http://www.unpan.org/

Santana, M. (2009). A preliminary assessment of the development of e-government in a local government in Peru. *Journal of Asia-Pacific Studies*, *12*, 75–89.

Scott, J. K. (2006). "E" the people: Do U.S. municipal government websites support public involvement? *Public Administration Review*, *66*(3), 341–353. doi:10.1111/j.1540-6210.2006.00593.x

Seifert, J. W., & Petersen, R. E. (2002). The promise of all things E? Expectations and challenges of emergent electronic government. *Perspectives on Global Development and Technology*, *1*(2), 193–212. doi:10.1163/156915002100419808

Siau, K., & Long, Y. (2005). Synthesizing e-government stage models – A meta-synthesis based on meta-ethnography approach. *Industrial Management & Data Systems*, *105*(4), 443–458. doi:10.1108/02635570510592352

Stowers, G. N. L. (1999). Becoming cyberactive: State and local governments on the World Wide Web. *Government Information Quarterly*, *16*(2), 111–127. doi:10.1016/S0740-624X(99)80003-3

Streib, G. D., & Willoughby, K. G. (2005). Local governments as e-governments: Meeting the implementation challenge. *Public Administration Quarterly*, *29*(1), 78-110.

United Nations. (UN). (2005). *Global e-government readiness report 2005*. New York, NY: United Nations Department of Economic and Social Affairs Division for Public Administration and Development Management. Retrieved from http://unpan1.un.org/intradoc /groups/public/ documents/un/ unpan021888.pdf

United Nations. (UN). (2008). *UN e-government survey 2008: From e-government to connected governance*. United Nations Department of Economic and Social Affairs, Division for Public Administration and Development Management. Retrieved from http://unpan1.un.org/intradoc/ groups/public/documents /un/unpan028607.pdf

United Nations. (UN). (2010). *United Nations e-government survey 2010*. New York, NY: United Nations Department of Economic and Social Affairs. Retrieved April 30, 2010, from http://www2. unpan.org/egovkb /global_reports/10report.htm

United Nations and the American Society for Public Administration (UN & ASPA). (2002). *Benchmarking e-government: A global perspective*: United Nations Division for Public Economics and Public Administration and American Society for Public Administration. Retrieved from http://unpan1.un.org/intradoc /groups/public/ documents /UN/UNPAN021547.pdf

U.S. Office of Management and Budget (U.S. OMB). (2005). *FY 2004 report to Congress on implementation of the E-Government Act of 2002*. Office of Management and Budget. Retrieved December 7, 2007, from http://www.whitehouse. gov /omb/inforeg/ 2004_egov_report.pdf

West, D. M. (2004). E-government and the transformation of service delivery and citizen attitudes. *Public Administration Review*, *64*(1), 15–27. doi:10.1111/j.1540-6210.2004.00343.x

West, D. M. (2006). *State and federal e-government in the United States, 2006*. Retrieved July 7, 2007, from http://www.insidepolitics.org / egovt06us.pdf

Wilkinson, V. O., & Cappel, J. J. (2005). Impact of economic prosperity and population on e-government involvement. *Issues in Information Systems*, *6*(2), 204–209.

Wood, L., Bernt, P., & Ting, C. (2009). Implementing public utility commission websites: Targeting audiences, missing opportunities. *Public Administration Review*, *69*(4), 753–763. doi:10.1111/j.1540-6210.2009.02022.x

Ya Ni, A. (2006). *What drives the development of e-government? An analysis of U.S. county government's adoption of e-government services*. Paper Presented at the Association for Public Policy Analysis and management 2006 Fall Conference.

Yang, J., & Paul, S. (2005). E-government application at local level: Issues and challenges: An empirical study. *Electronic Government*, *2*(1), 56–76. doi:10.1504/EG.2005.006648

ENDNOTE

1. Readers are encouraged to contact the author if they would like a list of the counties included in the analysis.

Section 4
Institutional and Political Aspects of E-Governance

Chapter 13
Institutions of Information Access and Constraint:
The Cases of China and India

Jeannine E. Relly
University of Arizona, USA

ABSTRACT

This chapter examines institutions of information access and the potential for information asymmetry in China and India, both of which have recently adopted access-to-information regulations and legislation, respectively. An examination of these two countries largely is a study of most-different cases. The chapter uses the framework of institutionalism to follow the history of government information policy in both nations and to examine measurements of the political, cultural, and economic environments in which access-to-information legislation is adopted, implemented, enforced, and used by the public.

INTRODUCTION

The two Asian nations described as "continental-sized economies" joined a minority of developing nations in the world in adopting access-to-information legislation and regulations in the new millennium (Goswani, 2006, p.77; Relly, 2009). Though China's Open Government Information regulations (2007) and India's Right to Information Act (Gazette of India, 2005) may differ in what they propose and deliver, both governments had, to an extent, informing the public, combating corruption, and economic development as motives for adopting the laws that signal governmental openness (Banisar, 2006; Horsley, 2007a, 2007b; Guha Thakurta, 2009; Zhiyong, 2008). The two nations joined a club of more than six dozen nations and territories with access-to-information laws, regulations, ordinances, and codes, in what has been described as a global diffusion of information policy (Relly, 2009).

DOI: 10.4018/978-1-60960-753-1.ch013

Yale legal scholar Jamie P. Horsley wrote that China's open-government regulations "mark a turning point away from the deeply ingrained culture of government secrecy toward making Chinese government operations and information more transparent" (2007b, p.1). Scholar Alasdair Roberts (2010) wrote that the activity in India around the Right to Information Act is "the most exciting experiment with [Freedom of Information Act-style] laws in the world today" (p. 27).

This comparative study is the first to examine the similarities and differences in the political, cultural, and economic institutions of access to public information and governmental openness in China and India, nations that together account for more than a third of the world's 6.8 billion people and half of the poorest (U.S. Census, 2010; Guha Thakurta, 2009; Zhiyong, 2008; The Economist, 2009), which in itself provides strong potential for an enormous information-access divide.

There are numerous reasons to study access to information in these two nations. Access to information has become a social, political and economic issue in both nations. The two nations' economies are neck and neck in growth, and interest in information from these nations is insatiable, given that the two have expanded in dismal economic times and amidst a global recession at the end of the first decade of the new millennium, when other nations had declined in growth (Guha Thakurta, 2009, p. 1). Like India, which had state-level access-to-information laws before the legislation was adopted on the national level, China began adopting access-to-information legislation at the municipal and provincial levels before the Open Government Information regulations were adopted (Horsley, 2006; Snell & Xiao, 2007, p. 46).

Historically, the two nations have had different approaches to government-held information and access to it, which provides for markedly varied contrasts. China has the largest population in the world with one-party rule and India has the second largest number of citizens and is the world's largest democracy. The two nations also have very different narratives when it comes to their histories of governmental reform toward increased accountability in governance and the driving forces behind the adoption of access-to-information legislation and regulations.

Globalization has advanced a host of institutions that have spread in structure, if not spirit, from country to country (Banisar, 2006; Relly, 2009). Though access-to-information legislation is among the institutions that are being adopted in dozens of countries to advance the practice of governmental openness to varying degrees, this chapter suggests there are other institutions to be taken into consideration when examining citizens' access to government information and the prospects for political and economic openness in nations.

With the cases of China and India, as with all nations, there are unique institutions and factors that ultimately shape how access-to-information legislation is used and how it develops. As a number of scholars have pointed out, the mere presence of any type of institution, in this case access-to-information legislation and regulations, does not serve in any way as a guarantee that a nation will incorporate the norms that long have been embedded with each institution (North, 2004; Hall and Taylor, 1996; Pierson, 2004).

The following sections outline the framework of the chapter, the history of governmental reform related to access to information in China and India, the institutions of information access and the potential for information asymmetry, and the prospects for research areas in the future.

FRAMEWORK

This chapter uses the framework of institutionalism to study the context for access to information in China and India. As proposed by Hall and Taylor (1996), the three institutionalism schools – historical institutionalism, sociological institutionalism, and rational-choice institutionalism -- are used to complement the analytical strengths and constraints of each framework. Though there are a number of definitions of institutions, the chapter uses Douglass North's (2004) delineation of formal and informal institutions because of their fit with the three schools of institutionalism in this study. Formal institutions are defined as laws, regulations, constitutions, ordinances, policies and programs; and informal institutions are represented by that which is transmitted through cultural systems, such as traditions and customs (North, 2004, pp. 3, 46).

The framework of rational-choice institutionalism is employed because, to an extent, adopting the formal institutions of access-to-information legislation has the means-end objective of increasing transparency and reducing public uncertainty about governmental rules, regulations, policies, and activities, and ultimately reducing transaction costs. However, as scholars have noted, the rational-choice orientation is highly structural and depends on rational actors adhering to the constraints and rules of the game (Hay and Wincott, 1998). And it has been noted that formal and informal institutions and factors in the political, social, and economic environment of a nation weigh into the development of institutions and their capacity.

Given the limitations of the instrumental approach of rational-choice institutionalism, the chapter research is strengthened by considering the historical context and cultural institutions in which access legislation is embedded. Historical institutionalism in this study serves as a framework to examine the information policy context leading up to and following the adoption of access-to-information legislation in China and India. Historical events mark "critical junctures" whereby some form of institutional development transpires along the path in time (p. 950).

Further, sociological institutionalism was included as a framework for the precise points outlined by sociologists Walter Powell and Paul DiMaggio who have noted, "Institutions are a phenomenological process by which social relationships and actions come to be taken for granted" (Powell & DiMaggio cited in Sangmpam, 2007, p. 202). In choosing to use sociological institutionalism as a framework, the chapter acknowledges that while formal institutions, such as access-to-information legislation, may contribute to an environment that would support governmental openness and public knowledge of government activity, the informal institutions of culture and tradition play a role in the extent to which the laws and policies are effective.

Thus, the following sections examine the historical context in China and India that led up to the adoption of access-to-information legislation. The remaining sections examine new and old[1] political, cultural, and economic institutions and factors that the literature indicates are considered necessary for nations attempting to advance transparency policies, such as information-access legislation (Camerer, 2006; Grigorescu, 2002, Islam, 2006; Relly & Sabharwal, 2009; Roberts, 2006).

BACKGROUND

As historical institutionalists (Skocpol & Somers, 1980; Thelen, 1999; Thelen, 2000) would point out, the history leading up to China and India adopting access-to-information legislation will impact the development of institutions that support information access. Before examining the current status of new and old institutions of information access, the following two sections outline the paths that China and India have taken toward government information policy in the last several decades.

Development of Information Policy in China

It was in 1978 that China began to move toward an open-door policy to spur international investment in a nation that was devastated by the Cultural Revolution (Horsley, 2007a, 2007b; Yang, 2009). In this post-Mao period of the late 1970s, elite political figures determined that economic development was an essential priority for the state (Holzer & Zhang, 2009, p. 56).

Though the constitution of the People's Republic of China, adopted in 1982, does not provide for information rights, there are provisions within the constitution that lay a legal foundation for openness in government (Horsley, 2007a, p. 67). Open government at the village level began in the early 1980s, well after the Cultural Revolution. The village-level program began with farmers in rural sections of China who started a system with the support of national party branches that provided a legal foundation for publicizing information about the flow of income for public goods (Piotrowski, Zhang, Yu, & Lin, 2009; Zhou, 2009, p. 93). Horsley (2007a) suggests that a 1993 law adopted to protect consumers was the first to provide "'a right to know'" (pp. 67-68).

By the late 1990s, the Chinese Communist Party and a state council office issued a document titled "Joint Opinions on Perfecting Systems of Transparency in Village Affairs and a Democratic Administration System"(Carter & Yanbin, 2007, pp. 11-12). From the late 1990s into the new millennium, other laws required that government statistics would be published, environmental information would be shared with the public, and government licensing information would be open to the public (Horsley, 2007a, pp. 67-68).

The access-to-information ideology was developed further in the year 2000 and five years later, when the government expanded on the village level ideal in the advancement of publications with titles such as "Opinions Regarding Further Steps to Promote Transparency of Government Affairs in Local Government at Town and Village Level" and "Opinions on Further Enforcing Government Administration Publication," which focused in large part on access-to-government information, corruption abatement, developing government with respect for rule of law, and advancing the ideal of social democracy (Carter & Yanbin, 2007, p. 12).

The commitments made by China for accession into the World Trade Organization in 2001, which were made in order to open the nation's market to international services and products, included a number of transparency agreements with policies related to industry, trade, agriculture as well as regulations related to imports (U.S. General Accounting Office, 2002, p. 48). When it was requested, China committed to publishing information and providing clarification on information about laws, processes and rules to members of the World Trade Organization (WTO) (GAO, 2002, p. 9). At the beginning of the third year of WTO membership, many said the government had made progress in its transparency policies. However, a survey of member companies of the U.S.-China Business Council, in which 30 percent of the 208 members responded, it was clear that issues included poor access to information about the process of making rules in China (Walton, 2004, p. 6).

The drafters of China's Open Government Information regulations consulted with foreign experts during the drafting of the legislation (Horsley, 2007b, p.1). Because drafting laws and discussing them take more time than regulations in China, national open government regulations were drafted because it was more expedient, even though regulations do not have the status of laws (Horsley, 2007a, p. 69, 2007b, p.1).

Horsley (2007a) points out that information is not available about any grassroots movement, if such groups did spawn access-to-information legislation in China. However, it does appear that leadership within the government and academics in the nation carried the torch for increasing governmental openness through legislation (pp. 62-63). So, by all accounts, China's movement toward access-to-information regulations did not rise up from a grassroots push or social movement as in India and a number of other countries.

The adoption of the Open Government Information regulations was, in part, to satisfy international commitments. But according to Horsley (2007a), the move was largely for domestic reasons that included fighting government corruption, promoting economic development, and building trust in government (p. 1).

The Regulations of the People's Republic of China on Open Government Information (2007) were adopted in 2007 and went into effect on May 1, 2008. Eleven days later, the Sichuan earthquake struck and the government appeared to be more open with the public than with previous disasters; and a number of scholars, medical professionals, columnists and others commented on how different the level of governmental openness was from a major earthquake in 1976 (China Digital Times, 2008; Piotrowski et al., 2009). However, some argued that this, in the initial stages at least, could have been because the event was not politically threatening.

The Road to Adopting the Right to Information Act in India

Though the Supreme Court of India ruled in 1975 that the right to information is protected in the constitution, it would be nearly three decades later that a law would be adopted (Puddephatt, 2009; Rodrigues & Slough, 2005).

The right-to-information grassroots movement rose out of the Indian state of Rajasthan in the western side of the nation. Since the latter half of the 1980s, the Mazdoor Kisan Shakti Sangathan (MKSS) nongovernmental group in India has focused its agenda on the poor in the nation and corrupt government practices (Jenkins & Goetz, 1999), which led to the access-to-information campaign beginning in 1990.

Puddephatt (2009) writes that the coalition that has campaigned for access to information in India differs from those in other parts of the world in that the rural poor played a large role in the movement. The MKSS, comprised largely of rural agriculture workers who were illiterate and poor, staged marches, hunger strikes, protests and rallies under the banner "Our Money, Our Accounts" and "The Right to Know, the Right to Live," voicing disapproval about government activity on issues that included drought-relief assistance, minimum wages, working environments and pressing the government for access-to-information legislation (pp. 22-23).

According to Jenkins & Goetz (1999), the grassroots group received a broad network of support that included a few New-Delhi-based elites. The media increasingly paid attention to the public hearings and focused its attention on right to information for the poor who were seeking information from public authorities (Puddephatt, 2009). Prominent lawyers, retired bureaucrats, news media professionals, and others joined the struggle. Inspired by the grassroots movement, the National Campaign for People's Right to Information formed in 1996 in the capitol to press for access-to-information legislation. The group would not accept funding from any international donors or other institutional funders to preserve independence (p. 25).

By 1996, an access-to-information bill was drafted; however it was not introduced into the Indian parliament until 2002. It was approved that year in a watered-down version. By the time that the national law was adopted, there were nine states that had adopted the legislation (Rodrigues & Slough, 2005, p. 2). But the law never was implemented because a date was not set for the legislation to go into force. By 2005, both parliamentary houses had adopted the legislation and that same year the legislation entered into force (Puddephatt, 2009, pp. 24-26).

In the two and a half years following the law's adoption, citizens around the country had placed some 2 million requests for government information under the law (RTI Assessment & Analysis Group, 2009; Roberts (2010, p. 6).

POLITICAL, CULTURAL, & ECONOMIC INSTITUTIONS OF INFORMATION ACCESS

Given that access-to-information legislation could be one of the first steps toward a nation's government providing an institutional commitment to transparency policy and that the institutions in the environment in which the law or regulations are adopted will shape how effectively the law is implemented and used, the chapter examines old and new economic, political, and cultural institutions and factors that the literature indicates are considered necessary for nations to be ready for information-access legislation and the capacity to use it (Camerer, 2006; Grigorescu, 2002, Islam, 2006; Relly & Sabharwal, 2009; Roberts, 2006). As noted, some institutions are formal in structure, such as legal protections, policies, and programs; and some institutions are less structured yet are embedded in tradition. Both are critical to information access.

POLITICAL INSTITUTIONS AND ACCESS TO INFORMATION

In the global realm, access to information has been linked to freedom of expression in international declarations and covenants (United Nations, 1948; United Nations, 1966). Grigorescu (2002) argues that in addition to the institution of access-to-information legislation, the institution of a news media that is independent and free and an independent ombudsman are key to supporting governmental transparency (p. 469).A large body of normative and empirical literature also presents an argument for the institutions of a free news media and a robust civil society that would utilize the access-to-information legislation; this may include seeking government information on the Internet (Balkin, 1999; Besley & Burgess, 2001; Djankov, McLiesh, Nenova, & Shleifer, 2003; Donohue, Tichener, & Olien, 1995; Grigorescu, 2003; Price, Davis, Noll, & DeLuce, 2002; Relly & Sabharwal, 2009).

Among the international standards for effective implementation of access-to-information legislation, it has been suggested that an independent commissioner or ombudsman, or some type of independent body for oversight, would be designated to examine denials of information requests. According to these international standards, this office would, ideally, be involved in programming to advance knowledge and awareness of access legislation (Banisar, 2006; Council of Europe Committee of Ministers, 2002; Darbishire & Carson, 2006; Mendel, 2008). The ombudsman system has been among other international governance trends for several decades and is designed on a national level to offer an office that is independent so that it can investigate complaints that may arise within a government agency (Michael, 1982).

Based on this literature, the chapter utilizes secondary data to examine the measurements of political institutions and other factors in China and India that support information access (Freedom House, 2009a, 2009b; Global Public Integrity, 2009a, 2009b).

Effectiveness of Information Access Legislation and Civil Liberties

When the researchers scored public access to information, civil society and news media together, China received a "very weak" score of 50 and India received a moderate score of 72 (see Table 1) (Global Public Integrity, 2009a, 2009b). Both nations' scores largely were impacted by the scores for the strength of civil society and news media. It is important to note that both nations received a "strong" score for "public access to information" because of the adopted legislation. But when examining each nation for the effectiveness of the law in practice, there was more nuance.

In Table 1, the data indicate that the effectiveness for the institution of the "right to access information" in India was stronger than China

(Global Public Integrity, 2009a, 2009b). For China, the researchers found that although the Open Government Information regulations are useful for citizens as an instrument to access government information, and improvements have been made in implementation, there is a need for the government to improve the quality of the information that it is provided and for the government to limit how sensitive information is defined. The researchers who examined the implementation of the information-access regulations in China found that areas needing improvement also included: providing information requesters with reasons for denial and responding to appeals in a consistent manner. Interestingly, it was noted that the number of appeals to information request denials were not large (Global Public Integrity, 2009a).

In India, analysts with Global Public Integrity (2009b) calculated measurements for the information access environment primarily through using reports from nongovernmental and governmental surveys. These surveys indicated requesters stated that they obtained information from the government half of the time; the reporting from nongovernmental organization requesters was similar (40 percent of the time) while the government stated that it furnished information 90 percent of the time (p. 2). The main areas researchers cited for ineffectiveness in India's access to information program were that the government had issues with responding to requests within the time required by law and that the quality of the information received was considered unsatisfactory three-quarters of the time (Global Public Integrity, 2009b, p. 3).

Not surprisingly, as Table 1 notes, China and India had significantly different scores for the indictor for Civil Liberties, which ranged from 1 to 7 when recoded, with the highest number representing the strongest civil liberties (Freedom House, 2009a, 2009b, 2009c). The chapter uses the Civil Liberties indicator because it represents citizens' abilities to associate, assemble, express, and share information.

In its explanatory note on the Civil Liberties score, Freedom House (2009a) states that although China guarantees free speech in the constitution, government authorities control information flow through the news media, especially in areas that are deemed sensitive. The state also must approve of material that will go out for publication. Nongovernmental organizations must register with authorities in the government and must follow guidelines that limit activity that would cause public dissent (Freedom House, 2009a).

The tens of thousands of protests around the country in China in the last half of the past decade have led some scholars to note that President Hu Jintao's administration has recognized that issues, such as those related to the environment and social

Table 1. Political institutions for access to information

Country	Right to Access Information Effectiveness (2009)	Civil Liberties[1] (2009)	Online Information Access Obstacles[2] (2009)	Ombudsman Protected from Political Interference[3] (2009)
Indicator range	**0-100**	**1-7**	**0-100**	**0-100**
China	63	2	78	25
India	71	5	34	50

[1] The 1-to-7 scale for Civil Liberties scores were reverse coded so that the highest numbers now represent the strongest score.
[2] The highest end of the 0-to-100 scale represents the greatest amount of online information access Obstacles.
[3] The highest end of the 0-to-100 scale represents the greatest amount of protection from political interference for the ombudsman.
Sources: Freedom House (2009), Global Integrity (2009a, 2009b)

inequities, have caused these tensions. According to Holzer & Zhang (2009), this progression has led to newfound reform in the political agenda, which previously had largely focused on efficiency to promote economic development, toward striving to include values of governmental effectiveness, including social equity, governmental accountability, and democratic participation (p. S7). It will be of great interest to many just how this plays out in the most populated nation in the world with a recognized value for political stability.

In India, the constitution protects freedom of expression and speech. The news media is vibrant, though journalists in the nation are constrained in some cases when the Indian government censors articles that are related to security; also, laws related to criminal defamation or charges related to contempt of court have been used to quiet criticism (Freedom House, 2009a).

Online Information Access Issues

China's scores were three times higher than India's for issues with Online Information Access, a measurement that represents information access obstacles, content limitations, and user-right violations (see Table 1) (Deutsch Karlekar & Cook, 2009a). The reports that accompany the secondary data used in this chapter indicate that China has one of the most tightly controlled environments for Internet use of any state in the world. The report notes that the government of China has used a system that is multilayered in nature to monitor, censor, and control information used both on cellular telephones and on the Internet (p.1). In one pilot study of 15 nations, China was one of three countries that used systematic methods of filtering users' political content on the Internet through a centralized infrastructure system that allowed constraints on service providers and the quantity of gateways. China also was cited for filtering users' cellular text messages in a systematic manner (Deutsch Karlekar & Cook, 2009a, 2009c).

The same report on India notes the explosion in Internet and mobile phone use that started in the mid-1990s after the government opened the provider sector for Internet services. Overall, India's "Internet freedom" score was slightly depressed because of issues with citizens' access to technology because of its large number of poor citizens (low per capita income), rather than governmental controls and obstacles (Deutsch Karlekar & Cook, 2009b, pp.1-3).

Interestingly, China has more than three times the number of Internet users (298 million people) compared with India (82 million users) and just under double the mobile phone user penetration (347 million in India and 633 million in China in 2008) (Deutsch Karlekar & Cook, 2009a, 2009b), which is a direct measure of potential for information access.

Ombudsman Protected from Political Interference

The national ombudsman is used as a proxy measurement in this chapter because, more and more, an independent entity that monitors the appeal process when information requests are denied in nations with new access-to-information laws. According to the data, China scored moderate for the oversight and regulation of national ombudsman and India scored strong when laws requiring a national ombudsman were taken into consideration. However, both countries had issues when rated for the office being protected, in practice, from political interference (see Table 1) (Global Integrity, 2009a, 2009b). However, it is interesting to note that the Indian Right to Information Act takes great pains to ensure that the central and state information commissioners who oversee the implementation of the law are autonomous (The Gazette of India, 2005).

CULTURAL INSTITUTIONS AND INFORMATION ACCESS

According to the work of sociologist Talcott Parsons (1965), cultural norms interpenetrate social systems (p. 990). It also has been noted that the institution of culture, in some cases, may hold more power than formal arrangements (Puddephatt, 2006, p.10). This chapter acknowledges this could be the case in nations that recently have adopted access-to-information legislation. Kaldor, & Vejvoda (1997) note that some nations do not embrace a "rights culture" for a number of reasons, including a history of governmental traditions that have focused on "a communitarian outlook" without a "tradition of community policing" (pp. 67-68).

The literature also has linked access to information and the culture of corruption (Florini, 1999; Stiglitz, 2003; United Nations Development Program, 2004), inequities among citizens of a nation and access to information (Darbishire & Carson, 2006; Darch & Underwood, 2005), and ineffectiveness in governance and information access (Darbishire and Carson, 2006; Islam, 2006). Based on this literature, the study examines institutions of culture measurements for corruption, whistle-blower protection, enforcement of the law, and gender equity in education in China and India.

Corruption, Whistleblower Protection, Law Enforcement, and Gender Equity

The study used Transparency International's (2009) measurement of perception of corruption in this chapter about institutions of access to information because both India and China adopted access-to-information legislation and regulations, in part, as a means of enabling the public to have a way to check government activity in a push to curb corruption. On the 0-to-10 scale with the highest number indicating the highest level of perceived corruption after recoding, both nations scored similarly high (Table 2).

The reform policies in China that began after the Cultural Revolution unleashed potential for corruption. The Chinese government acknowledged that the social system was challenged during this period in that the bureaucratic structure had been weakened and the institutions available to deal with corruption were weakened by private interests (Yang, 2009, p. S144). The literature also has noted that the civil service in India has a weak system of monitoring performance and that worker apathy is embedded in Indian public worker culture, as are issues related to corruption in the form of nepotism, wielding influence, and bribery (Soni, 2008, p. 1159).

Transparency International noted in its 2009 report that China "has launched a sustained anti-

Table 2. Cultural institutions for information access

Country category	Perceptions of Corruption Index (2009)	Whistle-blowing Measures (2009)	Law Enforcement (2009)	Education Enrollment Ratio – Females as Percentage of Males (2007)
Indicator range	**0-10**	**0-100**	**0-100**	**0-100**
China	6.4	79 (moderate)	67 (weak)	100
India	6.6	69 (weak)	58 (very weak)	70

Sources: Global Integrity (2009a,2009b), Transparency International (2009), United Nations Development Program (2007), World Bank (2007)

corruption drive and intensified a crackdown on corruption in the public sector, investigating and prosecuting ministers, public officials and employees" (2009, p.2). In another report for the same year, India's issues with widespread corruption were described as one of the areas that undermined governmental accountability and government effectiveness (Freedom House, 2009b, p. 3).

To examine the culture of enforcement of the implementation of access-to-information legislation and regulations, the chapter included secondary data sources for the institution of law enforcement. China and India were shown to have "weak" and "very weak" law enforcement, respectively, and "weak" rule of law (Global Integrity, 2009a, 2009b).

Generally, the institution of whistleblower protection through legislation is designed to allow citizens or government employees to disclose information about issues, such as corruption, without suffering a penalty (Michaels, 1982). Both China and India have legal measures in place to protect civil servants who blow the whistle on authorities for abuse of power, graft, and corruption (Global Integrity, 2009a, 2009b). During the study period in China, researchers found that there were institutions in place to protect whistleblowers and there were some cases where these individuals were protected. However some cases of whistle-blowing were ignored because the government stated that the information was unverifiable. It was reported that more than half (60 percent) of the sources for corruption cases in China were from whistleblowers and that a national hotline has been set up for reports on public-sector corruption (Global Integrity, 2009a). In India, the researchers found that protection for public-service workers who are whistleblowers is present in a resolution but not in statute, though reports indicate legislation is being drafted (Global Integrity, 2009b).

Though it does appear that China's law enforcement scores and whistle-blower protection measurements are slightly stronger than India's scores for these measures, it is unclear how this will impact accountability in the area of access to information legislation because China is in transition from being a rule *by* law nation (Peerenboom, 2002). It also is unclear the extent to which information disclosed by whistleblowers about corrupt activity is shared with the public.

There are a number of institutions that could serve as proxies for examining equity and the potential for information access. The chapter used the measurement of gender equity in primary, secondary, and tertiary education enrollment of females as a percentage of males (United Nations Development Program, 2007). Data indicate there is near parity for access to education for both males and females in China, while India is behind China by 10 percent (Table 2). According to a study conducted by PricewaterhouseCoopers (2009), more than double the percentage of men (26 percent) than women (12 percent) knew about the access-to-information law in India (p.6). In two and a half years after the Right to Information Act was implemented, about 400,000 applications were filed for information in villages around the country (RTI Assessment, 2009). Surprisingly, most of the applicants were men (more than 90 percent in rural areas were men and 85 percent in urban locations were men who filed applications) (pp.7-8).

ECONOMIC INSTITUTIONS AND GOVERNMENT INFORMATION ACCESS

In an effort to compete in the globalized world and to augment economic development, a number of developing nations have adopted transparency policies, such as access-to-information legislation, ordinances, and regulations. In addition to access-to-information legislation, enhanced E-government programs (Banisar, 2006; Florini, 2007; Relly & Sabharwal, 2009) are used, in part, as a signal to business that a government is open about its policies and activities, an information environment that companies favor for investment and that donor nations prefer when providing aid. The programs also are used, in many countries, to inform the citizenry. However, building the infrastructure and human capacity that is necessary to respond to information requests in developing nations with newly adopted access legislation is a challenge (Grigorescu, 2003; Neuman & Calland, 2007; Roberts, 2004, 2006).

As Table 3 shows, China scored higher than India on all of the economic indicators of access capacity and information-access infrastructure. Given that the literature has pointed to the issue of the cost in developing nations of setting up the infrastructure for records and personnel in order to administer the implementation and enforcement of access-to-information legislation, constraints on budgets could be an issue. India's per capita income is less than half (43 percent) that of China (see Table 3). China's development of E-government measured here by the Web index also slightly exceeds that in quality of India. As Table 3 shows, China's telecommunication infrastructure was four times that of India's. And the capacity to read government information on the Web was nearly one-third higher in China than India.

Interestingly, electrical power capacity issues continue to hobble India. This directly impacts telecommunication infrastructure and access to information. In 2003, the government adopted a much needed Electricity Act in a year in which the nation had a 7.1 percent energy shortfall and the system has been described as having inadequate capacity to transmit power at affordable prices (Panagariya, 2005; Goswani, 2006).

One of India's infrastructural bright spots has been the mobile telephony, which has boomed with subscribers. However, in 2005, services in the information technology field, though a traded service, represented less than 2 percent of the Gross Domestic Product of the nation (Panagariya, 2005, 35).

In one of the many audits conducted around the implementation and use of the Right to Information Act in India, most of the more than 200 information officers in the government did not maintain electronic applications for information requests (PricewaterhouseCoopers, 2009, p. 4, 47). According to the responses from the survey, there was not an electronic management system of documents for this purpose in government offices (p. 47).

THE STRENGHTHS AND CONSTRAINTS OF INFORMATION ACCESS IN CHINA AND INDIA

As the history of China and India's information policies in the second half of the 20th century indicate, both countries have had a host of formal institutions suggesting information access, with one of the most recent examples being the institution of access to information in statute.

Table 3. Economic indicators and institutions of information-access infrastructure and access capacity

Country category	GDP per capita (2007)	Web Index [1] (2008)	Telecommunication Infrastructure Index[1] (2008)	Adult Literacy[2] (2007)
Indicator range	--	**0-1**	**0-1**	**0-100**
China	$2,432	.5084	.16	93.3%
India	$1,046	.4783	.0435	66%

[1] On the 0-to-1 index, the 1 represents the strongest E-Government presence represented in the Web Index and Telecommunication Infrastructure.

[2] Percentage of those 15 years and older who can read.

Sources: United Nations Development Program (2007a, 2007b) United Nations (2008)

Further, as the indicators of the new and old political, cultural, and economic institutions of these countries demonstrate, there are many variables that are involved in determining how equitable, effective, and efficient the environment is for fostering access to information.

Given the longstanding access-to-information and freedom of expression paradigm in democratic and industrialized nations, it will be an object lesson for researchers and practitioners to observe how the implementation, use, and enforcement of the access legislation will develop with the institutions that are in place in China and India. From the perspective of institutions of political openness, it is clear from the most recent literature that close to a dozen nations that are not electoral democracies have adopted access-to-information legislation (Relly & Cuillier, 2010; Grigorescu, 2003; Relly & Sabharwal, 2009; Roberts, 2006; Szekely, 2007; Vleugels, 2009). So China is not alone among the nations with some form of the legislation in an environment with constraints on civil liberties and other political rights. It does appear that the concept of the "ideal" context for access-to-information legislation may have shifted with one fourth of the developing nations that have adopted some form of information access legislation not being electoral democracies (Relly & Cuillier, 2010).

In the case of China, which clearly is operating under a different paradigm than India with the concept of public access to information, there are a number of considerations to keep in mind. A recent academic study using a convenience sample of 128 government functionaries in China found that nearly three-fourths (72%) of those surveyed had a "generally open" attitude about releasing government information under the regulations (Piotrowski et al., 2009, S132); it is not clear to what extent social desirability may have played a role in responses. And as Scotton and Hachten (2010) noted, the news media in China are seeking independence and increased rights and the public is reaching for more civil liberties. Still, Horsley (2007a) noted, China's government holds a "monopoly on political power today" that was born out of the founding of the People's Republic of China in 1949 as a "dictatorship of the people" (Horsley, 2007a, p. 55; People's Daily Online, 1982).

With cultural institutions, such as corrupt government activity, the literature indicates that China and India do not have a monopoly on dealing with corruption issues nor are these nations the only ones to use the institution of access-to-information legislation as an instrument to curb it. However, previous research has shown that China has adopted a number of laws to deal with corruption, in addition to the Open Government Information regulations, which are instrumental approaches toward attempting to constrain corrupt acts. Despite these legal measures to promote the flow of information about government activity, Yang (2009) suggests that corruption still remains an issue in China (p. S145-S146). And from the cultural standpoint, others point out that in India, because of the residual of colonial traditions from British rule in the bureaucracy (Roberts, 2010; Maheshwari, 2005), it will take a number of years to ascertain the effectiveness of the nation's information-access law (Roberts, 2010, p. 25-27).

In examining economic institutions and factors associated with information access, it is important to note that both China and India face challenges inherent in the course of development. Both nations show promise in specific instrumental areas of government information policy, and, though this study would not argue economic determinism, implementing access-to-information legislation and E-government programs effectively in the long term will require a commitment of financial resources by both nations. As Roberts (2004) suggests, governments in some poor countries will have to make challenging decisions when deciding upon programs to allocate funds.

China has invested more than $100 billion (U.S.) in projects related to information technology, more than any developing nation (Kluver, 2005). In China, E-government and access-to-information legislation are considered to be interrelated (Kluver, 2005, p. 75; Snell & Xiao, 2007, p. 45). And in India, though the country likely is the most monitored nation for implementation and use of its new Right to Information law (Roberts, 2010, p.3), the majority of information officers still do not use electronic applications for Right to Information Act requests (PricewaterhouseCoopers, 2009).

Researchers have previously reported a correlation between income per capita and telecommunications infrastructure (Relly & Sabharwal, 2009). As the figures in this chapter show, China has somewhat of an economic edge with its GDP per capita that is more than double that of India. China's investment in E-government, telecommunication infrastructure, and education is evident from the data examined in this chapter. However, in one of the few studies of the perceptions of information officers in China about the implementation of the nascent Open Government Information regulations, nearly two-thirds of the government employee respondents believed that records systems were not sufficient for dealing with public information requests, leading the researchers to conclude: "Current record management and organizational incentive systems in Chinese government agencies are important constraints on [Open Government Information] implementation" (Piotrowski et al., S132).

These issues are not idiosyncratic to China. Similarly, an audit report on India stated that information commission members in that nation suggested that to improve the system for implementing the Right to Information Act, the government should increase its budget, training, and management of records (RTI Assessment and Analysis Group, 2009, p.30). However, the auditors found that the government of India was not at risk, at the time, for being overwhelmed with information requests.

As the data in this chapter show, the high rate of illiteracy in India may inhibit expedient use of the Right to Information Act in the country. As India's population has grown, the proportion of the gross domestic product that the government has spent on higher education has dropped each decade (Panagariya, 2005). Goswani (2006) suggests that India's greatest challenge to development is that the nation does not have basic educational infrastructure in place for one-third of a billion people under 20 years old (p. 110).

In India, however, the government and information access advocates have attempted to deal with the illiteracy issue with a remarkable amount of innovation. The Right to Information Act has a section that specifies a government officer must render assistance to those who cannot write (The Gazette of India, 2005). The Indian government and others also have been credited for creative methods of reaching out to sectors of the public in access-to-information awareness campaigns. In the state of Kerala, for example, a top literacy official has held classes about the Right to Information Act for nearly 300,000 citizens (Roberts, 2010, p. 23). A festival for films also was held to exclusively address the right to information (p.23).

Nonetheless, issues related to access to information are not limited to citizens' capacity to read. Moon et al. (2005) found that a measurement that included literacy served as a predictor of a country's ability to effectively implement E-Government and for the public to access government information on the Web (p. 7). It has been noted that India's "bottleneck" in the information technology sector largely is because of the small percentage of citizens who attend college (Panagariya, 2005, p. 37). In 2005 those who were from 18 to 24 years attending Indian universities represented only 6 percent of that category of citizens (p. 37). And thus, the limits on the capacity to develop and maintain E-government programs may impede information access.

In both the cases of China and India, it will take time to ascertain how the design for implementation and utilization of access-to-information legislation and other formal and informal institutions of information access will take shape. Further, as Pierson (2004) wisely points out, there are alternatives to the institutional change focus that examine not only one grouping of institutional arrangements but the interaction effects from the perspective of institutional development.

FUTURE RESEARCH

The relative newness of the implementation of the Right to Information Act in India and the Open Government Regulations in China make the future for research on information access in these nations wide open. The political, cultural, and economic institutions associated with the capacity to effectively use access to information legislation, such as the ones outlined in this chapter and elsewhere, could be examined in time to gain a deeper understanding of the direction and level of commitment to public access in each nation. Pierson (2004) argues for observing how institutions develop rather than change because the study of institutional development "encourages scholars to remain attentive to the ways in which previous institutional outcomes can channel and constrain later efforts at institutional innovation" (p. 133).

Given that previous studies have indicated that records management and public sector worker training in both China and India appeared to be a potential limiting factor for implementing the access-to-information legislation in both countries (Roberts, 2010; Piotrowski et al., 2009), future studies in this area could produce important findings in the field. Similarly, both the popular and academic literature has hinted at issues in both nations with E-government. In China, the quality of information on government Web sites has been questioned (Fletcher, 2008). In India, the lack of information posted on government Web sites, in itself, has been cited as an issue (RTI Assessment & Analysis Group, 2009). Because these nations appear to be distances apart in this area in terms of making E-government a priority for government investment and determining what type of information would be made available to the public, each would make interesting case studies.

CONCLUSION

This chapter examined new and old institutions related to information access and information asymmetry in both China and India. An examination of these two countries, in many ways, is largely a study of most-different cases. Similar to the evolution of other policies in China, the Open Government Information regulations, in many ways, were born through governmental actors and academics rather than being generated from the grassroots up (Horsley, 2007a). In China, there have been a limited number of studies (Piotrowski et al., 2009; Horsley, 2010). In India, because of the grassroots movement that grew up around the introduction of the access-to-information legislation, journalists, civil society organizations, prominent lawyers and others, there is monitoring of the implementation and use of the law from many sectors of society (Puddephatt, 2009).

Interestingly, the countries are far apart in communication infrastructure and policies and practices toward access to information. Though China only had a slightly higher score than India for government information on the Web, India's income per capita was less than half that of China's and telecommunication infrastructure was one-fourth that of China, which some research indicates could impact the capacity for a government to provide information when there is political will to do so (Grigorescu, 2003; Neuman & Calland, 2007; Roberts, 2004, 2006).

Although China has invested billions of dollars in information technology for a number of years and has come close to approaching educational equity for women and men, the government limits access to information that would lead to social or political instability. In short, it still appears to place primary value on information access as it relates to economic development rather than information access as a human right, as reflected in some of the data examined in this chapter. India, on the other hand, considers access to information to be a right, as demonstrated by its Right to Information Act.

Given China's current focus on curbing corruption and economic development, it will be interesting to continue studies of the political institutions associated with information access in that nation, for numerous studies have shown that independent and free news media and voting and public participation rights have a curbing effect on corruption as measured by public perception (Brunetti & Weder, 2003; Triesman, 2000; Xin & Rudel, 2004). Though China scores consistently lower than India on the indicator for freedom of the news media and freedom of speech (Civil Liberties) and scores double India's score for online obstacles to information access, it has been noted that there have been subtle changes in China in these areas over the years (Scotton & Hachten, 2010; Yin, 2008), including that China paradoxically has a more socially connected online community than in the United States (Barboza, 2010, B1). And, as Horsley (2010) noted, citizens from all economic backgrounds have been filing requests for government information since the regulations went into effect; and the news media, which has not been active in making information requests under the regulations, has reported fervently on the use of them (p. 2).

As India's 44 percent illiteracy rate demonstrates, the financial and political commitment to the institution of education and literacy in India could serve as stumbling block for the capacity of the government to integrate technology and access to information and true public information access for the disadvantaged or underrepresented in society, though those who worked on the 2005 Right to Information Act were keenly aware of this issue and made certain that there is a provision in the law that allows assistance for those not able to file written requests. Other innovations are under way and one audit showed that 2 percent of the 400,000 village information requesters were illiterate (RTI Assessment & Analysis Group, 2009, pp. 7, 9).

As scholar Alasdair Roberts (2010) suggested, there are "daunting barriers" to the Right to Information Act in India fully reaching its potential with the mounting number of appeals and issues with enforcement (p.4). However, as Roberts notes, "It's worth remembering that the scale on which [the Right To Information Act] is being implemented is unprecedented" (p.2). And though less than one-fourth of China's central government's agencies received a score that was passing on a report card on implementation of the Open Government Information regulations, legal scholar Jamie Horsley (2010, p. 1) notes "the widespread and assertive citizen utilization of the fledgling [Open Government Information] system bodes well for the continued, if uneven, development of a more open and responsive Chinese government and realization of the Chinese people's right to know."

REFERENCES

RTI Assessment & Analysis Group and National Campaign for People's Right to Information. (2009, July). *Safeguarding the right to information – Report of the people's RTI assessment2008.*

Balkin, J. M. (1999). How mass media simulate political transparency. *Cultural Values*, *3*(4), 393–413.

Banisar, D. (2006). *Freedom of information around the world 2006: A global survey of access to government information laws*. London, UK: Privacy International.

Barboza, D. (2010, April 19). For Chinese, Web is the way to entertainment. *The New York Times,* B1, B8.

Besley, T., & Burgess, R. (2001). Political agency, government responsiveness and the role of the media. *European Economic Review*, *45*, 629–640. doi:10.1016/S0014-2921(01)00133-7

Brunetti, A., & Weder, B. (2003). A free press is bad news for corruption. *Journal of Public Economics, 87*, 1801–1824. doi:10.1016/S0047-2727(01)00186-4

Camerer, M. I. (2006). Measuring public integrity. *Journal of Democracy, 17*(1), 152–165. doi:10.1353/jod.2006.0004

Carter, M., & Yanbin, L. (2007). *EU-China Information Society Project – Access to government information in Europe and China: What lessons to be learned?*London, UK: The EU-China Information Society.

China Digital Times. (2008). *Chinese intellectuals contemplate the earthquake: Lessons we are learning*. Retrieved February 22, 2010, from http://chinadigitaltimes.net/ 2008/05/chinese-intellectuals- contemplate-on-earthquake- lessons-we-are-learning/

Council of Europe Committee of Ministers. (2002). *Recommendation of the Committee of Ministers to member states o access to official documents*. Retrieved March 1, 2010, from https://wcd.coe.int/ ViewDoc.jsp?id=262135&BackColorInternet=B9BDEE&BackColorIntranet=FFCD4F&BackColorLogged=FFC679

Darbishire, H., & Carson, T. (2006). *Transparency & silence: A survey of access to information laws and practices in 14 countries*. New York, NY: Open Society Institute.

Darch, C., & Underwood, P. G. (2005). Freedom of information legislation, state compliance and the discourse of knowledge: The South African experience. *The International Information & Library Review, 37*, 77–86. doi:10.1016/j.iilr.2005.05.003

Deutsch Karlekar, K., & Cook, S. G. (2009a). *Freedom on the net: A global assessment of Internet and digital media – China*. Washington, DC: Freedom House.

Djankov, S., McLiesh, C., Nenova, T., & Shleifer, A. (2003). Who owns the media? *The Journal of Law & Economics, 46*, 341–381. doi:10.1086/377116

Donohue, G. A., Tichenor, P. J., & Olien, C. N. (1995). A guard dog perspective on the role of media. *The Journal of Communication, 45*(2), 115–132. doi:10.1111/j.1460-2466.1995.tb00732.x

Fletcher, O. (2008, September 12). China's transparency is just thin air. *Online Asia Times*. Retrieved February 13, 2010, from http://www.atimes.com/atimes /China/J112Ad01.html

Florini, A. (1999). *Does the invisible hand need a transparent glove? The politics of transparency*. Washington, DC: Annual World Bank Conference on Development Economics.

Florini, A. (2007). The battle over transparency. In Florini, A. (Ed.), *The right to know: Transparency for an open world* (pp. 1–16). New York, NY: Columbia University Press.

Freedom House. (2009a). *Freedom in the world – China*. Washington, DC: Freedom House.

Freedom House. (2009b). *Freedom in the world – India*. Washington, DC: Freedom House.

Freedom House. (2009c). *Freedom in the world methodology*. Washington, DC: Freedom House.

Global Integrity. (2009a). *China: Integrity indicators scorecard*. Retrieved March 10, 2010, from http://report.globalintegrity.org /China/2009/scorecard/print

Global Integrity. (2009b). India: Integrity indicators scorecard. Retrieved March 10, 2010, from http://report.globalintegrity.org /India/2009/scorecard/print

Goswani, O. (2006). Elephants can dance: India's response to globalization and the challenges she faces. In Kelly, D. A., Rajan, R. S., & Goh, G. H. L. (Eds.), *Managing globalization: Lessons from China and India* (pp. 75–113). London, UK: World Scientific. doi:10.1142/9789812774729_0004

Grigorescu, A. (2002). European institutions and unsuccessful norm transmission: The case of transparency. *International Politics*, *39*, 467–489. doi:10.1057/palgrave.ip.8892005

Grigorescu, A. (2003). International organizations and government transparency: Linking the international development realms. *International Studies Quarterly*, *47*, 643–667. doi:10.1046/j.0020-8833.2003.04704003.x

Guha Thakurta, P. (2009, October 3). Can India's economy overtake China? *BBC News.* Retrieved on February 20, 2010, from http://news.bbc.co.uk/2/hi/8273464.stm

Hall, P. A., & Taylor, C. R. (1996). Political science and the three new institutionalisms. *Political Studies*, *44*(5), 936–957. doi:10.1111/j.1467-9248.1996.tb00343.x

Hay, C., & Wincott, D. (1998). Structure, agency and historical institutionalism. *Political Studies*, *46*, 951–957. doi:10.1111/1467-9248.00177

Holzer, M., & Zhang, M. (2009). Introduction to the special issue on comparative Chinese/American public administration. *Public Administration Review*, S5–S12. doi:10.1111/j.1540-6210.2009.02083.x

Horsley, J. P. (2006). Introduction on open government information implementation. *Government Information Quarterly*, *23*(1), 5–10. doi:10.1016/j.giq.2006.02.007

Horsley, J. P. (2007a). Toward an open China? In Florini, A. (Ed.), *The right to know: Transparency in an open world* (pp. 54–91). New York, NY: Columbia University Press.

Horsley, J. P. (2007b). *China adopts first nation-wide open government information regulations*. Retrieved February 9, 2010, from freedominfo.org/features /20070509.htm

Horsley, J. P. (2010, April 23). *Update on China's open government information regulations: Surprising public demand yielding some positive results*. Washington, DC: FreedomInfo.org. Retrieved on April 23, 2010, from http://www.freedominfo.org/ 2010/04/update-on-china -open-government-information -regulations

Islam, R. (2006). Does more transparency go along with better governance? *Economics and Politics*, *18*(2), 121–167. doi:10.1111/j.1468-0343.2006.00166.x

Jenkins, R., & Goetz, A. M. (1999). Accounts and accountability: Theoretical implications of the right–to–information movement in India. *Third World Quarterly*, *20*(3), 603–622. doi:10.1080/01436599913712

Kaldor, M., & Vejvoda, I. (1997). Democratization in East and Central European countries. *International Affairs*, *73*(1), 59–83. doi:10.2307/2623550

Kluver, R. (2005). The architecture of control: A Chinese strategy for e-governance. *Journal of Public Policy*, *25*(1), 75–97. doi:10.1017/S0143814X05000218

Maheshwari, S. R. (2005). *Public administration in India – The higher civil service*. New Delhi, India: Oxford University Press.

Mendel, T. (2008). *Freedom of information: A comparative legal survey* (2nd ed.). Paris, France: UNESCO.

Michael, J. (1982). *The politics of secrecy: Confidential government and the right to know*. New York, NY: Penguin Books.

Moon, M. J., Welch, E. W., & Wong, W. (2005). What drives global governance? An exploratory study at a macro level. *Proceedings of the 38th Hawaii International Conference on System Sciences, 2005.*

Neuman, L., & Calland, R. (2007). Making the law work - The challenges of implementation. In Florini, A. (Ed.), *The right to know: Transparency for an open world* (pp. 179–213). New York, NY: Columbia University Press.

North, D. (2004). *Institutions, institutional change and economic performance*. Cambridge, United Kingdom: Cambridge University Press.

Panagariya, A. (2005, July/August). A passage to prosperity. *Far Eastern Economic Review*, 35–38.

Parsons, T. (1965). Culture and the social system. In Parsons, T., Shils, E., Naegele, K. D., & Pitts, J. R. (Eds.), *Theories of society – Foundations of modern sociological theory* (pp. 963–993). New York, NY: MacMillan Publishing Co., Inc.

Peerenboom, R. (2002). *China's long march toward rule of law*. Cambridge, UK: Cambridge University Press. doi:10.1017/CBO9780511493737

People's Daily Online. (1982, December 4). *The constitution of the People's Republic of China*. Retrieved February 20, 2010, from http://english.peopledaily.com.cn /constitution/constitution.html

People's Republic of China Open Government Information. (2007). *Regulations translated into English*. The China Law Center, Yale Law School. Retrieved on February 20, 2010, from http://www.law.yale.edu/ documents/pdf/Intellectual_Life / Ch_OGI_Regualtions_Eng_ Final_051607.pdf

Pierson, P. (2004). *Politics in time*. Princeton, NJ: Princeton University Press.

Piotrowski, S. J., Zhang, Y., Yu, W., & Lin, W. (2009). Issues for implementation of the Chinese open government information regulations. *Public Administration Review*, *1*(69), S129–S135. doi:10.1111/j.1540-6210.2009.02100.x

Price, M. E., Davis Noll, B., & De Luce, D. (2002). *Mapping media assistance*. The Program in Comparative media Law & Policy, Center for Socio–Legal Studies, University of Oxford. Retrieved December 22, 2004, from www.undp.org/oslocentre/ docs04/A21%20Literature%REVIEW.doc

PricewaterhouseCooper. (2009, June). *Final report: Understanding the key issues and constraints in implementation the RTI Act*. New Delhi, India.

Puddephatt, A. (2006, April). *A guide to measuring the impact of right to information programs - Practical guidance note*. Oslo, Norway: United Nations Development Program.

Puddephatt, A. (2009). *Exploring the role of civil society in the formulation and adoption of access to information laws: The cases of Bulgaria, India, Mexico, South Africa, and the United Kingdom*. Washington, DC: World Bank Institute.

Relly, J. E. (2009). *The diffusion of access-to-information legislation: A cross-national contextual analysis*. Paper presented at the annual meeting of the International Communication Association, Chicago.

Relly, J. E., & Cuillier, D. (2010). A comparison of political, cultural, and economic indicators of access to information in Arab and non-Arab states. [special issue on Open Government]. *Government Information Quarterly*, *27*(4), 360–370. doi:10.1016/j.giq.2010.04.004

Relly, J. E., & Sabharwal, M. (2009). Perceptions of transparency of government policymaking: A cross-national study. *Government Information Quarterly*, *26*(1), 148–157. doi:10.1016/j.giq.2008.04.002

Roberts, A. (2004). A partial revolution: The diplomatic ethos and transparency in intergovernmental organizations. *Public Administration Review*, *64*(4), 410–424. doi:10.1111/j.1540-6210.2004.00388.x

Roberts, A. (2006). *Blacked out: Government secrecy in the information age*. New York, NY: Cambridge University Press.

Roberts, A. (2010). A great and revolutionary law? The first four years of India's Right to Information Act. *Public Administration Review, 70*(6), 925-933. Retrieved on April 29, 2010, from http://papers.ssrn.com/sol3/cf_dev /AbsByAuth.cfm?per_id=383666

Roberts, A. (2010, January 13). *India's Right to Information Act: The first four years*. Retrieved January 13, 2010, from Freedominfo.org/features /20100113.htm

Rodrigues, C., & Slough, P. (2005). India's right to information movement makes a breakthrough. *Open Government: A Journal of Freedom of Information, 1*(1), 1–13.

Sangmpam, S. N. (2007). Political rules: The false primacy of institutions in developing countries. *Political Studies*, *55*(1), 201–224. doi:10.1111/j.1467-9248.2007.00650.x

Skocpol, T., & Somers, M. (1980). The use of comparative history in macrosocial inquiry. *Comparative Studies in Society and History*, *22*(2), 174–197. doi:10.1017/S0010417500009282

Snell, R., & Xiao, W. (2007, January–March). Freedom of Information returns to China. *Public Administration Today*, 44-47.

Soni, V. (2008). A portrait of public administration in India: Challenges of governance in the world's largest democracy. *Public Administration Review*, (special issue), 1158–1161. doi:10.1111/j.1540-6210.2008.00965.x

Stiglitz, J. E. (2003). *Globalization and its discontents*. New York, NY: W.W. Norton & Co. Inc.

Szekely, I. (2007). Central and Eastern Europe – Starting from scratch. In Florini, A. (Ed.), *The right to know: Transparency for an open world* (pp. 116–142). New York, NY: Columbia University Press.

The Economist. (2009, November 26). *The gloves go on: Lessons from Brazil, China and India*. Retrieved February 20, 2010, from http://www.economist.com/ world/international/displaystory.cfm?story_id=14979330

The Gazette of India. (2005, June 15). *The Right to Information Act*, 2005. Retrieved February 28, 2010, from http://righttoinformation.gov.in /rti-act.pdf

Thelen, K. (1999). Historical institutionalism and comparative politics. *Annual Review of Political Science*, *2*, 369–404. doi:10.1146/annurev.polisci.2.1.369

Thelen, K. (2000). Timing and temporality in the analysis of institutional evolution and change. *Studies in American Political Development*, *14*(1), 101–108. doi:10.1017/S0898588X00213035

Transparency International. (2009). *Corruption perceptions index 2009 – Regional highlights: Asia-Pacific*. Berlin, Germany: Transparency International.

Treisman, D. (2000). The causes of corruption: A cross-national study. *Journal of Public Economics*, *76*, 399–457. doi:10.1016/S0047-2727(99)00092-4

United Nations Development Program. (2007a). *Human development report 2007/2008*. New York, NY: Palgrave Macmillan.

United Nations Development Program. (2007b). *Human development report 2009 – Statistics*. Retrieved on April 28, 2010, from http://hdrstats.undp.org/ en/indicators/#G

United Nations Development Programme. (2004). *Anti–corruption final version: Practice note*. Retrieved April 15, 2004, from http://www.uneca.org/itca/ governance /Documents/ Anti%20 Corruption%20Note%20FINAL%20VERSION %20031704.pdf

United Nations General Assembly. (1948). *Universal declaration of human rights*. Retrieved on March 29, 2010, from http://www.un.org/en/ documents/udhr/

United Nations General Assembly. (1966). *International covenant on civil and political rights*. Retrieved March 29, 2010, from http://www1.umn.edu/humanrts/ instree/b3ccpr.htm

U.S. Census Bureau. (2010). *US & world population clocks*. Retrieved March 17, 2010, from http:// www.census.gov/ main/www/popclock.html

U.S. General Accounting Office. (2002). *World Trade Organization analysis of China's commitments to other members, report to Congressional committees*. Washington, DC: U.S General Accounting Office.

Walton, J. (2004, January-February). WTO: China enters year three. *The China Business Review Online*. Retrieved February 20, 2010, from http:// www.chinabusinessreview.com/ public/0401/01.html

World Bank. (2007). *Databank*. Retrieved on August 13, 2010, from http://databank.worldbank.org /ddp/home.do?Step=3&id=4

Xin, X., & Rudel, T. K. (2004). The context for political corruption: A cross-national analysis. *Social Science Quarterly*, *85*(2), 294–309. doi:10.1111/j.0038-4941.2004.08502005.x

Yang, K. (2009). Institutional congruence, ideas, and anticorruption policy: The case of China and the United States. *Public Administration Review*, (special issue), S142–S150. doi:10.1111/j.1540-6210.2009.02102.x

Yin, J. (2008). Beyond the four theories of the press: A new model for the Asian & the world press. *Journalism & Communication Monographs*, *10*(1), 3–62.

Zhou, H. (2007). Open government in China – Practices and problems. In Florini, A. (Ed.), *The right to know: Transparency in an open world* (pp. 92–115). New York, NY: Columbia University Press.

ADDITIONAL READING

Ackerman, J. M., & Sandoval-Ballesteros, I. E. (2006). The global explosion of freedom of information laws. *Administrative Law Review*, *58*(85), 85–130.

Bennett, C. J. (1997). Understanding ripple effects: The cross-national adoption of policy instruments for bureaucratic accountability. *Governance: An International Journal of Policy and Administration*, *10*(3), 212–233.

Binder, C. (1952). Freedom of information and the United Nations. *International Organization*, *6*(2), 210–226. doi:10.1017/S0020818300016507

Blanton, T. (2003). Beyond the balancing test: National security and open government in the United States. In Walawender, B. D., & Colonna, A. (Eds.), *National security and open government: Striking the right balance* (pp. 33–73). Syracuse, NY: Campbell Public Affairs Institute.

Blanton, T. S. (2002, July/August). The world's right to know. *Foreign Policy*, *131*, 50–58. doi:10.2307/3183417

Chongkittavorn, K. (2002). The media and access to information in Thailand. In Islam, R., Djankov, S., McLeish, C., & Faintich, A. (Eds.), *The right to tell: The role of mass media in economic development* (pp. 255–265). Washington, D.C.: The World Bank.

Coronel, S. S. (2001). Fighting for the right to know. In S.S. Coronel (Ed.) (Ed.), *The right to know: Access to information in Southeast Asia* (pp. 1–19). Bangkok: Raintree Publishing Inc.

Cuillier, D. (2008). Access attitudes: A social learning approach to examining community engagement and support for press access to government records. *Journalism & Mass Communication Quarterly*, *85*(3), 551–578.

Darch, C., & Underwoord, P. G. (2010). *Freedom of information and the developing world: The citizen, the state and models of openness*. Oxford: Chandos Publishing.

Driscoll, P. D., Splichal, S. L., Salwen, M. B., & Garrison, B. (2000). Public support for access to government records: A national survey. In Davis, C. N., & Splichal, S. L. (Eds.), *Access denied: Freedom-of-information in the information age* (pp. 23–36). Ames, IA: Iowa State University Press.

Evans, B. (2003). The use by journalists of the Australian freedom of information regime. *Freedom of Information Review*, *103*, 8–16.

Feinberg, L. E. (1997). In Cooper, P. J., & Newland, C. A. (Eds.), *Open government and freedom of information: fishbowl accountability. Handbook of public law and administration* (pp. 376–399). San Francisco: Jossey-Bass Publishers.

Finel, B. I., & Lord, K. M. (1999). The surprising logic of transparency. *International Studies Quarterly*, *43*(2), 315–339. doi:10.1111/0020-8833.00122

Foerstel, H. N. (1999). *Freedom of information and the right to know - The origins and application of the Freedom of Information Act*. Westport, CT: Greenwood Press.

Gill, J., & Hughes, S. (2005). Bureaucratic compliance with Mexico's new access to information law. *Critical Studies in Media Communication*, *22*(2), 121–137. doi:10.1080/07393180500072038

Halstuk, M. (2000). Speed bumps on the information superhighway: A study of federal agency compliance with the Electronic Freedom-of-Information Act of 1996. *Communication Law and Policy*, *5*(4), 423–468. doi:10.1207/S15326926CLP0504_01

Halstuk, M. (2008). Freedom of information. In Donsbach, W. (Ed.), *The international encyclopedia of communication* (pp. 1889–1892). Malden, MA: Blackwell Publishing.

Horsley, J. P. (2003, July-August). Guangzhou's pioneering foray into open government. *The China Business Review Online.* Retrieved February 20, 2010, from http://www.chinabusinessreview.com/public/0307/horsley.html

Iyer, V. (2001). Opportunities, challenges and principles for legislation. In V. Iyer, *Freedom of Information: An Asian survey* (pp. 1–17). Singapore: Asian Media Information and Communication Center and the School of Communication Studies, Nanyang Technological University.

Jaeger, P. T. (2007). Information policy, information access, and democratic participation: The national and international implications of the Bush administration's information politics. *Government Information Quarterly*, *24*(4), 840–859. doi:10.1016/j.giq.2007.01.004

Lamble, S. (2002). Freedom of information, a Finnish clergyman's gift to democracy. *Freedom of Information Review*, *97*, 2–8.

Mehra, A. (1986). *Free flow of information: A new paradigm*. New York: Greenwood Press.

Perritt, H. H. Jr, & Rustad, Z. (2000). Freedom of information spreads to Europe. *Government Information Quarterly*, *17*(4), 403–417. doi:10.1016/S0740-624X(00)00050-2

Piotrowski, S. J. (2007). *Governmental transparency in the path of administrative reform*. Albany, NY: State University of New York Press.

Piotrowski, S. J., & Rosenbloom, D. H. (2002). Nonmission–based values in results–oriented public management: The case of freedom of information. *Public Administration Review*, *62*(6), 643–656. doi:10.1111/1540-6210.00247

Roberts, A. (2001). Structural pluralism and the right to know. *The University of Toronto Law Journal*, *51*(3), 243–271. doi:10.2307/825940

Roberts, A. (2002). Administrative discretion and the Access to Information Act: An "internal law" on open government. *Canadian Public Administration*, *45*(2), 175–194. doi:10.1111/j.1754-7121.2002.tb01079.x

Roberts, A. (2004). A partial revolution: The diplomatic ethos and transparency in intergovernmental organizations. *Public Administration Review*, *64*(4), 410–424. doi:10.1111/j.1540-6210.2004.00388.x

Roberts, A. (2007). Transparency in the security sector. In Florini, A. (Ed.), *The right to know: Transparency for an open world* (pp. 309–336). New York: Columbia University Press.

Roberts, A. S. (2000). Less government, more secrecy: Reinvention and the weakening of freedom of information law. *Public Administration Review*, *60*(4), 308–320. doi:10.1111/0033-3352.00093

Scotton, J. F., & Hachten, W. A. (2010). Introduction. In Scotton, J. F., & Hachten, W. A. (Eds.), *New media for a new China*. Malden, MA: Wiley-Blackwell.

Shrivastava, K. M. (2009). *The right to information: A global perspective*. New Delhi: Lancer Publishers.

Snell, R. (2001). Administrative compliance – evaluating the effectiveness of freedom of information. *Freedom of Information Review*, *93*, 2–8.

Snell, R. (2002a). FoI officers – a constituency in decline? *Freedom of Information Review*, *102*, 69–72.

Snell, R. (2006). Freedom of information practices. *Agenda (Durban, South Africa)*, *13*(4), 291–307.

United Nations Development Program. (2007). *Human development report 2007/2008*. New York: Palgrave Macmillan.

Zhiyong, X. (2008, May 20). Comparing information openness in China and India. The Economic Observer Online. Retrieved December 29, 2009, from http://www.eeo.com.cn/ens/Observer/2008/05/20/100365.html

KEY TERMS AND DEFINITIONS

Access-to-Information Legislation: The legal right for the public to request and obtain information that is in possession of the government.

Diffusion of Information Policy: Process where ideals about policies related to government information management or information access are spread from one country to another at a rapid rate.

Formal Institutions: Constitutions, contracts, laws, ordinances, programs, policies, rulings of the court, and other rules of the game that are backed by and enforced by the state.

Informal Institutions: Cultural information that is expressed through traditions and customs that tend to be unwritten.

Information Asymmetry: One individual, group, government or other entity has more information or more complete information than the other individual, group, government or other entity.

New Institutions: Formal and informal institutions that are related to new technologies or policies that have been developed in the last 20 years.

Old Institutions: Formal and informal institutions, such as civil liberties and corruption, which are older than 20 years.

ENDNOTE

1 The chapter defines new institutions as formal and informal institutions that are related to technology or policies that have been developed in the last 20 years; the remaining institutions, such as literacy; corruption; and civil liberties, are considered old institutions.

Chapter 14
Transparency in Electronic Governance:
Freedom of Information via Governmental Website

Jing Shiang
Tunghai University & Taiwan E-Governance Research Center, Taiwan

Jin Lo
National Chengchi University & Taiwan E-Governance Research Center, Taiwan

Hui-Ju Wang
National Chengchi University & Taiwan E-Governance Research Center, Taiwan

ABSTRACT

With widespread use and application of modern information and communication technology (ICT), especially computers and the Internet, the realization of government informational transparency through digital channels has been at the core of contemporary democratic governance. This chapter examines public transparency in Taiwan as seen in its development of electronic government, especially in the construction and use of public websites, which in recent years has received significant approbation in various international evaluations. It has been noted that most of its public agencies have established websites that designate sections for freedom of information (FOI) purposes. Of all the kinds of information seen in the public website sections, "policy white papers, statistics and reports" are the most abundant, are updated most frequently, and are most browsed by site visitors. Governments in Taiwan have also implemented back-office procedures and system applications for FOI purposes through the use of websites. Though only half of the surveyed public agencies provide online FOI request forms, most agencies rely on their agency-head e-mail boxes as main channels for receiving and processing citizen FOI requests. As e-transparency is a critical way of governing and a basis for governing legitimacy, the experiences and developments seen in the Taiwan case can serve as important references for international comparisons and further understanding.

DOI: 10.4018/978-1-60960-753-1.ch014

INTRODUCTION

With widespread use and application of modern information and communication technology (ICT), especially computers and the Internet, the realization of government informational transparency through digital channels has been at the core of contemporary democratic governance. In Taiwan, the performance of electronic government (e-government) development, especially in the construction and use of public websites, has in recent years received significant approbation in various international evaluations by, for example, Brown University and the World Economic Forum. On the other hand, Taiwan is one of the most democratic nations among the Chinese people. Hence, it is worthwhile to investigate how public institutions in Taiwan put transparency into practice through electronic channels and media (i.e., through official websites).

This chapter presents the findings of a research study which explored the ways Taiwan's governments provide public information through websites. The purposes of the research are to understand the contents of publicized information in governmental websites (or public websites) and the provision of online freedom of information applications, and to investigate the supporting back-office procedures and systems used in providing electronic transparency. This research was conducted by surveying chief information officers (CIOs) of 137 main public agencies from central and local governments in Taiwan in 2009.

The findings indicate that over 70% of the public agencies surveyed have established sections on their websites focused on FOI purposes. While public information can still be found in other parts of public agency websites, these sections are especially for publication of government information specifically mandated in Taiwan's Openness of Government Information Act enacted in 2005. Of all the kinds of information seen in the sections, "policy white papers, statistics and reports" are the most abundant, are updated most frequently, and are most browsed by site visitors. The study also found that information in the assigned sections is collected, maintained, and uploaded primarily by related units, while IT units play a supporting role in designing websites and integrating publicized information.

Governments in Taiwan also implement back-office procedures and system applications for FOI purposes through their websites. Though only half of the surveyed public agencies provide online FOI applications, most agencies rely on their chief e-mail boxes as the main channels for receiving and processing citizen FOI requests. While currently there are few such requests or applications, once such applications or requests are received, officials will process them as official issues. The applications are processed through organizational bureaucratic procedures to determine approval status. Central government agencies, as opposed to local ones, have established official and comprehensive procedures and measures for fulfilling the mandates of FOI.

BACKGROUND

Information Technology and Open Government Information

Modern ICTs not only enable more efficient and effective public management, but they also improve administration by making it more transparent, democratic, participatory and responsive to social needs. ICTs are becoming an increasingly important means of improving access to government services and information. These processes are called e-government. Many public agencies are using modern ICTs both to offer the digitalization of public services and provide greater government transparency, which would allow users free, easy, and appropriate access to administrative information. In light of the multiple possibilities of new technologies, this chapter focuses on the transparency of governmental websites, one of the tools most widely used by administrative agencies to provide online access to government information (Mitchell, 1998; Pérez, Bolívar, & Hernández, 2008).

In the twenty-first century, one of the challenges to government is the promotion of people's trust in government. Electronic government and governmental websites have already been considered an important mechanism by which to offer public services effectively and to extensively promote public participation. However, most existing studies still focus on government electronic delivery services. There has been insufficient assessment of the transparency and democratization of governmental websites (Lo, 2008b).

The disclosure of public sector information has helped inform society about public sector policies, activities and their contributions to social and economic development (Pina, Torres, & Royo, 2007; Pérez et al., 2008). In the wake of democratization and the information revolution, there has been demand for reforming the government disclosure mechanism and the public service system, both of which used to be dispersed and thus user-unfriendly (Yeh, 2007). Governmental websites can function as fundamental mechanisms for public information disclosure, which stands as the cornerstone of democratic governance. Internet use is expected to result in government services becoming directly and easily accessible to the public, meaning public information will be more widely disseminated and of greater public use.

Open Government Information Status and Problems in Taiwan

The due process requirements of the modern government administration can be roughly divided into three categories: "impartiality, openness and participation." The first two requirements have been codified in Taiwan's "Administrative Procedure Act" (APA) of 1999, while "openness" was formed by the "Freedom of Government Information Act" (FOIA, or FOI law), which was promulgated and has been enforced since December 28, 2005 (Tang, 2005). Taiwan's FOIA was enacted to "establish the institution for the publication of government information, facilitate people to share and fairly utilize government information, protect people's right to know, further people's understanding, trust and overseeing of public affairs, and encourage public participation in democracy (Article 1)." Taiwan's FOIA protects the people's right to know, understand, trust and oversee public affairs and establishes procedures for citizens to request access to government information. The laws place the burden on the government to make public its treaties, correspondence with foreign countries, laws, administrative decisions, administrative reports, budgets, research papers, procurement contracts and meeting records. It is now essential for government entities in their day-to-day operations to understand and integrate regulations stipulated in the Acts (Shin, 2007).

According to Taiwan's FOIA, open government information is provided by means of two main approaches: (1) "Active Disclosure of Information" includes the scope of information and the means of disclosure;" (2) "Passive Disclosure of Information" includes the applicant processing (see Article 11, 12), cost sharing, methods of communication (Article 13, 14, 15) and access to personal information (Article 16, 17) by subject. With the exception of information that might violate personal privacy, personal rights or national secrets (see Article 18), the government shall actively make these types of information available to the public (Article 7):

1. Treaties, diplomatic documents, laws, Emergency Orders, regulations and orders which are made in accordance with the Central Regulatory Standardization Law, and local autonomous laws and regulations.
2. The interpretary orders and discretionary standards made by government agencies for helping lower government agencies or

subordinates interpret laws consistently, find facts, and exercise discretionary power.
3. The structures, duties, addresses, telephone numbers, fax numbers, websites and e-mail addresses of government agencies.
4. Documents about administrative guidance.
5. Administrative plans, statistics and research reports.
6. Budgets and audits.
7. The results of petitions and the decisions of administrative appeals.
8. Documents related to public works and procurements.
9. Subsidies that are paid or accepted.
10. Meeting records of the agencies based on a collegiate system.

Moreover, FOIA also sets out certain "Exemptions from Disclosure", such as information deemed as matters of national security, law enforcement, internal communication, and confidentiality (see Article18, 19). Government information classified as national secrets, intellectual property, and professional and trade secrets will not be publicly available. In addition, information that would compromise a criminal investigation, disrupt government work or invade personal privacy will not be accessible.

Taiwan's FOIA belongs to a larger trend in the digital age, especially in terms of the public ways and means of global e-government. Article 3 defines "government information" as information that a government agency produces or acquires within its respective authority and is saved in the form of documents, pictures, photos, magnetic disks, magnetic tapes, optical disks, microfilm, integrated circuit chips or other media which can be read, seen, made audible or understood with the assistance of technology or auxiliary methods. Therefore, Taiwan's FOIA has already integrated modern ICTs into its scope of application. While the democratic transition is the critical driving force behind Taiwan's institutionalization of information disclosure, there is a secondary effect seen in the drive towards a better government information system that can reduce the cost of gathering information for decision making and facilitating meaningful citizen participation (Yeh, 2007). An integrated government website also serves to change the legitimacy of government, changing it from a "congressional transmission belt" model to a participatory model.

A domestic literature review (Lin, 1993; Shiang, 2001; RDEC, 1996; RDEC, 2008; Chen, 2006; Wu, 2008; Lo, 2008b; Hsiao & Lo, 2010) indicates that the actual implementation of Taiwan's FOI is very limited. There are two notable reasons. First, the supervisory authorities are not clear. In other words, there is no single FOI oversight body to enforce the FOIA. The Ministry of Justice enforces the Act for government agencies, and the Research, Development, and Evaluation Commission (RDEC) is in charge of e-government and e-transparency for the public sectors. Most government agencies usually do not know which sector to follow to enforce compliance. Second, Taiwan's FOIA does not come with specific enforcement rules. Moreover, the above mentioned articles and regulations are too broad and vague, leading to a situation in which all executive authorities have different standards in approving or rejecting requests for government information. This confusion results in ineffective implementation of government information disclosure (RDEC, 1996; Chen, 2006; Chen, 2006; Wu, 2008).

For these reasons, we have to look beyond the legal system. We have to focus on the actual operation and execution in terms of strategic planning, management, administrative procedures and results of evaluations of the current FOI status. Hence, the main purpose of this chapter is to examine the e-transparency of Taiwan's central and local governmental websites in implementing the FOIA, especially in the following three aspects: planning, implementation and evaluation.

Figure 1. Active Online Publication of Information

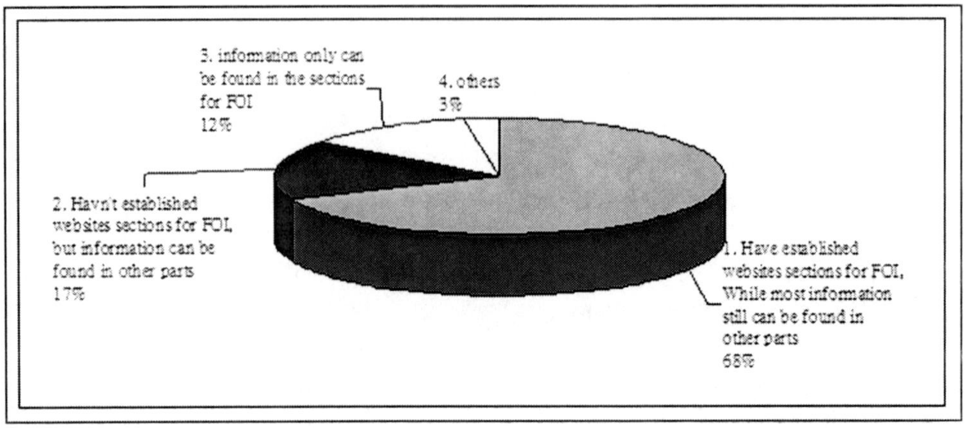

MAIN FOCUS

As an applied policy research, this study aims to obtain insights into the execution of online FOI among governmental websites through conducting interviews with five agencies. The results offer a foundation for developing a survey questionnaire and further policy suggestions. Our study is based on a comprehensive questionnaire survey which targets public officials who are responsible for managing affairs of governmental websites and who come from 87 central agencies, 25 local governments and 25 local councils.

The survey was conducted during October 2009. Questionnaire items were designed in terms of three dimensions of online FOI: planning, execution, and evaluation. Of all 137 questionnaires distributed, 115 valid questionnaires were returned, with an effective response rate of 83.9%.

Plan-Active Approaches to Publicize Online Information

For active online publication of information, as indicated in Figure 1, 68.7% of agencies have built websites sections for FOI, and most information still can be searched in other sections. 16.5% of agencies have not established website sections for FOI, but information is still available in other sections. In addition, only 12.2% of agencies have publicized information in the main sections for FOI. There remain 3% of agencies with websites under construction.

Further looking at the type of agencies and FOI, information mostly publicized by central agencies is not only available in the FOI main sections but also in alternative areas. Due to the execution of FOIA, most central agencies, direct-controlled municipalities, and county-controlled cities have established sections for FOI, with a few exceptions. Furthermore, a considerable number of local council agencies have not built sections for FOI, resulting in diffused information throughout the websites.

Administrative agencies are not the only entities responsible for FOIA in Taiwan. Promotion and evaluation of FOI should also be further executed by legislative agencies. The FOI online sections offering regular information are able to help citizens, despite diverse templates among governmental websites. This research suggests that governmental agencies of every level should set up online FOI sections and identify the mechanisms for accountability and further evaluation and management.

Figure 2. Comparisons among Ten Items of Active Publication in the FOI Sections of Governmental Websites

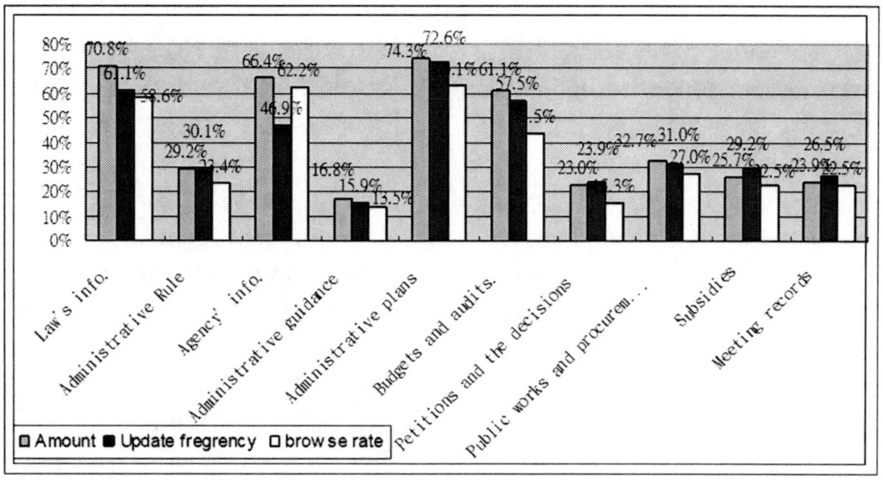

Execution-Operation and Management of FIO

Active Publication of Main Information Items, Update Rate, and Click Rate in Governmental Websites

According to article 7 of the FOIA, there are ten items of government information that should be actively published and contained in FOI sections of governmental websites. Based on these ten items of open information, Figure 2 summarizes overall comparisons with regard to amount of open information, update frequency, and click rate in the FOI sections of governmental websites.

First, in terms of the amount of publicized information (Figure 2), the results indicate a maximum of 74.3% of administrative plans, statistics and research report, 70.8% of treaties, diplomatic documents, laws, Emergency Orders, regulations and orders which are made in accordance with the Central Regulatory Standardization Law, and local autonomous laws and regulations, 66.4% of the structures, duties, addresses, telephone numbers, fax numbers, websites and e-mail addresses of government agencies, 61.1% of budgets and audits, and other items numbering under 30%, including a minimum of 16.8% of documents about administrative guidance.

Second, comparing update frequency (Figure 2), the study findings indicate a maximum of nearly 73% of administrative plans, statistics and research reports, 61.1% of treaties, diplomatic documents, laws, Emergency Orders, regulations and orders which are made in accordance with the Central Regulatory Standardization Law, and local autonomous laws and regulations, and 57.5% of budgets and audits. The other seven items have lower update rates relative to those just mentioned, and among them documents about administrative guidance is the item with the lowest update rate.

Passive Application Mechanism of Online Information

Application Mechanisms

Of all 111 valid questionnaires returned, only 47.7% of agencies have created online service system applications that let citizens download application forms for information, and use "mayor boxes" to request for public information. Among the agencies which provide online application services, over the past half year, less than an average of 50 users have been drawn by 43.1%

of agencies per month, more than 201 users by 25.5% of agencies, and no statistical results for 19.6% of agencies.

Overall, each governmental website has a passive mechanism used to respond to applicants, and a large gap of use frequency does currently exist. This may be related to existing business characteristics, business scopes, crowd serving, and the use of substantial application mechanisms.

The factors affecting this type of mechanism, and the long-term traces and statistics of quantities, therefore, need to be heavily emphasized. Making comparisons between different levels of the agencies and their online response mechanisms reveals that more than half of the total agencies have established mechanisms in response to citizen requests for information: 56.3% of central agencies websites and 61.1% of directly-controlled municipality websites, contrasting against 9.1% of council websites. Compared to active publication, the above response mechanisms, passively set for applications, should be of greater concern to central and local government agencies. Moreover, there is a considerable opportunity for local council agencies to improve their websites in terms of active and passive publication of information.

Application via Email

The agencies offering citizens ways to request for information via e-mail, mostly known as "mayor boxes" or opinion boxes, made up 31.6% of the total 114 agencies. Among them, less than 50 applicants per month during the past half year have been drawn by 46.7% of agencies, 201 applicants by 26.7% of agencies, and no statistical result for 10% of agencies.

Similarly, comparing 36 governmental websites with e-mail requests for information and their types of governmental levels reveals that the agencies allowing citizens to ask for information through e-mail are mostly central agencies, followed by local agencies, and their distributions are 80.6% and 16.7%, respectively.

Performance-Evaluation of Online Information Publication

Management Rules and Quality Assurance of Online Information Publication

Management Rules

In terms of management practices for online FOI, there are 48.6% of agencies without specific rules for online information publication. Conversely, 27.1% of agencies have made related rules for online information FOI such as the charge standard, operating instructions, or privacy protection. Without specific rules, there remain 24.3% of agencies mostly depending on the Information Law as reference.

Quality Assurance

First, there are 66.7% of agencies mainly assuring the enrichment and quality of online information via the inner-guard cross units. This has two causes. One is because the information units are incapable of totally controlling the complicated, multiple activities involved within every agency. On the other hand, based on the immediate update of information, the information units often play roles as assistants and maintainers of an open information system, namely as possessors of the leading control rights over the diffusion of open information. Moreover, the agencies report that the quality of online information is also guaranteed by the evaluation of inner-directed units, and internal inspection or regular meetings, and their distributions are 17.6% and 11.1%, respectively.

The Extent to Which the Information Should be Publicized on Governmental Websites

15.3% of agencies report that information publicized on their websites is definitely an imperative for the agencies. 45.9% of agencies indicate that information publicized on their websites must contribute over 80% to all FOI requirements. Moreover, a contribution between 60% and 80% is suggested by 18.9% of agencies and a contribution of less than 60% by 20% of agencies. Overall, more than 80% of agencies demonstrate that the proportion of open information required in governmental websites at least should reach over 60%.

FUTURE RESEARCH DIRECTIONS

To better serve citizens in terms of providing governmental information online, several research directions are suggested. First, studies can focus on designing a more specific way or system of information classification. This system is required due to the ambiguity in the nature of information. Although the FOIA specifies ten categories of information to be released by public agencies, no further detail or guidance of what information these categories would encompass is provided. This leaves public agencies plenty of room to claim that they adhere to the law while failing to meet citizen requests for information.

Second, future studies may also explore how to establish a comprehensive index of information that a public agency owns or holds. Without such indices, normal citizens will never know what public information that may be valuable to them is actually available and accessible.

The third direction for future research can focus on evaluation activities. Research should pay more attention to the demand side of FOI. Citizen requirements in receiving and using public information must be solicited and public agencies may accordingly manage their information resources. Research should also evaluate the actual usage of online public information as a way to adjust and adapt to citizen needs.

The last suggestion is to concentrate more on how intra-agency and inter-agency integration and collaboration can be made to facilitate a full capacity online provision of governmental information. As FOIA implementation is still in it infancy in Taiwan, such necessary mechanisms are still absent, which hinders a high-scale e-transparency.

CONCLUSION

While international evaluations of e-governments have existed for many years, assessment of meeting FOI through government websites in order to realize democratic governance has generally been ignored. As e-transparency is a critical way of governing and a basis for governing legitimacy, experiences and developments in Taiwan can serve as important references for international comparison and understanding.

This chapter presents the current situation of online public information provision in Taiwan. It has been shown that, under the provision of the FOI Act established in 2005, most public agencies have designated FOI sections on their official websites. On these websites and designated sections, users can access a variety of governmental information specified in the FOIA. Of all the categories of public information, "policy white papers, statistics, and research reports" are the most abundant, most frequently updated, and most viewed.

Though required by the FOIA, most agencies in Taiwan do not provide information request forms or related mechanisms, online or offline. Most agencies still only allow citizens to make such requests online through using opinion e-mail boxes or agency-head e-mailboxes provided on agency websites. As such, agencies do receive and process such requests, but such requests have been very rare over the past few years.

Combining ICTs and websites to publicize governmental information is seen as benefiting agencies in collecting, integrating and cataloging their existing data and information. However, changes in information management for FOI seem not to be affecting organizational structure, nor ways of functioning and management practices. On the other hand, privacy and security issues are the main concerns for these agencies. Because sensitive-data leaking is also one of the major concerns in implementing the online FOI and information categories have not yet been made completely clear, agencies are therefore not actively engaged in fully realizing the letter and spirit of the FOIA online. At the same time, intra-agency and inter-unit information collaboration and integration are seen as a major challenge in implementing FOI online.

Overall, most agencies in Taiwan have not established FOI-specific formal procedures and rules for controlling and checking their information dissemination practices. Most agencies have followed existing ways of conducting business and have simply slipped FOI requests into these existing processes. As a result, there is no designated person responsible for overseeing FOI at the agency level, and there is no one person who knows whether FOI is fully implemented, online or offline, in the respective agencies.

Several lines for future research have been suggested, including, designing a more specific way or system of information classification, establishing the possibility of a comprehensive index of public information, evaluating citizen online FOI needs and actual usage, and finding mechanisms for intra-agency and inter-agency integration and collaboration for FOI purposes.

REFERENCES

Chen, C. C. (2005). Freedom of information: A survey of current status. [in Chinese]. *Yan Kao Shuang Yue Kan*, *29*(3), 73–87.

Chen, Y. H. (2006). A survey on the impact and yield following Taiwan's implementing administration information disclosure. [in Chinese]. *Yan Kao Shuang Yue Kan*, *30*(1), 86–98.

Hsiao, N. Y., & Lo, J. (2010). An value-chain evaluation framework for electronic government. [in Chinese]. *Journal of Public Administration*, *35*(1), 1–37.

Lee, J., & Kim, J. (2007). Grounded theory analysis of e-government initiatives: Exploring perceptions of government authorities. *Government Information Quarterly*, *24*(1), 135–147. doi:10.1016/j.giq.2006.05.001

Legislative Yuan. (2006). *The Freedom of Government Information Law*. Taipei, Taiwan: RDEC, Legislative Yuan.

Lin, M. C. (1993). Das amtsgeheimnis und recht auf information. [in Chinese]. *National Taiwan University Law Journal*, *23*(1), 51–86.

Lo, J. (2008a). Benefit and risk of electronic participation: Exploring citizen's cognitive attitude and behavior of using governmental websites. [in Chinese]. *Journal of Cyber Culture and Information Society*, *15*, 181–208.

Lo, J. (2008b). Towards an electronic democracy? Setting up the indicators for evaluating the democratization of the governmental websites in Taiwan. [in Chinese]. *Soochow Journal of Political Science*, *26*(1), 143–198.

Mitchell, G. R. (1998). Pedagogical possibilities for argumentative agency in academic debate. *Argumentation and Advocacy*, *35*, 41–60.

Pérez, C. C., Bolívar, M. P., & Hernández, A. M. L. (2008). E-government process and incentives for online public financial information. *Online Information Review*, *32*(3), 379–400. doi:10.1108/14684520810889682

Pina, V., Torres, L., & Royo, S. (2007). Are ICT's improving transparency and accountability in the EU regional and local governments? An empirical study. *Public Administration*, *85*(2), 449–472. doi:10.1111/j.1467-9299.2007.00654.x

Research, Development, and Evaluation Commission (RDEC). (1996). *A study of government open information*. Taipei, Taiwan: RDEC, Executive Yuan. (in Chinese)

Research, Development, and Evaluation Commission (RDEC). (2008). *A framework for analyzing the transparency in government*. Taipei, Taiwan: RDEC, Executive Yuan. (in Chinese)

Shiang, J. (2001). A study of public employees' perception of the freedom of government information policy. [in Chinese]. *Journal of Law and Political Science, 12*, 1–52.

Shin, H. F. (2007). Operation of the Freedom of Government Information Act in current legal system. [in Chinese]. *Yan Kao Shuang Yue Kan, 31*(3), 15–30.

Tang, D. T. C. (2006). A comparative analysis of Taiwan's freedom of Information Act 2005. [in Chinese]. *National Taiwan University Law Journal, 35*(6), 37–115.

Wu, H. C. (2008). *The study of e-information of the government administration - An example from Taipei county*. Unpublished Master's thesis, Department of Public Administration, National Chengchi University, Taipei. (in Chinese)

Yeh, J. R. (2007). The government gazette system reform and freedom of government information. [in Chinese]. *Yan Kao Shuang Yue Kan, 31*(3), 3–14.

KEY TERMS AND DEFINTIONS

e-Governance: Definitions for e-Government and *e-Governance* range from the working definitions like "the ability for anyone visiting the city website to communicate and/or interact with the city via the Internet in any way more sophisticated than a simple email letter to the generic city (or webmaster) email address provided at the site"(1) to "the use of technology to enhance the access to and delivery of government services to benefit citizens, business partners and employees".(2) Focus of these definitions range from those focusing on ICT to those focusing on ICT-enabled government and governance transformation.

Freedom of Information (FOI): *Freedom of information* (or information freedom) refers to the protection of the right to freedom of expression with regards to the Internet and information technology (see also, digital rights). Freedom of information may also concern censorship in an information technology context, i.e. the ability to access Web content, without censorship or restrictions. *Freedom of information* is an extension of freedom of speech, a fundamental human right recognised in international law, which is today understood more generally as freedom of expression in any medium, be it orally, in writing, print, through the Internet or through art forms. This means that the protection of freedom of speech as a right includes not only the content, but also the means of expression.[1] Freedom of information may also refer to the right to privacy in the context of the Internet and information technology. As with the right to freedom of expression, the right to privacy is a recognised human right and freedom of information acts as an extension to this right.

Freedom of Information Legislation: *Freedom of information legislation* also called Freedom of Government Information Act (FOIA) are rules that guarantee access to data held by the state. They establish a "right-to-know" legal process by which requests may be made for government-held information, to be received freely or at minimal cost, barring standard exceptions. Also variously referred to as open records or (especially in the United States) sunshine laws, governments are also typically bound by a duty to publish and promote openness. In many countries there are constitutional guarantees for the right of access to information, but usually these are unused if specific support legislation does not exist.

Governmental Website: Governmental website also called governmental website, A website made by the local, state, department or national government of a country. Usually these sites also operate websites that are intended to inform tourists or support tourism. For example, MyEGov is the central governmental website for Taiwan.

Information and Communication Technology: usually called ICT, is often used as a synonym for information technology (IT) but is usually a more general term that stresses the role of communications (telephone lines and wireless signals) in modern information technology. ICT consists of all technical means used to handle information and aid communication, including computer and network hardware as well as necessary software. In other words, ICT consists of IT as well as telephony, broadcast media, and all types of audio and video processing and transmission.

Open Government: *Open government* is the governing doctrine which holds that the business of government and state administration should be opened at all levels to effective public scrutiny and oversight. In its broadest construction it opposes reason of state and national security considerations, which have tended to legitimize extensive state secrecy. The origins of open government arguments can be dated to the time of the European Enlightenment: to debates about the proper construction of a then nascent civil society.

Transparency: *Transparency* is a general quality. It is implemented by a set of policies, practices and procedures that allow citizens to have accessibility, usability, informativeness, understandability and audit ability of information and process held by centers of authority (society or organizations). Feedback mechanisms are necessary to fulfill the goal of transparency.

Whilst e-Government has traditionally been understood as being centered around the operations of government: e-Governance is understood to extend the scope by including citizen engagement and participation in governance. As such, following in line with the OECD definition of e-Government, e-Governance can be defined as the use of ICT as a tool to achieve better governance.

Chapter 15
The Use of Internet by Diasporic Communities for Political Mobilization

Maricarmen Sanchez
Florida International University, USA

Sukumar Ganapati
Florida International University, USA

ABSTRACT

This chapter analyzes how the Internet enables social and political mobilization of diasporic communities. Two diasporic communities—the Eritreans and the Iranians—form the empirical basis. The Eritrean diasporic community has used the Internet in their fight against Ethiopia and in their efforts to establish Eritrea as an independent country. The Iranian diasporic community used social networking, blogging, and other methods to politically mobilize amongst themselves in the host society and to mobilize their fellow countrymen in their homeland in the recent 2009 elections. The case studies illustrate how the Internet enables political mobilization that transcends time and space. Yet, the success of political mobilization depends on the diaspora's relationship with the homeland's government, their ability to create linkages, and their power relations.

INTRODUCTION

I've been waiting a long time for this moment: to be able to sit down at my work table (a wobbly little table underneath a mango tree, at the rear of the yard) and speak calmly of Haiti, at length. Better yet: to speak of Haiti in Haiti.

DOI: 10.4018/978-1-60960-753-1.ch015

The above quote from the novel *Down Among the Dead,* by the Haitian-Quebecois author, Dany Laferriere, describes the writer's feelings of nostalgia for his homeland while visiting Haiti for the first time in twenty years (as cited in Braziel & Mannur, 2003, p. 10). The nostalgic sentiment is a common feeling exhibited by many in the diaspora. Internet and related communication technologies have enabled the diasporic communities to fulfill such nostalgia virtually by keeping in touch with their homeland. Diasporic communities are able to communicate with their fellow countrymen regardless of location. This is a significant change from the traditional mediums of communication (i.e. letter, telephone, etc.) that were prevalent before the Internet revolution. The Internet enables people of common interest to unite, communicate with one another, and exchange ideas and information across a mass of people regardless of location, thus "breaking the bond of geography" (Issa-Salwe, 2006, p.55). The Internet is a venue in which diasporic communities are able to construct political identities and "social meaning by articulating and identifying with alternative discourses" (Issa-Salwe, 2006, p. 54). The use of Internet and other communications technologies by the diaspora to construct political identities and mobilize collective action is illustrative of cross-boundary collaboration to influence political processes in the homeland. The diaspora could be an engine to foster e-government through financial and technical assistance, despite limited Internet availability within the country (e.g. Rwanda, see Mwangi (2006)). Yet, extant literature on e-government exploring the role of the diaspora's influence on cross-boundary collaboration of governance processes is limited. Examining the diaspora's role is significant since they maintain intimate ties with the home country, partly emanating from their political identities.

This chapter analyzes the role of the Internet in enabling social and political mobilization of diasporic communities to influence the governance processes in their home country. Social and political mobilization involves the collective action effort of the diasporic communities to influence the social and political processes in their country. The expatriates' deep interest is partly a result of the nostalgia referenced above for development of the country. The Internet enables collective mobilization by transcending time and space that distances the diaspora. Two diasporic communities—the Eritreans and the Iranians—form the empirical basis for the chapter. The Eritrean diasporic community has used the Internet in their fight against Ethiopia and in their efforts to establish Eritrea as an independent country. The Iranian diasporic community used social networking, blogging, and other methods to politically mobilize amongst themselves in the host society and to mobilize their fellow countrymen in their homeland in the recent 2009 elections. The case studies illustrate how the Internet enables political mobilization that transcends time and space. We argue that a successful political mobilization depends on the diaspora's relationship with the homeland government, their ability to create linkages, and their power relations.

The rest of the chapter is organized as follows. The next section provides a literature review of the use of the Internet in establishing identities of diasporic communities, particularly with respect to social and political mobilization. This is followed by a brief background on the historical context of Eritrean and Iranian diaspora. After this, the use of Internet for social and political mobilization of the Eritrean and Iranian diaspora is analyzed. The last section concludes with the lessons of the study for the role of the Internet in mobilizing collective action.

DIASPORIC IDENTITIES AND THE INTERNET

The etymological root of diaspora is *diasperien*, where "*dia* means across and *-sperien* is to sow or scatter seeds", (Braziel & Mannur, 2008, p. 1). Diaspora refers to a group of people scattered throughout the world. The term "diaspora" was first used in "the Greek translation of the Hebrew scriptures" whose intended readers were the "Hellenic Jewish community in Alexandria" (Braziel & Mannur, 2003, p. 1). Greeks used *diaspora* to refer to "Jews living in exile" from Palestine. Subsequently, the term was used to describe Jewish population outside of Palestine addressing specifically the struggles of Jewish people throughout the world (Braziel & Mannur, 2003). In its current form, the term diaspora is not only used to describe Jews but other communities as well, such as the Caribbean diaspora, the African diaspora, the Armenian diaspora, the Cuban diaspora, and so forth. In this context, diaspora is a community that is displaced from its country of origin through "migration, immigration, or exile to one or more countries" (Braziel & Mannur, 2003, p. 2).

Our theoretical framework for the chapter draws on Anderson's (1983) notion of the diaspora's imagined community and their consequent political identity with their homeland. Diasporic communities are often nostalgic about their homeland (Braziel & Mannur, 2003). They yearn to feel, smell, see, and taste things that are native to the homeland. As diasporic communities spend time away from their country of origin and idealize about it, the differences between the host society and the country of origin increase, giving rise to an "imagined community" of the country of origin, quite similar to Edward Said's "imaginary geography and history" (cited in Hall, 2003, p. 241). The formation of "imagined communities" intensifies the connections that diasporic communities have with their homeland. Whether the diaspora will identify themselves with the host society, their homeland, or both is quite complex (Hiller & Franz, 2004; Parham, 2005). Radhakrishnan (2003) identifies three distinct identities of the diaspora: (1) assimilation, where the diaspora identifies with the host society, (2) reclaiming ethnicity, where the diaspora identifies with the homeland, and (3) hyphenated identity, where the diaspora identifies with both the host society and the homeland. Of course, the diaspora may adopt certain values from their host society, but nevertheless maintain close ties with the homeland roots (Radhakrishnan, 2003).

The close ties of the diaspora with the homeland are both cultural and political. Modern electronic communications and technology—in particular, the Internet—have enabled the diaspora to communicate with family and friends (Elkins, 1997). Diasporic communities are able to exchange their ideas with others through virtual and social communities (but are not limited to them). The Internet has become a means for diasporic groups to establish and maintain their cultural and political identities (Holmes, 2007; Issa-Salwe, 2006). The falling prices in communications have facilitated the diasporic communities to maintain their linkages with their homeland. The communications enable the diaspora to keep themselves up to date with respect to events in the homeland (Bernal, 2005). Moreover, the Internet is a less expensive and more cost efficient medium for disseminating information than the traditional mediums of publishing (Issa-Salwe, 2006). Online information is dynamic and real time, enabling the diaspora to be active participants in the events affecting their homeland, thus facilitating better political mobilization (Castells, 2007).

Several studies have revealed that immigrants use the Internet to obtain information regarding politics in their homeland. In her study of immigrants from the former Soviet Union, Turkey, and of Kurdish ethnicity in Germany, Kissau (2009, p. 84) concludes that "the Internet can contribute to the strengthening of ethnic and diversity media." Internet affords greater access to information than other offline forms of media. It allows for collaboration between "mainstream and minority media" through the exchange of information (Kissau, 2009, p. 84). Immigrants can communicate with each other and the homeland at relatively low costs. Furthermore, the Internet provides immigrants/diasporic groups a venue to express themselves without restrictions. The Internet expands the space of migrant and diasporic communities to participate in the public sphere (Kissau, 2009). Of course, there are issues of digital divide. Typically, developing countries have low levels of Internet penetration as compared to developed countries. Migrants from developing countries do not have full access to the public sphere of their homeland through the mainstream and minority media. Yet, the Internet enables diasporic populations that were once voiceless in homeland events to have a voice (Whitaker, 2004).

The voice that the Internet provides to the diasporic communities challenges the traditional construct of nations because citizens can spread information globally. In this, the state is continuously being challenged through transnationalism. Transnationalism is "the flow of people, ideas, goods, and capital across national territories in a way that undermines nationality and nationalism as discrete categories of identification, economic organization, and political constitution" (Braziel & Mannur, 2003, p.8). Although the two concepts of diaspora and transnationalism are distinct, there are overlaps. Diaspora refers mainly to people, but trasnationalism refers to an array of concrete and non-concrete phenomena and processes. Diaspora, then, is the human agency for effecting transnationalism, wherein the immigrant communities influence the social and political processes in the homeland. National politics is internationalized by the diaspora, partly enabled by the modern electronic communications.

The Internet is not merely an information dissemination mechanism in this sense—it is a powerful medium to mobilize collective action among the diasporic communities. Internet along with the mobile phone enables political mobilization through blogs, social networks, and podcasts (Castells, 2007). Bernal (2005) observes that the diaspora and the Internet share commonalities. The Internet does not belong to a concrete space and place, such space and place is a conceptually constructed one. Similarly, the diasporic population does not perceive as belonging to a particular place; they are constantly in the search for a sense of belonging. The consequent virtual communities formed by the diaspora also transcend space and time. As Elkins (1997) argues, virtual communities form when people share common interests. In the diasporic virtual communities, the common interest is the homeland bonds that tie the diasporic groups and people in their country of origin. People of a diasporic community identify themselves with the situations and experiences of their fellow countrymen, thus forming potential alliances (Bernal, 2005). Diasporic communities influence the ideas of their fellow countrymen and vice-versa (Castells, 2007). Political debates and actions in virtual communities influence the political processes and phenomena in the homeland. As the Internet is not location specific, it expands the public sphere of the political dialogs from national to international. The specific dynamics of how the imagined community and the political identities of the transnational diaspora result in the political mobilization are examined below with respect to the Eritrean and Iranian diaspora.

ERITREAN AND IRANIAN DIASPORA

The Eritrean and Iranian diaspora are good cases to examine since both used the Internet to influence political processes in their homeland. The Internet has been used by both diasporic groups to exchange information, thoughts, and ideas, and to bring their issues to the forefront. In the case of the Eritrean diaspora, the Internet became a platform to politically mobilize and participate in the process of establishing their country. In the case of the Iranian diaspora, the Internet became a collaborative medium with Iranians at home to give international exposure to Iran's election process. A brief background of the Eritrean and Iranian diaspora follows to provide the historical context of how they used the Internet for political mobilization.

Table 1 gives the key indicators of the Eritrea and Iran and their diaspora. As the table indicates, Iran is a much larger country in terms of population, is far more affluent, and has more urban population than Eritrea. The inward remittance flow from the Iranian diaspora is also larger than that of Eritrean diaspora. However, the stock of emigrants as a percentage of the population is

Table 1. Key indicators of Eritrea and Iran and their diaspora

	Eritrea	Iran
Population (millions, 2006)	5	69
Gross National Income per capita (US$, 2006)	3,000	200
Urban population (% of population, 2006)	19.8%	67.4%
Inward remittance flow (US$ million, 2000)	3	536
Stock of emigrants (2005)	848,815	969,920
Stock of emigrants as percentage of population (2005)	19.3%	1.4%
Emigration rate of tertiary educated	45.8%	13.1%
Top 10 destination countries	Sudan, Ethiopia, Saudi Arabia, United States, Italy, United Kingdom, Germany, Canada, Sweden, Australia	United States, Germany, Canada, Israel, Sweden, United Kingdom, Netherlands, France, Australia, Austria

Source: World Bank (2008a)

much larger for Eritrea than Iran; the emigrants are largely the educated middle class, as indicated by the emigration rate of those with tertiary education. The top 10 countries for emigration are mainly the U.S. and European countries for both Eritrea and Iran, although Eritrean emigrants also move to nearby African and Middle Eastern countries.

Eritrea and Eritrean Diaspora

Along with Ethiopia, Eritrea was a part of the Italian colony from 1886 to 1942 (Bernal, 2004). The Italians carved out Eritrea as a "colonial territory along the western shores of the Red Sea" (Bernal, 2004, p. 7). The Eritrean population was distinctive from the Ethiopians, which in the future would lead to conflict between the two groups. After Italian rule, Eritrea came under the trusteeship of the British during the World War II. In 1952, Eritrea was made an autonomous unit federated to Ethiopia, controlled by local authority. However, the autonomy was short-lived as Ethiopia formally annexed Eritrea as a part of its territory in 1962. After nearly three decades of war, Eritrea gained independence to become an independent nation in 1993.

The political struggle for independence had begun as a resistance to the despotic rule of Ethiopian rulers, including Haile Selassie and Colonel Mengistu Hailemariam (Bernal, 2004, p.7) The Eritrean Liberation Front (ELF) had been formed in 1961. Subsequently, the Eritrean People's Liberation Front (EPLF) was formed in 1971 as a breakaway revolutionary group from the EPF to liberate Eritrea (Bernal, 2004, p. 8). The EPLF became the primary vehicle in Eritrea's struggle for nationhood since 1974, gaining military victory from Ethiopia and eventual independence in 1993. Despite the common cultural roots with the Ethiopians, the long political struggle resulted in the Eritreans trying to carve out a separate national identity, distinct from Ethiopians. The EPLF has been broadly acclaimed for its role in liberating Eritrea. However, since Eritrea's independence, the EPLF (renamed People's Front for Democracy and Justice (PFDJ) in 1994) has been the ruling party in a one-party system (Bernal, 2004, p.9). Müller (2008) argues that "until the 1998–2000 Eritrea–Ethiopian war, the PFDJ-led government commanded significant capital of popular legitimacy." The border wars have persisted since then despite mediation efforts by the United Nations. Strong government controls with militarization resulted in loss of political freedom and human rights in the 2000s. Although the 1997 constitution required democratic elections to be held, no such elections have taken place—the election scheduled in 2002 was canceled. Myers (2010) recently termed Eritrea as Africa's North Korea due to the strong armed state militarism.

Many Eritreans fled Ethiopia due to the wars and the political struggles. The neighboring Sudan was a major destination for the refugees, where the Eritreans faced the harshest conditions. Eritrean Muslims who moved to Saudi Arabia found service sector jobs (Bernal, 2004). Many also moved to North America and Europe as refugees or political exiles. Most Eritreans in the United States first came for educational purposes. The diaspora, however, had deep nationalistic links with the Eritrean political struggles in general, and the EPLF in particular. The EPLF received funding for war by mobilizing the diaspora (Bernal, 2004). After Independence, the Eritrean government went into great lengths to incorporate Eritreans living abroad in the politics of the homeland, thus maintaining a strong political identity with the Eritrean diaspora (Bernal, 2004). The Eritrean diaspora has concrete links to Eritrean identity through dual citizenship (they are given national identity cards) and are also required to pay income tax (Bernal, 2006). The diaspora is also enfranchised since the Eritrean constitution states that if the mother or father is Eritrean, the child is Eritrean. Bernal (2004, p. 10) terms the strong state efforts to maintain the links with the diaspora as "nationalizing the transnational."

Iran and Iranian Diaspora

Iran was ruled by the Qajar Dynasty from 1795 to 1925, during which time, the deep Islamic religious roots of Persia (as it was historically known) came into contention with the Western culture and society (Shahideh, 2004, p. 23). In 1925, Iran came under the control of the Pahlavi Dynasty after an army coup in 1921. Reza Shah Pahlavi, the founder of the Pahlavi dynasty, jump-started modernization and secularization in Iran. He abolished the wearing of the veil by Muslim women. He also changed the country's name from Persia to Iran in 1935 to highlight the country's Aryan roots. The Pahlavi dynasty remained in power between 1925 and 1979, except for a brief period during the early 1950s following the World War II. Under the Pahlavi dynasty, Iran prospered economically due to its oil reserves. The rulers also implemented many social and administrative reforms (the White Revolution) that resulted in the country's modernization and economic growth. At the same time, however, civil liberties were negatively affected with the Shah's autocratic rule. In particular, the practices of SAVAK, "a secret police trained and formed by the British, United States, and Israeli intelligence" were abusive to the point of infringing on human rights (Sullivan, 2001, p. xxiii). The Pahlavis alienated large sections of Iranian population, particularly the Shia clerics. Protests by clerics such as Ayatollah Khomeini began as early as 1963. Other groups, including the nationalists, left wing Marxists, and students joined in the late 1970s, leading to the ouster of the Shah's government in 1979 (Sullivan, 2001). Iran became a theocratic state guided by Islamic principles.

The Iranian history is an important background for analyzing the political identity of the Iranian diaspora. Three waves of emigration from Iran could be identified (Hakimzadeh, 2006). The first two waves were during the Shah's rule and the third wave occurred after the Ayatollah took power. During the first two waves of emigration, mostly upper and middle class Iranians left the country. In the first wave, Iranians sent their children to study in United States and Europe, and once the Shah left power, parents and relatives joined them. The second wave of migration took place immediately after the political revolution, and mostly consisted of professionals. This group included families with women who were feared the imposition of the strict Muslim dress codes of the new Islamic regime and young men who would otherwise have to serve in the Iraq-Iran war. The third wave of emigration is from 1995 to current day, and it consists of a combination of professionals and lower skilled labor (Hakimzadeh, 2006). The emigrants have been mainly the middle class, intelligentsia, and artists (i.e. movie producers). They left Iran because of religious and/or ethnic persecution (i.e. Kurdish, Jewish, etc) and censorship. Iranians that left after the fall of the Shah thought that they were leaving Iran for a short while and would return with the fall of an Islamic government. However, most did not return home. In the U.S., while most Iranians adapted the new country as their home, with their children adopting a hyphenated nationality, many others have expressed a willingness to return home and lack a sense of belongingness (Sullivan, 2001). Moreover, older Iranians in the diaspora idealize about Iran under the Shah regime, and oppose the Islamic government that followed (Orr, 2004). Unlike the Eritrean concentration in Washington, D.C. in the United States, most Iranians settled down in Los Angeles.

USE OF INTERNET BY ERITREAN AND IRANIAN DIASPORA

The rise of the Internet and other allied communications technologies in the 1990s provided additional scope for political mobilization and organization among the Eritrean and Iranian diaspora. The Eritrean diaspora used the Internet as a platform to be actively involved in the new state formation since 1993. Eritrean diaspora influenced the political processes and raised funds using web technologies. More recently, the Eritrean diaspora have organized on the web and used other communications technologies to mobilize against the U.N. sanctions imposed on Eritrea. The Iranian diaspora also used the Internet to mobilize politically and to influence the political processes in Iran. Such mobilization is particularly evident in the recent 2008 elections held in Iran. However, the Iranian diaspora have been much less powerful in influencing the outcomes.

Use of Internet by Eritrean Diaspora

Bernal (2006, p. 161) argues that the Eritrean diaspora organized themselves on the web, using it as a forum for debating the "history, culture, democracy and identity." She (2006, p. 161) maintains that by using the Internet, the diaspora "mobilized demonstrators, amassed funds for war, debated the formulation of the constitution, and influenced the government of Eritrea." An early forum in this context is the Dehai (www.dehai.org), whose roots date back to 1992. It was established by Eritreans living in Washington, D.C. as a reaction to the negative messages about Eritrea that were being posted in a listserv called *socioculturalafrica* (Bernal, 2005, p. 664). Dehai followed the model of *socialculturalafrica*, in which people posted their ideas and debates transpired. The initial users of the Dehai were mostly those in the hi-tech industry and universities who had access to the Internet. The site then expanded to include professionals. Debates on the site have been in English, to unite Eritrean diaspora living across different countries. Although the site has been mainly concerned with Eritrea, anyone can subscribe and post messages to generate ideas (Bernal, 2005).

Dehai is not an organization that only uses the Internet to mobilize but subscribers also meet in person and converse on the phone, particularly in Eritrea (Bernal, 2005). Eritrea's Internet outreach and mobile subscription was low even during the mid-2000s, even by African standards. According to the World Bank (2008b), the mobile phone subscribers were 2.2% of the population and Internet users were 4.1%; its overall e-government web measure index was a very low 0.06. The only Eritreans that had access to the Internet were the elite, usually politicians, who signed on to Dehai using fictional names (Bernal, 2005). Through the debates on Dehai, the Eritrean diaspora were able to influence the constitution, laws, and the construction of Eritrea as a nation. As Bernal (2006, p. 162) argues, "Cyberspace has facilitated the participation of the diaspora in the formation of Eritrea's national institutions and political culture." Moreover, the Internet became a forum for raising funds for political activities, particularly during the 1998-2000 border wars with Ethiopia. Postings on the Dehai recorded various donations during this time, such as the one thousand dollars per household pledge in Copenhagen in 1998, one month salary pledge in Riyadh, twenty-six thousand dollars raised "on the spot" in one meeting in Edomonton, Canada, etc. (Bernal, 2005, p. 671).

While Dehai was an early forum and still continues to be active as of this writing, many other sites have also arisen for the participation of the Eritrean diaspora. Some of the sites are oriented toward protesting the United Nations Security Council resolution No. 1907 entitled "Peace and Security in Africa" in December 2009. Adopted in the wake of Eritrea's alleged activities to support Somali insurgents, the resolution imposed arms ban, travel prohibitions, and froze assets of Eritrean businesses and senior government officials. The principal site which has been actively protesting the sanctions as illegal and "unjust" is the E-SMART (Eritrean Sanctions Must be Annulled and Repealed Today!). Its website, http://www.eritrean-smart.org/, purports to be a public forum for discussion and political action against the UN Security Council resolution. Other similar sites have arisen around the world to protest the resolution: raimoq.com (in Germany); beilul.com (in Sweden); meadna.com; ertra.com; alenalki.com; biddho.com. Protests against the resolution were organized in a number of cities across the United States, United Kingdom, Switzerland, Australia, and others. While these websites are largely sympathetic to the Eritrean government, other sites are more varied, carrying different shades of debates. Such sites include: awate.com; asmarino.com. These sites have included critical views of the Eritrean strong state, prompting Eritrean government officials to be wary of the Eritrean diasporic media's influence on the country's political processes (British Broadcasting Corporation, 2008).

Use of Internet by Iranian Diaspora

Ghorashi and Boersma (2009) argue that the Iranian diaspora has evolved from an exclusive form of transnational exilic communities in the 1980s to an inclusive network of transnational connections with Iranians in Iran in the 2000s. This evolution of the use of cyberspace and other media by the Iranian diaspora to connect with the Iranians is set in the historical context of the three waves of the diaspora. Consequently, unlike the Eritrean diaspora, which has been largely supportive of Eritrean government and its political struggle against Ethiopia, the Iranian diaspora, is quite diverse (Graham & Khosravi, 2002; McAuliffe, 2008). Political views and identities among the three waves do not coincide well. This is partly reflected in Naficy's (2001) depiction of cinema by Iranian diaspora, where he argues that the diaspora construct and express their identities through "accented" films, where their experiences are translated through open- and closed-form aesthetics and alternative production modes. They reflect Anderson's "imagined community" of Iran through their nostalgic and memory-driven multilingual narratives.

The Iranian diaspora's use of Internet in influencing political processes in Iran is particularly evident in the presidential elections. In 2005, Mahmoud Ahmadinejad won the presidential election. However, his presidential term had been marked with remarkable controversies, principally emanating from his rigid Islamic rule. Very few in the Iranian diaspora were supportive of his rule. The 2009 elections were mired in conflict when he ran against Mir Hussein Moussavi. Although Moussavi announced that he won the elections on June 12th, 2009, Ahmadinejad declared that he had won the election with 69% majority vote. Violent protests erupted on Iranian streets, which drew the Iranian diaspora into the fray. The Iranian national elections became internationalized with the use of Internet. The diaspora became critical of Ahmadinejad and politically mobilized to support the opposition movements within Iran.

The close connection between the Iranian diaspora and Iranians in Iran was facilitated by the better development of Internet infrastructure in Iran (as compared to Eritrea, where the diaspora had to depend on phone connections to make the linkages). Rahimi (2008, p.40) argues that the level of Internet in Iran has developed "to a level of sophistication which exceeds that of some European nations." Information and communications technologies grew with government support from 1994 to 2003, after which the Iranian government began to control the spread of new technologies and systematically blocked access to Internet sites or filtered the sites (Rahimi, 2008). As per the World Bank (2008b), the mobile phone subscribers were nearly 60% of the population and Internet users were 32%; the country's overall e-government web measure index was comparatively higher than Eritrea (0.26). Persian ranks as the third most popular language in the world of blogs (Rahimi, 2008). Iranian blogs in Persian, called Weblogistan, form the virtual public sphere for young Iranians (especially students) to air their political views and participate in political debates (Rahimi, 2008; Bucar and Fozaeli, 2008).

In the 2009 elections, besides the blogs, Web 2.0 tools such as Twitter, Facebook and Myspace became instrumental in the involvement of the Iranian diaspora. Since the international press could not report on what was occurring in Iran, Iranians themselves turned to report the events through such tools (Cohen, 2009). Twitter, in particular, became a major mechanism for reporting from Iran and internationalizing the Iranian election coverage. Text messaging and websites in Farsi were also used to organize protests (Cohen, 2009). In solidarity with the protestors in Iran, the Iranian diaspora also carried out protests in many cities around the world, including Amsterdam, Berlin, Hamburg, London, Los Angeles, Munich, Paris, San Francisco and Washington, D.C. (Fassihi & Rhodes, 2009). In the end, however, the Ahmadinejad regime prevailed, with its severe restrictions on the Internet, including blocking and filtering websites and cracking down on protestors. Morozov (2009, p.13) argues that the "Twitter revolution" in Iran also had a dark side, in which misinformation mislead activists, and the enormous volume of tweets "slowed down the entire Iranian Internet, making it difficult to obtain any (even non-government) information or upload photos or videos from the protests." The Iranian government curbed dissent by using the new media to identify and punish the protesters: "Relying on photos and videos uploaded to Flickr and YouTube by protesters and their Western sympathizers, the secret police now have a large pool of incriminating evidence" (Morozov, 2010, "Undermine Dictators", para. 2).

COMPARISON BETWEEN ERITREAN AND IRANIAN DIASPORA'S INTERNET USE IN POLITICAL MOBILIZATION

The cases of Eritrean and Iranian diaspora's use of the Internet for political mobilization offers interesting comparative insights. Three major insights could be drawn from the comparison. First, the relationship between the government and the diaspora is important for the diaspora to influence political processes in the homeland. Second, the Internet technologies could both assist and hinder in the political mobilization depending on whether it creates network linkages or generates misinformation. Third, the power relations between the diaspora and the homeland's population matter for whether the diaspora can influence the political processes.

Relationship Between Government and the Diaspora

The Eritrean diaspora has been largely more successful than the Iranian diaspora in influencing political processes in the homeland. This has been so despite Eritrea's lower infrastructure levels with respect to information and communication technologies, and relatively low use of Internet within the country. The rationale for such difference is that the Eritrean diaspora have been largely supportive of the Eritrean government functions until the 1990s. The Eritrean diaspora mobilized politically and provided funding in support of Eritrea's fight for independence and in border wars with Ethiopia. Such support is also evident in the volume of online sites that are oriented toward annulment of the 2009 U.N. Security Council sanctions on Eritrea. However, this does not imply that the diaspora is uniform in its support; indeed, voices critical of the Eritrean strong government tactics in the 2000s have also arisen. The Iranian diaspora, on the other hand, have generally deviated from the Iranian government. The Iranian government has also followed an authoritarian rule, subduing dissent within the country. Although the ICT infrastructure is better developed, the Iranian government controls Internet communication. The diaspora has had little effect and Iran has largely ignored international warnings on its activities.

Network Linkages or Misinformation?

In the case study of Eritrea, the Internet played a major role in the formation of the country by creating linkages among the Eritrean diaspora distributed all over the world. The Dehai emerged as a common platform for the Eritrean diaspora to undertake political debates, establish their identities, and to raise the required funding to maintain Eritrean nationalism. Eritrean politicians also joined in the debates. The crucial aspect of the linkage between the diaspora and the Eritrean population is the large extent of remittances that flowed into the country, thus making the diaspora a key economic entity required for the country's development. Eritrea has also recognized the diaspora's influence and importance by encouraging the diaspora to buy land in the country; the diaspora's income is also double taxed. The Internet did create similar linkages among the Iranian diaspora living across the world; they also connected with the Iranians in Iran through Internet networks. However, the Iranian diaspora is more diverse than the Eritrean diaspora, having emigrated in three distinct waves that have different political views. Funding from the Iranian diaspora has also not been key to the Iranian government; Iran's economic development has been mainly due to its oil reserves. Although the Internet did enable linkages between the Iranian diaspora and the Iranians in Iran, such linkages were effectively thwarted by the Iranian government. Moreover, as Morozov (2009) argues, the Twitter revolution in Iran had the dark side in which misinformation mislead the activists and the enormous volume clogged the networks.

Power Relationships

The Eritrean diaspora were generally quite powerful to influence the political process in Eritrea. They influenced policies, laws, regulation, and development (Bernal, 2005). Diasporic Eritreans provided the financial backing for both wars and paid taxes. When diasporic Eritreans criticized Eritrean government policies on Dehai, the Eritrean government would take notice and address such policy concerns. In Castells's terms (2006), the Eritrean state is being continuously challenged through transnationalism; Bernal (2004) goes further to argue that the Eritrean state nationalized the transnational. However, the emerging power relationship between the strong government and the emerging critical voices of the diaspora remains to be seen. The Iranian diaspora, on the other hand, did not have equivalent power to influence political processes in the country. The Iranian diaspora played a secondary role in the protest and events that transpired after the elections. In other words, the role of diasporic Iranians was to aid Iranians within the country in promulgating the cause of the Iranian protestors. The protestors were quickly stifled by the Iranian government, which has been unfazed by international criticism.

CONCLUSION

This chapter analyzed how the Internet enables social and political mobilization of Eritrean and Iranian diasporic communities. The Internet was used by both diasporic groups to exchange information, thoughts, and ideas, and to bring their issues to the forefront. The Eritrean diasporic community used the Internet in their fight against Ethiopia and in their efforts to establish Eritrea as an independent country. The Iranian diasporic community used social networking, blogging, and other methods to politically mobilize amongst themselves in the host society and to mobilize their fellow countrymen in their homeland in the recent 2009 elections.

The cases of the Eritrean and Iranian diaspora's use of the Internet for political mobilization, however, illustrate distinctive differences. First, the relationship between the government and the diaspora is important for the diaspora to influence political processes in the homeland. The Eritrean diaspora has been largely more successful than the Iranian diaspora in influencing political processes despite Eritrea's lower infrastructure levels with respect to information and communication technologies. Second, the Internet technologies could both assist and hinder in the political mobilization depending on whether it creates network linkages or generates misinformation. Linkages were created among both the Eritrean and Iranian diaspora; however, the dark side of misinformation and other problems also surfaced in Iran. Third, the power relations between the diaspora and the homeland's population matter for whether the diaspora can influence the political processes. Whereas the Eritrean diaspora were generally quite powerful to influence the political process in Eritrea, the Iranian diaspora has had little influence.

REFERENCES

Anderson, B. (1983). *Imagined communities: Reflections on the origins and spread of nationalism*. London, UK: Verso.

Bernal, V. (2004). Eritrea goes global: Reflections on nationalism in a transnational era. *Cultural Anthropology*, *19*(1), 3–25. doi:10.1525/can.2004.19.1.3

Bernal, V. (2005). Eritrea on-line: Diaspora, cyberspace, and the public sphere. *American Ethnologist*, *32*(4), 660–675. doi:10.1525/ae.2005.32.4.660

Bernal, V. (2006). Diaspora, cyberspace, and political imagination: The Eritrean diaspora online. *Global Networks*, *6*(2), 161–179. doi:10.1111/j.1471-0374.2006.00139.x

Braziel, J. E., & Mannur, A. (2003) Nation, migration, globalization: Point of contention in diaspora studies. In J. E. Braziel & A. Mannur (Ed), *Theorizing diaspora* (1-22). Oxford, UK: Blackwell Publishing Ltd.

British Broadcasting Corporation. (2008). *Government concerned on influence of diaspora media over public*. Eritrea.

Bucar, E. M., & Fazaeli, R. (2008). Free speech in Weblogistan? The offline consequences of online communication. *International Journal of Middle East Studies*, *40*(3), 403–419. doi:10.1017/S0020743808080999

Castells, M. (2007) Communication, power and counter-power in the network society. *International Journal of Communication, 1*, 238-266. Retrieved May 1, 2010, from http://ijoc.org/ojs/index.php /ijoc/article/view/46/35

Cohen, N. (2009, June 21). Twitter on the barricades: Six lessons learned. *New York Times*. Retrieved May 1, 2010, from http://www.nytimes.com/ 2/06/21/weekinreview/ 21cohenweb.html?_r=1

Elkins, D. J. (1997). Globalization, telecommunication, and virtual ethnic communities. *International Political Science Review, 18*(2), 139–152. doi:10.1177/019251297018002002

Fassihi, F., & Rhoads, C. (2009, September 18). Iranian diaspora joins to protest Ahmadinejad. *Wall Street Journal*. Retrieved May 1, 2010 from http://online.wsj.com/article/ SB125322907482521229.html

Ghorashi, H., & Boersma, K. (2009). The Iranian Diaspora and the new media: From political action to humanitarian help. *Development and Change, 40*(4), 667–691. doi:10.1111/j.1467-7660.2009.01567.x

Graham, M., & Khosravi, S. (2002). Reordering public and private in Iranian cyberspace: Identity, politics, and mobilization. *Identities (Yverdon), 9*(2), 219–246. doi:10.1080/10702890212204

Hakimzadeh, S. (2006). *Iran: A vast diaspora abroad and millions of refugees at home*. Migration Policy Institute. Retrieved May 1, 2010, from http://www.migrationinformation.org/ Profiles/display.cfm?ID=424

Hall, S. (2003). Cultural identity and diaspora. In J. E. Braziel & A. Mannur (Ed), *Theorizing diaspora* (233-246). Oxford, UK: Blackwell Publishing Ltd.

Hiller, H. H., & Franz, T. M. (2004). New ties, old ties and lost ties: The use of the Internet in diaspora. *New Media & Society, 6*(6), 731–752. doi:10.1177/146144804044327

Holmes, M. (2007). Culture without the state? Reinvigorating Ukrainian culture with diasporic efforts. *Review of Policy Research, 24*(2), 133–154. doi:10.1111/j.1541-1338.2007.00273.x

Issa-Salwe, A. (2006). The Internet and Somali diaspora-The Web as a means of expression. *Bildham: An International Journal for Somali Studies, 6*, 54-67. Retrieved from http://digitalcommons.macalester.edu /cgi/viewcontent.cgi?article=1056

Kissau, K. (2009). Online spheres of migrants in Germany: How and why migrants use the Internet. In C. Dietz & P. Stammen, *Media on the move: Migrants and minorities and the media* (pp. 80-84). 4th Symposium on Forum Media and Development, held in Bonn, 2008. Aachen, Germany: Catholic Media Council (CAMECO). Retrieved May 1, 2010, from http://www.cameco.org/files /mediaonthemove_ complete_1.pdf

McAuliffe, C. (2008). Transnationalism within: Internal diversity in the Iranian diaspora. *The Australian Geographer, 39*(1), 63–80. doi:10.1080/00049180701877436

Morozov, E. (2009). Iran: Downside to the Twitter revolution. *Dissent, 56*(4), 10–14. doi:10.1353/dss.0.0092

Morozov, E. (2010). Think again: The Internet. *Foreign Policy*. Retrieved August 25, 2010 from http://www.foreignpolicy.com/ articles/2010/04/26/ think_again_the_Internet

Mwangi, W. (2006). The social relations of e-government diffusion in developing countries: The case of Rwanda. *Proceedings of the 2006 International Conference on Digital Government Research* (pp. 199-208). Los Angeles, CA: Digital Government Research Center. Retrieved May 1, 2010, from http://portal.acm.org/ citation.cfm?id=1146658

Myers, N. (2010). Africa's North Korea. *Foreign Policy*. Retrieved August 25, 2010, from http://www.foreignpolicy.com/ articles/2010/06/21/africas_north_korea?page=full

Naficy, H. (2001). *An accented cinema: Exilic and diasporic filmmaking*. Princeton, NJ: Princeton University Press.

Orr, H. C. (2004). Tehrangeles: L.A. The Iranian expatriate capital abroad. *The Raw Story*. Retrieved May 1, 2010, from http://rawstory.com/exclusives/ orr/tehrangeles_iran_capital_expatriates_812.htm

Parham, A. A. (2005). Internet, place, and public sphere in diaspora communities. *Diaspora, 14*(2/3), 349–380.

Radhakrishnan, R. (2003). Ethnicity in the age of diaspora. In J. E. Braziel & A. Mannur (Eds.), *Theorizing diaspora* (119-131). Oxford, UK: Blackwell Publishing Ltd.

Rahimi, B. (2008). Politics of the Internet in Iran. In Semati, M. (Ed.), *Media, culture and society in Iran: Living with globalization and the Islamic state* (pp. 37–56). Oxon, UK: Routledge.

Shahideh, L. (2004). *The power of Iranian narratives*. Lanham, MD: University Press of America.

Sullivan, Z. (2001). *Exiled memories stories of the Iranian diaspora*. Philadelphia, PA: Temple University Press.

Whitaker, M. P. (2004). Some reflections on popular anthropology, nationalism, and the Internet. *Anthropological Quarterly, 77*(3), 469–498. doi:10.1353/anq.2004.0034

World Bank. (2008a). *Migration and remittances factbook 2008*. Retrieved May 1, 2010, from http://go.worldbank.org/ QGUCPJTOR0

World Bank. (2008b). *Information and communication technologies tables*. Washington, DC: World Bank. Retrieved May 1, 2010, from http://go.worldbank.org/ 7S1VU9WNZ0

KEY TERMS AND DEFINITIONS

Blog: Short for "web log", blog refers to an online commentary on issues (e.g. political, cultural, social issues relating to the home country) that are of common interest to the community (e.g. the diaspora).

Diaspora: Diaspora is a community that is displaced from its country of origin through "migration, immigration, or exile to one or more countries" (Braziel & Mannur, 2003, p. 2).

Diaspora's Political Identity: The political self definition of the diasporic community, wherein they could identify themselves with the host society, the homeland society, or both (i.e. have dual identities).

Imagined Community: A concept originated by Benedict Anderson (1983) to describe the perceived socio-political relationships of people who identify themselves with a group.

Transnationalism: Transnationalism is "the flow of people, ideas, goods, and capital across national territories in a way that undermines nationality and nationalism as discrete categories of identification, economic organization, and political constitution" (Braziel & Mannur, 2003, p.8).

Virtual Communities: Virtual communities are the Internet enabled communities, typically formed by people who share common interests.

Web 2.0: Web 2.0 refers to a range of Internet tools that are dynamic and interactive, where the web is used as a platform (e.g. Twitter, Facebook).

Chapter 16
Government Capacity Enhancement and Political Progress:
Chinese E-Government Effectiveness and Value Assessment

Feng-Chun Yang
Peking University, China

ABSTRACT

This study focuses on e-government development progress in China, examining how China's e-government building and implementation are impacting government and society to reveal its inner values. China's e-government building and development have mainly focused on enhancing government capacity and this has eventually led to the imbalance between government and society. At the same time, it has also neglected government public service provision and the interactive capacity to link government and the public. This situation contributes to the persistence of the prevailing government management and control modes and the ignoring of the demands for social change and demands of the public will, thus setting aside political and social reform. This study also notes that government and internet users are engaging in increasingly fierce fights over the power of discourse power in a networked world and power over political resources. This will become the new variable that influences China's e-government building and development.

DOI: 10.4018/978-1-60960-753-1.ch016

INTRODUCTION

The Chinese government initiated information technology and computer applications in the 1980s. In 1986, China got access to the Internet. In 1998, Qingdao City in Shandong Province set up a web page on the Internet and this was the beginning of online Chinese government. From 1999-2000, the State Economic and Trade Commission and China's largest telecom operator co-operated to set up the Government Online Project (Wu, 2004). The central government's website was launched in 2006. By 2008, the percentage of all levels of government bodies with websites was as follows: 96.1% of ministries, 100% of provincial local governments and 99.1% of municipal governments (Ministry of Industry and Information Technology of China, Department of Information, 2009). All levels of government websites feature, to some extent, certain functions such as government information publications, online work, communication and interaction, and so forth. Governments at all levels have established, are establishing or will establish various types of applications, including office, macroeconomic, fiscal, taxation, finance, customs, public security, social security, agriculture, quality supervision, inspection and quarantine, flood control, land resources, personnel and human resources, journalism, publishing, environmental protection, urban management, state-owned assets supervision, corporate credit monitoring, drug regulation and so forth. In addition to e-government at all levels of administrative organs, e-government has also become the office and performance platforms of certain agencies, including all levels of committees of the Chinese Communist Party, the National People's Conference (NPC), the Chinese People's Political Consultative Conference (CPPCC), the courts, and the Procurate (State Council Information Work Office[SCIWO], 2006).

With regard to the difference between the level of e-government development in China and advanced international levels, some data from international agencies indicate that the overall level of development of China's e-government is above the world average, and is increasing annually. For example, the *2005 Global E-government Readiness Report* of the United Nations Economic and Social Affairs (2005) show that the Chinese e-government readiness index is at 0.5078, or ranking fifty-seventh in the world. This is an improvement of 10 points compared with the data for 2004 (United Nations, 2004). Moreover, the *Global E-government Report* of Brown University notes that in 2003 China ranked eleventh in the world and jumped to fifth by 2005 (Wang, 2006). Yang Xueshan, the Vice Minister of Industry and Information Technology, has indicated that the application system construction and practical application of some departments and local governments have been world leaders (Yang, 2009).

Surveying the brief history of the development of Chinese e-government, it is not difficult to see that development and construction have been rapid and comprehensive. Moreover, currently, e-government has come to serve as an important infrastructure and means of supporting China's economic growth, governance, and social control (Communist Party of China Central Committee General Office, 2002). At the same time, it has been noted that the expanded e-government applications initiated government information disclosure and generated some new government concepts. A series of changes was initiated in terms of the government management system and the adjustment of relations between the government and the public, such as providing public services through the Internet. These examples can be considered, to some extent, as government management and institutional changes. In that sense, the construction and application of e-government, in fact, have been successful changes of substantive significance in the Chinese government over the recent thirty years (Communist Party of China Central Committee General Office & State Council General Office, 2006).

From around the late 1980s China basically terminated the substantive reform of the government system. Thus, reform of government and politics was not the focus of government attention, (Yan, 2008) during the large scale building of the Chinese government information infrastructure which started in the 1990s (Zeng, 2004). Clearly, in a period in which the Chinese government was rejecting government reforms it was impossible to introduce e-government as government reform. Thus, this is the most noteworthy issue: If the Chinese government has not had much interest in reforming government nor the government system, why has it been so eager to promote e-government construction?

Upon examining the development of Chinese e-government it is clear that the reason that e-government has been able to survive and develop in China is because of a choice made by the government. The Chinese e-government construction and application has been a capacity strengthening top-down campaign by the government, one which has had clear targets and which has been directly promoted and implemented by high levels within the central government. These high levels aim to improve government management and enhance management "effectiveness" (Communist Party of China Central Committee General Office, 2002). This embodies the distinctive government-centered characteristic which targets the enhancement of government capacity.

THE ESSENCE OF E-GOVERNMENT IN CHINA: MANAGEMENT AND CONTROL

Prior to the early 1980s China had adopted a planned economy and government management capacity and efficiency depended largely on whether it was able to calculate in real time and with accuracy a large amount of national economic data. Before the introduction of the computer, the calculation of economic data was done by hand and this restricted the ability and any efficiency improvements within the government. In 1975 the State Council decided to establish the State Planning Commission Computing Centre and set up corresponding terminals in every local government. The aim was to quickly and accurately collect and process a large amount of statistical information, check the implementation of plans, quickly schedule production; arrange population, materials, equipment and other major economic census data collection, and establish ready access to information databases (Zhou & Tang, 2002). In 1980 China began to introduce international loans and bought computers for the data calculation of the national economy. With computers, the government data processing capacity was greatly improved and the processing time significantly shortened (Zhou & Tang, 2002). As a result, government departments and senior leaders saw the important roles that computer and information technology could serve. With the direct support of the top leaders of the central government, the central government and local governments at all levels began to establish the economic information system using computer applications. Since the 1990s, over 1,600 governments above the county level have established Economic Information Centers. The Economic Information Center has not only become an important decision support agency at all levels of government economic management, but also, some local economic information centers in some places have undertaken functions that promote and coordinate government information technology management at the same time (see State Information Center Website, http://www.sic.gov.cn/web/Column.asp?ColumnId=1).

During the 1990s the pace of market reform in China accelerated, various markets expanded, economic activities gradually became active, and wealth increased greatly. Government leaders began seeking to expand government share, especially the central government share in the proportion of the growth in the national wealth. Central government leaders began adjusting the central and local fiscal distribution relations, aiming to raise the central government's allocation of shares. However, at the management level, not only was there the expanding scale and impact of smuggling, tax evasion, business fraud and other illegal or irregular conduct which interfered with and eroded government tax revenue, but also there was the conventional manual production process which made it difficult for the government to get timely access to a variety of central government macroeconomic data. This was not good in light of the central government's hold over wealth. These management difficulties underscored the urgent need for the construction of an information technology infrastructure. From 1993, customs, taxation, business, banking, auditing and other departments began establishing a large-scale information construction project in order to plug loopholes in management. The information technology projects in these areas--such as the so-called "gold tax", "gold customs", "gold card" projects--basically centered on improving the government, in particular, the central government's fiscal extracting capacity. (Wang & Hu, 1993) The Gold Tax Project began in 1993 and the second phase of the project was completed in 2004. The project basically suppressed the use of VAT invoices to curb taxes and to plug tax loopholes, among which the violation of invoices through the authentication system had greatly reduced the proportion of total certified invoices. From January 2001, in pilot cities, the rate of 0.227% was reduced to 0.002% by July 2004. The total proportion of violation invoices in the total number of audit was reduced from 8.5% to 0.053%. The Gold Customs Project, which began in the 1990s, has played an important supporting role in customs revenue increase. In 2004, customs revenue reached 474.4 billion yuan, an increase of 103.2 billion yuan compared with the previous year, or about a one-third increase. In the same year, 12,939 smuggling cases were detected, with a combined value of 9.93 billion yuan. From January to August 2004, the national customs office helped tax authorities seize 4,972 counterfeit payment books, reflecting approximately 789 million yuan in tax evasion (SCIWO, 2005). Jinan, Shandong income tax information project compared the local taxation date with national data and found about 25,000 data differences, which resulted in 5000 companies having to pay taxes, and about 2,700 million in back taxes (SCIWO, 2006b). Thus, these golden projects not only established a technical and management web that could solve tax evasion, smuggling, and enhance government revenue management capabilities, but they also enabled the government to easily achieve its tax management objectives (Han, 2001, 2002). This web woven by e-government, which helped to increase government tax revenue, played a direct role in the Chinese government's rapid accumulation of wealth (Xie, 2006).

With the beginning of twenty-first century, intensifying social conflict and increasing instability, the government's new task and objective is to achieve social and political stability (Communist Party of China Central Committee General Office, 2002; Li, & Wu, 2009). Since the government does not intend to carry out substantial adjustment in relationships between social interests nor in political democratic reform, to maintain social and political stability depends more on the government's enhanced control. This control and management thinking has given rise to various application projects designed to help identify and prevent destabilizing persons and events. An example is the Gold Shield Project, which is a community public opinion management system, municipal management, and crisis management system. It has become a new hot spot of e-government construction at all levels. These projects, which feature substantial increases in government control capacity, have played important roles in the management of unexpected events characterized by certain destabilizing social and political properties. The Gold Shield Project, for example, currently has established a database containing 1.3 billion permanent residents, with which the police can easily locate and obtain relevant information on any specific person. In 2007, the public security organs throughout the country captured 390 thousand persons at-large (Ministry of Industry and Information Technology of China, Department of Information, 2009). The national crime scene fingerprint system realized an automatic comparison network. In 2005, about 56,765 criminal cases underwent comparison, 58,499 cases were solved, of which 461 involved murders (SCIWO, 2006b). In urban management, in 2005, each city was divided into small blocks to implement precise management projects. The project began to spread all over the country. It is used not only for maintenance and management of urban facilities, but also it can be used to acquire information and management of unexpected events, such as demonstrations, crowd gathering and so forth (Jiang & Chen, 2007). In 2008, a series of security protection, monitoring and identification system projects to raise the level of the security of the Beijing Olympic Games was completed and implemented (Sun, 2008), including the facial-recognition monitoring system used to identify dangerous persons (Lin, 2007). As for the management of public opinion through monitoring information transmissions, in recent years the regulation of the Internet has allowed for successful information monitoring and filtering. And when necessary, shutting down the Internet has also become an important part of government network management (such as Shi Shou, Hubei and Xinjiang off line).

FROM GOVERNMENT-CENTRIC TO CITIZEN-CENTRIC E-GOVERNMENT

Since its origin, the Chinese e-government construction has reflected the pursuit of the government to enhance its capacity. Through e-government, by means of enhanced government management and control, the government has gradually formed the e-political construction concept and strategy in e-government planning, construction and application. That is, e-government has been government-centered, centered less on political improvement and public participation, with the relative neglect of public service provision and a lack of interaction between the government and the public. This way of thinking and strategy are reflected in various aspects of the Chinese e-government content, network settings, policy planning and so forth.

The 2006 framework of the national e-government development stipulates: Chinese e-government shall consist of a government intranet and extranet, the former composed of networks connected with each other, including the party committees, people's congress, government, CPPCC, the court, and the Procurate, mainly to meet the needs of all levels of government departments, especially the need of office, management, coordination, supervision and decision-making government bodies above the provincial level. The e-government extranet is designed to meet the needs of social management and public services government departments at all levels (SCIWO, 2006a). Thus, according to this framework, the Chinese e-government network is divided into two parts, an intranet and an extranet. High-level government agencies and their functions, most government activities, and resources all comprise the intranet. The extranet is only an interface for internet resources and activity output. It is the carrier for government office, management, coordination, supervision and decision-making activities, which are converted into social management and public service output. With regard to interaction between the public and the government, the extranet serves as the point of public access to government. But the extranet is not the most important area of government activities. Thus, the interaction between the public and the government seldom reaches the government. Which is to say, there is a lack of direct and fundamental interaction. The extranet enhances the government's capacity, technically speaking, but it does not necessarily promote the government's public service synchronization and interaction capabilities. This maintains the social isolation of government (Zhou & Liu, 2009).

In 2006 China released its information strategy. The strategy stated that the following items would be the focus of government information construction by 2020: improving public services, strengthening public administration, strengthening and improving macroeconomic regulation and control of consolidated supervision. Although the goal of public service is listed as a strategic focus, compared with the other three items of focus, the goal of improving public service objectives, tasks and requirements are comparatively flexible and some are conceptual (Communist Party of China Central Committee General Office & State Council General Office, 2006). By comparison, then, the other three items of focus are all related to enhancing government capacity, and they have targets, tasks, and implementation requirements that are much clearer and more specific than those of public service provision (Communist Party of China Central Committee General Office & State Council General Office, 2006).

Promulgated in 2006, an overall framework of national e-government was put forward to support government business applications, including: office, financial management, tax management, financial regulation, import and export management, and agriculture-related management and services, food and drug safety monitoring, credit monitoring, resource management, environmental protection, public safety management, social protection, judicial protection and other services (SCIWO, 2006a). The applications of these items encompass the main departments.

Article seventeen of the Central Committee of the Communist Party of China in 2002 planned the systematic construction of twelve priority business missions. Henceforth, more businesses began entering the "gold projects". Projects relating to the people's livelihood and public services were few (Wang, 2006). In 2008 the official connected to the reform committee consciously revealed country development: in constructed e-government projects the public service application constituted less than three percent. The effect on e-administration to improve government administrative ability and substantive public efficiency is not sufficiently evident (Gu, 2008).

The concept of providing public service e-government with theoretical and system support (such as service-oriented government) and the concept of public service itself appeared in the remarks on developing e-government of Chinese government leaders only very late. As the first to vigorously promote the construction of China's e-government, Premier Zhu Rongji very seldom mentioned e-government provision of public services or expansion of public interaction, despite a great amount of information on e-government and official statements. His successor, Premier Wen Jiabao put forward formally the service-oriented government until in February 21, 2004 in the Third Session of the Tenth National People's Congress. His government report noted the need to create new government management with service management in order to better serve the public, businesses and public services (Wen, 2004). In a targeted promotion campaign, the central government administrative affairs office of the State Department for the Electronic Information Office launched nationwide action, known as "online 100 case dealing," which began throughout China through August 2007. The campaign proposed that government websites should be strengthened to meet people's living needs while also providing public services through the internet, services such as civic education, health care, social security, transportation and public utilities (SCIWO, 2007). However, the so-called "online 100 case dealing" consisted of just some items, such as information queries, forms, file downloads and so forth.

With regards to achieving interaction between the public and government through e-government, strengthening public participation, and raising public influence on government, in such areas progress has been quite limited. Nevertheless, as early as 1998, some local governments had already established government portal sites. After 2000, the government embarked on a massive network project. By 2007, over 80% of Chinese government websites had channels for public participation, among which 82.6% had public mailboxes. Moreover, 52.4% of government websites established and improved on-line survey projects and 21.6% of government websites organized an online interview, 17.7% of government websites had set up administrative forums. However, the real interactive effect has been far from ideal. The total interactive letters and messages in China is only 30,000, online interviews number about 1,800, and online surveys and public participation in government activities of internet users also only number about a hundred million. Thus, only a very small percentage of internet users has posted to government sites concerning government work (China Software Testing Center, 2007). This situation relative to government sites spending a large amount of resources is negligible. Increasing data on government websites is showing that despite the growing number of government websites featuring interactive components, the interaction effects and actual significance are not substantive. In recent years, the actual impact of some local official sites, personal web pages, and blogs have proven to be very weak (Li, 2009).

Thus, the singular focus on government management and control ability, the relative neglect of public service provision, and the conceptual and strategic lack of emphasis on interaction between government and public, can all rapidly advance the construction of government departments and increase greatly government management and control. However, this fact has had neither impact on promoting the public good, enhancing the capability for public participation and influence in government, nor contributing to progress in the social and political systems. In short, a purely government-based e-government construction, in essence, lacks adequate value in terms of public service provision and political progress.

Thus, China's e-government needs to strengthen the promotion of the public good and the support of political democratization if it aims to form and enhance the value of e-government construction. This is the most basic and most important task to keep government balanced and to protect the public good and rights, especially in light of realizing enhanced government management and control ability. Only in this way will e-government truly become a means and carrier for improving government administration and political progress.

FUTURE CHALLENGES TO E-GOVERNMENT IN CHINA: PUBLIC PARTICIPATION

The government-centered tendency of the construction and applications of e-government means that information has improved government management only in a very limited fashion. Government has expanded the resources and enhanced the status of information, but at the same time, it neglects to use information technology to allow the public to participate in and influence government political conditions and channels. This, to some extent, further exacerbates the original isolation of government from society, and the opposition between officials and the public. It can be said from this perspective that the Chinese e-government is a campaign of government management improvement which lacks public participation. China's e-government is a kind of government management improvement in which there are internet users but no electronic citizens and there is management but no participation. Thus, the clear way forward consists in realizing the public good and rights, and expanding government political resources.

The public's alienation from e-government development and the lack of participation do not mean that the Chinese public lacks the basis and conditions for government development (China Internet Network Information Center, [CINIC], 2008). Rather, the alienation is caused by the construction and application of concepts of e-government, as well as institutional and resource allocation conditions. In fact, in recent years, China has made rapid progress in information technology development, and networks have spread throughout all aspects of social life. Internet users have increased, and China has become the country with the most users. The web life of internet users, subject to various conditions, shows more entertainment and social life features. But for more and more internet users, even within the limited open spaces of the Internet, there area important places for entering social and political life (CINIC, 2009). Internet users, speakers, web forum members, and the concerned citizen criticize government work and policies through web and web forums, which have become one of the most important scenes in China's internet life (Zhu, Shan, & Hu, 2008). Public participation in government cannot be institutionalized under the conditions and public opinion is still the way through the network. The public may influence local policies and behavior, whether major or minor, and sometimes it may even be able to amend or overthrow government policy (Zhu, Hu, & Sun, 2007). Sometimes it has played a role in political participation and public opinion.

The reason that the public has been separated from the construction and application of e-government is because the Chinese government's conceptual application has been established for reasons not specifically related to e-government construction and application. This has made the potential and positive functions of e-government unable to be realized while improving government management and services and the government system. On the other hand, with the increase in e-government management and control capabilities, the government has further strengthened its dominant position and resources compared with the case of society and the public. This exacerbates the existing imbalance. This can be said to be the fundamental flaw of Chinese e-government construction and application. In fact, in terms of the political reality, China should try to realize improvements in political participation and government system rationalization through information technology.

It should be noted that the development of China's information technology and the internet users passion for the rights of the public and their desire for their government to improve participation have provided the chance to optimize politics and government, if the government were to grasp this opportunity. This would serve as a fundamental basis for realizing the balance between government and society, for realizing the social harmony wished for by the government. Obviously this requires that the government open up more public spaces for speech and action, that it have more courage and wisdom to allow for more public voices. But, in fact, in so far as e-government strengthens the ability of the government (its ability to access resources), it actually enables the government to continue to extend the prevailing capital management and control model, ignoring social changes and public demands (Communist Party of China Central Committee, 2004). Obviously, this is the reality of e-government and the political reality, two new phenomena in government relations.

In fact, from a political viewpoint, the strengthening of government capacity has created a new imbalance with society and the public and social problems and conflicts cannot be simply erased. The legitimacy of the government and it's ruling political stability, therefore, cannot be enhanced. In recent years, an increasing amount of data indicates that through information technology, the public is gaining access to relatively greater freedoms and mobility, and it still doggedly is trying to influence government decision-making, monitoring government actions, or even pushing governments with its own agenda. But usually such wishes and demands do not get attention, or any effective response. In such cases, internet users specifically and the public in general are easily lead to emotionally and morally resent and have contempt towards the government and its officials.

The legal and moral criticism of internet users and the public easily evolve into major and minor conflicts between the government and the public. When conflicts between officials and the public arise, up to now, internet users and the public have remained in the relatively weak position. The government's control of internet users is usually more intense and more multifarious. Notably, in the last few years when China's e-government development and applications have made further progress, the government increasingly controlled with more strictness the behavior of internet users and cyberspace. A host of restrictions on internet use, implementation of network management, monitoring policies, attempts and practical measures have continuously appeared on the agenda of government at all levels, some of which have already been implemented. It can be expected that the fierce competition between the government and internet users for political resources and for the internet-based voice may come to serve as a prelude to a breakthrough construction and application of e-government, one that is based solely on limited government and more centered on public service provision and political progress.

REFERENCES

China Internet Network Information Center. (2008, July). *The 22nd Statistical Survey Reports on Internet Development in China*. Retrieved from http://www.cnnic.net.cn/ uploadfiles/ doc/2008/7/23/ 170424.doc

China Internet Network Information Center. (2009, July). *The 24th Statistical Survey Reports on Internet Development in China*, Retrieved from http://www.cernet.com/ news/chinacngi.pdf

China Software Testing Center. (2007). *The 2007 China Government Website Performance Evaluation Report*, Retrieved from http://www.ccidjianli. com/ 2007wzpg/07jixiao/untitled /xinindex.htm

Communist Party of China Central Committee. (2004, September 27th). Decision on Building up the Party's Governing Capacity *People's Daily*, pp. A1.

Communist Party of China Central Committee General Office. (2002). *No.17 Guideline of National E-government Construction*. Retrieved from http://news.xinhuanet.com/ it/2005-05/19/ content_2974699.htm

Communist Party of China Central Committee General Office and State Council General Office. (2006). *2006-2020 National Informatization Development Strategy*. Retrieved from http:// news.xinhuanet.com/ newscenter/2006-05/08/ content_4522878_16.htm

Gu, D. W. (2008). China E-government Current Stage and Development Trend Speech on 2008 China E-government Forum. Retrieved from http://www.ccidit.com/ readthread-175.html

Han, Z. J. (2001, December 1st). Li Lanqing Emphasize in a National Tax Work Conference that We Should Improve Tax Supervision through Tax Informatization Construction. *People's Daily*, pp. A1.

Han, Z. J. (2002, July 1st). Zhu Rongji Emphasized Facing New Situations and Score New Achievements. *People's Daily*, pp. A1.

Jiang, A. L., & Chen, Z. R. (2007). Research on Grid Municipal Management Mode. *Modern Urban Research.*

Li, C. X. (2009). *Quantitative Research on JiangXi Province Officials Blogs*. Unpublished doctoral dissertation, Peking University, Beijing.

Li, J., & Wu, Q. C. (2009). *The First Sino-us Economic Dialogue: All the important problems has been talked about except landing on the Moon*. Retrieved from http://www.chinanews.com.cn/ gn/news/2009/07-29/ 1794984.shtml

Lin, H. (2007, April 3rd). Automatic Human Face Recognition System Make a First Appearance in Beijing: it can recognize 500 thousand faces a second. *China Youth Daily*. Retrieved from http://zqb.cyol.com/content/ 2007-04/03/ content_1720026.htm

Ministry of Industry and Information Technology of China, Department of Information. (2009). *Stride and Integration: China Informatization Development Report*. Beijing: Publishing House of Electronics Industry.

State Council Information Work Office. (2005). *China Informatization Development Report 2005*. Beijing: Publishing House of Electronics Industry.

State Council Information Work Office. (2006a). *No.2 The Notice on Printing the National Overall Framework of E-government.*

State Council Information Work Office. (2006b). *China Informatization Development Report 2006*. Beijing: Publishing House of Electronics Industry.

State Council Information Work Office. (2007). *No.126 The Notice on the Government 100 Case Dealing in Internet through Government Website*.

Sun, R. (2008). The Chief Expert on Olympic Games Security Reveals how to build Beijing into a iron bastion. *China News Week*, *26*, 38–40.

United Nations. (2004). *Global E-Government Development Report 2004.* Retrieved from http://www2.unpan.org/egovkb/ global_reports/04report.htm

United Nations. (2005). *Global E-Government Development Report 2005,* Retrieved from http://www2.unpan.org/egovkb/ global_reports/05report.htm

Wang, C. S. (Ed.). (2006). *China E-government Development Report*. Beijing: Social Science Academic Press.

Wang, S. G., & Hu, A. G. (Eds.). (1993). *China State Capacity Report*. Shenyang: Liaoning People's Press.

Wen, J. B. (2004, March 5th). Report on Government Work at the Second Session of the Tenth National People's Congress, *People's Daily*, pp. A1.

Wu, A. M. (Ed.). (2004). *China E-government: Theory and Practice*. Beijing: People's Press.

Xie, X. R. (2006, July 28th). Speech in National Tax Informatizaiton Construction Conference (Summary). Retrieved from http://202.108.90.130/ n8136506/ n8136563/n8193451/n8193496/ n8194115/8243310.html

Yan, Z. C. (2008). Decipherment: The Four Modernizations is the Biggest Policy in China. *Political Science Research*, *10*, 38–43.

Yang, X. S. (2009, February 23th). Information development in rural areas and E-government Building. Message posted to http://www.xinhuanet.com/ xhft/20090223/wz.htm

Zeng, P. Y. (Ed.). (2004). *Informatization and E-government*. Beijing: People's Press.

Zhou, H. H., & Tang, T. H. (Eds.). (2002). *The Theory and Practice of E-government*. Beijing: Chinese Academy of Governance Press.

Zhou, M., & Liu, Z. M. (2009). Vigorously Promote Administration Extranets, Build E-government Public Service System. In Changsheng, W. (Ed.), *China E-government Development Report,* 196-197. Beijing: Social Science Academic Press.

Zhu, H. X., Hu, J. C., & Sun, W. T. (2007). *The Report on 2007 China Internet Public Sentiment Analysis*. Retrieved from http://www.china.com.cn/ aboutchina/zhuanti/08zgshxs/ 2008-04/02/ content_14098960.htm

Zhu, H. X., Shan, X. G., & Hu, J. C. (2008). *The Report on 2008 China Internet Public Sentiment Analysis*. Retrieved from http://caofeidian.china.com.cn/ aboutchina/zhuanti/09zgshxs/ content_17100922_4.htm

Section 5
New Frontier in E-Governance

Chapter 17
Internet Use and Governance in China

Kaifeng Yang
Florida State University, USA

Chengfu Zhang
Renmin University of China, China

Jun Tang
Renmin University of China, China

ABSTRACT

As Internet use increases rapidly in China, its governance implications have been debated among researchers. This chapter provides a brief discussion of the complex relationship between Chinese Internet use and Chinese governance regarding the development of the Internet infrastructure, the level and form of Internet use, the "dark" side of the Internet and its control, and the provision of electronic government services. We argue that Internet use in China has been shaped by China's governance structure, but at the same time it is changing, albeit slowly, that structure.

INTRODUCTION

Internet use--the use of the Internet in political, social, organizational, and individual lives--has received significant attention from researchers, as the Internet has transformed and is still transforming human life across the globe. While there exists large variation in the rates of interest use between developed and developing countries and even among the developing countries, countries lagging behind are quickly catching up and there seems to be a rapid conversion to long-run equilibrium (Chinn & Fairlie, 2010). In China, the Internet has become increasingly popular among citizens due to its widespread and timely information dissemination, convergent information formation, unconstrained usage and diverse contents. The Internet has also become an inseparable part of the economic development and business innovation in this fast growing economy. Thus, there has been a rise of Chinese "Internet studies" that discuss the development and consequences of the Internet in China (e.g., Harwit & Clark, 2001; Holliday & Yep, 2005; Kluver & Yang, 2005; Ma, Chung

DOI: 10.4018/978-1-60960-753-1.ch017

& Thorson, 2005; Qiu & Chan, 2004; Shi, 2006; Yang, G., 2003; Yang & Xu, 2010).

This chapter discusses Internet use and governance in China. While there is no doubt that internet use for various purposes has been rapidly increasing, its political or governance consequence is still being debated. On the one hand, there is a widespread belief among political leaders (e.g., Bill Clinton and George W. Bush) and commentators that the Internet will bring freedom and democracy to China and other authoritarian regimes (Taubman, 1998). This is partly the reason why there has been great interest in the Chinese Internet practice. On the other hand, there is disappointment among many observers that democratization has not been achieved in China and the political control and censorship over the Internet has yet to be loosened (Chung, 2008; Liang & Lu, 2010; McNally & Wright, 2010). Given the space limit, this chapter provides only a brief overview of the issue, demonstrating the complex relationship between Internet use and Chinese governance regarding four aspects: the development of the Internet infrastructure; the level and form of Internet use; the "dark" side of the Internet and its control; and the provision of electronic government services.

THEORETICAL BACKGROUND

Internet use has gained significant attention from policy makers and researchers because of its potentially huge impact on economic development, social structure, information flow, political dynamics, and democratization. This is not only true for internet use in the political and administrative arenas, such as online political participation and the use of e-government services, but also true for internet use in civic and personal arenas, such as reading online news, publishing blogs, using emails, and visiting social networking sites. The impact of the latter on the economy, social interactions, and information flow is more immediate than on politics and democratization (e.g., via the change of social structure, the rise of social movements, and the improvement of citizenship, etc.), which requires a long-term incremental perspective.

A long-term perspective is required in thinking about the impact of Internet use on governance (social and political) also because the relationship between the two is not one-way but two-way. Governance can be viewed as a set of institutions that regulate or enable actors who interact with one another in social and political relationships. Democratic governance, ultimately, is a set of democratic institutions that define the actions and interactions between citizens and their representatives (or those who make decisions for the state). Therefore, the relationship between governance and internet use can be explained with the general theory about the relationship between institutions and technology, which depicts institutions and technology as shaping each other (Fountain 2001; Singh, 2002; Yang, K., 2003). If the effects of the Internet are affected by the past or current governing institutions, then its potential in leading to a transformed governance cannot be realized overnight. What we observe will be a long-term co-evolution of the Internet and governance.

The belief that internet use will necessarily bring out democratization and political change in China reflects a perspective of technological determinism. Technological determinism states that the effect of technologies cannot be resisted and will necessarily occur given the technologies' autonomous, exogenous, and transforming influence on individuals, institutions, and society (Bekker & Homberg, 2005; Fountain, 2001). Technological determinists consider the Internet the most important development in our lifetimes that allows more opportunities for citizen participation, direct decision making, and democracy, with an impact on society comparable to that of the alphabet (Castell, 1996; Norris, 2001). On its extreme, technological determinism may become technological utopianism, which submits that information technology will enable a utopian vision for public administration (Margetts, 1999). Taubman (1998) writes that the Internet will empower citizens and undermine authoritarian regimes like China because the Internet makes it more difficult for such regimes to maintain hegemony over the supply of information or to block political pluralism.

Unlike technological determinists who are overoptimistic, social determinists are more pessimistic about the impact of technology (Barber, 1998; Miles et al., 1988). For them, it is structures and institutions that shape technologies, not the other way around. Technologies are neutral and "do not in themselves tilt in the direction of any particular values" (Rosenau, 2002, p. 275). Barber (1998) points out that "where technology takes our political and social institutions will depend, in part, on where we take technology" (p. 575). A somewhat more extreme view argues that current technologies are not neutral but already reflecting the past social structures and values. Technologies are social artifacts or social constructions that have different meanings to different social groups, and the interaction between those groups eventually determines the evolution of the technologies (Bijker, 1995; Williams & Edge, 1996). Therefore, the Internet could be used by authoritarian regimes to strengthen their control and maintain their legitimacy.

Our perspective is that technologies and institutions shape each other. We acknowledge that the Internet, without doubt, changes the way people seek, use, distribute, and exchange information, as well as the way they interact and socialize. In the same time, we acknowledge that the current social and political institutions affect how the Internet is used. The Internet does provide opportunities for change, but any institutional change is subject to path dependence (North, 1990). Ultimately, actors' action is shaped by institutions and structures while at the same time shaping institutions and structures (Giddens, 1984).

Institutions can be defined in various ways. We follow North (1990) and consider a broad conception: institutions as rules of the game. Thus, institutions include both formal and informal rules, as well as ideologies, discourses, and norms. In this chapter we consider the following three aspects: a socialist regime with Chinese characteristics and seeking to maintain its political legitimacy; a political discourse that places economic development at the core of the state's responsibility; and a unitary government with the central government largely determines government agenda across government levels. Given the three institutional aspects, China's policy development over the issue of Internet use and e-government is largely decided at the national level; Internet use is not allowed to harm the socialist regime or diminish the legitimacy of the Chinese Communist Party (CCP); and the Internet should be utilized to facilitate economic development. As a result, the Chinese leadership has a paradoxical love-hate relationship with the Internet: it expects the Internet to help China's reform and modernization, but also fears that it may threaten political stability (Zhang, 2002). The effects of the above institutional aspects, as well as how they are shaped by the Internet, can be illustrated in discussing the issues that follow.

INFRASTRUCTURE DEVELOPMENT

The increasingly strong internet infrastructure lays a great foundation for and drives individuals' and organizations' internet use. According to the *25th Statistical Survey Report on Internet Development in China*, issued by the Chinese Internet Network Information Center (CNNIC) in January 2010, by the end of 2009, the number of IPv4 addresses had reached 230 million, ranked second in the world and right after the United States (see Table 1). The number of IPv4 address has been and is still increasing rapidly, with an annual growth rate at 28.2%. The total amount of domain names is

Table 1. Comparison of Internet-based resources in China between 2008.12 and 2009.12

	December 2008	December 2009	Annual Growth	Annual Growth Rate
IPv4	181,273,344	232,446,464	51,173,120	28.2%
Domain name	16,826,198	16,818,401	-7,797	-0.05%
.cn domain name	13,572,326	13,459,133	-113,193	-0.83%
Website	2,878,000	3,231,838	353,838	12.3%
Website affiliated with.cn	2,216,400	2,501,308	284,908	12.9%
International export bandwidth(Mbps)	640,286.67	866,367.20	226,080.53	35.3%

Data sources: CNNIC. *Statistical Survey Report on Internet Development in China*, 2001-2010

16.82 million, among which 80% are.cn domain names. While the number of domain names has remained relatively stable, their utilization rate has been increasing. The number of websites has reached 3.23 million and is steadily growing. The amount of international export bandwidth has increased to 866,367Mbps, with a high annual growth rate at 35.3%.

The 2010 CNNIC report also shows that in 2009 the use of laptops and cell phones for internet access continued its rapid growth, while the use of desktops increased slowly. In 2009, the number of WAP (Wireless Application Protocol) phones increased 98.3%, laptop with internet modems increased 42.4%, and desktop with internet modem increased 5.8%. The rapid growth of cell phone internet users highlights the need for internet access at any time and any place.

Table 2. Size and Growth of Netizens (Internet Users) in China

Year	Size of Netizens (10 Thousand)	Growth Rate
2000	2250	—
2001	3370	49.8%
2002	5910	75.4%
2003	7950	34.5%
2000	9400	18.2%
2005	11100	18.1%
2006	13700	23.4%
2007	21000	53.3%
2008	29800	41.9%
2009	38400	28.9%

Data Source: CNNIC. *Statistical Survey Report on Internet Development in China*, 2001-2010

Relatedly, the 2010 CNNIC report shows that the number of Chinese netizens has been soaring and the Internet prospect is very bright. The scale of Chinese netizens surpassed the United States in June 2008 and became number one in the world. In 2009, the internet penetration rate had a great leap, exceeding the global average. By the end of 2009, the number of Chinese netizens had reached 384 million and the penetration rate had reached 28.9%. The number of netiznes increased 86 million as compared with the end of 2008. As shown in Tables 2 and 3, although the growth of netizens has slowed down, the trend of growth remains and the current growth rate is still high (Figure 1).

The reason for the fast growing Internet infrastructure is the support from the national government through the state-owned telecommunication industry. For example, in January 1999, China Telecom and the Economic Information Center of the State Economic and Trade Commission jointly organized a meeting to promote "government online projects" (Loverlock & Ure, 2003). To support the project, the National Bureau of Telecommunication required its branches at all levels to assist, mobilize, and coordinate the information industry and the media. Facilitating

Table 3. The Use of Web Applications

Type	Application	2007		2008		Annual Change		2009年		Annual Change	
		Rate of use	Size of netizen (10,000)	Rate of use	Size of netizen (10,000)	Growth (10,000)	Growth rate	Rate of use	Size of netizen (10,000)	Growth (10,000)	Growth rate
Information Access	Online News	73.6%	15,500	78.5%	23,400	7,900	51.0%	80.1%	30769	7834	31.5%
	Search Engine	72.4%	15,200	68.0%	20,300	5,100	33.6%	73.3%	28134	7369	38.6%
	Online Job Seeking	10.4%	2,200	18.6%	5,500	3,300	150.0%	-	-	-	-
Online Entertainment	Online Music	86.6%	18,200	83.7%	24,900	6,700	36.8%	83.5%	32074	7174	28.8%
	Online Game	59.3%	12,500	62.8%	18,700	6,200	49.6%	68.8%	26454	7754	41.5%
	Online Video	76.9%	16,100	67.7%	20,200	4,100	25.5%	62.6%	24044	3844	19.0%
	Online Literature	-	-	-	-	-	-	42.3%	16261	-	-
Communication	Instant Messaging	81.4%	17,100	75.3%	22,400	5,300	31.0%	70.9%	27233	4833	21.6%
	Blog	-	-	54.3%	16,200	-	-	57.7%	22140	5940	36.7%
	Email	56.5%	11,900	56.8%	16,900	5,000	42.0%	56.8%	21797	4897	29.0%
	Social Networking Site	-	-	19.3%	5,800	-	-	45.8%	17587	11787	203.22%
	Forum/BBS	-	-	30.7%	9,100	-	-	30.5%	11701	2601	28.6%
E-Commerce	Online Shopping	22.1%	4,600	24.8%	7,400	2,800	60.9%	28.1%	10800	3400	45.9%
	E-Bank	19.2%	4,000	19.3%	5,800	1,800	45.0%	24.5%	9412	3612	62.3%
	Online payment	15.8%	3,300	17.6%	5,200	1,900	57.6%	24.5%	9406	4206	80.9%
	Internet Stocking	18.2%	3,800	11.4%	3,400	-400	-10.5%	14.8%	5678	2278	67.0%
	Travel Booking	-	-	5.6%	1,700	-	-	7.9%	3024	1324	77.9%
Others	Online education	16.6%	3,500	16.5%	4,900	1,400	40.0%	-	-	-	-

Data sources: CNNIC. *Statistical Survey Report on Internet Development in China*, 2001-2010

Figure 1. Size and Growth of Chinese Netizens. (Data Source: CNNIC. Statistical Survey Report on Internet Development in China, 2001-2010)

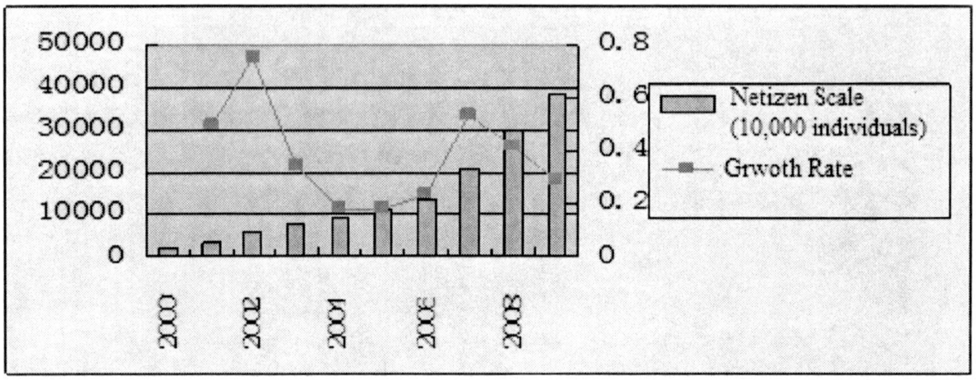

internet use is often related by officials to Deng Xiaopin's support of informatization, Jiang Zemin's emphasis on e-government in the 16th CCP Report in 2002, and President Hu Jintao's and Premier Wen Jiabao's attention to e-government (Holliday & Yep, 2005; Ma, Chung & Thorson, 2005).

The state-owned telecommunication companies seek to heavily invest in the Internet not only because it is in line with the central government policy, but also because they are under pressure to grow in an increasingly competitive market. The Internet economy has attracted both public and private capital, but only the state-own companies were allowed to invest in the infrastructure. In late 2000, three new networks were created to boost internet use: China Mobile launched the CMNet that targeted for wireless Internet users; China Great Wall created the CGWNet that aimed for military users; and the Ministry of Foreign Trade and Economic Cooperation established CIETNet that focused on international e-commerce (see a detailed review in Harwit & Clark, 2001).

The state support has enabled the fast infrastructure growth, but it also means that the state has control over the physical hardware and access of the Internet. For example, China's Internet services are based on a number of major interconnecting networks including ChinaNet, China 169, China Science and Technology Network (CSTNet), China Education and Research Network (CERNet), CMNET, CGWNet, CIETNet, and China Golden Bridge Network (China GBN). China's Internet service providers (ISPs) must obtain permission from one of these networks to connect international networks. Since all of the networks must go through the Ministry of Information Industry (MII)'s international gateway, MII can effectively control the information flow between individuals inside and outside of China. It can also block access to sites and delete individual web pages (Chung, 2008).

LEVEL AND FORM OF INTERNET USE

China is undergoing an e-boom era, and Chinese people use various web applications to obtain information, communicate, entertain, educate, and transact. First, the use of web applications has been increasing. Web applications include web-based media, internet information retrieval, web-based communication, online community, online entertainment, electronic commerce, internet finance, among others. These web applications provide adequate action space for netizens. Generally, netizens obtain information mainly through web-based media, internet information retrieval, and online community. They satisfy their needs in communication, entertainment, and business through other applications such as web-based communication, online entertainment, electronic commerce, and internet finance.

The 2010 CNNIC *China Internet Development Statistics Report* shows that at the end of 2009, internet music (83.5%), internet news(80.1%), and search engine 73.3%) were the top 3 Internet applications (see Table 3). However, as to growth rate, e-commerce applications were far ahead of others with an average annual growth rate at 68%, and online payment users had increased 80.9%, and ranked first among all web applications. It is clear that the dominant internet use among Chinese netizens is transitioning from e-entertainment to e-business. Table 3 shows that utilization rate, netizen scale, growth, and growth rate for 18 web applications from 2007 to 2009. Among them, the application that had the lowest utilization rate in 2009 was travel booking (7.9%) and the application that had the lowest growth rate in 2009 was internet video conferencing (19.0%).

Second, obtaining information has always been the main form of online participation. Internet media, online news and online community can contain large volume of information. Once an individual enters a website, he/she can obtain information without additional operations, which is a good way to get timely news information. Table 4 shows that 80.1% of the netizens used online news applications in 2009, a 31.5% increase from 2008. Interactivity is one of the most important features of online news, which changes the traditional one-way relationship between media and audience to a two-way or multi-way communicational relationship. Online news integrates multi-media functions so that it has stronger expressiveness and appeal. In recent years, online media has become as important as traditional media in reporting major political and social events.

Another popular online participation activity is to use search engines. With search engines

Table 4. Forms of Information Access Online

Application	2007		2008		Annual Change		2009		annualchange	
	Rate of Use	Size of Netizens (10,000)	Rate of Use	Size of Netizens (10,000)	Growth (10,000)	Growth Rate	Rate of Use	Size of Netizens (10,000)	Growth (10,000)	Growth Rate
Online News	73.6%	15,500	78.5%	23,400	7,900	51.0%	80.1%	30769	7834	31.5%
Search Engines	72.4%	15,200	68.0%	20,300	5,100	33.6%	73.3%	28134	7369	38.6%
Online Job Seeking	10.4%	2,200	18.6%	5,500	3,300	150.0%	-	-	-	-

Data sources: CNNIC. *Statistical Survey Report on Internet Development in China*, 2001-2010

netizens can input keywords or other labels to filter and search for particular information. Search engines are not as intuitive as online media and online news in terms of the process of information access, but they can meet the specific needs of different users. Table 4 shows that 73.3% of the netizens used search engines in 2009, a 38.6% increase from 2008. Another increasingly-used application in the information access category is job seeking. While it started later than online news and search engines, it has grown very fast. In 2008, while 78.5% of the netizens used online news and 68% used search engines, only 18.6% used online job seeking applications. However, in comparison to 2007, the use of online job seeking increased 150%, a much higher growth rate than online news (51%) and search engines (33.6%).

Third, online communication and exchange has been increasingly used. Among online communication applications, instant messaging has been the most popular one. As Table 5 shows, in 2009, 70.9% of the netizens (or 272 million) used instant messaging, a 21.6% increase from 2008. The second most popular application is blogging. In 2009, 57.7% of the netizens (or 221 million) owned a blog, a 36.7% increase from 2008. Notably, active blogs increased 37.9% from 2008, reaching about 145 million (or 37.7% of the netizens). The role of blogs in online participation and expression has increased to a notable degree. By the end of 2009, the percentage of netizens who owned a blog (57.7%) had even surpassed the percentage of netizens who used emails (56.8%). From 2008 to 2009, the percentage of netizens who used emails remained the same (56.8%), but the absolute number of email users increased from 169 million to 218 million (a 29% increase).

Forums and BBS have also been an important mechanism for public debates and viewed as e-civil society (Yang, 2003). For example, online chat rooms often serve as barometers for public opinions on some political issues such as international relations, environmental disasters, and important political events (McNally, 2005). One famous forum is the *Strong Nation Forum* (*qiangguo* luntan) under the *People's Daily,* which had about 100,000 hits and 1,000 postings per day in 2000 (Yang, 2003). The contents on the forum are more liberal than the *People's Daily* (Zheng & Wu, 2005), which is the master mouthpiece of the Chinese government.

Fourth, compared with 2008, the age structure of Chinese netizens in 2009 was more streamlined and balanced. The number of netizens above 30 years old was on the rise and accounted for 38.5% of the whole netizen population. Being more mature and with stronger purchasing capacity, this part of the population is the most important user group for e-economic development. As Table 6

Table 5. 2008-2009 Comparison of the Use of Online Communication Applications

	2008		2009		annualchange	
	Rate of Use	**Size of Netizens (10,000)**	**Rate of Use**	**Size of Netizens (10,000)**	**Growth (10,000)**	**Growth Rate**
Instant Message	75.3%	22,400	70.9%	27,233	4,833	21.6%
Own a Blog	54.3%	16,200	57.7%	22,140	5,940	36.7%
Update Blog	35.2%	10,500	37.7%	14,477	3,977	37.9%
Forum/BBS	30.7%	9,100	30.5%	11,701	2,601	28.6%
Social Networking	--	--	45.8%	17,587	--	--
Email	56.8%	16,900	56.8%	21,797	4,897	29%

Data sources: CNNIC. *Statistical Survey Report on Internet Development in China*, 2001-2010

Table 6. 2007—2009 Netizens' Age Distribution

year	Under 10	10-19	20-29	30-39	40-49	50-59	Above 60
2007	0.8%	27.8%	38.1%	20.5%	8.1%	3.3%	1.4%
2008	0.4%	35.2%	31.5%	17.6%	9.6%	4.2%	1.5%
2009	1.1%	31.8%	28.6%	21.5%	10.7%	4.5%	1.9%

Data sources: CNNIC. *Statistical Survey Report on Internet Development in China*, 2001-2010

shows, the percentage of netizens in their forties was 8.1% in 2007, 9.6% in 2008, and 10.7% in 2009; the percentage of netizens in their fifties was 3.3% in 2007, 4.2% in 2008, and 4.5% in 2009.

Similar to the investment in the Internet infrastructure, the fast growth in internet use is also facilitated by the partnership between government agencies and state-owned telecommunication companies that strive for more profits. For example, the percentage of netizens under 10 years old increased slightly in 2009: from 0.4% in 2008 to 1.1% in 2009. This was partly due to the implementation of the "School Link" Project, which helped a majority of primary and secondary schools establish a fairly comprehensive online educational program. Meanwhile, the Ministry of Education, the Ministry of Finance, the Ministry of Industry and Information Technology, and the State Council Information Office have launched measures to clean the campus network environment. They offer free internet filtering software for computer terminals of primary and secondary schools in order to protect the teenagers from unhealthy information.

The data above suggest that the primary internet use by Chinese people is not political mobilization, which is also reflected in how advocacy groups/organizations utilize their websites. For example, environmental NGOs, the most active NGOs in China, have "simulated the civil movements in China" (Lee, 2007, p. 270). This is partly because environmental activities are viewed as less politically sensitive and face fewer regulation barriers. Yang and Taylor (2010) find that 45% of these NGOs have set up their own websites. Even for these NGOs, however, the websites "do little to organize their publics to participate in environmental social movements" although they do provide information to members, the public and the media (Yang & Taylor, 2010, p. 1).

Nevertheless, the Internet use has helped citizens to increase social capital, develop trust, and collaborate with others (Yang, K. 2003). For example, while the environment NGOs' website plays primarily an educational role, Sullivan and Xie (2009) find extensive linkages between Chinese environmental actors--state and non-state--online, which suggests that there is a network of environmental actors connected via the Internet. Such a network is of great importance for any social movement to occur. Another example is that, in the aftermath of the Sichuan Earthquake in 2008, millions of volunteers were mobilized online.

Moreover, it should be pointed out that sometimes attention to a social problem may lead to policy changes. For instance, the Internet helped educate Chinese netizens about AIDS and its response in China, creating pressure for a real policy change--from denial and inaction to a more aggressive and humanitarian policy based on international best practices (Kaufman, 2010). In fact, both President Hu Jintao and Premier Wen Jiabao admitted that they learned from the Internet about public opinion. The 4th Plenary Session of the 16th CCP Central Committee in 2004 decided that "much attention should be paid to the influence of some new media like the Internet on public opinion." The government started to use the Internet to gauge public opinion. The Information Section of the First Secretariat

Bureau under the General Office of the State Council began to edit *E excerpts of Online Information* for the State Council leaders on a daily basis (Dong & Yang, 2006). Some public issues were quickly reported to the leadership through this channel, such as the fake powered milk case in Fuyang, Anhui Province, the case of migrant workers coming under attack while demanding payment of overdue wages from their employers in Guangzhou, and the case of the illegal pulling down and removal of a residential community in Jiayang, Hunan Province (Chen & Dong, 2005).

Given the increasing importance of public opinion online to government agenda setting, Wang (2008) contends that while a western style democratization has not occurred, China's political system has changed. The Internet has helped Chinese citizens become more engaged in social and political discussion than they would otherwise. Wang (2008) concludes: "today the public is not an ignored bystander but is seriously involved in the agenda-setting process and that there is an impressive congruence between the priorities of the public and the priorities of the Chinese government...agenda setting is 'becoming a more and more scientific and democratic process'" (p. 81).

THE "DARK SIDE" AND ITS CONTROL

For many observers, Chinese government uses the Internet as a tool for informing citizens of what it wants them to know, but has also been extremely sensitive to the potential of the Internet to mobilize mass actions (Chung, 2008). Fountain(2001) writes that "the central government of the People's Republic of China(PRC) enacts networked computing as an instrument of social control and surveillance. Technologies used for jamming, blocking, and filtering information dominate"(p. 33). Indeed, WebPages that are reported to threaten social order and national security have been blocked or deleted, such as those relating to the Falun Gong movement, the Tiananmen Square incident, and the independence of Taiwan and Tibet. Television channels such as CNN and BBC World News are monitored and regularly blocked, as well as social networking sites such as Facebook and LinkedIn. Table 7 lists the forbidden online content as defined by the State Council News Office and the Ministry of Information Industry in the "Rules on Regulating Internet News Information Services," enacted in 2005.

According to Chung (2008), China has about 30,000 "cyber-cops" who "selectively block foreign news sites and terminate domestic sites publishing politically sensitive information" (p. 735). For example, in September 2004, officials from the State Council's News Office, the MII, and Ministry of Education shut down a very popular BBSs, *Yi Ta Hu Tu*, which originated from the Beijing University and became the largest BBS in the education network at the time. Users of the BBS include mostly professors, researchers, and students at universities and research institutes. A law professor of Beijing University issued an open letter to the university president asserting that shutting down the BBS without proper procedure violates the users' constitutional rights.

Online journalists and common Internet users are also required to practice self-censorship online. The foundation for self-censorship was established in March 2002, when the Internet Society of China issued a "Public Pledge on Self-Discipline for the China Internet Industry" (Liang & Lu, 2010). All website hosting services have to install keyword filtering software and hire people to monitor information on their websites. Even foreign Internet companies often cooperate with the Chinese government on this matter. For example, Yahoo! gave out information about Shi Tao as the government learned of Shi's email to *Asia Democracy Foundation* an internal CCP document that "warned journalists of the dangers of social unrest resulting from the dissidents on the 15th anniversary of the Tiananmen Square massacre" (BBC News 2005).

Table 7. List of Forbidden Content on the Internet in China

	When posting or transmitting news or contents on current affairs, Internet news information service providers are prohibited from including any of the following materials
1	Violating the basic Constitutional principles
2	Endangering national security, disclosing state secrets, subverting the regime, or undermining national unification
3	Harming the dignity or interest of the state
4	Instigating ethnic hatred or discrimination, or undermining ethnic solidarity
5	Breaking state policies on religion, or diffusing evil cults or feudal superstition
6	Spreading rumors to disturb social order or destroy social stability
7	Spreading obscenity, pornography, gambling, violence, terror, or abetting criminal conduct
8	Insulting or slandering others, or infringing upon others' legitimate rights and interests
9	Inciting illegal assemblies, associations, marches, or demonstration, or assembling a crowd to disturb social order
10	Conducting activities in the name of an illegal civil organization
11	Any other content prohibited by law or administrative regulations

Source: The State Council News Office and the Ministry of Information Industry, "Rules on Regulating Internet News Information Services," Section 3, Article 19, translated by the author. Accessed on November 7, 2010 at: http://news.xinhuanet.com/politics/2005-09/25/content_3538899.htm

In the mean time, there are other dark sides of the Internet that do not directly relate to political matters and that the government can find more support from its citizens. For example, "Internet suicide" and "Internet addiction" have become an important social problem, which is part of an moral crisis faced by Chinese (Golub & Lingley, 2008). A report in 2007 listed China as the second largest cyber crime nation in the world, only behind the U.S. (Liang & Lu, 2010). Online fraud, selling illegal goods online, invasion of personal privacy, online gambling, and pornography are all crimes targeted by the Chinese authority. The latter two are particularly monitored as they are often considered serious challenges to socialist order. For example, pornographic information may impact teenagers in a very bad way. Cyberspace is open to pornographic and violent information which can undermine adolescent health and social values. According to Ministry of Public Security, among the imprisoned young offenders in China, 80% of them had bad Internet use records, 60% of crime activities involve the Internet and Internet cafes. The Internet, particularly online games and bad websites, provide pornographic and violent scenes that lead teenagers into an abnormal development track. The pursuit of sensation and fashion becomes an important factor for teenagers to consider in their daily lives. Imitating the plots on the web has also become a major factor for juvenile delinquency and the lack of communication barrier between teenagers and other people.

The anonymity, non-restrictiveness, and other features of the Internet have made it an important and attractive tool for many netizens to express their ideas and influence public opinions. On the other hand, however, the anonymity and non-restrictiveness have also caused problems in what's express on the web. And opinions on the web are sometimes seriously biased, reflecting only the ideas of particular groups of netizens and leading to Internet disorder. This has become a real problem in online participation in China. As psychological experiments have shown, humans in anonymous circumstances tend to show "animal" behavior. Cyberspace provides sufficient condition for anonymity, so people under the protection of anonymity tend to express irrational and immoral comments. Anonymity allows such comments to be publicized promptly and widely, which may bring out large-scale intensification of social conflicts and negative impacts on the government. Specially, the anonymity on the Internet enhances the "animal" tendency of netizens. Evidences include the gradual increase of the number of anonymous spaces, and the increase of the impact brought by these spaces. Second, the effects brought by anonymity become greater. In addition to using pseudonyms and being anonymous on the web, the Diving law further enhances the anonymous sense of the netizens. Diving means that individuals can view online information without being knowing by others, revealing their own identities, publishing information, or replying any messages. As a result, what is expressed on the web can be rapidly and widely distributed and shared.

In order to effectively manage internet use, the Chinese government is trying to introduce a real name system on the Internet that requires netizens to reveal their real identities when expressing their opinions, spreading information, or obtaining information on the web. Such a system can avoid the spread of fake information, the formation of harmful public opinions, and disputes caused by the anonymity. However, the real name system may, to some extent, violate the privacy of netizens and reduce their enthusiasm in online participation. When privacy becomes semi-privacy or no privacy, netizens may be unwilling to participate online or express their opinions freely due to the fear of being punished or prosecuted.

To sum up, while strong censorship exists, it serves some positive purposes and its negative effects on democratization cannot be overstated. If the government control prevented all social mobilization via the Internet, it would have proved the social determinism. In many occasions, policy entrepreneurs or active citizens have tried to use the Internet to communicate policy information or mobilize public opinion. Sometimes they fail but other times they succeed. Institutional change may occur during this trial and error process. A case in point is the *Sun Zhigang* incident. Sun Zhigang, a graphic designer in Wuhan, was beaten to death in the Custody and Repatriation Center of Guangzhou City after being detained for not carrying a temporary residence permit in March 2003. Such tragedy was nothing new under the Measures for Internment and Deportation of Urban Vagrants and Beggars, which was enacted twenty years ago. In the initial stage of Sun's case, it seemed that the incident would again produce no policy change--the mainstream Chinese media was warned not to report on the case after the *Southern Metropolis Daily* and several other small newspapers picked up the story. One different thing this time is that the story had already spread around the country on the Internet. For example, within two hours since it was posted on Sina.com, the largest Chinese news portal, about 4,000 comments were generated (Xiao, 2003). Hundreds of scholars and lawyers sent letters to the Standing Committee of the National People's Congress calling for the eradication of the temporary residence permits. Eventually, the State Council on June 22 abolished the temporary permit system and started to transform those detention centers into relief care facilities for migrants, vagrants, and the homeless.

Even for censoring itself, there have been occasional successes where Internet users have changed government policies. One case is the proposed installation of Green Dam-Youth Escort software, which was funded by the government's treasury and said to block children from viewing online pornography and other harmful content. The Ministry of Industry and Information Technology required all personal computer sold in China be installed with the software. Many internet users believed that the project was to monitor their internet habits and was an intrusion into their privacy. With the help of lawyers and local civil right organizations, the public eventually forced the government to terminate the project (Yang, K. 2010). At the micro level, there always seems to be a continuing struggle between internet monitors and internet users. A survey of internet users by the

Global Communication Association in 2007 found that 94% of the respondents knew the censorship issue, over 79% disagreed on the practices, and about 79% reported using anti-blocking software everyday (Chinascope, 2007).

While the censorship and self-censorship are in place, "those willing to meet in virtual arenas and daring enough to air their discontent with social and political problems are definitely on the increase" (Lagerkvist, 2005, p. 123). It is now internet news forums that usually first circulate or report on more critical, sensitive, controversial policy news or issues. Partly because of the more effective government control over the traditional media, the Internet starts to serve as an alternative means of agenda setting. In addition, communication between citizens and the government has been enhanced via digital networking, and information technology does enable citizens to participate in the implementation of policies (Zhang, 2002). Overall, as Lagerkvist (2005, p. 126) concludes, "internet opinion is gaining a certain influence over how Chinese leaders can act and present themselves in the international arena."

Provision of E-Government Services

E-government services help government understand citizen needs, obtain public information, increase trust in government, and improve quality of life. Almost all Chinese city governments have created their own websites since May 18, 1998, when the city of Qindao established the first Chinese government website—Qindao Government Information Public Network. Chinese city governments follow the trend of web applications to display government image, distribute government information, introduce public participation, and provide public services. However, government websites are deficient in the areas such as open information and public participation.

On January 22, 1999, the China Telecom and the Economic Information Center of the State Economic and Trade Commission jointly organized a meeting to promote "Government Online Projects." The goal of the project was to have over 60% of central government agencies and provincial and local governments to go online in 1999 and raise the percentage to over 80% in 2000 (Lovelock & Ure, 2003). In February 2003, the Government Online Project Service Center organized a meeting in Beijing to release its survey results and further promote the project. According to its statistics, within the past three years, the number of government websites had reached more than 10, 000, and online business and online approval had been gradually implemented. Almost all central government agencies went online. The Golden Projects also continued and expanded. In addition to Golden Bridge, Golden Customs, and Golden Card, other projects have been started:

- **Golden Sea:** To build a data network linking top government leaders with other institutions, organizations and offices under the direct jurisdiction of the CCP Central Committee. Main participants include the State Statistical Bureau and the State Information Center.
- **Golden Macro:** To develop a state economic and policy support system by setting up databases unifying industries, taxation, prices, investments, resources, energy, transportation and information exchange. The main participants include China Import-Export Bank, the Ministry of Finance, and the State Information Center.
- **Golden Tax:** To make use of computerized tax receipts and direct bank connections to aid the flow and the use of funds across China. The main participants include the Ministry of Finance, the Ministry of Information Industry, the State Taxation Bureau, and the Great Wall Computer Coorporation.
- **Golden Intelligence:** To enable teachers and researchers to have timely information and to enable international and lo-

cal communication and cooperation. The main participant is the State Education Commission.

- **Golden Enterprise:** To design and build an integrated enterprise quota and distribution system and to build a country-wide enterprise and product database. The main participant is the State Economic and Trade Commission.
- **Golden Agriculture:** To develop and monitor agricultural supervisory committees and the calculation and forecasting system. The main participant is the Ministry of Agriculture.
- **Golden Health:** To develop and apply computer technology, communications technology, and scientific information distribution in the medical sector. The main participant is the Ministry of Health.
- **Golden Information:** To develop real-time information flows by the State Statistics Bureau.
- **Golden Housing:** To create a property information network.
- **Golden Switch:** To build China's domestic digital switch manufacturing industry by the Ministry of Information Industry.
- **Golden Cellular:** To provide the basis for a coordinated mobile communications strategy and to develop national roaming standards and systems by the Ministry of Information Industry.

In 2001, the State Council issued the *Announcement about the 2001-2005 Planning Guideline for Government Informatization* (State Council, 2001), in order to deal with the problems in China's e-government. In January 2002, the State Standardization Commission and the State Council's Informatization Office announced *A Framework for E-Government Standards*, proposing to design six types of standards about overall standard, application, application support, information security, network infrastructure, and management, respecively. In July 2002, the Informatization Leadership Team and the State Council specified the goal and the development strategy for China's e-government during the Tenth Five-Year period. By the end of 2005, the standardization of e-government development had progressed significantly. Nine documents were made public to seek public comments:

- E-Government Standardization Guideline (2nd version; 1st version in 2002)
- E-Government Standards for Network Technology and Application Management
- E-Government Standards for Comprehensive System Design
- Standards for Electronic Government Documents based on XML
- E-Government Terms
- Monitoring Standards for Information Projects
- E-Government Data Elements
- Government Information Exchange System
- Government Information Catalog System

With the great attention by the central government, China's e-government initiative has made notable progress. According to the State Council's Informatization Office (2006), an preliminary framework for e-government has emerged: the percentage of governments with websites significantly increased; there is widespread attention to developing online public participation channels; online service has become a popular topic; online approval and service capacity has been strengthened; intergovernmental information sharing and collaboration though ICTs have gained steady progress; major operational systems such as Golden Shield and Golden Tax have had clear effects; e-government information security has been strengthened, and local governments have had increasingly positive experience with e-government. There are many success stories such as the Golden Projects and Guangdong Province's

Transportation Safety Information Sharing System (State Council, 2006).

Nevertheless, China's government websites have their limitations. Holliday and Yep (2005) surveyed 616 Chinese government websites in 2004 and found that most of them were "brochure" sites offering only static information about the government agency without dynamic or interactive functions. For example, in 2004 most government websites posted governments' mission statement (85%), legal responsibilities (78%), supervising departments (73%), supervised departments (64%), divisions (75%), press releases (90%), what's new (87%), and list of publications (84%). Very few websites, however, provided options to order publications by email (1%), make purchases (2%), or email named officials (9%). The majority of the websites did not have information about last update (6%), current activities (29%), annual reports (9%), briefings (11%), or chat rooms (5%). Holliday and Yep concluded that "Chinese e-government at the start of 2004 fell well short of the benchmark established by English e-government towards the end of 2001" (247). Lollar (2006) found a similar pattern and further pointed out that China's government websites tend to post "good" news and government success. Holliday and Yep (2005) and Lollar (2006) found that very few websites had executable services, which was consistent with a 2004 State Council report that observed that nearly half of the government websites were simply one-way information distributor (China Daily, 2004).

Even for information disclosure, Chinese government websites still have many shortcomings. First, the information disclosure is not complete. The *Regulation on Open Government Information* was put into effect in May 2008, which requires that government websites include open information sections to publicize and regularly update open information catalogues and guidelines. In practice, however, these catalogues and guidelines are not complete. Second, information disclosure is not in time. A sense of urgency is a notable characteristic of the cyberspace. Chinese government websites always fail to disclose and update information in time, so they often lose the opportunity to lead public opinion in the very beginning and end up struggling with policy implementation. It also leads to the lack of timely responses to major emergencies or crises. Third, the information on government websites tends to lack authority and originality. A common concern of government websites is the source of information which always comes from news media even without making sure if it is trustworthy. Because information from news media is not always first-hand government information and may lack authority and accuracy, it sometimes undermines the credibility of government websites. Information on government websites should be "few but good," using only verified and authoritative materials. Forth, information is disclosed in a single form and lacks innovation. The disclosure is confined to thinking from the governments' perspective, not the perspective of the general public. And finally, there is a lack of integration across government websites. Redundant construction is fairly common in government websites. At the same time, there is often inconsistency between government websites, reducing their credibility.

There are other problems with Chinese government websites as well. One is that the web design needs improvement. Problems such as lack of connectivity between website components and not-well-arranged website outlays are often seen in government websites, which make the websites messy and difficult for citizens to find the information they want. Another is that the search function is not strong or available. A good search function can ensure citizens find the particular information they need, but most government websites do not offer this function. A third issue is the interactive communication between government and citizens via the websites is not well managed. Although interactional programs such as message board have been set up, governments often fails to respond to the questions in time. The design, reply, and management of message boards have problems, hindering the interaction between governments and citizens.

Finally, Chinese government websites lacks standardization. Chinese government websites do not have uniform domain names. In May 2007, for example, among 95 websites owned by the county level governments in Shanxi province, 65 websites (68.4%) used gov.cn as their domain name and had relatively strong standards and abundant contents; 17 websites were affiliated with the Xinhua website (13.7%) and at a primitive stage with relatively simple contents; 13 websites used other domain names (Xu, 2008). In addition, the intro-government and inter-government online systems are not well connected. While many government websites and sizeable Internet infrastructure have been established, they are not connected in a way to achieve communication and resource sharing. E-government development requires multiple levels of governments to integrate their web platforms, but China has not built a common platform for different levels of government and government agencies in different geographic areas, which leads to repetitive construction and waste (Zhang & Ye, 2005).

CONCLUSION

The Internet has changed and is still changing how Chinese citizens and government conduct their lives or operations. With the support from the leadership and the mobilization ability of the state, China is determined to take advantage of the Web-based technologies to achieve its modernization and reform agenda. It is reasonable to expect that citizens' use of the Internet will continue to increase in areas such as obtaining information, communicating ideas, and doing businesses. The use of the Internet for political and administrative participation, however, has a less certain future--it depends on China's democratization process and how the role of government evolves, and it also depends on how active citizens or policy entrepreneurs make strategic moves and thus shape institutional changes. Future studies may start to examine the successes and failures of such citizens or entrepreneurs in order to find out under what circumstances their actions are more likely to cause real policy or institutional change. This type of change may not be grand, but it accumulates momentum for more fundamental changes.

REFERENCES

Barber, B. (1998). Three scenarios for the future of technology and strong democracy. *Political Science Quarterly, 113*(4), 573–589. doi:10.2307/2658245

Bekkers, V., & Homburg, V. (2005). E-government as an information ecology: Backgrounds and concepts. In Bekkers, V., & Homburg, V. (Eds.), *The information ecology of e-government*. Amsterdam, The Netherlands: IOS Press.

Bijker, W. E. (1995). *Of bicycles, bakelites, and bulbs: Toward a theory of sociotechnical change*. Cambridge, MA: MIT.

Castell, M. (1996). *The rise of the network society*. Malden, MA: Blackwell Publishers.

Chen, L., & Dong, X. (2005, March 31). Hulianwang Zhongguo de xin minyi shidai: yijian yeshi caifu. (Opinions are treasure: the new era of public opinion in networked China). *Hulianwang Zhoukan* (Internet Weekly). Retrieved from http://media.163.com/05/0331/ 11/1G5T8FDT00141E7P.html

China Daily. (2004, April 5). *Nation quickens spread of e-government*.

China International Network Information Center (CNNIC). (2001). *The 9th statistical survey report on the Internet development in China*. Retrieved on June 15, 2010, from http://www.cnnic.net.cn/download/manual/ en-reports/9.pdf

China International Network Information Center (CNNIC). (2002). *The 10th statistical survey report on the Internet development in China*. Retrieved on June 15, 2010, from http://www.cnnic.net.cn/download/manual/ en-reports/10.pdf

China International Network Information Center (CNNIC). (2003). *The 12th statistical survey report on the Internet development in China*. Retrieved on June 15, 2010, from http://www.cnnic.net.cn/download/manual/ en-reports/12.pdf

China International Network Information Center (CNNIC). (2005). *The 16th statistical survey report on the Internet development in China*. Retrieved on June 15, 2010, from http://www.cnnic.net.cn /download/2005/ 2005072601.pdf

China International Network Information Center (CNNIC). (2006). *The 18th statistical survey report on the Internet development in China*. Retrieved on June 15, 2010, from http://www.cnnic.net.cn/download/2006/ 18threport-en.pdf

China International Network Information Center (CNNIC). (2007). *The 19th statistical survey report on the Internet development in China*. Retrieved on June 15, 2010, from http://www.cnnic.net.cn/html/Dir/2007/02/ 05/4432.htm

China International Network Information Center (CNNIC). (2008). *The 21st statistical survey report on the Internet development in China*. Retrieved on June 15, 2010, from http://www.cnnic.net.cn/uploadfiles/pdf/2008 /2/29/104126.pdf

China International Network Information Center (CNNIC). (2009). *The 23rd statistical survey report on the Internet development in China*. Beijing: Ministry of Information Industry. Retrieved on June 15, 2010, from http://www.cnnic.net.cn/uploadfiles/pdf/2009/ 3/23/153540.pdf

China International Network Information Center (CNNIC). (2010). *The 25th statistical survey report on the Internet development in China*. Beijing, China: Ministry of Information Industry. Retrieved on June 15, 2010, from http://www.cnnic.net.cn/uploadfiles/pdf/2010/3/ 15/142705.pdf

Chinascope. (2007). *A survey of mainland Chinese's view on Internet censorship*.

Chinn, M., & Fairlie, R. (2010). ICT use in the developing world: An analysis of differences in computer and Internet penetration. *Review of International Economics*, *18*(1), 153–167. doi:10.1111/j.1467-9396.2009.00861.x

Chung, J. (2008). Comparing online activities in China and South Korea. *Asian Survey*, *48*(5), 727–751. doi:10.1525/AS.2008.48.5.727

Dong, R., & Yang, T. (2006). Wangshang yizheng cuisheng minyi shengchanli (Political workshops on the Internet boost the production of public opinion). Liaowang Zhoukan, 11. Retrieved from http://news.xinhuanet.com/ misc/2006-03/13/content_4297654.htm

Fountain, J. (2001). *Building the virtual state: Information Technology and institutional change*. Washington, DC: Brookings Institution.

Giddens, A. (1984). *The constitution of society: Outline of the theory of Structuration*. Berkeley, CA: University of California Press.

Golub, A., & Lingley, K. (2008). Just like the Qing empire: Internet addiction, MMOGs, and moral crisis in contemporary China. *Games and Culture*, *3*(1), 59–75. doi:10.1177/1555412007309526

Harwit, E., & Clark, D. (2001). Shaping the Internet in China: Evolution of political control over network infrastructure and content. *Asian Survey*, *41*, 377–408. doi:10.1525/as.2001.41.3.377

Holliday, I., & Yep, R. (2005). E-government in China. *Public Administration and Development, 25*, 239–249. doi:10.1002/pad.361

Kaufman, J. (2010). Turning points in China's AIDS response. *China. International Journal (Toronto, Ont.), 8*(1), 63–84.

Kluver, R., & Yang, C. (2005). The Internet in China: A meta-review of research. *The Information Society, 21*, 301–308. doi:10.1080/01972240591007616

Lagerkvist, J. (2005). The rise of online public opinion in the People's Republic of China. *China. International Journal (Toronto, Ont.), 3*(1), 119–130.

Lee, S. (2007). Environmental movements and social organizations in Shanghai. *China Information, 21*, 269–298. doi:10.1177/0920203X07079647

Liang, B., & Lu, H. (2010). Internet development, censorship, and cyber crimes in China. *Journal of Contemporary Justice, 26*(1), 103–120. doi:10.1177/1043986209350437

Lollar, X. (2006). Assessing China's e-government: Information, service, transparency, and citizen outreach of government websites. *Journal of Contemporary China, 15*(46), 31–41. doi:10.1080/10670560500331682

Lovelock, P., & Ure, J. (2003). E-government in China. Retrieved June 10, 2007, from http://www.trp.hku.hk/ publications/e_gov_china.pdf

Ma, L., Chung, J., & Thorson, S. (2005). E-government in China: Bringing economic development through administrative reform. *Government Information Quarterly, 22*, 20–37. doi:10.1016/j.giq.2004.10.001

Margetts, H. (1999). *Information Technology in government: Britain and America*. London, UK: Routledge.

McNally, C. (2005). Global capitalism vs. Leninist controls: "Informatization" and e-government in the People's Republic of China. *Journal of E-Government, 2*(4), 3–14. doi:10.1300/J399v02n04_02

Miles, I., Rush, H., Turner, K., & Bessant, J. (1988). *Information horizons: The long-term social implications of new Information Technology*. London, UK: Edward Elgar.

Norris, P. (2001). *Digital divide: Civic engagement, information poverty, and the Internet worldwide*. Cambridge, UK: Cambridge University Press.

North, D. (1990). *Institutions, institutional change, and economic performance*. New York, NY: Cambridge University Press.

Qiu, J., & Chan, M. (2004). China Internet studies: A review of the field. In Nissenbaum, H., & Price, M. (Eds.), *The academy & the Internet* (pp. 275–307). New York, NY: Peter Lang.

Rosenau, J. (2002). Information Technologies and the skills, networks, and structures that sustain world affairs. In Rosenau, J., & Singh, J. P. (Eds.), *Information Technologies and global politics*. Albany, NY: State University of New York Press.

Shi, Y. (2006). E-government website accessibility in Australia and China: A longitudinal study. *Social Science Computer Review, 24*(3), 378–385. doi:10.1177/0894439305283707

Singh, J. (2002). Information Technologies and the changing scope of global power and governance. In Rosenau, J., & Singh, J. P. (Eds.), *Information Technologies and global politics*. Albany, NY: State University of New York Press.

State Council. (2001). *Announcement about the 2001-1005 planning guideline for government informatization. Beijing, China*. China: Author.

State Council's Informatization Office. (2006). *China's informatization development report 2006*. Beijing, China: State Council.

Sullivan, J., & Xie, L. (2009). Environmental activism, social networks, and the Internet. *The China Quarterly*, 422–432. doi:10.1017/S0305741009000381

Taubman, G. (1998). A not-so World Wide Web: The Internet, China, and the challenges to non-democratic rule. *Political Communication*, *15*(2), 255–272.

Wang, S. (2008). Changing models of China's policy agenda setting. *Modern China*, *34*(1), 56–87. doi:10.1177/0097700407308169

Williams, R., & Edge, D. (1996). The social shaping of technology. In W. H. Dutton with M. Peltu (Ed.), *Information and communication technologies: Visions and realities* (pp. 53-67). Oxford, UK: Oxford University Press.

Xiao, Q. (2003). Cyber speech: Catalyzing free expression and civil society (China). *Harvard International Review*, *25*(2), 70–75.

Xu, Y. (2008). The problems and policy recommendations in the construction of websites for county level governments: The case of Shanxi. [in Chinese]. *Theory Exploration*, *4*, 133–134.

Yang, A., & Taylor, M. (2010). (forthcoming). Relation-building by Chinese ENGOs' websites: Education, not activation. *Public Relations Review*, 1–10.

Yang, G. (2003). The co-evolution of the Internet and civil society in China. *Asian Survey*, *43*(3), 405–422. doi:10.1525/as.2003.43.3.405

Yang, K. (2003). Neoinstitutionalism and e-government: Beyond Jane Fountain. *Social Science Computer Review*, *21*, 432–442. doi:10.1177/0894439303256508

Yang, K. (2010). (forthcoming). The aborted green dam-youth escort censor-ware in China: A case study of emerging civic participation in China's Internet policy-making process. *Telematics and Informatics*, 1–10.

Yang, K., & Xu, X. (2010). E-government in mainland China. In Berman, E., Moon, J., & Choi, H. (Eds.), *Public administration in East Asia* (pp. 165–194). New York, NY: CRC Press. doi:10.1201/EBK1420051902-c8

Yang, Y. (2010). A Chinese way of democratization? *China. International Journal (Toronto, Ont.)*, *8*(2), 330–345.

Zhang, B., & Ye, H. (2005). China's e-government development: Problems and policy recommendations. [in Chinese]. *Journal of the Hunan Mass Media Technology College*, *5*(5).

Zhang, J. (2002). Will the government serve the people? *New Media & Society*, *4*(2), 163–184. doi:10.1177/146144402222226325

Zheng, Y., & Wu, G. (2005). Information Technology, public space, and collective action in China. *Comparative Political Studies*, *38*(5), 507–536. doi:10.1177/0010414004273505

KEY TERMS AND DEFINITIONS

Democratization: the transition to a more democratic political regime.

Governance: an institutional framework that defines, enables, and constrains the relationships, responsibilities, and accountabilities between actors, organizations, or other entities.

Institution: rules of the game, or any structure or mechanism that governs the behavior of a set of individuals who are bounded within a given community.

Internet Use: the use of the Internet by various actors in political, social, organizational, and/or individual lives.

Netizen: an individual who is actively involved in online communities.

Social Determinism: a theoretical perspective that assumes that social structures and interactions alone determine individual behavior and technology development.

Technological Determinism: a theoretical perspective that assumes that technology drives the development of a society's social structure and cultural values.

Chapter 18
Vision 2020:
A Case Study of Web 2.0 Application to Public Governance in Taiwan

Ching-Heng Pan
National Chung-Hsing University & Taiwan E-Governance Research Center, Taiwan

Don-Yun Chen
National Cheng-Chi University & Taiwan E-Governance Research Center, Taiwan

Chian-Wen Wang
National Cheng-Chi University & Taiwan E-Governance Research Center, Taiwan

ABSTRACT

There has been a noticeable change in the roadmap for e-governance development in recent years. In accordance with recent public reforms targeted at achieving good governance, the focal areas of e-governance have started to shift from improving provider-centered services, readiness of tangible infrastructure, and administration reengineering to developing citizen-centered initiatives, information disclosure, and public participation. Recent developments in Web technologies offer opportunities as well as challenges for government to address these emerging issues. Web technologies and applications have entered the phase identified more generally under the conceptual umbrella of Web 2.0. The core value propositions of Web 2.0 are multifaceted, such as using the Web as a single platform for versatile interactions, users also serving as producers, facilitating collective intelligence with greater ease, richer user experiences, and continuous upgrade of applications based on user feedback. These features are considered facilitative of a bottom-up, decentralized, deliberative, and participatory governance structure.

In 2008, a website named Vision 2020 was launched by the Taiwan central government. The website was designed with Web 2.0 features, aimed at encouraging interaction between the elite and the general public in order to build vision of what the country should be like in the year 2020. Since Web 2.0 technologies facilitate participation, this chapter attempts to examine Vision 2020 features, such as its "Web 2.0-ness," levels of e-participation, and the relationship between the two.

DOI: 10.4018/978-1-60960-753-1.ch018

The chapter introduces a novel website model adopted in Vision 2020. An evaluation framework is presented for assessing the extent to which a website facilitates electronic participation via Web 2.0 technologies. Then, the Vision 2020 website is thoroughly examined in terms of the evaluation framework. Recommendations for the design and implementation strategies of government websites aimed to increase e-participation are offered.

INTRODUCTION

In conjunction with the recent trend of pursuing good governance, building a more citizen-centric government has become increasingly important for democratic governments around the globe. How to utilize internet technologies to make the policy process more bottom-up, deliberative and boundary-spanning is a great challenge to many governments. This challenge is driven by the need for government to accommodate diverse and evolving social demands. Among various efforts toward citizen-centric reforms, the positive experience of Web 2.0 applications that encourage participation in market and political campaigns has drawn the attention of e-government reformers, who have been seeking remedies for the relatively low rate of on-line participation via government websites.

Since the bursting of the dot-com bubble in the early 2000s, the concept of Web 2.0 has taken the lead in Internet development. The core values of Web 2.0 are: the web as platform, user as producer, collective intelligence, rich user experience, and perpetual beta status. Through two-way interactions between user-user and user-website, individuals can collaborate, share and exchange critical information to ensure viable mutual participation and create virtual social networks that influence opinion formation and even coordinate action in the real-world (O'Reilly, 2005; Osimo, 2008).

According to a recent digital-divide survey, about 40% of internet users in Taiwan read public news on line.[1] This signals the importance of the Web as a public arena waiting for the government actors to take proactive measures. Under the recent trend of Web 2.0, the government is increasingly thinking of using Web 2.0 applications to further develop citizen-centered e-government initiatives. In November 2008, a Web 2.0 inspired website named "Vision 2020" was established by the central government. It was designed to attract ordinary citizens to participate in the cause of building a common vision for Taiwan. However, as the government has shown increasing interest in adopting Web 2.0 applications, it is becoming more urgent to evaluate the effects of adopting this new technology. In this chapter, the authors introduce the new business model underlying Vision 2020 and we provide a preliminary performance evaluation report. In light of the assumption that Web 2.0 technologies promote bottom-up participation, our objectives are to examine Vision 2020's features, such as its "web 2.0-ness," levels of e-participation, and the relationship between the two.

BACKGROUND

In the Time of Rebuilding Participatory Democracy

Throughout the evolution of representative democracy, the governance structure has encountered a serious challenge in that citizens are becoming increasingly indifferent to democratic procedures. Mitigating people's alienation from public affairs has been a critical issue faced by democratic regimes (Fraunholz & Unnithan, 2008). Since the 1980s, democratization in Taiwan has moved from the transition stage to habitualization stage (Rustow, 1973). Citizens should not be considered merely as voters or consumers. Instead, they should be viewed as participants, partners and co-inventors of public policy that seeks not only efficiency but also more inclusive, legitimate citizen participation (Smith & Ingram, 1993). The government ought to include public opinion in the political process by creating diverse participative mechanisms in order to build a responsive, legitimate and "strong democracy" (Barber, 1984).

Adoption of information and communication technologies (ICTs) in government should not simply seek to achieve more efficient service delivery. It is equally important to press for participatory democracy. A recently emerging trend is the urge to free e-governance from managerialism and seeing ICTs as ways to strengthen democratic governance (Caldow, 2004; Chadwick, 2003; Lenihan, 2002; Macintosh, 2004). At the core of this effort is a response to the criticism that citizens are treated as customers, resulting in the demand that policy makers refocus on public service and civic engagement. "Public servants do not deliver public services; they deliver democracy" (Denhardt & Denhardt, 2007: xi). The development of e-governance should therefore respond to the call for the reaffirmation of democratic values, citizenship and service in public interest.

ICTs and Civic Engagement

From a narrower perspective, Diller (2001) argues that civic engagement is like a community service; community members are all responsible for volunteer work, participation in community activities, etc. Cooper (2005) equates civic engagement with citizens' participation in deliberative procedures and collective actions for common interests and institutional networks, with which the general public may become an indispensable element of public governance. Park (2006) specifically points to individual efforts applied to public affairs such as voting, hearings and volunteer activities. From a broader perspective, Putnam (1995) considers civic engagement an important foundation for building social capital that includes formal and informal social activities. Using a typological approach, Norris (2001) construes the concept according to three aspects: political knowledge of public affairs, trust in the political system, and the impact of participation on policy decisions. Jennings and Zeitner (2003) measures the concept with three sub-constructs: media attentiveness, political involvement, and volunteerism. Although the definitions may appear diverse, they point to the fact that civic engagement is not merely observable actions but also cognition, knowledge and attitude. It differs from citizen participation, which mostly implies observable activities in which citizens engage.

Skocpol and Fiorina (1999) list three important schools of thought on the issue of civic engagement in American democracy. The social capital approach stresses that it is through regular face-to-face interactions that individuals learn to cooperate with one another to solve public problems and develop the social trust which forms the basis for efficient government and social institutions. Putnam (1995), an important scholar in this camp, argues that the levels of social trust and civic engagement sharply decreased in the late twentieth century, connecting the issue to modern technologies, such as television, video games and the Internet, which are said to promote individual isolation. The second camp is the rational choice theorists, who are more skeptical about the viability of creating effective incentives for individuals to participate in public affairs. An individuals' self-interest driven behavior, in the context of civic engagement, oftentimes may not add up to a socially optimal outcome. How significantly can ICTs change the incentive structure remains uncertain. The third approach is historical institutionalism. The decline of civic engagement results from changes in organizational structures, relationships between political elites and citizens, and the shifting of resources among social and political activities. New advocacy groups representing new voices in politics increased after the 1950s, while cross-class voluntary federations have been in decline. Such changes in social infrastructure may have compromised the political leverage held by average citizens, thus impairing citizen involvement in public affairs (Skocpol & Fiorina, 1999). Does the Web help facilitate new voices, converge cross-class voices, or segmentalize voices? The answer is neither as clear nor simple as it may appear.

Optimists in the 1990s believed that ICTs would enhance civic engagement (Kim, 2006); even a genuine form of direct democracy could be realized with the fast developing technologies (Grossman, 1955). Empirical research suggests that the effectiveness of e-governance initiatives and level of civic engagement are positively related (Coleman & Gotze, 2002; Chen & Dimitrova, 2006). Although the optimist views may be debatable, it is recognized that civic engagement may be enhanced through ICTs.

ICTs Substantiate Deliberative Democracy

Engaging citizens does not necessarily imply realization of constructive inputs for policy making. The ultimate goal of civic engagement is to involve citizens in the political process to achieve deliberative democracy. The main difference between deliberative democracy and the dominant liberal democracy or representative democracy is that in liberal democracy, citizen preferences are assumed constant and the political process mainly aims to reflect the accumulation of preferences; the main role of the citizens is as voters only. By contrast, in deliberative democracy, preferences are assumed to be time varying and, therefore, citizens are not merely voters; they may experience self-transformation in the deliberative process of seeking the common good (Warren, 1992). The process of information collection, rational debate, persuasion, and dialectical dialogue are the points of emphasis in a deliberative democracy. Votes are supplementary in this regard (Bessette, 1994; Elster, 1998).

As a consequence of the advent of e-governance, the synthesis of ICTs and deliberative democracy has become an approach for realizing e-democracy. The United Nations (2003) proposed a method for evaluating citizen participation in three dimensions: e-information, e-consultation and e-decision making. The typology is similar to OECD's framework of evaluating government-citizen relations: information, consultation and public participation in policy making (OECD, 2001). Chen, Huang, and Hsiao (2004) integrated the above indicators with Arnstein's "ladder of citizen participation" (see Table 1). According to Arnstein's (1969) ladder of citizen participation, the bottom two rungs are manipulation and therapy. Their real objective is not to enable people to participate in planning or conducting programs, but to enable power holders to "educate" or "cure" the participants. Rung 3 and 4, informing and consultation, allow the have-nots to hear and to have a voice. In this situation, citizens may indeed hear and be heard, but they still lack the power to ensure that their views will be heeded by the powerful. Rung 5 is placation, which refers to the levels of citizen empowerment entailing increasing degrees of impact on decision-making. Citizens enter into the partnership rung that enables them to negotiate and engage in trade-offs with traditional power holders. At the topmost rungs, 7 and 8 (delegated power and citizen control), citizens obtain the majority of decision-making or full managerial power (Arnstein, 1969).

Opportunities and Challenges for ICTs on Deliberative Democracy

ICTs facilitate deliberative democracy in several ways. First, ICTs make it possible for the citizen to interact with the government virtually at any time and place, and therefore encourage broader

Table 1. Levels of e-Participation – a synthesis (adapted from Chen, Huang, and Hsaio, 2004:40).

<table>
<tr><th>Arnstein:
Ladder of citizen participation</th><th>OECD:
Government-citizen relations</th><th>United Nations</th></tr>
<tr><td>Citizen control</td><td rowspan="2">Public participation:
A bilateral partnership where citizens actively participate in policy agenda setting and policy discourses, but the ultimate accountability is of the government.</td><td rowspan="2">e-Decision making</td></tr>
<tr><td>Delegated power</td></tr>
<tr><td>Partnership</td><td rowspan="3">Consultation:
A bilateral relation based on available channels for citizens to comment on public policies</td><td rowspan="3">e-Consultation</td></tr>
<tr><td>Placation</td></tr>
<tr><td>Consultation</td></tr>
<tr><td>Informing</td><td rowspan="3">Information:
A unilateral relation based on the information produced and delivered by the government to the citizens</td><td rowspan="3">e-Information</td></tr>
<tr><td>Therapy</td></tr>
<tr><td>Manipulation</td></tr>
</table>

and more equitable participation. Second, advanced multimedia and other communication technologies increase the accessibility and richness of information used during the process of deliberation. Third, user anonymity reduces the psychological barriers to participation caused by socio-economic disparities (Witschge, 2002; Gastil, 2000; Stomer-Galley, 2002). Four, simultaneous interactions facilitate immediate mutual understanding, while non-simultaneous interactions increase deliberation.

However, ICT is a double edged sword for deliberative democracy. Bimber (2000) argues about a general trade-off between civil liberties and achievement of a deliberative common good. There will be the decreasing cost and increasing accessibility of political information enabled by the fast and integrated development of Web technology. On the one hand, lower costs and greater accessibility reduce the need for large, bureaucratic, institutionalized organizations to manage and communicate information, permitting flexible, specialized, fast and fragmented communication. As a result, increased political equality, acceleration of political processes, and more rapid cycling of the political agenda all become more attainable. On the other hand, however, since individuals can easily perform unlimited filtering, dialogues or interactions occur only among individuals of the same camp (Sunstein, 2001). Deinstitutionalized politics, fragmented communication, and accelerated pace of public agenda building and decision making may undermine the coherence of the debate and the dialogue, and reduce the deliberativeness of democracy. Anonymity gives rise to another dilemma between ensuring equal participation and holding participants accountable for their acts. Hiding behind the computer screen is not consistent with the spirit of rational and responsible interactions in deliberative democracy. Therefore, the question is what are the principles of using ICTs to practice deliberative democracy so that Habermas' (1987) "ideal speech situation" is achieved? Week (2000) argues that broad, informed, deliberative and credible results should be followed to evaluate participation. ICTs should at least help the participant access information and its interpretation (Webler, 1995).

Furthermore, the digital divide is increasingly being viewed as a common barrier that denies access to the "have-nots" as they lack the necessary skill or incentive for ICT-based participation. Demographic disparities and social inequalities such as ethnicity, income, and education often result in some sections of the society being denied access to information and participation in decision making. These inequalities are reinforced by digital divides, which could further deprive the have-nots of the opportunity to participate in the process of policy making (Norris, 2001).

WEB 2.0 AND E-GOVERNANCE

E-governance initiatives in the 1990s by and large followed the managerialism perspective that viewed citizens as customers and saw ICTs as business tools to be used by the government to deliver public services and to increase customer satisfaction. In the era of Web 2.0, which began in the early 2000s, the notion of e-governance has expanded to encompass e-citizenship and e-democracy, both of which involve the general public in the policy process through e-engagement and e-participation (Misra, 2008). If Web 2.0 applications – characterized by participation, collaboration and network effects – are effectively adopted to connect government and citizens, it will help reshape the governance structure and turn people from inert stakeholders to proactive designers and co-innovators of public policies (Tapscott & Williams, 2006).

Furthermore, if the potential benefits of Web 2.0 can be fully realized, the agency problem doomed in representative democracy may be alleviated by reducing the functional role of the political representative or "middle-man" (Accenture, 2005). Web 2.0 technologies reduce the costs of generating knowledge, adding value to information, and distributing information in the decision making process, and in turn lower the most important barrier to public participation: the "professional asymmetry" separating the political profession and the general public in the policy process. The governance structure could thus start to experience a fundamental change catalyzed by Web 2.0 technologies.

The Values of Web 2.0 to Public Governance

Web 2.0 is drawing growing attention among scholars in academia and practitioners of e-governance. However, the term "Web 2.0" does not seem to have a succinct and universally-accepted definition. O'Reilly (2005), pushing the concept front stage, proposes the following definition:

Web 2.0 is the network as [a] platform spanning all connected devices; Web 2.0 applications are those that make the most of the intrinsic advantages of that platform: delivering software as a continually-updated service that gets better the more people use it, consuming and remixing data from multiple sources, including individual users, while providing their own data and services in a form that allows remixing by others, creating network effects through an "architecture of participation," and going beyond the page metaphor of Web 1.0 to deliver rich user experiences.

The concept of Web 2.0 is broad and diverse. From both the business and technological viewpoints, the term may refer to different things, such as a platform of Internet technology (AJAX and XML) or a business operation model in the sense of e-commerce. In terms of user behavior, the ideas of social software, social computing, and participative website are all related to certain aspects of Web 2.0. These ideas are centered on the concept of "the Web as the platform" on which all users, including program developers and corporate personnel, interact with one another for pursuing their respective interests. Table 2 summarizes the concept of Web 2.0 from three dimensions, each representing a certain aspect of Web 2.0 (Downes, 2004; O'Reilly, 2005; Anderson, 2007; Osimo, 2008). The Web 2.0 applications listed in Table 2 are not exhaustive; they only outline what the term usually refers to. Web 2.0 technologies are used to develop web applications for users to

Table 2. Three dimensions of Web 2.0

Dimension	Construct	Source
Value	User as producer	Downes (2004); O'Reilly (2005); Osimo (2008)
	Collective intelligence	O'Reilly (2005); Osimo (2008)
	Perpetual beta	O'Reilly (2005); Osimo (2008)
	Extreme ease of use	Osimo (2008)
Application	Blog, Wiki, Podcast RSS feeds, Tagging, Search engine	O'Reilly (2005); Anderson (2007); Osimo (2008)
Technology	Ajax	O'Reilly (2005); Anderson (2007); Osimo (2008)
	Open API Microformats	Anderson (2007); Osimo (2008)
	XML Flash/Flex	Osimo (2008)

easily interact with the webpage and take more control over the page.

For the purpose of this study, we extend the discussion to values offered by Web 2.0 technologies and applications. Ease of sharing and ease of interaction have become vital parts of today's Internet usage. The earlier Web users' role of information producer or consumer was relatively easier to define, especially in terms of their actions of putting content on the Web or "consuming" information from the Web. Most content users simply browsed websites to receive information of interest in a uni-directional flow. Information was made available online through technology-based actions usually conducted by information technology (IT) persons. Thanks to Web 2.0 technologies, today's Web users need not be IT-savvy to simultaneously provide information to other users and benefit from other users' inputs. Web 2.0 applications usually provide a web-based platform where users can easily share content with one another. The applications or web services get better as more people use them and they can even enable the user to build a service. The boundary line between consumer and producer becomes thin and blurred. Consider blogging as an example: when users produce content on their weblog out of their own interests, this creates value for other interested users as a spillover of the original value of writing a weblog. Through mashups and hyperlinks, blog content may be referenced, reused and reassembled in novel ways to produce another webpage belonging to another user. Other examples such as interactive maps, search engines, videos and web syndication are all common components for mashups or reassembling. Seamless interconnection, interactive participation and continuous value adding to data have become the cornerstones of today's Web architecture.

In the same way, the more users participate in the process of quick information exchange, the higher the likelihood of achieving quality collaboration through the process of establishing inter-subjectivity and consensus. A typical example of collective intelligence is Wikipedia, the free and open-access encyclopedia that relies on over 13,000 volunteer contributors to edit submitted articles and has become a crucial source of knowledge. Its accuracy of information is considered competitive with the authoritative scholarly reference work *Encyclopedia Britannica* (Giles, 2005).

Web 2.0 service providers compete on the usability of applications more than ever before; this is because the user is the key contributor to a successful Web 2.0 operation. User feedback is therefore the crucial element in building organizational competency for technology development. As a result, web-based applications are being continuously released in beta version to reflect continuing improvements, instead of following the traditional start-end process from beta to final release.

It follows, then, that only the most user-friendly, intuitive and simple applications are likely to remain competitive. Many of the popular Web 2.0 applications today are not developed by large corporate entities but often by under-funded individuals. Usually applications are built with lightweight programming and simple interfaces that allow remixing and syndication.

AN EVALUATION FRAMEWORK FOR WEB 2.0 ON E-PARTICIPATION

The strategies of providing more interaction channels between the government and citizens and opening policy discussions to citizens can reduce political alienation. Recent research indicates that the use of Web 2.0 applications is maturing and has become an influential factor in political participation (Kohut, 2008). This study looks into the Vision 2020 initiative and attempts to discover whether a public website's "Web 2.0-ness" is positively correlated to user levels of e-participation.

This research adopts a definition of Web 2.0 that emphasizes its value in four ways: user as producer, collective intelligence, perpetual beta, and extreme ease of use. The three constructs of e-participation were derived from the indicators of e-participation, which includes e-information, e-consultation and e-decision-making (United Nations, 2003; OECD, 2001).

The idea of *user as producer* refers to users generating website content, sharing user experiences and opinions on issues at stake, and facilitating proper dialogue between end users or between end users and government decision-makers. Users do not necessarily consider themselves producers, but they are if they upload data onto the Web and make them available for others to use (e.g., a video clip, a travel journal, a food criticism, or just a short comment on a forum). When a user puts one of these on the Web for his/her own interest, he or she is an information producer as long as other users find the information useful. The more frequently or actively a user shares information on the Web, the higher the level of "user-as-producer."

Collective intelligence gauges the extent to which network effects of dialogues inspire new ideas or debates that lead to constructive convergence of opinions or knowledge. A quite common Web experience is that the quantity of information on the Web is abundant and perhaps even overwhelming; efficiently finding the most useful information can be quite a challenge. Creating tags or labels on website content by the general user/producer of the website certainly helps other users meet the challenge. This bottom-up collaborative work can be better achieved by involving as many users as possible. The term *folksonomy* is now commonly used to refer to the collaborative social classification created by ordinary folks (Vander Wal, 2007).[2] User-generated tags also can be displayed with a visual "tag cloud" or weighted list of words to show the popular words of a website (Bausch & Bumgardner, 2006). There are other collaborative works seen on *wiki* websites, which are "often used to power community websites, for personal note taking, in corporate intranets, and in knowledge management systems."[3] A crucially conducive factor of online collaboration and in turn collective intelligence is the user's sense of belonging to the community. If the user develops psychological attachment to an online group or community that he or she feels comfortable with, it is more likely that the user's willingness to share, to actively participate, will be stronger. The user's sense of belonging to the community is therefore a useful construct of online participation, regardless of whether the user's motive to participate in the online community is to receive information in return, to build personal reputation, or to feel that a contribution has an impact (Kollock, 1999; Bishop, 2007). Therefore, the user's perception of some other users as acquaintances should give the user the sense of belonging to the community that facilitates the generation of collective intelligence.

Perpetual beta means the website system and functional designs get continuously adjusted or upgraded based on user constant feedback on preferences and experiences (O'Reilly, 2005; Osimo, 2008). In this case, the website will likely provide a forum or area with similar functions for users to openly exchange experiences and communicate with the website service provider. In addition, the user should be aware of periodical notices of new releases available for download.

Extreme ease of use looks at the ease of acquiring information, providing customized functionality, and the richness of user experiences that raise the desire to revisit the website. In other words, a website is considered extremely easy to use when the user perceives that (1) the website information is sufficient, appropriate and useful; (2) the website designs are harmonious and easy to navigate; (3) the data transmission speed is stable and fast; (4) the website attends to the issue of security and privacy; and (5) the user's request is quickly responded to (Wolfinbarger & Gilly, 2003; Colier & Bienstock, 2006; Loiacono, Watson, & Goodhue, 2007; Sahadev & Purani, 2008). Table 3 summarizes the constructs and indicators for assessing the utilities of Web 2.0 adopted in this study.

There are three levels in the construct for online participation: e-information, e-consultation and e-decision making (United Nations, 2008). E-information is assessed by asking whether the website adequately provides participation information and actively promotes online events. E-consultation means whether the website has a strategic plan for public consultation recognized by the user, whether the plan is systematically implemented, and whether users are satisfied with the consultation process (Macintosh & Whyte, 2002). The main purpose of public consultation is to strengthen the legitimacy of public policy in democracy. The consultation process should be socially inclusive so that people of different socioeconomic status, ethnicity, geographic areas, etc., have their say in the policy making process. ICTs make it more feasible to organize dialogue on public affairs among ordinary citizens at lower costs. A Web 2.0 website must be able to facilitate multilateral dialogue, and this certainly includes government feedback responding to citizen opinions. The deepest level of citizen participation is when citizens have substantial influence on policy decisions. When users perceive that their opinions have or can have an actual impact on policy decisions, their motivation to participate will be further reinforced (Kollock, 1999). The user's sense of self-efficacy will be developed if the government website promises to weigh the user's opinion seriously. Table 4 summarizes the constructs and indicators of e-participation.

THE CASE OF VISION 2020

In November 2008, the RDEC of the central government created a website called "Vision 2020" to involve ordinary citizens in the process of envisioning what Taiwan should be like in the year 2020 (http://www.vision2020.tw). This one-year project concluded at the end of 2009. The website was designed to take advantage of the openness of the Web and to encourage participants to freely share their opinions on eleven social issues with other participants and designated "issue-masters." The underpinning notion is that the country's future development should be based on the deliberative consensus of ordinary citizens, rather than on the will of the elites in a top-down manner. The elites and grass-roots citizens, regardless of their age, gender, or socio-economic status, should collaborate on formulating the vision for Taiwan in 2020.

Table 3. Constructs and Indicators of Web 2.0 Values

Construct	Indicator
User as producer	1. User's motives to participate; 2. Sharing behaviors of participants: frequencies of sharing information; 3. Extent of participation: take initiative in raising policy issue for discussion, actively joining discussions.
Collective intelligence	1. Folksonomy - Whether the user can mark keywords or tags on his/her own or others' posts for searching; - Searching keywords or tags will lead to intended information; - Identify issue trends through keywords or tags searching.
	2. Collaborative work online 3. Social networking - Virtual social bonding: consider some other user acquaintances, perception of the sense of community
Perpetual beta	1. Functional Service - Whether the system adopts user feedback and continues to improve, revise, or upgrade
Extreme ease of use	1. Information content - Whether the website data is sufficient - Whether the website data is appropriate - Whether the website data is useful
	2. Interface design - Whether the interface layout is consistent (in symbols, background, layout, and color) - Whether the design is harmonious - Whether the interface is succinct and vivid
	3. Ease of use - Whether it is easy to learn - Whether it is easy to use - Whether website design is easy to follow
	4. Efficiency - Whether website data search is satisfying - Whether website download speed is satisfying - Whether the system is stable
	5. Security/Privacy - Whether the website has a security policy. - Whether the website has a privacy protection policy
	6. Responsiveness - Whether the website quickly responds to user requests

The operation of Vision 2020 was outsourced to private vendors. The RDEC first selected eleven issues and divided the website into eleven blog-like "arenas" or channels. And then eleven real world renowned opinion-leaders were contracted with RDEC to serve as the "issue-masters." Each issue master was responsible for hosting his or her blog channel by providing information and moderating public debate. The website adopted this novel design in an attempt to attract more online participation. The eleven channels were: education, human rights, thought, culture, environment, cross-strait relations, health, home, society, life style and family. The activities in which users could participate included a front page for each issue on which users could express (PK voting) their preference by casting votes, use the "Discuss with us" option to post and read opinions, and use the "Photo books" option to post visual materials to share with other users.[4]

For each issue, the issue master was responsible for posting keynote articles on his/her blog,

Table 4. Constructs and indicators of e-Participation

Construct	Indicator
E-Information	1. Providing information about e-participation: - Website has clear and explicit policy or mission statement for e-participation. - Website uses emails asking members to join online forums. - Web calendar announces upcoming participatory activities
E-Consultation	1. Conducted as planned - Whether the process of consultation is systematic and structured as planned - Degree of user satisfaction with the process 2. Consultation objectives - What is the purpose of consultation and what policy is made known to citizens? 3. Target audience - Whether consultation is inclusive 4. Responsiveness among participants - Whether one's opinion on a policy is known to others to initiate dialogue 5. Responsiveness of the government - Whether government promptly provides feedback to users' opinion
E-Decision-Making	1. Impacts on policy content - The online discussions between me and government agencies will affect the direction of policy-making. - Government agencies promise me that my suggestions expressed on website are examined when formulating the policy

responding to opinions, and coordinating discussions online. Users could easily do "mash-up" or redirect Vision 2020 to and from other websites with hyperlinks. This was designed to facilitate network broadcasting to ensure that dissemination can reach a wider audience, for greater impact. The issue master and participants could also create sub-categories under each main issue. For example, in the education arena, there were sub-categories such as "equality in education," "recent reforms in education policy," and "the problem of population and education." Among eleven channels, the highest number of sub-categories was seen under the health issue channel. On the front page, as a measure to increase user-friendliness, more recent or popular posts were marked to suggest reading priority.

The "PK voting" section of the website features items that could be voted upon, which originated in the blog or discussion arenas. First, the qualification to vote was not very strict. An intending voter only needed to file his or her name and e-mail address in order to vote. Second, pros and cons of the issue were presented side by side for voters to carefully consider. Also, users not only could cast votes but also post opinions explaining their viewpoints or simply mark their support of allies. Finally, PK voting allowed cross-issues voting, keyword searching, and highlighting of "hot voting issues" on each front page to attract more votes.

In the "Discuss with us" section, there were two areas in which users could participate: current issues and opinion exchange. This section was similar to other online forums where participants could publish, search, subscribe, and quick-jump to a certain opinion. The webmaster would announce the automatic counts for sub-issues, published articles, readership, and responses so participants could judge the popularity of each discussed matter. In terms of the website's openness, the original version of Vision 2020 did not require members to register in order to participate. However, in order to mitigate deviant online behavior, the later version required participants to become registered members to participate.

METHODS

Given the lack of a common definition of Web 2.0, this research adopted seven in-depth interviews and a focus group session for the purpose of better framing the theoretical constructs of the evaluation framework. The gathered information was also supplementary to the survey data for research findings. Two interviewees, coded A1 and B1, were government officials from the RDEC responsible for supervising the entire Vision 2020 initiative. One interviewee, coded C1, is a professor specializing in e-commerce and Web 2.0 research. Four interviewees were senior executives from Web-related companies including Google Taiwan (D1), the contractor of Vision 2020 (D2), the publicly funded Institute for Information Industry (D3), and a Web-marketing consulting firm (D4). The guidelines of the semi-structured interviews were centered on three main questions: (1) what are the scopes and values of Web 2.0? (2) How would the government and citizens use Web 2.0 applications to improve information dissemination, policy consultation and decision-making? (3) What dimensions ought to be included in evaluating a Web 2.0 website? A tentative evaluation framework and a survey questionnaire were developed after the in-depth interviews. Afterwards, a focus group consisting of researchers and practitioners of Web 2.0 was conducted. During the session, the aforementioned questions were posed. The panelists were also requested to examine the face-validity of the tentative evaluation framework and survey questions. Subsequently the framework and survey questions were revised accordingly.

Content analysis was adopted to analyze opinions posted on Vision 2020 forums. Opinions were categorized, coded and statistically analyzed. The codebook is shown in Appendix I. The research team also examined objectively observable web content such as page design, layout and available functionality. NVivio_8 and SPSS 17 were used to analyze qualitative and quantitative data, respectively.

The structure of the online questionnaire was designed on the basis of the four value dimensions of Web 2.0 and the three aspects of e-participation. The survey subjects were all registered members of Vision 2020. The member roster was obtained from RDEC after meeting the requirements of administrative procedures and research ethics. An email was sent to each member on the roster to obtain consent to participate in the survey. After deleting duplicate email addresses, there was a total of 614 members on the roster. A pilot test was conducted to ascertain the questionnaire's validity and reliability. The final questionnaire was administered in September 2009. After three follow-ups, 89 questionnaires were returned, representing a response rate of 15%. The main drawbacks of this survey were self-selection and non-random samples.

The survey first inquired into the respondent's motivation for participating in online forums, using a question with 14 answers to choose from, including an open-ended item. The respondents were allowed to choose up to three answers. The motivation question was followed by three sets of multiple choice questions. The first set of questions measured the respondent's perception of the extent to which Vision 2020 achieved the four Web 2.0 values, namely, user as producer, collective intelligence, perpetual beta, and extreme ease of use. The second set of questions measured the respondent's perception of the website's performance in providing information, facilitating public consultation, and including public opinion into the policy shaping process. A 5-point Likert scale was used for the first two sets of questions. The third set of questions requested the respondent's demographic information and web user experiences.

DATA ANALYSIS

Findings from the Qualitative Data

The qualitative data show that several issues need to be addressed if Web 2.0 technologies are to be applied to government websites as a means to establish "good e-governance." A few general observations concerning the current website operation are provided below.

Lack of a Long-Term Road Map

In contrast to the private sector, the public sector is relatively unaware of the potentials of Web 2.0 and lacks long-term planning for utilizing the technology.

The government lacks a long term road map for adopting Web 2.0 applications, in part because politically appointed officials usually do not consider their postings long term. A four-year projection, consistent with the election cycle, is the most common time span. It's a pity! (D1)

Lack of Responsiveness: Contract Management and Precaution

A common criticism of the government is its slow responsiveness to citizen needs. This is sometimes caused by ill-defined and ill-managed government contracts. There were two major types of contracts in the Vision 2020 initiative, one signed with each issue master or blog channel host, and the other with a private vendor responsible for system operation and maintenance. The RDEC, the issue masters, and the web service vendors would have joint meetings on a regular basis. Usually the service company could provide timely technical support to issue masters when some new functionality was needed. The contracts were able to meet this need. This was considered advantageous in comparison to some other government website contracts. An interviewee mentioned a contract restriction in another project that kept the government from making timely adjustments to a website.

We came up with a few nice proposals but failed to implement not because the RDEC did not provide support but because either the contract or the budget was not flexible enough to carry out the new ideas. The contractor would not add new features to the website unless a new contract was signed. (D2)

However, signing a new contract has to go through the procedures prescribed by the Government Procurement Law, which means that the original vendor would not necessarily win the new bid. An interviewee from the RDEC mentioned:

We thought about collaborating with organizations that were already maintaining websites or forums on certain issues such as public health or education. It seemed an efficient way of allocating resources. Unfortunately, if we sign a contract with them with funding, we may be questioned about benefiting the organizations and get ourselves into the trouble of illegality. (A1)

The government is slow to respond in public forums due in part to government employees' hesitation in responding quickly. Any response from the government side is considered an official statement. Speed may not be the first priority to the government compared to accuracy or politics.

Particularly in the case of controversial issues, media reporters may enthusiastically quote and interpret what the agency has to say about the issue in debate; and sometimes it does not turn out pretty. They have to be very cautious about their responses to public opinions. (D3)

Web 2.0 in G2G

Attention seemed to be focused more on utilizing the Web 2.0 technologies for managing government to citizen (G2C) relationships. There seemed to be less effort made for marketing Web 2.0 applications among the internal customers (i.e., government employees). Government employees needed a better understanding of Web 2.0 features in order to make the best use of the applications.

Web 2.0 is all about interaction. It is not limited to interaction between the government and individual citizens but also between organizations. I think it deserves more attention from the government. (D2)

Directions for the Future

In order to tackle these problems, the government needs to carry out some infrastructural reforms. First, government employees must be aware of the important role of ICTs in a governance structure. For a government Web initiative to be successful, government employees need to change their mindset first, for they are the architects, builders and maintainers of the website. If they do not pay serious attention to the fast changing environment, it is unlikely that the citizens by themselves can make the e-governance structure work.

If you want to see any change, change the mindset first. This is what the government needs to do from within. (D1)

Second, institutional barriers, such as red tape and factionalism in government, can hinder effective responses to inter-departmental issues. Removing these barriers has been a crucial part of government reforms in the last two decades, but it is even more critical now since we are coming closer to responding to demands for integrating government functionalities that can offer a seamless online service platform.

I am confident that there are talented persons in the government. My experience tells me that it is the red tape or turf concerns that keep people or agencies from working together to solve problems. (D1)

The potential benefits of Web 2.0 applications are promising, but it is also true that Web 2.0 will not be the cure for all governance problems. Therefore, strategic planning that sets reasonable goals and implementation phases, and carefully selects target populations and website functionalities is essential to Web 2.0 adoption.

Website Content

The main materials for content analysis are posts on the website, including articles posted by the blog channel hosts or issue masters and user posts on discussion forums. The earliest post dated back to January 3, 2009. After that there were 538 posts on record available for further analysis. As Table 5 shows, health ranks the first among all issues with 165 posts in total, while the life issue came in last with only 16 posts. However, in terms of average number of responses or the average word counts of the responses to blog articles written by the issue master, the life issue interestingly ranked number one in both cases. Among free discussion forums, the health issue still attracted the maximum number of responses while the human rights issue had the maximum average word count of posts.

Overall, the health issue attracted the highest number of responses. Perhaps this was because the health channel was considered "softer" and more focused. The health issue is soft relative to some other issues because the possibility of this issue involving a clash of political ideologies is low. It is focused because its subcategories or subtopics on this channel appear more organized; discussions could be better framed or moderated. Although the life channel could also be considered

Table 5. Description of posts by issue

Issue	Total	Blog (n, x_1, x_2)* / Forum (n, x_1, x_2)*			Issue	Count	Blog (n, x_1, x_2)* / Forum (n, x_1, x_2)*		
Health	**165**	72	**6.64**	1074.86	Thought	33	25	**7.24**	892.28
		93	3.80	361.81			8	1.38	283.00
Education	**91**	34	2.88	1580.74	Social affairs	23	15	1.20	1058.33
		57	1.82	505.81			8	0.38	331.88
Cross-strait	**46**	44	1.61	1724.91	Family	22	15	0.67	591.00
		2	1.00	603.05			7	1.00	74.00
Human rights	41	31	3.13	**3030.00**	Culture	20	19	0.84	1070.89
		10	2.20	935.20			1	1.00	25.00
Land	41	38	0.53	**2766.39**	Life	16	11	**10.64**	**3707.46**
		3	2.33	642.33			5	0	483.20
Environment	40	36	1.19	1432.36					
		4	0.25	65.75					

* n denotes the number of posts; x_1 is the number of average responses; x_2 is the average word counts of the posts. Highlighted numbers are the first three places in each category, where the blog section is marked in boldface and the forum section in shade.

"soft," discussions seemed less focused than those in the health channel.

I think people tend to be more concerned about issues relevant to their daily routines such as food, clothing, housing and transportation, etc. These are good entry points for developing theme-based marketing on government websites. (C1)

Table 6. The demographics of survey respondents

Demographics		N*	%
Sex	Male	43	55.8
	Female	34	44.2
Age	19 or below	5	6.5
	20-29	42	54.5
	30-39	17	22.1
	40-49	7	9.1
	50-59	3	3.9
	60 or above	2	2.6
Education	Junior high school or less	0	0
	Senior high school	3	3.9
	College	47	61.0
	Graduate school	25	32.5

*Missing values excluded

Survey Data

The survey population consisted of all 614 registered members of Vision 2020. Among the 89 respondents, 56% were male, 76% aged 20 to 39, and almost 96% held college or graduate degrees. Table 6 shows demographic statistics. It is obvious that most respondents were young and well educated.

Table 7 shows that to further discuss a policy issue was the most important motive for visiting the website, representing 53.2% of all respondents. To voice oneself on a policy issue, acquire more policy information, and encounter the viewpoints of other users were other secondary motives for website visits.

In terms of user behavior, about 66% of users visited the website at least once or twice a month; 58 (76%) respondents stayed on the website for less than 30 minutes on average. Most respondents (87%) posted 0 to 1 article per week on average.

Table 7. Motive to visit Vision 2020

Motive to participate *	n	%
To further discuss policy issues	41	53.2
To voice myself	39	50.6
To acquire more policy information	30	39.0
To learn about other people's viewpoints	24	31.2
To monitor the government's implementation	23	29.9
To see the government's responses	18	23.4
To try out this new venue of political participation	7	9.1
To advocate	5	6.5
Curiosity	4	5.2
Desire to publish	3	3.9
Job requirement	2	2.6
Sense of self-accomplishment	0	0.0

* N = 77. Multiple answers allowed; the total percentage may exceed 100%

Table 8. Frequency of visit

Frequency of visits to Vision 2020 in the past year	N	%
Once or more than once a day	0	0.0
Two or three times a week	10	13.2
Once a week	15	19.7
Once or twice a month	25	32.9
Once a quarter	9	11.8
Once in half-a-year	5	6.6
Once a year	1	1.3
None in the past year	11	14.5
Total	76	100

Table 8 and Table 9 show the frequency of visits and the number of posts per week, respectively.

With regard to evaluating the value propositions of Web 2.0, respondents showed positive inclination toward *user as producer*. More than half of respondents agreed or strongly agreed that they would share policy opinions with other users. However, they were less likely to initiate an issue on the forum (28.6%). Regarding *collective intelligence*, there was no such function as *folksonomy* or tagging on Vision 2020. On being asked whether they developed virtual acquaintance with other members, 30% agreed and 51% disagreed. This suggests that the sense of belonging to the online community was present, but the level of repeated interaction among members was not high enough to develop familiarity with other users. *Perpetual beta* aims to measure user perceptions of the degree of continuous upgrades in system and website functions. Most respondents were neutral (44.2%) in this regard. As for *extreme ease of use*, several indicators were measured. Most respondents felt positively towards the richness and sufficiency of website content (45.5%), harmonious interface design (58.4%), design in accordance with user expectations (58.4%), ease of use (55.9%), and the speed and stability of download (61%), while they remained neutral on the security/ privacy issue (55.8%) and on the speed of response to requests (60%).

Under the construct of electronic participation, three levels of participation were measured. At the *e-information* level, most respondents agreed that the website actively promoted various participatory activities (52%) but somehow were less inclined to agree that the website actively provided policy information (37.4%). Perhaps this was because Vision 2020 was mainly designed to allow the public to take part in envisioning the future rather than debating present policies. In addition, maintenance of the website was contracted to eleven hosts, who were by and large in control of moderating the issues, content, and discussions. Providing policy information, therefore, might not have been a focal function of the website.

At the *e-consultation* level, members were generally positive toward the website design in terms of facilitating discussions (45.5%), helping to clarify policy content (52%), sufficiently allowing stakeholders to voice themselves (53.3%), and other people's feedbacks were constructive (42.9%). As for the indicator of government responsiveness, most respondents held a negative attitude, disagreeing that the government responded

Table 9. Number of post per week

Number of posts per week	N	%
0~1	65	86.7
2~4	7	9.3
5~10	2	2.7
11~15	0	0
16 or more	1	1.3
Total	75	100

to their opinions (30%). Besides the common sentiment of the government being unresponsive, we conjecture that the business model of Vision 2020 might have caused the government attitude to appear even worse when gauging responsiveness. Vision 2020 took the form of multiple blog channels hosted by eleven non-governmental "celebrities" (so to speak) who did not officially represent the government and could not have responded to opinions and suggestions officially. Yet, knowing the website was established and supervised by the government, the user would sense an even higher level of discrepancy between the expected and actual responses received, and in turn felt more unsatisfied.

Finally, *e-decision making*, the most difficult level of e-participation, aimed to measure the degree of impact of online forums on policy content. Most respondents were neutral (49%), but the percentage of negative responses (29%) was higher than positive responses (22%).

We performed a correlation test between the value constructs and the participation constructs by converting the 5-point Likert scale into scores. From strongly disagree to strongly agree, the survey responses were converted into scores of 1 to 5 assuming equal intervals. It appears that those respondents' perceptions of Web 2.0 values and the levels of e-participation on the Vision 2020 website were at most moderately correlated. *User as producer*, arguably the most important value construct of Web 2.0, did not appear correlated with any of the three e-participation constructs. *Collective intelligence* had low to moderate correlation with e-participation, while *perpetual beta* and *extreme ease of use* had slightly stronger correlation with e-participation. Although Vision 2020 did adopt some Web applications such as blog and interactive forums, it was not yet a full-blown Web 2.0 website. The statistics show that system upgrades and maintaining user-friendly environment appear to have been the advantage of the Vision 2020 model, as indicated by the higher correlations of *perpetual beta* and *extreme ease of use*. However, it still lacked a more participatory and collaborative architecture to facilitate *user as producer* and *collective intelligence* features that Web 2.0 applications ultimately pursue.

Note that the preliminary results have limited validity for generalization in that the survey samples were voluntary respondents, the sampling frame was confined to the 614 registered members of Vision 2020, and no demographic information of the population was available for testing the respondent representativeness. Given that Vision 2020 is a novel government attempt to incorporate Web 2.0 concepts in policy forums through using

Table 10. Pearson's correlation between Web 2.0 values and e-participation

value of Web 2.0 e-Participation	User as producer	Collective intelligence	Perpetual beta	Extreme ease of use
e-Information	.064	.248*	.359**	.421***
e-Consultation	.164	.296**	.527***	.647***
e-Decision making	.040	.412***	.417***	.476***

* $p < 0.05$, ** $p < 0.01$, *** $p < 0.001$ (2-tailed).

multiple blog channels, the findings shed light on the perspective of "governance 2.0" – it is worthwhile to pursue new forms of online participation enabled by ICTs, and the attention must not be diverted from the basic value proposition. That is, maintaining an attractive and convenient user environment is still the cornerstone of more sophisticated venues of public participation via Web 2.0 features.

SOLUTIONS AND RECOMMENDATIONS

Though the current implementation of *e-consultation* does not appear to have been successful, it is worth exploring the potential of ICTs in pursuit of realizing participatory democracy. Political scientists are also working toward this end in order to resolve the paradox of representative democracy. Our "two cents worth" regarding how to incorporate Web 2.0 in future websites is twofold. One is for public institutions and the other for website operation.

Pursue Democratic Governance by Adopting Web 2.0 Technologies, Applications, and Values

In order to realize the value propositions of Web 2.0, technical issues and selection of applications need to be addressed first. Through strategic planning and evaluation in line with the guidance of the threefold Web 2.0 concept, it is hoped that democratic governance would be improved by offering the general public new Web venues to participate in the political process. On the one hand, *user as producer* and *collective intelligence* are the core values of a Web 2.0 platform characterized by collaboration and participation. On the other hand, the survey data indicate that *perpetual beta* and *extreme ease of use* have strong correlation to e-participation. To enhance democracy with ICTs, we suggest that the government should set the goal of pursuing the core value propositions of Web 2.0 while pragmatically maintaining a constantly updated and user-friendly online environment to keep the user from losing interest.

Remove Red Tape and Break Factionalism to Build Collaborative Governance

Almost all interviewees pointed out that a major barrier to government responsiveness is red tape. Hierarchical procedures and bureaucratic approvals are unavoidably counterproductive to responsiveness. In turn, they hinder quick exchange of opinion, which is necessary for multiplying the benefits of information and forming collective intelligence. Furthermore, most public organizations are horizontally divided by functionalities and end up being unconnected departmental silos. Besides the benefits such as professionalism, expertise, and clearly defined responsibilities, it is also a breeding ground for factionalism. For a Web 2.0 website to run successfully, leadership must be determined to take on the challenge of inter-departmental collaboration.

Identify the Modules of Web 2.0 Applications for Democratic Governance

We identify two basic modules of applying Web 2.0 to government websites designated for democratic governance – a marketing module and a radical module. The marketing module utilizes Web 2.0 applications to promote governmental affairs and public policies, manage public relations, and facilitate political campaigns. Therefore, the strategies of policy marketing are at the center of planning. In a sense, the agenda for this module is more under the government's control. The radical module, on the other hand, stresses the grass-roots and gives much weight to the deliberative element of the policy formulation process. Providing channels for citizens to access information, voice themselves, and participate in policy formation are thus the focal points of this module. The two modules are not necessarily mutually exclusive, but the government needs to seriously consider how much control it is willing to cede and allow the public to shape policy agenda. As today's public problems oftentimes cross jurisdictions and authorities, collaboration across departments and functionalities is more important than ever before. A good governance structure has to be inclusive and receptive. This is where Web 2.0 can help. But, the government needs to change its mindset to accept some unfamiliar phenomena that the new technologies may bring.

Continuous Upgrades and Extreme Ease of Use

The survey data suggest that maintaining an attractive Web interface has high correlation to e-participation. While this is not surprising, the website should perform continuous beta testing and system upgrades to meet evolving user needs. Government contracts should remain flexible to the extent that continuous upgrades and revisions are not completely constrained. The government should make the website extremely easy to use in terms of information access, customization of functions and services, and richness of user experience. These are the basics of encouraging users to revisit, and are as important as pursuing other Web 2.0 value propositions.

FUTURE RESEARCH DIRECTIONS

As a new field of research, Web 2.0 is full of promise but still short of empirically sound theories, particularly in the field of political science and public administration. The effects of the ever changing and improved ICTs on political participation are and will always be intriguing to researchers in the foreseeable future. Both researchers and practitioners are in the stage of groping for strategies that can make the best of the newly developing Web applications. In the hope of serving as a starting point, this study makes a bold attempt to establish a framework for evaluating the impact on e-participation of Web 2.0 sites. From the research objectives and findings, we have made it clear that evaluation is important in that the legitimacy of modern democracy is losing its foothold due to the decreasing trust of the people. Meanwhile, anticipated solutions to the legitimacy problem offered by Web 2.0 have not been fully embodied in current government initiatives. This is because, at least in part, government agencies are inclined to be risk averse. It is would be considered highly risky to adopt initiatives without clear roadmaps and fine-tuned assessment tools. Therefore, more and deeper empirical research on the effects of Web 2.0 is imperative, so that the government will have reliable tools for strategic planning and implementation of its initiatives.

Specifically, the effort of establishing an effective evaluation framework for Web 2.0 applications in e-governance should continue. As an early research attempt, our study certainly runs the risk of oversimplifying the value propositions of Web 2.0. Nevertheless, we are confident that the concept of Web 2.0 will become clearer and more definite as the collective intelligence in this research arena comes into effect. Future research should first work on the typology of what Web 2.0 may bring to civic engagement, and then measures for each typological construct should be developed.

Future research should also place Web 2.0 in the context of government reforms. What does Web 2.0 mean to interagency collaboration, for example? How to reform public institutions so that barriers to collaboration such as red tape and departmentalism can be removed to create an institutional environment consistent with realizing Web 2.0 value propositions? To answer the questions, research areas such as organizational change, bureaucratic politics, administrative reform, etc., all have insights to offer. Among other things, the Web 2.0 readiness of bureaucrats is another concern that might stand in the way of realizing Web 2.0 benefits. It takes strong leadership and commitment to overcome the bureaucrat's negative attitudes toward a more transparent, open and responsive online government.

Understanding user behavior on Web 2.0 applications is by all means the most fundamental work for establishing e-governance initiatives. The private sector is quickly adopting social networking services to its favor in areas such as marketing and customer relation management. The public sector may be willing to catch up, but it still lacks a full understanding of what users expect from Web 2.0 government websites. This calls for more observations, descriptions and experiments to fill the knowledge gap.

CONCLUSION

Governments around the globe are looking for favorable applications of Web 2.0 technologies. The new technologies do offer opportunities for advancing public governance in terms of operations within the government (G2G), as well as interactions between the government and citizens (G2C). While some countries are quick to adopt Web 2.0 applications in their government websites, others are more cautious about the possible annoyance that Web 2.0 applications might bring about. The objective of this research is to develop an evaluation framework for assessing the relationship between Web 2.0 value propositions and e-participation from the user perspective. The concept of Web 2.0 adopted in this study is a useful base model for future research. Using the Vision 2020 initiative as an example, the preliminary findings suggest that the core value propositions of Web 2.0, namely, user as producer and collective intelligence, were either minimal on the website or were not perceived by the users to be conducive to e-participation. The other two value aspects of Web 2.0, perpetual beta and extreme ease of use, were perceived to be more related to e-participation. The Vision 2020 initiative was an attempt to leverage the core of Web 2.0. The findings from the qualitative data suggest that institutional barriers would be the first target of reform if a Web 2.0-friendly environment should be created.

ICTs and Web 2.0 in particular offer great opportunities for improving the quality of public services and strengthening democratic governance. The call for descriptive analysis and theory building are equally important cornerstones of realizing latent potentials. The government is now at the crossroads of deciding whether to adopt or avoid Web 2.0 applications. A possible scenario is that the already unsatisfied public would not patiently wait for the government to think through whether using Web 2.0 technology, such as social networking applications for policy making, would be detrimental to bureaucratic control and professionalism. The government would appear even more sluggish if various Web 2.0 applications were to become even more widely used in the private sector and citizens come to expect equivalent convenience and efficiency offered by the government. Holding on to bureaucratic control at the cost of public participation risks losing the opportunity for regaining public trust. Transforming the mindset of the decision makers is probably the most critical task for those who are eager to see e-governance leap forward.

REFERENCES

Adler, R. P., & Goggin, J. (2005). What do we mean by civic engagement? *Journal of Transformative Education*, *3*(3), 236–253. doi:10.1177/1541344605276792

Anderson, P. (2007). *What is Web 2.0? Ideas, technologies and implications for education*. Bristol, UK: JISC Technology and Standards Watch. Retrieved April 13, 2009, from http://www.jisc.ac.uk/media/documents/techwatch/tsw0701b.pdf

Arnstein, S. (1969). A ladder of citizen participation. *American Institute of Planners Journal*, *35*, 216–224. doi:10.1080/01944366908977225

Barber, B. R. (1984). *Strong democracy: Participatory politics for a new age*. Berkley, CA: University of California Press.

Bausch, P., & Bumgardner, J. (2006). *Flickr hacks*. Sebastopol, CA: O'Reilly Press. Retrieved August 1, 2010, from http://www.oreilly.com /catalog/flickrhks/chapter/ hack14.pdf

Bessette, J. M. (1994). *The mild voice of reason: Deliberative democracy and American national government*. Chicago, IL & London, UK: Chicago University Press.

Bimber, B. (2000). The study of Information Technology and civic engagement. *Political Communication*, *17*, 329–333. doi:10.1080/10584600050178924

Bishop, J. (2007). Increasing participation in online communities: A framework for human–computer interaction. *Computers in Human Behavior*, *23*(4), 1881–1893. doi:10.1016/j.chb.2005.11.004

Caldow, J. (2004). *E-democracy: Putting down global roots*. Armonk, NY: Institute for Electronic Government, IBM. Retrieved April 28, 2009, from http://www-1.ibm.com/industries /government/ieg/pdf/ e-democracy%20putting %20down%20 roots.pdf

Carpini, M. X. (2000). Gen.com: Youth, civic engagement, and the new information environment. *Political Communication*, *17*, 341–349. doi:10.1080/10584600050178942

Chadwick, A. (2003). Bringing e-democracy back in: Why it matters for future research on e-government. *Social Science Computer Review*, *21*(4), 443–455. doi:10.1177/0894439303256372

Chen, D. Y., Huang, D. Y., & Hsiao, N. (2004). E-participation: Internet and citizen participation in policy making process. [in Chinese]. *Research and Evaluation Bimonthly*, *28*(4), 36–51.

Chen, Y. C., & Dimitrova, D. V. (2006). Electronic government and online engagement: Citizen interaction with government via Web portals. *International Journal of Electronic Government*, *2*(1), 54–76. doi:10.4018/jegr.2006010104

Colier, J. E., & Bienstock, C. C. (2006). Measuring service quality in e-retailing. *Journal of Service Research*, *8*(3), 260–275. doi:10.1177/1094670505278867

Cooper, T. L. (2005). Civic engagement in the twenty-first century: Toward a scholarly and practical agenda. *Public Administration Review*, *65*(5), 534–535. doi:10.1111/j.1540-6210.2005.00480.x

Denhardt, R., & Denhardt, J. (2007). *The new public service: Serving, not steering*. New York, NY: M. E. Sharpe Inc.

Diller, E. C. (2001). *Citizens in service: The challenge of delivering civic engagement training to national service programs*. Washington, DC: Corporation for National Service. Retrieved April 28, 2009, from http://www.nationalservice-resources.org/ files/legacy/filemanager/download /457/diller.pdf

Downes, S. (2004). Educational blogging. *EDUCAUSE Review*, *9*(5), 14–26.

Elster, J. (1998). Introduction. In Elster, J. (Ed.), *Deliberative democracy* (pp. 1–18). New York, NY: Cambridge University Press.

Fraunholz, B., & Unnithan, C. (2008). E-governance: Enabling the French Web 2.0 revolution? In A. Agarwal & V. V. Ramana (Eds.), *Foundations of e-government* (pp. 344-359). Retrieved January 18, 2009, from http://www.iceg.net/2007/books/1/36_363.pdf

Gastil, J. (2000). Face-to-face citizen deliberation: A luxury or necessity? *Political Communication*, *17*, 357–361. doi:10.1080/10584600050178960

Giles, J. (2005). Internet encyclopaedias go head to head. *Nature*, *438*, 900–901. doi:10.1038/438900a

Golding, P. (1996). World wide wedge: Division and contradiction in the global information infrastructure. *Monthly Review (New York, N.Y.), 48*(3), 70–85.

Habermas, J. (1984. 1987). *Theory of communicative action,* vols. 1 and 2. Boston, MA: Beacon Press.

Huang, M., Li, X., & Zeng, X. (2007, May). *Service quality in Web 2.0 electronic commerce: An integrative perspective from typical service and technique-adoption.* Paper presented at the meeting of the International Conference on Wireless Communications, Networking and Mobile Computing, Shanghai, China.

Jennings, M. K., & Zeitner, V. (2003). Internet use and civic engagement. *Public Opinion Quarterly, 67*(3), 311–334. doi:10.1086/376947

Kim, J. (2006). The impact of Internet use patterns on political engagement: A focus on online deliberation and virtual social capital. *Information Polity, 11*, 35–49. doi:10.1108/09593840610700800

Koh, J., & Kim, Y. G. (2004). Knowledge sharing in virtual communities: An e-business perspective. *Expert Systems with Applications, 26*, 155–166. doi:10.1016/S0957-4174(03)00116-7

Kollock, P. (1999). The economies of online cooperation: Gifts and public goods in cyberspace. In Smith, M., & Kollock, P. (Eds.), *Communities in cyberspace* (pp. 220–239). London, UK: Routledge.

Lenihan, D. G. (2002). *E-government, federalism and democracy: The new governance.* Ottawa, Canada: Center for Collaborative Government. Retrieved June 14, 2009, from http://www-it.fmi.uni-sofia.bg/eg/ res/ktapublication_vol9e.pdf

Loiacono, E. T., Watson, R. T., & Goodhue, D. L. (2007). WebQual: An instrument for consumer evaluation of websites. *International Journal of Electronic Commerce, 11*(3), 51–87. doi:10.2753/JEC1086-4415110302

Macintosh, A. (2004, January). Characterizing e-participation in policy-making. *Proceedings of the 37th Hawaii International Conference on System Sciences,* Hawaii. Retrieved June 14, 2009, from http://csdl.computer.org/comp/ proceedings/hicss/2004/2056/05 /205650117a.pdf

Macintosh, A., & Whyte, A. (2002, August). *An evaluation framework for e-consultations?* Paper presented at the meeting of the International Association for Official Statistics conference, London, UK. Retrieved April 28, 2009, from http://www.statistics.gov.uk/ iaoslondon2002/contributed_papers /downloads/IP_Macintosh.doc

Misra, D. C. (2008). *Ten guiding principles for e-civil service.* Retrieved June 14, 2009, from http://egov-india.blogspot.com/ 2008/12/ten-guiding- principles-for-e-civil.html

Norris, P. (2001). *Digital divide: Civic engagement, information poverty, and the Internet worldwide.* New York, NY: Cambridge University Press.

O'Reilly, T. E. (2005). *What is Web 2.0?* Retrieved February 18, 2009, from http://www.oreillynet.com/pub /a/oreilly/tim/news/2005/09/ 30/what-is-web-20.html

OECD. (2001). *Citizens as partners: Information consultation, and public participation in policy making.* Paris, France: OECD. Retrieved June 14, 2009, from http://books.google.com.tw/ books?id=0pVGmUxcQgEC&printsec=frontcover&dq=Citizens+as+Partners:+Information+Consultation,+and+Public+Participation+ in+Policy+Making&source=bl&ots=T_CjioU_-T &sig=LgG2T52bnFBFelPP4bRSgoFfZ9s &hl=zh-TW& ei=kF7k S4ewLMgkQX8uNES&sa =X &oi= book_result&ct=result& resnum=1&ved=0CCUQ6AEwAA#v=onepage&q&f=false

OECD. (2003). *Promise and problems of e-democracy: Challenges of online citizen engagement*. Paris, France: OECD. Retrieved June 14, 2009, from http://www.oecd.org/dataoecd /9/11/35176328.pdf

Osimo, D. (2008). *Web 2.0 in government: Why and how?* Luxembourg: Office for Official Publications of the European Communities. Retrieved February 18, 2009, from http://documentostics.com/ component/option,com_docman /task,doc_download/ gid,1417/Itemid,4

Parasuraman, A., Zeithmal, V. A., & Malhotra, A. (2005). E-S-Qual: A multiple-item scale for assessing electronic service quality. *Journal of Service Research*, *7*(3), 213–233. doi:10.1177/1094670504271156

Park, H. M. (2006, May). The impact of digital government on civic engagement: A typological approach. *Proceedings of the 7th Annual International Conference on Digital Government Research*, San Diego, CA.

Putnam, R. D. (1995). Bowling alone: America's declining social capital. *Journal of Democracy*, *6*(1), 65–78. doi:10.1353/jod.1995.0002

Sahadev, S., & Purani, K. (2008). Modeling the consequences of e-service quality. *Marketing Intelligence & Planning*, *26*(6), 605–620. doi:10.1108/02634500810902857

Skocpol, T., & Fiorina, M. P. (1999). *Civic engagement in American democracy*. Washington, DC: Brookings Institution Press.

Smith, S. R., & Ingram, H. (1993). Public policy and democracy. In Ingram, H., & Smith, S. (Eds.), *Public policy and democracy* (pp. 1–14). Washington, DC: Brookings Institution Press.

Stromer-Galley, J. (2002). New voices in the political sphere: A comparative analysis of interpersonal and online political talk. *Javnost/The Public*, *9*, 23-42.

Sunstein, C. (2001). *Republic.com*. Princeton, NJ: Princeton University Press.

Tapscott, D., & Williams, A. D. (2006). *Wikinomics: How mass collaboration changes everything*. London, UK: Penguin Books Ltd.

The United Nations. (2008). *E-government survey 2008: From e-government to connected governance*. New York, NY: United Nations Publications. Retrieved April 28, 2009, from http://www.unpan.org/egovkb/ global_reports/08report.htm

Vander Wal, T. (2007). *Folksonomy*. Retrieved August 2, 2010, from http://vanderwal.net/ folksonomy.html

Warren, M. (1992). Democratic theory and self-transformation. *The American Political Science Review*, *86*(1), 8–23. doi:10.2307/1964012

Week, E. C. (2000). The practice of deliberative democracy: Results from four large-scale trails. *Public Administration Review*, *60*(4), 360–372. doi:10.1111/0033-3352.00098

Welber, T. (1995). Right discourse in citizen participation: An evaluative yardstick. In Renn, O., Welber, T., & Wiedemann, P. (Eds.), *Fairness and competence in citizen participation: Technology, risk and society* (pp. 35–86). Boston, MA: Kluwer.

West, D. M. (2005). *Global e-government 2005*. Providence, RI: Center for Public Policy, Brown University. Retrieved January 18, 2009, from http://www.insidepolitics.org /egovt05int.pdf

Witschge, T. (2002, October). *On-line deliberation: Possibilities of the Internet for deliberative democracy*. Paper presented at the meeting of Euricom Colloquium Electronic Networks & Democratic Engagement, Nijmegen, The Netherlands. Retrieved June 14, 2009, from http://java.cs.vt.edu/public /projects/digitalgov/ papers/ onlinedeliberation_Nl.pdf

Wolfinbarger, M., & Gilly, M. C. (2003). Etailq: Dimensionaling, measuring and predicting, e-tail quality. *Journal of Retailing, 79*(3), 183–198. doi:10.1016/S0022-4359(03)00034-4

ADDITIONAL READING SECTION

Chen, Y. C., & Dimitrova, D. V. (2006). Electronic government and online engagement: Citizen Interaction with government via web portals. *International Journal of Electronic Government, 2*(1), 54–76. doi:10.4018/jegr.2006010104

O'Reilly, T. E. (2005). *What is web 2.0?* Retrieved February 18, 2009, from http://www.oreillynet.com/pub /a/oreilly/tim/news/2005 /09/30/what-is-web-20.html

Osimo, D. (2008). *Web 2.0 in government: Why and how?* Luxembourg: Office for Official Publications of the European Communities. Retrieved February 18, 2009, from http://documentostics.com /component/option,com_docman /task,doc_download/gid,1417/ Itemid,4

KEY TERMS AND DEFINITIONS

Information and Communication Technologies (ICTs): A general term that refers to modern technologies handling information and communication, such as telephony, cable, satellite and radio, as well as digital technologies, such as computers, information network hardware and software, and include all types of audio and video processing and transmission. Recent development has focuses on applications related to the Internet and the World Wide Web.

Web 2.0: A broad concept referring to recently developed Web applications characterized by "network as platform" and "architecture of participation" where users may remix data to create new services.

e-Governance: The use of ICTs, and particularly the Internet, as a tool to achieve better governance by continuous optimization of service delivery, citizen participation and engagement, and public-private relationships.

e-Participation: Citizen participation through the mediation of information and communication technologies, particularly the Internet and the Web.

Deliberative Democracy: a form of democracy that emphasizes dialectical discourse, persuasion, and rational communication on public issues.

Civic Engagement: Citizens' participation in deliberative procedures and collective actions for common interests and institutional networks, with which the general public may become an vital element of public governance.

Vision 2020: A website launched by the Taiwan central government in 2008, designed with Web 2.0 features, aimed at encouraging public participation in discussing public affairs.

ENDNOTES

1 Data taken from the 2008 Digital Divide Survey by the Research, Development, and Evaluation Commission (RDEC) of the Executive Yuan, Taiwan.

2 *Folksonomy,* coined by Thomas Vander Wal in 2004, is a portmanteau of *folk* and *taxonomy* referring to the practice and method of Web users collaboratively creating and managing tags to annotate and categorize Web content.

3 Wiki. (2010, August 26). In *Wikipedia, The Free Encyclopedia*. Retrieved September 5, 2010, from http://en.wikipedia.org/w/index.php?title=Wiki&oldid=381162710

4 PK, an abbreviation of Penalty Kick from soccer game rule, refers to one-on-one challenge.

APPENDIX

Codebook for website content analysis

Variable	*Column*	*Description*	*Value*
Issue	01	issue areas	01 education 02 human rights 03 thought 04 culture 05 ecology 06 cross-strait issues 07 health 08 land 09 society 10 life 11 family
Discussion Area	02	postings/articles in forum	Yes, 1; No, 0
Host's Blog	03	articles in blog	Yes, 1; No, 0
Responses	04	counts of responses	--
Words	05	counts of words	--
Recommendations	06	counts of recommendations	--
Browse times	07	counts of readership	--
Post year	08	year of publication	xxxx
Post month	09	month of publication	xx
Post day	10	day of publication	xx
Sharing video or photo	11	function of media or photo sharing	0 no 1 yes

Chapter 19
A Framework for Government 2.0 Development and Implementation:
The Case of U.S. Federal Government

Yu-Che Chen
Northern Illinois University, USA

ABSTRACT

This book chapter formulates a framework for Government 2.0 development and implementation, drawing from literature on collaborative public management, public sector knowledge management, management Information Systems, innovation, and e-governance. This framework encompasses policy/managerial, organizational, and technological dimensions and identifies factors for success, such as supporting policy guidance and institutions, providing incentives and resources, and developing and promoting technical standards. Using the proposed framework, this chapter critically analyzes the possibility of Government 2.0 for the case of the United States. The analysis underscores the importance of institutional support, management commitment, and development of data standards and resource framework documents. The analysis also points to the need for improvement in the areas of provision of policy and management guidance, sustaining resource commitment, and expanding technical standards development and usability. The conclusion will summarize main points and make note of future research opportunities.

INTRODUCTION

One of the central issues that electronic governance and cross-boundary collaboration need to confront in the next decade is the rise of Government 2.0. The emergence of Government 2.0 results from the rapid growth of Web 2.0 technologies and the government deployment of these technologies for creating public value. The last two to three years have witnessed rapid growth in the use of Web 2.0 technologies. Web 2.0 technologies, broadly defined, include RSS, video-sharing, wikis, blogs, mash-ups, social networking, twittering,

DOI: 10.4018/978-1-60960-753-1.ch019

and virtual worlds, among others. The popularity of social networking sites, where many Web 2.0 technologies are being deployed, is indicative of the general trend. For example, by the end of 2009, the number of registered Facebook users in the United States reached 100 million, in a country of 310 million.[1] The use of social networking sites has been gaining momentum outside the United States, with the number reaching 250 million by the end of 2009.[2] The number of registered Facebook users grew to 500 million by the end of July, 2010,[3] which is a growth of over 40 percent within a six–month period. In China, which in June 2008 became the country with the largest Internet population, the number of Internet users reached 384 million by the end of 2009.[4] There are no official statistics on the number of users for social networking sites in China. However, some statistics suggest a strong presence of social networking activities in China. There are over 100 million users of RenRen and over 300 million users of Qzone.[5]

The government use of Web 2.0 is also on the rise as citizens and businesses adopt Web 2.0 technologies to interact with one another. The title of the United Nations' 2008 e-government survey report, "Connected Governance", captured the essence of this new chapter in interactivity and engagement. It is where all stakeholders involved in public affairs are connected. However, Government 2.0 goes beyond simple applications of Web 2.0 technologies in government. What makes these applications work is a fundamental shift in beliefs concerning the role of government. These beliefs include (a) that governmental action should be open and transparent and citizens should be informed about government programs and their effects; and (b) that government should collaborate with citizens and businesses when trying to solve public policy and services problems.[6]

Progress toward Government 2.0 is a journey that various national governments have recently begun to consider, and some have even begun to undertake. As of summer 2010, most countries that have embarked on the journey of Government 2.0 are still in the early phases of experimenting. This early effort has focused on the public value created by Government 2.0. For example, Australia has considered combining public sector information with government openness and collaboration with citizens.[7] And the European Commission has researched the potential use of Web 2.0 for government functions, such as regulation and service provision (Osimo, 2008). These two examples of movement towards Government 2.0 also highlight the importance of transparency, collaboration, and innovation as core cultural elements of government.

With regards to Government 2.0 implementation, the United States is leading the effort, and it is uniquely positioned to do so for the following reasons. First, it has a long institutional tradition of open government, specifically with regulations such as the Freedom of Information Act and the Administrative Procedure Act. A comparative analysis has highlighted the uniqueness of such an institutional tradition (Chen & Hsieh, 2009). Second, the United States has an active and large population that is already using Web 2.0 technologies. Lastly, the Obama Administration's commitment to open government as articulated in its Open Government Initiative has mobilized the resources for Government 2.0 implementation.

Government 2.0 has met with many challenges even with its short history of experimentation and implementation. On a deeper level are institutional and infrastructure issues. A country needs to have supporting laws, regulations, and political institutions that can facilitate an open exchange between government and citizens, as well as among citizens. A critical mass of online population with access to Web 2.0 technologies is the basic infrastructure requirement. As a new paradigm, a successful Government 2.0 program requires significant changes in organizational culture and business practices--in short, sustained political and managerial support is necessary. Finding the resources to produce Government

2.0 content and manage interactivity is a significant challenge. Moreover, the legal, policy, and technical infrastructure implications are still under debate. For example, public managers are concerned about the legal ramifications of Government 2.0; the very notion of "public record" has become blurred as more user content is being generated, shared, and manipulated.

A survey of public administration and public management literature suggests only scant research conducted on Government 2.0. The limited number of existing studies discuss the potential and practice of Government 2.0 (i.e. Osimo (2008) and report by Australian Government 2.0 Taskforce) or point out critical elements for realizing the potential of Government 2.0, such as information design (Zappen, Harrison, & Watson, 2008) and the alignment of Web 2.0 technology to organizational strategies (Meijer & Thaens, 2010). And yet, clearly, the significance of Government 2.0 as briefly described above calls for increased scholarly attention. At this early stage, research on Government 2.0 needs to build on relevant bodies of literature to develop a coherent research framework and accurate analysis of best practices.

To meet this need, this chapter aims to develop a conceptual framework for Government 2.0 implementation. The proposed framework draws from the literatures on collaborative public management, knowledge network management, management information systems (MIS), innovation, and electronic governance. This framework offers scholars a list of research propositions for empirical investigation. It provides public managers a framework for Government 2.0 development and implementation. Moreover, this chapter will use the experience of the United States to illustrate various components of the proposed framework. As a leading nation in the effort of applying Web 2.0 technologies in government, the U.S. experience is instructive for both practitioners and scholars alike. The following section will outline policy and management recommendations as well as opportunities for future research. The concluding section will reiterate the main points of this chapter.

A FRAMEWORK FOR GOVERNMENT 2.0 DEVELOPMENT AND IMPLEMENTATION

Relevant Bodies of Literature

The study of Government 2.0 can benefit from insights gleaned from existing relevant bodies of literature. Relevance is established through connecting the characteristics of Government 2.0 to the themes of these literatures. These insights will serve as guidelines for the development and further empirical research on Government 2.0. For example, one defining feature of Web 2.0 is the collaborative nature of exchange. The Ideascale project conducted by the U.S. federal government worked with citizens to gather the best ideas for improving public services. The collaborative public management literature assists in identifying the conditions for collaboration and its processes (Goldsmith, 2004; Gray, Jenkins, Leeuw, & Mayne, 2003; McGuire & Silvia, 2010; O'Leary & Bingham, 2009; O'Toole, 1997; Thomson & Perry, 2006; Wood & Gray, 1991). Shared values and goals, trust and social capital, high level of interdependence, managerial and organizational capacity, are some of the conditions that have been specified.

One main goal of Government 2.0 is to create, disseminate, and store knowledge. For example, government employees can use a Wiki environment to collaborate on generating ideas for better public services. Thus, the knowledge network management literature is relevant; it can illuminate the organizational and interpersonal processes underlying knowledge sharing and creation, the main activity involved in the use of Web 2.0 tools. The issue of data ownership and turf needs to be resolved for information sharing cross organizational boundaries (Dawes, 1996).

To overcome barriers to information sharing, leadership is necessary (Dawes, Cresswell, & Pardo, 2009; Pardo & Tayi, 2007). The tacit nature of some public sector knowledge requires a careful design of structures and processes to facilitate knowledge sharing (Agranoff, 2007).

The proposed framework also leverages research on management information system, specifically studies on the use of collaborative information technology, such as group decision support systems and virtual teams. The perspective is socio-technical: the appropriation of technology is a combination of the characteristics of technology and configuration of organizational and individual traits (Laudon & Laudon, 2010). One of the core arguments is fitness: collaborative information technology makes the most impact when it accentuates an underlying incentive system supported by management (Daft, Lengel, & Trevino, 1987; Kahai & Cooper, 2003). For example, matching information richness requirement to the level of complexity in tasks is critical, as stated in McGrath and Hollingshead's (1994) time, interaction, and performance (TIP) theory. Put another way, more complex task requires the use of information technology that is capable of carrying richer information.

The innovation literature is used to identify the factors related to the adoption and use of innovative technologies. Web 2.0, in essence, embodies a set of innovative technologies. The larger notion of organizational capacity for innovation is one of the main conditions for learning and using new and innovative technologies (Cohen & Levinthal, 1990). Managerial innovativeness is also one of the key factors for using new technologies (Moon & Norris, 2005). Moreover, the innovation literature suggests that the diffusion of innovation is possible where a social system plays a role in initial adoption (Rogers, 2003). The lessons learned from innovations in government underscore the importance of interagency and intersector collaboration, market incentive, and flexible management techniques (Borins, 2008).

Lastly, e-governance literature draws from various theoretical traditions in its effort to understand the use of information technology in providing public services and improving policy-making processes. The political dimension of e-government is worth noting as political support is critical to government adoption of e-government (Ho, 2004). Online civic engagement is likely an extension of off-line civic engagement (Dimitrova and Chen, 2006). One of the main theoretical traditions that e-governance studies rest on is theories of how individuals make decisions whether to adopt and use new technology. These theories include the theory of planned behavior (Ajzen, 1991), the technology acceptance model (TAM) (Davis, 1989; Venkatesh & Davis, 2000), and United Theory for Adoption and Use of Technology (UTAUT) (Venkatesh, Morris, Davis, & Davis, 2003). These theories address social pressure, organizational incentives, technical capacity, information system design among many other factors.

Government 2.0 embodies various dimensions that support its use and development. An integrative framework is a productive avenue for drawing insights from various bodies of literature and for presenting a coherent framework for theory and practice. Here, the proposed framework has three main categories: policy and management, organization, and technologies. The policy and management factor refers to the broad policy context and management considerations. The organization factor is concerned with characteristics that influence the adoption and use of information technologies, and the technologies factor is concerned with the characteristics of the technology in question and how technology fits in the context of policy, management, and organizational considerations. The next three sections will discuss each factor in depth and ground the arguments in the insights from the relevant bodies of literature identified above.

Policy and Management for Successful Government 2.0

A successful Government 2.0 implementation is likely to require a supportive policy and institutional context. Fountain (2001) articulated the need for supportive institutions for technology enactment in her study of federal agencies' adoption of information technology in the United States. The technology enacted is usually a function of institutional and managerial preference, rather than that of technical characteristics. With regards to the use of Web 2.0 technologies that are premised on open government, supporting laws and regulations for open government serve as an important institutional condition. An example of open government regulations is the U.S. Administrative Procedure Act, which mandates a public commenting period for proposed federal rules. Information technology, on the other hand, has limited impact on institutional arrangements. As Kraemer and King (2008) argue, it is not that information technology can reform government; rather, it is government reforms that can have a technology component.

A comparative perspective brings a sharper focus on the need for supporting institutions in successful e-government. Heeks' (1999) survey of e-government practices highlights the importance of certain societal forces, such as democratic practices, that can induce advances in e-government. The e-government surveys published by the United Nations over the past few years also echo the need for laying the institutional foundation for e-government (United Nations, 2005, 2008, 2010). A direct comparison between Taiwan, a new democracy, and the United States, reveals the critical role of supporting institutions in the area of e-participation (Chen & Hsieh, 2009). Moreover, the level of civic engagement off-line is a strong predictor of online civic engagement (Dimitrova & Chen, 2006). Technology is probably seen and used as an extension of available tools that people in various communities use to engage policy issues and concerns.

Top management support is critical for successful e-government projects. The need for top management support has been noted in studies of information systems projects in the private sector. Complex information systems such as Enterprise Resource Planning systems usually cite top management support as a requirement for successful implementation (Bingi, Sharma, & Godla, 1999; Willcocks & Sykes, 2000). This level of support provides the needed resources (human, financial, and technical) for implementation. The e-governance literature also supports the notion of top management support. This support can be grounded in managerial innovativeness when managerial innovativeness believes in the potential of innovative technologies for delivering better public services (Moon & Norris, 2005).

Broad executive support is also critical for collaborative Web 2.0 projects. Managerial support is one of the necessary ingredients for cross-boundary collaborations. This broad-based support can be used to overcome conflicts among participating organizations, especially when they disagree over policy priorities and the distribution of benefits (Agranoff, 2007; O'Leary & Bingham, 2009). This broad-based support can take the form of a high level of trust among participating organizations in informal exchange of resources (Thurmaier & Wood, 2002). Such collaboration is voluntary and emerges from the ground up. Broad executive support can also take the form of a mandate. In the context of public sector knowledge management systems, Dawes et al. (2009) have noted how a legal mandate can garner the necessary support for implementation of a system that cuts across multiple jurisdictions. Government 2.0 projects would likely see the need for broad-based and high-level support as the number of participating agencies increases. This could be challenging, as not all governmental agencies are comfortable with the high level of transparency which Government 2.0 requires.

Thus, a strategic management orientation is likely to bring success to Government 2.0 implementation.

The Australian Working Group on Web 2.0 in government offers an encompassing strategic notion of Government 2.0 as an integral part of the strategic management of public sector information (Australian Government 2.0 Taskforce, 2009). Traditionally, government is the sole producer and distributor of public sector information. However, the era of Government 2.0 includes citizens and other stakeholders in the process of generating knowledge and insights about public affairs. This strategic orientation aligns well with the new paradigm of government-citizen relationships as envisioned by the proponents of Government 2.0. In a cross-boundary setting, empirical evidence supports the strategic alignment of information systems to match up with organizational goals that can facilitate implementation (Meijer & Thaens, 2010).

Policy and management support in the form of an incentive system can motivate participants to consider both individual and collective interests. The literature on knowledge management has long argued for a well-structured incentive system that can encourage individuals to create and share knowledge (Agranoff, 2007). Cross-boundary collaboration can work when the benefits of collaboration outweigh its costs. Citizen participation in online government activities, an important part of Government 2.0, would likely increase with incentives.

Organizational Factors for Government 2.0

Organizational culture plays a critical role in the government adoption and use of Web 2.0 technologies. Dawes et al (2009) identify a culture of collaboration as a key ingredient for knowledge sharing across government agencies. The use of Web 2.0 is premised on collaboration where a supporting organizational culture is the underlying foundation. An organizational culture that values citizen-centric services also goes a long way in deploying inter-departmental information systems (Chen, 2010a). Such organizational culture would be conducive to applications of Government 2.0 to further collaborate with citizens, business, and non-profit organizations.

An organizational culture of transparency and open communication is likely to support Government 2.0 activities. Online civic engagement requires government to be open and transparent in the first place. Without relevant government information available online, citizens could not engage in meaningful exchange and collaboration with government. A rigorous analysis of organizational culture for Government 2.0 needs to examine formal and informal organizational rules and procedures that can codify organizational culture.

The complexity of interorganizational information sharing and flow would also affect the ease of Government 2.0 implementation. The degree of coordination is an important consideration when making available citizen-centric or issue-specific information for the public. In this regard, studies of 311 systems which require coordination and collaboration of multiple departments in a local government have proven instructive (Reddick, 2009; Schellong & Langenberg, 2006).

The amount of effort required in standardizing government information for meaningful comparison is likely to correlate with difficulty in Government 2.0 implementation. Citizens' involvement in deliberating public policy issues depends on having comparative and meaningful policy information available to them. However, the experience of recent financial crises has shown that such information is difficult to generate. The effort by the U.S. Securities and Exchange Commission (SEC) to phase in the implementation of eXtensible Business Reporting Language (XBRL) is focused on bringing standardization to financial data, making them machine readable and comparable. Such foundational work is needed for government or sector-wide Government 2.0 projects.

Organizational technical capacity is likely to impact the adoption and use of Government 2.0. Technical capacity is a significant barrier to the adoption of e-government in general. ICMA surveys have documented the lack of technical capacity as one of the top two reasons for not engaging in e-government practices (International City/County Management, 2002; International City/County Management Association (ICMA), 2004). Moreover, organizational technical capacity extends beyond the technical aspect of building and maintaining information systems; it includes also the ability to manage technology projects. Melitski (2003) argues the importance of such management capacity in successful implementation of e-government projects. Given the important role played by technology service firms in the development and implementation of e-government projects in the U.S. government, Chen and Perry (2003) along with Brown and Brudney (1998) have emphasized the importance of IT management capacity in improving the performance of e-government projects.

Moreover, the level of organizational resources committed to Web 2.0 project is also relevant.

Managing communication in a Web 2.0 context takes a large amount of resources, at least at the initial stages. The responsible agency needs to modify its content for the Web 2.0 audience; Twitter only allows 140 characters and blog readers shy away from long paragraphs. Production resources need to invest in design and graphics, to increase impact. Moreover, the responsible agency needs to budget resources for maintaining and managing the interactivity that Web 2.0 promises. As the Director of the USA.gov and Web Best Practices has noted, it takes significant commitment of time and resources to maintain interactivity (General Service Administration, 2008).

Technology Factors

The sustainability of Government 2.0 depends on, in large part, the development and use of Web 2.0 technologies. Web 2.0 applications and use have seen rapid growth over the past few years. Government 2.0 is likely to follow Web 2.0 just as e-government followed the development of e-commerce. The growth of Government 2.0 in part will depend on the growth of analytics applications which are able to analyze the large number of inputs from various Web 2.0 outlets, such as blogs, interactive portals, Facebook sites, and more. The development of blog mining software and other analytics is critical as public managers need to make sense of mountains of data. One of the information management challenges associated with a wide use of Web 2.0 applications is the ability to use machine/software to sift through hundreds or even thousands of pages of information and distill clear messages out of these posts. Moreover, the development of the semantic web is likely to aid in the effort to make sense of the plethora of user generated content related to a particular topic. For example, recently the SEC issued a mandate requiring the use of XBRL for financial transparency and to improve government transparency in general (Chen, 2010b).

The future success of Government 2.0 also hinges on the maturing of technologies to facilitate collaboration. Media richness theory suggests the importance of presence for collaboration (Daft & Lengel, 1986; Kahai & Cooper, 2003). The more non-verbal cues that can be shared via the media, the more effective the communication is. The technology of projecting life-size individuals onto a screen in a conference room is available. The immersive nature of 3D virtual environments such as SecondLife offers an alternative venue for training and simulations. With maturing teleconference capabilities, group-decision support systems are maturing.

Time, interaction, and performance (TIP) theory (McGrath & Hollingshead, 1994) highlights the importance of paying attention to group processes and technical capacities of participants and utilizing technologies to enable a productive exchange. The use of interactive social media Web sites needs to be subject to testing and analysis in order to shed light on how to best utilize various capabilities. For example, a three-stage process is commonly found in Web 2.0 sites that solicit user input. The first stage is open submission of ideas; the second stage is voting and commenting, and the third stage is dissemination and updating on the implementation of ideas. Rigorous research on the OpenSource movement has been conducted, focusing especially on how the processes and rules of engagement should be structured to leverage technologies for open collaboration.[8]

Technology plays a critical role in improving the ease of use of Government 2.0 applications. Long established models such as TAM and UTAUT both speak to the critical role that usability plays in adoption and use. The success of the i-Phone and i-Pod illustrates the relevance of usability. With regards to e-government applications, empirical studies support the importance of ease of use in the intention of adoption and use of e-government applications (Wang & Shih, 2009). In short, the more technology development can address usability issues, particularly in mobile devices, the more likely we will see wide adoption of Government 2.0.

UNITED STATES' GOVERNMENT 2.0

The proposed framework offers an analytical lens through which the federal government's effort to implement Government 2.0 can be analyzed. The focus here is on the federal government, as opposed to state and local governments, because of the federal government's leading role in the move to Government 2.0. The various efforts of state and local governments in implementing Government 2.0 lay outside the scope of the present research. After a brief description of some recent efforts, the following sections will describe and analyze Government 2.0 efforts by examining all three key dimensions of the framework discussed above.

For the Obama Administration, Government 2.0 activities have been seen mostly in the General Service Administration's efforts to modernize federal government websites and engage citizens online. The usability of federal government websites has been improved by featuring high impact photos, simplifying navigation, removing clutter, and shortening some links to various federal government websites (General Service Administration, 2010).

Making government information accessible and understandable is an integral part of Government 2.0. Any meaningful collaboration between government and citizens rests on citizens' access to government and policy information. The Obama Administration emphasizes transparency. High profile projects include data.gov and recovery.gov. The former, data.gov, promotes participatory democracy by making high value, machine readable raw data available to the public.[9] It also offers a platform for developers to make use of a web of linked data (semantic web) to "mash up" data sets and visualize public affairs information such as clean air status, broadband adoption, and global aid.[10] Recovery.gov is designed to provide transparency in how money allocated to the American Recovery and Reinvestment Act is being spent. This website offers geographic analysis of recovery money spending as well as other perspectives. It offers an unprecedented level of access and detail on accountability information, down to the level of each funding recipient.

The citizen engagement office of the GSA has launched several projects during the first year of the Obama Administration. The Ideascale project encouraged American citizens to provide policy and management ideas for the federal government during the end of 2009 and the beginning of 2010. This project utilized Web 2.0 technologies to foster collaboration among various federal agencies, citizens, and citizen groups. Citizens were at the center of this collaborative effort; they proposed, voted, and commented on policy ideas. Federal agencies were committed to implementing some of the top-rated ideas. The more recent effort known as "Challenges and Prizes" continues the platform of open innovation; federal agencies pose a challenge to the public and offer prizes to engage citizens in solving public problems (General Service Administration, 2010).

Policy and Management Context of U.S. Federal Government 2.0

The U.S. has a long tradition of supporting laws and institutions for electronic participation, and this is a cornerstone of Government 2.0. The Administrative Procedure Act lets citizens participate in the policy-making process by allowing them to comment on proposed regulations. Regulatory agencies are mandated to respond and address the comments. More recently, the e-rulemaking process allows citizens and interest groups to comment on proposed regulations electronically. The U.S. received high marks on e-participation in the United Nations' 2008 E-government Survey. The U.S. government was cited for providing official channels for citizens to participate in the policy-making process and its efforts at making this participation meaningful by requiring regulatory agencies to respond as part of the public record.

Availability and access to government information are an integral part of supporting Government 2.0. The Freedom of Information Act gives private citizens access to government documents pertaining to their interest. The Electronic Freedom of Information Act (E-FOIA) extends such access, encompassing electronic files and information that have been growing fast with the popularity of the internet and advances in communication networks and devices.

Moreover, the Obama Administration provides a supportive institutional, policy, and management framework for the implementation of Government 2.0. The main policy framework is the Open Government Initiative announced within the first few weeks of the administration's inauguration in 2009. The Open Government Initiative has three pillars: transparency, participation, and collaboration. Transparency ensures that citizens have access to policy-related government information. Portals such as recovery.gov and data.gov were established for improving transparency. Participation encourages and engages citizens in solving public problems. It builds on the U.S.'s strength in e-participation and incorporates the Web 2.0 dimension, which will allow the government and citizens to collaborate on problem solving. The Challenge and Prizes project is an example of such an online platform. Collaboration, the last pillar, represents a new orientation; government seeks open innovation as well as partnership with organizations from the public and private sectors. This Open Government Initiative specifies an implementation timetable for making information available online (Orszag, 2009). For example, federal agencies need to have the top three high-impact data sets published online and registered them via data.gov within 45 days of the date of the memorandum (Orszag, 2009). These efforts are focused on ensuring that relevant government information is readily available for citizens.

Utilizing the proposed framework to take an assessment of these efforts to date suggests the following: First, the United States does have a supporting institutional framework for making information accessible to citizens as well as allowing citizens to participate in the policy making process. Nonetheless, the existing institutional framework lags behind when it comes to certain emerging issues brought on by Government 2.0. One example of this can be seen in the very definition of "public records." As public websites and user generated content get "mashed up" the definition of "public records" begins to blur. Thus, there is a need for forward-looking institutional and policy initiatives. Next, though there is a high-level executive support for Government 2.0, there is not enough emphasis on concrete incentives or penalties for lack of action. Indeed, the Open Government Directive, with its specific deadlines, is unprecedented in terms of its level of commitment from the Executive Office, but this commitment stops short of having either real penalties for lack of action or real incentives for federal agencies to move quickly. Unlike the case of Australia, there is presently no policy document from the U.S. Office of E-government and Information Technology on its use of Government 2.0 information. Lastly, there does not seem to be a clear strategic direction guiding the move to Government 2.0 and there are no concrete measures of performance. So far, most of the Government 2.0 advances have been focused on generating policy solutions. There is less evidence of how the ultimate impact of these ideas may or may not result in efficiency improvements or whether they are changing the culture of civic engagement, though both goals are touted in Government 2.0 initiatives.

Organizational Factors

The Obama Administration has been promoting a culture of openness and use of innovative technologies, both of which are conducive to Government 2.0. Such promotion is documented in the President's address on openness,[11] which declares that openness must prevail. We have begun to see some initial evidence of the administration's commitment to addressing policy issues related to openness. Such commitment moves the federal government one step closer to the institutionalization of an openness culture. For example, specific policy documents have been developed to support open innovation, and one strategy has involved giving prizes to citizens who contribute to the solution of public policy problems (Zients, 2010). Actually, this openness culture is also rooted in the history of garnering political support for the administration. Appealing directly to the American public has been pivotal in the Obama Administration's effort to gain public support for major policy initiatives, such as health care reform and financial recovery.

The organizational effort to integrate federal government information can be seen in the use of portals. Portals such as data.gov or recovery.gov aggregate information from multiple agencies to allow for information search and use. The dominant approach is geared more towards providing access to data sets than towards addressing more fundamental issues of data standards or improving the business practices of data sharing.

The U.S. government provides technical resources for Government 2.0 via the General Service Administration, which is responsible for the developing and implementing federal government web portals, among many other service responsibilities. The GSA provides technical resources on government 2.0 initiatives for various federal agencies. The apps.gov portal run by the GSA provides access to solutions for cloud IT, social media, business, and productivity applications. Certain fees are associated with these solutions, whether they are designed by the government or a software company.

The assessment of the U.S. government's Government 2.0 effort is still preliminary, and such an assessment would focus more on outlining the challenges ahead. The development of an organizational culture usually takes several years. Presently, it has been less than eighteen months into the Obama Administration, whereas an organizational culture typically takes three to four years to take root (Khademian, 2002). Openness, of course, seems to concentrate on less controversial issues. In the area of national security, for example, openness and transparency seem not highly pressing.

Moreover, the business process involved in providing citizen-centric services has only begun to address more difficult issues of data standardization. Much of the effort so far, specifically in financial transparency, has been overseen by single agencies, such as the FDIC and the SEC. However, the federal government needs to plan for government-wide data standards. So far, the technical resources provided for improving citizen-centric service via GSA have not seen active purchase and utilization. Too much of the focus has been on improving the user interface. Another larger issue yet to be addressed is concerned with building technical capacity to implement large complex interagency projects to provide citizen-centric services online.

Technological Elements

The U.S. federal government has made a conscious effort to increase the use of the semantic web via the provision of resource documentation and demonstration projects. The main information dissemination portal of the U.S. federal government is data.gov. As of July 2010, it featured semantic web as the creative and productive method by which raw government information is made available online. This site provides examples of how raw data can be "mashed up" to answer enduring or new policy questions for ordinary citizens to understand. Examples include the "Clean Air Status and Trends Network", which shows the status of clean air around the country and features trend information on a dynamic map. Moreover, this web site disseminates the "Resource Description Framework" (RDF), which features documents that show how developers and users can "mash up" information resources from various sources. These RDF documents are foundational for combining information resources to address a particular topic.

The U.S. federal government helps identify and promote the use of business analytics via the website apps.gov. Business intelligence is one of the business application categories available on apps.gov. The IT industry is mostly responsible for developing business analytics applications and implementation. Business analytics would be more useful as the semantic web continues to grow. A web-based open-source version of business analytics applications could help build online communities focused on various policy issues and provide useful policy information.

Social media is one of the main application service areas available to the Government Service Administration. Various social media applications are available to federal agencies. As part of the Challenges and Prizes program, for example, federal agencies are experimenting with innovative portals that use the interactivity provided by social media. Moreover, the U.S. government has an active blog for the White House and a channel on YouTube. The Obama administration also tweets via Twitter to keep the press and citizens informed about its policy ideas and positions. It has become standard for main federal government websites to have a social media component, such as a "follow us" option for Facebook or blog updates. The use of social media among citizens is likely to drive its application in government. The continuing shift of demographics, as more of people in the "net generation" enter the workforce and engage in public affairs, will increasingly require government to use social media.

Currently, the U.S. federal government deals with access issue on two fronts. First, it aims to design Web sites with a high level of usability. The Official White House Web site has an increased level of usability resulting from the use of photos, videos, blogs, and dynamically generated lists of items of interest. It is a significant improvement over a cluttered homepage that is a result of agencies trying to fit too much information on one page. Various federal agency websites are still in the process of becoming more user-friendly. On the second front, the government aims to enact the rural broadband initiative, which is designed to connect rural communities via broadband. Currently, this initiative is aimed at covering the communities underserved by telecommunication companies. This grant program is a part of the American Recovery and Reinvestment Act administered via the U.S. Department of Agriculture.

A review of the technological aspects of Government 2.0 suggests that the federal government has made a conscious effort to promote and use relevant technologies. The efforts as seen in data.gov on semantic web and the promotion of business analytics on apps.gov are particularly illustrative. However, the emphasis should be placed more on policies and standards. As software services move to the "cloud", the federal government adoption of Web 2.0 needs to address issues such as public records, privacy and security. Relevant technologies are in most cases readily available. The main barrier lies in getting clear policy guidance for implementation. It is noteworthy that the GSA's CIO also recognizes the continuing challenges of federal policies keeping pace with technology advances.[12]

Currently, data standards are falling behind the increasing availability of machine readable data that cut across multiple federal agencies. The standardization of data definitions across government agencies has been touted as a way to reduce the administrative burden of businesses and citizens meeting reporting standards. XBRL efforts in countries like Australia and the Netherlands have been designed to address such data standardization issues. However, the U.S. federal government is falling behind; it does not have a comprehensive government-wide implementation. As of the writing of this chapter, data standardization is seen only in a single-agency (i.e. SEC) or a single project (recovery.gov), rather than government-wide. Enterprise data standards are foundational for interoperability and comparability of government information resources coming from various agencies. More emphasis should be put on developing and implementing these standards to lay the foundation for the semantic web.

The technical aspect of Government 2.0 requires the development of performance measures and evaluation frameworks. The core issue is the return on investment for the deployment of these technologies. A quick survey of U.S. federal government websites does not reveal an articulation of performance measures associated with the use of Government 2.0. A cursory look may focus on the number of ideas or comments provided by citizens, and this may be used as a rough measure of effectiveness. However, more comprehensive and comparable performance measures should be developed for these new initiatives; this would drive performance enhancement and accountability simultaneously.

Policy and Management Recommendations for Government 2.0

The recommendations below focus on the experiences of the U.S. federal government's Government 2.0 efforts; they are based on a critical review using the framework proposed above. The initial evidence of the impact of the effort to increase transparency is encouraging as part of the survey conducted by the Pew Internet and American Life at the end of 2009. The results of the survey indicate about 40 percent of adult internet users have accessed raw data about government spending and activities. About 16 percent of them visited a website, such as data.gov, to access government data.[13]

The U.S. federal government can further improve the policy and management effort undergirding Government 2.0 by taking the following steps: First, the White House can work with key lawmakers to keep legislation and regulations at pace with the development and use of Government 2.0. A better definition of public records and more proper response to the Freedom of Information request in the world of social media would be useful. Second, the White House (via the General Service Administration) could provide policy guidance for the adoption and implementation of Government 2.0. A critical piece of policy document would incorporate a good set of performance matrices that track the progress of Government 2.0.

Moreover, on the policy and management front, the White House needs to sustain its support for the Open Government Initiative. Such support can take the form of committing and allocating needed resources to support the interactivity components of Government 2.0. The White House also needs to provide incentives for federal agencies and government employees to take advantage of Government 2.0 applications. Two possible incentives include making Government 2.0 a strategic component of government operation and including the successful use of Government 2.0 in performance reviews.

On the organizational front, the nurturing of an openness culture is fundamental. Such an openness culture should go beyond making government information and actions more transparent to citizens. It should also be concerned with nurturing a culture of collaboration among government agencies which share the same public service goals (e.g. national defense for the intelligence community). Moreover, the federal government should bring the same rigor of open innovation initiatives (i.e. Ideascale) to government-wide collaborations. A cursory survey of collaborative projects indicates a small number of federal government initiatives.[14] The problem of stove-piping has become more serious as contemporary public problems, such as national security, require an ever-increasing level of coordination and collaboration. The federal government should double its effort in creating virtual communities that can generate public values; one example is Intellipedia, which encompasses sixteen intelligence agencies (General Service Administration, 2008).

Building organizational capacity to implement technology is also a critical component of a successful strategy. The current effort of apps.gov is laudable. However, more organizational resources should be committed to capacity building. One bright spot is the effort to leverage applications developed by non-profit organizations. It is necessary, however, to build the management capacity for such a partnership directly into Web 2.0 technologies for government.

The federal government's leadership in building and providing standard documents for the semantic web is a critical step in the right direction. The next logical step is to provide more of such documents for high value data sets. The U.S. federal government can also provide some technical guidelines on how to utilize Government 2.0 technologies. These documents should provide federal agencies with a template and process model, showing how to utilize these technologies. Moreover, the federal government should continue to improve the usability and access to government information. The White House website is a significant and productive step in that direction. But the government needs to expand that effort to improve other federal government agency websites.

FUTURE RESEARCH DIRECTIONS AND OPPORTUNITIES

Electronic governance is likely to see more applications of Web 2.0 technologies. Government 2.0 is at the core of electronic governance; it provides connectedness and collaboration, both of which signal a gradual shift in the paradigm of government-citizen relationships. Due to the newness of the applications of Web 2.0 in government, research opportunities abound. Practitioners and researchers alike can formulate a normative standard on the nature and purposes of Government 2.0. For example, some would argue that the purpose of Web 2.0 is to foster participatory democracy and its performance would need to be measured accordingly (Hilbert, 2009). Others may contend that Government 2.0 has a broader impact; it adds to the public good, as seen, for example, in increased civic engagement, effectiveness and efficiency of public services, as well as increased creation of public sector information as a strategic resource (Australian Government 2.0 Taskforce, 2009; Osimo, 2008). A clear stand on these goals will help formulate the performance measures for Government 2.0 successes.

The institutional/managerial, organizational, and technology factors for the success of Government 2.0, drawn from various literatures, suggests some future possibilities for rigorous empirical investigation. An active Web 2.0 population, strong civic engagement culture and practices, and supportive laws and regulations, are all likely to be positively associated with Government 2.0 successes. The experience of the U.S. federal government underscores the relevance of all three factors. An international/comparative investigation examining variations in these conditions would provide stronger empirical evidence on the impact of these factors.

Moreover, top management support is likely to be one of the critical factors for Government 2.0 success. Such support would need to be translated into concrete resource commitment specific to Government 2.0 and the development of a nurturing culture of civic engagement and collaboration. These managerial factors can be investigated within a context of one country and one level of government, which would control for the larger national institutional context. Local governments in the United States, given their large number and varied uses of Web 2.0, are prime targets for research. In this way, the relative importance of various managerial factors in implementing Web 2.0 can be teased out.

The organizational aspect of Government 2.0 and its management is another productive avenue of future research. This dimension speaks to the complexity of collaboration and coordination across government agencies and service areas. This line of future research can draw from collaborative public management, networked organizations, and bureaucratic politics. The core question is how to structure organizational processes and identify and deploy enabling technologies for delivering public values associated with Government 2.0. Another related research opportunity is the development of performance measures for Government 2.0 that can help in the management of organizational resources to increase accountability. Once performance measures are developed, practitioners and scholars can examine the incentive structures that drive performance. To understand the organizational and structural dimensions of Government 2.0, future research should examine a variety of organizational settings that vary in complexity and level of integration.

Future research into the relationship between building technology and data standards and the use of Web 2.0 (or 3.0) for government will likely prove fruitful for the technical dimension of empirical investigation. Government is in a unique position for building public sector data standards. Such standards and resource documents are likely to help further democratize government information and unleash more and better use of public sector information. An important case to follow is the U.S. government's involvement in the development and use of XBRL for the FDIC, SEC, and future reporting of government activities. Another case is the preparation of the Resource Description Framework documents that allow for "mashing up" government information resources.

CONCLUSION

Government 2.0 is a critical component in the effort to improve electronic governance, achieve transparency in government information and increase effectiveness in citizen participation in public policy and services. Moreover, Government 2.0 allows for cross-boundary collaboration and can form virtual communities of participants from the public, non-profit, and private sectors. Indeed, Government 2.0 is the new frontier of e-governance, and it deserves serious attention from both scholars and practitioners.

This chapter has offered a framework that can help scholars better understand the development and implementation of Government 2.0. The proposed framework draw from several bodies of relevant literature: collaborative public management, public sector knowledge network management, management information systems, innovation, and e-governance. This framework identifies policy and managerial, organizational, and technological factors as critical for Government 2.0 success. Supportive laws and regulations, top management support, and strategic Web 2.0 information resource management coupled with incentives are the key policy and management elements. Critical organizational factors encompass an organizational culture which is based on open government and collaboration, matching organizational resource commitment to the complexity of collaborative processes, and building an organization's technical and technology management capacity. Relevant technological factors encompass the development of analytics applications for making sense of inputs from Web 2.0, enhancing the orchestration of the intricate processes involved in utilizing Web 2.0 in varying contexts, developing and using data standards for the semantic web, and improving the usability of Government 2.0 to foster wider adoption.

The description and analysis of the U.S. federal government's Government 2.0 experiences also provide policy and management lessons. The above discussion underscores the importance of supportive laws and regulations and the role of the Open Government Initiative in providing the overall policy framework for Government 2.0. Moreover, the above analysis shows the importance of a sustained commitment to keeping laws and regulations in pace with the application of Web 2.0 functionalities to government. The U.S. has already seen the initial positive impacts of the Open Government Directive; this directive has fostered a culture of open government. However, this cultivation will take time and sustained effort if it is to serve as a foundation for Government 2.0. The initiatives of the General Service Administration offer a platform for a wider and deeper utilization of Web 2.0. However, the actual level of utilization can only be driven by a set of concrete incentives. Laying the technological foundation, such as the Resource Description Framework documents, is an important step in the right direction. Marked improvements in the usability of the White House website is also another good beginning. Nonetheless, more effort such as these, particularly in developing data standards and improving usability, is needed to meet future technical challenges.

Opportunities for future research abound because Government 2.0 is still at an early stage of development. An international/comparative study can help examine the role that institutions, policy, and management commitment play. Promising research opportunities will arise as a growing number of countries begin to experiment with Government 2.0. Management strategies that fit a particular Government 2.0 organizational implementation context are worth exploring. Examining U.S. local governments will help scholars understand variations in implementation while controlling for national laws and regulations. The relevance of various recommendations for the technological aspect of Government 2.0 can be examined in more detail, even on a per-project or per-program basis. Finally, evaluating Government 2.0 initiatives with a coherent set of performance measures (such as effectiveness of civic engagement in knowledge creation) will help improve the theory and practice of Government 2.0.

REFERENCES

Agranoff, R. (2007). *Managing within networks: Adding value to public organizations*. Washington, DC: Georgetown University Press.

Ajzen, I. (1991). The theory of planned behavior. *Organizational Behavior and Human Decision Processes*, *50*(2), 179–211. doi:10.1016/0749-5978(91)90020-T

Australian Government 2.0 Taskforce. (2009). *Draft report of the government 2.0 taskforce*. Online Service Branch, Australian Government Information Management Office, Department of Finance and Deregulation.

Bingi, P., Sharma, M. K., & Godla, J. (1999). Critical issues affecting an ERP implementation. *Information Systems Management, 16*(3), 7–14. doi:10.1201/1078/43197.16.3.19990601/31310.2

Borins, S. (Ed.). (2008). *Innovations in government: Research, recognition, and replication*. Washington, DC: Brookings Institution Press and Ash Institute For Democratic Governance And Innovation.

Brown, M. M., & Brudney, J. L. (1998). A smarter, better, faster, and cheaper government: Contracting and Geographic Information Systems. *Public Administration Review*, *58*(4), 335–345. doi:10.2307/977563

Chen, Y.-C. (2010a). Citizen-centric e-government services: Understanding integrated citizen service Information Systems. *Social Science Computer Review*..doi:10.1177/0894439309359050

Chen, Y.-C. (2010b). *Realizing the full potential of XBRL in government: Case studies of XBRL implementation*. Washington, DC: IBM Center for the Business of Government.

Chen, Y.-C., & Hsieh, J.-Y. (2009). Advancing e-governance: Comparing Taiwan and the United States. *Public Administration Review, 69*(Supplement 1).

Chen, Y.-C., & Perry, J. (2003). Outsourcing for e-government: Managing for success. *Public Performance & Management Review*, *26*(4), 404–421. doi:10.1177/1530957603026004007

Cohen, W. M., & Levinthal, D. A. (1990). Absorptive capacity: A new perspective on learning and innovation. *Administrative Science Quarterly*, *35*, 128–152. doi:10.2307/2393553

Daft, R. L., & Lengel, R. H. (1986). Organizational information requirements, media richness, and structural design. *Management Science*, *32*(5), 554–571. doi:10.1287/mnsc.32.5.554

Daft, R. L., Lengel, R. H., & Trevino, L. K. (1987). Message equivocality, media selection, and manager performance: Implications for Information Systems. *Management Information Systems Quarterly*, *11*(3), 355–366. doi:10.2307/248682

Davis, F. D. (1989). Perceived usefulness, perceived ease of use, and user Acceptance of Information Technology. *Management Information Systems Quarterly*, *13*(3), 319–339. doi:10.2307/249008

Dawes, S. (1996). Interagency information sharing: Expected benefits, manageable risks. *Journal of Policy Analysis and Management*, *15*(3), 377–394. doi:10.1002/(SICI)1520-6688(199622)15:3<377::AID-PAM3>3.0.CO;2-F

Dawes, S., Cresswell, A., & Pardo, T. (2009). From need to know to need to share: Tangled problems, information boundaries, and the building of public sector knowledge networks. *Public Administration Review*, *69*(3), 392–402. doi:10.1111/j.1540-6210.2009.01987_2.x

Dimitrova, D., & Chen, Y.-C. (2006). Profiling the adopters of e-government information and services: The influence of psychological characteristics, civic mindedness, and information channels. *Social Science Computer Review*, *24*(2), 172–188. doi:10.1177/0894439305281517

Fountain, J. (2001). *Building the virtual state: Information Technology and institutional change*. Washington, DC: Brookings Institution Press.

General Service Administration. (2008). *Government and social media*. Washington, DC: Office of Citizen Services, General Service Administration.

General Service Administration. (2010). *A 25-minute morning with the Center for New Media and Citizen Engagement*. Washington, DC: The Center for New Media and Citizen Engagement, U.S. General Service Administration.

Goldsmith, S. E. W. (2004). *Governing by network: The new shape of the public sector*. Boston, MA & Washington, DC: Innovations in American Government, John F. Kennedy School of Government; Brookings Institution Press.

Gray, A., Jenkins, B., Leeuw, F., & Mayne, J. (2003). *Collaboration in public services (Vol. 10)*. New Brunswick, NJ & London, UK: Transaction Publishers.

Heeks, R. (1999). *Reinventing government in the information age: International practice in IT-enabled public sector reform*. London, UK & New York, NY: Routledge. doi:10.4324/9780203204962

Hilbert, M. (2009). The maturing concept of e-democracy: From e-voting and online consultations to democratic value out of jumbled online chatter. *Journal of Information Technology & Politics*, *6*(2), 87–110. doi:10.1080/19331680802715242

International City/County Management Association. (2002). *Electronic government 2002*. Washington, DC: International City/County Management Association.

International City/County Management Association. (2004). *2004 e-government survey*. Washington, DC: International City/County Management Association.

Kahai, S. S., & Cooper, R. B. (2003). Exploring the core concepts of media richness theory: The impact of cue multiplicity and feedback immediacy on decision quality. *Journal of Management Information Systems*, *20*(1), 263–299.

Khademian, A. (2002). *Working with culture: The way the job gets done in public programs*. Washington, DC: CQ Press.

Kraemer, K., & King, J. L. (2008). Information Technology and administrative reform: Will e-government be different? In Norris, D. (Ed.), *E-government research: Policy and management* (pp. 1–20). Hersey, PA: IGI Global.

Laudon, K. C., & Laudon, J. P. (2010). *Management Information Systems: Managing the digital firm* (11th ed.). Upper Saddle River, New Jersey.

McGrath, J. E., & Hollingshead, A. B. (1994). *Groups interacting with technology: Ideas, evidence, issues, and an agenda*. Thousand Oaks, CA: Sage Publications.

McGuire, M., & Silvia, C. (2010). The effect of problem severity, managerial and organizational capacity, and agency structure on intergovernmental collaboration: Evidence from local emergency management. *Public Administration Review*, *70*(2). doi:10.1111/j.1540-6210.2010.02134.x

Meijer, A., & Thaens, M. (2010). Alignment 2.0: Strategic use of new Internet technologies in government. *Government Information Quarterly*, *27*, 113–121. doi:10.1016/j.giq.2009.12.001

Melitski, J. (2003). Capacity and e-government performance: An analysis based on early adopters of Internet technologies in New Jersey. *Public Performance and Management Review*, *26*(4), 376–390. doi:10.1177/1530957603026004005

Moon, J., & Norris, D. (2005). Does managerial orientation matter? The adoption of reinventing government and e-government at the municipal level. *Information Systems Journal*, *15*, 43–60. doi:10.1111/j.1365-2575.2005.00185.x

O'Leary, R., & Bingham, L. B. (Eds.). (2009). *The collaborative public manager: New ideas for the twenty-first century*. Washington, DC: Georgetown University Press.

O'Toole, L. (1997). Implementing public innovations in network settings. *Administration & Society*, *29*(2), 115–134. doi:10.1177/009539979702900201

Orszag, P. R. (2009). *Open government directive, memorandum for the heads of executive departments and agencies*. Retrieved from http://www.whitehouse.gov /omb/assets/memoranda_2010 / m10-06.pdf

Osimo, D. (2008). *Web 2.0 in government: Why and how?*Luxembourg: Office for Official Publications of the European Communities.

Pardo, T. A., & Tayi, G. K. (2007). Interorganizational information integration: A key enabler for digital government. *Government Information Quarterly*, *24*(4), 691–715. doi:10.1016/j.giq.2007.08.004

Reddick, C. (2009). The adoption of centralized customer service systems: A survey of local governments. *Government Information Quarterly*, *26*(1), 219–226. doi:10.1016/j.giq.2008.03.005

Rogers, E. M. (2003). *Diffusion of innovations* (5th ed.). New York, NY: Free Press.

Schellong, A., & Langenberg, T. (2006). *Effective citizen relationship management: Hurricane Wilma and Miami-Dade County 311*. Paper presented at the 2006 International Conference on Digital Government Research.

Thomson, A. M., & Perry, J. (2006). Collaboration processes: Inside the black box. *Public Administration Review*, *66*(6), 20–32. doi:10.1111/j.1540-6210.2006.00663.x

Thurmaier, K., & Wood, C. (2002). Interlocal agreements as overlapping social networks: Picket-fence regionalism in metropolitan Kansas City. *Public Administration Review*, *62*(5), 585–598. doi:10.1111/1540-6210.00239

United Nations. (2005). *Global e-government readiness report 2005: From e-government to e-inclusion*. New York.

United Nations. (2008). *UN e-government survey 2008: From e-government to connected governance*. New York.

United Nations. (2010). *United Nations 2010 global e-government survey: Leveraging e-government at a time of financial and economic crisis*. New York, NY: United Nations.

Venkatesh, V., & Davis, F. D. (2000). A theoretical extension of the technology acceptance model: Four longitudinal field studies. *Management Science*, *46*(2), 186–204. doi:10.1287/mnsc.46.2.186.11926

Venkatesh, V., Morris, M., Davis, G., & Davis, F. (2003). User acceptance of Information Technology: Toward a unified view. *Management Information Systems Quarterly*, *27*(3), 425–478.

Wang, Y.-S., & Shih, Y.-W. (2009). Why do people use information kiosks? A validation of the united theory of acceptance and use of technology. *Government Information Quarterly*, *26*, 158–165. doi:10.1016/j.giq.2008.07.001

Willcocks, L., & Sykes, R. (2000). The role of the CIO and IT function in ERP. *Communications of the ACM*, *43*(4), 32–38. doi:10.1145/332051.332065

Wood, D., & Gray, B. (1991). Toward a comprehensive theory of collaboration. *The Journal of Applied Behavioral Science*, *27*(2), 139–162. doi:10.1177/0021886391272001

Zappen, J. P., Harrison, T. M., & Watson, D. (2008). *A new paradigm for designing e-government: Web 2.0 and experience design*. Paper presented at the 9th Annual International Digital Government Research Conference, Montreal.

Zients, J. (2010). *Guidance on the use of challenges and prizes to promote open government*. Office of Management and Budget.

KEY TERMS AND DEFINITIONS

E-Governance: A more progressive and advanced form of e-government with the emphasis on online citizen participation and on integration of government information systems for citizen-centric services.

E-Government: Government use of information and communication technologies to provide information and services to citizens, businesses, and other stakeholders.

Government 2.0: Government use of Web 2.0 technologies to inform citizens about government actions to promote openness and transparency as well as to collaborate with citizens, businesses, and non-profit organizations to solve public problems.

Open Government Initiative: A main policy framework for the implementation of Government 2.0 by the Obama Administration with three pillars: transparency, participation, and collaboration.

Semantic Web: Also known as Web 3.0, which improves information quality and data availability by enabling better organization and codification of data around topics of interest.

Web 2.0: Use of technologies that promote interactivity and user involvement, including examples such as RSS, video-sharing, wikis, blogs, mash-ups, social networking, twittering, and virtual worlds, among others.

XBRL (eXtensible Business Reporting Language): An example of Web 3.0. The language provides a common set of data definitions for the use and development of applications that make financial and business information machine-readable and comparable.

ENDNOTES

1 This number was quoted from the page 5 of the special report on social networking in the Economist published on January 30, 2010. The original source cited by is Facebook.

2 Ibid.

3 Social Network and Statehood, The Future is Another Country. July 22, 2010. The Economist.

4 Page 3, http://www.cnnic.cn/uploadfiles/pdf/2010/3/15/142705.pdf, accessed July 22, 2010.

5 http://social.venturebeat.com/2010/04/07/china%E2%80%99s-top-4-social-networks-renren-kaixin001-qzone-and-51-com/, accessed July 25, 2010. Note that Facebook is blocked in China.

6 Australian Government 2.0 Taskforce, Engage: Getting on with Government 2.0, Government 2.0 Taskforce 2009 Draft Report, Australia, pp. 4-6.

7 Australian Government 2.0 Taskforce.

8 Charlie Schweik at University of Massachusetts at Amherst is one of the leading scholars working on this topic.

9 For details, visit http://www.data.gov/about. The information was accessed July 22, 2010.

10 For more details, visit http://www.data.gov/semantic/index. The information was accessed July 27, 2010.

11 This is prominently featured on the home (blog) page for the Administration's Open Government Initiative http://www.whitehouse.gov/Open. This page was accessed on July 29, 2010.

12 The interview was conducted by Michael Krigsman and an excerpt of the transcript is available on http://www.zdnet.com/blog/projectfailures/cio-interview-casey-coleman-of-the-general-services-administration/7166 (accessed July 20, 2010).

13 For details, visit the Pew Internet and American Life Project Web site and search for "Government Online." The direct URL for the press release with all the numbers is http://www.pewinternet.org/Press-Releases/2010/Government-Online.aspx (accessed July 21, 2010).

14 It was based on the review of the Collaboration Project web site that catalogues Government 2.0 projects and White house Web site that features recent Government 2.0 projects. This review was conducted in July, 2010.

Compilation of References

Accenture Institute for Health & Public Service Value Project Team. (2009, November 12). *From e-government to e-governance: Using new technologies to strengthen relationships with citizens*. Retrieved September 15, 2010, from http://www.accenture.com/Global/Research_and_Insights/Institute_For_Public_Service_Value/From-e-Government-to-e-Governance.htm

Accenture. (2003). *El liderazgo de la administración electrónica-Desarrollo de una visión estratégica*. Retrieved February 2004 from http://www.accenture.com

Adler, R. P., & Goggin, J. (2005). What do we mean by "civic engagement"? *Journal of Transformative Education, 3*(3), 236–253. doi:10.1177/1541344605276792

Adler, R. P., & Goggin, J. (2005). What do we mean by civic engagement? *Journal of Transformative Education, 3*(3), 236–253. doi:10.1177/1541344605276792

Agranoff, R. (2007). *Managing within networks: Adding value to public organizations*. Washington, DC: Georgetown University Press.

Ahituv, N. (1980). A systematic approach toward assessing the value of an information system. *Management Information Systems Quarterly, 4*(4), 61–75. doi:10.2307/248961

Ajzen, I. (1991). The theory of planned behavior. *Organizational Behavior and Human Decision Processes, 50*(2), 179–211. doi:10.1016/0749-5978(91)90020-T

Ajzen, I. (2002). Perceived behavioral control, self-efficacy, locus of control, and the theory of planned behavior. *Journal of Applied Social Psychology, 32*, 665–683. doi:10.1111/j.1559-1816.2002.tb00236.x

Ajzen, I. (1991). The theory of planned behavior. *Organizational Behavior and Human Decision Processes, 50*(2), 179–211. doi:10.1016/0749-5978(91)90020-T

Akesson, M., & Edvardsson, B. (2008). Effects of e-government on service design as perceived by employees. *Managing Service Quality, 18*(5), 457–478. doi:10.1108/09604520810898839

Akhavan, P., Jafari, M., & Ali-Ahmadi, A. (2006). Exploring the interdependency between reengineering and Information Technology by developing a conceptual model. *Business Process Management Journal, 12*(4), 517–534. doi:10.1108/14637150610678104

Alexander, E. R. (1995). *How organizations act together: Interorganizational coordination in theory and practice*. Philadelphia, PA: Gordon and Breach.

Allen, B. A., Juillet, L., Paquet, G., & Roy, J. (2001). E-governance & government online in Canada: Partnerships, people, & prospects. *Government Information Quarterly, 18*, 94–104. doi:10.1016/S0740-624X(01)00063-6

Almarabeh, T., & AbuAli, A. (2010). A general framework for e-government: Definition maturity challenges, opportunities, and success. [from http://www.eurojournals.com/ejsr.htm]. *European Journal of Scientific Research, 39*(1), 29–42. Retrieved September 15, 2010.

Alshawi, S., & Alalwany, H. (2009). E-government evaluation: Citizen's perspective in developing countries. *Information Technology for Development, 15*(3), 193–208. doi:10.1002/itdj.20125

Alter, C., & Hage, J. (1993). *Organizations working together*. Los Angeles, CA: Sage.

Anderson, J. C., & Gerbing, D. W. (1988). Structural equation modeling in practice: A review and recommended two-step approach. *Psychological Bulletin, 103*(3), 411–423. doi:10.1037/0033-2909.103.3.411

Anderson, B. (1983). *Imagined communities: Reflections on the origins and spread of nationalism*. London, UK: Verso.

Anderson, K. (1999). Reengineering public sector organizations using information technology. In Heeks, R. (Ed.), *Reinventing government in the information age* (pp. 312–330). New York, NY: Routledge.

Anderson, P. (2007). *What is Web 2.0? Ideas, technologies and implications for education*. Bristol, UK: JISC Technology and Standards Watch. Retrieved April 13, 2009, from http://www.jisc.ac.uk/media /documents/ techwatch/ tsw0701b.pdf

Archmann, S., & Castillo, J. (2009). *E-inclusion: Paving the way for e-participation.* Retrieved August 2010 from http://www.epractice.eu/files /eGov.%202.0-pave%20 the%20 way%20for%20e-Participation %20-%202009. pdf

Arnstein, S. (1969). A ladder of citizen participation. *American Institute of Planners Journal*, *35*, 216–224. doi:10.1080/01944366908977225

Attaran, M. (2004). Exploring the relationship between information technology and business process reengineering. *Information & Management*, *41*, 585–596. doi:10.1016/ S0378-7206(03)00098-3

Auffret, J. P. (2010). Rural and municipal e-government initiatives in developing countries: Best practices and a framework for success. *Journal of E-Governance*, *33*(3), 139–143.

Australian Government Information Management Office. (2005, July). *Australian government technical interoperability framework*. Retrieved August 27, 2010, http://www.finance.gov.au/ publications/ australian-government-technical-interoperability-framework/ docs/ AGTIF_V2_-_FINAL.pdf

Australian Government Information Management Office. (2006, April). *Australian government information interoperability framework - Sharing information across boundaries.* Retrieved August 27, 2010, from http://www. finance.gov.au/ publications/ agimo/ docs/ Information_Interoperability_Framework.pdf

Australian Government Information Management Office. (2009, August). *National government information sharing strategy - Unlocking government assets to benefit the broader community.* Retrieved August 27, 2010, from http://www.finance.gov.au/ publications/national-government-information-sharing-strategy/ docs/ ngiss.pdf

Australian Government Information Management Office. (2007, July). *The Australian government business process interoperability framework: Enabling seamless service delivery.* Retrieved Auguust 27, 2010, from http://www. finance.gov.au/ publications/ agimo/ docs/ Business_Process_Interoeprabiltiy_Framework.pdf

Australian Government 2.0 Taskforce. (2009). *Draft report of the government 2.0 taskforce*. Online Service Branch, Australian Government Information Management Office, Department of Finance and Deregulation.

Backus, M. (2001). E-governance and developing countries: Introduction and examples. *IICD Research Report, 3.* Retrieved April 30, 2010, from http://www.ftpiicd.org/ files/ research/reports/report3.doc

Bagozzi, R., & Yi, Y. (1998). On the evaluation of structural equation models. *Journal of the Academy of Marketing Science*, *16*(1), 74–94. doi:10.1007/BF02723327

Bailey, J. E., & Pearson, S. W. (1983). Development of a tool for measuring and analyzing computer user satisfaction. *Management Science*, *29*(5), 530–545. doi:10.1287/ mnsc.29.5.530

Balkin, J. M. (1999). How mass media simulate political transparency. *Cultural Values*, *3*(4), 393–413.

Ballard, C., & Prine, R. (2002). Citizen perceptions of community policing: Comparing Internet and mail survey responses. *Social Science Computer Review*, *20*(4), 485–493. doi:10.1177/089443902237324

Ballard, T. N. (2001). *All e-government is local, tech leaders say.* Retrieved September 10, 2010, from http:// www.Govexec.com

Bandura, A. (1994). Self-efficacy. In Ramachaudran, V. S. (Ed.), *Encyclopedia of human behavior* (*Vol. 4*, pp. 71–81). New York, NY: Academic Press.

Banisar, D. (2006). *Freedom of information around the world 2006: A global survey of access to government information laws*. London, UK: Privacy International.

Barber, B. (1998). Three scenarios for the future of technology and strong democracy. *Political Science Quarterly*, *113*(4), 573–589. doi:10.2307/2658245

Barber, B. R. (1984). *Strong democracy: Participatory politics for a new age*. Berkley, CA: University of California Press.

Barboza, D. (2010, April 19). For Chinese, Web is the way to entertainment. *The New York Times,* B1, B8.

Barnes, S. J., & Vidgen, R. (2003). Measuring website quality improvements: A case study of the forum on strategic management knowledge exchange. *Industrial Management & Data Systems*, *103*(5), 297–309. doi:10.1108/02635570310477352

Barnes, S. J., & Vidgen, R. (2006). Data triangulation and Web quality metrics: A case study in e-government. *Information & Management*, *43*, 767–777. doi:10.1016/j.im.2006.06.001

Barnes, S. J., & Vidgen, R. (2007). Interactive e-government: Evaluating the website of the UK inland revenue. *International Journal of Electronic Government Research*, *3*(1), 19–37. doi:10.4018/jegr.2007010102

Barnes, S. J., & Vidgen, R. (2004). Evaluating the website of the UK inland revenue. *Journal of Electronic Commerce in Organizations*, *2*(1), 42–63. doi:10.4018/jeco.2004010104

Bateson, J. E. G. (1985). Self-service consumer: An exploratory study. *Journal of Retailing*, *61*(3), 49–76.

Batson, C., & Coke, J. (1981). *A source of altruism and helping behavior: Social, personality and developmental perspective*. New Jersey: Erlbaum.

Bauer, R. A. (1960). Consumer behavior as risk taking. In Hancock, R. S. (Ed.), *Dynamic marketing for a changing world* (pp. 389–393). Chicago, IL: American Marketing Association.

Baum, C. H., & Maio, A. D. (2000). *Gartner's four phases of e-government model*. Retrieved December 3, 2007, from http://www.gartner.com

Bausch, P., & Bumgardner, J. (2006). *Flickr hacks*. Sebastopol, CA: O'Reilly Press. Retrieved August 1, 2010, from http://www.oreilly.com /catalog/flickrhks/chapter/ hack14.pdf

Becker, J., Algermissen, L., & Niehaves, B. (2006). A procedure model for process oriented e-government projects. *Business Process Management Journal*, *12*(1), 61–75. doi:10.1108/14637150610643760

Behn, R. (2003). Why measure performance? Different purposes require different measures. *Public Administration Review*, *63*(5), 586–606. doi:10.1111/1540-6210.00322

Bekkers, V., & Homburg, V. (2005). E-government as an information ecology: Backgrounds and concepts. In Bekkers, V., & Homburg, V. (Eds.), *The information ecology of e-government*. Amsterdam, The Netherlands: IOS Press.

Benbasat, I., & Barki, H. (2007). Quo vadis TAM. *Journal of the Association for Information Systems*, *8*(4), 211–218.

Bensaou, M. (1997). Interorganizational cooperation: The role of information technology. An empirical comparison of U.S. and Japanese supplier relations. *Information Systems Research*, *8*(2), 107–124. doi:10.1287/isre.8.2.107

Bentler, P. M. (1990). Comparative fit indexes in structural models. *Psychological Bulletin*, *107*(2), 238–246. doi:10.1037/0033-2909.107.2.238

Bernal, V. (2004). Eritrea goes global: Reflections on nationalism in a transnational era. *Cultural Anthropology*, *19*(1), 3–25. doi:10.1525/can.2004.19.1.3

Bernal, V. (2005). Eritrea on-line: Diaspora, cyberspace, and the public sphere. *American Ethnologist*, *32*(4), 660–675. doi:10.1525/ae.2005.32.4.660

Bernal, V. (2006). Diaspora, cyberspace, and political imagination: The Eritrean diaspora online. *Global Networks*, *6*(2), 161–179. doi:10.1111/j.1471-0374.2006.00139.x

Bertot, J. C., & Jaeger, P. T. (2006). User-centered e-government: Challenges and benefits for government websites. *Government Information Quarterly*, *23*, 163–168. doi:10.1016/j.giq.2006.02.001

Bertot, J. C., Jaeger, P. T., & McClure, C. R. (2008). Citizen-centered e-government services: Benefits, costs, and research needs. In S. A. Chun, M. Janssen, & J. R. Gil-Garcia (Eds.), *The Proceedings of the 9th Annual International Digital Government Research Conference: Partnerships for Public Innovation* (pp.137-142). Montreal, Canada: Digital Government Society of North America.

Besley, T., & Burgess, R. (2001). Political agency, government responsiveness and the role of the media. *European Economic Review*, *45*, 629–640. doi:10.1016/S0014-2921(01)00133-7

Bessette, J. M. (1994). *The mild voice of reason: Deliberative democracy and American national government*. Chicago, IL & London, UK: Chicago University Press.

Betancourt, V. (2006). *E-government: An opportunity for citizen participation in the era of digital development*. Retrieved April, 14, 2009, from http://www.apc.org/en/news/ all/world/e-government- opportunity-citizen-participation-era

Beynon-Davies, P. (2005). Constructing electronic government: The case of the UK inland revenue. *International Journal of Information Management*, *25*, 3–20. doi:10.1016/j.ijinfomgt.2004.08.002

Bhatnagar, S. (2007). *Impact assessment study of computerized services delivery projects from India and Chile*. IT@WEB Staff working Papers. Retrieved April 28, 2009, from http://www.iimahd.ernet.in/ egov/documents/impact-assessment-study-wbr.pdf

Bijker, W. E. (1995). *Of bicycles, bakelites, and bulbs: Toward a theory of sociotechnical change*. Cambridge, MA: MIT.

Bimber, B. (2000). The study of Information Technology and civic engagement. *Political Communication*, *17*, 329–333. doi:10.1080/10584600050178924

Bingi, P., Sharma, M. K., & Godla, J. (1999). Critical issues affecting an ERP implementation. *Information Systems Management*, *16*(3), 7–14. doi:10.1201/1078/43197.16.3.19990601/31310.2

Bishop, J. (2007). Increasing participation in online communities: A framework for human–computer interaction. *Computers in Human Behavior*, *23*(4), 1881–1893. doi:10.1016/j.chb.2005.11.004

Bishop, P., & Anderson, L. (2004). *E-government to e-democracy: High tech solutions to no tech problems*. Paper presented at the Australian Electronic Governance Conference, Centre for Public Policy, University of Melbourne, Melbourne Victoria.

Bitner, M. J., Booms, B. H., & Tetreault, M. S. (1990). The service encounter: Diagnosing favorable and unfavorable incidents. *Journal of Marketing*, *54*(1), 71–84. doi:10.2307/1252174

Bonham, G. M., Seifert, J. W., & Thorson, S. J. (2001). *The transformational potential of e-government: the role of political leadership*. Paper presented at the Electronic Governance and Information Policy (Panel 9-1), 4th Pan-European International Relations Conference of the European Consortium for Political Research, University of Kent, Canterbury.

Bonsón, E., Escobar, T., & Flores, F. (2006). Online transparency of the banking sector. *Online Information Review*, *30*(6), 714–730. doi:10.1108/14684520610716180

Boonstra, A., & de Vries, J. (2005). Analyzing inter-organizational systems from a power and interest perspective. *International Journal of Information Management*, *25*, 485–501. doi:10.1016/j.ijinfomgt.2005.08.006

Borins, S. (2001). Public management innovation: Toward a global perspective. *American Review of Public Administration*, *31*(1), 5–21. doi:10.1177/02750740122064802

Borins, S. (2002). On the frontiers of electronic governance: A report on the United States and Canada. *International Review of Administrative Science*, *68*(2), 199–211. doi:10.1177/0020852302682003

Borins, S. (Ed.). (2008). *Innovations in government: Research, recognition, and replication*. Washington, DC: Brookings Institution Press and Ash Institute For Democratic Governance And Innovation.

Bouckaert, G., & Van de Walle, S. (2003). Comparing measures of citizen trust and user satisfaction as indicators of "good governance": Difficulties in linking trust and satisfaction indicators. *International Review of Administrative Sciences*, *69*(3), 329–344.

Boyer, K. K., Hallowell, R., & Roth, A. V. (2002). E-service: Operation strategy - A case study and method for analyzing operational benefits. *Journal of Operations Management*, *20*(2), 175–188. doi:10.1016/S0272-6963(01)00093-6

Bozeman, B. (2000). *Bureaucracy and red tape*. Upper Saddle River, NJ: Prentice Hall.

Braziel, J. E., & Mannur, A. (2003) Nation, migration, globalization: Point of contention in diaspora studies. In J. E. Braziel & A. Mannur (Ed), *Theorizing diaspora* (1-22). Oxford, UK: Blackwell Publishing Ltd.

British Broadcasting Corporation. (2008). *Government concerned on influence of diaspora media over public*. Eritrea.

Brown, S. A., Chervany, N. L., & Reinicke, B. A. (2007). What matters when introducing new Information Technology. *Communications of the ACM*, *50*(9), 91–96. doi:10.1145/1284621.1284625

Brown, K., & Coulter, P. (1983). Subjective and objective measures of police service delivery. *Public Administration Review*, *43*(1), 50–58. doi:10.2307/975299

Brown, M. M. (2007). Understanding e-government benefits: An examination of leading-edge local governments. *American Review of Public Administration*, *37*(2), 178–197. doi:10.1177/0275074006291635

Brown, M. M., & Brudney, J. L. (1998). A smarter, better, faster, and cheaper government: Contracting and Geographic Information Systems. *Public Administration Review*, *58*(4), 335–345. doi:10.2307/977563

Brown, D. (1999). Information Systems for improved performance management: Development approaches in U.S public agencies. In Heeks, R. (Ed.), *Reinventing government in the information age* (pp. 113–134). New York, NY: Routledge.

Brunetti, A., & Weder, B. (2003). A free press is bad news for corruption. *Journal of Public Economics*, *87*, 1801–1824. doi:10.1016/S0047-2727(01)00186-4

Bucar, E. M., & Fazaeli, R. (2008). Free speech in Weblogistan? The offline consequences of online communication. *International Journal of Middle East Studies*, *40*(3), 403–419. doi:10.1017/S0020743808080999

Cabinet Office. (2010, May 29). *Gov talk*. Retrieved August 30, 2010, from http://www.cabinetoffice.gov.uk/ govtalk.aspx

Caldow, J. (2004). *E-democracy: Putting down global roots*. Armonk, NY: Institute for Electronic Government, IBM. Retrieved April 28, 2009, from http://www-1.ibm.com/industries /government/ieg/pdf/ e-democracy%20 putting %20down%20roots.pdf

Camerer, M. I. (2006). Measuring public integrity. *Journal of Democracy*, *17*(1), 152–165. doi:10.1353/jod.2006.0004

Capgemini. (2005). *Online availability of public services: How is Europe progressing?* Capgemini for the European Commission Directorate General. Information and Society Media. Retrieved December 3, 2007, from http://ec.europa.eu/ information_society/soccul/ egov/ egov_benchmarking_2005.pdf

CapGemini. (2007). *The user challenge- Benchmarking the supply of online public services, 7th measurement*. European Commission, General Direction of Information Society and Media. Retrieved January 2008 from http:// ec.europa.eu/ information_society/ eeurope/i2010/docs/ benchmarking/ egov_benchmark_2007.pdf

CapGemini. (2009). *Smarter, faster, better e-government*. 8th Benchmark Measurement.

Carpini, M. X. D. (2000). Gen.com: Youth, civic engagement, and the new information environment. *Political Communication*, *17*, 341–349. doi:10.1080/10584600050178942

Carpini, M. X. (2000). Gen.com: Youth, civic engagement, and the new information environment. *Political Communication*, *17*, 341–349. doi:10.1080/10584600050178942

Carter, L. (2008). E-government diffusion: A comparison of adoption constructs. *Transforming Government: People. Process and Policy*, *2*(3), 147–161.

Carter, M., & Yanbin, L. (2007). *EU-China Information Society Project – Access to government information in Europe and China: What lessons to be learned?* London, UK: The EU-China Information Society.

Castell, M. (1996). *The rise of the network society*. Malden, MA: Blackwell Publishers.

Castells, M. (2007) Communication, power and counter-power in the network society. *International Journal of Communication*, *1*, 238-266. Retrieved May 1, 2010, from http://ijoc.org/ojs/index.php/ijoc/article/view/46/35

Census, U. S. (2008). *Metropolitan and micropolitan statistical areas*. Retrieved June 2, 2007, from http://www.census.gov/ population/www/metroareas /metroarea.html

Center for Digital Government (CDG). (2006). *Digital counties survey*. Folsom, CA: The Center for Digital Government. Retrieved June 7, 2007, from http://www.centerdigitalgov.com/ contact.php.

Center for Technology in Government. (1999, October 1). *What rules govern the use of information?* Retrieved August 27, 2010, from http://www.ctg.albany.edu/ publications/ reports/ what_rules_govern/ what_rules_govern.pdf

Center for Technology in Government. (2001, April 10). *Insider's guide to using information in government, policy area.* Retrieved August 27, 2010, from http://www.ctg.albany.edu/ static/ usinginfo/ Policy/ policy.htm

CESG - The National Technical Authority for Information Assurance. (2010, May). *HMG IA maturity model.* Retrieved August 30, 2010, from http://www.cesg.gov.uk/ products_services/ iacs/ iamm/ index.shtml

Chadwick, D. W., & Basden, A. (2001). Evaluating trust in a public key certification authority. *Computers & Security, 20*(7), 592–611. doi:10.1016/S0167-4048(01)00710-6

Chadwick, A., & May, C. (2003). Interaction between states and citizens in the age of the Internet: E-government in the United States, Britain, and the European Union. *Governance: An International Journal of Policy and Administration, 16*(2), 271–300.

Chadwick, A. (2003). Bringing e-democracy back in: Why it matters for future research on e-government. *Social Science Computer Review, 21*(4), 443–455. doi:10.1177/0894439303256372

Chan, H. S., & Chow, K. W. (2007). Public management policy and practice in Western China: Metapolicy, tacit knowledge, and implications for management innovation transfer. *American Review of Public Administration, 37*(4), 479–497. doi:10.1177/0275074006297552

Chanley, Virginia, A., Thomas, J. R., & Wendy, M.R. (2000). The origins and consequences of public trust in government: A time serious analysis. *Public Opinion Quarterly, 64*, 239–256. doi:10.1086/317987

Chatfield, A. T., & Alhujran, O. (2008). A cross-country comparative analysis of e-government service delivery among Arab countries. *Information Technology for Development, 15*(3), 151–170. doi:10.1002/itdj.20124

Chen, C. D., Fan, Y. W., & Farn, C. K. (2007). Predicting electronic toll collection service adoption: An integration of the technology acceptance model and the theory of planned behavior. *Transportation Research Part C, Emerging Technologies, 15*, 300–311. doi:10.1016/j.trc.2007.04.004

Chen, S. C., Chen, H. H., & Chen, M. F. (2009). Determinants of satisfaction and continuance intention towards self-service technologies. *Industrial Management & Data Systems, 109*(8-9), 1248–1263. doi:10.1108/02635570911002306

Chen, Y.-C., & Thurmaier, K. (2008). Advancing e-government: Financing challenges and opportunities. *Public Administration Review, 68*(3), 537–548. doi:10.1111/j.1540-6210.2008.00889.x

Chen, Y., & Gant, J. (2001). Transforming local e-government services: The use of application service providers. *Government Information Quarterly, 18*(4), 343–355. doi:10.1016/S0740-624X(01)00090-9

Chen, Y., & Hsieh, J. (2009). Advancing e-governance: Comparing Taiwan and the United States. *Public Administration Review, 69*, s151–s158. doi:10.1111/j.1540-6210.2009.02103.x

Chen, C. C. (2005). Freedom of information: A survey of current status. [in Chinese]. *Yan Kao Shuang Yue Kan, 29*(3), 73–87.

Chen, Y. H. (2006). A survey on the impact and yield following Taiwan's implementing administration information disclosure. [in Chinese]. *Yan Kao Shuang Yue Kan, 30*(1), 86–98.

Chen, D. Y., Huang, D. Y., & Hsiao, N. (2004). E-participation: Internet and citizen participation in policy making process. [in Chinese]. *Research and Evaluation Bimonthly, 28*(4), 36–51.

Chen, Y. C., & Dimitrova, D. V. (2006). Electronic government and online engagement: Citizen interaction with government via Web portals. *International Journal of Electronic Government, 2*(1), 54–76. doi:10.4018/jegr.2006010104

Chen, Y.-C. (2010a). Citizen-centric e-government services: Understanding integrated citizen service Information Systems. *Social Science Computer Review*.. doi:10.1177/0894439309359050

Chen, Y.-C. (2010b). *Realizing the full potential of XBRL in government: Case studies of XBRL implementation*. Washington, DC: IBM Center for the Business of Government.

Chen, Y.-C., & Perry, J. (2003). Outsourcing for e-government: Managing for success. *Public Performance & Management Review*, *26*(4), 404–421. doi:10.1177/1530957603026004007

Chen, Y.-C., & Knepper, R. (2005). Digital government development strategies: Lessons for policy makers from a comparative perspective. In Huang, W., Siau, K., & Wei, K. K. (Eds.), *Electronic government strategies and implementation* (pp. 394–420). Hershey, PA: Idea Group.

Chen, L., & Dong, X. (2005, March 31). Hulianwang Zhongguo de xin minyi shidai: yijian yeshi caifu. (Opinions are treasure: the new era of public opinion in networked China). *Hulianwang Zhoukan* (Internet Weekly). Retrieved from http://media.163.com/05/0331/11/1G5T8FDT00141E7P.html

Chen, Y.-C., & Hsieh, J.-Y. (2009). Advancing e-governance: Comparing Taiwan and the United States. *Public Administration Review, 69*(Supplement 1).

Chiang, M. S., Chen, T. Y., Huang, D. Y., Chung, K. J., & Hsiao, N. Y. (2004). *Utilizing ICTs to realize citizen participation: Vision, cases, and strategies*. Institute for the Information Industry.

Chin, W. W., & Newsted, P. R. (1999). Structural equation modeling analysis with small samples using partial least squares. In Hoyle, R. H. (Ed.), *Statistical strategies for small sample research* (pp. 307–341). Thousand Oaks, CA: SAGE Publications.

China Daily. (2004, April 5). *Nation quickens spread of e-government*.

China Digital Times. (2008). *Chinese intellectuals contemplate the earthquake: Lessons we are learning*. Retrieved February 22, 2010, from http://chinadigitaltimes.net/ 2008/05/chinese-intellectuals- contemplate-on-earthquake- lessons-we-are-learning/

China International Network Information Center (CNNIC). (2001). *The 9th statistical survey report on the Internet development in China*. Retrieved on June 15, 2010, from http://www.cnnic.net.cn/ download/manual/en-reports/9.pdf

China International Network Information Center (CNNIC). (2002). *The 10th statistical survey report on the Internet development in China*. Retrieved on June 15, 2010, from http://www.cnnic.net.cn/ download/manual/en-reports/10.pdf

China International Network Information Center (CNNIC). (2003). *The 12th statistical survey report on the Internet development in China*. Retrieved on June 15, 2010, from http://www.cnnic.net.cn/ download/manual/en-reports/12.pdf

China International Network Information Center (CNNIC). (2005). *The 16th statistical survey report on the Internet development in China*. Retrieved on June 15, 2010, from http://www.cnnic.net.cn /download/2005/2005072601.pdf

China International Network Information Center (CNNIC). (2006). *The 18th statistical survey report on the Internet development in China*. Retrieved on June 15, 2010, from http://www.cnnic.net.cn/ download/2006/18threport-en.pdf

China International Network Information Center (CNNIC). (2007). *The 19th statistical survey report on the Internet development in China*. Retrieved on June 15, 2010, from http://www.cnnic.net.cn/ html/Dir/2007/02/05/4432.htm

China International Network Information Center (CNNIC). (2008). *The 21st statistical survey report on the Internet development in China*. Retrieved on June 15, 2010, from http://www.cnnic.net.cn/ uploadfiles/pdf/2008 /2/29/104126.pdf

China International Network Information Center (CNNIC). (2009). *The 23rd statistical survey report on the Internet development in China*. Beijing: Ministry of Information Industry. Retrieved on June 15, 2010, from http://www.cnnic.net.cn/ uploadfiles/pdf/2009/3/23/153540.pdf

China International Network Information Center (CNNIC). (2010). *The 25th statistical survey report on the Internet development in China*. Beijing, China: Ministry of Information Industry. Retrieved on June 15, 2010, from http://www.cnnic.net.cn/ uploadfiles/pdf/2010/3/15/142705.pdf

China Internet Network Information Center. (2008, July). *The 22nd Statistical Survey Reports on Internet Development in China*. Retrieved from http://www.cnnic.net.cn/uploadfiles/doc/2008/7/23/ 170424.doc

China Internet Network Information Center. (2009, July). *The 24th Statistical Survey Reports on Internet Development in China*, Retrieved from http://www.cernet.com/news/chinacngi.pdf

China Software Testing Center. (2007). *The 2007 China Government Website Performance Evaluation Report*, Retrieved from http://www.ccidjianli.com/2007wzpg/07jixiao/untitled /xinindex.htm

Chinascope. (2007). *A survey of mainland Chinese's view on Internet censorship.*

Chinn, M., & Fairlie, R. (2010). ICT use in the developing world: An analysis of differences in computer and Internet penetration. *Review of International Economics*, *18*(1), 153–167. doi:10.1111/j.1467-9396.2009.00861.x

Cho, H., & LaRose, R. (1999). Privacy issues in Internet surveys. *Social Science Computer Review*, *17*(4), 421–434. doi:10.1177/089443939901700402

Choudrie, J., & Weerrakody, V. (2007). Horizontal process integration: The perspective of a UK local authority. *International Journal of Electronic Government Research*, *3*(3), 22–39. doi:10.4018/jegr.2007070102

Choudrie, J., Weerakkody, V., & Jones, S. (2005). Realising e-government in the UK: Rural and urban challenges. *The Journal of Enterprise Information Management*, *18*(5), 568–585. doi:10.1108/17410390510624016

Christensen, T., & Laegreid, P. (2005). Trust in government: The relative importance of service satisfaction, political factors, and demography. *Public Performance & Management Review*, *28*(4), 487–511.

Christian, L. M., Dillman, D. A., & Smyth, J. D. (2007). Helping respondents get it right the first time: The influence of words, symbols, and graphics in Web surveys. *Public Opinion Quarterly*, *71*(1), 113–125. doi:10.1093/poq/nfl039

Chung, J. (2008). Comparing online activities in China and South Korea. *Asian Survey*, *48*(5), 727–751. doi:10.1525/AS.2008.48.5.727

Citrin, A. V., Sprott, D. E., Silverman, S. N., & Stem, D. E. Jr. (2000). Adoption of Internet shopping: The role of consumer innovativeness. *Industrial Management & Data Systems*, *100*(7), 294–301. doi:10.1108/02635570010304806

Claver-Cortés, E., Juana-Espinosa, S., & Tarí, J. J. (2008). E-government maturity at Spanish local levels. *International Journal of Value Chain Management*, *2*(1), 4–17. doi:10.1504/IJVCM.2008.016115

Cohen, W. M., & Levinthal, D. A. (1990). Absorptive capacity: A new perspective on learning and innovation. *Administrative Science Quarterly*, *35*, 128–152. doi:10.2307/2393553

Cohen, N. (2009, June 21). Twitter on the barricades: Six lessons learned. *New York Times*. Retrieved May 1, 2010, from http://www.nytimes.com/ 2/06/21/weekinreview/21cohenweb.html?_r=1

Colier, J. E., & Bienstock, C. C. (2006). Measuring service quality in e-retailing. *Journal of Service Research*, *8*(3), 260–275. doi:10.1177/1094670505278867

Communist Party of China Central Committee. (2004, September 27th). Decision on Building up the Party's Governing Capacity *People's Daily*, pp. A1.

Communist Party of China Central Committee General Office. (2002). *No.17 Guideline of National E-government Construction*. Retrieved from http://news.xinhuanet.com/it/2005-05/19/ content_2974699.htm

Communist Party of China Central Committee General Office and State Council General Office. (2006). *2006-2020 National Informatization Development Strategy*. Retrieved from http://news.xinhuanet.com/ newscenter/2006-05/08/ content_4522878_16.htm

Cook, L. S., Bowen, D. E., Chase, R. B., Dasu, S., Stewart, D. M., & Tansik, D. A. (2002). Human issues in service design. *Journal of Operations Management*, *20*(2), 159–174. doi:10.1016/S0272-6963(01)00094-8

Cooper, T. L. (2005). Civic engagement in the twenty-first century: Toward a scholarly and practical agenda. *Public Administration Review*, *65*(5), 534–535. doi:10.1111/j.1540-6210.2005.00480.x

Corbin, J., & Strauss, A. (2008). *Basics of qualitative research* (3rd ed.). Los Angeles, CA: Sage.

Council of Europe Committee of Ministers. (2002). *Recommendation of the Committee of Ministers to member states o access to official documents*. Retrieved March 1, 2010, from https://wcd.coe.int/ ViewDoc.jsp?id=262135&BackColorInternet=B9BDEE&BackColorIntranet=FFCD4F&BackColorLogged=FFC679

Couper, M. P. (2000). Web surveys: A review of issues and approaches. *Public Opinion Quarterly*, *64*(4), 464–494. doi:10.1086/318641

Couper, M. P., Kapteyn, A., Schonlau, M., & Winter, J. (2007). Noncoverage and nonresponse in an Internet survey. *Social Science Research*, *36*(1), 131–148. doi:10.1016/j.ssresearch.2005.10.002

Couper, M. P., Traugott, M. W., & Lamias, M. J. (2001). Web survey design and administration. *Public Opinion Quarterly*, *65*(2), 230–253. doi:10.1086/322199

Coursey, D., & Norris, D. F. (2008). Models of e-government: Are they correct? An empirical assessment. *Public Administration Review*, *68*(3), 523–536. doi:10.1111/j.1540-6210.2008.00888.x

Coursey, D. H., & Killingsworth, J. (2005). Managing e-government in Florida: Further lessons from transition and maturity. In Garson, G. D. (Ed.), *Handbook of public Information Systems* (2nd ed., pp. 335–351). New York, NY: Marcel Dekker/CRC.

Crawford, S. D., Couper, M. P., & Lamias, M. J. (2001). Web surveys: Perceptions of burden. *Social Science Computer Review*, *19*(2), 146–162. doi:10.1177/089443930101900202

Cresswell, A. M., & Pardo, T. A. (2001). Implications of legal and organizational issues for urban digital government development. *Government Information Quarterly*, *18*(4), 269–278. doi:10.1016/S0740-624X(01)00086-7

Cristiano, C., & Wimmer, M. A. (Eds.). (2007). Roadmapping e-government research: Visions and measures towards innovative governments in 2020. *EC-funded Project eGovRTD2020.* Retrieved July 19, 2010, from http://www.egovrtd2020.org/ EGOVRTD2020/FinalBook.pdf

Cunningham, S. M. (1967). The major dimensions of perceived risk. In Cox, D. F. (Ed.), *Risk-taking and information handling in consumer behavior* (pp. 82–108). Boston, MA: Harvard University Press.

Dabholkar, P. A. (1996). Consumer evaluations of new technology-based self-service options: An investigation of alternative models of service quality. *International Journal of Research in Marketing*, *13*, 29–51. doi:10.1016/0167-8116(95)00027-5

Dabholkar, P. A., & Bagozzi, R. P. (2002). An attitudinal model of technology-based self-service: Moderating effects of consumer traits and situational factors. *Journal of the Academy of Marketing Science*, *30*(3), 184–202.

Daft, R. L., & Lengel, R. H. (1986). Organizational information requirements, media richness, and structural design. *Management Science*, *32*(5), 554–571. doi:10.1287/mnsc.32.5.554

Daft, R. L., Lengel, R. H., & Trevino, L. K. (1987). Message equivocality, media selection, and manager performance: Implications for Information Systems. *Management Information Systems Quarterly*, *11*(3), 355–366. doi:10.2307/248682

Darbishire, H., & Carson, T. (2006). *Transparency & silence: A survey of access to information laws and practices in 14 countries*. New York, NY: Open Society Institute.

Darch, C., & Underwood, P. G. (2005). Freedom of information legislation, state compliance and the discourse of knowledge: The South African experience. *The International Information & Library Review*, *37*, 77–86. doi:10.1016/j.iilr.2005.05.003

Davis, F. D. (1989). Perceived usefulness, perceived ease of use, and user acceptance of Information Technology. *Management Information Systems Quarterly*, *13*(3), 319–340. doi:10.2307/249008

Davis, F. D., Bagozzi, R. P., & Warshaw, P. R. (1989). User acceptance of Information Technology: A comparison of two theoretical models. *Management Science*, *35*(8), 982–1003. doi:10.1287/mnsc.35.8.982

Davis, F. D. (1989). Perceived usefulness, perceived ease of use and user acceptance of Information Technology. *Management Information Systems Quarterly*, *13*(3), 318–339. doi:10.2307/249008

Dawes, S. (1996). Interagency information sharing: Expected benefits, manageable risks. *Journal of Policy Analysis and Management*, *15*(3), 377–394. doi:10.1002/(SICI)1520-6688(199622)15:3<377::AID-PAM3>3.0.CO;2-F

Dawes, S. S. (2008). The evolution and continuing challenges of e-governance. *Public Administration Review*, *68*(s1), s86–s102. doi:10.1111/j.1540-6210.2008.00981.x

Dawes, S. (1996). Interagency information sharing: Expected benefits, manageable risks. *Journal of Policy Analysis and Management*, *15*(3), 377–394. doi:10.1002/(SICI)1520-6688(199622)15:3<377::AID-PAM3>3.0.CO;2-F

Dawes, S., Cresswell, A., & Pardo, T. (2009). From need to know to need to share: Tangled problems, information boundaries, and the building of public sector knowledge networks. *Public Administration Review*, *69*(3), 392–402. doi:10.1111/j.1540-6210.2009.01987_2.x

Deloitte, R. (2000). *At the dawn of e-government: The citizen as customer*. New York, NY: Deloitte Research.

DeLone, W. H., & McLean, E. R. (1992). Information System success: The quest for the dependent variable. *Information Systems Research*, *3*(1), 60–95. doi:10.1287/isre.3.1.60

DeLone, W. H., & McLean, E. R. (2003). The DeLone and McLean model of Information System success: A ten-year update. *Journal of Management Information Systems*, *19*(4), 9–30.

Denhardt, R., & Denhardt, J. (2007). *The new public service: Serving, not steering*. New York, NY: M. E. Sharpe Inc.

Der Beauftragte der Bundesregierung für Informationstechnik. (2008, August 24). *Standards and architecture for e-government*. Retrieved August 30, 2010, from http:// www.CIO.bund.de/ cln_164/ DE/ Standards/ SAGA/ saga_node.html

Deutsch Karlekar, K., & Cook, S. G. (2009a). *Freedom on the net: A global assessment of Internet and digital media – China*. Washington, DC: Freedom House.

Diller, E. C. (2001). *Citizens in service: The challenge of delivering civic engagement training to national service programs*. Washington, DC: Corporation for National Service. Retrieved April 28, 2009, from http://www.nationalserviceresources.org/ files/legacy/filemanager/ download /457/diller.pdf

Dimitrova, D., & Chen, Y.-C. (2006). Profiling the adopters of e-government information and services: The influence of psychological characteristics, civic mindedness, and information channels. *Social Science Computer Review*, *24*(2), 172–188. doi:10.1177/0894439305281517

Djankov, S., McLiesh, C., Nenova, T., & Shleifer, A. (2003). Who owns the media? *The Journal of Law & Economics*, *46*, 341–381. doi:10.1086/377116

Dong, R., & Yang, T. (2006). Wangshang yizheng cuisheng minyi shengchanli (Political workshops on the Internet boost the production of public opinion). Liaowang Zhoukan, 11. Retrieved from http://news.xinhuanet.com/misc/2006-03/13/ content_4297654.htm

Donohue, G. A., Tichenor, P. J., & Olien, C. N. (1995). A guard dog perspective on the role of media. *The Journal of Communication*, *45*(2), 115–132. doi:10.1111/j.1460-2466.1995.tb00732.x

Downes, S. (2004). Educational blogging. *EDUCAUSE Review*, *9*(5), 14–26.

Dublin Core Metadata Initiative. (1995-2010). *DCMI home: Dublic Core (R) metadata initiative*. Retrieved August 30, 2010, from http://dublincore.org

Dugdale, A., Daly, A., Papandrea, F., & Maley, M. (2005). Acessing e-government: Challenges for citizens and organizations. *International Review of Administrative Science, 71*(1), 109–118. doi:10.1177/0020852305051687

Edmiston, K. D. (2003). State and local e-government: Prospects and challenges. *American Review of Public Administration, 33*(1), 20–45. doi:10.1177/0275074002250255

E-Government Act. (2002). *E-Government Act.* (Pub. L. No. 107-347, 116 Stat. 2899).

Elkins, D. J. (1997). Globalization, telecommunication, and virtual ethnic communities. *International Political Science Review, 18*(2), 139–152. doi:10.1177/019251297018002002

Elliott, K. M., Hall, M. C., & Meng, J. (2008). Student technology readiness and its impact on cultural competency. *College Teaching Methods & Styles Journal, 4*(6), 11–22.

Elster, J. (1998). Introduction. In Elster, J. (Ed.), *Deliberative democracy* (pp. 1–18). New York, NY: Cambridge University Press.

Estevez, E., Fillottrani, P., & Janowski, T. (2010). *Information sharing in government - Conceptual model for policy formulation.* 10th European Conference on eGovernment, Limerick, Ireland.

European Commission. (2009a). *E-government: E-participation.* Retrieved August 2010 from http://ec.europa.eu/ information_society /activities/egovernment/ policy/ eparticipation /index_en.htm

European Commission. (2009b). *E-inclusion.* Retrieved August 2010 from http://ec.europa.eu/ information_society/ activities/einclusion/ index_en.htm

Eyob, E. (2004). E-government: Breaking the frontier of inefficiencies in the public sector. *Electronic Government, 1*(1), 107–114. doi:10.1504/EG.2004.004140

Fagan, J. C., & Fagan, B. D. (2001). Citizens access to on-line legislative documents. *Government Information Quarterly, 18*, 105–121. doi:10.1016/S0740-624X(01)00064-8

Fassihi, F., & Rhoads, C. (2009, September 18). Iranian diaspora joins to protest Ahmadinejad. *Wall Street Journal.* Retrieved May 1, 2010 from http://online.wsj.com/ article/ SB125322907482521229.html

Featherman, M. S., & Pavlou, P. A. (2003). Predicting e-service adoption: A perceived risk facets perspective. *International Journal of Human-Computer Studies, 59*, 451–474. doi:10.1016/S1071-5819(03)00111-3

Federal Geographic Data Committee. (2006, September 29). *Benefits - Federal Geographic Data Committee.* Retrieved August 30, 2010, from http://www.fgdc.gov/ framework/ handbook/ benefits

Fedorowicz, J., Gogan, J. L., & Williams, C. B. (2007). A collaborative network for first responders: Lessions from the CapWIN case. *Government Information Quarterly, 24*, 785–807. doi:10.1016/j.giq.2007.06.001

Ferber, P., Foltz, F., & Pugliese, R. (2004). *Cyberdemocracy v. e-government: The degree of interactivity on state legislative websites.* Paper presented at the 2004 Meeting of the American Political Science Association, Chicago, IL.

Fieldman, M. S., & Khademian, A. M. (2007). The role of public management in inclusion: Creating communities of participation. *Governance: An International Journal of Policy. Administration and Institution, 20*(2), 305–324.

Finger, M., & Pecoud, G. (2003). *From e-government to e-governance? Towards a model of e-governance.* Paper presented at the 3rd European Conference on e-Government, Trinity College Dublin, Ireland.

Fishbein, M., & Ajzen, I. (1975). *Belief, attitude, intention, and behavior: An introduction to theory and research.* Reading, MA: Addison-Wesley.

Fisher, D. (2004, September). *The business process maturity model - A practical approach for identifying opportunities for optimization.* Retrieved August 27, 2010, from http://www.bptrends.com/publicationfiles/ 10-04% 20ART% 20BP%20 Maturity%20 Model%20 -%20 Fisher.pdf

Flak, F., Olsen, D. H., & Wolcott, P. (2005). Local e-government in Norway. Current status and emerging issues. *Scandinavian Journal of Information Systems, 17*(2), 41–84.

Fletcher, O. (2008, September 12). China's transparency is just thin air. *Online Asia Times.* Retrieved February 13, 2010, from http://www.atimes.com/atimes /China/ J112Ad01.html

Florini, A. (2007). The battle over transparency. In Florini, A. (Ed.), *The right to know: Transparency for an open world* (pp. 1–16). New York, NY: Columbia University Press.

Florini, A. (1999). *Does the invisible hand need a transparent glove? The politics of transparency.* Washington, DC: Annual World Bank Conference on Development Economics.

Fornell, C. (2007). *The satisfied customer: Winners and losers in the battle for buyer preference.* New York, NY: Palgrave Macmillan.

Fornell, C., Johnson, M. D., Anderson, E. W., Cha, J., & Bryant, B. E. (1996). The American customer satisfaction index: Nature, purpose and findings. *Journal of Marketing, 60*(4), 7–18. doi:10.2307/1251898

Fornell, C., Van Amburg, D., Morgeson, F. V. III, Bryant, B., Anderson, G., & Johnson, M. (2005). *The American customer satisfaction index at 10 years.* Ann Arbor, MI: The Stephen M. Ross School of Business.

Fountain, J. E. (2001). *Building the virtual state: Information Technology and institutional change.* Washington, DC: Brookings Institution Press.

Fountain, J. E. (2001). *Building the virtual state: Information Technology and institutional change.* Washington, DC: Brookings Institution Press.

Fraunholz, B., & Unnithan, C. (2008). E-governance: Enabling the French Web 2.0 revolution? In A. Agarwal & V. V. Ramana (Eds.), *Foundations of e-government* (pp. 344-359). Retrieved January 18, 2009, from http:// www.iceg.net/2007/ books/1/36_363.pdf

Freedom House. (2009a). *Freedom in the world – China.* Washington, DC: Freedom House.

Freedom House. (2009b). *Freedom in the world – India.* Washington, DC: Freedom House.

Freedom House. (2009c). *Freedom in the world methodology.* Washington, DC: Freedom House.

FreshMinds. (2009). *Understanding digital inclusion - A research summary* [Electronic Version]. Retrieved August 2010 from http://research.freshminds.co.uk/ files/ u1/shminds_report_ understandingdigitalinclusion.pdf

Fricker, R. D., & Schonlau, M. (2002). Advantages and disadvantages of Internet research surveys: Evidence from the literature. *Field Methods, 14*(4), 347–367. doi:10.1177/152582202237725

Fricker, S., Galesic, M., Tourangeau, R., & Yan, T. (2005). An experimental comparison of Web and telephone surveys. *Public Opinion Quarterly, 69*(3), 370–392. doi:10.1093/poq/nfi027

Fullenbaum, R., & McNeill, M. (1995). *Survey and comparison of distressed area definitions.* Washington, DC: Appalachian Regional Commission.

G-7. (1997). *Government strategies and the new Information Technologies.* Retrieved December 3, 2009, from http://www.open.gov.uk/ govonline/golint ro.htm

Garthwaite, P. H. (1994). An interpretation of partial least squares. *Journal of the American Statistical Association, 89*(425), 122–127. doi:10.2307/2291207

Gastil, J. (2000). Face-to-face citizen deliberation: A luxury or necessity? *Political Communication, 17*, 357–361. doi:10.1080/10584600050178960

Gefen, D., Karahanna, E., & Straub, D. W. (2003). Trust and TAM in online shopping: An integrated model. *Management Information Systems Quarterly, 27*(1), 51–90.

General Service Administration. (2008). *Government and social media.* Washington, DC: Office of Citizen Services, General Service Administration.

General Service Administration. (2010). *A 25-minute morning with the Center for New Media and Citizen Engagement.* Washington, DC: The Center for New Media and Citizen Engagement, U.S. General Service Administration.

Ghorashi, H., & Boersma, K. (2009). The Iranian Diaspora and the new media: From political action to humanitarian help. *Development and Change, 40*(4), 667–691. doi:10.1111/j.1467-7660.2009.01567.x

Giddens, A. (1984). *The constitution of society: Outline of the theory of Structuration*. Berkeley, CA: University of California Press.

Gilbert, D., Balestrini, P., & Littleboy, D. (2004). Barriers and benefits in the adoption of e-government. *International Journal of Public Sector Management, 17*(4), 286–301. doi:10.1108/09513550410539794

Giles, J. (2005). Internet encyclopaedias go head to head. *Nature, 438*, 900–901. doi:10.1038/438900a

Gil-Garcia, J. R., Chengalur-Smith, I., & Duchessi, P. (2007). Collaborative e-government: Impediments and benefits of information-sharing projects in the public sector. *European Journal of Information Systems, 16*, 121–133. doi:10.1057/palgrave.ejis.3000673

Gil-Garcia, J. R., Pardo, T. A., & Burke, B. (2010). Conceptualizing information integration in government. In Scholl, J. (Ed.), *Electronic government, information, technology and transformation*. M.E. Sharpe.

Gil-Garcia, J. R., Chun, S. A., & Janssen, M. (2009). Government information sharing and integration: Combining the social and the technical. *Information Polity, 14*(2).

Gil-Garcia, J. R., Schneider, C. A., Pardo, T. A., & Cresswell, A. M. (2005). *Interorganizational information integration in the criminal justice enterprise: Preliminary lessons from state and county initiatives*. 38th Hawaii International Conference on System Sciences (p. 8). IEEE Computer Society.

Gisler, M., & Spahni, D. (2001). *E-government*. Haupt.

Global Integrity. (2009a). *China: Integrity indicators scorecard*. Retrieved March 10, 2010, from http://report.globalintegrity.org /China/2009/scorecard/print

Global Integrity. (2009b). India: Integrity indicators scorecard. Retrieved March 10, 2010, from http://report.globalintegrity.org /India/2009/scorecard/print

Global Privacy and Information Quality Working Group (GPIQWG). (2010). *Privacy and information quality*. Retrieved August 30, 2010, from http://www.it.ojp.gov/default.aspx? area=globalJustice& page=1151

Golding, P. (1996). World wide wedge: Division and contradiction in the global information infrastructure. *Monthly Review (New York, N.Y.), 48*(3), 70–85.

Goldkuhl, G., & Persson, A. (2006). *From e-ladder to e-diamond - Re-conceptualizing models for public e-services*. Paper presented at the 14th European Conference on Information Systems, June 2006.

Goldsmith, S. E. W. (2004). *Governing by network: The new shape of the public sector*. Boston, MA & Washington, DC: Innovations in American Government, John F. Kennedy School of Government; Brookings Institution Press.

Golub, A., & Lingley, K. (2008). Just like the Qing empire: Internet addiction, MMOGs, and moral crisis in contemporary China. *Games and Culture, 3*(1), 59–75. doi:10.1177/1555412007309526

González, R., Gasco, J., & Llopis, J. (2007). E-government success. Some principles from a Spanish case study. *Industrial Management and Data, 107*(6), 845–867. doi:10.1108/02635570710758752

Goswani, O. (2006). Elephants can dance: India's response to globalization and the challenges she faces. In Kelly, D. A., Rajan, R. S., & Goh, G. H. L. (Eds.), *Managing globalization: Lessons from China and India* (pp. 75–113). London, UK: World Scientific. doi:10.1142/9789812774729_0004

GovDex Team. (2010). *The Australian government collaborative workspace - Govdex*. Retrieved August 27, 2010, from http://www.govdex.gov.au/

Government Reform and Innovation. (n. d.). Retrieved September 1, 2010, from http://www.rdec.gov.tw/ mp.asp?mp=14

Graham, M., & Khosravi, S. (2002). Reordering public and private in Iranian cyberspace: Identity, politics, and mobilization. *Identities (Yverdon), 9*(2), 219–246. doi:10.1080/10702890212204

Gray, A., Jenkins, B., Leeuw, F., & Mayne, J. (2003). *Collaboration in public services* (*Vol. 10*). New Brunswick, NJ & London, UK: Transaction Publishers.

Greenberg, S. R. (2006). *State e-government strategies: Identifying best practices and applications*. Report for the Congressional Research Service. Retrieved June 14, 2007, from http://www.utexas.edu/lbj /pubs/isbn/egovernment

Grigorescu, A. (2002). European institutions and unsuccessful norm transmission: The case of transparency. *International Politics*, *39*, 467–489. doi:10.1057/palgrave.ip.8892005

Grigorescu, A. (2003). International organizations and government transparency: Linking the international development realms. *International Studies Quarterly*, *47*, 643–667. doi:10.1046/j.0020-8833.2003.04704003.x

Gronroos, C. (1990). *Service management and marketing: Managing the moments of truth in service competition*. Lexington, MA: Lexington Books.

Gu, D. W. (2008). China E-government Current Stage and Development Trend Speech on 2008 China E-government Forum. Retrieved from http://www.ccidit.com/ readthread-175.html

Guha Thakurta, P. (2009, October 3). Can India's economy overtake China? *BBC News*. Retrieved on February 20, 2010, from http://news.bbc.co.uk/ 2/hi/8273464.stm

Habermas, J. (1996). *Between facts and norms: Contributions to a discourse theory of law and democracy*. Cambridge, MA: MIT Press.

Habermas, J. (1984. 1987). *Theory of communicative action*, vols. 1 and 2. Boston, MA: Beacon Press.

Hair, F. Jr, Anderson, R. E., Tatham, R. L., & Black, W. C. (1998). *Multivariate data analysis* (5th ed.). Basingstoke, UK: Macmillan.

Hakimzadeh, S. (2006). *Iran: A vast diaspora abroad and millions of refugees at home*. Migration Policy Institute. Retrieved May 1, 2010, from http://www.migrationinformation.org/ Profiles/display.cfm?ID=424

Halachmi, A. (2004). *E-government theory and practice: The evidence from Tennessee (USA)*. Retrieved September 28, 2010, from http://unpan1.un.org/intradoc/groups/public/documents/un/unpan019248.pdf

Hale, M., Musso, J., & Weare, C. (1999). Developing digital democracy: Evidence from Californian municipal Web pages. In Hague, B. N., & Loader, B. D. (Eds.), *Digital democracy: Discourse and decision making in the information age* (pp. 96–115). London, UK: Routledge.

Hall, P. A., & Taylor, C. R. (1996). Political science and the three new institutionalisms. *Political Studies*, *44*(5), 936–957. doi:10.1111/j.1467-9248.1996.tb00343.x

Hall, S. (2003). Cultural identity and diaspora. In J. E. Braziel & A. Mannur (Ed), *Theorizing diaspora* (233-246). Oxford, UK: Blackwell Publishing Ltd.

Hammer, M., & Champy, J. (1993). *Reengineering the corporation*. London, UK: Nicholas Brealy.

Han, Z. J. (2001, December 1st). Li Lanqing Emphasize in a National Tax Work Conference that We Should Improve Tax Supervision through Tax Informatization Construction. *People's Daily*, pp. A1.

Han, Z. J. (2002, July 1st). Zhu Rongji Emphasized Facing New Situations and Score New Achievements. *People's Daily*, pp. A1.

Hartley, J. (2005). Innovation in governance and public services: Past and present. *Public Money and Management*, *25*(1), 27–34.

Harwit, E., & Clark, D. (2001). Shaping the Internet in China: Evolution of political control over network infrastructure and content. *Asian Survey*, *41*, 377–408. doi:10.1525/as.2001.41.3.377

Hatry, H. P. (2006). *Performance measurement: Getting results*. Washington, DC: Urban Institute Press.

Hay, C., & Wincott, D. (1998). Structure, agency and historical institutionalism. *Political Studies*, *46*, 951–957. doi:10.1111/1467-9248.00177

Heeks, R., & Bailur, S. (2007). Analyzing e-government research: Perspectives, philosophies, theories, methods, and practice. *Government Information Quarterly*, *24*, 243–265. doi:10.1016/j.giq.2006.06.005

Heeks, R. (1999). *Reinventing government in the information age: International practice in IT-enabled public sector reform*. London, UK & New York, NY: Routledge. doi:10.4324/9780203204962

Heeks, R. (2006). *Benchmarking e-government: Improving the national and international measurement, evaluation and comparison of e-government*. Paper presented at iGovernment Working Paper, 18, Manchester, UK: University of Manchester.

Hertfordshire Constabulary. (2008, October). *Standard operating procedure title: Information sharing - Procedure number: P60105_1.* Retrieved August 30, 2010, from http://www.herts.police.uk/ FOI/ corporate_support_policies/ P60105_Procedure.pdf

Hesson, M., & Al-Ameed, H. (2007). Business process reengineering in UAE public sector: A town planning case study. *Business Process Management Journal, 13*(3), 348–378. doi:10.1108/14637150710752281

Hilbert, M. (2009). The maturing concept of e-democracy: From e-voting and online consultations to democratic value out of jumbled online chatter. *Journal of Information Technology & Politics, 6*(2), 87–110. doi:10.1080/19331680802715242

Hiller, H. H., & Franz, T. M. (2004). New ties, old ties and lost ties: The use of the Internet in diaspora. *New Media & Society, 6*(6), 731–752. doi:10.1177/146144804044327

Hiller, J. S., & Belanger, F. (2001). *Privacy strategies for electronic government.* The PricewaterhouseCoopers Endowment for The Business of Government, Arlington, VA. Retrieved June 19, 2007, from http://www.businessofgovernment.org /pdfs/HillerReport.pdf

Ho, A., & Ni, A. Y. (2004). Explaining the adoption of e-government features: A case study of Iowa County Treasurers' offices. *American Review of Public Administration, 34*(2), 164–180. doi:10.1177/0275074004264355

Ho, A. T. K. (2002). Reinventing local governments and the e-government initiative. *Public Administration Review, 62*(4), 434–444. doi:10.1111/0033-3352.00197

Holden, S. H., Norris, D. F., & Fletcher, P. D. (2002, January). Electronic government at the grass roots: Contemporary evidence and future trends. *Proceedings of the 36th Hawaii International Conference on System Sciences*, Hawaii.

Holliday, I., & Yep, R. (2005). E-government in China. *Public Administration and Development, 25*, 239–249. doi:10.1002/pad.361

Holmes, M. (2007). Culture without the state? Reinvigorating Ukrainian culture with diasporic efforts. *Review of Policy Research, 24*(2), 133–154. doi:10.1111/j.1541-1338.2007.00273.x

Holzer, M., & Yang, K. (2004). Performance measurement and improvement: An assessment of the state of the art. *International Review of the Administrative Sciences, 70*(1), 15–31. doi:10.1177/0020852304041228

Holzer, M., & Kim, S. T. (2006). *Digital governance in municipalities worldwide (2005): A longitudinal assessment of municipal websites throughout the world.* The E-Governance Institute National Center for Public Performance.

Holzer, M., & Kim, S. T. (2008). *Digital governance in municipalities worldwide (2007): A longitudinal assessment of municipal websites throughout the world.* The E-Governance Institute National Center for Public Performance.

Holzer, M., & Zhang, M. (2009). Introduction to the special issue on comparative Chinese/American public administration. *Public Administration Review*, S5–S12. doi:10.1111/j.1540-6210.2009.02083.x

Holzer, M. (2007). Global trends in municipal e-government: An online assessment of worldwide municipal Web portals. In Agarwal, A., & Ramana, V. V. (Eds.), *Foundations of e-government.* Computer Society of India.

Holzer, M. (2004, May). *Restoring trust in government: The potential of digital citizen participation.* Paper presented at the Second Sino-U.S. International Conference: Public Administration in the Changing World? China, Beijing.

Holzer, M., & Kim, S. (2007). *Digital governance in municipalities worldwide -- A longitudinal assessment of municipal websites throughout the world.* Paper presented at The e-governance Institute, National Center for Public Performance, Rutgers, the State University of New Jersey, Campus at Newark.

Homburg, V. (2000). The political economy of information exchange politics and property rights in the development and use of interorganizational Information Systems. *Knowledge, Technology, &. Policy, 13*(3), 49–66.

Hong, I. B. (2002). A new framework for interorganizational systems based on the linkage of participants' roles. *Information & Management, 39*, 261–270. doi:10.1016/S0378-7206(01)00095-7

Hoonakker, P., & Carayon, P. (2009). Questionnaire survey nonresponse: A comparison of postal mail and Internet surveys. *International Journal of Human-Computer Interaction*, *25*(5), 348–373. doi:10.1080/10447310902864951

Horan, T. A., Abhichandani, T., & Rayalu, R. (2006). *Assessing user satisfaction of e-government services: Development and testing of quality-in-use satisfaction with Advanced Traveler Information System (ATIS)*. Paper presented at the 39th Hawaii International Conference on System Sciences, Hawaii.

Horsley, J. P. (2006). Introduction on open government information implementation. *Government Information Quarterly*, *23*(1), 5–10. doi:10.1016/j.giq.2006.02.007

Horsley, J. P. (2007a). Toward an open China? In Florini, A. (Ed.), *The right to know: Transparency in an open world* (pp. 54–91). New York, NY: Columbia University Press.

Horsley, J. P. (2007b). *China adopts first nationwide open government information regulations*. Retrieved February 9, 2010, from freedominfo.org/features /20070509.htm

Horsley, J. P. (2010, April 23). *Update on China's open government information regulations: Surprising public demand yielding some positive results*. Washington, DC: FreedomInfo.org. Retrieved on April 23, 2010, from http://www.freedominfo.org/ 2010/04/update-on-china -open-government-information -regulations

Horst, M., Kuttschreuter, M., & Gutteling, G. M. (2007). Perceived usefulness, personal experiences, risk perception and trust as determinants of adoption of e-government services in The Netherlands. *Computers in Human Behavior*, *23*(4), 1838–1852. doi:10.1016/j.chb.2005.11.003

Howard, M. (2001). E-government across the globe: How will "e" change government? *Government Finance Review*, *17*(4), 6–9.

Hsiao, N. Y., & Lo, J. (2010). An value-chain evaluation framework for electronic government. [in Chinese]. *Journal of Public Administration*, *35*(1), 1–37.

Hu, L., & Bentler, P. M. (1995). Evaluating model fit. In Hoyle, R. H. (Ed.), *Structural equation modeling: Concepts, issues, and applications* (pp. 76–99). Thousand Oaks, CA: SAGE.

Huang, C. J., & Chao, M.-H. (2001). Managing WWW in public administration: Uses and misuses. *Government Information Quarterly*, *18*(4), 357–373. doi:10.1016/S0740-624X(01)00085-5

Huang, Z. (2006). E-government practices at local levels: An analysis of U.S. counties websites. *Issues in Information Systems*, *7*(2), 165–170.

Huang, M., Li, X., & Zeng, X. (2007, May). *Service quality in Web 2.0 electronic commerce: An integrative perspective from typical service and technique-adoption*. Paper presented at the meeting of the International Conference on Wireless Communications, Networking and Mobile Computing, Shanghai, China.

Hughes, M., Scott, M., & Golden, W. (2006). The role of business process redesign in creating e-government in Ireland. *Business Process Management Journal*, *12*(1), 76–87. doi:10.1108/14637150610643779

Hunag, T. Y., & Lee, C. P. (2010). Evaluating the impact of e-government on citizens: A cost-benefit analysis. In Reddick, C. G. (Ed.), *Citizens and e-government: Evaluating policy and management* (pp. 37–52). Hershey, PA: IGI Global. doi:10.4018/978-1-61520-931-6.ch003

Hunag, C. M., Chu, P. Y., & Huang, T. Y. (2008). *Evaluation and analysis of e-governance in Taiwan* (G2G, G2E). Taiwan e-Governance Research Center. Taipei. Retrieved August 27, 2010, from http://www.teg.org.tw/research / view.do?id=24&language=en

Hung, S. Y., & Chang, C. M. (2005). User acceptance of WAP services: Test of competing theories. *Computer Standards & Interfaces*, *27*(4), 359–370. doi:10.1016/j.csi.2004.10.004

Hung, S. Y., Chang, C. M., & Yua, T. J. (2006). Determinants of user acceptance of the e-government services: The case of online tax filing and payment system. *Government Information Quarterly*, *23*(1), 97–122. doi:10.1016/j.giq.2005.11.005

ICMA. (2005). *The municipality yearbook 2005*. Washington, DC: International City/County Management Association (ICMA).

Igbaria, M., Guimaraes, T., & Davis, G. B. (1995). Testing the determinants of microcomputer usage via a structural equation model. *Journal of Management Information Systems, 11*(4), 87–114.

Information Sharing Environment Office of the Director of National Intelligence. (2010). *Information sharing environment*. Retrieved August 30, 2010, from http://www.ise.gov/Homepage.aspx

Internal Revenue Service. (2009, December 22). *Fed/State information sharing*. Retrieved August 30, 2010, from http://www.irs.gov/ govt/ liaisons/ article/ 0,id=133087,00.html

International City/County Management Association. (2002). *Electronic government 2002*. Washington, DC: International City/County Management Association.

International City/County Management Association. (2004). *2004 e-government survey*. Washington, DC: International City/County Management Association.

International Organization for Standardization. (1999). *ISO 3166 code lists*. Retrieved August 30, 2010, from http://www.iso.org/ iso/ country_codes/ iso_3166_code_lists.htm

Irani, Z., Al-Sebie, M., & Elliman, T. (2006). Transaction stage of e-government systems: Identification of its location & importance. *Proceedings of the 39th Hawaii International Conference on System Sciences, 2006.*

Islam, R. (2006). Does more transparency go along with better governance? *Economics and Politics, 18*(2), 121–167. doi:10.1111/j.1468-0343.2006.00166.x

Issa-Salwe, A. (2006). The Internet and Somali diaspora-The Web as a means of expression. *Bildham: An International Journal for Somali Studies, 6*, 54-67. Retrieved from http://digitalcommons.macalester.edu /cgi/viewcontent.cgi?article=1056

ITACG. (2010, September 03). *Interagency thread assessment and coordination group*. Retrieved August 30, 2010, from http://www.ise.gov/ITACG.aspx

ITU. (2005, August). *X.509*. Retrieved August 29, 2010, from http://www.itu.int/ itu-t/ recommendations/ rec.aspx?rec=X.509

Jaeger, P. T. (2003). The endless wire: E-government as global phenomenon. *Government Information Quarterly, 20*(4), 323–331. doi:10.1016/j.giq.2003.08.003

James, J. (2008). The digital divide across all citizens of the world: A new concept. *Social Indicators Research, 89*(2), 275–282. doi:10.1007/s11205-007-9156-9

James, Y. (2003). *E-government in Asia: Enabling public service innovation in the 21st century*. Times Edition.

Janssen, D., Rotthier, S., & Snijkers, K. (2004). If you measure it they will score: An assessment of international e-government benchmarking. *Information Polity, 9*, 121–130.

Janssen, M., & Veenstra, A. F. v. (2005). Stages of growth in e-government: An architectural approach. *The Electronic. Journal of E-Government, 3*(4), 193–200.

Jarboe, G. (April 8, 2010). Rip Van Winkle: "Things change fast in today's world." Retrieved from http://blog.searchenginewatch.com/100408-093526.

Jenkins, R., & Goetz, A. M. (1999). Accounts and accountability: Theoretical implications of the right–to–information movement in India. *Third World Quarterly, 20*(3), 603–622. doi:10.1080/01436599913712

Jennings, M. K., & Zeitner, V. (2003). Internet use and civic engagement. *Public Opinion Quarterly, 67*(3), 311–334. doi:10.1086/376947

Jiang, A. L., & Chen, Z. R. (2007). *Research on Grid Municipal Management Mode*. Modern Urban Research.

Jing, F., & Zhang, P. (2009). *A field study of G2G information sharing in Chinese context based on the layered behavioral model*. 42st Hawaii International International Conference on Systems Science (HICSS-42 2009). IEEE Computer Society.

Joseph, R. C., & Jeffers, P. I. (2009). E-government in the Caribbean nations. *Journal of Global Information Technology Management, 12*(1), 52–70.

Kaaya, J. (2004). Implementing e-government services in East Africa: Assessing status through content analysis of government websites. *The Electronic. Journal of E-Government, 2*(1), 39–54.

Kahai, S. S., & Cooper, R. B. (2003). Exploring the core concepts of media richness theory: The impact of cue multiplicity and feedback immediacy on decision quality. *Journal of Management Information Systems*, *20*(1), 263–299.

Kahne, J., Chi, B., & Middaugh, E. (2002). *City works evaluation summary*. Los Angeles, CA: Constitutional Rights Foundation.

Kaldor, M., & Vejvoda, I. (1997). Democratization in East and Central European countries. *International Affairs*, *73*(1), 59–83. doi:10.2307/2623550

Kaplowitz, M. D., Hadlock, T. D., & Levine, R. (2004). A comparison of Web and mail survey response rates. *Public Opinion Quarterly*, *68*(1), 94–101. doi:10.1093/poq/nfh006

Kaufman, H. (1977). *Red tape: Its origins, uses, and abuses*. Washington, DC: Brookings Institution.

Kaufman, J. (2010). Turning points in China's AIDS response. *China. International Journal (Toronto, Ont.)*, *8*(1), 63–84.

Kaylor, C., Deshazo, R., & Van Eck, D. (2001). Gauging e-government: A report on implementing services among American cities. *Government Information Quarterly*, *18*(4), 293–307. doi:10.1016/S0740-624X(01)00089-2

Keehley, P. S., Medlin, S., MacBride, S., & Longmire, L. (1996). *Benchmarking for best practices in the public sector*. San Francisco, CA: Jossey-Bass.

Kelly, J., & Swindell, D. (2002). A multiple indicator approach to municipal service evaluation: Correlating performance and citizen satisfaction across jurisdictions. *Public Administration Review*, *62*(5), 610–621. doi:10.1111/1540-6210.00241

Kelly, J. M., & Swindell, D. (2002). Service quality variation across urban space: First steps towards a model of citizen satisfaction. *Journal of Urban Affairs*, *24*(3), 271–288. doi:10.1111/1467-9906.00127

Kettinger, W. J., Teng, T. C., & Guha, S. (1997). Business process change: A study of methodologies, techniques, and tools. *Management Information Systems Quarterly*, *21*(1), 55–81. doi:10.2307/249742

Khademian, A. (2002). *Working with culture: The way the job gets done in public programs*. Washington, DC: CQ Press.

Kim, J. (2006). The impact of Internet use patterns on political engagement: A focus on online deliberation and virtual social capital. *Information Polity*, *11*, 35–49. doi:10.1108/09593840610700800

Kinder, T. (2002). Vote early, vote often? Democracy in European cities. *Public Administration*, *8*(3), 557–582. doi:10.1111/1467-9299.00318

Kissau, K. (2009). Online spheres of migrants in Germany: How and why migrants use the Internet. In C. Dietz & P. Stammen, *Media on the move: Migrants and minorities and the media* (pp. 80-84). 4th Symposium on Forum Media and Development, held in Bonn, 2008. Aachen, Germany: Catholic Media Council (CAMECO). Retrieved May 1, 2010, from http://www.cameco.org/files/mediaonthemove_ complete_1.pdf

Klievink, B., & Janssen, M. (2009). Realizing joined-up government: Dynamic capabilities and stage models for transformation. *Government Information Quarterly*, *26*, 275–284. doi:10.1016/j.giq.2008.12.007

Kluver, R. (2005). The architecture of control: A Chinese strategy for e-governance. *Journal of Public Policy*, *25*(1), 75–97. doi:10.1017/S0143814X05000218

Kluver, R., & Yang, C. (2005). The Internet in China: A meta-review of research. *The Information Society*, *21*, 301–308. doi:10.1080/01972240591007616

Koh, J., & Kim, Y. G. (2004). Knowledge sharing in virtual communities: An e-business perspective. *Expert Systems with Applications*, *26*, 155–166. doi:10.1016/S0957-4174(03)00116-7

Kollock, P. (1999). The economies of online cooperation: Gifts and public goods in cyberspace. In Smith, M., & Kollock, P. (Eds.), *Communities in cyberspace* (pp. 220–239). London, UK: Routledge.

Korteland, E., & Bekkers, V. (2007). Diffusion of e-government innovations in the Dutch public sector: The case of digital community policing. *Information Polity*, *12*, 139–150.

Kotler, P. (Ed.). (1994). *Marketing management: Analysis, planning, implementation and control*. Englewood Cliffs, NJ: Prentice-Hall.

Kouzmin, A., Loffler, E., Klages, H., & Kakabadse, N. (1999). Benchmarking and performance measurement in public sectors. *International Journal of Public Sector Management*, *12*(2), 121–144. doi:10.1108/09513559910263462

Kraemer, K., & King, J. L. (2008). Information Technology and administrative reform: Will e-government be different? In Norris, D. (Ed.), *E-government research: Policy and management* (pp. 1–20). Hersey, PA: IGI Global.

Krueger, R. A., & Casey, M. A. (2009). *Focus groups: A practical guide for applied research*. Thousand Oaks, CA: Sage Publications.

Kumar, K., & van Dissel, H. G. (1996). Sustainable collaboration: Managing conflict and cooperation in interorganizational systems. *Management Information Systems Quarterly*, *20*(3), 279–300. doi:10.2307/249657

Lagerkvist, J. (2005). The rise of online public opinion in the People's Republic of China. *China. International Journal (Toronto, Ont.)*, *3*(1), 119–130.

Lam, W. (2005). Barriers to e-government integration. *The Journal of Enterprise Information Management*, *18*(5), 511–530. doi:10.1108/17410390510623981

Landsbergen, D. Jr, & Wolken, G. Jr. (2001). Realizing the promise: Government Information Systems and the fourth generation of Information Technology. *Public Administration Review*, *61*, 206–220. doi:10.1111/0033-3352.00023

Laudon, K. C., & Laudon, J. P. (2010). *Management Information Systems: Managing the digital firm* (11th ed.). Upper Saddle River, New Jersey.

Lawson-Body, A., Keengwe, J., Mukankusi, L., Illia, A., & Miller, G. (2008). E-government service delivery performance: An adaptation of the balanced scorecard to the public sector. *Journal of Electronic Commerce in Organizations*, *6*(2), 11–28. doi:10.4018/jeco.2008040102

Layne, K., & Lee, J. (2001). Developing fully functional e-government: A four stage model. *Government Information Quarterly*, *18*(1), 122–136. doi:10.1016/S0740-624X(01)00066-1

Lee, S. M., Kim, I., Rhee, S., & Trimi, S. (2006). The role of exogenous factors in technology acceptance: The case of object-oriented technology. *Information & Management*, *43*(4), 469–480. doi:10.1016/j.im.2005.11.004

Lee, J. (2010). 10 year retrospect on stage models of e-government: A qualitative meta-synthesis. *Government Information Quarterly*, *27*(3), 220–230. doi:10.1016/j.giq.2009.12.009

Lee, J., & Kim, J. (2007). Grounded theory analysis of e-government initiatives: Exploring perceptions of government authorities. *Government Information Quarterly*, *24*(1), 135–147. doi:10.1016/j.giq.2006.05.001

Lee, S. (2007). Environmental movements and social organizations in Shanghai. *China Information*, *21*, 269–298. doi:10.1177/0920203X07079647

Legislative Yuan. (2006). *The Freedom of Government Information Law*. Taipei, Taiwan: RDEC, Legislative Yuan.

Lekkas, D. (2003). Establishing and managing trust within the public key infrastructure. *Computer Communications*, *26*, 1815–1825. doi:10.1016/S0140-3664(03)00077-X

Lenihan, D. G. (2002). *E-government, federalism and democracy: The new governance*. Ottawa, Canada: Center for Collaborative Government. Retrieved June 14, 2009, from http://www-it.fmi.uni-sofia.bg/eg/ res/ktapublication_vol9e.pdf

Lenk, K., & Traunmuller, R. (2002). Preface to the focus theme on e-government. *Electronic Markets*, *12*, 145–147. doi:10.1080/101967802320245901

Lenk, K., & Traunmüller, R. (2002). Electronic government: Where are we heading? In Lenk, K., & Traunmüller, R. (Eds.), *Electronic government: First international conference, EGOV 2002* (pp. 1–9). New York, NY: Springer.

Li, C. X. (2009). *Quantitative Research on JiangXi Province Officials Blogs*. Unpublished doctoral dissertation, Peking University, Beijing.

Li, J., & Wu, Q. C. (2009). *The First Sino-us Economic Dialogue: All the important problems has been talked about except landing on the Moon*. Retrieved from http://www.chinanews.com.cn/ gn/news/2009/07-29/1794984.shtml

Liang, B., & Lu, H. (2010). Internet development, censorship, and cyber crimes in China. *Journal of Contemporary Justice*, *26*(1), 103–120. doi:10.1177/1043986209350437

Liljander, V., Gillberg, F., & Van Riel, A. (2006). Technology readiness and the evaluation and adoption of self-service technologies. *Journal of Retailing and Consumer Services*, *13*(3), 177–191. doi:10.1016/j.jretconser.2005.08.004

Lin, J. C., & Hsieh, P. L. (2006). The role of technology readiness in customers, perception and adoption of self-service technologies. *International Journal of Service Industry Management*, *17*(5), 497–517. doi:10.1108/09564230610689795

Lin, J. C., & Hsieh, P. L. (2007). The influence of technology readiness on satisfaction and behavioral intentions toward self-service technologies. *Computers in Human Behavior*, *23*(3), 1597–1615. doi:10.1016/j.chb.2005.07.006

Lin, M. C. (1993). Das amtsgeheimnis und recht auf information. [in Chinese]. *National Taiwan University Law Journal*, *23*(1), 51–86.

Lin, H. (2007, April 3rd). Automatic Human Face Recognition System Make a First Appearance in Beijing: it can recognize 500 thousand faces a second. *China Youth Daily*. Retrieved from http://zqb.cyol.com/content/ 2007-04/03/ content_1720026.htm

Linden, R. M. (2010). *Leading across boundaries: Creating collaborative agencies in a networked world.* San Francisco, CA: Jossey-Bass.

Lo, J. (2008a). Benefit and risk of electronic participation: Exploring citizen's cognitive attitude and behavior of using governmental websites. [in Chinese]. *Journal of Cyber Culture and Information Society*, *15*, 181–208.

Lo, J. (2008b). Towards an electronic democracy? Setting up the indicators for evaluating the democratization of the governmental websites in Taiwan. [in Chinese]. *Soochow Journal of Political Science*, *26*(1), 143–198.

Lociacano, E., Watson, R. T., & Goodhue, D. (2002). WebQUAL: A measure of website quality. *Marketing Educators' Conference. Marketing Theory and Applications*, *13*, 432–437.

Löfstedt, U. (2007). E-government services in local governments- A study of development in Swedish municipalities. *Journal of Organizational Transformation and Social Change*, *4*(2), 157–176. doi:10.1386/jots.4.2.157_1

Loiacono, E. T., Watson, R. T., & Goodhue, D. L. (2007). WebQual: An instrument for consumer evaluation of websites. *International Journal of Electronic Commerce*, *11*(3), 51–87. doi:10.2753/JEC1086-4415110302

Lollar, X. (2006). Assessing China's e-government: Information, service, transparency, and citizen outreach of government websites. *Journal of Contemporary China*, *15*(46), 31–41. doi:10.1080/10670560500331682

Lovelock, P., & Ure, J. (2003). E-government in China. Retrieved June 10, 2007, from http://www.trp.hku.hk/publications/e_gov_china.pdf

Lu, Y. B., Zhou, T., & Wang, B. (2009). Exploring Chinese users' acceptance of instant messaging using the theory of planned behavior, the technology acceptance model, and the flow theory. *Computers in Human Behavior*, *25*(1), 29–39. doi:10.1016/j.chb.2008.06.002

Luna-Reyes, L. F., Gil-Garcia, J. R., & Cruz, C. B. (2007). Collaborative digital government in Mexico: Some lesions from federal Web-based interorganizational information integration initiatives. *Government Information Quarterly*, *24*, 808–826. doi:10.1016/j.giq.2007.04.003

Ma, L., Chung, J., & Thorson, S. (2005). E-government in China: Bringing economic development through administrative reform. *Government Information Quarterly*, *22*, 20–37. doi:10.1016/j.giq.2004.10.001

Macintosh, A. (2006). E-participation in policy-making: The research and the challenges. In Cunningham, P., & Cunningham, M. (Eds.), *Exploiting the knowledge economy: Issues, applications and case studies*. Amsterdam, Netherlands & Washington, DC: IOS Press.

Macintosh, A. (2004, January). Characterizing e-participation in policy-making. *Proceedings of the 37th Hawaii International Conference on System Sciences,* Hawaii. Retrieved June 14, 2009, from http://csdl.computer.org/comp/ proceedings/hicss/2004/2056/05 /205650117a.pdf

Macintosh, A., & Whyte, A. (2002, August). *An evaluation framework for e-consultations?* Paper presented at the meeting of the International Association for Official Statistics conference, London, UK. Retrieved April 28, 2009, from http://www.statistics.gov.uk/ iaoslondon2002/ contributed_papers /downloads/IP_Macintosh.doc

Madlberger, M., & Kotzab, H. (2001). Adapting the Internet as distribution channel for stationary retailers: The American case. *Electronic Markets, 11*(1), 64–74. doi:10.1080/10196780151105465

Maheshwari, S. R. (2005). *Public administration in India – The higher civil service*. New Delhi, India: Oxford University Press.

Mahler, J. (2004). Influences of organizational culture on learning in public agencies. *Journal of Public Administration: Research and Theory, 7*(4), 519–540.

Mahrer, H., & Krimmer, R. (2005). Towards the enhancement of e-democracy: Identifying the notion of the "middleman paradox". *Information Systems Journal, 15*(1), 27–42. doi:10.1111/j.1365-2575.2005.00184.x

Marche, S., & McNiven, J. D. (2003). E-government and e-governance: The future isn't what it used to be. *Canadian Journal of Administrative Sciences, 20*(1), 74–86. doi:10.1111/j.1936-4490.2003.tb00306.x

Margetts, H. (1999). *Information Technology in government: Britain and America*. London, UK: Routledge.

McAdam, R., & Donaghy, J. (1999). Business process reengineering in the public sector: A study of staff perceptions and critical success factors. *Business Process Management Journal, 5*(1), 33–49. doi:10.1108/14637159910249135

McAuliffe, C. (2008). Transnationalism within: Internal diversity in the Iranian diaspora. *The Australian Geographer, 39*(1), 63–80. doi:10.1080/00049180701877436

McCarthy, R. V., & Aronson, J. E. (2000/2001). Activating consumer response: A model for website design strategy. *Journal of Computer Information Systems, 41*(2), 2–9.

McClure, C. R. (1994). Network literacy: A role for libraries? *Information Technology and Libraries, 13*(2), 116–117.

McDonagh, M. (2002). E-government in Australia: The challenge to privacy of personal information. *International Journal of Law and Information Technology, 10*(3), 327–343. doi:10.1093/ijlit/10.3.327

McGrath, J. E., & Hollingshead, A. B. (1994). *Groups interacting with technology: Ideas, evidence, issues, and an agenda*. Thousand Oaks, CA: Sage Publications.

McGuire, M., & Silvia, C. (2010). The effect of problem severity, managerial and organizational capacity, and agency structure on intergovernmental collaboration: Evidence from local emergency management. *Public Administration Review, 70*(2). doi:10.1111/j.1540-6210.2010.02134.x

McLachlan, G. J., & Peel, D. (2000). Mixtures of factor analyzers. In P. Langley (Ed.), *Proceedings of the Seventeenth International Conference on Machine Learning* (pp.599-606). San Francisco, CA: Morgan Kaufmann.

McNally, C. (2005). Global capitalism vs. Leninist controls: "Informatization" and e-government in the People's Republic of China. *Journal of E-Government, 2*(4), 3–14. doi:10.1300/J399v02n04_02

Meijer, A., & Thaens, M. (2010). Alignment 2.0: Strategic use of new Internet technologies in government. *Government Information Quarterly, 27*, 113–121. doi:10.1016/j.giq.2009.12.001

Mele, V. (2005). Paradigm and practice: The innovative organization to deal with e-government. In Khosrow-Pour, M. (Ed.), *Practicing e-government: A global perspective* (pp. 289–309). Hershey, PA: Idea Group. doi:10.4018/978-1-59140-637-2.ch013

Melitski, J. (2003). Capacity and e-government performance: An analysis based on early adopters of Internet technologies in New Jersey. *Public Performance and Management Review, 26*(4), 376–390. doi:10.1177/1530957603026004005

Mendel, T. (2008). *Freedom of information: A comparative legal survey* (2nd ed.). Paris, France: UNESCO.

Meuter, M. L., Ostrom, A. L., Bitner, M. J., & Roundtree, R. (2003). The influence of technology anxiety on consumer use and experiences with self-service technologies. *Journal of Business Research, 56*(11), 899–906. doi:10.1016/S0148-2963(01)00276-4

Meuter, M. L., Ostrom, A. L., Roundtree, R. I., & Bitner, M. J. (2000). Self-service technologies: Understanding customer satisfaction with technology-based service encounters. *Journal of Marketing*, *64*, 50–64. doi:10.1509/jmkg.64.3.50.18024

Michael, J. (1982). *The politics of secrecy: Confidential government and the right to know*. New York, NY: Penguin Books.

Miles, I., Rush, H., Turner, K., & Bessant, J. (1988). *Information horizons: The long-term social implications of new Information Technology*. London, UK: Edward Elgar.

Mills, R. T., & Krantz, D. S. (1979). Information, choice, and reactions to stress: A field experiment in a blood bank with laboratory analogue. *Journal of Personality and Social Psychology*, *37*(4), 608–620. doi:10.1037/0022-3514.37.4.608

Ministerio para las Administraciones Públicas (MAP). (2007). *Ley de acceso electrónico de los ciudadanos a los servicios públicos. Plan de actuación*. Madrid, Espana: Ministerio par alas Administraciones Públicas.

Ministry of Economic Affairs and Communication, Department of State Information Systems. (2007a, February 25). *Instructions for the semantic description of databases and operations performed by databases*, version 1.1. Retrieved August 30, 2010, from http://www.riso.ee/ en/ files/ EstonianGov_Semantic_Description-Instructions_v1.1c.pdf

Ministry of Economic Affairs and Communication, Department of State Information Systems. (2007b, April 08). *Methodology for the semantic interoperability of databases and operations performed by databases.* Retrieved August 30, 2010, from http://www.riso.ee/ en/ files/ EstonianGov_Semantic_Description-Methodology_v1.2.pdf

Ministry of Economic Affairs and Communications, Department of State Information Systems. (2005). *Estonian IT interoperability framework.* Retrieved August 30, 2010, from http://www.riso.ee/ en/ files/ framework_2005.pdf

Ministry of Industry and Information Technology of China, Department of Information. (2009). *Stride and Integration: China Informatization Development Report*. Beijing: Publishing House of Electronics Industry.

Ministry of Information and Communication Technology. (2010, April 28). *Thailand ICT master plan 2*. Retrieved September 15, 2010, from http://www.mict.go.th/ewt_news.php?nid=74

Misra, D. C. (2008). *Ten guiding principles for e-civil service*. Retrieved June 14, 2009, from http://egov-india.blogspot.com/ 2008/12/ten-guiding- principles-for-e-civil.html

Mitchell, G. R. (1998). Pedagogical possibilities for argumentative agency in academic debate. *Argumentation and Advocacy*, *35*, 41–60.

Moon, M. J. (2002). The evolution of e-government among municipalities: rhetoric or reality? *Public Administration Review*, *62*(4), 424–433. doi:10.1111/0033-3352.00196

Moon, M. J., & Norris, D. F. (2005). Does managerial orientation matter? The adoption of reinventing government and e-government at the municipal level. *Information Systems Journal*, *15*, 43–60. doi:10.1111/j.1365-2575.2005.00185.x

Moon, M. J. (2002). The evolution of e-government among municipalities: Rhetoric or reality? *Public Administration Review*, *62*(4), 424–433. doi:10.1111/0033-3352.00196

Moon, M. J. (2003). *Can IT help government to restore public trust? Declining public trust and potential prospects of IT in the public sector.* Paper presented at the 36th Hawaii International Conference on System Sciences.

Moon, M. J., Welch, E. W., & Wong, W. (2005). What drives global governance? An exploratory study at a macro level. *Proceedings of the 38th Hawaii International Conference on System Sciences, 2005.*

Morgeson, F. V. III. (2011). Comparing determinants of website satisfaction and loyalty across the e-government and e-business domain. *Electronic Government: An International Journal*, *8*(2/3), 164–184. doi:10.1504/EG.2011.039835

Morgeson, F. V. III, & Mithas, S. (2009). Does e-government measure up to e-business? Comparing end-user perceptions of U.S. federal government and e-business websites. *Public Administration Review*, *69*(4), 740–752. doi:10.1111/j.1540-6210.2009.02021.x

Morgeson, F. V. III, VanAmburg, D., & Mithas, S. (2011). Misplaced trust? Exploring the structure of the e-government-citizen trust relationship. *Journal of Public Administration: Research and Theory*, *21*(2), 257–283. doi:10.1093/jopart/muq006

Morgeson, F. V., III, VanAmburg, D., & Mithas, S. (2010, April). Misplaced trust? Exploring the structure of the e-government-citizen trust relationship. *Journal of Public Administration Research and Theory Advance Access*. Retrieved from http://jpart.oxfordjournals.org/ content/ early/2010/04/25/ jopart.muq006.abstract

Morgeson, F. V., III. (2005). Reconciling democracy and bureaucracy: Towards a deliberative-democratic model of bureaucratic accountability. (Doctoral dissertation, University of Pittsburgh, 28 March 2005).

Morozov, E. (2009). Iran: Downside to the Twitter revolution. *Dissent*, *56*(4), 10–14. doi:10.1353/dss.0.0092

Morozov, E. (2010). Think again: The Internet. *Foreign Policy*. Retrieved August 25, 2010 from http://www.foreignpolicy.com/ articles/2010/04/26/ think_again_the_Internet

Moya Martinez, G. (2003). La administración pública en línea: Estudio sobre servicios públicos de los ayuntamientos de la región de Murcia basados en Web. *Anales de Documentación*, *6*, 187–202.

Mwangi, W. (2006). The social relations of e-government diffusion in developing countries: The case of Rwanda. *Proceedings of the 2006 International Conference on Digital Government Research* (pp. 199-208). Los Angeles, CA: Digital Government Research Center. Retrieved May 1, 2010, from http://portal.acm.org/ citation.cfm?id=1146658

Myers, N. (2010). Africa's North Korea. *Foreign Policy*. Retrieved August 25, 2010, from http://www.foreignpolicy.com/ articles/2010/06/21/ africas_north_korea?page=full

Naficy, H. (2001). *An accented cinema: Exilic and diasporic filmmaking*. Princeton, NJ: Princeton University Press.

Nagesh, G. (February 7, 2008). *OMB touts savings from e-gov initiatives*. GovExec.com. Retrieved from http://www.govexec.com/dailyfed/0208/020708n1.htm

National Aeronautics and Space Administration. (2008, June 24). *Minimum hardware configurations*. Retrieved August 28, 2010, from http://www.nasa.gov/ pdf/ 324312main_STD-2805L.pdf

National Association of Counties (NACO). (2000). *2000 e-government survey*. Washington, DC: National Association of Counties.

National Collaboration Program Team. (2005, May 05). *The National Collaboration Framework (NCF) - An introduction*. Retrieved August 27, 2010, from http://www2.finance.gov.au/ e-government/ service-improvement-and-delivery/ national-collaboration-framework/ docs/ NCP-Overview_Document_-_5_tiers.pdf

National Electronics and Computer Technology Center (NECTEC). (2001). *E-government project 2002-2003*. Ratchathewi, Thailand: NECTEC. Retrieved September 15, 2010, from http://www.nectec.or.th

National Electronics and Computer Technology Center (NECTEC). National Science and Technology Development Agency (NSTDA), & Ministry of Science and Technology (MOST). (2003). *Thailand Information and Communication Technology (ICT): Master plan (2002-2006)*. Ratchathewi, Thailand: National Electronics and Computer Technology Center. Retrieved September 15, 2010, from http://www.mict.go.th

National Electronics and Computer Technology Center (NECTEC). (2010). *Website*. Retrieved September 15, 2010, from http://www.nectec.or.th

Neuman, L., & Calland, R. (2007). Making the law work - The challenges of implementation. In Florini, A. (Ed.), *The right to know: Transparency for an open world* (pp. 179–213). New York, NY: Columbia University Press.

NIEM Program Management Office - NPMO. (2007, January 9). *NIEM concepts of operations*. Retrieved August 30, 2010, from http://www.niem.gov/ files/ NIEM_Concept_of_Operations.pdf

NIEM Technical Architecture Committee - NTAC. (2008, October 31). *National information exchange model naming and design rules*. Retrieved August 30, 2010, from http://www.niem.gov/ pdf/ NIEM-NDR-1-3.pdf

NIEM. (2009, August). *NIEM newsletter*. Retrieved August 31, 2010, from http://www.niem.gov/ newsletter200908-2.php

NIEM. (2010). *The NIEM practical implementer's course*. Retrieved August 29, 2010, from http://www.niem.gov/ elearning.php

Norris, P. (2001). *Digital divide: Civic engagement, information poverty, and the Internet worldwide*. Cambridge, UK: Cambridge University Press.

Norris, D. F., & Lloyd, B. A. (2006). The scholarly literature on e-government: Characterizing a nascent field. *International Journal of Electronic Government Research*, *2*(4), 40–56. doi:10.4018/jegr.2006100103

Norris, P. (2001). *Digital divide: Citizen engagement, information poverty and the Internet worldwide*. New York, NY: Cambridge University Press.

Norris, D. F., & Moon, M. J. (2005). Advancing e-government at the grassroots: Tortoise or hare? *Public Administration Review*, *65*(1), 65–75.

Norris, P. (2001). *Digital divide: Civic engagement, information poverty, and the Internet worldwide*. Cambridge, UK: Cambridge University Press.

Norris, D. F. (2007). Electronic democracy at the American grassroots. In Norris, D. F. (Ed.), *Current issues and trends in e-government research*. Baltimore, MD: University of Maryland. doi:10.4018/9781599042831.ch008

Norris, D. F., Fletcher, P. D., & Holden, S. H. (2001). *Is your local government plugged in? Highlights of the PTI/ICMA 2000 electronic government survey*. Retrieved April 6, 2009, from http://www.ipa.udel.edu/ localgovt/ training/web/ egov2000survey_results.pdf

North, D. (2004). *Institutions, institutional change and economic performance*. Cambridge, United Kingdom: Cambridge University Press.

North, D. (1990). *Institutions, institutional change, and economic performance*. New York, NY: Cambridge University Press.

Nye, J. S. Jr. (1999). Information technology and democratic governance. In Kamarck, E. C., & Nye, J. S. Jr., (Eds.), *Democracy.com? Governance in networked world* (pp. 1–18). Hollis, UK: Hollis Publishing Company.

O'Reilly, T. E. (2005). *What is Web 2.0?* Retrieved February 18, 2009, from http://www.oreillynet.com/pub /a/ oreilly/tim/news/2005/09/ 30/what-is-web-20.html

OASIS. (2002). *OASIS Web services security (WSS)*. Retrieved August 30, 2010, from http://www.oasis-open.org/ committees/ tc_home.php? wg_abbrev=wss

OASIS. (2007, April 11). *OASIS Web services business process execution language (WSBPEL) TC*. Retrieved August 27, 2010, from http://www.oasis-open.org/ committees/ tc_home.php? wg_abbrev=wsbpel

Obi, T. (2009). Waseda University international e-government rankings. *I-Ways: The Journal of E-Government Policy and Regulation*, *32*(3), 129.

OECD e-Government Studies. (2003). *The e-government imperative*. OECD Publishing.

OECD. (2001). *Citizens as partners: Information consultation, and public participation in policy making*. Paris, France: OECD. Retrieved June 14, 2009, from http:// books.google.com.tw/ books?id=0pVGmUxcQgEC& printsec=frontcover&dq=Citizens +as+Partners:+Information+ Consultation,+and+Public+ Participation+in+Policy+Making &source=bl&ots=T_ CjioU_-T &sig=LgG2T52bnFBFelPP4bR SgoFfZ9s&hl=zh-TW&ei=kF7k S4ew-LM-gkQX8uNES&sa=X &oi=book_ result&ct=result& resnum=1&ved=0CCUQ6AEw AA#v=onepage&q&f=false

OECD. (2003). *Promise and problems of e-democracy: Challenges of online citizen engagement*. Paris, France: OECD. Retrieved June 14, 2009, from http://www.oecd.org/dataoecd /9/11/35176328.pdf

OECD. (2005a). *E-government for better government*. OECD publishing.

OECD. (2005b). *Proposed outline for accessing e-government benefits*. OECD publishing. Retrieved February 18, 2008, from http://webdomino1.oecd.org/ COMNET/ PUM/egovproweb.nsf/ viewHtml/index/$FILE/ GOV.PGC.EGOV.2006.1.doc

OECD. (2008). *OECD e-government studies: Belgium*. Paris, France: Organization for Economic Co-operation and Development.

Office of Juvenile Justice and Delinquency Prevention. (2006, October). *Guidelines for juvenile information sharing*. Retrieved August 30, 2010, from http://www.ncjrs.gov/ pdffiles1/ ojjdp/ 215786.pdf

Office of Management and Budget. USA. (n.d.). *Federal Enterprise Architecture (FEA)*. Retrieved August 30, 2010, from http://www.whitehouse.gov/ omb/ e-gov/ fea/

Office of Management and Budget. (2008). *Program assessment rating tool, guidance no. 2008-01*. Retrieved from http://www.whitehouse.gov/omb/assets/performance_pdfs/part_guid_2008.pdf

Office of Science Policy - National Insitute of Health. (2010, June 10). *NIH public private partnerships program*. Retrieved August 30, 2010, from http://ppp.od.nih.gov/

Office of the Director of National Intelligence. (2009, January 21). *IC directive 501 - Discovery and dissemination or retrieval of information within the intelligence community*. Retrieved August 30, 2010, from http://www.dni.gov/ electronic _reading_room/ ICD_501.pdf

Office of the Director of National Intelligence, United States of America. (2008, February 22). *United States intelligence community - Information sharing strategy*. Retrieved August 27, 2010, from http://www.dni.gov/reports/ IC_Information_Sharing_Strategy.pdf

Olalla, M. F. (2006). Information technology in business process reengineering. *International Advances in Economic Research*, *6*(3), 581–589. doi:10.1007/BF02294975

O'Leary, R., & Bingham, L. B. (Eds.). (2009). *The collaborative public manager: New ideas for the twenty-first century*. Washington, DC: Georgetown University Press.

Oliver, R. L. (1980). A cognitive model of the antecedents and consequences of satisfaction decisions. *JMR, Journal of Marketing Research*, *17*, 460–469. doi:10.2307/3150499

OMG. (1997-2010). *Object Management Group - UML*. Retrieved August 27, 2010, from http://www.uml.org/

OMG. (1997-2010). *Object Management Group/Business process management Initiative*. Retrieved August 27, 2010, from http://www.bpmn.org

Organization for Economic Co-operation and Development (OECD). (1998). *Information Technology as an instrument of public management reform*. Madrid, Espana: Ministerio para las Administraciones Públicas.

Orr, S. K. (2005). New technology and research: An analysis of Internet survey methodology in political science. *Political Science and Politics*, *38*(2), 263–267.

Orr, H. C. (2004). Tehrangeles: L.A. The Iranian expatriate capital abroad. *The Raw Story*. Retrieved May 1, 2010, from http://rawstory.com/exclusives/ orr/tehrangeles_iran_capital_ expatriates_812.htm

Orszag, P. R. (2009). *Open government directive, memorandum for the heads of executive departments and agencies*. Retrieved from http://www.whitehouse.gov /omb/assets/memoranda_2010 /m10-06.pdf

Osimo, D. (2008). *Web 2.0 in government: Why and how?* Luxembourg: Office for Official Publications of the European Communities. Retrieved February 18, 2009, from http://documentostics.com/ component/option,com_docman /task,doc_download/ gid,1417/Itemid,4

Ostrom, E. (1973). The need for multiple indicators in measuring the output of public agencies. *Policy Studies Journal: the Journal of the Policy Studies Organization*, *2*, 85–91. doi:10.1111/j.1541-0072.1973.tb00132.x

Ostrom, E. (1999). Why do we need multiple indicators of public service outputs? In McGinnis, M. D. (Ed.), *Polycentricity and local public economies*. Ann Arbor, MI: University of Michigan Press.

O'Toole, L. (1997). Implementing public innovations in network settings. *Administration & Society*, *29*(2), 115–134. doi:10.1177/009539979702900201

Ouadahi, J. (2008). A qualitative analysis of factors associated with user acceptance and rejection of a new workplace Information System in the public sector: A conceptual model. *Canadian Journal of Administrative Sciences*, *25*(3), 201–213. doi:10.1002/cjas.65

Ozimek, J. (Novermber 9, 2008). Finland's flawed e-voting scheme - Blame the voters? *The Register*. Retrieved from http://www.theregister.co.uk/2008/11/09/finland_evoting/

P. (2004). Joined-up government in the western world in comparative perspective: A preliminary literature review and exploration. *Journal of Public Administration Research and Theory, 14*(1), 103-138.

Panagariya, A. (2005, July/August). A passage to prosperity. *Far Eastern Economic Review*, 35–38.

Panopoulou, E., Tambouris, E., & Tarabanis, K. (2008). A framework for evaluating websites of public authorities. *Aslib Proceedings*, *60*(5), 517–546. doi:10.1108/00012530810908229

Parasuraman, A., & Colby, C. (2003). *Techno-ready marketing: How and why customers adopt technology*. New York, NY: The Free Press.

Parasuraman, A., & Grewal, D. (2000). The impact of technology on the quality-value-loyalty chain: A research agenda. *Journal of the Academy of Marketing Science*, *28*(1), 168–174. doi:10.1177/0092070300281015

Parasuraman, A., Zeithaml, V. A., & Berry, L. L. (1985). A conceptual model of service quality and its implications for future research. *Journal of Marketing*, *49*(Fall), 41–50. doi:10.2307/1251430

Parasuraman, A., Zeithaml, V. A., & Berry, L. L. (1988). SERVQUAL: A multiple-item scale for measuring consumer perceptions of service quality. *Journal of Retailing*, *64*(1), 12–40.

Parasuraman, A., Zeithaml, V. A., & Malhotra, A. (2005). E-S-QUAL: A multiple-item scale for assessing electronic service quality. *Journal of Service Research*, *7*(3), 213–233. doi:10.1177/1094670504271156

Pardo, T. A., & Tayi, G. K. (2007). Interorganizational information integration: A key enabler for digital government. *Government Information Quarterly*, *24*(4), 691–715. doi:10.1016/j.giq.2007.08.004

Pardo, T. A., Burke, B., Gil-Garcia, J. R., & Guler, A. (2009). Clarity of roles and responsibilities in government cross-boundary information sharing initiatives: Identifying the determinants. *Proceedings of 5th International Conference on e-Government,* (pp. 148-155). Boston, MA: Academic Publishing Limited.

Pardo, T. A., Cresswell, A. M., Dawes, S. S., & Burke, G. B. (2004). Modeling the social & technical processes of interorganizational information integration. *Proceedings of the 37th Hawaii International Conference on System Sciences - 2004* (pp. 1-8). IEEE.

Parent, M., Vandebeek, C. A., & Gemino, A. C. (2005). Building citizen trust through e-government. *Government Information Quarterly*, *22*, 720–736. doi:10.1016/j.giq.2005.10.001

Parent, M., Vandebeek, C. A., & Gemino, A. C. (2004). *Building citizen trust through e-government*. Paper presented at the 37th Hawaii International Conference on System Sciences. Retrieved February 18, 2008, from http://csdl2.computer.org/ comp/proceedings/hicss/2004/2056/05/205650119a.pdf

Parham, A. A. (2005). Internet, place, and public sphere in diaspora communities. *Diaspora*, *14*(2/3), 349–380.

Paris, M. (2005). Local e-government and devolution: Electronic service delivery in Northern Ireland. *Local Government Studies*, *31*(3), 307–319. doi:10.1080/03003930500095137

Park, H. M. (2006, May). The impact of digital government on civic engagement: A typological approach. *Proceedings of the 7th Annual International Conference on Digital Government Research*, San Diego, CA.

Parks, J. D., & Schelin, S. H. (2005). Assessing e-government innovation. In Garson, G. D. (Ed.), *Handbook of public Information Systems* (2nd ed., pp. 615–630). New York, NY: Marcel Dekker/CRC.

Parsons, T. (1965). Culture and the social system. In Parsons, T., Shils, E., Naegele, K. D., & Pitts, J. R. (Eds.), *Theories of society – Foundations of modern sociological theory* (pp. 963–993). New York, NY: MacMillan Publishing Co., Inc.

Parusuraman, A. (1996, October). *Understanding and leveraging the role of customer service in external, interactive, and internal marketing*. Paper presented at the meeting of the Frontiers in Service Conference, Nashville, TN.

Peerenboom, R. (2002). *China's long march toward rule of law*. Cambridge, UK: Cambridge University Press. doi:10.1017/CBO9780511493737

People's Daily Online. (1982, December 4). *The constitution of the People's Republic of China*. Retrieved February 20, 2010, from http://english.peopledaily.com.cn /constitution/constitution.html

People's Republic of China Open Government Information. (2007). *Regulations translated into English*. The China Law Center, Yale Law School. Retrieved on February 20, 2010, from http://www.law.yale.edu/ documents/pdf/Intellectual_Life/Ch_OGI_Regualtions_Eng_Final_051607.pdf

Pérez, C. C., Bolívar, M. P., & Hernández, A. M. L. (2008). E-government process and incentives for online public financial information. *Online Information Review, 32*(3), 379–400. doi:10.1108/14684520810889682

Peters, B. G. (1998). Managing horizontal government: The politics of co-ordination. *Public Administration, 76*, 295–311. doi:10.1111/1467-9299.00102

Petter, S., & Ephraim, R. M. (2009, April). A meta-analytic assessment of the DeLone and McLean IS success model: An examination of IS success at the individual level. *Information & Management, 46*(3), 159–166. doi:10.1016/j.im.2008.12.006

Piaget, J. (1954). *The construction of reality in the child*. New York, NY: Basic Books. doi:10.1037/11168-000

Pierson, P. (2004). *Politics in time*. Princeton, NJ: Princeton University Press.

Pina, V., Torres, L., & Royo, S. (2007). Are ICT's improving transparency and accountability in the EU regional and local governments? An empirical study. *Public Administration, 85*(2), 449–472. doi:10.1111/j.1467-9299.2007.00654.x

Piotrowski, S. J., & Van Ryzing, G. G. (2007). Citizen attitudes toward transparency in local government. *American Review of Public Administration, 37*(3), 306–323. doi:10.1177/0275074006296777

Piotrowski, S. J., Zhang, Y., Yu, W., & Lin, W. (2009). Issues for implementation of the Chinese open government information regulations. *Public Administration Review, 1*(69), S129–S135. doi:10.1111/j.1540-6210.2009.02100.x

Pollitt, C. (2003). Joined-up government: A survey. *Political Studies Review, 1*, 34–49. doi:10.1111/1478-9299.00004

Potter, A. (2002). Accessibility of Alabama government websites. *Journal of Government Information, 29*(5), 303–317. doi:10.1016/S1352-0237(03)00053-4

Premkumar, G., Ramamurthy, K., & Liu, H. N. (2008). Internet messaging: An examination of the impact of attitudinal, normative, and control belief systems. *Information & Management, 45*(7), 451–457. doi:10.1016/j.im.2008.06.008

Price, M. E., Davis Noll, B., & De Luce, D. (2002). *Mapping media assistance*. The Program in Comparative media Law & Policy, Center for Socio–Legal Studies, University of Oxford. Retrieved December 22, 2004, from www.undp.org/oslocentre/ docs04/A21%20 Literature%REVIEW.doc

PricewaterhouseCooper. (2009, June). *Final report: Understanding the key issues and constraints in implementation the RTI Act*. New Delhi, India.

Public Sector Website Survey Project. (2004). *Website*. Retrieved September 15, 2010, from http://www.mict.go.th

Puddephatt, A. (2009). *Exploring the role of civil society in the formulation and adoption of access to information laws: The cases of Bulgaria, India, Mexico, South Africa, and the United Kingdom*. Washington, DC: World Bank Institute.

Puddephatt, A. (2006, April). *A guide to measuring the impact of right to information programs - Practical guidance note*. Oslo, Norway: United Nations Development Program.

Putnam, R. D. (2000). *Bowling alone: The collapse and revival of American community*. New York, NY: Simon & Schuster Inc.

Putnam, R. D. (1995). Bowling alone: America's declining social capital. *Journal of Democracy, 6*(1), 65–78. doi:10.1353/jod.1995.0002

Qiu, J., & Chan, M. (2004). China Internet studies: A review of the field. In Nissenbaum, H., & Price, M. (Eds.), *The academy & the Internet* (pp. 275–307). New York, NY: Peter Lang.

Queensland Government Chief Information Officer. (2010, February 08). *Information asset custodianship (IS44) - Current information standards*. Retrieved August 30, 2010, from http://www.qgcio.qld.gov.au/ QGCIO/ architectureandstandards/ informationstandards/ current/ Pages/ InformationAssetCustodianship.aspx

Radhakrishnan, R. (2003). Ethnicity in the age of diaspora. In J. E. Braziel & A. Mannur (Eds.), *Theorizing diaspora* (119-131). Oxford, UK: Blackwell Publishing Ltd.

Rahimi, B. (2008). Politics of the Internet in Iran. In Semati, M. (Ed.), *Media, culture and society in Iran: Living with globalization and the Islamic state* (pp. 37–56). Oxon, UK: Routledge.

Ramió, C. (2001). The problems of implementing new public management in Latin American administrations: State model and institutional culture. *Revista del CLAD Reforma y Democracia, 21*(Octubre). Retrieved December 3, 2009, from www.clad.org

Rao, S. S., & Metts, G. (2003). Electronic commerce development in small and medium sized enterprises: A stage model and its implications. *Business Process Management, 9*(1), 11–32. doi:10.1108/14637150310461378

Reddick, C. G. (2005). Citizen interaction with e-government: From the streets to servers? *Government Information Quarterly, 22*, 38–57. doi:10.1016/j.giq.2004.10.003

Reddick, C. G. (2004). A two-stage model of e-government growth: Theories and empirical evidence for U.S. cities. *Government Information Quarterly, 21*(1), 51–64. doi:10.1016/j.giq.2003.11.004

Reddick, C. (2009). The adoption of centralized customer service systems: A survey of local governments. *Government Information Quarterly, 26*(1), 219–226. doi:10.1016/j.giq.2008.03.005

Regional Office for Latin America and the Caribbean (ROLAC). (2007). *Participación municipal en la gestión de los servicios públicos, equipamientos sociales y tributos para alcanzar los OMD's en América Latina y el Caribe*. Río de Janeiro, Brasil: ROLAC, United Nations Human Settlements Programme.

Relly, J. E., & Cuillier, D. (2010). A comparison of political, cultural, and economic indicators of access to information in Arab and non-Arab states. [special issue on Open Government]. *Government Information Quarterly, 27*(4), 360–370. doi:10.1016/j.giq.2010.04.004

Relly, J. E., & Sabharwal, M. (2009). Perceptions of transparency of government policymaking: A cross-national study. *Government Information Quarterly, 26*(1), 148–157. doi:10.1016/j.giq.2008.04.002

Relly, J. E. (2009). *The diffusion of access-to-information legislation: A cross-national contextual analysis*. Paper presented at the annual meeting of the International Communication Association, Chicago.

Research, Development, and Evaluation Commission (RDEC). (1996). *A study of government open information*. Taipei, Taiwan: RDEC, Executive Yuan. (in Chinese)

Research, Development, and Evaluation Commission (RDEC). (2008). *A framework for analyzing the transparency in government*. Taipei, Taiwan: RDEC, Executive Yuan. (in Chinese)

Ringle, C. M., Wende, S., & Will, A. (2005). *SmartPLS 2.0*. Retrieved September 1, 2010, from http://www.smartpls.de

Roberts, A. (2004). A partial revolution: The diplomatic ethos and transparency in intergovernmental organizations. *Public Administration Review, 64*(4), 410–424. doi:10.1111/j.1540-6210.2004.00388.x

Roberts, A. (2006). *Blacked out: Government secrecy in the information age*. New York, NY: Cambridge University Press.

Roberts, A. (2010). A great and revolutionary law? The first four years of India's Right to Information Act. *Public Administration Review, 70*(6), 925-933. Retrieved on April 29, 2010, from http://papers.ssrn.com/sol3/cf_dev /AbsByAuth.cfm?per_id=383666

Roberts, A. (2010, January 13). *India's Right to Information Act: The first four years*. Retrieved January 13, 2010, from Freedominfo.org/features /20100113.htm

Rocheleau, B., & Wu, L. (2002). Public versus private Information Systems. Do they differ in important ways? A review and empirical test. *American Review of Public Administration, 32*(4), 349–397. doi:10.1177/027507402237866

Rodrigues, C., & Slough, P. (2005). India's right to information movement makes a breakthrough. *Open Government: A Journal of Freedom of Information, 1*(1), 1–13.

Rodríguez Bolívar, M. P., Caba, C., & López, A. M. (2007). E-government and public financial reporting. The case of Spanish regional governments. *American Review of Public Administration, 37*(2), 142–177. doi:10.1177/0275074006293193

Rogers, E. M. (1995). *Diffusion of innovation* (4th ed.). New York, NY: The Free Press.

Rogers, E. M. (2003). *Diffusion of innovations* (5th ed.). New York, NY: Free Press.

Rosenau, J. (2002). Information Technologies and the skills, networks, and structures that sustain world affairs. In Rosenau, J., & Singh, J. P. (Eds.), *Information Technologies and global politics*. Albany, NY: State University of New York Press.

Rostow, W. W. (1960). *The stages of economic growth: A non-Communist manifesto*. Cambridge, UK: University Press.

RTI Assessment & Analysis Group and National Campaign for People's Right to Information. (2009, July). *Safeguarding the right to information – Report of the people's RTI assessment2008*.

Ryder, G. (2007). Debunking the optimists - An evaluation of conventional wisdom about the digital divide and e-government in the British Isles. *Transforming Government: People. Process and Policy, 1*(2), 112–130.

Saanen, Y. A., Sol, H. G., & Verbraeck, A. (1999). Snapshots of e-commerce's opportunities and threats. *Electronic Markets, 9*(3), 181–189. doi:10.1080/101967899359085

Sahadev, S., & Purani, K. (2008). Modeling the consequences of e-service quality. *Marketing Intelligence & Planning, 26*(6), 605–620. doi:10.1108/02634500810902857

Sakowicz, M. (2004). *How to evaluate e-government? Different methodologies and methods*. United Nations Online Network in Public Administration and Finance. Retrieved December 2, 2007, from http://www.unpan.org/

Sangmpam, S. N. (2007). Political rules: The false primacy of institutions in developing countries. *Political Studies, 55*(1), 201–224. doi:10.1111/j.1467-9248.2007.00650.x

Santana, M. (2009). A preliminary assessment of the development of e-government in a local government in Peru. *Journal of Asia-Pacific Studies, 12*, 75–89.

Saxena, K. B. C. (2005). Towards excellence in e-governance. *International Journal of Public Sector Management, 18*(6), 498–513. doi:10.1108/09513550510616733

Schedler, K., & Summermatter, L. (2007). Customer orientation in electronic government: Motives and effects. *Government Information Quarterly, 24*(2), 291–311. doi:10.1016/j.giq.2006.05.005

Schellong, A., & Langenberg, T. (2006). *Effective citizen relationship management: Hurricane Wilma and Miami-Dade County 311*. Paper presented at the 2006 International Conference on Digital Government Research.

Schlosberg, D., Zavestoski, S., & Shulman, S. W. (2007). Democracy and e-rulemaking: Web-based technologies, participation, and the potential for deliberation. *Journal of Information Technology & Politics, 4*(1), 37–55. doi:10.1300/J516v04n01_04

Scholl, H. J., & Klischewski, R. (2007). E-government integration and interoperability: Framing the research agenda. *International Journal of Public Administration, 30*, 889–920. doi:10.1080/01900690701402668

Schooley, B. L., & Horan, T. A. (2007). Towards end-to-end government performance management: Case study of interorganizational information integration in emergency medical services (EMS). *Government Information Quarterly, 24*(4), 755–784. doi:10.1016/j.giq.2007.04.001

Scott, J. K. (2006). "E" the people: Do U.S. municipal government websites support public involvement? *Public Administration Review, 66*(3), 341–353. doi:10.1111/j.1540-6210.2006.00593.x

Seifert, J. W., & Petersen, R. E. (2002). The promise of all things E? Expectations and challenges of emergent electronic government. *Perspectives on Global Development and Technology, 1*(2), 193–212. doi:10.1163/156915002100419808

Shackleton, P., Fisher, J., & Dawson, L. (2004). E-government services: One local government's approach. In Linger, H. (Eds.), *Constructing the infrastructure for the knowledge economy: Methods and tools, theory and practice* (pp. 581–592). Melbourne, VIC, Australia: Kluwer Academic/Plenum Publishers.

Shahideh, L. (2004). *The power of Iranian narratives.* Lanham, MD: University Press of America.

Shi, Y. (2006). E-government website accessibility in Australia and China: A longitudinal study. *Social Science Computer Review, 24*(3), 378–385. doi:10.1177/0894439305283707

Shiang, J. (2001). A study of public employees' perception of the freedom of government information policy. [in Chinese]. *Journal of Law and Political Science, 12*, 1–52.

Shin, H. F. (2007). Operation of the Freedom of Government Information Act in current legal system. [in Chinese]. *Yan Kao Shuang Yue Kan, 31*(3), 15–30.

Siau, K., & Long, Y. (2005). Synthesizing e-government stage models – A meta-synthesis based on meta-ethnography approach. *Industrial Management & Data Systems, 105*(4), 443–458. doi:10.1108/02635570510592352

Sin, C. Y. (2007). *Foundation of effective e-government: The Singapore experience. Harvard University: Belfer Center for Science and International Affairs (BCSIA).* John F. Kennedy School of Government.

Singh, J. (2002). Information Technologies and the changing scope of global power and governance. In Rosenau, J., & Singh, J. P. (Eds.), *Information Technologies and global politics.* Albany, NY: State University of New York Press.

Skocpol, T., & Somers, M. (1980). The use of comparative history in macrosocial inquiry. *Comparative Studies in Society and History, 22*(2), 174–197. doi:10.1017/S0010417500009282

Skocpol, T., & Fiorina, M. P. (1999). *Civic engagement in American democracy.* Washington, DC: Brookings Institution Press.

Smith, A. G. (2001). Applying evaluation criteria to New Zealand government websites. *International Journal of Information Management, 21*(2), 137–149. doi:10.1016/S0268-4012(01)00006-8

Smith, S. R., & Ingram, H. (1993). Public policy and democracy. In Ingram, H., & Smith, S. (Eds.), *Public policy and democracy* (pp. 1–14). Washington, DC: Brookings Institution Press.

Smyth, J., Dillman, D., Christian, L., & O'Neill, A. (2010). Using the Internet to survey small towns and communities: Limitations and possibilities in the early 21st century. *The American Behavioral Scientist, 53*(9), 1423–1488. doi:10.1177/0002764210361695

Snavely, K. (1991). Marketing in government sector: A public policy model. *American Review of Public Administration, 21*(4), 311–326. doi:10.1177/027507409102100403

Snell, R., & Xiao, W. (2007, January–March). Freedom of Information returns to China. *Public Administration Today*, 44-47.

Soni, V. (2008). A portrait of public administration in India: Challenges of governance in the world's largest democracy. *Public Administration Review*, (special issue), 1158–1161. doi:10.1111/j.1540-6210.2008.00965.x

State Council. (2001). *Announcement about the 2001-1005 planning guideline for government informatization. Beijing, China.* China: Author.

State Council Information Work Office. (2005). *China Informatization Development Report 2005.* Beijing: Publishing House of Electronics Industry.

State Council Information Work Office. (2006). *No.2 The Notice on Printing the National Overall Framework of E-government.*

State Council Information Work Office. (2006). *China Informatization Development Report 2006.* Beijing: Publishing House of Electronics Industry.

State Council Information Work Office. (2007). *No.126 The Notice on the Government 100 Case Dealing in Internet through Government Website.*

State Council's Informatization Office. (2006). *China's informatization development report 2006.* Beijing, China: State Council.

State Services Commission. (2008, February). *New Zealand e-government interoperability framework (NZ e-GIF),* version 3.3. Retrieved August 30, 2010, from http://www.e.govt.nz/ library/ e-gif-v-3-3-complete.pdf

State Services Commission. (2009). *Web standards - E-government in New Zealand.* Retrieved August 30, 2010, from http://www.e.govt.nz/ standards/ web-standards

Stemberger, I. M., & Jaklic, J. (2007). Towards e-government by business process change: A methodology for public sector. *International Journal of Information Management, 27*, 221–232. doi:10.1016/j.ijinfomgt.2007.02.006

Stiglitz, J. E. (2003). *Globalization and its discontents*. New York, NY: W.W. Norton & Co. Inc.

Stowers, G. N. L. (1999). Becoming cyberactive: State and local governments on the World Wide Web. *Government Information Quarterly, 16*(2), 111–127. doi:10.1016/S0740-624X(99)80003-3

Streib, G. D., & Willoughby, K. G. (2005). Local governments as e-governments: Meeting the implementation challenge. *Public Administration Quarterly, 29*(1), 78–110.

Streib, G. D., & Willoughby, K. G. (2005). Local governments as e-governments: Meeting the implementation challenge. *Public Administration Quarterly, 29*(1), 78-110.

Stromer-Galley, J. (2002). New voices in the political sphere: A comparative analysis of interpersonal and online political talk. *Javnost/The Public, 9*, 23-42.

Sudan, R. (2008). *Next generation organization models for e-government*. Washington, DC: The World Bank's Development Bookstore. Retrieved September 15, 2010, from http://web.worldbank.org/

Sullivan, Z. (2001). *Exiled memories stories of the Iranian diaspora*. Philadelphia, PA: Temple University Press.

Sullivan, J., & Xie, L. (2009). Environmental activism, social networks, and the Internet. *The China Quarterly*, 422–432. doi:10.1017/S0305741009000381

Sun, R. (2008). The Chief Expert on Olympic Games Security Reveals how to build Beijing into a iron bastion. *China News Week, 26*, 38–40.

Sunalai, A., & Tubtimhin, J. (2009). Thailand e-government: A step forward into the right track. In J. Tubtimhin, & R. Pipe (Eds.), *Global e-governance - Advancing e-governance through innovation and leadership, volume 2: Global e- governance series* (pp. 3-25). Fairfax, VA: IOS Press.

Sung, Y. H. (2006). Reforming government organization and information system to provide integrated services. [RDEC]. *Research, Development and Evaluation Commission Bi-monthly, 30*(6), 35–43.

Sung, Y. H. (2008). *Digital government*. Lujhou, China: National Open University.

Sung, Y. H. (2009). Service quality between e-government users and administrators. *Journal of E-Government Policy and Regulation, 32*, 241–248.

Sung, Y. H. (2007). How has Taiwan achieved the world highest e-government standard? In Obi, T. (Ed.), *E-governance: A global perspective on a new paradigm* (pp. 75–80). Tokyo, Japan: IOS Press.

Sunstein, C. (2001). *Republic.com*. Princeton, NJ: Princeton University Press.

Survey Report of e-Government Survey Project. (2008). *Survey report*. Retrieved September 15, 2010, from http://www.mict.go.th

Swiss, J. (2005). A framework for assessing incentives in results-based management. *Public Administration Review, 65*(5), 592–602. doi:10.1111/j.1540-6210.2005.00486.x

Szekely, I. (2007). Central and Eastern Europe – Starting from scratch. In Florini, A. (Ed.), *The right to know: Transparency for an open world* (pp. 116–142). New York, NY: Columbia University Press.

T.Obi Research Office. (2010). *The 2010 Waseda University world e-government ranking*. Tokyo, Japan: T.Obi Research Office.

Tang, D. T. C. (2006). A comparative analysis of Taiwan's freedom of Information Act 2005. [in Chinese]. *National Taiwan University Law Journal, 35*(6), 37–115.

Tapscott, D., & Williams, A. D. (2006). *Wikinomics: How mass collaboration changes everything*. London, UK: Penguin Books Ltd.

Tassabehji, R., Elliman, T., & Mellor, J. (2007). Generating citizen trust in e-government security: Challenging perceptions international. *Journal of Cases on Electronic Commerce, 3*(3), 1–17.

Taubman, G. (1998). A not-so World Wide Web: The Internet, China, and the challenges to nondemocratic rule. *Political Communication*, *15*(2), 255–272.

Taylor, S., & Todd, P. A. (1995). Understanding Information Technology usage: A test of competing models. *Information Systems Research*, *6*(2), 144–176. doi:10.1287/isre.6.2.144

Teo, H. H., Wei, K. K., & Benbasat, I. (2003). Predicting intention to adopt interorganizational linkages: An institutional perspective. *Management Information Systems Quarterly*, *27*(1), 19–49.

Thai Telecentre. (n.d.). *The origin of a community telecenter project.* Retrieved September 15, 2010, from http://www.thaitelecentre.org/thai/index.php?option=com_content&view=article&id=44&Itemid=54&lang=en

The 9/11 Commission. (2004, July 22). *The 9/11 Commission report.* Retrieved August 30, 2010, from http://www.9-11commission.gov/ report/ 911Report.pdf

The Economist. (2009, November 26). *The gloves go on: Lessons from Brazil, China and India.* Retrieved February 20, 2010, from http://www.economist.com/ world/international/displaystory.cfm?story_id=14979330

The Gazette of India. (2005, June 15). *The Right to Information Act*, 2005. Retrieved February 28, 2010, from http://righttoinformation.gov.in /rti-act.pdf

The Internet Engineering Taskforce - IETF. (1985). *File transfer protocol (FTP).* Retrieved August 30, 2010, from http://tools.ietf.org/ html/rfc959

The Markle Foundation. (2006, October). *A model contract for health information exchange.* Retrieved August 30, 2010, from http://www.connectingforhealth.org/ commonframework/ docs/ M2_ModelContract.pdf

The United Nations /ASPA. (2001). *Benchmarking e-government: A global perspective.* Retrieved April 30, 2010, from http://unpan1.un.org/intradoc/ groups/public/documents/un/ unpan021547.pdf

The United Nations. (2008). UN e-government survey 2008: From e-government to connected governance. New York, NY: UN Publishing Section. Retrieved May 26, 2010, from http://unpan1.un.org/intradoc/groups/public/documents/un/unpan028607.pdf

The United Nations. (2008). *E-government survey 2008: From e-government to connected governance.* New York, NY: UN Publishing Section. Retrieved September 15, 2010, from http://unpan1.un.org/intradoc/groups/public/documents/un/unpan028607.pdf

The United Nations. (2010). *United Nations e-government survey 2010: Leveraging e-government at a time of financial and economic crisis.* New York, NY: UN Publishing Section. Retrieved September 15, 2010, from http://www2.unpan.org/egovkb/global_reports/10report.htm

The United Nations. (2003). *World public sector report 2003: E-government at the crossroads.* New York, NY: UN.

The United Nations. (2008). *United Nations e-government survey 2008: From e-government to connected governance.* New York, NY: UN.

The United Nations. (2003). *Global E-Government Survey 2003.* Retrieved from http://www2.unpan.org/egovkb/global_reports/03survey.htm

The United Nations. (2004). *Global E-Government Development Report 2004.* Retrieved from http://www2.unpan.org/egovkb/ global_reports/04report.htm

The United Nations. (2005). *Global E-Government Development Report 2005,* Retrieved from http://www2.unpan.org/egovkb/ global_reports/05report.htm

The United Nations. (2008). *E-government survey 2008: From e-government to connected governance.* New York, NY: United Nations Publications. Retrieved April 28, 2009, from http://www.unpan.org/egovkb/global_reports/08report.htm

Thelen, K. (1999). Historical institutionalism and comparative politics. *Annual Review of Political Science*, *2*, 369–404. doi:10.1146/annurev.polisci.2.1.369

Thelen, K. (2000). Timing and temporality in the analysis of institutional evolution and change. *Studies in American Political Development*, *14*(1), 101–108. doi:10.1017/S0898588X00213035

Thomas, C. W. (1998). Maintaining and restoring public trust in government agencies and their employees. *Administration & Society*, *30*(2), 166–193. doi:10.1177/0095399798302003

Thomas, J. C., & Streib, G. (2003). The new face of government: Citizen-initiated contacts in the era of e-government. *Journal of Public Administration: Research and Theory, 13*, 83–102. doi:10.1093/jpart/mug010

Thompson, J. (1967). *Organizations in action*. New York, NY: McGraw-Hill.

Thomson, A. M., & Perry, J. (2006). Collaboration processes: Inside the black box. *Public Administration Review, 66*(6), 20–32. doi:10.1111/j.1540-6210.2006.00663.x

Thorson, S., Chung, J., & Ma, L. (2005). E-government in China: Bringing economic development through administrative reform. *Government Information Quarterly, 22*(1), 20–37. doi:10.1016/j.giq.2004.10.001

Thurmaier, K., & Wood, C. (2002). Interlocal agreements as overlapping social networks: Picket-fence regionalism in metropolitan Kansas City. *Public Administration Review, 62*(5), 585–598. doi:10.1111/1540-6210.00239

Tolberg, C. J., & Mossberger, K. (2006). The effects of e-government on trust and confidence in government. *Public Administration Review, 66*(3), 354–369. doi:10.1111/j.1540-6210.2006.00594.x

Transparency International. (2009). *Corruption perceptions index 2009 – Regional highlights: Asia-Pacific*. Berlin, Germany: Transparency International.

Trechsel, A., & Mendez, F. (Eds.). (2005). *The European Union and e-voting: Addressing the European Parliament's Internet voting challenge*. London, UK: Routledge.

Treisman, D. (2000). The causes of corruption: A cross-national study. *Journal of Public Economics, 76*, 399–457. doi:10.1016/S0047-2727(99)00092-4

Tubtimhin, J. (2010). Community driven healthcare service, a case study of Nakhonchaisi hospital in Thailand. In Pipe, R. (Ed.), *Journal of E-Governance*. Fairfax, VA: IOS Press.

U.S. Census Bureau. (2010). *US & world population clocks*. Retrieved March 17, 2010, from http://www.census.gov/ main/www/popclock.html

U.S. General Accounting Office. (2002). *World Trade Organization analysis of China's commitments to other members, report to Congressional committees*. Washington, DC: U.S General Accounting Office.

U.S. Office of Management and Budget (U.S. OMB). (2005). *FY 2004 report to Congress on implementation of the E-Government Act of 2002*. Office of Management and Budget. Retrieved December 7, 2007, from http://www.whitehouse.gov /omb/inforeg/ 2004_egov_report.pdf

United Kingdom. (1998). *Data Protection Act*. Retrieved August 30, 2010, from http://www.opsi.gov.uk/ acts/ acts1998/ ukpga_19980029_en_1

United Nations & American Society for Public Administration. (2002). *Benchmarking e-government. A global perspective*. Retrieved November 10, 2002, from http:// www.npan.org/ egovernment2.asp

United Nations. (2010). *United Nations 2010 global e-government survey: Leveraging e-government at a time of financial and economic crisis*. New York, NY: United Nations.

United Nations and the American Society for Public Administration (UN & ASPA). (2002). *Benchmarking e-government: A global perspective*: United Nations Division for Public Economics and Public Administration and American Society for Public Administration. Retrieved from http://unpan1.un.org/intradoc /groups/ public/documents /UN/UNPAN021547.pdf

United Nations Department of Economic and Social Affairs. (2010). *United Nations e-government survey 2010: Leveraging e-government at a time of financial and economic crisis*. New York, NY: UN Publishing Section.

United Nations Development Program. (2007a). *Human development report 2007/2008*. New York, NY: Palgrave Macmillan.

United Nations Development Program. (2007b). *Human development report 2009 – Statistics*. Retrieved on April 28, 2010, from http://hdrstats.undp.org/ en/indicators/#G

United Nations Development Programme. (2004). *Anti–corruption final version: Practice note*. Retrieved April 15, 2004, from http://www.uneca.org/itca/ governance /Documents/ Anti%20Corruption%20Note %20 FINAL%20VERSION %20031704.pdf

United Nations General Assembly. (1948). *Universal declaration of human rights*. Retrieved on March 29, 2010, from http://www.un.org/en/ documents/udhr/

United Nations General Assembly. (1966). *International covenant on civil and political rights*. Retrieved March 29, 2010, from http://www1.umn.edu/humanrts/ instree/ b3ccpr.htm

United Nations. (2005). *Global e-government readiness report 2005: From e-government to e-inclusion*. New York.

United Nations. (2008). *E-government survey 2008. From e-government to connected governance*. Retrieved April 14, 2009, from http://unpan1.un.org/intradoc/ groups/ public/documents/ UN/UNPAN028607.pdf

United Nations. (2008). *UN e-government survey 2008: From e-government to connected governance*. New York.

United Nations. (2010). *United Nations e-government survey 2010. Leveraging e-government at a time of financial and economic crisis*. Retrieved April 24, 2010, from http:// www2.unpan.org/ egovkb/global_reports/ 10report.htm

United Nations. (UN). (2005). *Global e-government readiness report 2005*. New York, NY: United Nations Department of Economic and Social Affairs Division for Public Administration and Development Management. Retrieved from http://unpan1.un.org/intradoc /groups/ public/ documents/un/ unpan021888.pdf

United Nations. (UN). (2008). *UN e-government survey 2008: From e-government to connected governance*. United Nations Department of Economic and Social Affairs, Division for Public Administration and Development Management. Retrieved from http://unpan1.un.org/ intradoc/ groups/public/documents /un/unpan028607.pdf

United Nations. (UN). (2010). *United Nations e-government survey 2010*. New York, NY: United Nations Department of Economic and Social Affairs. Retrieved April 30, 2010, from http://www2.unpan.org/egovkb / global_reports/10report.htm

United States Intelligence Community. (2008, February 22). *Information sharing strategy*. Retrieved August 30, 2010, from http://www.dni.gov/ reports/ IC_Information_Sharing_Strategy.pdf

US Department of Defense. (2005, August 20). *DoD enterprise architecture data reference model*, v 0.04. Retrieved August 30, 2010, from http://cio-nii.defense.gov/ docs/ DoD_DRM_v04_5Aug.pdf

US Department of Homeland Security. (2008, December 12). *Statement on information sharing and personal data protection between the European Union and the United States of America*. Retrieved August 30, 2010, from http:// www.dhs.gov/xlibrary/assets/usa_statement_data_privacy_protection_eu_12122008.pdf

US Department of Homeland Security. (2009). *The blog @ Homeland Security*. Retrieved August 30, 2010, from http://blog.dhs.gov

US Department of Homeland Security. (2009). *Information sharing mechanisms to improve homeland security*. Retrieved August 30, 2010, from http://www.whitehouse.gov/ omb/expectmore/ issue_summary/ issueDetailedPlan_24.pdf

US Department of Homeland Security. (2010). *Lessons learnt-Information sharing*. Retrieved August 30, 2010, from https://www.llis.dhs.gov/index.do

US Department of Justice and US Department of Homeland Security. (2010, August 19). *National information exchange model (NIEM)*. Retrieved August 29, 2010, from http://www.niem.gov/ index.php

US Department of Justice, Office of Justice Programs. (2004, October). *Justice information sharing initiative*. Retrieved August 30, 2010, from http://it.ojp.gov/documents/ Infoshare_102004 _PlusAcronymGlossary.pdf

US Department of Justice, Office of Justice Programs. (2010). *Global justice information sharing initiative*. Retrieved August 30, 2010, from http://www.it.ojp.gov/ global

US Department of Treasury. (1990). *Financial crimes enforcement network*. Retrieved August 30, 2010, from http://www.fincen.gov/ about_fincen/wwd/

van Beuningen, J., de Ruyter, K., Wetzels, M., & Streukens, S. (2009). Customer self-efficacy in technology-based self-service assessing between- and within-person differences. *Journal of Service Research*, *11*(4), 407–428. doi:10.1177/1094670509333237

van de Donk, W. B. H. J., & Snellen, I. Th. M. (1998). Towards a theory of pubic administration in an information age? In Snellen, I. Th. M., & van de Donk, W. B. H. J. (Eds.), *Public administration in information age: A handbook* (pp. 3–19). Amsterdam, The Netherlands: IOS Press.

Van de Walle, S., & Bouckaert, G. (2003). Public service performance and trust in government: The problem of causality. *International Journal of Public Administration*, *26*(8-9), 891–913. doi:10.1081/PAD-120019352

Van Riel, A., Semeijn, J., & Janssen, W. (2003). E-service quality expectations: A case study. *Total Quality Management*, *14*(4), 437–450. doi:10.1080/1478336032000047255

Van Ryzin, G. G. (2005). Testing the expectancy disconfirmation model of citizen satisfaction with local government. *Journal of Public Administration: Research and Theory*, *16*, 599–611. doi:10.1093/jopart/mui058

Van Ryzin, G. G., & Immerwahr, S. (2007). Importance-performance analysis of citizen satisfaction surveys. *Public Administration*, *85*(1), 215–226. doi:10.1111/j.1467-9299.2007.00641.x

Vander Wal, T. (2007). *Folksonomy*. Retrieved August 2, 2010, from http://vanderwal.net/ folksonomy.html

Venkatesh, V., Morris, M. G., Davis, G. B., & Davis, M. D. (2003). User acceptance of Information Technology: Toward a unified view. *Management Information Systems Quarterly*, *27*(3), 425–478.

Venkatesh, V., & Davis, F. D. (2000). A theoretical extension of the technology acceptance model: Four longitudinal field studies. *Management Science*, *46*(2), 186–204. doi:10.1287/mnsc.46.2.186.11926

Venkatesh, V., Morris, M., Davis, G., & Davis, F. (2003). User acceptance of Information Technology: Toward a unified view. *Management Information Systems Quarterly*, *27*(3), 425–478.

Volkoff, O., Chan, Y. E., & Newson, E. F. P. (1999). Leading the development and implementation of collaborative interorganizational systems. *Information & Management*, *35*, 63–75. doi:10.1016/S0378-7206(98)00087-1

W3C. (2001, March 15). *Web services description language (WSDL) 1.1.* Retrieved August 30, 2010, from http://www.w3.org/TR/wsdl

W3C. (2004, February 10). *OWL Web ontology language.* Retrieved August 30, 2010, from http://www.w3.org/ TR/ 2004/ REC-owl-features-20040210/

Walczuch, R., Lemmink, J., & Streukens, S. (2007). The effect of service employees' technology readiness on technology acceptance. *Information & Management*, *44*(2), 206–215. doi:10.1016/j.im.2006.12.005

Walton, J. (2004, January-February). WTO: China enters year three. *The China Business Review Online*. Retrieved February 20, 2010, from http://www.chinabusinessreview.com/ public/0401/01.html

Wang, Y. S., & Liao, Y. W. (2008, October). Assessing e-government systems success: A validation of the DeLone and McLean model of Information Systems success. *Government Information Quarterly*, *25*(4), 717–733. doi:10.1016/j.giq.2007.06.002

Wang, C. S. (Ed.). (2006). *China E-government Development Report*. Beijing: Social Science Academic Press.

Wang, S. G., & Hu, A. G. (Eds.). (1993). *China State Capacity Report*. Shenyang: Liaoning People's Press.

Wang, S. (2008). Changing models of China's policy agenda setting. *Modern China*, *34*(1), 56–87. doi:10.1177/0097700407308169

Wang, Y.-S., & Shih, Y.-W. (2009). Why do people use information kiosks? A validation of the united theory of acceptance and use of technology. *Government Information Quarterly*, *26*, 158–165. doi:10.1016/j.giq.2008.07.001

Warren, M. (1992). Democratic theory and self-transformation. *The American Political Science Review*, *86*(1), 8–23. doi:10.2307/1964012

Week, E. C. (2000). The practice of deliberative democracy: Results from four large-scale trails. *Public Administration Review*, *60*(4), 360–372. doi:10.1111/0033-3352.00098

Weerakkody, V., Baire, S., & Choudrie, J. (2006). E-government: The need for effective process management in the public sector. In R. H. Sprague, Jr. (Ed.), *Proceedings of the 39th Hawaii International Conference on System Sciences - Volume 04* (pp. 74-83). Los Alamitos, CA: IEEE.

Welber, T. (1995). Right discourse in citizen participation: An evaluative yardstick. In Renn, O., Welber, T., & Wiedemann, P. (Eds.), *Fairness and competence in citizen participation: Technology, risk and society* (pp. 35–86). Boston, MA: Kluwer.

Welch, E. W., Hinnant, C. C., & Moon, M. J. (2004). Linking citizen satisfaction with e-government and trust in government. *Journal of Public Administration: Research and Theory*, *15*(3), 371–391. doi:10.1093/jopart/mui021

Welch, E. W., Hinnant, C. C., & Moon, M. J. (2005). Linking citizen satisfaction with e-government and trust in government. *Journal of Public Administration: Research and Theory*, *15*(3), 371–391. doi:10.1093/jopart/mui021

Welch, E. W., & Hinnant, C. C. (2003). *Internet use, transparency, and interactivity effects on trust in government.* Paper presented at the 36th Annual Hawaii International Conference on System Sciences (HICSS'03), Hawaii, USA.

Welch, E. W., & Hinnant, C. C. (2002). *Internet use, transparency, and interactivity effects on trust in government.* Paper presented at the 36th Hawaii International Conference on System Sciences–2003, Hawaii, USA.

Welp, Y. (2008). América Latina en la era del gobierno electrónico. Análisis de la introducción de nuevas tecnologías para la mejora de la democracia y el gobierno. *Revista CLAD Reforma y Democracia*, *41*, 42–57.

Wen, J. B. (2004, March 5th). Report on Government Work at the Second Session of the Tenth National People's Congress, *People's Daily*, pp. A1.

West, D. M. (2004). E-government and the transformation of service delivery and citizen attitudes. *Public Administration Review*, *64*(1), 15–27. doi:10.1111/j.1540-6210.2004.00343.x

West, D. M. (2004). E-government and the transformation of service delivery and citizen attitudes. *Public Administration Review*, *64*(1), 15–27. doi:10.1111/j.1540-6210.2004.00343.x

West, D. (2008). *The Brookings Institution.* Retrieved September 1, 2010, from http://www.brookings.edu/

West, D. M. (2005). *Global e-government 2005.* Providence, RI: Center for Public Policy, Brown University. Retrieved January 18, 2009, from http://www.insidepolitics.org /egovt05int.pdf

West, D. M. (2006). *State and federal e-government in the United States, 2006.* Retrieved July 7, 2007, from http://www.insidepolitics.org /egovt06us.pdf

West, D. M. (2008). *Improving technology utilization in electronic government around the world.* Retrieved April 30, 2010, from http://psiplatform.net/content/ download/14972/187426/file/ 0817_egovernment_west.pdf

Whitaker, M. P. (2004). Some reflections on popular anthropology, nationalism, and the Internet. *Anthropological Quarterly*, *77*(3), 469–498. doi:10.1353/anq.2004.0034

Wholey, J. S., & Hatry, H. (1992). The case for performance monitoring. *Public Administration Review*, *52*(6), 604–610. doi:10.2307/977173

Wholey, J. S., & Newcomer, K. E. (1997). Clarifying goals, reporting results. In Newcomer, K. E. (Ed.), *Using performance measurement to improve public and non-profit programs*. San Francisco, CA: Jossey-Bass.

Wilkinson, V. O., & Cappel, J. J. (2005). Impact of economic prosperity and population on e-government involvement. *Issues in Information Systems*, *6*(2), 204–209.

Willcocks, L., & Sykes, R. (2000). The role of the CIO and IT function in ERP. *Communications of the ACM*, *43*(4), 32–38. doi:10.1145/332051.332065

Willcoeks, L., & Smith, G. (1995). IT-enabled business process reengineering: Organizational and human resource dimensions. *The Journal of Strategic Information Systems*, *4*(3), 279–301. doi:10.1016/0963-8687(95)96806-J

Williams, R., & Edge, D. (1996). The social shaping of technology. In W. H. Dutton with M. Peltu (Ed.), *Information and communication technologies: Visions and realities* (pp. 53-67). Oxford, UK: Oxford University Press.

Wilson, J. Q. (1989). *Bureaucracy: What government agencies do and why they do it.* New York, NY: Basic Books.

Witschge, T. (2002, October). *On-line deliberation: Possibilities of the Internet for deliberative democracy.* Paper presented at the meeting of Euricom Colloquium Electronic Networks & Democratic Engagement, Nijmegen, The Netherlands. Retrieved June 14, 2009, from http://java.cs.vt.edu/public /projects/digitalgov/ papers/ onlinedeliberation_Nl.pdf

Wixom, B. H., & Todd, P. A. (2005). A theoretical integration of user satisfaction and technology acceptance. *Information Systems Research*, *16*(1), 85–102. doi:10.1287/isre.1050.0042

Wold, H. (1985). Systems analysis by partial least squares. In Nijkamp, P., Leitner, H., & Wrigley, N. (Eds.), *Measuring the unmeasurable* (pp. 221–251). Boston, MA: Martinus Nijhoff.

Wolfinbarger, M. F., & Gilly, M. C. (2003). eTailQ: Dimensionalizing, measuring, and predicting e-tail quality. *Journal of Retailing, 79*(3), 183–198. doi:10.1016/S0022-4359(03)00034-4

Wong, W., & Welch, E. (2004). Does e-government promote accountability? A comparative analysis of website openness and government accountability. *Governance: An International Journal of Policy. Administration and Institutions, 17*(2), 275–297.

Wood, L., Bernt, P., & Ting, C. (2009). Implementing public utility commission websites: Targeting audiences, missing opportunities. *Public Administration Review, 69*(4), 753–763. doi:10.1111/j.1540-6210.2009.02022.x

Wood, L., Bernt, P., & Ting, C. (2009). Implementing public utility commission websites: Targeting audiences, missing opportunities. *Public Administration Review, 69*(4), 753–763. doi:10.1111/j.1540-6210.2009.02022.x

Wood, D., & Gray, B. (1991). Toward a comprehensive theory of collaboration. *The Journal of Applied Behavioral Science, 27*(2), 139–162. doi:10.1177/0021886391272001

World Bank. (2007). *Databank.* Retrieved on August 13, 2010, from http://databank.worldbank.org /ddp/home.do?Step=3&id=4

World Bank. (2008a). *Migration and remittances factbook 2008.* Retrieved May 1, 2010, from http://go.worldbank.org/ QGUCPJTOR0

World Bank. (2008b). *Information and communication technologies tables*. Washington, DC: World Bank. Retrieved May 1, 2010, from http://go.worldbank.org/7S1VU9WNZ0

WS BPEL TC. (2003, May). *Business process execution language for Web services,* version 1.1. Retrieved August 30, 2010, from http://www.ibm.com/ developerworks/library/ specification/ ws-bpel/

Wu, I. L., & Chen, E. L. (2005). An extension of trust and TAM model with TPB in the initial adoption of online tax: An empirical study. *International Journal of Human-Computer Studies, 62*(6), 784–808. doi:10.1016/j.ijhcs.2005.03.003

Wu, A. M. (Ed.). (2004). *China E-government: Theory and Practice*. Beijing: People's Press.

Wu, H. C. (2008). *The study of e-information of the government administration - An example from Taipei county*. Unpublished Master's thesis, Department of Public Administration, National Chengchi University, Taipei. (in Chinese)

Xiao, Q. (2003). Cyber speech: Catalyzing free expression and civil society (China). *Harvard International Review, 25*(2), 70–75.

Xie, X. R. (2006, July 28th). Speech in National Tax Informatizaiton Construction Conference (Summary). Retrieved from http://202.108.90.130/n8136506/ n8136563/n8193451/n8193496/ n8194115/8243310.html

Xin, X., & Rudel, T. K. (2004). The context for political corruption: A cross-national analysis. *Social Science Quarterly, 85*(2), 294–309. doi:10.1111/j.0038-4941.2004.08502005.x

Xu, Y. (2008). The problems and policy recommendations in the construction of websites for county level governments: The case of Shanxi. [in Chinese]. *Theory Exploration, 4*, 133–134.

Ya Ni, A., & Tat-Kei Ho, A. (2005). Challenges in e-government development: Lessons from two information kiosk projects. *Government Information Quarterly, 22*(1), 58–74. doi:10.1016/j.giq.2004.10.005

Ya Ni, A. (2006). *What drives the development of e-government? An analysis of U.S. county government's adoption of e-government services*. Paper Presented at the Association for Public Policy Analysis and management 2006 Fall Conference.

Yan, Z. C. (2008). Decipherment: The Four Modernizations is the Biggest Policy in China. *Political Science Research, 10*, 38–43.

Yang, J., & Paul, S. (2005). E-government application at local level: Issues and challenges: An empirical study. *Electronic Government*, *2*(1), 56–76. doi:10.1504/EG.2005.006648

Yang, K. (2009). Institutional congruence, ideas, and anticorruption policy: The case of China and the United States. *Public Administration Review*, (special issue), S142–S150. doi:10.1111/j.1540-6210.2009.02102.x

Yang, A., & Taylor, M. (2010). (forthcoming). Relation-building by Chinese ENGOs' websites: Education, not activation. *Public Relations Review*, 1–10.

Yang, G. (2003). The co-evolution of the Internet and civil society in China. *Asian Survey*, *43*(3), 405–422. doi:10.1525/as.2003.43.3.405

Yang, K. (2003). Neoinstitutionalism and e-government: Beyond Jane Fountain. *Social Science Computer Review*, *21*, 432–442. doi:10.1177/0894439303256508

Yang, K. (2010). (forthcoming). The aborted green dam-youth escort censor-ware in China: A case study of emerging civic participation in China's Internet policy-making process. *Telematics and Informatics*, 1–10.

Yang, Y. (2010). A Chinese way of democratization? *China. International Journal (Toronto, Ont.)*, *8*(2), 330–345.

Yang, K., & Xu, X. (2010). E-government in mainland China. In Berman, E., Moon, J., & Choi, H. (Eds.), *Public administration in East Asia* (pp. 165–194). New York, NY: CRC Press. doi:10.1201/EBK1420051902-c8

Yang, X. S. (2009, February 23th). Information development in rural areas and E-government Building. Message posted to http://www.xinhuanet.com/ xhft/20090223/wz.htm

Yeh, J. R. (2007). The government gazette system reform and freedom of government information. [in Chinese]. *Yan Kao Shuang Yue Kan*, *31*(3), 3–14.

Yen, D. C., & Evans, D. (2005). E-government: An analysis for implementation: Framework for understanding cultural and social impact. *Government Information Quarterly*, *22*(3), 354–375. doi:10.1016/j.giq.2005.05.007

Yi, M. Y., & Hwang, Y. (2003). Predicting the use of Web-based Information Systems: Self-efficacy, enjoyment, learning goal orientation, and the technology acceptance model. *International Journal of Human-Computer Studies*, *59*, 431–449. doi:10.1016/S1071-5819(03)00114-9

Yin, J. (2008). Beyond the four theories of the press: A new model for the Asian & the world press. *Journalism & Communication Monographs*, *10*(1), 3–62.

Zappen, J. P., Harrison, T. M., & Watson, D. (2008). *A new paradigm for designing e-government: Web 2.0 and experience design.* Paper presented at the 9th Annual International Digital Government Research Conference, Montreal.

Zeithaml, V. A., Parasuraman, A., & Malhotra, A. (2002). Service quality delivery through websites: A critical review of extant knowledge. *Academy of Marketing Science Journal*, *30*(4), 362–375. doi:10.1177/009207002236911

Zeng, P. Y. (Ed.). (2004). *Informatization and E-government*. Beijing: People's Press.

Zhang, B., & Ye, H. (2005). China's e-government development: Problems and policy recommendations. [in Chinese]. *Journal of the Hunan Mass Media Technology College*, *5*(5).

Zhang, J. (2002). Will the government serve the people? *New Media & Society*, *4*(2), 163–184. doi:10.1177/14614440222226325

Zheng, Y., & Wu, G. (2005). Information Technology, public space, and collective action in China. *Comparative Political Studies*, *38*(5), 507–536. doi:10.1177/0010414004273505

Zheng, L., Yang, T.-M., Pardo, T. A., & Jiang, Y. (2009). Understanding the "boundary" in information sharing and integration. *Proceedings of the 42nd Hawaii International Conference on System Sciences - 2009* (pp. 1-10). IEEE.

Zhou, H. H., & Tang, T. H. (Eds.). (2002). *The Theory and Practice of E-government*. Beijing: Chinese Academy of Governance Press.

Zhou, M., & Liu, Z. M. (2009). Vigorously Promote Administration Extranets, Build E-government Public Service System. In Changsheng, W. (Ed.), *China E-government Development Report*. Beijing: Social Science Academic Press.

Zhou, H. (2007). Open government in China – Practices and problems. In Florini, A. (Ed.), *The right to know: Transparency in an open world* (pp. 92–115). New York, NY: Columbia University Press.

Zhu, H. X., Hu, J. C., & Sun, W. T. (2007). *The Report on 2007 China Internet Public Sentiment Analysis*. Retrieved from http://www.china.com.cn/ aboutchina/ zhuanti/08zgshxs/ 2008-04/02/content_14098960.htm

Zhu, H. X., Shan, X. G., & Hu, J. C. (2008). *The Report on 2008 China Internet Public Sentiment Analysis*. Retrieved from http://caofeidian.china.com.cn/ aboutchina/ zhuanti/09zgshxs/ content_17100922_4.htm

Zients, J. (2010). *Guidance on the use of challenges and prizes to promote open government*. Office of Management and Budget.

About the Contributors

Yu-Che Chen, Ph.D., is an Associate Professor of E-Government and Public Management in the Division of Public Administration at Northern Illinois University. He received his Master of Public Affairs and Ph.D. from Indiana University – Bloomington. Dr. Chen's research interests include international electronic governance, e-government implementation, and IT-enabled interorganizational collaboration. Chen's recent research publications can be found in journals such as *Public Administration Review*, *American Review of Public Administration*, *International Journal of Electronic Government Research*, *Government Information Quarterly*, *Public Performance & Management Review*, and *Social Science Computer Review*. His research has also appeared as book chapters in the *Encyclopedia of Digital Government*, *E-government Research*, and other books on electronic government. Additionally, he has published management reports with the IBM Center for the Business of Government on e-government XBRL implementation and IT outsourcing. Dr. Chen serves on the IT Committee of the National Association of Schools of Public Affairs and Administration and is the Chair for the Section on Science and Technology in Government for the American Society for Public Administration. He has also served on various editorial advisory boards for books and journals on e-governance and public administration.

Pin-Yu Chu, Ph.D., currently serves as Distinguished Professor of National Chengchi University, Taiwan. Dr. Chu holds a doctorate in Engineering-Economic Systems from Stanford University. Her research interests include technology development and management, digital governance, and conflict management. Her publications can be found in *Government Information Quarterly*, *Public Performance and Management Review*, *Omega: The International Journal of Management Science*, *Journal of Management & Organization*, *International Journal of Technology Management*, *Industrial Management Data Systems*, *Journal of Applied Social Psychology*, and *Electronic Government: An International Journal*. Dr. Chu serves on the Personnel Policy Council, Central Personnel Administration of Taiwan, the Committee of Government Technology Program Review, the Review Expert Board of Higher Education Evaluation & Accreditation Council of Taiwan, et cetera.

* * *

Maria del Carmen Caba Pérez, Ph. D. in Governmental Accounting, is Associate Professor at the Department of Accounting and Finance at the University of Almeria (Spain). She is a foundational member of the Spanish Association of Accounting University Teachers and member of European Accounting Association. She teaches Financial Accounting and Public Sector Management and control.

Her research interests are focused on the financial information disclosures on the Web (e-government), on the management system and financial information in the federal and local governments. She is author of numerous articles in national and international journals indexed at the ISI/JCR including *Government Information Quarterly, Online Information Review, International Review of Administrative Sciences, American Review of Public Administration, Public Administration and Development,* and *Public Management Review*. Also, she has written some chapters to books edited by prestigious international Editorials (Kluwer Academic Publishers; IGI Global; Springer) on different topics related to e-government.

Chih-Hao Chang is a Ph.D. candidate of Global Information and Telecommunication, Waseda University. He used to served as a researcher in a non-government organization in Taiwan called "Institute for Information Industry", which played the role of Government CIO and think tank of government in terms of making ICT policy. Mr. Chang's research interest is on e-governance, Information System, and service marketing. He is a member of the International Academy of CIO, and his papers have been published in the journal of IACIO. His research was awarded with honor by Okawa Isao scholarship in 2007. Besides this, he made a lot of contributions to improving research methodology of "Waseda e-government ranking" as the project leader from 2006 to 2008.

Don-Yun Chen holds a Ph.D. from Political Science of Rochester University, USA. He is Director of the Taiwan E-Governance Research Center (TEG) and Professor of the Department of Public Administration at National Chengchi University Taiwan. TEG was established in 2007, and is supported by the Research, Development and Evaluation Commission (RDEC) of the Executive Yuan, Taiwan, with an aim to provide an interactive channel and information sharing platform for international research institutions in e-governance related fields. Dr. Chen focuses on e-governance, democratic governance, bureaucratic politics, public policy analysis, and management. His practical experiences include Deputy Director of Public Management Consulting Center at Shih Hsin University, and member of the e-governance committee, Taiwan Association for Schools of Public Administration and Affairs (TASPAA). He also serves as a policy consultant on e-government for the Taipei City Government, and a principal evaluator of e-government applications for the National Service Quality Award issued by the RDEC.

Li-Chun Chiang, Ph.D., is an Associate Professor of the Department of Political Science at the National Cheng Kung University, Tainan, Taiwan, and also served as the Deputy Director of the Taiwan E-Governance Research Center (TEG). Her research interests include e-government, gender and Information Technology, public administration, and Information Technology. Dr. Chiang's recent research publications can be found in journals such as *Systems Research and Behavioral Science, Psychological Reports, Ethics & Behavior,* and *Educational Technology and Society.*

Elsa Estevez is a Senior Researcher in the Center for Electronic Governance at United Nations University - International Institute for Software Technology in Macao, and Assistant Professor at the National University of the South, Argentina. She has 25 years of experience in academia and software industry, including teaching e-government-related courses to government audiences around the world and courses on Software Engineering to university students. Her research interests include electronic services and software infrastructure for electronic governance, and software tools to enable communities of practice; she has a number of publications on these topics. She served as a Program Committee member and Chair at several national and international conferences, most recently a PC Co-Chair of I3E2010, and holds a PhD and MSc Degree in Computer Science from the National University of the South, Argentina and Licenciado Degree in Computer Science from the University of Buenos Aires.

Pablo Fillottrani is an Adjunct Researcher in the Commission of Scientific Research of Buenos Aires Province and an Associate Professor at the National University of the South, Bahía Blanca, Argentina. Previously he was a Research Associate at the KRDB group in the Free University of Bozen/Bolzano, Italy. His research interests include formal languages for knowledge representation and reasoning, conceptual modeling with applications to databases and Software Engineering, Semantic Web, and computational logic and logic programming. He currently serves as program committee member and chair of several international conferences. He holds a PhD and Msc Degree in Computer Science from National University of the South, Argentina.

Sukumar Ganapati is an Associate Professor in the Public Administration Department at Florida International University. He teaches courses in IT and E-government and local economic development. His research interests encompass housing, community development, and Information Technology applications.

Nai-yi Hsiao is an Associate Professor of the Department of Public Administration at National Chengchi University in Taipei, Taiwan, and received his Ph.D. in Public Administration and Policy at State University of New York at Albany, USA. His specialty includes electronic governance, IT governance, systems thinking and policy simulation, and judgment and decision-making. Dr. Hsiao's recent research publications can be found in journals such as *Government Information Quarterly, International Journal of Public Administration, Public Administration and Development,* and *Asian Social Policy Review*.

Lung-Teng Hu is the Deputy Director of the Taiwan e-Governance Research Center, which is sponsored by the Research, Development and Evaluation Commission (RDEC) of the Executive Yuan in Taiwanese central government. He is also an Associate Professor of the Department of Public Administration and Policy at National Taipei University in Taipei, Taiwan. He currently serves as the Vice Executive Director of the Transparency International's national chapter in Taiwan as well. He received his Ph.D. from the School of Public Affairs and Administration at Rutgers University at Newark, USA. His research interests include e-government and e-governance, knowledge management in the public sector, government performance measurement and management, as well as government transparency.

Tong-Yi Huang, Ph.D., is an Associate Professor of the Department of Public Administration at National Cheng-chi University in Taipei, Taiwan, where he teaches public administration, survey research methods, and citizen participation at undergraduate and graduate levels. Dr. Huang also serves as a Research Fellow of Taiwan e-Government Research Center. Dr. Huang received his Ph. D. from the Department of Government of the University of Texas at Austin. His recent research interests include e-government evaluation, e-democracy, and deliberative democracy. Dr. Huang's recent research publications can be found in journals such as *Public Administration and Development* and *International Journal of Public Administration*.

Tomasz Janowski is a Senior Research Fellow at United Nations University - International Institute for Software Technology in Macao (UNU-IIST) where he founded and heads the Center for Electronic Governance. His expertise is in foundations and frameworks for electronic governance, tools and applications of formal techniques, and rigorous development of enterprise systems, particularly systems for the public sector. He founded and coordinates a series of International Conferences on Theory and Practice of Electronic Governance (ICEGOV), and serves as an Editorial Board member and Programme Committee member and chair at various journals and conferences. As part of his contribution to international development, he assists several governments including Afghanistan, Argentina, Cameroon, China, Colombia, Costa Rica, Ecuador, Egypt, Jordan, Republic of Korea, Kyrgyzstan, Macao SAR, Maldives, Mongolia, Nepal, Nigeria, and Palestine on how to design and implement Electronic Governance programmes based on the rigorous framework EGOV that he developed in the Center. He has a PhD in Computer Science from the University of Warwick, UK.

Chung-pin Lee, Ph.D., is an Assistant Professor of the Department of Public Administration at Tamkang University in Taiwan, and also a research fellow of Taiwan E-Governance Research Center. In 2007-8, he was a Fulbright visiting scholar in the Askew School of Public Administration and Policy at Florida State University. His research interests are public innovation and diffusion, e-governance, and deliberative democracy. Dr. Lee's recent research publications can be found in journals such as *Public Administration Review*, *Journal of Public Administration* (published in Taiwan), and *Public Administration & Policy* (published in Taiwan).

Frank Leyman is the manager of international relations, FEDICT (the Federal Public Service for ICT). He holds a Master degree in Marketing and in Applied Economics from the University of Mons in Belgium. He started his career with IBM Belgium as a telecom Marketing specialist. After 6 years he joined the Belgian national Telecom operator BELGACOM where he was in charge of setting up the Corporate Services Sector. After 3 years he was appointed as Distribution Channels Director for the Belgacom Group. In 1999, Frank left Belgacom for a more international career by joining the company PROTON WORLD. This company is specialized in large scale smartcard based projects. He was in charge of business development in the Middle-East and African Region and co-developed the complete government offering. Since mid-2005, he has worked for FEDICT where he has managed international relations as well as the relations with European Commission, UN, and OECD. He was the Chairman (2009-2010) of the International Council for IT in Government Administration (ICA).

Jin Lo is a Ph. D. Candidate in Public Administration at National Chengchi University in Taiwan. He is a part-time Lecturer at both the Department of Public Management and Policy and the Department of Political Science Department at Tunghai University. His areas of expertise include e-government, deliberative democracy, and e-governance. In 2010, he obtained a Doctoral Dissertation Grant and Award of National Science Council.

Antonio M. López-Hernández is a Full Professor of Accounting at Granada University, Spain. He is a founding member of the Spanish Association of Accounting University Teachers and a member of the European Accounting Association. He teaches Public Sector Management and Control. His research interests are focused on the financial information disclosures on the Web (e-government), on the management system and financial information in the federal and local governments. He is an author of numerous articles in national and international journals indexed at the ISI/JCR including *International Public Management Journal, Government Information Quarterly, Online Information Review, International Review of Administrative Sciences, American Review of Public Administration, Public Administration and Development, Public Money & Management,* and *Public Management Review*. Also, he has written some chapters to books edited by prestigious international publishers (Kluwer Academic Publishers; IGI Global; Springer) on different topics related to e-government.

Forrest V. Morgeson III is a Research Scientist at the American Customer Satisfaction Index (ACSI) in Ann Arbor, Michigan. He received his Ph.D. in Political Science from the University of Pittsburgh. His recent research focuses on citizen satisfaction with U.S. federal government services, electronic government, and the financial impact of private sector consumer satisfaction, and has recently been published or is forthcoming in journals such as *Public Administration Review*, *Journal of Public Administration Research and Theory*, *Electronic Government: an International Journal*, *Journal of Marketing*, *Marketing Science*, and the *International Journal of Research in Marking*. In addition to his research activities, Dr. Morgeson has consulted with dozens of corporations and government agencies on customer and citizen satisfaction over the past decade, and has delivered lectures and presentations on a variety of topics in more than a dozen countries.

Adegboyega Ojo is a Research Fellow at the United Nations University – International Institute for Software Technology (UNU-IIST) located in Macao. At UNU-IIST, he belongs to the Electronic Governance Programme. Before joining UNU-IIST in May 2004 as a Postdoctoral Fellow, he was Senior Lecturer at the Department of Computer Sciences at the University of Lagos in Nigeria. His expertise lies in the domains of Electronic Governance, Technology Strategy and Architectures, Software Technology, and Computational Intelligence. His academic and professional career spans about two decades of teaching, research and capacity building in computing, e-governance, and related subjects. He has published several peer-reviewed papers as journal articles, book chapters, and contributions to conference proceedings. He currently serves as program committee member and chair of several international conferences in the area of e-governance and Information Systems. Adegboyega holds Ph.D. and B.Sc. degrees in Computer Science from the University of Lagos, Nigeria.

Ching-Heng Pan is currently an Assistant Professor at the Graduate Institute of National Policy and Public Affairs at National Chung Hsing University in Taiwan, and a research fellow at the Taiwan E-Governance Research Center. Dr. Pan received his MPA from Columbia University and earned his Ph.D. in Public Administration from the University of Southern California. His current research interests involve various aspects of e-governance, including Web 2.0 applications in the public sector, e-government evaluation, and reuse of public sector information. He teaches the courses in e-governance, organizational theory and behaviors, regulatory policy, public policy analysis, and public administration theories.

Jeannine E. Relly is an Assistant Professor in the School of Journalism at the University of Arizona, where she also is an affiliated faculty member with the Center for Latin American Studies. Her research largely focuses on political, cultural, legal, and economic institutions in developing nations with access-to-information legislation. Her recent research has examined the global diffusion of access-to-information legislation and e-governance in developing nations with and without access-to-information laws.

Manuel Pedro Rodríguez Bolívar is an Associate Professor at the University of Granada (Spain). He is a foundational member of the Spanish Association of Accounting University Teachers and of the European Accounting Association. His research interests are focused on e-government, the conceptual framework of accounting, the use of BSC in public administrations and public agencies, and on environmental accounting. He is the author of numerous articles in national and international journals indexed at the ISI/JCR list, including the *Government Information Quarterly, Public Administration and Development, Public Money & Management, Online Information Review, International Review of Administrative Sciences,* and *American Review of Public Administration*. Also, he has also contributed chapters to books edited by prestigious international publishers such as IGI Global, Springer, or Kluwer Academic Publishers on different topics related to e-government and he is author of books published by the Ministry of Economy and Ministry of Treasure in Spain.

Maricarmen A. Sanchez is a native of Miami, Florida. She is a graduate student in the Public Administration Department at Florida International University. Her research interest is mainly in anthropology.

Jing Shiang received his Ph.D. in Public Administration, the Ohio State University. He is Professor and Chair of Department of Public Management and Policy at Tunghai University, and he also serves as Chief Secretary of the University. His specialty includes information policies, e-government, and e-governance. In 1995, he was the recipient of Dissertation Award by National Association of Schools of Public Affairs and Administration (NASPAA). Furthermore, he also obtained Research Grant and Award of National Science Council in 1996 and 2000. He was the Chair of E-Governance Research Committee of Taiwan Association for Schools of Public Administration and Affairs (TASPAA).

Yu-Hsieh Sung is the Deputy Minister of the Research, Development and Evaluation Commission (RDEC) under the Cabinet. He also teaches as Adjunct Associate Professor at Chuan-Yuan University. Dr. Sung has been working for RDEC since 1985. His experience mainly includes e-government, government performance evaluation, and government reform. He was the key person to lead a group on developing, coordinating, and expediting the "Electronic Government" project in Taiwan started in 1996. In the past four years, he made his efforts in promoting the re-engineering of government organization that combines the strategic use of ICTs with government administration. Dr. Sung holds a B.S. degree from Chung-Hsing University, Taiwan, an M.P.P. degree from the University of Michigan, U.S.A., and a Ph.D. degree in Business Administration from Cheng-Chi University, Taiwan.

Jun Tang is an Associate Professor of the School of Public Administration, Renmin University of China. He is the director of the Institute of Crisis Management and deputy director of the Institute of Governance and Reform at Renmin University. His research interests include public management, crisis management, and e-government. He has widely published on those subjects.

Toshio Obi received his Ph.D. in Global Information and Telecommunications Studies of Waseda University. Currently, he is a Professor of Graduate School of GITS, Director of Institute of e-Government, Waseda University, and Director of APEC e-Government Research Center. He is also the Chair of National e-Government Promotion Council of Japan; Member of Prime Minister Committee on IT Strategy; President of International Academy of CIO; Chair of UNESCO UNITWIN Program on Disaster Management; Adviser of Communication and Information Network Industries Ass (CIAJ); and Chair of Broadband Committee of the Telecomm Association of Japan. His research focuses primarily on e-government, international ICT policy, CIO, and e-governance. He is also the author of "Global e-governance" (IOS Press, 2006 and 2010), "Mobile Internet" (PHP Press, 2000), "Mobile Government in Japan" (European Management Association, 2009), "NGN" (CIAJ, 2009), and he received Gold medal on International Contribution by ITU Association of Japan in 2005.

Kuan-Chiu Tseng is an Assistant Professor of the Department of Public Administration at the Tamkang University in Taipei, Taiwan. His areas of specialization are e-governance, government innovation, cross-boundary management and public bureaucracy. He works as a research fellow at the Taiwan e-Governance Research Center sponsored by the Research, Development and Evaluation Commission (RDEC) of the Executive Yuan.

Jirapon Tubtimhin is Senior Expert (e-Government), the previous Director of the project, Government Information Technology Infrastructure (GITI) under National Electronics and Computer Technology Center (NECTEC), National Science and Technology Development Agency (NSTDA), Ministry of Science and Technology (MOST). In an international arena, Mr. Tubtimbin is Secretary General of International Academy of CIO (IAC) and he was ex-Project Overseer of several APECTEL Projects in the area of CIO and e-government development. His recent career records include IT Consultant to IT Committees of various public agencies, guest lecturer & speaker in both local and international public & private institutions, universities, and conferences/seminars, member/editor of IPAIT 2004 Committee on Substances (2003-2004), Manager of Thailand e-Government Project under NECTEC (2001-2003), and Director of Bureau of e-Government Development, Ministry of ICT (2003), Thailand.

Chian-Wen Wang is a doctoral student research fellow of Taiwan e-Governance Research Center, which is sponsored by the Research, Development and Evaluation Commission (RDEC) of the Executive Yuan in Taiwanese central government. He is also a Ph.D. student of Department of Public Administration, National Chengchi University, Taiwan. His research interests include public-private partnerships, e-governance, and organizational behavior and management.

Hui-Ju Wang is a Ph. D. student of Business Administration department of National Chengchi University. Her specialized fields include cyber psychology and behavior, and marketing management. In 2007, she received Dissertation Award by Chinese Management Association.

Lawrence E. Wood is an Assistant Professor in the School of Media Arts and Studies in the Scripps College of Communication at Ohio University. He is also currently the Associate Director of the Communication and Development Studies master's program at Ohio University. His research and professional interests relate to the various dimensions of the digital divide, development in the U.S. as well as in international contexts, and public policy, including E-government. He has published articles about E-government in journals such as *Government Information Quarterly* and *Public Administration Review*.

Kaifeng Yang is an Associate Professor and Ph.D. program director of the Askew School of Public Administration and Policy, Florida State University. He is the managing editor of *Public Performance* *and Management Review* and has widely published in leading public administration journals such as *Public Administration Review* and *Journal of Public Administration Research and Theory*. His research interests include citizen participation, public management, and e-government.

Feng Chun Yang is the senior research fellow and dean of Academy of E-Government, Peking University. He started his teaching career in 1987 at Peking University. He was a visiting scholar from November, 1993 to March, 1994 at Michigan University and at Melborne University from July, 1999 to July, 2000. He founded E-Government Research Center of Peking University in 2001 and it was renamed to Academy of E-Government, Peking University in 2003. His current research interests include China e-government building pattern, e-government application of local governments, and the influence of ICT application on government. He has also provided e-government policy and technical consulting for central and local governments in China and served as expert at some related international organizations.

Chengfu Zhang is Professor and Vice Dean of the School of Public Administration, Renmin University of China. He is a council member of the Public Administration Academic Degree Commission of the Chinese State Council and the director of the Institute of Governance and Reform at Renmin University. His research interests include government reform, e-government, and crisis management. He has published a dozen of books and numerous articles on those subjects.

Index

Symbols

A

B

C

D

E

F

G

Q

R

S

T

U

V

W

Y

CPSIA information can be obtained at www.ICGtesting.com
265051BV00008B/195-248/P